NEGRO EMPLOYMENT IN BASIC INDUSTRY

A Study of Racial Policies in Six Industries

INDUSTRIAL RESEARCH UNIT

WHARTON SCHOOL OF FINANCE AND COMMERCE

UNIVERSITY OF PENNSYLVANIA

Founded in 1921 as a separate Wharton Department, the Industrial Research Unit has a long record of publication and research in the labor market, productivity, union relations, and business report fields. Major Industrial Research Unit studies are published as research projects are completed. Advanced research reports are issued as appropriate in a general or special series.

RECENT INDUSTRIAL RESEARCH UNIT STUDIES

(Available from the University of Pennsylvania Press or the Industrial Research Unit)

No. 40 Gladys L. Palmer, *et al.*, *The Reluctant Job Changer* (1962) $7.50.

No. 41 George M. Parks, *The Economics of Carpeting and Resilient Flooring: An Evaluation and Comparison* (1966) $5.00.

No. 42 Michael H. Moskow, *Teachers and Unions: The Applicability of Bargaining to Public Education* (1966) $8.50.

No. 43 F. Marion Fletcher, *Market Restraints in the Retail Drug Industry* (1967) $10.00.

No. 44 Herbert R. Northrup and Gordon R. Storholm, *Restrictive Labor Practices in the Supermarket Industry* (1967) $7.50.

No. 45 William N. Chernish, *Coalition Bargaining: A Study of Union Tactics and Public Policy* (1969) $7.95.

No. 46 Herbert R. Northrup, Richard L. Rowan, *et al.*, *Negro Employment in Basic Industry. A Study of Racial Policies in Six Industries* (Also Vol. I Studies of Negro Employment) 1970 $10.00.

Nos. 1-39 Available from Kraus Reprint Co.
16 East 46th St., New York, N.Y. 10017

NEGRO EMPLOYMENT IN BASIC INDUSTRY

A Study of Racial Policies in Six Industries

(Volume I – Studies of Negro Employment)

by

HERBERT R. NORTHRUP
Professor of Industry and Director,
Industrial Research Unit

CARL B. KING
WILLIAM H. QUAY, JR.
HOWARD W. RISHER, JR.
Research Associates

RICHARD L. ROWAN
Associate Professor of Industry
and Associate Director, Industrial
Research Unit

INDUSTRIAL RESEARCH UNIT
WHARTON SCHOOL OF FINANCE AND COMMERCE
UNIVERSITY OF PENNSYLVANIA

Library of Congress Catalog Card Number 79-128-607
MANUFACTURED IN THE UNITED STATES OF AMERICA
ISBN: 0-8122-7621-3

FOREWORD

In September 1966, the Ford Foundation began a series of major grants to the Industrial Research Unit of the Wharton School of Finance and Commerce to fund a series of studies of the Racial Policies of American Industry. The purpose has been to determine why some industries are more hospitable to the employment of Negroes than are others and why some companies within the same industry have vastly different racial employment policies.

Studies have proceeded on an industry-by-industry basis, under the direction of the undersigned, with Dr. Richard L. Rowan, Associate Professor of Industry, as Associate Director. As of March 1970, reports have been completed in twenty-one industries, and ten more are underway. Twelve industry studies have been published as reports: automobiles, aerospace, steel, hotels, petroleum, rubber tires, chemicals, paper, banking, insurance, public utilities, and meat packing. Others including motor truck, railroads, urban transit, coal mining, shipbuilding, textiles, and tobacco are being readied for publication.

With this volume, we inaugurate a series of books updating, revising, and combining our industry studies and analyzing the reasons for different racial policies and Negro employment representation in different industries. This book thus includes our previously published reports on automobiles, aerospace, steel, rubber tires, petroleum, and chemicals, with the first three which were published in 1968, updated, and all revised where deemed desirable. A final chapter analyzes and contrasts the situation in various industries. In addition, this volume, as the first in the series contains an introductory part, setting forth the purpose and hypotheses of the overall project, and a brief overview of the position of the Negro in industry.

Three additional volumes are now being prepared for publication and four or five others are planned. Volume II, entitled *Negro Employment in Finance;* Volume III, *Negro Employment in Public Utility Industries;* and Volume IV, *Negro Employment in Southern Industry* are all expected to be published in 1970. Somewhat later, five more volumes are due: *Negro Employment in Transportation Industries; Negro Employment in the Maritime Industries; Negro Employment in*

Selected Manufacturing Industries; Negro Employment in Service and Retail Trade; and *Negro Employment in Building Construction.* These nine volumes should contain the most thorough analysis of Negro employment now extant.

Volume I is the result of cooperative effort of several persons. Parts One and Eight were written by the undersigned after considerable and significant discussions with Dr. Rowan. Part Two (automobiles), Part Three (aerospace), and Part Five (rubber tires) are also the undersigned's work, with Professor Alan B. Batchelder of Kenyon College, assisting on Part Five. Professor Rowan wrote Part Four (steel). Part Six is the joint work of Carl B. King and Howard W. Risher, Jr. Mr. King, who already had a law degree from the University of Texas, made his contribution while a candidate for the M.B.A. degree at the Wharton School. Mr. Risher is currently a Ph.D. candidate at the University of Pennsylvania; Part Seven is the work of William H. Quay, like Mr. King, a former M.B.A. student, now in industry. Mr. Quay was assisted by our editor and proofreader extraordinary, Mrs. Marjorie C. Denison, who also did the principal editing, proofreading, and the index. She was, in turn, ably assisted by Miss Elsa Klemp, and with Miss Klemp compiled and checked tables, charts, and facts in general. Our administrative staff is headed by Mrs. Margaret E. Doyle, who has managed to keep our financial affairs sound, order our supplies, take care of our travel, maintain student relations, trouble shoot on a variety of problems, and manage the office and its personnel. Our secretaries and stenographers—Mrs. Marie P. Spence, Mrs. Veronica M. Kent, and Mrs. Rose Elkin—did the typing.

Many others have contributed to this volume. The extraordinary cooperation of numerous industry and government personnel made it possible to obtain material and data not otherwise available. Their request for anonymity precludes our recording individually the great debt which we obviously owe. Dr. John R. Coleman, President of Haverford College, made the initial grants possible as a staff member of the Ford Foundation, and later Mitchell Sviridoff, Vice-President and Basil T. Whiting, Project Officer, assured continued Foundation support and interest. In addition, Mr. Whiting arranged a special addition to the grant to make this publication possible. Numerous students added their help, questions, or discussions to improve our own understanding.

In most previous reports, as in this one, the data cited as "in the possession of the author," have been carefully authenticated and are on file in our Industrial Research Unit Library.

HERBERT R. NORTHRUP, *Director*
Industrial Research Unit
Wharton School of Finance and Commerce
University of Pennsylvania

Philadelphia
March 1970

TABLE OF CONTENTS

Part Three
THE NEGRO IN THE AEROSPACE INDUSTRY
Herbert R. Northrup

Part Four
THE NEGRO IN THE STEEL INDUSTRY
Richard L. Rowan

Part Five

THE NEGRO IN THE RUBBER TIRE INDUSTRY

Herbert R. Northrup

Part Six
THE NEGRO IN THE PETROLEUM INDUSTRY
Carl B. King and Howard W. Risher, Jr.

Part Seven

THE NEGRO IN THE CHEMICAL INDUSTRY

William Howard Quay, Jr.

Part Eight
CONCLUDING ANALYSIS
Herbert R. Northrup

Part One

INTRODUCTION AND OVERVIEW

by

HERBERT R. NORTHRUP

PART ONE: LIST OF TABLES

CHAPTER I.

The Approach and Some Hypotheses

The civil rights issue remains the number one social and economic problem in America today. Basic to this issue is the right and ability of citizens to earn a livelihood. Negroes, our largest minority, continue to represent a disproportionate share of unemployment, and are concentrated disproportionately in the unskilled and lower-paying jobs where employed. Other civil rights issues would undoubtedly not disappear if minority group employment problems were solved to the same extent as those of the white majority have been, but the opening of jobs on a truly fair and equal basis would be the most significant step toward eliminating racial inequities. A job with dignity and income stabilizes the family, permits the acquisition of decent housing, and enables a person otherwise to fend for himself even if he is socially unacceptable to others, or encounters invidious rebuffs.

Considerable detail concerning the Negro in the labor market is now available. Several studies have been made of union and government policies toward discrimination in employment. A number of case studies of particular employer racial employment policies are also available.[1] But employer policies have not been analyzed in depth to determine their rationale. Yet, employer policies will be the major determining factor in the course of minority group employment, even though union and government policies will interact with and affect such employer policies.

If economic conditions of minority groups are to continue to be improved, we must know why some industries are more hospitable to minority group employment than are others, and why some companies within the same industry have vastly different racial employment policies. What are the economic, institutional, and behavioral

1. See, for example, Herbert R. Northrup and Richard L. Rowan, eds., *The Negro and Employment Opportunity* (Ann Arbor, Bureau of Industrial Relations, University of Michigan, 1965), Chapters 5-10, 20, 22-23.

factors determining these policies? If these questions are capable of constructive analysis—as it is believed that they are—then it can be determined in what types of industries and companies the greatest potential for Negro employment exists, and in what types the most significant barriers to such employment are found. These findings, combined with labor market analysis and trends with business and job forecasting, will permit a more rational attack on discrimination in employment in terms of potential results for effort expended. They should also materially improve vocational guidance, the direction of training and development at all levels, and the utilization of legal means to overcome discrimination.

SOME HYPOTHESES WHICH ARE EXAMINED

The varying racial employment policies of American industry have been the study and practice of the senior author for more than twenty-five years.[2] During this period of sweeping change, several basic hypotheses have been developed which are examined in this and succeeding volumes. Some of the key hypotheses which our studies list and the questions test are set forth below.

(1) *The Demand for Labor*

Negroes have made their greatest employment gains in time of relatively full employment—World War I, World War II, and the 1960's are key examples of such periods. Does this pattern exist throughout each industry? Will it endure? In every industry examined in this and the other volumes in the series, the impact of the demand for labor and of labor market conditions are examined.

(2) *The Nature of the Work*

The availability of Negro labor—that is, the supply—is affected by numerous factors, most of which also affected demand. Thus Negroes were first employed in industry as unskilled laborers or in work which was dirty, unpleasant, or backbreaking. Their disadvantaged educational status, their lack of experience, and their over-supply relative to demand have all contributed to this situation. Industries which have traditionally needed such labor have employed large numbers of

2. For results of early efforts, see Herbert R. Northrup, *Organized Labor and the Negro* (New York: Harper and Brothers, 1944).

minority groups. Does this fix the status of the minority group and "disqualify" members of that group in the eyes of the employer for better jobs in such industries? This question takes on added significance in view of the heavy replacement of unskilled labor by mechanical devices and the relative decline in demand for unskilled labor since World War II. Do industries and companies which *traditionally* employed Negro labor in *traditional* jobs tend to be more discriminating employers of the future (or even the present)? Or does the presence of Negroes on the employment roles enable them to advance more easily to better jobs? Do both hypotheses have some validity in different circumstances and in different industries? The industries discussed in this volume include older ones like steel and relatively new ones like aerospace and therefore afford an opportunity to test aspects of these questions. Likewise, in nearly all the succeeding volumes, this hypothesis will be examined on an industry by industry basis.

(3) *The Time and Nature of the Industry's Development*

When an industry began may determine *how* its policies became institutionalized, what is required to change them, and under what circumstances they will in fact be changed. Thus the traditional white industry of the South is cotton textiles which developed there during post Civil War years in part as an economic restoration mechanism and a source of employment for poor whites. Negroes were excluded or confined to yard or janitorial work. It set the pattern for most new southern industries prior to World War II, and did not change until the mid-1960's.

In contrast, the tobacco industry which developed prior to the Civil War employed Negroes since its inception. But cigarette production which started in the 1870's like other post-civil war manufacturing, was worked on by whites only. Instead of exclusion, the tobacco industry developed a racial-occupational segregation pattern which remained until recent market and government pressures forced token integration.

Bituminous coal mining used Negroes as strike-breakers and a labor source after World War I ended immigration; but Negroes have been excluded from anthracite mining which reached maturity and was unionized before Negroes were brought into northern industry during World War I.

In 1942, a leading utility executive stated that Negroes were not qualified to operate trolley cars; it was difficult to say that about Negroes as bus drivers when the Negro applicant drove up in a car.

In this and all succeeding volumes, careful attention is paid to the timing of an industry's development and to the policies followed by industry in the South, as well as in other regions. The special cases of the textiles, tobacco, coal, and paper industries, along with lumber, will be analyzed in our forthcoming volume, *Negro Employment in Southern Industry.*

(4) *The Mores of the Community*

Industry does not operate in a vacuum. Generally, in fact, does not industry policy reflect the mores of the community? The development of industry in North v. South, in heavily minority group populated v. light minority group populated areas, etc., may provide the basis for quite different racial employment policies. When companies have expanded into new regions, do they follow community patterns? Or, do they adhere to what they were accustomed in their initial location? Are there consistent reasons for variations other than the convictions of managements? Each industry is examined in the light of history and community views to determine the answer to these questions.

(5) *The Relation of Racial Employment Policies and Consumer Market Orientation*

Are companies that produce products directly for the consumer market more likely to pursue more vigorous equal employment policies than those which make goods for other producers? Would, for example, the racial difficulties in some areas have been at least arrested if consumer goods industries had been the dominant employer? There are many facets to such a question. The diverse nature of an industry's customer orientation is examined in each of the industry studies in this and succeeding volumes.

(6) *The Concern of the Industry, or more likely, the Company with its Image is Significant*

Company or executive concern with its "image" involves more than consumer orientation. For example, it is possible to contrast companies in the business machine field and discover wide variation in interest in minority group employment. This observation may also be made with respect to other industries. What is the significance of executive interest in projecting a certain image of the company?

(7) *Ethnic Orientation of Management*

Do companies headed by individuals of minority ethnic stock or by those whose origin was somewhat outside the background from which most managers have developed initiate programs sympathetic to expanded minority group employment? To the extent that such information can be obtained, it is tested empirically.

(8) *Community Crises*

In recent years, company racial policies have been altered by such events as the southern school integration struggle and the Detroit riot. Nationally based companies located in the South found that they could not remain neutral because, if schools closed, they could not recruit key managerial or professional people to their southern locations. Southern banks, utilities, and financial institutions saw that school closings would thwart community industrial development. Likewise the major automobile companies understood that Detroit racial unrest threatened their capacity to produce. The impact of factors extraneous to industry's direct employment function, but closely related thereto, is examined wherever pertinent in each industry studied.

(9) *The Nature of Union Organization*

In general—although not always—older industries like railroads, printing, and building construction, are ones unionized on a craft basis with its concomitant job scarcity consciousness and antiminority group bias. A community of feeling between craftsmen and employers on racial employment matters exists in such industries. The interaction tends to strengthen discrimination. Moreover, the fragmentation of unions adds additional barriers which must be overcome if existing discriminatory patterns are to be modified. When a union comes in, does it tend to institutionalize the practices of a particular period and thus make progress in the future difficult? Does this occur with unions organized on an industrial basis as well as with those organized on a craft basis? Or is union policy largely a neutral factor? Each industry discussed in this and succeeding volumes carefully analyzes the impact of unions on the industry racial policies.

(10) *The Impact of Technology*

The concentration of Negroes in unskilled and service work makes them especially susceptible to replacement by machines; and their inferior educational background poses impediments when opportunities to operate new equipment are available. Of course, there are opposite experiences as the bus-trolley example indicates. But the relatively small ratio of Negroes in skilled jobs compared to unskilled, and their lack of background and training to operate complicated equipment continue as major problems.

Must the traditional impact of new technology always endure so that progress is partially at the expense of the black man? Do union policies play a significant role in racial aspects of technological displacement? The industries discussed in this volume demonstrate a surprising variation in this regard, as do some of those analyzed in succeeding volumes. Our analysis of the bituminous coal and railroad industries in later volumes—two industries in which technological displacement has been a major factor—will show that Negroes have been disproportionately affected.

(11) *The Service Industry Situation*

The service industries offer a fertile field for examination because some have been traditionally Negro, or minority group, some traditionally white, some segregated by establishment, some segregated by job (waiters v. busboys), and some mixed. Is there a hypothesis which can explain these varying employment patterns? In view of the continued expansion of this sector of the economy, the volumes examining financial institutions, hotels and retail trade, and transportation services are of added significance.

(12) *Industrial Location*

The location of a plant or industry, not only as to region, but also in relation to Negro residence is likely to be a significant determinant of the racial composition of the work force. It is likely that the less skilled the work, the less will people travel distances to the job. Commuting mores vary, however, from area to area so the locational impact must be examined in each instance.

(13) *The Role of the Government*

The impact of government on employer policies is, of course, a significant study in itself, but it must be dealt with in a study of employer policies. This involves not only procurement and fair employment commission activity, but also general standards setting government employment. The usual hypothesis is that the closer the company is to government supervision, the more it must follow government standards. Yet, a careful examination of the facts will demonstrate that this hypothesis is far too simple. The automobile industry, which sells primarily to the public, has a far higher percentage of Negroes than does the aerospace industry, which has the government as its principal, or in many cases, sole customer. Electric and gas utilities and the Bell System are regulated primarily by state public service commissions, but in many areas, the policies of these utilities differ. Airlines, maritime employers, truckers, and railroads also do not demonstrate too similar policies despite similar governmental relations; and there are other examples. Why these variations occur is obviously worth careful study, and will be examined carefully in our various volumes. Perhaps more significant is the question of whether government regulation is a requirement for progess toward equal employment, and the concomitant question of whether progress, even under government pressure, can be made if the demand for labor slackens. These questions are, of course, fundamental not only for an understanding of employer racial policies, but also for a rational prediction of future trends.

(14) *Managerial Action and Policy*

Managers are affected by the various factors playing upon them in their decision making, but their own ideas, feelings, background, concepts, and prejudices operate not only as a result of the various factors set forth above, but independently also. The differences in racial policies among companies similarly situated attest to this fact. Throughout our discussions, we shall attempt to assess the role played by managerial action and policy in affecting the extent and nature of Negro employment.

FINAL INTRODUCTORY COMMENTS

The racial policies of American industry are affected by numerous internal and external pressures and variables. By examining the history and present status of Negro employment in some thirty industries, we believe that these racial policies can be better understood, that public policy in regard to manpower, resource allocation, and fair employment can be more intelligently directed. The six key industries studied in this volume include 32 companies that rank among the top 50 in the *Fortune* directory and almost 20 percent of the top 500. Their policies are not only representative of America's major manufacturing corporations but help set the pace for all industry. Before examining the policies of the six industries, it is helpful to take a broad overview of the position of Negroes in industry.

CHAPTER II.

An Overview of Negro Employment

The overall position of Negroes in the economy provides the institutional background for the racial policies of industry. In this chapter, we take a broad look at Negro population and its regional and urban concentration; at relative Negro income, economic, and educational status; and at occupational change and status. A final section provides a brief review of government attempts to improve the job and occupational status of Negroes.

POPULATION AND CONCENTRATION

Negroes have comprised 10 to 12 percent of America's population since the turn of the century (Table 1). Initially the bulk of the black population lived in the South—as late as 1940, 77 percent resided in the one-time Confederate states and in the neighboring border

TABLE 1. *Total and Negro Population United States, 1900-1969*

	Population (millions) Total	Negro	Percent Negro
1900	76.0	8.8	12
1940	131.7	12.9	10
1950	150.5	15.0	10
1960	178.5	18.8	11
1968	198.2	22.0	11
1969	199.8	22.3	11

Source: U. S. Bureau of the Census

Note: Data exclude Alaska and Hawaii prior to 1960, armed forces overseas for all years and armed forces living in barracks for 1966-1969. 1969, 5-quarter average centered on January 1969.

areas.[3] Since 1940, the proportion of Negroes in the South has declined steadily, so that a bare majority now reside there.

The first mass migration of Negroes northward occurred during World War I. Prior to that time, those Negroes who did live in the North were primarily service employees in cities. In the South, however, Negroes (and whites) were mainly a rural population. Southern Negroes were traditionally employed in construction, including the skilled trowel trades (bricklaying, cement finishing, and plastering) and to a lesser extent, painting and carpentry, in tobacco factories, on the railroads, in forests product industries, in the southern Appalachian coal mines, and in the steel mills of the Birmingham area; for the most part, however, southern Negroes labored in the fields. When northern industry turned to the surplus labor pool of the South after World War I cut off the supply of immigrant labor, thousands of Negroes (and whites) moved from southern farms to northern cities and to urban living. In such industries as meat packing, steel, and automobiles, Negroes thus won their first foothold in northern manufacturing jobs.[4]

Migration continued throughout the 1920's as southern Negroes sought to escape the poverty and harshness of southern rural living, but slowed down considerably as a result of the depression of the 1930's. World War II, however, opened the doors for jobs for Negroes to a greater extent than ever before. Migration from the South reached a peak during this period as industries and jobs were opened to blacks in war material producing plants by a combination of patriotism, labor market needs, and increased government intervention.

Since World War II, the outmigration of Negroes from the South has continued, but at a slower pace. Moreover, despite the loss of three million blacks, between 1940 and 1964, in the South their number

3. Regional definitions in this chapter follow those of the Bureau of the Census. See Table 2 for details.

4. This chapter makes use of a number of studies of the U. S. Bureau of Census and the U.S. Bureau of Labor Statistics, particularly: *The Negroes in the United States,* Bulletin No. 1511, U.S. Bureau of Labor Statistics, 1966. *Social and Economic Conditions of Negroes in the United States,* jointly. (BLS) Report No. 332 and Census Current Population Report Series P-23, No. 24, 1967; *Recent Trends in Social and Economic Conditions of Negroes in the United States,* BLS Report No. 347 and Current Population Series P-23, No. 26, 1968, *The Social and Economic Status of Negroes in the United States, 1969,* BLS Report No. 375 and Current Population Series P-23, No. 29, 1969; all published in Washington, D. C., by the Government Printing Office; Claire C. Hodge, "The Negro Job Situation: Has It Improved?" *Monthly Labor Review,* Vol. XCII (January 1969), pp. 20-28.

has increased in recent years. The South, where 20 percent of the population is black, retains a narrow majority of the nation's Negroes (Table 2).

The overwhelming number of Negroes, both North and South, are city dwellers. By 1960, six cities—New York, Chicago, Philadelphia, Detroit, Washington, and Los Angeles—had approximately 20 percent of the nation's black population. Of these, only Washington, a

TABLE 2. *Percent Distribution of the Negro Population by Region United States, 1940-1969*

Region	1940	1950	1960	1966	1968	1969
United States	100	100	100	100	100	100
South	77	68	60	55	53	52
North	22	28	34	37	40	41
Northeast	11	13	16	17	18	19
North Central	11	15	18	20	22	21
West	1	4	6	8	8	7

Source: U.S. Bureau of the Census

Notes: Data before 1960 exclude Alaska and Hawaii. Percentages may not add to totals because of rounding. Regional definitions used in Part One are the standard Bureau of the Census definitions as follows:

Northeast:

New England: Connecticut, Massachusetts, Maine, New Hampshire, Rhode Island, Vermont.

Middle Atlantic: New Jersey, New York, Pennsylvania.

North Central:

East North Central: Illinois, Indiana, Michigan, Ohio, Wisconsin.

West North Central: Iowa, Kansas, Minnesota, Missouri, Nebraska, North Dakota, South Dakota.

South:

South Atlantic: Delaware, District of Columbia, Florida, Georgia, Maryland, North Carolina, South Carolina, Virginia, West Virginia.

East South Central: Alabama, Kentucky, Mississippi, Tennessee.

West South Central: Arkansas, Louisiana, Oklahoma, Texas.

West:

Mountain: Arizona, Colorado, Idaho, Montana, Nevada, New Mexico, Utah, Wyoming.

Pacific: Alaska, California, Hawaii, Oregon, Washington.

TABLE 3. *Population by Race, in Each of the Thirty Largest Cities in the United States 1950-1970*

(In Order of 1960 Negro Population)

City	United States Census						CRM Projection		
	1950			1960			1970		
	Total	Negro	Percent Negro	Total	Negro	Percent Negro	Total	Negro	Percent Negro
	Figures in Thousands								
New York City, N. Y.	7,892	748	9.5	7,782	1,088	14.0	8,100	1,500	18.5
Chicago, Illinois	3,621	492	13.6	3,550	813	22.9	3,610	1,150	31.9
Los Angeles, Calif.	1,970	171	8.7	2,479	335	13.5	3,000	700	23.3
Philadelphia, Pa.	2,072	376	18.1	2,003	529	26.4	2,200	700	31.8
Detroit, Michigan	1,850	301	16.3	1,670	482	28.9	1,700	800	47.1
Baltimore, Md.	950	225	23.7	939	326	34.7	920	432	47.0
Houston, Texas	596	125	21.0	938	215	22.9	1,140	310	27.2
Cleveland, Ohio	915	148	16.2	876	251	28.7	805	305	37.9
Washington, D. C.	802	281	35.0	764	412	53.9	840	574	68.3
St. Louis, Mo.	857	154	18.0	750	214	28.5	700	320	45.7
Milwaukee, Wisc.	637	22	3.5	741	63	8.5	800	146	18.2
San Francisco, Calif.	775	44	5.7	740	74	10.0	750	126	16.8
Boston, Mass.	801	40	5.0	697	63	9.0	675	85	12.6
Dallas, Texas	434	57	13.1	680	129	19.0	800	200	25.0
New Orleans, La.	570	182	31.9	628	234	37.3	680	303	44.6

Pittsburgh, Pa.	677	82	12.1	604	101	16.7	610	126	20.7
San Antonio, Texas	408	29	7.1	588	42	7.1	720	72	10.0
San Diego, Calif.	334	15	4.5	573	34	5.9	723	72	10.0
Seattle, Wash.	468	16	3.4	557	27	4.8	647	56	8.7
Buffalo, New York	580	37	6.4	533	71	13.3	510	114	22.4
Cincinnati, Ohio	504	78	15.5	503	109	21.7	470	150	31.9
Memphis, Tenn.	396	147	37.1	498	184	36.9	580	226	39.0
Denver, Colo.	416	15	3.6	494	30	6.1	510	51	10.0
Atlanta, Ga.	331	121	36.6	487	186	38.2	540	212	39.3
Minneapolis, Minn.	522	7	1.3	483	12	2.5	450	21	4.7
Indianapolis, Ind.	427	64	15.0	476	98	20.6	500	145	29.0
Kansas City, Mo.	451	56	12.4	476	83	17.4	500	120	24.0
Columbus, Ohio	376	47	12.5	471	77	16.3	525	167	31.8
Phoenix, Ariz.	107	5	4.7	439	21	4.8	600	60	10.0
Newark, N. J.	439	75	17.1	405	138	34.1	405	185	45.7

Source: *The Negro Population: 1965 Estimates and 1970 Projections* (Peekskill, N. Y.: The Center for Research in Marketing Incorporated, 1967), Table 1. (It is believed that these estimates for Negro city population in 1970 are conservative.)

border city which is now two-thirds Negro, is not clearly in the North or West. The 1970 census of population may show that the cities of Cleveland, Detroit, and Newark, New Jersey, Baltimore, St. Louis, Atlanta, Memphis, New Orleans, and Richmond have populations that are either majority black or very close thereto. Table 3 shows the Negro population for the thirty largest cities for 1950 and 1960, and estimates for 1970. The impression of the authors, after nearly four years of field work in many of these cities, is that, if anything, the estimates for 1970 are likely to underestimate the proportion of Negroes.

The movement toward black majorities in a number of key cities has occurred despite evidence of a slowing down of the Negro in-migration.[5] This is because whites have been flocking into the suburbs almost without pause since World War II. Thus in 1966, 56 percent of all Negroes lived in central cities. On the other hand, whites live predominantly outside of metropolitan central cities—either in suburbs or in small towns so that in 1966 only about 25 percent of the white population dwelt in the central city area.[6] Despite a leveling off of the Negro population in central cities between 1966 and 1968, and an increase in the number of Negroes in the suburbs, these concentrations are likely to endure for many years. (See Table 4.)

Negro population concentration is more intense than just in the center cities:

> Within the central cities, the main problem is not number or proportion of Negroes, but their spatial arrangement and economic status. In most large cities in 1960, half or more of the Negroes lived in census tracts in which the population was 90 percent or more Negro and in which population density per square mile was especially high. Besides being confined to a disproportionately small space within the city, the Negro tracts were usually contiguous or formed one or more pockets within the city. Color was the only common characteristic of these pockets of Negro residence. Other socioeconomic characteristics of the population were usually heterogeneous, for example, the range of income and education.
>
> The spatial confinement of urban Negroes to densely populated areas raises serious economic issues for the Nation. Because of segregation, the residents of Negro neighborhoods tend to be more socially and economically heterogeneous, but the choices available to them as consumers are more limited and more homo-

5. *Recent Trends in Social and Economic Conditions of Negroes . . ., op. cit.*, pp. 3-4.
6. *Social and Economic Conditions of Negroes . . ., op. cit.*, p. 9.

geneous than among whites. Segregation frequently limits the Negro consumer in his choice of such items as housing, public service, transportation, supermarket facilities, recreation, banking, insurance, medical and legal services, and many others. Such artificial narrowing of consumer choice can and often does drastically reduce real income and curtail important increments to human, business, and community resource development.[7]

From an employment point of view, the concentration of Negroes in the center city areas is no longer advantageous. Since World War II, industry, particularly manufacturing enterprise, has tended to move away from the older inner cities of the Northeast and Midwest, and to seek location either in other parts of the country or in the suburbs

TABLE 4. *Population and Population Change by Location Inside and Outside Metropolitan Areas, 1950-1969*

	Total Population (in millions)							
	Negro				White			
Region	1960	1966	1968	1969	1960	1966	1968	1969
United States	18.8	21.5	21.9	22.3	158.1	170.9	173.7	175.3
Metropolitan areas	12.2	14.8	15.0	15.6	99.2	109.3	110.7	111.7
Central cities	9.7	12.1	11.8	12.3	47.5	46.6	45.8	45.3
Suburbs[a]	2.5	2.7	3.2	3.3	51.7	62.7	64.9	66.4
Smaller cities, towns and rural	6.7	6.7	7.0	6.7	58.9	61.6	63.0	63.6

	Population Change, 1950-1969							
	Negro				White			
Region	1950-1960	1960-1966	1966-1968	1968-1969	1950-1960	1960-1966	1966-1968	1968-1969
United States	+3.8	+2.6	+0.4	+0.4	+23.7	+12.8	+2.8	+1.6
Metropolitan areas	+3.8	+2.6	+0.2	+0.6	+19.3	+10.2	+1.3	+1.0
Central cities	+3.2	+2.4	−0.2	+0.5	+ 2.2	− 0.8	−0.8	−0.5
Suburbs[a]	+0.6	+0.2	+0.4	+0.1	+17.2	+11.0	+2.2	+1.5
Smaller cities, towns and rural	[b]	[b]	+0.2	−0.3	+ 4.3	+ 2.7	+1.5	+0.6

Source: U.S. Bureau of the Census

a. Comprises the part of metropolitan area outside of central cities.

b. Less than 50,000

7. *The Negroes in the United States, op. cit.*, pp. 3 and 15.

or rural areas surrounding these cities.[8] Moreover, in other sections of the country, also, industry has tended to move away from cities or to locate new facilities in suburban or rural areas. Higher city taxes, the decline of urban transit, the difficulties and high costs of automobile operations and parking in cities, higher city labor costs, the need to abandon old, multi-story, high cost structures for more economical one story buildings, and the westward movement of the population, have all contributed to these changes.

A further disturbing factor related to the Negro inner city population concentration and the flight of jobs from the cities is the character of jobs which are expanding within cities. Such jobs tend to be those for which women are employed, particularly white collar jobs in such key service industries as banking, insurance, and real estate. The problems of the Negro family have been well recounted elsewhere.[9] In 1968, 26.4 percent of all nonwhite families had a female head whereas only 8.9 percent of all white families were so constituted.[10] The historic greater ease of Negro women than men to find jobs thus tends to be exacerbated by the concentration of Negroes in the cities and the character of jobs available therein.

INCOME, ECONOMIC AND EDUCATIONAL STATUS

In 1968, despite sharp rises in relative income, Negro families had median income equal to only 60 percent of white income. (Table 5.) The greatest disparity between Negro and white family income is in the South where it was 54 percent of white income in 1967 and 1968; the least disparity is found in the North Central and West where the Negro median is three-quarters or more of the white (Table 6).

A much greater percentage of Negroes than whites live in what Bureau of the Census terms a poverty situation (Table 7). A basic reason for this lower income situation is, of course, the relative disadvantaged educational status among Negroes. In 1870, the nonwhite[11] population was nearly 80 percent illiterate, as compared

8. For a thorough analysis of these trends, see Daniel Creamer, *Manufacturing Employment by Type of Location*. Studies in Business Economics No. 106 (New York: National Industrial Conference Board, No. 106, 1969).

9. *Ibid.*, and note 2, *supra*.

10. *Recent Trends . . ., op. cit.*, p. 22.

11. Negroes comprise about 92 percent of all nonwhites and nonwhite data are used for much statistical analysis relating to blacks.

TABLE 5. *Median Income of Nonwhite Families as a Percent of White Family Income, 1950-1968*

	All Nonwhite	Negro[a]
1950	54	a
1951	53	a
1952	57	a
1953	56	a
1954	56	a
1955	55	a
1956	53	a
1957	54	a
1958	51	a
1959	52	a
1960	55	a
1961	53	a
1962	53	a
1963	53	a
1964	56	54
1965	55	54
1966	60	58
1967	62	59
1968	63	60

Source: U.S. Bureau of the Census.

a. The annual figures shown are based on the Current Population Survey. The percent of Negro to white median family income (instead of the percent of nonwhite to white as shown) is available from this survey only from 1964.

TABLE 6. *Family Income in 1968, and Comparison of Negro and White Family Income, 1965, 1966, 1967, and 1968 by Region*

	Median family income, 1968		Negro income as a percent of white			
	Negro	White	1965	1966	1967	1968
United States	$5,359	$8,936	54	58	59	60
Northeast	6,460	9,318	64	68	66	69
North Central	6,910	9,259	74	74	78	75
South	4,278	7,963	49	50	54	54
West	7,506	9,462	69	72	74	80

Source: U.S. Bureau of the Census.

TABLE 7. *Persons Below the Poverty Level,[a] 1959-1968*

	Percent		Number (in millions)	
	Nonwhite	White	Nonwhite	White
1959	56	18	11.0	28.5
1960	56	18	11.5	28.3
1961	56	17	11.7	27.9
1962	56	16	12.0	26.7
1963	51	15	11.2	25.2
1964	50	15	11.1	25.0
1965	47	13	10.7	22.5
1966	42	12	9.7	20.8
Based on revised methodology:[b]				
1966	40	11	9.2	19.3
1967	37	11	8.8	19.0
1968	33	10	8.0	17.4

Source: U. S. Bureau of the Census.

a. The poverty concept is based on a revised definition adopted in 1969 (for a detailed explanation, see Special Studies, Series P-23, No. 28). As applied to 1968 incomes, the poverty threshold for a nonfarm family of four was $3,553.

b. Reflects improvements in statistical procedures used in processing the income data.

with 11.5 percent of the white population; by 1959, the figures were 7.5 percent for nonwhites, 1.6 percent for whites.[12] The sharp rise in nonwhite illiteracy has continued. Nevertheless, the white-nonwhite educational difference has persisted, even though it has decreased in recent years. Table 8 shows that among whites and nonwhites, median years of school completed was greater among those in the labor force than among persons not working or seeking work for both whites and nonwhites, but that in all cases, educational attainment, measured by years in school, was greater for whites than for nonwhites in 1965. Table 8 also shows that the disparities were greatest in farm areas and in the South.

Since 1965, Negroes have continued to improve their educational preparation and status, but their educational attainments continue to lag behind whites. Moreover, years of schooling alone do not tell the whole story. Still segregated southern schools, many of those in center cities of the North, and predominantly black colleges are, by and large, distinctly inferior to schools and colleges which most whites attend. The average Negro student in the final year of high school is

12. *The Negroes in the United States, op. cit.*, p. 194.

TABLE 8. *Educational Attainment of the Population 18 Years Old and Over, by Labor Force Status, Color, Sex, Residence, and Region, March 1965*

Years of school completed, residence, and region	Male: In labor force: Non-white	Male: In labor force: White	Male: Not in labor force: Non-white	Male: Not in labor force: White	Female: In labor force: Non-white	Female: In labor force: White	Female: Not in labor force: Non-white	Female: Not in labor force: White
	Percent distribution, by years of school completed							
Total								
Number (in thousands)	4,603	41,651	1,030	8,763	3,262	21,607	3,383	34,727
Percent	100.0	100.0	100.0	100.0	100.0	100.0	100.0	100.0
No. school years completed	2.1	0.5	12.6	4.8	0.9	0.3	5.0	1.8
Elementary:								
1 to 4 years	13.3	2.7	24.8	10.2	5.9	1.4	13.4	3.8
5 to 7 years	16.0	7.7	18.1	16.9	13.6	5.0	19.7	9.9
8 years	10.4	13.1	9.5	21.1	11.3	10.3	12.0	15.3
High school:								
1 to 3 years	24.4	18.8	16.1	14.4	25.7	17.7	25.8	19.3
4 years	21.4	33.2	11.2	14.7	28.6	43.9	18.0	34.8
College:								
1 to 3 years	6.0	11.0	5.6	12.8	6.3	11.0	4.4	10.2
4 years	3.7	7.7	1.1	2.9	5.6	7.1	1.4	4.1
5 years or more	2.7	5.4	1.0	2.2	2.2	3.3	0.4	0.9
	Median school years completed, by residence and region							
Total	10.0	12.2	7.1	8.9	11.1	12.3	9.0	12.0
Nonfarm	10.3	12.3	7.0	8.9	11.2	12.4	9.2	12.0
United States, excluding South	11.1	12.3	8.3	8.9	12.0	12.4	10.2	12.2
South	9.1	12.1	5.6	8.8	10.1	12.3	8.2	11.4
Farm	6.1	9.4	(1)	8.5	8.5	12.1	6.9	10.2

Source: U.S. Bureau of Labor Statistics. Data are unpublished from the March 1965 supplement to the Current Population Survey.

(1) Median not shown where base is less than 100,000.

Note: Because of rounding, sums of individual items may not equal totals.

TABLE 9. *Median Income of Men 25 to 54 Years Old by Educational Attainment, 1968*

		Median income, 1968		Negro income as a percent of white
		Negro	White	
Elementary:	Total	$3,900	$5,844	67
	Less than 8 years	3,558	5,131	69
	8 years	4,499	6,452	70
High school:	Total	5,580	7,852	71
	1 to 3 years	5,255	7,229	73
	4 years	5,801	8,154	71
College:	Total	7,481	10,149	74

Source: U.S. Bureau of the Census.

performing at a ninth grade level.[13] Our studies of racial employment problems in various industries in this and succeeding volumes will repeatedly note that lack of education and training continue to block opportunity and the fulfillment of greater equal employment goals and aspirations.

Moreover, where Negroes do attain education, it does not mean that income will be equalized. Table 9 shows that at each educational level, Negro men have less income than do white men. Moreover, the disparity is greatest at the college level. The reasons include the inferior character of much Negro education, discrimination in employment, and the fact that college educated Negroes are disproportionately underrepresented in high-paying jobs in industry and overrepresented in such lower-paying fields as teaching and the ministry.

EMPLOYMENT AND UNEMPLOYMENT

Despite great progress since 1960, nonwhite unemployment rates continue to average about double those of whites, as they have since 1954 (Table 10). Thus in 1958, the bottom of the most severe post-World War II recession, white unemployment averaged 6.1 percent of the civilian labor force, nonwhite 12.6 percent; in the very prosperous year of 1967, the percentages were 3.4 and 7.4 respectively. Among married men—the largest component of both the nonwhite and white labor force—who have the lowest unemployment rates, the

13. *Social and Economic Conditions of Negroes . . . , op. cit.*, p. 49.

ratio holds: 1.6 percent unemployed for whites in 1967, 3.2 percent for nonwhites. Among teenagers, who have the highest unemployment rates, the ratios in 1967 were 10.2 percent white unemployment, and an astronomical 26.4 percent nonwhite.[14] The double relationship of nonwhite unemployment to white endured through the decade of the 1960's.

The reasons for this disparity of joblessness are many. One—disadvantaged educational attainment—has just been noted. We have also pointed out that the center city concentration of Negroes is no longer advantageous to their search for work. In the following section we shall further note that Negroes are concentrated in those labor force occupations that are expanding the least. Throughout this and the succeeding volumes, we shall examine the role of discrimination in contributing to unequal employment opportunity, and hence

TABLE 10. *Unemployment Rates,[a] 1948-1969*

	Nonwhite	White	Ratio: nonwhite to white
1948	5.2	3.2	1.6
1949	8.9	5.6	1.6
1950	9.0	4.9	1.8
1951	5.3	3.1	1.7
1952	5.4	2.8	1.9
1953	4.5	2.7	1.7
1954	9.9	5.0	2.0
1955	8.7	3.9	2.2
1956	8.3	3.6	2.3
1957	7.9	3.8	2.1
1958	12.6	6.1	2.1
1959	10.7	4.8	2.2
1960	10.2	4.9	2.1
1961	12.4	6.0	2.1
1962	10.9	4.9	2.2
1963	10.8	5.0	2.2
1964	9.6	4.6	2.1
1965	8.1	4.1	2.0
1966	7.3	3.3	2.2
1967	7.4	3.4	2.2
1968	6.7	3.2	2.1
1969	6.5	3.2	2.0

Source: U.S. Bureau of Labor Statistics.
a. The unemployment rate is the percent unemployed in the civilian labor force.

14. *Recent Trends . . ., op. cit.*, pp. 12-13.

to the disparate unemployment rates. In addition, as explained by the U. S. Bureau of Labor Statistics:

> . . . [a] greater need for income keeps a higher proportion of nonwhite workers engaged in the search for work, even when conditions are not favorable for finding it. Nonwhite women are much more likely than are white women to be heads of their families. And in families with husbands at their head (the usual situation), nonwhite women tend to participate in the labor force at higher rates than white women, regardless of income.
>
> * * *
>
> . . . the growth of job opportunities has attracted many youths into seeking jobs, whether or not they are in school. The nonwhite youths are not as likely to be seeking work as the white youths. But when they are, they are more likely to need and hold full-time jobs or to work long hours. Well over one-third of the nonwhite teenagers lived in families with less than $3,000 income in March 1965. The median income for the families of unemployed nonwhite teenagers was $3,667. For the families of the employed youths, the median rose less than $1,000. Most white teenagers, in contrast, come from families with incomes above $7,000.
>
> Unemployment rates are especially high for all youths. When the disadvantages of inexperience and limited training are compounded by the results of discrimination and impoverishment, the barriers to employment become formidable. In the early months of 1966, for example, 25 to 30 percent of the nonwhite girls who sought work were unable to find it. This was the highest unemployment rate of any group in the labor force but it was scarcely more severe than the rate for the nonwhite boys, which ranged between 20 and 25 percent. These rates for nonwhite youngsters exceed those for white youths two- to three-fold. The difference was especially pronounced in the 18- and 19-year age groups.
>
> Despite the frustrations of the job search, few nonwhite teenagers withdraw from the job market. In 1965, only 57,000 were neither in school nor in the labor force. Of this group, many were girls who were married or working at home.[15]

In addition to being unemployed at twice the rates of whites, nonwhites are much more likely to be underemployed or, insofar as men are concerned, not working or looking for work. On the other hand, nonwhite women, who often must assume family support, are more likely than white women to be labor force participants.[16]

15. *The Negroes in the United States, op. cit.,* pp. 21-22.
16. *Social and Economic Conditions Among Negroes . . ., op. cit.,* pp. 34-36. *Recent Trends in Social and Economic Conditions . . .,* op. cit., p. 17.

Despite the persistence of the unfavorable white-nonwhite employment ratio, Negro employment, like total employment, made substantial gains during the 1960's, but Negro employment had a faster rate of growth. In 1967, employment of Negroes, age 16 and over averaged 8 million, a 20 percent increase over a decade earlier. The number of Negroes employed increased by about 400,000 or 5.4 percent from 1957 to 1962, and by approximately one million, or 14.4 percent from 1962 to 1967. In both periods, this represented a faster rate of growth than that of white workers.[17]

The major factors contributing to this sharp rise in Negro jobs were, first of all, the exceptional increase in the number of job opportunities which featured most of the decade of the 1960's; the emphasis on civil rights and training of the disadvantaged, especially since 1964; and the relative unavailability of white workers and the fact that, as a result of high nonwhite unemployment as late as 1962, the relative availability of Negroes to supply the accelerated demand for labor during this period.

There were other sanguine developments in the employment situation of Negroes during the 1960's. One was the drop in long term unemployment. In 1962, about 30 percent of the Negro unemployed —some 300,000 persons—were out of a job fifteen weeks or more. By 1967, the number of such long term unemployed had been reduced by two-thirds so that only one-sixth of the Negro unemployed were without jobs fifteen weeks or more. About the same number of white unemployed in 1967 were jobless for long terms also.[18]

Negroes also gained substantially as full-time workers, and those on short work weeks (less than 35 hours) declined substantially after 1962. More than 90 percent of the increase in the total number of Negroes at work occurred on full-time job schedules (35 hours or more). By 1967, the number of Negro nonagricultural workers on full-time schedules was 5.8 million, as compared with 4.7 million in 1962. Meanwhile the number of Negro nonagricultural workers employed part time because of economic reasons (excluding personal preference) declined from 615,000 to 475,000.[19]

The decade of the 1960's also saw Negroes move in large numbers into those industries which are generally considered to offer the best

17. Hodge, *op. cit.*, p. 20.
18. *Ibid.*
19. *Ibid.*, pp. 20-21.

jobs in terms either of pay, advancement, security, or status, or on all four criteria. For example, the number of Negroes in the fields of education, public administration, and durable goods manufacturing grew by one-third or more, rising from 1.3 million in 1962 to 2.1 million in 1967. This was an increase of nearly 60 percent as compared with an increase of only 25 percent for whites. During the same period, Negro employment in such traditional (and low pay, prestige, and status) areas as agricultural laborer and private household domestic service declined 46 percent and 19.7 percent respectively.[20]

OCCUPATIONAL STATUS

Between 1940 and 1960, Negroes made significant gains in improving their occupational status, but in some key areas they did not advance as rapidly as whites. For example, Negroes comprised 4.6 percent of salaried workers in 1940, but only 3.4 percent by 1960 despite the fact that over the twenty year period the number of Negro white collar persons increased by 75,000. The precipitous decline in Negro farmers, farm proprietors, and farm managers without a sufficiently offsetting increase in the other white collar areas in which Negroes, despite some gains in the clerical group, barely held their own accounts for this proportional loss. (See Tables 11, 12, 13.)

Between 1940 and 1960, Negro professionals and technical employees won their first foothold in industry, but most Negroes so classified were teachers, ministers, social workers, and to a lesser extent lawyers and medical doctors. The great expansion of engineers and scientists in industry during this period continued in an overwhelming ratio to be a source of white employment; and few Negroes took engineering degrees. Likewise, Negroes as late as 1960 were generally barred from the executive suite of large corporations so that their managerial positions were still heavily in Negro run enterprises and small business catering to a black clientele.

During these two decades, Negroes made much greater progress in the blue collar job sectors. Their percentage of craftsmen rose from 2.6 percent to 4.3 percent; and their share of operatives and other semiskilled workers almost doubled, going from 5.6 percent to 10.1 percent (Tables 11, 12, and 13). On the other hand, in 1960 Negroes

20. *Ibid.*, pp. 21-22.

TABLE 11. *Employed Persons by Race, Sex, and Occupational Group, United States, 1940*

Occupational Group	All Employees			Male			Female		
	Total	Negro	Percent Negro	Total	Negro	Percent Negro	Total	Negro	Percent Negro
Professional and technical	3,345,048	119,200	3.6	1,875,387	53,312	2.8	1,469,661	65,888	4.5
Managers, officials, and proprietors, incl. farm	8,892,901	714,849	8.0	8,317,482	657,719	7.9	575,419	57,130	9.9
Managers, off., and prop.	3,749,287	48,154	1.3	3,325,767	37,240	1.1	423,520	10,914	2.6
Farmers and managers	5,143,614	666,695	13.0	4,991,715	620,479	12.4	151,899	46,216	30.4
Clerical and sales	7,517,630	79,322	1.1	4,360,648	58,557	1.3	3,156,982	20,765	0.7
Total white collar	19,755,579	913,371	4.6	14,553,517	769,588	5.3	5,202,062	143,783	2.8
Craftsmen and foremen	5,055,722	132,110	2.6	4,949,132	129,736	2.6	106,590	2,374	2.2
Operatives	8,252,277	464,195	5.6	6,205,898	368,005	5.9	2,046,379	96,190	4.7
Service workers	5,569,648	1,525,737	27.4	2,338,926	447,990	19.2	3,230,722	1,077,747	33.4
Private household workers	2,111,314	1,003,508	47.5	142,231	85,566	60.2	1,969,083	917,942	46.6
Service workers, excl. private household	3,458,334	522,229	15.1	2,196,695	362,424	16.5	1,261,639	159,805	12.7
Laborers	6,154,138	1,416,912	23.0	5,735,698	1,205,404	21.0	418,440	211,508	50.5
Farm laborers and foremen	3,090,010	780,312	25.3	2,770,005	581,763	21.0	320,005	198,549	62.0
Others	3,064,128	636,600	20.8	2,965,693	623,641	21.0	98,435	12,959	13.2
Total blue collar	25,031,785	3,538,954	14.1	19,229,654	2,151,135	11.2	5,802,131	1,387,819	23.9
Occupations not reported	378,719	26,743	7.1	244,734	16,072	6.6	133,985	10,671	8.0
Total	45,166,083	4,479,068	9.9	34,027,905	2,936,795	8.6	11,138,178	1,542,273	13.8

Source: *U. S. Census of Population, 1940:* Vol. III, *The Labor Force,* Part 1, Table 62.

TABLE 12. *Employed Persons by Race, Sex, and Occupational Group, United States, 1950*

	All Employees			Male			Female		
Occupational Group	Total	Negro	Percent Negro	Total	Negro	Percent Negro	Total	Negro	Percent Negro
Professional and technical	4,909,241	180,164	3.7	2,970,256	75,436	2.5	1,938,985	104,728	5.4
Managers, officials, and proprietors, inc. farm	9,323,718	587,438	6.3	8,530,569	531,932	6.2	793,149	55,506	7.0
Managers, off., and prop.	5,017,465	92,070	1.8	4,340,687	67,513	1.6	676,778	24,557	3.6
Farmers and managers	4,306,253	495,368	11.5	4,189,882	464,419	11.1	116,371	30,949	26.6
Clerical	6,894,374	181,020	2.6	2,602,610	106,765	4.1	4,291,764	74,255	1.7
Salesworkers	3,926,510	64,186	1.6	2,596,786	38,694	1.5	1,329,724	25,492	1.9
Total white collar	25,053,843	1,012,808	4.0	16,700,221	752,827	4.5	8,353,622	259,981	3.1
Craftsmen and foremen	7,772,560	281,002	3.6	7,537,016	269,373	3.6	235,544	11,629	4.9
Operatives	11,146,220	1,012,362	9.1	8,127,433	738,362	9.1	3,018,787	274,000	9.1
Service workers	5,695,169	1,625,590	28.5	2,446,566	500,144	20.4	3,248,603	1,125,446	34.6
Private household workers	1,407,466	809,659	57.5	73,156	36,069	49.3	1,334,310	773,590	58.0
Service workers excl. private household	4,287,703	815,931	19.0	2,373,410	464,075	19.6	1,914,293	351,856	18.4
Laborers	5,817,026	1,356,357	23.3	5,240,711	1,188,286	22.7	576,315	168,071	29.2
Farm laborers and foremen	2,399,794	499,743	20.8	1,950,458	360,086	18.5	449,336	139,657	31.1
Others	3,417,232	856,614	25.1	3,290,253	828,200	25.2	126,979	28,414	22.4
Total blue collar	30,430,975	4,275,311	14.0	23,351,726	2,696,165	11.5	7,079,249	1,579,146	22.3
Occupations not reported	740,522	81,534	11.0	458,229	50,705	11.1	282,293	30,829	10.9
Total	56,225,340	5,369,653	9.6	40,510,176	3,499,697	8.6	15,715,164	1,869,956	11.9

Source: *U.S. Census of Population, 1950:* Vol. II, *Characteristics of the Population,* Part 1, Table 128.

TABLE 13. *Employed Persons by Race, Sex, and Occupational Group, United States, 1960*

	All Employees			Male			Female		
Occupational Group	Total	Negro	Percent Negro	Total	Negro	Percent Negro	Total	Negro	Percent Negro
Professional and technical	7,232,410	287,969	4.0	4,479,358	112,661	2.5	2,753,052	175,308	6.4
Managers, officials and proprietors, incl. farm	7,915,227	256,726	3.2	7,017,426	217,433	3.1	897,801	39,293	4.4
Managers, off., and prop.	5,409,543	87,950	1.6	4,629,842	63,193	1.4	779,701	24,757	3.2
Farmers and managers	2,505,684	168,776	6.7	2,387,584	154,240	6.5	118,100	14,536	12.3
Clerical	9,306,896	360,598	3.9	3,015,476	178,920	5.9	6,291,420	181,678	2.9
Sales workers	4,638,985	82,768	1.8	2,977,872	46,685	1.6	1,661,113	36,083	2.2
Total white collar	29,093,518	988,061	3.4	17,490,132	555,699	3.2	11,603,386	432,362	3.7
Craftsmen and foremen	8,741,292	372,463	4.3	8,488,777	356,586	4.2	252,515	15,877	6.3
Operatives	11,897,601	1,197,667	10.1	8,641,652	887,434	10.3	3,255,949	310,233	9.5
Service workers	7,170,788	1,943,259	27.1	2,659,736	535,230	20.1	4,511,052	1,408,029	31.2
Private household workers	1,725,826	915,494	53.0	61,063	27,288	44.7	1,664,763	888,206	53.4
Service workers, excl. private household	5,444,962	1,027,765	18.9	2,598,673	507,942	19.5	2,846,289	519,823	18.3
Laborers	4,552,338	1,094,814	24.0	4,199,707	1,001,692	23.9	352,631	93,122	26.4
Farm laborers and foremen	1,444,807	326,193	22.6	1,201,922	256,698	21.4	242,885	69,495	28.6
Laborers, exc. farm and mine	3,107,531	768,621	24.7	2,997,785	744,994	24.9	109,746	23,627	21.5
Total blue collar	32,362,019	4,608,203	14.2	23,989,872	2,780,942	11.6	8,372,147	1,827,261	21.8
Occupations not reported	3,183,719	502,825	15.8	1,986,951	307,308	15.5	1,196,768	195,517	16.3
Total	64,639,256	6,099,089	9.4	43,466,955	3,643,949	8.4	21,172,301	2,455,140	11.6

Source: *U.S. Census of Population, 1960:* PC(1) D, *Detailed Characteristics, U.S. Summary,* Table 205.

continued to be—as they had always been—overconcentrated as household domestics (53 percent) and as laborers (24 percent). In 1960 approximately 75 percent of all Negro employed persons were blue collar workers whereas less than 50 percent of the total work force was so classified. Yet it was the white collar areas that were expanding rapidly in the late 1940's and the 1950's.

The progress of Negro women paralleled that of Negro men between 1940 and 1960 in that they suffered severe losses in farming and continued to be over concentrated in household service and laboring jobs, and in blue collar as compared with white collar occupations. On the other hand, the large number of Negro teachers and those in clerical and in other heavily female occupations and professions rose sufficiently, in contrast to the situation for Negro males, so that proportion of Negro female white collar employees rose from 2.8 percent in 1940 to 3.7 in 1960. The Negro male salaried employee ratio, however, declined from 5.3 percent in 1940 to 3.2 percent in 1960, with the precipitous fall in the farm sector the prime factor.

The Negro Occupational Changes Since 1960

If progress was slow and uncertain between 1940 and 1960, it has been rapid and clear since then. Table 14 shows the annual average by occupation for nonwhite workers, 1957, 1962, and 1967. From 1962 to 1967, about one million nonwhite workers moved into the jobs that generally offer higher pay and status—professional, clerical, craftsmen, and operatives in the steel, automobile, and other durable goods manufacturing industries. In addition, there was a substantial increase in such semiskilled jobs as taxi drivers, deliverymen, and assemblers in nondurable goods industries—jobs which pay well and offer steady work.[21]

Many of the Negroes who achieved higher pay and status were upgraded from lower-paying jobs. In other cases, Negroes who formerly might have been compelled to settle for unskilled or menial work, were able to obtain better jobs. As a consequence, Negro employment in the less attractive, lower-paying, and less secure occupations declined by approximately 600,000 from 1962 to 1967. This included 200,000 household domestic laborers, 360,000 farm laborers, and 60,000 industrial laborers. In various service jobs, some more prestigious and skilled than others, Negro employment increased by about 230,000.

21. *Ibid.*, p. 21.

Negro men and women shared about equally in the gains among professionals. As would be expected, Negro women won most of the clerical gains and men those in managerial, craft, and durable goods occupations.

The gains made by Negroes since 1957 can be seen in Table 15, which sets forth the proportion of nonwhite workers by occupation for 1957, 1962, and 1967. Table 15 shows that Negroes made substantial progress in medical and health occupations and in the teaching profession, but experienced the least gains in managerial and sales occupations. Negroes also made substantial progress in the skilled crafts, in the protective services (policemen, firemen, and guards), and in operatives jobs. These data, of course, do not tell us whether Negroes are concentrated in the lower ranges of these occupational groups, or whether they are in the lower status and/or pay sectors of such groups. Even if that were the case, however, progress has been substantial.

Table 15 summarizes these changes since 1962 and relates them to the proportion of Negroes in the labor force. Before examining the data in Table 15, it is well to bear in mind the limits of this approach as set forth in a caveat published by the U.S. Bureau of Labor Statistics:

> The computation, of course, is useful only to provide a rough measure of relative gains in different occupations. There is no reason to expect the members of any one ethnic group to be distributed among occupations exactly like every other group; even if all racial discrimination in employment and all inequalities in educational and training opportunity were removed, the traditional interests, personal preferences, and geographic location of various ethnic groups might lead to a somewhat different mix of occupations. Keeping these qualifications in mind, however, one can compare the Negroes' proportion of jobs in each occupation with their proportion of total employment to give a rough measure of progress.[22]

Since two-thirds of the Negro increase in employment since 1962 was in the fast gaining white collar areas, the proportion of Negroes so-employed rose from 16.7 percent in 1962 to 22.9 percent in 1967. Nevertheless, Negroes still represented only 5.4 percent of all white collar workers in 1967, as compared with 4.0 percent in 1962, considerably below their proportionate share of such jobs.

22. *Ibid.*, pp. 21-22.

TABLE 14. *Nonwhite Workers by Occupation Annual Averages, 1957, 1962, and 1967*

(Numbers in thousands)

Occupation group	1957[1,2]	1962[1]	1967	Change Percent 1957-1962	Change Percent 1962-1967
Total, 16 years of age and over	6,647	7,004	8,011	5.4	14.4
Total, 14 years of age and over	6,749	7,097	—	5.2	12.9[3]
Professional, technical, and kindred	246	373	592	51.6	58.7
Medical and health	42	72	120	71.4	66.7
Teachers, excluding college	88	138	202	56.8	46.4
Other	116	163	271	40.5	66.3
Managers, officials, and proprietors	140	188	209	34.3	11.2
Salaried	35	77	115	120.0	49.4
Self-employed, retail trade	61	59	51	−3.3	−13.6
Self-employed, excluding retail trade	44	52	43	18.2	−17.3
Clerical	401	512	899	27.7	75.6
Stenographers, typists, and secretaries	80	95	163	18.8	71.6
Other	321	417	736	29.9	76.5
Sales	78	115	138	47.4	20.0
Retail trade	62	77	99	24.2	28.6
Other	16	38	39	137.5	2.6
Craftsmen and foremen	380	427	617	12.4	44.5
Carpenters	35	44	52	25.7	18.2
Construction excluding carpenters	92	111	157	20.7	41.4
Mechanics and repairmen	119	133	192	11.8	44.4
Metal craftsmen excluding mechanics	35	36	69	2.9	91.7
Other craftsmen	76	76	100	0.0	31.6
Foremen, not elsewhere classified	23	27	49	17.4	81.5
Operatives and kindred workers	1,411	1,412	1,882	0.1	33.3
Drivers and deliverymen	314	303	354	−3.5	16.8
Other	1,097	1,110	1,528	1.2	37.7
Durable goods manufacturing	342	359	575	5.0	60.2
Nondurable goods manufacturing	286	306	484	7.0	58.2
Other industries	469	445	469	−5.1	5.4
Nonfarm laborers	1,007	962	899	−4.5	−6.5
Construction	—	225	197	—	−12.4
Manufacturing	—	264	285	—	8.0
Other industries	—	473	416	—	−12.1

TABLE 14. *Nonwhite Workers by Occupation Annual Averages, 1957, 1962, and 1967 (continued)*

(Numbers in thousands)

Occupation group	1957[1,2]	1962[1]	1967	Change Percent 1957-1962	Change Percent 1962-1967
Service workers	2,159	2,326	2,353	7.7	1.2
Private households	1,008	1,040	835	3.2	−19.7
Service workers, excluding private household	1,151	1,286	1,519	11.7	18.1
Protective service workers	32	37	67	15.6	81.1
Waiters, cooks, bartenders	239	253	304	5.9	20.2
Other service workers	880	996	1,149	13.2	15.4
Farm workers	927	782	423	−15.6	−45.9
Farmers and farm managers	276	195	107	−29.3	−45.1
Farm laborers and foremen	651	587	317	−9.8	−46.0
Paid	463	444	281	−4.1	−36.7
Unpaid family workers	188	143	36	−23.9	−74.8

Source: *Monthly Labor Review,* Vol. XCII (January 1969), p. 22.

1. Beginning in 1967, occupational data cover persons 16 years of age and over. Prior to 1967, occupational data have not been revised to exclude persons 14-15 years of age except for the figures on total employment shown here for comparison with 1967 total employment.
2. 1957 averages based on observations for January, April, July, and October; 1962 and 1967 are based on 12-month averages.
3. Based on change between 1962 including persons 14 years of age and over, and 1967 including persons 16 years and over.

Note: Dashes indicate data not available.

Within the professional group, Negro advances were concentrated in the teaching and medical and health professions. Negro engineers and scientists are still quite scarce and therefore Negro professionals in industrial employment continue to be relatively scarce. On the other hand, Negro clerical employees more than doubled in these five years—from 400,000 to 900,000. These are found largely in industry, but government is also a major employer.

Little progress has been made in the managerial and sales field—about a 25,000 increase each since 1962. Both require experience and training not often found—but increasingly more so—among black people. In addition, we shall note in many of the industry studies in

TABLE 15. *Nonwhite Workers as a Proportion of All Workers in Higher Status Occupations*

Occupation	Nonwhite workers as a proportion of all workers in the occupation: Percent 1962	Percent 1967	Increase, 1962-67 (Percentage points)	Increase in proportion of nonwhite workers required to reach 10.8 percent of all workers in occupation[1] (Percentage points)	Actual increase, 1962-67, as a percent of the increase required to reach 10.8 percent (Percent)
Professional, technical, and kindred workers	4.6	6.0	1.4	6.2	23
Medical and health	5.3	7.6	2.3	5.5	42
Teachers, except college	8.1	9.4	1.3	2.7	48
Others	3.3	4.4	1.1	7.5	15
Managers, officials, and proprietors	2.5	2.8	0.3	8.3	4
Salaried	1.9	2.2	0.3	8.9	3
Self-employed, retail trade	3.7	4.7	1.0	7.1	14
Self-employed, other	2.9	3.8	0.9	7.9	11
Clerical and kindred workers	5.1	7.3	2.2	5.7	39
Stenographers, typists and secretaries	3.8	5.1	1.3	7.0	19
Others	5.5	8.0	2.5	5.3	47
Sales workers	2.6	3.0	0.4	8.2	5
Retail trade	3.0	3.6	0.6	7.8	8
Other	2.1	2.2	0.1	8.7	1
Craftsmen, foremen, and kindred workers	4.9	6.3	1.4	5.9	24
Carpenters	5.4	6.2	0.8	5.4	15
Construction craftsmen except carpenters	6.5	8.2	1.7	4.3	40
Mechanics and repairmen	6.2	7.6	1.4	4.6	30
Metal crafts except mechanics	3.4	5.5	2.1	7.4	28
Other craftsmen	4.3	5.4	1.1	6.5	17
Foremen, not elsewhere classified	2.2	3.4	1.2	8.6	14
Protective service workers	4.6	7.0	2.4	6.2	39

Source: *Monthly Labor Review,* Vol. XCII (January 1969), p. 24.

1. Difference between 1962 level and 10.8 percent (the proportion of Negroes in the employed labor force in 1967).

Note: Operatives and kindred workers are not included in this table because the nonwhite proportion was greater than 10.8 percent of all workers in the occupation in 1967. (See Table 14.)

this and subsequent volumes, that the social aspects of selling have often acted as a bar to Negro employment (or as an excuse to exercise such a bar).

Negroes won many high-paying blue collar jobs. They increased their numbers of craftsmen by 45 percent, but because of the many new jobs, their proportion did not change significantly. Construction craftsmen and mechanics provided most of the new jobs for blacks.

Negro operatives increased from 1.4 to 1.9 million so that by 1967, nearly 25 percent of all Negroes were employed as operatives. The proportion of Negroes in operative jobs increased to 19.9 percent in 1962 and to 23.5 percent in 1967 (Table 15).

Employment in Perspective

With all these gains in a short period, one must still end a summation of the Negro occupational picture by pointing out that in 1967, 41 percent of all Negro workers, as compared with only 15 percent of all white workers, were still employed in unskilled laborer or service jobs. Great gains toward occupational equality have been made; much inequality exists. Moreover, there remains great disparity in the position of Negroes from industry to industry. The extent of that disparity and the reasons therefor are best understood by examining the situation in each industry separately. This is done in the remainder of this book (and succeeding volumes) after a short review of governmental civil rights orders and legislation which are aimed at improving the position of black workers and of other minorities.

THE GOVERNMENT AND EQUAL EMPLOYMENT OPPORTUNITY

One reason for the improved status of Negroes in the 1960's has been the increased involvement of the federal government, through legislation, executive orders, and court cases, in seeking equal employment opportunity. Some government involvement is not new. Throughout the Civil War and its aftermath, the federal government actively sought a workable policy to assure employment for the freedmen.[23] After a long lapse, the exigencies of World War I led to the

23. See, for example, Bell Irvin Wiley, *Southern Negroes, 1861-1865* (New Haven: Yale University Press, 1938), especially Part II; Vernon Lane Wharton, *The Negro in Mississippi, 1865-1890* (New York: Harper & Row, 1965); and V. Jacque Voegeli, *Free but Not Equal* (Chicago: University of Chicago Press, 1967).

establishment of a Division of Negro Economics in the U.S. Department of Labor which studied employment problems of the new black industrial workers.[24] Again came a lapse of interest, but during the early New Deal of President Franklin D. Roosevelt, efforts were made to obtain a fair share of jobs for Negroes in relief work and on other public projects.[25]

It was during World War II, however, that the modern governmental approach toward securing equal employment opportunity commenced. President Roosevelt issued Executive Orders establishing the President's Committee on Fair Employment Practice to oversee the policy that there should be no discrimination in defense contracts.[26] Although this Committee had no power to enforce its orders, it did help to secure a number of gains for Negroes and to develop procedures in the handling of complaints that are still utilized.

Congress declined to enact legislation making the Roosevelt Committee a statutory body, but government interest in equal employment proceeded on two fronts: state and executive. Beginning with New York in 1945, almost all the states outside of the South, the District of Columbia, and Puerto Rico, as well as several cities, enacted "fair employment practice" laws which outlaw racial and other types of discrimination and which provide a means of enforcing that prohibition.[27]

When Congress failed to enact civil rights legislation recommended by him, President Truman issued Executive Order 10308 establishing a Committee on Government Contract Compliance which sought, without too much effectiveness, to insure nondiscrimination in companies having government contracts. President Eisenhower likewise established a committee, the President's Committee on Government Contracts (known as the "Nixon Committee" because it was chaired

24. The leading work of the Division was the significant study by George E. Haynes, *The Negro at Work During the World War and During Reconstruction* (Washington: Government Printing Office, 1921).

25. Robert C. Weaver, *Negro Labor: A National Problem* (New York: Harcourt, Brace & Company, 1946), Chapters I and IX.

26. Executive Order 8802 was issued on June 25, 1941, and 9346 on May 29, 1943. The latter reorganized and activated the President's Committee on Fair Employment Practice.

27. Evaluation of these laws is found in Paul H. Norgren and Samuel E. Hill, *Toward Fair Employment* (New York: Columbia University Press, 1964); and Michael I. Sovern, *Legal Restraints on Racial Discrimination in Employment* (New York: Twentieth Century Fund, Inc., 1966), Chapter 3.

by the then Vice-President), by Executive Order 10499. This Committee was notable for its expansion of the fact gathering and inspection procedure among government contractors, and for its constructive activity in a number of industries, particularly petroleum (see Part VI). Its budget was limited, however, and it lacked the broad powers conferred on its successors. Moreover, the rising tide of Negro unemployment which existed during its tenure (see Table 10) was not stemmed by government action at the federal or state level and led both to a determination of the new Kennedy Administration to act more vigorously, and undoubtedly to greater militancy on the part of Negroes to obtain an increased opportunity for jobs.

In March 1961, President Kennedy issued Executive Order 10925, which established a new committee, the President's Committee on Equal Employment Opportunity. As modified by Executive Order 11114, PCEEO was given a broad mandate, a larger budget than its predecessors, and government contractors were instructed to "take affirmative action to ensure that applicants are employed and that employees are treated during employment without regard to their race, creed, or national origin." This was the inception of "affirmative action"—the requirement that a company must do more than not discriminate—but must in effect reach out into the nation's labor markets to find qualified Negroes. This obligation was continued by President Johnson when he abolished PCEEO and set up the Office of Federal Contract Compliance in the Department of Labor by Executive Order 11246, where it has remained under the Nixon Administration. As in the past, noncompliance with the Executive Orders carries the threat of contract debarment—a threat which has never been carried out, but which, as our industry studies will show, has nonetheless had considerable impact, although quite varied from industry to industry.

Meanwhile Congress enacted the Civil Rights Act of 1964, Title VII of which outlawed discrimination in employment as of July 1965; established the five man Equal Employment Opportunity Commission to investigate and to attempt to settle complaints of discrimination; provided for the rights of individuals to bring suits in federal courts where their rights under this statute have been violated; and provided for the U.S. Attorney-General to bring suits where "a pattern of discrimination" was found to exist. Title VII applies to employers of over 25 persons, to unions, and to employment agencies, and also specifically gives concurrent jurisdiction to state laws of the same nature. In a number of industries, suits filed by the Attorney-General or by individuals have had wide impact.

An evaluation of the overall impact of these laws and regulations is not attempted here. Rather in the course of our analysis of each industry, we shall analyze the impact of the role of government on Negro employment opportunity, not only in the 1960's, but in earlier periods as well, as appropriate. In Part VIII, the concluding chapter assesses the overall impact of government action in the six industries studied.

Part Two

THE NEGRO IN THE AUTOMOBILE INDUSTRY

by

HERBERT R. NORTHRUP

PART TWO: LIST OF TABLES

CHAPTER I.

Introduction

The automobile industry provides the classic example of how the Negro has fared in a dynamic, volatile, yet expanding mass production industry. The extent of Negro employment in the industry is closely related to its growth, but many other factors have been involved: government policy, the impact of a powerful union, and the ideas of America's greatest individualistic entrepreneur, the late Henry Ford. Other influences are also at work. Negro employment in this industry, as in others, is a function of the interaction of numerous pressures which shape the resultant racial policies and alter them significantly over time.

This study is concerned with the development, status, and problems involved in racial employment practices in the automobile industry, and particularly in the three principal companies therein: General Motors, Ford, and Chrysler. Plant visits by the author and most of the research were accomplished during the latter part of 1966 and the first half of 1967. Interviews with a variety of persons accompanied these visits, and information was obtained and evaluated by the author to supplement his past experience studying the same subject in this industry. It is believed that the firsthand information and statistics thus obtained represent an accurate portrayal of the situation in the industry.

CHAPTER II.

The Industry Background

In many ways the automobile industry epitomizes the American economy. Geared to turn out millions of quality products at relatively reasonable prices, it has set the tone and pace for mass production not only in America, but in the world, and changed the lives of all of us who depend upon the motor vehicle. In 1968 the industry consumed 60 percent of all rubber, 20 percent of all steel, and sizeable proportions of other materials.[1] Nineteen percent of all retail sales were automotive, and one business in six was dependent on the manufacture, distribution, servicing, and use of motor vehicles. In 1968, there were 16,400,000 multicar households in the United States, and 79 percent of all American families owned at least one automobile. Americans traveled 1,010 billion automobile miles and consumed 81 billion gallons of highway motor fuel. A record 11 million motor vehicles—cars, trucks, and buses—produced in the United States were sold.

The automobile has thus taken over the transportation of people and goods. In so doing, it has created great new industries. Such mammoth industries as petroleum, flat glass, rubber, cement, and asphalt depend upon automobile production either for direct sales, or to create their markets. The rise or fall of automobile sales and production is both a barometer of, and an influential factor in, the state of business in America. Where we live and work, the character of our cities, suburbs, and country, the methods of purchasing and the financing of goods have all been significantly altered by the advent of automobile transportation. Its influence is pervasive indeed. Its potential, therefore, for impacting on Negro employment problems is obviously considerable.

---

1. Data on production, sales, etc. are based on figures supplied by the Automobile Manufacturers Association and by Ward's Automotive Reports. The Association prepares an annual "Automobile Facts and Figures" book which is very useful.

INDUSTRIAL STRUCTURE

Nearly 200 companies have been engaged in automotive production at one time or another, but today, as for many years, the industry is dominated by three great companies—General Motors Corporation, the Ford Motor Car Company, and the Chrysler Corporation. In 1966, these companies were respectively, the largest, second largest, and fifth largest manufacturing enterprises in the United States. General Motors and Chrysler maintain headquarters in Detroit, Ford in the Detroit suburb of Dearborn.

Over the years, there has been a steady decline in the number of companies in the passenger car business, with American Motors today the only significant domestic competition to the Big Three. Moreover, American has been in a precarious position, holding only 2.5 percent of the market and losing money in most periods since 1965. Somewhat greater competition exists in the motor truck and bus portion of the automotive industry. International Harvester, the farm equipment and road machinery manufacturer, is a strong factor in the truck business, as are two independents, White Motor of Cleveland, and Mack Trucks of Allentown, Pennsylvania. In addition, a number of companies manufacture automobile parts and thus compete with captive parts plants of the Big Three.

Nevertheless, the tremendous investments required in tooling, plant, equipment, manpower, and marketing, give the Big Three both awesome competitive advantages and probably preclude any full scale entry into the market. Such investments can probably be recouped only by capturing a greater share of the market than American Motors now holds. Table 1, which gives the basic industrial statistics for the Big Three, and for American Motors, emphasizes this fact. American Motors, which ranked No. 131 among American manufacturing companies in 1968, is not only dwarfed by the size of the Big Three, but had meager earnings, bolstered by special credits despite sales of $761,070,000, assets of $349,046,000, and 21,338 employees!

The automobile industry has retained its huge appetite for manpower despite its tremendous capital investment and despite the great strides in mechanization and automation which have occurred in recent years. In 1968, the United States Bureau of Labor Statistics reported that 867,800 persons were employed in

TABLE 1. *The Major Automobile Companies, 1968*[a]

Company and 1968 Rank Among Industrial Corporations	Sales	Assets	Net Income	Invested Capital	Number of Employees[b]	Net Income as a Percent of Sales	Net Income as a Percent of Invested capital
	(Thousands of Dollars)						
General Motors Corporation (1)	22,755,403	14,010,175	1,731,915	9,756,810	757,231	7.6	17.8
Ford Motor Company (3)	14,075,100	8,953,200	626,600	4,946,600	415,039	4.5	12.7
Chrysler Corporation (5)	7,445,251	4,398,092	290,729	2,066,324	231,089	3.9	14.1
American Motors Corporation (131)	761,070	349,046	11,762[c]	190,570	21,338	1.5	6.2

Source: *Fortune*, Vol. LXXIX (May 15, 1969), pp. 168-169, 172-173.

a. All four are headquartered in the Detroit area.

b. Includes foreign-based employees.

c. More than 10 percent attributable to a special credit.

Standard Industrial Classification No. 371—"Motor Vehicles and Equipment."[2] Actually the industrial classifications of the federal government are neither uniform as between agencies nor complete in terms of the basic parts plants of the companies. The Bureau of Labor Statistics does not include within SIC 371 automobile stamping, forge, tool and die, foundry castings, or trim shops; the Bureau of the Census includes stamping and trim, but excludes the others.[3]

Consequently, company reports or automobile association statistics provide a better picture of the number of employees who are affected by the racial policies of the companies involved. The data in Table 1, which demonstrate the tremendous size of the Big Three, include foreign based employees, and employees in electrical appliance, aerospace, and other nonautomotive operations of the four companies. The four automobile companies had approximately one million employees in the United States in 1968, the bulk of whom were engaged either in building motor vehicles or parts and equipment for such vehicles.[4] The size and visibility of this huge labor force obviously give its racial policies great significance.

OCCUPATIONAL DISTRIBUTION

The occupational distribution of employees in the automobile industry is significant for our study. Table 2 shows that distribution for domestic plants of the Big Three in 1966. More than one-half of the employees are classified as "operatives," a basically semiskilled group. Operatives include persons who perform very rudimentary jobs on assembly lines that require only the most meager of on the job instruction, others who perform assembly or machine attendant jobs that require a few weeks instruction before reasonable proficiency is obtained, and still others who work on jobs requiring several months instruction before the required performance and productivity may be expected. Basically, however, these jobs can be readily picked up and require less than a high school education for proficiency.

2. As published in *Employment and Earnings.*
3. I am indebted to Dr. Donald Irwin, formerly of Chrysler Corporation, for this summary of the deficiencies of SIC 371 for our purposes.
4. The companies are product integrated to various degrees. General Motors, for example, probably manufactures more of its own components than its competitors, but only Ford has its own steelmaking and glassmaking facilities, although Chrysler now has a glass plant.

TABLE 2. *Big Three Automobile Companies Total Employment by Occupational Group*

Domestic Plants, 1966

Occupational Group	Employees	Percent
Officials and managers	74,395	7.9
Professionals	51,053	5.4
Technicians	24,499	2.6
Sales, office and clerical	93,365	9.8
Total white collar	243,312	25.7
Craftsmen	129,123	13.6
Operatives	515,843	54.5
Laborers	32,352	3.4
Service workers	26,755	2.8
Total blue collar	704,073	74.3
Total	947,385	100.0

Source: Data in author's possession.

These data include most of the nonautomobile manufacturing of the Big Three. The differences in totals with those for 1966 found in Table 9 are probably attributable to differences in payroll week used. Only a few hundred persons classified as "sales" are included in the "sales, office, and clerical" group.

The next largest group—13.6 percent of the total—is the skilled tradesman. It includes a wide range of crafts requiring considerable training and skill. They are a blue collar elite, highly sought after by the companies. Skills range from the top flight diemaker, to the millwright and welder, and include the whole gamut of metal and woodworking crafts.

Office and clerical staffs are almost 10 percent of the total, and the professional and managerial groups continue to increase. Automobile companies employ few sales personnel directly, since selling is done by franchised dealers.[5]

The blue collar jobs thus continue to predominate in the occupational distribution in the automobile industry, in contrast to such industries as aerospace where salaried employment has equaled or outstripped the hourly work force. Moreover, the bulk of the jobs in the automobile plants lies within a narrow skill range. Essentially

5. *Automobile Facts and Figures, 1969,* reported that there were 31,649 retail passenger car dealers in 1967 including those selling all domestic and foreign manufactured cars, and 4,186 wholesale dealers.

unskilled and untried workers can be taken off the streets, with minimal educational, communication, and arithmetic backgrounds, and can be successfully utilized as assembly line workers or taught to be machine tenders in a short period. Of course such persons have limitations on the number and type of jobs that they can fill. Employees with better education, experience, and training have a decided advantage in being more trainable and able to adapt to change. Yet the fact remains that the automobile industry has a capacity far beyond that of many industries to utilize the poorly educated and inexperienced recruit. This, of course, has great significance for Negro workers who are disproportionately represented in the poorly educated strata of society, and who so often have had little prior plant work experience or even exposure to such experience.

Female Employment

Approximately 10 percent of the employees of the Big Three are female. Of these, the largest group work in the offices, but a sizable number of women are also employed on assembly line operations in the plants.[6] Because Negro women are underrepresented in the white collar occupations where most females are employed, we shall note in a subsequent chapter that the percentage of women employed by the Big Three who are Negroes is only sightly more than one-half the proportion of Negro men to total men.

WAGES AND EARNINGS

Although the automobile industry can utilize personnel with relatively poor educational and experience backgrounds, the jobs pay well. In 1968 hourly earnings for automotive production workers averaged \$3.89, and weekly earnings, \$167.66.[7] In the same year average weekly earnings of production workers in all manufacturing were \$122.51, for production workers in durable goods manufacturing, the weekly earnings averaged \$132.07. The average hourly earnings for all manufacturing production employees were \$3.01, for those in durable goods industries, \$3.19.[8]

6. Data in the author's possession.
7. U. S. Bureau of Labor Statistics, *Employment and Earnings,* Vol. 15 (March 1969), Table C-2.
8. *Ibid.*

In addition to wages that are among the highest in American industry, automobile workers receive the protection of a wide variety of fringe benefits, including generous pensions, hospitalization and medical insurance, and supplemental unemployment benefits. In 1967—and fringe benefits have been considerably improved since then—General Motors estimated that its employees had average fringe benefits worth $1.30 per hour.[9] In 1965, the top five cities in terms of average weekly earnings of production workers were Flint, Detroit, Lansing, Saginaw, and Ann Arbor—all in Michigan and in all of which automobile manufacturers were the major industrial employers.[10] There is little reason to believe that these cities have since been outranked, or that automobile workers' wages and fringe benefits will not continue to rank near the top among those paid in industrial employment.

UNIONIZATION

These high earnings reflect not only the success and productivity of the industry but also the strength of the union. Organized as the United Automobile Workers in the early 1930's, and now known as the United Automobile, Aerospace and Agricultural Implement Workers, the UAW had a membership of approximately 1,600,000 in 1967. All domestic manufacturing plants of the automobile producers were unionized by the UAW except those in other industries, for example, electrical appliances, which were organized by other unions. Despite energetic efforts by the UAW, the salaried employees of Ford and General Motors remain overwhelmingly nonunion, but many of Chrysler's are found in the UAW fold. The role of the UAW and its leadership in affecting the racial policies of the industry is discussed in later sections of this study.

9. *How Do GM Wages Stack Up?* Pamphlet issued by General Motors Corporation, July 1967.
10. U.S. Bureau of Labor Statistics, Bulletin No. 1370-3, June 1966.

CHAPTER III.

The Pre-World War II Period

In 1910, the U. S. Bureau of the Census reported that the fledgling "motor vehicle" and "motor vehicle bodies and parts" industries employed 105,758 persons, but only 569 Negroes. Twenty years later, total employment stood at 640,474, and Negro employment at 25,895, or 4 percent in 1930 as compared with 0.5 percent twenty years earlier.

The increase in the number and percentage of Negro automobile workers was the result of the shortage of labor which developed during and after World War I. With immigration cut off, first by the War, and later by restrictive legislation, automobile manufacturers, like those in many other industries, commenced extensive recruiting in the South. Thousands of Negroes, and many more southern whites, migrated North to find permanent jobs in automobile, steel, meat packing, and other industries. In many industries, Negro recruits were used as strike breakers. Unionization, however, despite a very brief flurry during World War I which did not affect the major producers, was not a serious threat to the automobile companies, prior to 1934.[11] Negroes were not, therefore, introduced into the industry under strike conditions.

EARLY AREA AND JOB CONCENTRATIONS

This early period also saw the beginning of a trend still extant—much heavier utilization of Negro labor in the Detroit area especially, but also in other urban Michigan plants, than in most plants in other states.[12] Thus, the 1930 census found Negroes comprised 8.7 percent

11. On this point, see Sidney Fine, *The Automobile Under the Blue Eagle* (Ann Arbor, Michigan: University of Michigan Press, 1963), pp. 21-30.
12. The story of this early period is based largely upon an unpublished manuscript in the author's possession which Dr. Lloyd H. Bailer prepared for the "Negro in America" study which was directed by Dr. Gunnar Myrdal; and on the author's field work in the Detroit area during World War II.

of Michigan's automobile labor force, 2.4 percent of Indiana's, 1.9 percent of Ohio's, and few elsewhere. The reasons for this early Michigan concentration appear to be (1) the location in that state of the type of work for which Negroes were utilized; (2) the fact that no labor shortage existed where plants in other states were built and staffed; and (3) the policies of Henry Ford, the bulk of whose operations were in the Detroit area.

In 1940, Dr. Lloyd H. Bailer, after a detailed study of Negroes in the automobile industry, reported that:

> . . . the vast majority of Negro automobile workers are employed in the foundry, paint, and maintenance departments (chiefly as janitors) or as general unskilled labor. Of these, . . . the foundry is the most important. In fact, one can be quite certain that an automobile plant employing a sizable portion of Negro labor has a foundry. In many large plants the foundry is known as a "black department." In general, foundry occupations are the most undesirable in the industry . . . hot, dirty, and demand exceptional strength. The accident rate is higher in the foundry than any other department. . . . These conditions are not restricted to foundries in the automobile industry but are characteristic of all foundries . . . automobile foundries are among the safest and most modern. . . . But . . . foundry work is extremely disagreeable and often dangerous.[13]

In addition to foundry work, Negroes were heavily concentrated as sanders and sprayers in paint departments. Again these were (and are) undesirable jobs, arduous and unpleasant. And, of course, Negroes were widely used as janitors, porters, laborers, cafeteria bus boys, etc.

Because most foundry and body plants of automobile companies were (and are) located in Michigan, this tended to increase the proportion of Negroes in this state's industry. Some companies, according to Bailer, used Negroes in Michigan foundries and body shop paint departments, but not in these jobs in other states. Even in Michigan, however, foundries and paint departments were not all Negro. A lot of Mexican and other foreign born whites were also employed in these jobs, which were often 30 to 50 percent Negro. Some jobs, for example, chippers and foundry laborers, were often very nearly all Negro.

Dr. Bailer also found, in plants other than those of Ford, which are treated separately below, six Negro foremen and a "few" Negro

13. *Ibid.*, pp. 43-45.

straw bosses. These Negro foremen supervised all Negro groups. In most cases, however, supervisors were white even when the force in the department was over one-half Negro.

GENERAL MOTORS AND CHRYSLER

Dr. Bailer found that Negroes were not used on the assembly lines prior to World War II even in Michigan, except at Ford as will be discussed below. The general occupational and plant employment patterns reserved the assembly line for whites and confined Negroes in assembly plants to janitors, cafeteria workers, or laborers off the line. The reasons seem to be the general feeling of the times that whites would not work with Negroes, unless the work was so unpleasant or degrading that only a very poor class of whites was involved, as in foundries; or that Negroes were incapable or unsuited to such work. In this regard, of course, the automobile industry was typical of industry in general of the period.

According to Mr. Louis G. Seaton, Vice-President, General Motors Corporation, Dr. Bailer's findings omitted some significant developments at General Motors:

> Negro employees were placed on inspection, machining and assembly operations in General Motors as early as 1933. Cadillac, Chevrolet, and Oldsmobile were leaders in this effort in Michigan. In 1936, for instance, 30% of the employees working on inspection and machining operations at the Chevrolet Gear & Axle Plant in Detroit were Negroes.
>
> Both Cadillac and Oldsmobile had Negro employees in skilled trades classifications prior to World War II and 4% of the Oldsmobile work force in Lansing was composed of Negroes who were employed on production jobs in the early 30's. A number of these Negroes were on higher rated jobs such as paint spray, dingman, sheet metal finisher, polisher, auto mechanic, auto repairman and final inspector. . . .[14]

It does appear that despite the interesting developments in the divisions noted by Mr. Seaton, Negroes at General Motors were heavily concentrated in the foundry departments. Thus Bailer estimated that about 2,500 of General Motors' 100,000 employees in Michigan and Indiana were Negroes, and that about 2,000 of these worked in foundries in Flint, Saginaw, and Pontiac. But General Motors obviously did not follow so strict a policy of confining Negroes to the

14. Letter to author from Mr. Louis G. Seaton, August 31, 1967.

traditional jobs which the industry reserved for them, as Bailer indicated, and permitted some mixing of the races on machines, and in departments.

Actually Negro employment policies at General Motors prior to World War II were apparently left at least largely to decentralized management decisions. As Mr. Seaton noted, Oldsmobile, Chevrolet, and Cadillac were willing to pioneer in several plants. On the other hand, the Fisher Body Division went to the other extreme. Its management apparently did not believe in employing Negroes, for its plants prior to World War II often did not have even a Negro janitor. The reasons for this wide divergency of practice during the 1930's, other than managerial policy of the various General Motors divisions and plants, are not apparent.

During the 1920's, the automobile industry established a number of assembly plants on the East Coast, in the South and Southwest, and on the Pacific Coast. These plants employed virtually no Negroes. In some areas, Negro labor was not available. In other areas, there was no labor shortage when plants were constructed, so that no practice of employing Negro labor was established. The plants built in the South and Southwest followed the practice initiated by the textile industry in the latter part of the nineteenth century: all basic factory jobs, mechanical or assembly, were manned by whites. A few Negroes were hired as janitors, outside laborers, or cafeteria bus boys, but basically the prewar automobile plants in the South employed whites only. General Motors, Chrysler, and Ford all followed the policy outside of Michigan and its contiguous areas of avoiding racial problems by not hiring Negroes except in the few service or laboring occupations. This policy was facilitated by the fact that nearly all foundries were located in Michigan or neighboring states.

The Chrysler Corporation had far fewer parts plants of its own prior to World War II than either of its major competitors. Dr. Bailer estimated that only 2,000 of its 50,000 employees in 1940 were Negroes, nearly all of whom were found in Michigan plants. Chrysler's Negro employees were then almost all confined to the traditional jobs reserved for them in the industry: the foundry, especially at the Main Dodge plant, and in painting and laboring jobs.[15]

Prior to World War II, Chrysler bought its bodies from the Briggs Manufacturing Corporation (which it acquired after World War II).

15. These data are all based on figures given to Dr. Bailer by company and plant managements.

TABLE 3. *Negro Workers in Major Automobile Companies*
First Quarter, 1940

Company	Total Hourly Workers	Negro Workers	Percent Negro
Ford Motor Company[a]	88,773	9,882	11.1
Briggs Mfg. Corporation[a]	14,000	3,000	21.4
General Motors Corporation[b]	100,000	2,500	2.5
Chrysler Corporation	50,000	2,000	4.0
Packard Motor Car Company	16,000	600	3.8

Source: Lloyd H. Bailer, 1940 unpublished MS, based on data given him by companies.
[a]Michigan plants only.
[b]Michigan and Indiana automobile and auto parts plants only.
Note: Briggs has since been acquired by Chrysler.

Briggs had the highest percentage of Negro employees in the industry —3,000 out of a total of 14,000, or 21.4 percent. (See Table 3.) All the Negro employees of Briggs were found in Michigan; it had no Negro employees in its Indiana plant.

MR. FORD WAS UNIQUE

As was the case in so many aspects of his business life, Henry Ford's policies toward Negro labor were unique. At the mammoth River Rouge plant in Dearborn, a Detroit suburb, Ford employed the largest number of Negro workers in the industry. Indeed, about 40 percent of all Negro automobile workers worked at River Rouge. And although there were similar overconcentrations of Negroes in the foundry, the paint department, and in unskilled jobs at River Rouge as existed elsewhere in the industry, Negroes were employed during this period in nearly all manufacturing departments as well.

Ford's Negro employment policies grew out of representations made to him by members of the Negro community, particularly Negro ministers, after World War I. During the 1921 depression, the Negro leaders saw workers of their race losing newly gained industrial jobs, and appealed to Mr. Ford to give consideration to the needs of Detroit's new Negro population. He responded by agreeing to keep the percentage of Negro factory workers in his main facility—then Highland Park, but soon thereafter River Rouge—roughly proportionate to the Negro population ratio in Detroit. When the great River Rouge works was opened in the twenties, Negroes moved with their jobs and more were hired.

TABLE 4. *Negro Workers in Ford Michigan Plants*
1939-1940

Plant	Total Hourly Workers	Negro Workers	Percent Negro
River Rouge	84,096	9,825	11.7
Lincoln	2,332	31	1.3
Highland Park	992	16	1.6
Ypsilanti	805	9	1.1
Flat Rock	548	1	0.2

Source: Lloyd H. Bailer, 1940 unpublished MS, based on data given him by Ford payroll department.

Note: Ford then had 14 other small Michigan plants, none of which employed Negroes.

Table 3 shows the automobile companies employing the largest number of Negroes in the 1934-1940 period. Over half were accounted for by Ford, although Briggs had the highest percentage. Table 4 shows the distribution as among Ford plants. River Rouge employed nearly all the Negroes in the company. Most Negroes once employed at Highland Park were moved to River Rouge; Ford did not change the policies of the Lincoln Company when he purchased it in the early 1920's; and Negroes were not recruited for assembly plants in Norfolk, Memphis, Atlanta, Dallas, St. Louis, the East Coast, or Northern Michigan. At River Rouge, however, Ford kept his bargain with the Negro community and kept it well.

TABLE 5. *Distribution of Negro Employees, Ford River Rouge Works*
October 1937

Division	Total Hourly Workers	Negro	Percent Negro
Foundry	12,254	4,659	38.0
Foundry Machine Shop	3,952	616	15.6
Motor Mfg. & Assembly	14,577	754	5.2
Chassis & Parts Mfg. & Assembly	9,468	564	6.0
Spring & Upset Machining	5,484	574	10.5
Steel Stamping	7,046	555	7.9
Rolling Mills & Blast Furnaces	8,193	1,182	14.4
Tool Rooms	5,131	51	1.0
Construction	3,515	232	6.6
Miscellaneous	14,476	638	4.4

Source: Lloyd H. Bailer, 1940 unpublished MS, from data given him by Ford payroll department.

Table 5 shows the distribution of Negroes working at River Rouge as of October 5, 1937. As already noted, Negroes were unduly concentrated in unskilled and foundry jobs, and received a smaller than proportionate share of some of the better jobs. But the significant fact is that the River Rouge plant was the key one in the industry where Negroes were given the opportunity to work on nearly all operations pertinent to the industry. At River Rouge Negroes worked on the assembly line in large numbers; there alone were Negro apprentices and trade school graduates accepted; River Rouge had the industry's only Negro tool and die mechanics; and it had the industry's largest and most significant aggregation of parts assemblers, and of machine and press operators. Moreover, River Rouge had more Negro supervisors than were found in the rest of the industry, and the only ones supervising racially mixed crews.

The significance of the River Rouge operation on Negro employment transcended the automobile industry. When Henry Ford built this huge complex, he determined to make his operations as self-sufficient as possible. The River Rouge operations include not only an engine plant, stamping and other parts plants, and an assembly plant, but also huge blast furnaces and rolling mills where Ford makes its own steel; later a glass plant (Ford is the third largest flat glass maker in the country); foundries, docks where Ford-owned Great Lakes carriers unload coal, iron ore, and other raw materials; and at one time a cement plant, a tire plant, a lumber mill, and a paper box factory. Negroes were employed in all these plants, although in some areas, such as the rolling mill and the glass plant, they were not working on key jobs. In addition, at Ford, Negroes and whites commonly worked together in mixed pairs on presses and on other machines, as well as on assembly and subassembly lines. In short, prior to World War II, Negroes came closer to job equality at the Ford River Rouge works than they did at any large enterprise known to the author or recorded in the literature.

Ford fostered racial job equality with his typical combination of authoritarianism and paternalism. If white workers did not like his racial employment policies, their only alternative was to leave. Having made up his mind that his policies were proper, he brooked no interference nor gave any heed to the racial antagonisms on account of which most other employers feared to mix races or to give Negroes opportunities for better jobs.

In order to see that his policies were carried out, two Negroes were attached to the Ford Service Department, a combination of plant personnel and security force. They were responsible for recruiting and employing Negroes, and Negroes who felt that they had been discriminated against or otherwise aggrieved or who had problems, could take their cases directly to their Service Department representatives. That the Negro representatives in the Service Department had authority to correct situations was demonstrated sufficiently well so that line supervisors tended to carry out the Ford policy.

The fact that Ford offered Negroes the best jobs in the Detroit area gave Ford not only the choice Negro applicants, but also tremendous community leverage. This became a matter of consequence with the use of unionism which Henry Ford fought with his typical determination.

THE INITIAL UNION IMPACT

After the election of Franklin D. Roosevelt and the passage of the National Industrial Recovery Act (NRA) in 1933, automobile workers attempted to form unions, but with limited success in the face of employer opposition, the insistence of the American Federation of Labor on organization along craft lines, the inexperience of the budding unionists, and the inability of NRA boards to enforce their orders. According to a careful history of the NRA period:

> . . . The presence of a considerable number of Negroes and foreign-born in the automobile plants, particularly in the Detroit area, also posed a problem for the A. F. of L. The opposition of the Negro to the Federation because of the racial discrimination practiced by some of its affiliates, the racial antagonism between Negro and white workers in the automobile plants, the Negro support for the antiunion Ford Motor Company, which employed more Negroes than any other automobile firm and discriminated against them less in the assignment of jobs, and the higher rate of unemployment among Negroes than among white automobile workers all deterred the Negroes from responding to union entreaties.[16]

The same historian reports that American Federation of Labor's chief Detroit organizer noted that Negroes "were not coming to his meetings and that it was a 'tremendous problem' to persuade them to join the [AFL] federal labor unions."[17]

16. Fine, *op. cit.*, p. 149.
17. *Ibid.*

When unionism did come to the automobile industry in the mid-1930's, Mr. Ford was again unique. He held out against acceptance after General Motors, Chrysler, and most independents had recognized the United Automobile Workers, then an affiliate of the new Committee for Industrial Organization, in the wake of sit-down strikes and government intervention. Unionism under the UAW banner officially accepted Negroes as members without discrimination, but did nothing immediately to alter racial employment trends. The UAW leadership, traditionally split before Walter Reuther achieved control in the late 1940's, was in no position to alter the employment *status quo.* Seniority agreements were largely based on departmental and occupational groupings, and hence did little to promote greater integration. In some southern and border state plants, the national union officials had all that they could do even to gain union membership for Negro laborers and janitors in the face of the opposition of white members and local union leadership.[18]

The campaign to unionize Ford put the spotlight on the race issue. As one of its responses to the union campaign, Ford stepped up its employment of Negroes, and made much of the fact that Negroes were in a superior position at River Rouge than elsewhere. When the UAW struck River Rouge in 1941, some violence occurred between Negroes loyal to Ford and white strikers. Later Negroes heavily supported Ford's attempted deal with a rival American Federation of Labor group, but the UAW won handily in an election conducted by the National Labor Relations Board.

Ford turned from bitter antiunionism to complete union acceptance with a compulsory union shop. For the first time, the bulk of Negro automobile workers became union members, and a significant force in the UAW. Yet as the war drew close, Negroes were far from integrated into the union. In a careful study, published in 1944, Dr. Bailer found that Negro participation in union affairs was considerably less than whites because of a variety of causes, the three most significant of which were their traditionally unhappy experience with the older craft unions, the seniority system, and the lack of social acceptance.[19]

The first point—traditional union opposition to Negro membership—is exemplified by the building and railroad union practices

18. A discussion of UAW policies toward Negroes in the immediate pre-World War II and early war period is found in Herbert R. Northrup, *Organized Labor and the Negro* (New York: Harper and Brothers, 1944), Chapter IX.
19. Lloyd H. Bailer, "The Automobile Unions and Negro Labor," *Political Science Quarterly*, Vol. LIX (December 1944), pp. 548-577; and especially pp. 556-562.

which are still antagonistic to Negro advancement.[20] UAW locals, of course, put no bars on Negro membership—except in the South. White members of the Atlanta, Georgia, local attempted to have all Negroes—then used only as laborers and janitors—discharged. The UAW national leadership found itself helpless to force the local to admit the Negroes, but stood firm against any demand for their discharge.[21]

The seniority system deserves further comment. Since Negroes were concentrated in the lower-rated jobs, they could be displaced by white workers with better jobs and higher seniority when the labor force contracted, as it did in 1938. But when expansion occurred, Negroes desiring upgrading found that union contracts were often ignored because to do otherwise would result in the admission of Negroes to existing all white occupations or departments or to jobs traditionally reserved for whites. Convention debates and other sources cited by Bailer or found by the present author leave no doubt that, although the national officers of the UAW were generally sympathetic to Negro advancement, local officials who needed white worker support for re-election, generally helped to maintain the *status quo,* and the national officers did not feel that they could intervene. It is, therefore, not surprising that Dr. Bailer found that the Negro automobile worker trusted Henry Ford more than the leaders of the UAW, or that Negroes on a number of occasions went through UAW picket lines during strikes at various companies.[22]

The economic situation was acerbated by social affronts. Local meetings and some national conventions were held where Negroes were denied service. Local union social affairs were held with Negroes snubbed, or affairs were cancelled if Negroes showed a disposition to attend.[23] Despite the firmest of resolutions annually enacted by the national UAW convention, and despite a firm commitment to nondiscrimination by R. J. Thomas, then president of the UAW, and if anything, a firmer belief in equality by his successor, and then a UAW vice-president, Walter Reuther, it was apparent that the racial employment pattern and race relations in the industry were at an uneasy *status quo* at the time that America was thrust into World War II.

---

20. See Northrup, *op. cit.*, Chapters II and III; and F. Ray Marshall, *The Negro and Organized Labor* (New York: John Wiley & Sons, Inc., 1965), *passim.*
21. Interview of this author with ex-UAW Atlanta local president, June 12, 1940.
22. Bailer, "Automobile Unions and Negro Labor," *op. cit.*, pp. 562-566 for discussion of seniority system, and pp. 550-556 for details of unrest.
23. *Ibid.*, pp. 560-562.

CHAPTER IV.

The World War II Period

The shift over of the automobile industry from passenger cars to aircraft, tanks, army trucks, and other ordnance threatened initially to be disadvantageous to Negro workers. Worker shortages occurred first in skilled and assembly jobs from which Negroes had been barred in most facilities and fear was expressed that foundry and paint work would be in less demand. Most managements were disinclined to train Negroes for new jobs. Past experience had taught them that white workers would not work with Negroes on assembly lines or machine jobs, and they felt that only trouble would result from attempts to mix the races. White dominated local union leadership often reinforced these prejudices.[24]

Ford, too, followed its traditional policies, which were, of course, quite different from those of the rest of the industry. Negro foundry workers were trained and upgraded at River Rouge without governmental prodding, as were other employees in that huge works. On the other hand, Ford also followed its non-River Rouge racial employment policies at the new Willow Run bomber plant. Located in what was then a rural area, and reachable only by car, with little housing then nearby, Willow Run employed few Negroes in any capacity.

WARTIME CHANGES IN MANAGEMENT POLICIES

Both the failure to upgrade Negroes, and more often, actually doing so, caused wartime work stoppages. Negro laborers and foundry workers at Chrysler's Dodge Main Plant struck in August 1941 because they were being passed over in transfers to the Chrysler

24. This section is based on Herbert R. Northrup, *Organized Labor and the Negro* (New York: Harper and Brothers, 1944), Chapter IX; and Lloyd H. Bailer, "Automobile Unions and Negro Labor," *Political Science Quarterly*, Vol. LIX (December 1944), pp. 548-577; and especially pp. 556-562.

Tank Arsenal. Governmental pressure forced both the company and the local union to change their attitudes and transfers were initiated.

Strikes occurred at Packard and Hudson, among other plants, over Negro upgrading. At first such strikes caused management to backtrack. But as the labor market tightened, government pressure increased, the national UAW obtained greater control over its locals and management became more experienced, such outbursts were dealt with more firmly. In mid-1942, for example, a demonstration against Negro employment and upgrading at the Dodge Main Plant resulted in no change of company policy—now committed to an expansion and upgrading of Negroes—and the discharge of the leaders of the agitation.

The worst racial strike occurred at the Packard plant, in the heart of Detroit in June 1943. It had been preceded by minor disturbances over Negro upgrading, and shut down the entire works. Although both national and local union leaders tried to control the situation, many shop stewards were among the strike leaders. Nevertheless, the united stand of unions, company, and government broke the strike in less than one week without concession.

On June 21 of the same year, the worst race riot in Detroit's history to that date commenced. No violence occurred in the plants —a tribute to both the industry and union leaders. Yet "unionists of both races did participate in the frenzy that raged in various parts of the city."[25] Unlike the similar horror 24 years later, this riot featured white males looting and beating in the Negro areas.

Despite the violence and obstacles, great progress occurred in the turbulent World War II days. Briggs, for example, then an independent company, but now part of the Chrysler organization, increased its percentage of Negroes and integrated them into all manufacturing jobs. Heretofore, they had been confined to paint departments or to unskilled work. Moreover, Briggs employed substantial numbers of Negro women, a group even Ford had not utilized. By a careful indoctrination program Briggs avoided major difficulties in achieving this goal.

Negroes made great progress in both Chrysler and General Motors. As they flocked into the motor city, they found the center city concentrated Chrysler plants the most accessible. Chrysler responded by

25. Bailer, *loc. cit.*, p. 571.

hiring and upgrading on a vast scale so that by the end of the war it was to have the highest proportion of Negroes in the industry.

At General Motors, large scale upgrading and new hiring also occurred. The traditionally more liberal components—Chevrolet, Cadillac, and Oldsmobile—expanded their programs. The first Negro apprentices of the Corporation were employed by Oldsmobile. Negroes emerged from their foundry and labor status at Buick and Pontiac to win other production jobs. The policies of the Fisher Body Division were also liberalized. Following a hearing of the President's Committee on Fair Employment Practice in Chicago in 1944, which found some discriminatory employment practices at General Motors facilities there, the Corporation adopted a much stronger corporate-wide stance on integration rather than leaving the problem totally to decentralized management.

At the River Rouge works, the situation also changed before the end of the war. The numbers and percentage of Negroes rose there too, as the labor market tightened, but Ford officials were clearly disenchanted by the caliber of Negro recruits available from 1943 until the end of the war. Previously, Ford could take its pick of one of every four Negroes who applied, but as barriers elsewhere dropped and the labor market tightened, all employers found only recent arrivals from the South available. For a time Ford ceased to employ Negroes; and its special Negro representatives in the service department were transferred and not replaced. Henceforth, Negroes at River Rouge were dependent on the union or outside civil rights organizations to handle their special problems when they felt management was unfair.

AREA DIFFERENCES

As before World War II, the greatest advances in Negro employment were made in the Detroit area, and in other Michigan communities. Likewise, in Chicago and Cleveland, considerable progress in overcoming barriers resulted from the combination of a tight labor market, Negro and governmental pressure, and general enlightening of management policies. Patterns of employment in the East and West Coast automobile plants changed less, and in the South very little. But the significant thing is that by the postwar conversion period, despite strife, some nasty incidents, and occasional local management or local union footdragging, Negroes were working on assembly lines, on machines, and in many other jobs alongside whites as a general practice rather than something which only Henry Ford dared to do prior to the war.

On the other hand, by the end of the war there was little progress toward integrating Negroes in white collar and professional positions, or as dealers or dealer salesmen. Moreover, the automobile companies did little, if any, pioneering in southern automobile plants in this period. Developments in these areas would have to wait another two decades.

CHAPTER V.

From Post-War Reconversion to 1960

Reconversion resulted in some layoffs and loss of employment for Negroes and whites in the automobile industry, but recovery was rapid as new prosperity and pent up consumer demand kept sales and employment in the industry high through the remainder of the 1940's. Employment was further buoyed by the Korean War demands on the industry in the early 1950's, but slackened demand in 1954 and a serious recession in 1958 cut deeply into employment and into Negro work opportunities for the final years of the decade. An examination of the experience of the major companies in employing Negroes highlights the events of these fifteen years.

THE CHRYSLER EXPERIENCE, 1946-1960

Chrysler emerged from World War II with the largest percentage of Negro employees in the industry. Its concentration in the central Detroit area, its acquisition of the Briggs plants also located there, and its successful integration of the work force during the war caused it to pass Ford in percentage of Negro employees, although not in total numbers of Negroes employed. In 1946, 17 percent of Chrysler's 71,000 employees were Negro.[26]

Negroes continued to gain at Chrysler in the prosperous years after World War II, especially in the Detroit area plants, although as was the case in most automobile plants, such gains were confined, with very few exceptions, to production jobs. A few Negroes were employed as skilled tradesmen or apprentices, and a handful in white collar occupations, but generally these jobs remained closed to Negroes during the 1950's.

In the Detroit area, Chrysler employed over 100,000 persons by the end of 1952, of whom 22 percent were Negroes. At this time, 13.5 percent of Detroit's population was nonwhite. The percentage

26. From a reply of Chrysler Corporation to an inquiry of the Social Science Department, Fisk University, September 1946.

of Negroes was less in Chrysler plants outside of the motor city; for example, it was 7.5 percent in the Plymouth assembly plant at Evansville, Indiana, in the late 1950's, where the Negro population ratio was 6 percent. Chrysler has no southern automobile plants, but in border areas such as Evansville, Newark, Delaware, or St. Louis, it did not hesitate to use Negroes in all production jobs.[27]

Chrysler had some difficult times in the 1950's. Corporate employment peaked at 176,356 in 1955, and had not risen that high by 1968. It fell 32,000 in 1956, and by the end of 1958 plummeted to 91,678. Negro employees, being relatively new, were hit disproportionately hard. In 1957, for example, employment at four Chrysler Detroit plants stood at 45,584, including 9,242 Negroes, or 20.3 percent Negro. The following year, these plants employed only 22,776 persons, of whom 3,345, or just 14.7 percent were Negro. Improvement in the Negro workers' status was obviously not possible in this situation until prosperity returned—and for Chrysler, it did not return on a lasting basis until 1962.

FORD IN THE FORTIES AND FIFTIES

The period after World War II was one in which the Ford Motor Company sought successfully to regroup and modernize its operations in order to regain the number two slot in the industry, and even to challenge General Motors for first place. Henry Ford's paternalism was replaced by modern managerial rule; the River Rouge complex was reduced drastically in size, and manufacturing operations decentralized; small assembly plants were closed and fewer larger ones built. The impact on Negro labor was mixed.

The reduction in size of the River Rouge works reduced the Negro percentage in the company, for although production operations in such states as Ohio were well integrated, Rouge had in the 1950's, as it does today, the largest number and percentage of Negroes in the Ford Company. On the other hand, the closing of the small assembly plants in Upper Michigan, which had no Negro employees, or the Memphis plant in which Negroes were confined to a few menial jobs, or of small assembly plants in the East, did not materially reduce Negro employment opportunities.

---

27. Data in this and the ensuing section, unless otherwise indicated, are based on a variety of sources including studies made by various governmental agencies for the President's Committee on Government Contracts (Nixon Committee) during the Eisenhower Administration.

TABLE 6. *Ford Motor Company Employment by Race*

Twelve Assembly Plants, 1957 and 1958

Plant Location and Date	All Employees Total	Negro	Percent Negro	Salaried Employees Total	Negro	Percent Negro	Hourly Employees Total	Negro	Percent Negro
Atlanta									
1957	1,588	21	1.3	227	—	—	1,361	21	1.5
1958	1,393	20	1.4	221	—	—	1,172	20	1.7
Chicago									
1957	2,230	745	33.4	390	70	17.9	1,840	675	36.7
1958	1,770	515	29.1	330	40	12.1	1,440	475	33.0
Dallas									
1957	2,991	9	0.3	491	—	—	2,500	9	0.4
1958	1,652	5	0.3	304	—	—	1,348	5	0.4
Detroit									
1957	5,300	807	15.2	1,300	7	0.5	4,000	800	20.0
1958	4,050	681	16.8	1,100	6	0.5	2,950	675	22.9
Los Angeles									
1957	1,715	110	6.4	182	3	1.6	1,533	107	7.0
1958	1,207	90	7.5	280	4	1.4	927	86	9.3
Louisville									
1957	3,525	197	5.6	425	1	0.2	3,100	196	6.3
1958	2,573	158	6.1	420	1	0.2	2,153	157	7.3
Mahwah, N. J.									
1957	5,400	1,160	21.5	650	33	5.1	4,750	1,127	23.7
1958	4,375	921	21.1	475	19	4.0	3,900	902	23.1
Memphis									
1957	1,458	35	2.4	219	—	—	1,239	35	2.8
1958	929	23	2.5	181	—	—	748	23	3.1
Norfolk									
1957	1,626	9	0.5	249	—	—	1,377	9	0.6
1958	1,487	9	0.6	238	—	—	1,249	9	0.7
Chester, Pa.									
1957	1,990	141	7.1	281	—	—	1,709	141	8.3
1958	1,460	160	11.0	231	—	—	1,229	160	13.0
10 Total									
1957	27,823	3,234	11.6	4,414	114	2.6	23,409	3,120	13.3
1958	20,896	2,582	12.4	3,780	70	1.9	17,116	2,512	14.7
Kansas City									
1957	2,250	200	8.9	250	—	—	2,000	200	10.0
Metuchen									
1957	1,838	135	7.3	328	—	—	1,500	135	9.0
12 Total									
1957	31,911	3,569	11.2	4,992	114	2.3	26,909	3,455	12.8

Source: Reports to the President's Committee on Government Contracts (Nixon Committee).

Note: There are obviously some small arithmetical errors in these data since they do not add up in both directions. These errors do not change the overall results.

Negroes gained some at Ford during the post-World War II period partially because Ford expanded sales and employment fairly steadily until 1957, when a pre-1964 peak of 191,759 employees was reported. But even with the 1958 recession, which caused a cutback of 50,000 employees, Negroes were not hurt disproportionately in many cases as Table 6 demonstrates.

In the ten assembly plants surveyed in both 1957 and 1958, the ratio of Negro employment to total employment shows a slight increase despite 7,000 layoffs. More likely, the ratio stayed about constant, for the reported increase in the number of Negroes in the Chester, Pennsylvania plant from 141 to 160 while employment in that plant (since abandoned) fell from 1,990 to 1,460, is more likely a reporting error than a fact. Table 6 does indicate, however, the strong seniority position of Negroes at Ford. At many of these plants, Negroes were either hired when they were opened in the post-World War II era, or for older plants, during the war. At River Rouge also, for which Negro employment exceeded 30 percent of the 35,000 employees, layoffs in the 1958 recession seemed to have affected Negroes about proportionately, rather than excessively, because of the Negroes' strong seniority position there.

Table 6 also reveals that Negroes had made gains as salaried workers in two plants—Chicago and Mahwah, New Jersey. Ford continued to have the most Negro supervisors in the industry, but like its principal competitors, had comparatively few other white collar workers.

Finally, data in Table 6 demonstrates that little progress had been made in opening employment opportunities for Negroes in Ford's southern assembly plants in this period.

GENERAL MOTORS, 1946-1960

General Motors employs the largest number of Negroes in the industry, but a smaller percentage than either Chrysler or Ford. It is likely that General Motors' domestic labor force of about 450,000 in the mid-1950's, was approximately 8 or 9 percent Negro.[28]

---

28. For a good statement of General Motors policy by the staff official responsible for it, see Harold S. McFarland, "Minority Group Employment at General Motors," in Herbert R. Northrup and Richard L. Rowan (eds.), *The Negro and Employment Opportunity* (Ann Arbor: Bureau of Industrial Relations, University of Michigan, 1965), pp. 131-136.

TABLE 7. *General Motors Corporation Employment by Race*

Twelve Assembly Plants, 1957 and 1958

Plant Location and Date	All Employees Total	All Employees Negro	All Employees Percent Negro	Salaried Employees Total	Salaried Employees Negro	Salaried Employees Percent Negro	Hourly Employees Total	Hourly Employees Negro	Hourly Employees Percent Negro
Atlanta									
1957	1,676	64	3.8	316	—	—	1,360	64	4.7
1958	1,349	50	3.7	340	—	—	1,009	50	5.0
Baltimore									
1957	1,775	400	22.5	175	—	—	1,600	400	25.0
1958	1,900	524	27.6	320	na	—	1,580	524	33.2
Cincinnati									
1957	1,350	243	18.0	235	—	—	1,115	243	21.8
1958	1,300	232	17.8	235	—	—	1,065	232	21.8
Dallas									
1957	1,961	160	8.2	na	—	—	na	160	—
1958	1,923	159	8.3	349	—	—	1,574	159	10.1
Detroit									
1957	9,066	na	—	2,533	na	—	6,533	na	—
1958	7,222	247	3.4	2,294	—	—	4,231	247	5.8
Los Angeles									
1957	1,978	12	0.6	503	—	—	1,475	12	0.8
1958	1,490	40	2.7	278	—	—	1,212	40	3.3
Tarrytown, N. Y.									
1957	2,196	684	31.1	156	—	—	2,040	684	33.5
1958	2,056	671	32.6	156	1	0.6	1,900	670	35.3
7 Total[a]									
1957	20,002	1,563	14.3	3,918	—	—	14,123	1,563	18.5
1958	17,240	1,923	11.2	3,972	1	*	12,571	1,922	15.3
Kansas City									
1957	1,692	115	6.8	250	—	—	1,442	115	8.0
Linden, N. J.									
1957	3,700	578	15.6	583	—	—	3,117	578	18.5
St. Louis									
1957	2,800	250	8.9	400	—	—	1,400	250	17.9
San Francisco									
1957	1,260	223	17.7	195	—	—	1,065	223	20.9
11 Total									
1957	29,454	2,729	9.3	5,346	—	—	21,147	2,729	12.9

Source: Reports to the President's Committee on Government Contracts (Nixon Committee).

[a] The totals for *all* plants exclude only figures where *not available* (na). The percent Negro figure is based on total employment and total Negro figures where *both* are given. For example, since the 1957 figure for total Negro employees in Detroit assembly is na, the 9066 total Detroit employees are excluded from the 7 Total figure *when computing* percent Negro.

*Less than 0.05 percent.

Note: There are obviously some small arithmetical errors in these data since they do not add up in both directions. These errors do not change the overall results.

One reason why General Motors has a smaller percentage of Negroes is because of the wide dispersion of its vast operations. General Motors has not only by far the most plants in the industry, but also many located in areas where few Negroes reside. In addition, General Motors is more diversified and product integrated than its two principal competitors, and some of its nonautomotive factories are less able than automotive plants to assimilate untrained labor.

Nevertheless, it is probably also true that General Motors adopted a fair employment program more slowly than did Ford or Chrysler and that it moved into affirmative action at a later date than did its competitors. As we shall see in the following section, General Motors is now firmly committed in this regard. General Motors also has moved vigorously on occasions in the past. It worked with the UAW to place Negroes in jobs other than laborers in Atlanta despite intense white employee opposition. It reacted strongly in overcoming local union leadership intimidation to accomplish the same in Kansas City. And it has operated under a strong policy on fair employment for many years. Yet it is the kind of company that moves slowly but surely. And its equal opportunity program reflects this managerial philosophy.

Table 7 shows the Negro employment in eleven General Motors plants in 1957 and 1958, as surveyed by a government procurement agency. These plants may not be representative. But they do illustrate the situation at General Motors plants in several parts of the country. For example, Negroes had sizable representation in the Baltimore, Maryland, Cincinnati, Ohio, Tarrytown, New York, Linden, New Jersey, and San Francisco plants. Only at the New York plant, however, were Negroes represented among salaried employees —and there just one was colored.

The low representation among Negroes in General Motors Detroit facilities listed in Table 7 pertains to the Detroit Diesel plant. This operation, for reasons which are not clear, had a substantially smaller percentage of Negroes than did most General Motors facilities in either the Detroit area, or in other Michigan centers.

Among the plants in border state areas, Cincinnati had the highest percentage of Negroes, Baltimore, the lowest. Again, the reasons for these disparities are not known, but the vagaries of local managerial policies are probable answers. The 6.8 percent Negro employment in Kansas City marked considerable progress from prewar years. Negroes had once been confined to laborer and janitorial jobs there. When General Motors changed its policy after the War and offered production jobs to Negroes, the local union president allegedly visited each Negro employee and "advised" him not to seek an upgrade. Thus intimidated, no Negro employee would accept a promotion. General Motors broke this jam successfully by offering production jobs to Negro job applicants who were not then employees. When several new Negro employees accepted such jobs without incident, the Negro laborers and janitors asked for, and were granted, a new opportunity for upgrading.[29]

In the South, General Motors plants had a far higher percentage of Negroes than did Ford in this period. The percentage of Negroes at the Dallas (actually Arlington), Texas, plant was the highest of any automobile concern in the South. This plant was built after World War II and was not hindered by customs and practices of an earlier period.

General Motors, Atlanta operation, in which Negroes were much better represented than they were at Ford's in the same area, was nevertheless burdened with problems for both company and union. The union difficulties, already noted in the discussion of the World War II period, were commented upon by Professor Marshall as follows:

> . . . The UAW also has had considerable trouble . . . with its oldest Southern local in Atlanta [the G.M. local]. Indeed, this local even barred the eight Negro janitors in the plant from membership until forced by the international to admit them in 1946. Even after the Negroes were admitted, however, seating was segregated. In 1962 a Negro who attempted to sit in the white section was hit over the head with a chair by a white member. In 1961 Negroes were upgraded for the first time in the auto plant represented by this local. This gain for the Negroes was partly offset, however, by the loss of twelve jobs from which Negroes were "bumped" by whites after production lines were integrated.[30] [When employment increased later, these jobs were restored.]

Some local company officials, although certainly not violent, were equally devoted to the *status quo*. The *Wall Street Journal* in 1957 noting that the plant "employs only a few Negroes mainly for

29. Based on interviews by the author, November 1966.
30. F. Ray Marshall, *The Negro and Organized Labor* (New York: John Wiley & Sons, Inc., 1965), p. 179.

janitorial work," quoted the General Motors' Atlanta plant manager as saying:

> When we moved into the South, we agreed to abide by local custom and not hire Negroes for production work. This is no time for social reforming in that area and we're not about to try it.[31]

Obviously company policy was subject to considerable area influence even in the late 1950's. Yet despite this, General Motors, as noted, led Ford by a good margin in Negro employment in the South.

A strong factor in maintaining the *status quo* in southern plants at this time was the practice of hiring through state employment services. These agencies, although funded by the federal government, were highly segregated. The Negro sections often provided referrals to unskilled and service jobs only. Negroes in Atlanta, Dallas, or in other communities who wanted production or skilled work were referred to the state employment agencies by companies including automobile companies; but the Negro sections of these state agencies would neither test nor refer Negroes to the better jobs. Title VII of the Civil Rights Act of 1964 recognized this problem by forbidding such segregation on the part of federally supported state agencies.

THE RECESSION IMPACT, 1957-1960

As already indicated, the recession which began in late 1957, hit the automobile industry hard. Motor vehicle factory sales, which had soared to 9.2 million in 1955, a record not heretofore achieved nor surpassed for nine years, and which stood at 7.2 million in 1957, fell to 5.1 million in 1958. Ford employment dropped from 191,759 in 1957 to 142,076 in 1958; General Motors (world wide) from 588,160 to 520,625; and Chrysler, which already had a substantial number of employees on layoff, from 136,185 to 91,678. Negroes were heavily laid off, and in Detroit, as elsewhere, made up a disproportionate share of the unemployment. Detroit was designated by the federal government as a depressed area—that is, unemployment in excess of 6 percent of the labor force. In 1958, Detroit unemployment was estimated at 16.7 percent of the labor force; Negro

31. *Wall Street Journal*, October 24, 1957.

unemployment at nearly twice this amount.[32] Since those on layoff had prior recall rights before new employees could be hired, it was in late 1962 or early 1963 before many plants in the industry again hired on the open market.

American Motors provided an exception to the industry's sales and employment problems. Capitalizing on the compact car, American consolidated its automotive operations in Kenosha and Milwaukee, Wisconsin, and proceeded to gain 7.2 percent of the new passenger car production in 1959 and 1960—the highest share of the market which American or its predecessor companies (Hudson and Nash) enjoyed since the war.

Negroes lost out when American closed the old Hudson Motor Car Company plants in Detroit between 1953 and 1957, for Negro employment at Hudson had averaged 10-15 percent of 25,330 production workers employed by that company in its postwar peak year of 1950. Employment did, however, steadily build up at American's Milwaukee and Kenosha plants, and the plants there which Dr. Bailer found employed no Negroes prior to World War II, had a Negro complement of about 6 percent of approximately 27,000 by 1960—nearly all in the basic production areas.[33]

Studebaker-Packard enjoyed no such resurgence in the late 1950's. Following the merger in 1954, this company's market share, which had stood at 6.5 percent in 1949 prior to the merger of the two companies, plunged steadily downward to 1.0 in 1958; it jumped back to 2.2 percent in 1959, but then declined until the company went out of the automobile business in the United States in December 1963, and in Canada, in March 1966.

Studebaker-Packard early in the merger abandoned the old Packard plants in Detroit, which even before World War II employed 600 Negroes out of a 16,000 labor force, and in which Negro employment stood at about 15 percent of the 16,818 in Packard's peak employment year of 1952.[34] In 1963, Studebaker also abandoned and sold off most of its South Bend, Indiana, works. This came at a time when employment was at peak levels in the South Bend area.

32. From reports of Michigan Unemployment Compensation Commission and Detroit Urban League.

33. Data estimated by author from various public and private sources.

34. For accounts of difficulties for Negro and white employees laid off by Packard in Detroit, see Michael Aiken and L. A. Ferman, "The Social and Political Reactions of Older Negroes to Unemployment," *Phylon*, Vol. XVII (Fourth Quarter 1966), pp. 333-346.

Studebaker employed 26,696 workers in its peak premerger year of 1952; when it ceased production at South Bend, its force stood at 8,800, about 12 percent of whom were Negroes. Many of the former Studebaker Negro employees, having less seniority, had been laid off before the company gave up automobile production in South Bend.[35] Said Studebaker's Director of Personnel in December 1967:

> Since our cessation of automobile production . . . we have done no hiring in South Bend. At that time, we had Negro personnel in our employment office, a Negro Supervisor of Industrial Relations, a draftsman, two secretaries, and a percentage in the factory well above the population ratio in the South Bend area. Due to a constant reduction in force, all have been laid off . . . only one Negro remains in the union because of his seniority.[36]

Despite the setbacks of the recession and plant closings, Negro employment in the industry experienced a definite upward trend in the 1950's, as in previous decades. Table 8 shows the decennial census reports since 1930 for Standard Industrial Classification 371—Motor Vehicles and Equipment. By 1960, nonwhites (nearly all Negro) comprised 9.1 percent of the labor force attached to that part of the industry included in the census version of SIC 371, as compared with 7.8 percent in 1950 and 3.7 percent in 1940. The greatest employment gains of Negroes were made during the World War II period. In the decade of the 1950's Negroes did slightly better than hold their own, but in view of the plant closings in the middle of the 1950's and the severe recession of 1958, these data make it obvious that Negro workers were a significant and permanent sector of the industry's work force by 1960 which would not be dislodged by economic misfortune.

The Negro automobile labor force in 1960 was, however, confined almost exclusively to production jobs. As late as 1962, Negroes comprised less than one percent of the white collar and professional

35. For the experiences in placing the older Studebaker employees, see *Project Able*, Final Report, Contract No. MDS 37-64, Older Worker Employment, United Community Services of St. Joseph County, Inc., 1965; and J. John Paley and Frank J. Paley, "Unemployment and Reemployment Success: An Analysis of the Studebaker Shutdown," *Industrial and Labor Relations Review*, Vol. XXI (January 1958), pp. 234-250.

36. *A Current Look At: (1) The Negro and Title VII, (2) Sex and Title VII*, Washington: Bureau of National Affairs, Inc., 1967, Personnel Policies Forum, Survey No. 82, p. 6.

employment and barely one-half of one percent of the skilled craftsmen in one of the Big Three companies; another had no nonwhite clerical employees throughout most of the 1950's; and the third made little progress in this area. Gains in these job categories would have to wait until the 1960's.

TABLE 8. *Motor Vehicles and Motor Vehicle Equipment (SIC 371)*[a] *Total Employed Persons by Color and Sex, 1930-1960*

	All Employees			Nonwhite[b]			Percent Nonwhite		
Year	Total	Male	Female	Total	Male	Female	Total	Male	Female
1930[c]	640,474	595,433	45,041	29,834	29,504	330	4.7	5.0	0.7
1940	574,931	525,010	49,921	21,005	20,794	211	3.7	4.0	0.4
1950	868,974	759,545	109,429	67,885	63,572	4,313	7.8	8.4	3.9
1960	836,681	745,260	91,421	76,296	71,594	4,702	9.1	9.6	5.1

Source: *U. S. Census of Population:*
1960: PC (2)7A, *Occupational Characteristics,* Table 37.
1950: Vol. II, *Characteristics of the Population,* Part 1, *United States Summary,* Table 133.
1940: Vol. III, *The Labor Force,* Table 76.
1930: Vol. V, *General Report on Occupations,* Table 2, p. 468.

[a] Comparability: 1930 category "Automobile Factories," 1940 category "Automobiles and Automobile Equipment," and 1950, 1960 category "Motor Vehicles and Motor Vehicle Equipment" appear to be comparable. These categories include firms which do one of the following: (a) assemble or manufacture completed autos, trucks, and buses; (b) manufacture truck or auto bodies; (c) manufacture automobile parts and accessories.

[b] Nonwhite includes very small numbers of Orientals and American Indians.

[c] 1930 census compiled employment data differently than did later censuses. 1930 collected data on "gainful workers" which, unlike later censuses, did not distinguish between persons employed and persons unemployed but seeking work. The inclusion of the latter category tends to inflate employment statistics for a given industry. Also 1930 census includes workers 10 years and older; 1940-1960, 14 years and older.

CHAPTER VI.

Industrial Expansion and Civil Rights 1960-1968

The rise in civil rights emphasis in the 1960's, by a happy coincidence, came at a time of great prosperity in the automobile industry. Moreover, it happened when a natural turnover was occurring in the industry. Many employees hired around World War II, or earlier, were seeking retirement under the liberalized early, and regular retirement programs in the industry. Between 1962 and 1967, the United Automobile Workers took in 842,000 new workers—more than one-half of its total membership.[37] The need for Negroes to obtain jobs and the need of an industry for new workers were never better coordinated.

RECESSION AND PROSPERITY

The decade of the 1960's did not commence so propitiously. Although 1960 was a fairly good sales year for the industry, it was below the previous decade peak year of 1955. Then came another downturn in 1961, in which Chrysler was hit especially hard by lack of sales. But thereafter, sales rose, and as Table 9 shows, employment followed suit, with one record year following another through 1968, and with 1968 second only to 1965 in unit sales.

As already noted, the Big Three companies began the decade of the 1960's with substantial layoff lists, dating back to the 1958 recession mainly, but Chrysler in many cases to the early 1950's. The recession of 1961, following on the heels of the more severe one of 1958, forced such cutbacks that in some plants it required twenty-five years seniority to hold a job. Chrysler was forced to lay off 49,000 employees, including 7,000 white collar ones, because of the sales decline and the need to reduce costs in 1961. Thereafter,

37. *Wall Street Journal*, July 6, 1967, p. 1.

TABLE 9. *Big Three Automobile Companies Domestic Employment, 1960-1968*

Year	Company: General Motors	Company: Ford	Company: Chrysler	Total Three Companies
1960	457,965	160,181	105,410	723,556
1961	464,150	154,659	74,377	693,186
1962	486,869	186,640	77,194	750,703
1963	499,818	187,428	90,752	777,998
1964	545,347	197,578	104,845	847,770
1965	580,451	217,741	126,000	924,192
1966	586,622	233,849	133,114	953,585
1967	584,895	238,834	142,550	966,279
1968	621,991	244,819	153,973	1,020,783

Source: Company annual and other reports. Ford data excludes Philco-Ford and other subsidiary companies; General Motors and Chrysler data include non-automotive operations such as appliances, locomotives, and aerospace products.

however, Chrysler surged forward to regain much of its market position, and eventually to expand employment well beyond 1960 levels, but so far, not up to the peak years of the 1950's.

The prosperity of the 1960's was not shared by the independents. As already noted, Studebaker went out of the business altogether. From a share of 7.2 percent in 1960, American Motors lost position slowly for three years, and then more rapidly until by 1966 it held only 2.5 percent of the market. Negro employment in its Milwaukee and Kenosha plants dropped at least proportionately, remaining at approximately 6 percent, while total employment in these plants dipped from a peak of approximately 27,000 in 1960 to less than 18,000 in 1966, where it tended to stabilize.

NEGRO EMPLOYMENT IN THE 1960's—THE GENERAL PICTURE

There is no doubt that Negroes were the biggest gainers as employment rose in the 1960's following the surge in automobile sales. From a depressed area with a labor surplus and unemployment in excess of 16 percent, Detroit turned into a highly prosperous one, importing workers to overcome a critical labor shortage. Anyone willing and able to work could find it—and with earnings which in 1968 averaged in excess of $150 per week.

At the same time that sales and employment began to rise, greater emphasis on the need for Negro employment commenced. The Kennedy Administration reorganized and greatly strengthened the equal opportunity work done by the procurement agencies and the President's Committee on Equal Employment Opportunity (now the Office of Federal Contract Compliance). In addition, major corporations, including the Big Three automobile companies, were invited to join the Plans for Progress Program, in which the companies pledge themselves to work actively and affirmatively to further minority group employment.

Once the laid off workers of the 1950's and the 1961 recession were recalled, the Big Three automobile companies had little difficulty living up to their Plans for Progress pledges insofar as production workers in the northern industrial centers were concerned. The Detroit area, in particular, saw Negroes emerge as the dominant group in production in many plants. A tour of blue collar employment offices in Detroit any time since 1965 would reveal very few white applicants except at the time of school closings, or summer vacation, or unless the applicant was qualified for a skilled trade. In other parts of the country also Negro employment in the industry rose faster than total employment.

Tables 10 and 11 show the number and percentage of Negroes by occupational groupings for the Big Three companies, 1966 and 1968. Negroes made up 13.6 percent of the labor force of the Big Three by the end of 1966, a percentage slightly larger than their ratio in the general population, and 14.5 percent in 1968. In production operations, Negroes comprised about 25 percent of the work force—more than twice the percentage of Negroes to whites in the total labor force. In production operations, Negroes are, moreover, not confined to any particular type jobs or departments. Although they are slightly more concentrated in service and laborers jobs than as operatives, the difference in job rates or types of jobs among these groups is not great. Negroes work side by side with whites on all jobs in assembly plants, stamping and other manufacturing plants, and in all types of jobs associated with production in these areas. It is doubtful if Negroes have so large a share of production jobs in any other major industry.

TABLE 10. *Big Three Automobile Companies*
Employment by Race, Sex, and Occupational Group, 1966

Occupational Group	All Employees			Male			Female		
	Total	Negro	Percent Negro	Total	Negro	Percent Negro	Total	Negro	Percent Negro
Officials and managers	74,395	903	1.2	74,061	903	1.2	334	—	—
Professionals	51,053	301	0.6	50,380	287	0.6	673	14	2.1
Technicians	24,499	297	1.2	23,316	268	1.1	1,183	29	2.5
Sales, office, and clerical	93,365	3,545	3.8	57,650	2,768	4.8	35,715	777	2.2
Total white collar	243,312	5,046	2.1	205,407	4,226	2.1	37,905	820	2.2
Craftsmen	129,123	3,846	3.0	129,042	3,842	3.0	81	4	4.9
Operatives	515,843	104,112	20.2	460,702	98,313	21.3	55,141	5,799	10.5
Laborers	32,352	8,922	27.6	31,649	8,826	27.9	703	96	13.7
Service workers	26,755	7,269	27.2	24,898	6,855	27.5	1,857	414	22.3
Total blue collar	704,073	124,149	17.6	646,291	117,836	18.2	57,782	6,313	10.9
Total	947,385	129,195	13.6	851,698	122,062	14.3	95,687	7,133	7.5

Source: Data in author's possession.

Note: Two of the three companies report no sales personnel and one but a few. Hence they are combined with office and clerical throughout Part Two.

TABLE 11. *Big Three Automobile Companies Employment by Race, Sex, and Occupational Group, 1968*

	All Employees			Male			Female		
Occupational Group	Total	Negro	Percent Negro	Total	Negro	Percent Negro	Total	Negro	Percent Negro
Officials and managers	74,814	1,026	1.4	74,459	1,024	1.4	355	2	0.6
Professionals	51,817	367	0.7	51,027	344	0.7	790	23	2.9
Technicians	23,155	350	1.5	22,004	316	1.4	1,151	34	3.0
Sales, office, and clerical	91,504	4,014	4.4	57,168	3,152	5.5	34,336	862	2.5
Total white collar	241,290	5,757	2.4	204,658	4,836	2.4	36,632	921	2.5
Craftsmen	128,601	4,191	3.3	128,498	4,190	3.3	103	1	1.0
Operatives	522,197	111,066	21.3	463,487	103,819	22.4	58,710	7,247	12.3
Laborers	32,798	9,541	29.1	31,999	9,407	29.4	799	134	16.8
Service workers	26,672	7,274	27.3	24,785	6,863	27.7	1,887	411	21.8
Total blue collar	710,268	132,072	18.6	648,769	124,279	19.2	61,499	7,793	12.7
Total	951,558	137,829	14.5	853,427	129,115	15.1	98,131	8,714	8.9

Source: Data in author's possession.

THE CRAFTSMEN PROBLEM

Insofar as craftsmen are concerned, the situation is quite different. In 1966, Negroes comprised only 3 percent of the 129,123 skilled personnel in this group in Big Three plants, and in 1968, 3.3 percent of the 128,601 so classified. Despite a shortage of craftsmen and energetic efforts on the part of the companies to recruit personnel, this situation has been difficult to change for several reasons.

Traditionally, skilled craftsmen in the automobile industry have come from three sources: company apprentice programs; employment of those who learned their skills elsewhere, including immigrants; and upgraders or learners trained on the job after production experience.

The apprentice programs have always attracted a high type person —the high school graduate with good mechanical and mathematical aptitude who did not make it to college because of family attitudes or finances. They have traditionally been the "middle class" of automobile workers—a white elite who did not associate with the producation men.[38] Like building tradesmen, the skilled trades group have been antagonistic toward accepting Negroes into their group. Moreover, supervisory personnel in the skilled trades area have traditionally come up through the ranks, and undoubtedly share the general attitudes attributed to the rank and file. As will be discussed below, the UAW does not seem to have made great progress in changing attitudes or policies among the skilled trades.[39]

Since, with rare exceptions, only Ford accepted Negroes as apprentices prior to World War II, and since progress made by the industry prior to 1960 in attracting Negro apprentices was rather limited, the exclusionist attitudes of the skilled trades groups have been reinforced by industry experience. Historically, most Negroes have come to regard all apprenticeship programs as closed to them. There is little reason to believe that this feeling has been substantially overcome in the automobile industry.

Now that the automobile companies have not only opened their ranks to Negroes, but have been eagerly seeking apprentice candi-

---

38. For a good discussion of the social and ethnic backgrounds of the craftsmen, which tend to separate them from the production personnel, see Stanley H. Brown, "Walter Reuther: 'He's Got to Walk That Last Mile,'" *Fortune*, Vol. LXXVI (July 1967), pp. 89, 141-142.

39. F. Ray Marshall, *The Negro and Organized Labor* (New York: John Wiley & Sons, Inc., 1965), pp. 68-69.

dates, other factors mitigate against success for Negroes in these jobs. Negroes who apply find that they are less proficient in mathematics and score lower as a group in tests than do whites. Most of the Negroes applying come either from southern segregated institutions or from less desirable areas of the cities. In either case, their training is likely to compare unfavorably with that of whites from better surroundings. For example, in a sampling of applicants of one company in early 1967, only four Negroes of a total of 267 who took the preapprentice admission test passed the mathematics examination. Moreover, these four had scores that were marginal and therefore, in competition for openings in the apprentice program, were unlikely to gain admittance. Whenever apprentice openings occur, it has been the policy in at least one company to select those with the highest scores regardless of when the test was taken. Hence low scores may never be admitted. (The companies are limited by union contract on the number of apprentices in relation to journeymen whom they may employ. The General Motors contract, for example, limits the apprentice ratio to one per eight journeymen in a given craft. The contract permits flexibility, however, depending on the local area and/or craft skill supply and demand situation. Ratios as low as one for one have been negotiated for recent periods.)

The failure of Negroes to qualify for apprenticeship programs is a persistent problem. The same company from which the test score sample was taken now finds about 25 percent of its applicants for apprenticeship are Negroes, but only about 12 percent of those qualifying are Negroes. Moreover, those qualifying are on the low side. They find openings in apprentice classes for millwrights, pipe fitters, and welders. The tool and die and electrical trades take those with the highest scores, and few Negroes now make up these groups or qualify for them.

Tests, of course, are not identical among the three companies, and are never the only criteria for determining acceptance into apprenticeship programs. Tests are designed to determine whether the applicant is capable of handling high school mathematics, a prerequisite for comprehension of shop mathematics. The Ford program requires that an applicant be 18-27 years of age, have a tenth grade education, with a C average, and a successful joint union-management interview. The General Motors rules require that applicants be 18-26 years of age, and be a high school graduate or have equivalent education.

General Motors neither requires nor suggests a joint union-management interview. The key elements, in all cases, are mathematical aptitude and comprehension, and a high school education. Those who score high in the premployment tests are eagerly sought after and readily accepted.

Most Negroes who now meet these criteria, like most whites, go to college instead of into an apprentice program. Since proportionately fewer Negroes are available, their disproportionate showing among the apprentice applicants is likely to continue.

Ford and the UAW agreed in the 1967 negotiations to an experiment to try and break the testing cycle which has kept Negro representation in the apprentice program so low. Forty colored and forty white low scorers—that is, those who passed the tests, but with marginal performances—were accepted into the apprentice program ahead of high scorers. Their progress is being watched carefully to determine whether low scorers can become satisfactory apprentices and craftsmen, and therefore whether the tests need restructuring or reinterpreting. Ford is also having its tests thoroughly re-examined and restudied to determine whether built-in bias is influencing results.

Company apprenticeship programs in the automobile industry are not limited to new or to youthful applicants. For example, at General Motors, for those already on the company rolls, the age requirement is greatly expanded. General Motors will accept into the apprenticeship program employees in the 27-40 age group. Where qualifications "of the employe-applicant and non-employe-applicant are equal, the employe-applicant will be given preference." The General Motors agreement with the UAW also provides that "For all applicants placed on apprentice training in any given year, the ratio of those in the 27-40 age group to those under 27 years of age shall in no event exceed one to two in the particular trade involved."

Employees who demonstrate competence can be given credit for previous experience and can thus shorten the four-year apprentice training period and also receive wage rate adjustments. Employees transferred into apprentice training continue to accumulate seniority in the seniority group from which they transfer, as well as begin to accumulate seniority as an apprentice in a particular craft.

Applicants for apprentice training among Negro employees have always been markedly less than their proportion in the work force.

There are several reasons for this. The first, of course, is that Negroes are less well educated and more likely to be deficient in mathematical comprehension and general educational requirements. Moreover, these jobs have traditionally been closed to Negroes—except at Ford's River Rouge plant and a few others. To apply for apprentice training has been to "go out of bounds," as a Negro assembly line worker told the author.[40] Now that such job training is available, past practices and customs are difficult to overcome. The fact that so few Negroes are in the skilled crafts, discourages others from trying. It is more compatible to be where fellow members of one's race are clearly accepted and already found in large numbers.

Because of the high pay of production workers, a temporary sacrifice in earnings is likely to be required to enter the apprentice training program. This demands both a long-run view, strong motivation, and confidence in the future. Such apprentice candidates do not sacrifice their seniority, but apparently this is not enough motivation. Discrimination and motivation go hand in hand. Because of the pervasiveness of the former in the life of Negroes, the latter is often lacking. Opportunities for training which require sacrifice for eventual improvement are not grasped. Inexperience in industry, lack of family help in setting goals, the absence of similar opportunities in previous generations, and the difficulty of breaking with the past all continue to reduce the number of Negroes who grasp the opportunities for skilled trades training.

It is expecting much to believe that Negroes will take advantage of such training opportunities without special effort. If the number of Negro apprentices applying from existing employees is to be increased, it appears obvious that special motivational and training efforts will have to be made. Educational and motivational deficiencies must be overcome if qualifications are to be raised and if the desire is to be created to acquire the skills which both pay very well and provide a trade that will likely always be useful. There have been efforts to encourage Negro employees to go into the apprentice programs, but they have been neither massive nor particularly successful thus far. Whether with greater effort on the part of the companies, greater success would result cannot be predicted, but such efforts would at least provide the answer for the industry and its critics.

40. Interview, eastern automobile plant, November 1967.

Negroes are largely unrepresented among those craftsmen who enter the automobile industry after training in other industries or countries. Detroit's skilled craftsmen have always included a sizable number trained abroad, including many who make their way from the metals industries of Europe and Britain, through Canada, or directly. The high wages also attract craftsmen from other industries. Since few industries have been as willing to hire Negroes as has the automobile industry, and since no Negroes are found among the skilled immigrants, these recruits to the industry are virtually all white.

Upgraders or learners represent the most likely source of skilled Negro craftsmen for the future. They are production workers who are given training, first as helpers, and then as skilled workers, and thus learn a trade without a formal apprenticeship program, and without sacrificing their pay scale. In the past, both companies and the UAW Skilled Trades Department have been accused of reluctance to open up opportunities to Negroes.[41] This is certainly no longer so, but again the problem of background and education limits the number of Negroes who can handle these skills. In addition, companies cite a discouraging number of cases in which Negroes with requisite backgrounds preferred to stay on production jobs and not take the necessary training. Given, however, the tremendous size of the Negro labor force in the industry, it is likely that a slow but steady increase in their representation among skilled craftsmen should result *via* the upgrading route. Progress is likely to be slow because, again, of the educational, motivational, and in a steadily declining proportion, discriminatory barriers. The expanding Negro production labor force, however, would seem to insure an increasing spillover into skilled trade upgrading promotions, and it is likely that affirmative action on the part of the companies to expand their Negro skilled trades force will somewhat accelerate the pace.

MANAGERS, PROFESSIONALS, AND TECHNICAL EMPLOYEES

Progress in the salaried area has been slow, but since 1962 the major companies have been making a determined effort to recruit Negro professionals, technicians, and office workers. There are a limited number of Negroes with sufficient training for professional

41. Marshall, *supra,* note 39.

and technical jobs and not only automobile companies, but in fact companies in almost every major industry are attempting to recruit them. Consequently, the number of Negroes in these jobs is certain to rise but to increase slowly.

A number of changes have occurred in company policy in regard to professional and technical personnel. Most noteworthy was the decision of General Motors to open the General Motors Institute to Negroes, and to recruit Negroes intensively to attend the Institute. The General Motors Institute is an accredited five-year college at Flint, Michigan, which is a training ground for future General Motors executives. In 1967, the company reported that there were 18 Negroes among the 3,000 students, and that for the first time Negroes in 1967 would be in the graduating class.[42]

In the officials and managers group are included supervisory personnel. Most Negroes in this group are line supervisors or foremen, but a few have made it farther up the ladder. Negroes are beginning to appear in personnel and other staff positions, in accounting departments, and less frequently in line operations above the general foreman classification. Again progress is likely to be slow because of the few Negroes who are qualified for higher management jobs, the intense competition among various industries and companies to recruit qualified Negroes, and the equally intense internal competition in the automobile companies for managerial positions which offer rich pecuniary and status rewards.

DEALERS AND SALESMEN

Automobile companies do not have sales personnel in the traditional sense. Salesmen work for dealers who are independent businessmen operating company-awarded franchises. For many years, Edward B. Davis, a Detroit Negro, was the only Negro franchised dealer. He held a Studebaker franchise for 17 years, and then in 1962, became a Chrysler dealer.[43] Not until 1967, did Ford and General Motors announce the awarding of dealerships to Negroes. By 1969, Chrysler had about a dozen dealers, Ford, General Motors, and American Motors also had a few.

42. *New York Times*, July 16, 1967, p. 53.
43. *Detroit News*, August 31, 1967; *Detroit Free Press*, September 1, 1967; and *New York Times*, September 2, 1967.

Having so few Negroes among the approximately 30,000 franchised dealers in domestic automobiles is scarcely an outstanding record. The companies point out that they have had great difficulty in finding a Negro entrepreneur with the requisite business background, ability, who has also the necessary access to capital and credit resources. "The companies insist that they are not discriminatory and would be willing to sign up Negroes who know the auto business and have the financial backing necessary."[44]

Merely desiring to have a Negro dealer, and waiting for one to come along, proved insufficient. In August 1957, Mr. Virgil E. Boyd, president of Chrysler, announced a program of direct recruitment and training designed to set up in business Negroes who want to be car dealers as "the only way to get these people placed." Mr. Boyd's program calls for recruiting prospects from among "several hundred Negroes who now hold jobs as salesmen or sales managers in white-owned dealerships. . . ."[45]

Chrysler started a program several years ago when Mr. Boyd was sales vice-president to expand Negro representation among the sales force of the company and its dealers. The number of Negroes in these groups rose from 11 to 400 in two years. According to Mr. Boyd, a number of Negro salesmen have progressed to sales manager positions. They and other candidates are being considered for the Chrysler Institute, a special six-months course in dealer business operations, which traditionally has been operated as a training course for sons of Chrysler dealers. After six months at the Institute, trainees are given field instruction at dealerships. Negro candidates will train at both the Davis dealership and at white-owned dealerships. The first Negro graduate of the Institute, Donald Thomas, entered after working in Chrysler's personnel department. Prospective dealers, once trained, will be backed financially by the company if they can "come up with a nominal investment."[46]

Although all companies are, as Mr. Davis, the pioneer Negro automobile dealer, has stated, "now earnestly trying to get qualified men as dealers" without discrimination, it has required programs like Chrysler's to achieve solid results, and Ford and General Motors have now established their own. Developments like the Chrysler plan,

44. *Ibid.*
45. *Ibid.*
46. *Ibid.*

which commenced with six candidates at one time, will not show dramatic results for a number of years. The opportunities are there, and, as Chrysler has recognized, successful Negro dealers in many metropolitan areas which have sizeable Negro population, are certain both to attract business and to provide leadership and inspiration for Negroes interested in business opportunities.

Chrysler's program should also have salutory results on Negro representation among regional officers and dealer salesmen. As already noted, Chrysler has already moved to strengthen Negro participation in these areas. The other companies have likewise done so. All the Big Three have successfully encouraged and assisted dealers in recruiting Negro salesmen, particularly in the large cities where Negro population is now a significant source of sales. No data are available on the number or percentage of Negro salesmen other than the Chrysler figures already cited, but the author has found them with increasing frequency in big city dealerships in the East and Midwest.

On the other hand, regional and district offices typically have few Negroes. The industry does not list such regional and district personnel as salesmen, for they do not sell to the consumer. They aid and oversee dealers, handle customer and public relations problems, and generally look out for the interests of the companies. This is an area in which Negroes in nearly every industry are poorly represented, and the automobile industry is no significant exception.

OFFICE AND CLERICAL

In the office and clerical group, the fact that Negroes represented only 4.4 percent of the total in 1968 indicates the late start in hiring such Negro personnel, the progress during the 1960's when the bulk of the industry's 4,000 Negroes were employed in offices, and certain locational difficulties. Because of its late start in employing Negroes in clerical and white collar jobs, the industry must now compete for a scarce supply of qualified personnel. Moreover, employment habits have been slow to change, despite changes in company policies. Given the greater training of whites and the superiority of the schools which they are likely to attend, special programs and training are likely to be required to increase substantially Negro participation in clerical and office jobs. Since, in addition, turnover in accounting, sales office, and other jobs is not high among male office and clerical employees, the representation of Negroes is not likely to increase rapidly.

As we shall note below in our discussion of regional and locational difficulties, where plants and offices are located in suburbs or in other areas outside of Detroit or other cities, where Negroes cannot find housing, Negro males are willing to commute long distances, but females are not. Like most women who have households to care for, Negro females want work close to home. The general offices of Chrysler and General Motors are located in the heart of the Detroit area; Ford is at Dearborn, an outlying area; and many plant locations and their offices are farther out of Detroit or other metropolitan areas. Where potential Negro clerical help cannot live close by, it is difficult to obtain.

REGIONAL AND LOCATIONAL FACTORS

Developments in the 1960's have varied by region and by company, as they have in the past. Detroit in particular, and Michigan in general, continue to have the highest concentration of Negroes in the industry. Like many northern industrial centers, Detroit has had a heavy inmigration of Negroes, and an even heavier outmigration of whites. The Negro percentage of the population in other Michigan automotive centers is also substantial. The estimated ratio of Negro population for Detroit in 1965 was 39 percent; of Flint, 22 percent; Grand Rapids, 11 percent; Pontiac, 21 percent; and Saginaw, 24 percent. Projections for these areas indicate a continued rise in the ratio of Negroes to whites, with Detroit expected to be about 50 percent Negro by 1970.[47]

Negro representation in production operations has more than kept pace with the Negro population growth in the greater Detroit area. Some downtown Chrysler plants, for example, have a majority of Negro hourly employees; on the second shift (shift preference is by seniority), the ratio has been as high as 85 percent Negro. The Ford River Rouge works is about 42 percent Negro in total and with much higher Negro ratios in some production areas. Plants 30 to 70

47. Data from U. S. Census. See also *The Negro Population: 1965 Estimates and 1970 Projections* (Peekskill, N. Y.: The Center for Research in Marketing, Inc., February 1966).

percent Negro are quite common throughout the Greater Detroit area.[48]

An interesting aspect of Detroit area Negro automobile employment is the relatively high percentage in suburban areas where housing is completely closed to Negroes. An assembly plant, for example, twenty miles from center city, which can be reached only by car traveling on a turnpike that bisects several all-white communities, is 26 percent Negro. A prime reason is that employees who once worked closer to midtown Detroit transferred with their work when the new suburban assembly plant was built, and the plant became known as a place where Negroes were well received.

Where new plants have been built in the suburbs, Negroes have found work there despite the absence of housing open to them. For example, in a new stamping plant, which is also located in a suburban area, 18 percent of the labor force is Negro. The absence of housing for Negroes in such areas, however, insures that very few Negro females will be employed in such plants.

Seniority provisions have been of considerable aid in helping Negroes find work throughout the Detroit area, or in other areas where a number of plants of one company are located. When openings occur, the Chrysler agreement, for example, provides that preference be given, first, to qualified laid off employees of other departments in the plant, and second, to such employees who have been laid off by other Chrysler plants in the area. Employees do not lose their seniority if they refuse such job offers, but they then cannot collect supplemental unemployment benefits. With such provisions, it is not possible to confine Negroes to particular departments or plants because in effect a general labor pool is created, which has first chance at openings at any area plant or department covered by the agreement.

Like Ford and Chrysler, General Motors has a high concentration of Negro production workers in the greater Detroit area, where 25 to 45 percent of its employees in these categories are Negro. In Flint, Pontiac, Lansing, Grand Rapids, and Saginaw, General Motors plants with 15-25 percent Negro employment, or occasionally even higher, are typical.

In other eastern and midwestern cities, the percentage of Negroes in assembly and manufacturing plants varies considerably. Chicago

48. All data are the author's estimates based on information in his possession.

plants range from 13 to 60 percent Negro; Cleveland plants from 20 to 50 percent; and those in the New York City area, from 12 to 60 percent. In areas where few Negroes reside, for example, Wisconsin, very few are found in automotive plants. Except in the New York area, where housing nearby outlying plants is available to Negroes, plants in suburban areas do not have a high Negro complement as they do in Detroit. The sight of Negroes traveling toward, and working in automobile plants, far out of center city, and far from Negro housing opportunities, is much more common in Detroit than elsewhere.

In California plants, Negroes comprised 12.8 percent of the Big Three total employment and 17.2 of the operatives in 1966 and 13.4 percent of the total and 18.1 percent of the operatives in 1968; but, as usual, substantially smaller percentages of the craftsmen and salaried personnel. These data are found in Tables 12 and 13. Although California was estimated to have only a 6 percent Negro population in 1965, Los Angeles was estimated at 18 percent, Oakland at 31 percent, San Francisco at 14 percent.[49] Since most automobile plants are in or nearby these cities, Negro representation in these areas has about kept pace with the population.

In border cities, such as Wilmington, Delaware, Baltimore, St. Louis, Kansas City, Cincinnati, and Louisville, Negro employment varies considerably, with the percentage of production employees anywhere from 10 to 50 percent, but with very few Negro white collar employees or craftsmen. The Indianapolis area plants follow a similar pattern. Automobile plants located in smaller Ohio, Illinois, or Indiana communities do not generally employ a high percentage of Negroes, particularly if they are on the southern borders of these states.

The situation in the South is the weakest in terms of Negro employment. Tables 14 and 15 show that approximately 10 percent of the total employment in southern automobile plants both in 1966 and 1968, was Negro, with heavy concentration in the lowest job brackets. These plants were generally operated on a strictly segregated basis until 1961, with separate seniority lines in some cases that confined Negroes to the service and laboring jobs. The pioneering which Henry Ford did at River Rouge was not repeated by Ford or his successors

49. See note 47 for sources.

TABLE 12. *Big Three Automobile Companies Employment by Race, Sex, and Occupational Group California Plants, 1966*

Occupational Group	All Employees			Male			Female		
	Total	Negro	Percent Negro	Total	Negro	Percent Negro	Total	Negro	Percent Negro
Officials and managers	2,036	35	1.7	2,036	35	1.7	—	—	—
Professionals	765	4	0.5	748	4	0.5	17	—	—
Technicians	341	7	2.1	308	7	2.3	33	—	—
Sales, office, and clerical	3,168	183	5.8	2,325	177	7.6	843	6	0.7
Total white collar	6,310	229	3.6	5,417	223	4.1	893	6	0.7
Craftsmen	1,518	39	2.6	1,518	39	2.6	—	—	—
Operatives	15,929	2,739	17.2	15,891	2,739	17.2	38	—	—
Laborers	1,186	159	13.4	1,180	158	13.4	6	1	16.7
Service workers	841	137	16.3	841	137	16.3	—	—	—
Total blue collar	19,474	3,074	15.8	19,430	3,073	15.8	44	1	2.3
Total	25,784	3,303	12.8	24,847	3,296	13.3	937	7	0.7

Source: Data in author's possession.

TABLE 13. *Big Three Automobile Companies*
Employment by Race, Sex, and Occupational Group
California Plants, 1968

Occupational Group	All Employees			Male			Female		
	Total	Negro	Percent Negro	Total	Negro	Percent Negro	Total	Negro	Percent Negro
Officials and managers	2,032	41	2.0	2,031	41	2.0	1	—	—
Professionals	755	5	0.7	739	5	0.7	16	—	—
Technicians	298	10	3.4	272	9	3.3	26	1	3.8
Sales, office, and clerical	3,196	191	6.0	2,459	185	7.5	737	6	0.8
Total white collar	6,281	247	3.9	5,501	240	4.4	780	7	0.9
Craftsmen	1,453	35	2.4	1,453	35	2.4	—	—	—
Operatives	15,548	2,808	18.1	15,513	2,807	18.1	35	1	2.9
Laborers	1,353	206	15.2	1,348	205	15.2	5	1	20.0
Service workers	774	111	14.3	773	111	14.4	1	—	—
Total blue collar	19,128	3,160	16.5	19,087	3,158	16.5	41	2	4.9
Total	25,409	3,407	13.4	24,588	3,398	13.8	821	9	1.1

Source: Data in author's possession.

TABLE 14. *General Motors and Ford*
Employment by Race, Sex, and Occupational Group
Southern Plants, 1966

Occupational Group	All Employees			Male			Female		
	Total	Negro	Percent Negro	Total	Negro	Percent Negro	Total	Negro	Percent Negro
Officials and managers	3,512	28	0.8	3,511	28	0.8	1	—	—
Professionals	1,280	8	0.6	1,263	7	0.6	17	1	5.9
Technicians	260	7	2.7	220	6	2.7	40	1	2.5
Sales, office, and clerical	5,798	166	2.9	4,702	155	3.3	1,096	11	1.0
Total white collar	10,850	209	1.9	9,696	196	2.0	1,154	13	1.1
Craftsmen	2,786	12	0.4	2,786	12	0.4	—	—	—
Operatives	26,008	3,232	12.4	25,983	3,231	12.4	25	1	4.0
Laborers	2,992	447	14.9	2,990	447	14.9	2	—	—
Service workers	1,470	359	24.4	1,469	358	24.4	1	1	100.0
Total blue collar	33,256	4,050	12.2	33,228	4,048	12.2	28	2	7.1
Total	44,106	4,259	9.7	42,924	4,244	9.9	1,182	15	1.3

Source: Data in author's possession.

TABLE 15. *General Motors and Ford Employment by Race, Sex, and Occupational Group Southern Plants, 1968*

Occupational Group	All Employees			Male			Female		
	Total	Negro	Percent Negro	Total	Negro	Percent Negro	Total	Negro	Percent Negro
Officials and managers	4,705	27	0.6	4,703	27	0.6	2	—	—
Professionals	1,199	8	0.7	1,183	7	0.6	16	1	6.2
Technicians	226	7	3.1	188	7	3.7	38	—	—
Sales, office, and clerical	5,693	187	3.3	4,718	176	3.7	975	11	1.1
Total white collar	11,823	229	1.9	10,792	217	2.0	1,031	12	1.2
Craftsmen	2,845	11	0.4	2,845	11	0.4	—	—	—
Operatives	26,517	3,598	13.6	26,490	3,597	13.6	27	1	3.7
Laborers	3,016	488	16.2	3,012	488	16.2	4	—	—
Service workers	1,400	356	25.4	1,399	355	25.4	1	1	100.0
Total blue collar	33,778	4,453	13.2	33,746	4,451	13.2	32	2	6.2
Total	45,601	4,682	10.3	44,538	4,668	10.5	1,063	14	1.3

Source: Data in author's possession.

in the South. Nor did General Motors fill the breach, and Chrysler has no southern automotive plants.

The UAW likewise, as we have already noted, has not been much of a pioneer in southern automotive plants. In contrast to the record of both companies and the union in the automotive plants at Atlanta, Norfolk, and Dallas, have been the efforts of the International Harvester Company and the same UAW in Memphis, Tennessee and at other locations. International Harvester abolished separate facilities and integrated the work force in southern plants in the immediate post-World War II period, and the UAW put a rebellious local in trusteeship when it attempted to challenge that company's racial policies.[50]

In contrast, Ford and General Motors were slow to buck southern custom. Apparently, they feared a white reaction which might have harmed sales. Yet if *both* had moved, it is unlikely that customer reaction could have damaged *both* companies, especially since Chrysler, the main alternative for the consumer, remained the employer with the largest proportion of Negroes in its work force. Finally in 1961 the companies, with UAW cooperation, put an end to sanctioned discrimination and segregation. Progress in upgrading and hiring has followed, but has been slowed, especially in the Ford plants, because some of the facilities have had only limited expansion and relatively small turnover.

COMPANY DIFFERENCES

Chrysler continues to lead in the ratio of Negroes employed. Again a principal reason appears to be locational, since Chrysler remains the most concentrated in the central Detroit area, and has no plants in the South where equal employment opportunity in the industry has progressed the least, and very few plants in areas where Negro population is a very small ratio. In 1968, 25 percent of Chrysler's total work force and 32 percent of its blue collar workers were Negroes.[51]

50. On the International Harvester experience, see John Hope II, *Negro Employment in 3 Southern Plants of International Harvester Company* (Washington, D. C.: National Planning Association, 1953), Committee of the South Report No. 6; Robert Ozanne, *A Century of Labor Management Relations at McCormick and International Harvester* (Madison, Wis.: University of Wisconsin Press, 1967), pp. 183-193; and Marshall, *op. cit.*, pp. 178-179.

51. All data in this section, unless otherwise noted, are the author's estimates based upon data in his possession.

Chrysler's favorable position in regard to Negroes is bolstered by a very strong managerial attitude. Company officials, starting with the Chief Executive, have made the Company's position very clear. It has been in the forefront on a variety of special training projects such as the already noted one for potential Negro dealers, which are designed to improve Negro educational opportunities and to open up new vistas for Negroes. Its border city plants in Delaware and St. Louis have a substantially higher percentage of Negro employees than do comparable plants of other companies. And like its two bigger competitors, it strives hard to recruit Negroes for its managerial, professional, and technical positions.

Chrysler also leads its competitors in the percentage of Negro officials and managers. Nearly 5 percent of this important category at Chrysler are Negro. Most of those in this category are supervisors and foremen, but some higher-rated officials and staff members are involved. With its high percentage of Negroes, Chrysler has had, and accepted, the opportunity to upgrade Negroes to supervisory positions with considerable success. In all three companies, Negro foremen supervised mixed crews.

At the professional and technical levels, Chrysler is also slightly ahead of its competitors, but the percentage differences among the three companies are too small to be significant. All three companies, as noted, are, with most other large concerns, avidly recruiting eligible Negroes in these categories, but the very small number of qualified Negroes, particularly in engineering, is a major obstacle to overcome.

Chrysler's marketing policies, including its pioneering with the first Negro dealer, and with the program to increase dealer opportunities for Negroes, go hand in hand with its employment policies. Advertising in the Negro press and to the Negro communities not only attempts to capitalize on its employment policies, but further stresses the record of Chrysler as an equal opportunity employer, and probably the company with the highest ratio of Negro employees among major American Corporations.

Ford's total Negro employment ratio in 1968 was 18 percent, with nearly 24 percent of its blue collar workers Negro. As already noted, the huge River Rouge complex has a substantially higher Negro proportion.

Ford leads the industry in both the skilled craftsmen and office and clerical ratio of Negroes. In 1968, nearly 6 percent of Ford's skilled craftsmen and nearly 9 percent of its office and clerical workers were Negro. The historic willingness of Ford to utilize Negroes in all skills, and the fact that it has been well-known in the Detroit Negro community for several generations, that Ford accepts applications for its apprenticeship program from Negroes, undoubtedly go far to explain Ford's superior progress in this category.

Ford's top showing in the office and clerical field is of particular interest because its headquarters is farther from the center of Detroit's Negro population than are either General Motors' or Chrysler's. One reason is the large representation of Negroes in the plant offices in Chicago and New Jersey, as already noted in Table 6. Another is the traditional appeal of Ford to Negroes which aids in recruiting. And a third is the sincere effort in recent years of Ford officials to increase Negro representation in all salaried positions.

In 1968, General Motors employed 79,193 Negroes in the United States—probably the largest number employed by any company but a smaller percentage—12.7—than either of its major competitors. We have already noted several reasons for General Motors ratio lag. For one thing, General Motors is less concentrated in the Detroit area, and has numerous plants in areas where few Negroes live. In addition, General Motors' many plants in nonautomotive products include operations with a higher overall skill content than do basic automotive plants. In view of the disproportionate lack of skills among Negroes, this, of course, hinders their employment.

General Motors maintains a tremendous number of offices in cities throughout the country in order to care for its various business activities. Slowness in recruiting Negroes for regional sales work and for office and clerical jobs in general, and difficulties in finding qualified personnel in recent years are significant factors in holding down General Motors' proportion of Negroes.

A historic problem for General Motors was the reluctance of some decentralized managers to give effect to equal employment opportunity. The Corporation then adopted a strong policy which reduced local managerial discretion in this regard, and then brought it under even stricter central office control. Progress in the 1960's has been noteworthy. For example, in 1963, General Motors' domestic employment increased 2.7 percent over the previous year, but nonwhite employment increased 9.8 percent; in 1965, General Motors' domestic employment increase 6.4 percent, nonwhite employment

14.5 percent; in 1966, the figures were a 1.1 percent in total employment, and a 9.3 percent increase in nonwhite employment. By 1969, the nonwhite employment at General Motors had exceeded 15 percent.

Judged by recent events, it is reasonable to expect that the country's employer of the largest number of Negroes will continue to increase the percentage of Negroes in its employee force.

THE NEGRO AND THE UAW

Employment policies in the automobile industry are primarily management functions, but a union as powerful as the United Automobile, Aerospace and Agricultural Implement Workers plays a significant role. Hiring is done by management. If, however, discrimination is exercised in promotion, or if opportunities are denied to Negroes, the grievance machinery is available for redress and union officials, local and national, are expected to assess the grievance and to press it if it has a basis in fact.

The UAW has always prided itself on its nondiscriminatory stance. During World War II, for example, as already noted, although considerably less powerful than today, UAW officers vigorously opposed strikes aimed at preventing the upgrading of Negroes, and strongly supported the demands of Negroes for expanded employment opportunities. The seniority rules now extant in the industry permit as wide opportunities as exist anywhere in industry for intraplant and area interplant movement. There can be no doubt that these seniority regulations have been a significant factor in the expansion of Negro production jobs. Moreover, except at Chrysler, the UAW does not have any significant bargaining rights among salaried personnel; hence it cannot be charged with responsibility in this area of employment, although, among clerical groups, nonunion Ford, not partially unionized Chrysler, is the leading employer of Negroes.

The international UAW officials, and particularly President Walter Reuther, have always also been strong supporters of such Negro aspirations as equality in jobs, housing, and in other economic, political, and social activities, both within and outside of union affairs. Negroes have been appointed to a variety of union offices in the UAW, and have won numerous local elective offices. Few unions have made equality of opportunity and union performance so significant a union policy and activity as has the UAW. Nevertheless, Professor F. Ray Marshall, certainly a friendly observer of the UAW, found considerable dissatisfaction among Negro union members about the effectiveness of the UAW stance in the late 1950's and early 1960's.[52] The roots of the problem go back to World War II, or even earlier.

In our discussion of the early period, it was noted that the attitude of Negroes toward the UAW was initially one of watchful waiting and suspicion. Then after Ford was unionized, Negroes became a force strong enough to demand redress of their special problems in UAW conventions. The strikes incident to Negro upgrading during World War II convinced Negro UAW members that they needed a Negro on the UAW international executive board to protect their interests. At this time, the UAW was split into two factions: the Reuther and the Addes or left wing group. Mr. Reuther refused to support the creation of a "Negro job"; Addes did, and Negroes provided his margin of re-election in 1943, but the provision for a Negro executive board member was defeated.[53]

The fight over group Negroes' special representation on the UAW board continued until 1962, when two at large members were elected, one Negro and one Canadian. In the meantime, Mr. Reuther eliminated his rivals and won complete control of the UAW. As a compromise, a UAW Fair Practices and Anti-Discrimination Department was established in 1946, and Mr. Reuther and other top union officials continued to give their unqualified support to full equality and treatment for Negro union members.

Negro dissatisfaction, however, remained. It apparently was based upon the failure to achieve a number of objectives, and the feeling among some Negroes that the union Fair Practices and Anti-Discrimination Department was, as some put it, "ceremonial and symbolic."[54]

Some of the Negro UAW members' dissatisfaction undoubtedly came from the fact that their leverage as a minority was reduced after the war when Mr. Reuther swept his opposition out of office. For a time prior to that, Negroes controlled a balance of power bloc at

52. Marshall, *op. cit.*, pp. 68-69, 83-84, and 178-179.
53. Lloyd H. Bailer, "The Automobile Unions and Negro Labor," *Political Science Quarterly*, Vol. LIX (December 1944), pp. 572-575; Marshall, *op. cit.*, pp. 83-84; and Irving Howe and B. J. Widick, *The UAW and Walter Reuther* (New York: Random House, 1949), pp. 207-234.
54. Marshall, *op. cit.*, p. 69.

UAW conventions, and in some key locals. After the Reuther victory, this no longer was true. Moreover, in local elections at Ford Local 600 as well as elsewhere, race bloc voting seems to have increased racial tension and not been too successful from the Negro point of view.[55] Of course, as the proportion of Negroes tends to increase in many plants, such voting can insure the election of Negroes to local offices. Bloc voting, however, seems certain to worsen race relations in the union.

Particular dissatisfaction for Negroes in the period prior to 1963 was the failure of the UAW to insist in integrating southern locals, especially the General Motors local in Atlanta. The tensions there have already been noted, and contrasted with the International Harvester situation at Memphis.

The UAW, strangely enough, has acted more vigorously in opposing southern local segregation and discrimination among nonautomobile locals than among automobile locals. Besides trusteeing the Harvester local at Memphis, it revoked the charter of a Dallas local in 1952 composed of Braniff Airline mechanical employees.[56] The latter action proved largely futile. The Braniff employees obtained a charter from the International Association of Machinists, which then won bargaining rights, and the Negro employees involved ended up with a union definitely less interested in altering the *status quo*.

Obviously, the UAW went along with discrimination in Atlanta. Yet unless the company takes the lead, as Harvester did at Memphis, or as General Motors did later in Atlanta, the union cannot do the job. Its role is largely supportive in such a situation, but its support can, of course, also be crucial or even necessary.

Another Negro grievance is based upon the belief that the UAW skilled trades group has limited Negro employment opportunities. This charge is more difficult to assess, although the widespread claim that discrimination existed and the absence of Negroes from any large-scale participation in apprentice training gives some credence to their charges.

The skilled trades group has always been a problem to the UAW because of its strategic significance in bargaining and strike situations and its uneasy alliance with production workers. Essentially craft minded, and considering themselves socially above the production workers, the skilled trades group has often threatened to secede from

55. *Ibid.*
56. *Ibid.*, p. 178; and personal investigation, October 1967.

the UAW and join various craft unions. The ideology of the group, like that of the building trades craftsmen, essentially rejects equality of opportunity in favor of an elite corps maintained in part by excluding "undesirables" and limiting entrance to trades.

The skilled trades group has power in the UAW beyond numbers. They have now even been acceded the right to reject contracts and make that rejection binding on the majority—a UAW constitutional provision of questionable legality.[57] UAW leadership has been forced to tread lightly in forcing its views on the skilled craftsmen who historically at least have not as a group been committed to equality of opportunity.

The UAW's Fair Practices and Anti-Discrimination Department, which was established in 1946, is supported by a special fund of 1 percent per member per month. According to Professor Marshall, Negro UAW members have had mixed feelings concerning the Department.[58] Proponents felt that the Department symbolized the UAW's interest and good intentions and attracted race relations experts to work on problems. Opponents felt that the Department was "window dressing" that excused the union from acting.

In fact, the Fair Practices Department seems to have dramatized the UAW's commitment, and to have provided the UAW leadership with facts and programs. Its role has been more educational than action-oriented.

Negroes aggrieved over alleged discriminatory employment practices—as differentiated from union practices—need not utilize the Fair Practices Department, but can rather (and generally do) process their complaint through the regular grievance machinery. All automobile-company-UAW contracts contain an antidiscrimination clause similar to the one found in the General Motors contract:

> It is the policy of General Motors and the UAW-AFL-CIO that the provisions of this Agreement be applied to all employees covered by this Agreement without regard to race, color, creed or national origin. Any claims of violation of this policy may be taken up as a grievance, provided that any such claim must be supported by written evidence by the time it is presented by the Shop Committee at a meeting with Management.

57. Should a contract be rejected because the skilled trades reject it even though a majority in the bargaining unit accepts it, it is possible that the UAW can be charged with bargaining in bad faith—a violation of Section 8(b)(3) of the Taft-Hartley Act.

58. Marshall, *op. cit.*, pp. 83-84.

Of course, if a company official is discriminatory, and the local union committeemen and officials condone or support such discrimination, even such a clause as this may not be helpful. Its very existence, however, provides the opportunity to redress wrongs.

Although the function of the Fair Practices Department is, in fact, primarily educational, this is, indeed, a prime need. As Howe and Widick stated: "The blunt truth is that the bulk of the prejudice in the UAW is to be found in the ranks. . . ."[59] The same men who work next to Negroes in a plant may refuse to socialize with them on the outside or live in areas which have Negroes. The fact that Negroes must commute long distances to work in suburban plants because of such housing discrimination embitters relations within the plants; it also keeps down Negro participation in union affairs for local union halls are found near the place of work. Commuting long distances can insure lack of attendance at meetings. Negro spokesmen have expressed concern at the "apathy" of a large percentage of Negro union members.[60] Undoubtedly, disinterest is furthered by social rebuffs and by obstacles such as lack of housing near plants and union meeting halls.

Beginning in 1967, a new situation developed in Negro-UAW relations with the advent of self-styled revolutionary Negro groups, such as the Dodge Revolutionary Union Movement, or "DRUM," claiming membership in the Detroit Dodge Division plants of Chrysler. In the vilest of language, these groups have demanded control of both companies and unions ("a black chairman of Chrysler's board and a black president of the UAW), and have resorted to strikes and violence on a number of occasions. In one case in New Jersey, a Ford plant was struck by a radical black group and the strikers were supported by members of the Students for Democratic Action (SDS), the extreme left-wing (and very undemocratic) student group.

In other plants, Negro workers have formed "black coalitions" as a means of making their wishes known. Such groups operate both within and outside of existing collective bargaining relationships. Moreover, extremism is no monopoly of black automobile workers. In some plants, whites walked out when the flag was lowered in honor of the late Dr. Martin Luther King, Jr., and walked out again when companies refused so to honor the demise of Governor Lurleen Wallace

59. Howe and Widick, *op. cit.*, p. 228.
60. See, e.g., the comments of A. Philip Randolph, quoted by Marshall, *op. cit.*, p. 72.

of Alabama. That tensions have risen between white and black employees and fellow union members can be amply demonstrated. Yet by and large, thanks to the good sense of most company and union officials, it has been kept under control, and not exacerbated.

In the spring of 1969, local union elections occurred in the principal Chrysler plants in the Detroit area where Negroes have become a majority of the blue collar work force. As expected, most of the local offices were swept by black candidates, but the militant and revolutionary groups won few if any offices. Apparently, the Negro unionists, like the whites, wanted no part of black separatism which might risk the loss of UAW wages and benefits.[61]

It is easy to criticize the UAW, as it is the companies, for failing to eliminate discrimination. Yet given the political realities in which the national union officials must operate, and considering the accomplishments to date, one must conclude that they have led, not followed the membership, toward equal employment opportunity. It is also not surprising that local officials, coming themselves from the rank and file, and subject to re-election by that rank and file, have often stood with their constituents against progress. By and large, however, despite shortcomings, the UAW has remained throughout its existence a constructive force in the drive to reduce prejudice and to further equal employment opportunity in the industry.

---

61. See *Business Week,* May 24, 1969, pp. 54-56; and *Detroit Free Press,* May 20, 1969, p. A-4. The author has a collection of "DRUM" and "ELDRUM" leaflets in his possession.

CHAPTER VII.

Some Personnel Problems of the New Era

It is obvious that Negroes are now a significant and permanent part of the automobile industry work force, and that the number and percentage of Negroes have not only increased substantially in recent years, but are very likely to continue to do so. This raises the question of what problems have occurred as a result of the changing racial employment composition in the industry. At least three deserve special analysis: the impact on white employees, the effect on efficiency and turnover, and the discipline problem.

Detroit in 1967, as in 1943, was the scene of a destructive and senseless riot. The impact of this riot on Negro employment opportunities and company personnel policies is also discussed in this chapter.

IMPACT ON WHITE EMPLOYEES

Employers have found that when a department or plant becomes heavily Negro, whites no longer seek employment there. There is an analogy to housing. As more Negroes move in, fewer whites seek to live in a neighborhood. The high wages of the automobile industry hold the white workers already in plants, but as the percentage of Negroes approaches one half, new white worker applications decline and those who apply tend not to stay long. Progressively, the operation becomes more heavily Negro. This is a phenomenon which this author has observed in a number of plants in various industries.

The difficulties which Negroes often encounter in trying to break into formerly all white jobs are well-known. They have been brutalized, jostled, socially ostracized, and made the butt of jokes, horseplay, and vicious behavior. Such things have occurred in the automobile industry and could even occur today in subtle forms. Now in some plants the shoe is on the other foot. Jostling of white workers by the Negro majority has induced white workers to leave some plants, and fear of such behavior keeps other whites from applying.

But jostling is probably not the basic reason why some plants, particularly in the Detroit area, will continue to become more heavily Negro. When plants move toward a Negro majority, this fact becomes known and whites do not apply, or do not stay if they are hired. In a tight labor market this is accentuated. With plants located both in suburbs and city, as is the case of the Detroit area, the suburban dwelling whites can seek employment near their homes, the city dwelling Negroes near theirs. Interplant labor pool arrangements offset these movements somewhat; but the city plants, or particular departments which reach a high percentage of Negroes, continue to have a declining white ratio.

Managements are, of course, concerned about this trend. They have been working assiduously for equal employment opportunity, especially since 1960, but the tendency of some plants and departments to become overwhelmingly Negro, is a trend toward segregation. Moreover, it also narrows the labor market from which employees may be drawn as whites are eliminated as contenders for some jobs, the labor force potential is downgraded because of the disadvantaged educational backgrounds of Negroes, and the large numbers of Negro applicants without industrial experience.

This situation should not be overstressed in so far as the automobile industry is concerned. It is mainly a Detroit area phenomenon now, although a few plants in Chicago, Cleveland, and the East are moving in the same direction. Negroes are overall still a minority of the production workers in the industry as a whole. Moreover, the plants in Detroit are among the oldest in the industry. As new ones are built, they will be most probably located in outlying areas. Negroes will continue to work in such plants, but a substantial white local force will be available also. Nevertheless, the reluctance of white workers to work in plants which become known as "Negro plants," is likely to continue.

EFFICIENCY AND TURNOVER

The automobile industry added nearly 200,000 persons to its rolls between 1960 and 1968, but to do so it employed probably about 1.5 million persons. A sizable proportion of these more than one million hires are Negroes. Data concerning the relative efficiency of Negroes and whites are not available, but such problems as turnover, sickness and accident claims, seem to point in one direction—a higher turnover of Negroes, much greater incidence of claims, and a variety of problems related thereto.

Management personnel questioned were unanimous that the turnover of Negroes was much higher than whites, but they also stressed that this was particularly the case with the newly hired. The Negro employees who had been with the companies for a number of years were fairly stable. If a person remained more than one year he usually settled down. For example, Ford officials report that turnover, absenteeism, and other problems at the River Rouge foundry, where a great majority of the employees are colored, are well within reasonable bounds. Here the labor force is older, and young persons added to the labor force have ample opportunity to observe good working habits and attitudes of older persons of their own race. In addition a very competent plant personnel manager, himself a Negro, is given considerable credit for the stability of the operation. Yet despite such exceptions, turnover and absenteeism have remained excessive. To obtain one permanent employee since 1965, companies have been compelled to hire four or six.

In suburban plants, some of the same problems occurred with young white workers. "They looked at this pretty new plant, and applied for work. Then they found out that they were expected to work hard; they often lasted only a few weeks." Thus did a plant manager comment on some of his new white employees in March 1967. Said the personnel man in the same plant: "In Detroit, the heavy turnover, the Monday absentees, and the sickness and accident claims were dominated by Negroes; in this suburban paradise, the young white boys give them competition for these dubious traits."[62]

It is difficult to distinguish the youth trait from the Negro one, for young Negroes are heavily represented in the new labor force in the Detroit area. Most management personnel contacted felt, however, that jobs with high earnings were so new to the young Negroes, who had rarely seen such earning capacity in their families or in their neighborhoods that they easily enjoyed it and spent it loosely, often becoming either incapacitated for Monday work, or felt that they were so rich that they stayed off the job for days after payday. Said one labor relations official: "If we disciplined for days off and tardiness like we should, we would not have a labor force."

62. Interviews were conducted during November and December 1966, during the first half of 1967, and in January 1968.

Moreover, since work has not been available to young Negroes heretofore, especially with the pace, discipline, and need for physical stamina of an automotive factory, they often easily decide that the work is too rigorous and quit. The resultant turnover is enormous. To add one hundred, meant hiring four hundred, and in some plants, six hundred. The high turnover continues.

Of particular interest, was the belief among management personnel that newly arrived Negro migrants from the South were turning out to be superior employees to those who grew up in the cities. It is customary to blame inferior southern conditions for much of the employment and social problems which Negroes encounter in industry and in city living. Certainly this is often a correct analysis. But the automobile companies have found that many southern Negroes, for all their disabilities, are able and willing to work for a day's pay, whereas the city-bred Negroes are less likely to have this trait.

The same distinction was noted by a suburban Detroit plant manager between white youths raised in suburbia and those raised on farms or in small towns. The latter were inevitably the best workers and the ones with the least turnover. Modern city life can discourage work aptitude and good work habits. And since Negroes tend more and more to be concentrated in the worst parts of the cities, the effect on their potential as employees is serious.

DISCIPLINE PROBLEMS

The introduction of large numbers of Negroes into huge automobile plants has brought with it the mores of the slums—violence, gambling, lawlessness—which have proved difficult to control. Although the companies are understandably reticent on this subject, some plant managers and personnel officials indicated the concern felt. In one plant, there have been knifings, three shootings, and numerous thefts. Gambling is a constant problem. Parking lot thefts are so bad in some plants that the UAW has become interested in a group automobile insurance program to offset rising insurance rates. With so many new employees, and so many of these never before holding good jobs and being associated with relative prosperity and material well-being, the behavior and actions represent from whence they have come not where they are. The rising crime rate in our cities, particularly in the slum areas, is thus being carried into the plants.

Under these circumstances, it is no wonder that plant discipline and efficiency have suffered, and that quality has been hurt. Lack of experience, and lack of association directly or through the work of parents, with machinery and with industrial behavior, a poor education in northern city slums or in southern segregated schools, all greatly complicate the Negro automobile workers' learning experiences. Long hours—six and seven days a week, nine and ten hours a day—inflate workers' earnings, but add to the fatigue, absenteeism, and general disinterest, which hurt efficiency and quality. Moreover, the expansion of employment has resulted in the upgrading to supervision of thousands who are inexperienced at managing. Supervisors, on occasion, faced with violent reactions of employees fresh from the slums, have backed down in fear and discipline has suffered.

In time, the situation in some of these automobile plants will undoubtedly achieve a reasonable equilibrium. High earnings seem certain to stabilize the lives and habits of young Negro employees who grew up on relief or on southern farms, and without hopes of achieving what is already theirs. Nevertheless, the companies now realize that they must face up to new discipline problems before they become even more serious.

One must conclude, therefore, that the current employment of large numbers of Negroes has hurt efficiency and quality. In perspective, however, one may also hope that like all other newcomers to the industry, including the Negroes who joined the automobile labor force during World War II period, the new-Negro automobile workers will settle down to productive efficiency and stable employment. If that occurs, the Negroes in America will have achieved even greater progress and a stabilizing influence.

THE IMPACT OF THE 1967 RIOT

The horrible riot which shook Detroit and the country in July 1967, had a profound effect on the automobile manufacturers. Looting occurred near Chrysler headquarters and plants, and within easy range of the General Motors headquarters. Plants were shut down or nearly so because personnel feared to traverse riot-torn areas. As in 1943, no disturbances occurred in any plants, nor in or around the suburban headquarters of Ford at Dearborn, but Ford also lost production because of absenteeism.

Although looting and rioting remained outside of factory walls, some automobile workers, again as in 1943, were involved and arrested as looters. That such rioting and looting occurred in the city where Negroes have as good, if not better, industrial employment opportunities than anywhere in the world seemed surprising. Yet the riot of 1943 also occurred in a period of relatively full employment and expanding job opportunities.

High employment and expanding job opportunities affect race relations in contradictory ways. The tensions over job competition recede when work is plentiful for all. But new job opportunities expand the horizons and aspirations of Negro workers and at least temporarily create new crises by altering the *status quo*. Racial antagonism can then easily surface. Detroit has had two horrible race riots in times of relatively full employment—none in a recession.

Immediately after the rioting ended, all the automobile companies began not only to cooperate with government and UAW officials to try to prevent a recurrence of lawlessness, but also to re-examine hiring policies. Despite the fact that their hiring standards have encouraged the employment of unskilled in very large numbers, all companies have since made their standards even more flexible. Chrysler, for example, dropped previous barriers against persons with nondangerous or minor police records in order to open up jobs to Negroes who had had scrapes with the law. Chrysler "adopted" a high school in center city Detroit, in order to aid in instruction and to encourage students to stay in school and to look to the automobile industry for employment. Chrysler also stepped up its Detroit hiring and adopted and publicized its new policy to expand the number of Negro dealers.

In three months after the riot, General Motors hired 12,200 in the Detroit and Pontiac areas, 5,300 of whom were Negroes. For the first time General Motors went into Negro areas and hired on the spot, and also took referrals from government manpower and antipoverty agencies. According to General Motors Chairman, James M. Roche, continued adherence to a nondiscriminatory employment policy was not enough. More had to be done than "to wait for the qualified applicant to present himself at our employment office."

In addition, General Motors also instructed its employment personnel to utilize a "rule of reason" in taking men with police records. Special programs were initiated at Chevrolet Gear and Axle in Detroit, and at Pontiac and Fisher Body plants in Pontiac "to locate those individuals previously considered unhirable and to hire them." In Pontiac, of the first 250 hired, 182 were able to complete their probationary period, "90 percent of whom are described by supervision as 'competent' while the others need additional training."[63]

Ford also reacted energetically. It sent its employment interviewers into inner city areas and employed persons on the spot. Those that needed it were given a week's worth of bus tickets free of charge and lunch tickets for one hot meal, the cost of which is deducted from the second and third pay check. Some 3,000 Negroes were thus hired by the end of January 1968, nearly all of them at the River Rouge works. Of the 3,000, 1,600 were on the job; 600 were awaiting job assignment; 425 were rejected after physical examinations or were found to have major or habitual criminal records; and 375 who were hired either never showed up or "are taking their time about showing up for work."[64]

In addition to those hired by interviewers within the inner city, Ford hired some 2,800 persons—walk-in hires—at Detroit area employment offices during the same period. Of these 1,460 are considered to have been from among the hard-core unemployed, undoubtedly motivated by the publicity over the Ford program.[65]

The success of these programs will depend on many things, not the least of which is continued high sales and employment which will avoid layoffs, and the ability of the companies to overcome the turnover and discipline problems incident to the introduction of large numbers of unskilled and inexperienced personnel. To emphasize the company's commitment, Mr. Henry Ford II wrote all supervisors and executives on January 17, 1968, asking for their "full and active support" for equal opportunity in "one of Ford Motor Company's oldest, firmest and most basic policies." In this letter, Mr. Ford stated the inner-city hiring program's aim "is not only to offer employment opportunities, but actively to invite the interest of people who would not normally come to us—not to screen *out* doubtful applicants but to screen *in* if possible—and not merely to hire, but to help them make the grade after they are hired."

63. See *New York Times,* November 10, 1967; *Daily Labor Report,* No. 220, November 15, 1967, pp. A-7-8.
64. On the Ford program, see Gertrude Samuels, "Help Wanted: The Hard-Core Unemployed," *New York Times Magazine,* January 28, 1968, pp. 26-27, 42-50.
65. *Ibid.*

When the National Alliance of Businessmen program was launched as a joint industry-government effort to employ "hard-core" unemployed personnel, the automobile companies again took the lead. Henry Ford II chaired the program during its first year, and the River Rouge complex, as well as many other Ford plants, increased efforts to employ those previously thought "unemployable." In May 1969, Chrysler signed a contract with the United States Department of Labor to train 4,450 hard-core unemployed at a cost of $13.8 million to the government—the largest such contract let by the Labor Department. Then, as Chrysler's fortunes decline, in the early 1970's, this contract was cancelled. Meanwhile, General Motors was continuing its policy of doing all such training at its own expense and greatly increasing its minority employment.

The automobile industry's program to work hard-core unemployed into jobs is possible because of the large number of unskilled entry positions which its processes can utilize. Its experience will be valuable in determining America's capacity to rehabilitate through employment. Those who were hired and remained on the job for a reasonable time became immensely more capable of shifting for themselves. When automobile sales declined and layoffs occurred, they were more likely to find other jobs.

The policies put into effect by the automobile companies involve a complete reversal of traditional industrial hiring practices. Employment policies have stressed the hiring of the fittest and best personnel obtainable in the labor market; later the companies were literally searching for the most marginal that possibly can be utilized. That Mr. Ford wrote his executives and supervisors stressing the change and asking their assistance is indeed understandable. Such a policy change requires complete management support if it is to be successful. And to be successful in the long run, it requires not only that support, but favorable economic conditions. The layoffs which occurred in early 1970 have set back the program. The lowest on the seniority list are the first to go, and although now Negroes are found in abundance in the long, as well as in the short-service automobile employee groups, the hard-core are concentrated in the shortest-service group. The extent of Negro employment is, however, so great that the percentage of blacks will not be substantially reduced by the 1970 layoffs.

CHAPTER VIII.

Determinants of Industry Policy

In the course of this analysis, a number of factors have been discussed which have contributed to the racial employment policies of the automobile industry. These and others should be noted again in these concluding remarks.

THE NEED FOR EMPLOYEES

Negroes have made their greatest gains in three periods of tight labor markets—World War I, World War II, and 1962-1966. The availability of Negro labor to a growing automobile industry at critical moments in the history of both the Negro worker and the industry has provided an extraordinary mutual advantage. There can be no doubt that the industry's need and their availability are the most significant facts in Negroes becoming such an important part of the industry's labor force.

THE CHARACTER OF THE WORK

In the first part of this section (Table 2) it was noted that semiskilled operatives comprise more than one-half of the labor force, and that with laborers and service workers, an even greater majority. In few industries can inexperienced workers be utilized to such an advantage and at such attractive wages. A grade school education is usually sufficient, and sometimes not even necessary, for work on the assembly line. The industry affords an excellent opportunity for those without industrial experience. The nature of the work has permitted the assimilation into the work force of thousands of unskilled Negroes. In industries in which a much higher proportion of skilled employees or better educated workers are needed, for example, aerospace, this is not possible.

INDUSTRIAL LOCATION

Automobile plants tend to be concentrated in or nearby, centers of population. This is where the market is, and happily for Negroes where the centers of Negro population are. The tendency today is for large assembly plants with multiple shifts in order to reduce the plant fixed costs per unit. Moreover, the development of the fifteen automobile carrying rail car has permitted companies to increase their concentrations around Detroit and in Michigan rather than to disperse plants further. This has aided Negro employment.

Some of the oldest plants are in Detroit and some may be moved out in the future. Industry policy is to transfer workers with their plants. Such movements could, however, reduce the growth in the percentage of Negroes, but it is not likely to occur rapidly nor to have immediate significance. Plant locations are likely to continue to favor increased Negro employment, as they have in the past several years, by being reasonably near the centers of Negro population in the North and Midwest.

MANAGERIAL POLICY

One wonders how much the policies of Henry Ford account for the great advances made by Negroes in the industry. When others said Negroes could not handle skilled jobs, or whites and Negroes would not work together, he demonstrated that they were wrong. When World War II came, his example had proved what was possible. The Negro automobile worker owes much to this great pioneer.

Managerial policy between 1940 and 1960 demonstrates more of a tendency to associate itself with community mores than to stride out ahead. When World War II demanded, both for labor utilization and public policy, that all citizens be given an opportunity to work, the automobile companies easily fell into step. In the postwar years, they also stayed well within the practices of the times. Negroes held on to their gains in the industry, except where layoff or plant closings hurt all workers. In states having fair employment practice legislation, such as New York or New Jersey, the automobile companies set good examples of equal opportunity for production workers and opened up some jobs for Negro white collar personnel. These laws also emphasized the need for firm company policies rather than leaving the issue to local managerial discretion, and the companies in time adopted strong policies. In general, however, the automobile companies did little pioneering in opening up salaried jobs or in integrating southern plants prior to 1960.

The new post-1967 riot programs of the automobile companies contain some of the innovative flavor of the first Henry Ford. Here the experiment of utilizing the hard-core unemployed and the very marginal worker is being attempted. Given the industry's ability to utilize unskilled personnel, this experiment could be a very important contribution toward developing ways of alleviating the problem of unemployment in our central city slums.

Automobile companies feel strongly that they must examine all policies in terms of what they perceive as marketing realities. The race issue can put a company in the center of a controversy and cost it sales. Boycotts of one company by Negroes or segregationists can do just that. The Ford Motor Company is apparently most vulnerable to such action because of the close association of the Ford family with the company. According to one business journal: "Every time Henry Ford II has made a pronouncement in behalf of Negro rights, Ford Motor Co. sales have tumbled in the South."[66] It is doubtful if the impact has been either severe or permanent thus far. None of the companies show any desire to let up on their affirmative action programs however hesitant they once might have been. After Plans for Progress was inaugurated, all three companies joined. It would be difficult today to assail one company over another on this issue. Their efforts differ, and results vary some; but the commitment to equal opportunity and the need to utilize Negro labor are similar for all three.

The alignment of marketing policies and equal employment opportunity does not imply any lack of sincerity on the part of the companies. The author has talked with numerous officials in the industry who are dedicated to improvement of the Negro's status. Rather it means that the industry has a tendency, with such exceptions as Henry Ford's innovations, to stay within the country's mood in a given period. In general, the results appear to have been quite

66. "Business and the Urban Community," an insert into *Business Week,* February 2, 1968, p. c4.

salutary for Negro employment; but during the late 1940's and 1950's, the company's racial policies were quite cautious.

A feature of management policy in the automobile industry today is the strong central staff direction of equal employment opportunity policy. Just as the plant manager's labor relations actions are circumscribed by company policies and monitored and carefully tutored by the central staff, so equal employment opportunity has become a key central personnel staff activity. The plant managers and their staffs and the line organizations are given direct authority for seeing that equal opportunity policies are effectuated and are held responsible for the results. They are assisted, counseled, and policed by the central staff. In each company, the "word from above" is that equal employment opportunity is important, that the job must be done, and that affirmative and innovative actions are to be encouraged. There is no reason to believe that these policies will not be continued. Sound performance in civil rights matters, like sound performance in labor relations, are now part of the line managers' jobs. Experts on the staff responsible for minority employment appear to be as permanent a fixture as the labor relations group grew to be twenty-five years ago. In the automobile industry, the companies obviously expect to be able to be concerned constructively with minority group employment in the years ahead.

GOVERNMENT POLICY

Government policy has been an important factor in strengthening Negro labor utilization in the industry. Governmental insistence on progress during World War II both prodded the companies and gave them backing for action. State fair employment practice laws, and the threat of more, helped to keep policies reasonably liberal between 1945 and 1960. The contract compliance work, Plans for Progress, and Civil Rights laws of the 1960's have insured further action since then. Government encouragement and cooperation with industry after the July 1967 riot further encouraged and aided the programs for employment of the inner city and marginal Negroes.

We have already noted the importance of government policy in eliminating distinction among companies. Ending segregation in southern plants when the school integration crisis remained heated, further offended local white citizens, employees, and often local union officials, with local management personnel sometimes joining the footdragging. It was important that this be done by all companies at once. Having Negro performers star on their television shows, or in the case of Ford, publicity about grants of the Ford Foundation (totally unrelated to the company in management but not in people's minds) to a Negro group, or statements by Henry Ford II, evoked threats of boycotts. With all major companies following government policies, such threats are much less effective, even granting Mr. Ford's visibility.

Regular government inspections also keep the issue in the forefront. Some method of coordinating procurement agency, Equal Employment Opportunity Commission, and state agency inspections would decrease much lost time without diminishing the reminder that equal opportunity is the law. Yet plant inspections bring home to local managers the importance of the issue, for managers do not gain merit by inducing adverse rulings or publicity.

UNION POLICY

The industry is fortunate, first, in that unionization has occurred on an industrial basis and second, that its equal opportunity stance has strong support from the top officials of the UAW. Because unionization has occurred on an industrial basis, and because a majority of jobs in the plants are within a narrow spectrum of skill, seniority districts tend to become wide and in addition provide for transfer not only among departments, but among plants as well. If unionism were organized on a craft basis, or if progressions among jobs were established on long narrow bases, this would not be possible. The lack of union fragmentation, and the fluidity within the plants and among the plants provided in the union agreements have been major factors in expanding employment opportunities for Negroes.

In policy matters, Mr. Reuther and other top union officials have worked sincerely and assiduously for equal opportunity, cooperating with management officials where such cooperation was needed. There can be little doubt of their commitment.

Of course, it must be emphasized that the UAW is a labor union, not a civil rights organization. Demands, for example, that Negroes be given "superseniority" to compensate for past injustices are unthinkable for the union leadership and unsupportable by the membership which is predominantly white. Likewise attempts of the late Dr. Martin Luther King to win union support for a boycott against General Motors because, in his opinion, General Motors is not doing enough for civil rights, evoked instead praise for General Motors' nondiscrimination efforts from the UAW.[67] The UAW has been of definite aid in the progress of Negro automobile workers, but its prime interests remain those of a union and must be such if it is to survive, just as the prime aim of each company must be that of a profit-making corporation if it is to perform the functions of producing automobiles and providing employment. With the large mass of Negro workers now employed in automobile plants, they can be expected to increase their pressures for more representation in the governing bodies of the UAW, just as they are increasing their pressure for more and better jobs. Their success in obtaining both through existing and regular industrial relations channels can well determine whether the radical groups of either race will increase their strength and disruption potential.

67. Leonard Woodcock, UAW Vice-President, and chief negotiator in General Motors matters, was quoted in answer to Dr. King, that General Motors "had made an honest effort to practice nondiscrimination and offer opportunities to Negroes." *New York Times*, July 16, 1967.

CHAPTER IX.

Concluding Remarks

Negro workers play a major role in the automobile industry. Moreover, the situation remains very favorable not only for a continuation but an improvement in this situation. Of course there are problems involved and obstacles to overcome. A downturn in the industry's sales could reduce the proportion of Negroes at least temporarily, and so could a movement away from cities. Neither appears likely, however, to offset the great increases of the last several years. Cutbacks in early 1967, for example, resulted in layoffs of several thousand, about 80 percent of whom were low seniority Negroes. Attrition and turnover, however, soon returned many of these to jobs. As Negroes continue to hold down jobs in large numbers, their confidence and abilities will grow, and they will progress despite any temporary setback. It would appear, therefore, that the years ahead will see increased participation of Negroes in skilled, office, and salaried positions while they increase their share of production jobs.

PART THREE

THE NEGRO IN THE AEROSPACE INDUSTRY

by

Herbert R. Northrup

PART THREE: LIST OF TABLES

LIST OF FIGURES

CHAPTER I.

Introduction

Aerospace provides the best example of how the Negro has fared in an industry which is overwhelmingly dependent upon government as its principal customer. Yet the extent of Negro employment and upgrading in the industry is affected by a number of factors other than the pressures of the prime customer, such as industrial location and skill requirements. Moreover, the pressures of the government as customer are not unilateral, but must consider besides racial employment, such significant matters as delivery dates, labor force quality as it relates to reliability and safety of product performance, and military security. As a result, a complex of governmental-customer pressures bears upon the industry's racial employment policies.

This study is concerned with the development, status, and problems involved in racial employment policies in the aerospace industry, and in the principal companies therein. Basic to an understanding of these policies is the nature of the industry which is the subject of the next section of the study.

CHAPTER II.

The Aerospace Industry

The aerospace industry is actually a vast grouping of industries and companies rather than an industry in the strict sense of the term. It is basically an outgrowth of the aircraft industry, and reflects the dynamic changes which have occurred in the reorientation of that industry to missile, space, and to advanced research and development in the manned aircraft and outerspace fields. By the very nature of the requirements for production of sophisticated manned and unmanned aircraft, companies in aerospace have developed increasing need for and competence in electronics. Several, such as United Aircraft, General Dynamics, Northrop, or Hughes, have either purchased electronics companies, have built up their own electronic divisions, or have done both. In turn, major electronic companies have become big factors in both aircraft and space development and manufacturing. Thus the General Electric Company is both one of the two major builders of jet engines and one of the leading developers and builders of space vehicles and apparatus. Radio Corporation of America and Westinghouse Electric are also large space contractors.

The manufacture of large and complicated hardware and equipment has attracted other major concerns. Chrysler is a principal fabricator of the Saturn missile; General Motors manufactures engines and components used in flight; and numerous companies, large and small, contribute to the making of manned and unmanned air and space vehicles, communication satellites, aircraft, and other items.

The capacities developed by aerospace companies and their desire to diversify have led them into nonaerospace ventures. Lockheed Aircraft purchased and now operates a shipbuilding concern; General Dynamics operates shipyards, an electronics firm, and a host of other businesses. In 1967 North America Aviation merged with Rockwell-Standard, a conglomerate company primarily in nonaerospace operations.

TABLE 1. *Aerospace Industry*
Employment by Standard Industrial Classifications
1958 and 1963

SIC No.	Industry Sector	1958	1963
37211	Complete aircraft, military type	322,079	147,763
37214	Modifications, conversions and overhaul of aircraft	17,485	29,683
37216	Other aeronautical services for aircraft	9,717	72,947
37221	Aircraft engines for U. S. military	n.a.	66,618
37223	Research and development on aircraft engines	33,488	7,552
37224	Aircraft engine parts and accessories	63,185	39,227
37225	Complete missile or space vehicle engines and/or propulsion units	n.a.	17,716
37226	Research and development on complete missile or space vehicle engines and/or propulsion units	n.a.	51,773
37228	Missile and space vehicle engines and/or propulsion units parts or accessories	n.a.	5,377
37291	Other aircraft parts and auxiliary equipment	195,027	106,799
37292	Guided missile components and subassemblies, n.e.c.	n.a.	40,267
37293	Research and development on aircraft parts	n.a.	1,159
37294	Research and development on missile parts and components, n.e.c.	n.a.	21,990
38111	Aircraft flight, nautical, and navigational instruments and automatic pilots	45,957	15,490
38211	Aircraft engine instruments, except flight	1,256	5,299
	Total	688,194	629,660

Source: *Compendium of Manufacturing Production Statistics for the United States, 1947-1965* (Washington, D. C., Georgetown Economic Data Library, Georgetown University, 1967), pp. 264-268.

The complexities of the industry, therefore, do not lend themselves to easy statistical collection, especially since the mid-1950's and the development of the outerspace research and exploration programs, which required new hardware, techniques, and company capabilities. The governmental standard industrial classification system (SIC) now recognizes a variety of divisions in the industry, as set forth in Table 1, with the employment for 1958 and 1963. These data, however, greatly understate the numbers of people involved who are subject to the policies of aerospace companies and work directly in, or closely related to, basic aerospace activity.

Since the prime purpose of this study is an analysis of an industry's racial policies, and those of its major component companies, the data developed by the Aerospace Industries Association of America, Inc., more accurately reflect the numbers of employees who are affected by aerospace company policies. The Association data are based upon both government statistics and direct reports from the companies to the Association, and are utilized here to describe the industry for the purposes of this study.

In terms of company policies, emphasis in this study will be on those concerns which are primarily aerospace. Thus although some employment data of Chrysler or General Electric, for example, will undoubtedly be included in the general aerospace figures, discussions of policies of such companies, or those similarly situated, will be found in other parts of this book or in other volumes in the series.[1]

SALES AND STRUCTURE

The aerospace industry, as defined herein, is the largest manufacturing industry in the United States. The Aerospace Industries Association, Inc., reported that in 1968, total sales of the aerospace industry reached a post-World War II high of 29.5 billion, and that 2.6 billion of these sales were of nonaerospace products sold by the industry from plants where aerospace manufacturing or research was the prime business. According to this same source, aerospace sales in 1968 were 3.4 percent of gross national product, 4.9 percent of manufacturing sales, and 8.9 percent of durable goods sales.[2] Table 2 summarizes the industry's sales data for the years 1960-1968.

Table 3 lists the ten largest companies whose principal products are in the aerospace industry as of 1968. All are billion dollar sales companies and eight have more than 50,000 employees. Such giants as General Electric Company, Radio Corporation of America, Textron, and Westinghouse Electric undoubtedly have aerospace product sales and employment equal to, or greater than, some of the companies listed here but these companies do not publish data by product or divisions.

The industry is one which is dominated by large corporations, although many small concerns provide needed services and products.

1. See, for example, part two for an analysis of the automobile companies' racial policies.
2. The Aerospace Industries Association of America, Inc., publishes an annual book, *Aerospace Facts and Figures.* These data are found in the 1969 edition.

TABLE 2. *Aerospace Sales and the National Economy 1960-1968*

(Billions of dollars)

Year	Total Gross National Product	Sales of Manufacturing Industries	Sales of Durable Goods Industry	Sales of Aerospace Industry	Aerospace Sales as Percent of GNP	Aerospace Sales as Percent of Manufacturing Industries	Aerospace Sales as Percent of Durable Goods
1960	503.7	368.7	189.5	17.3	3.4	4.7	9.1
1961	520.1	370.7	186.5	18.0	3.5	4.9	9.7
1962	560.3	397.4	205.2	19.2	3.4	4.8	9.4
1963	590.5	420.4	219.0	20.1	3.4	4.8	9.2
1964	632.4	448.0	235.6	20.6	3.3	4.6	8.7
1965	684.9	492.0	266.6	20.7	3.0	4.2	7.8
1966	747.6	538.5	295.6	24.6	3.3	4.6	8.3
1967	789.7	548.5	299.7	27.3	3.4	5.0	9.1
1968	860.6	603.7	331.0	29.5	3.4	4.9	8.9

Source: Manufacturing and Durable Goods Industries; Department of Commerce, Bureau of the Census, "Manufacturers' Shipments, Inventories, and Orders, Series M-3" (Monthly). Gross National Product; Department of Commerce, "Survey of Current Business," (Monthly). Aerospace; Aerospace Industries Association estimates, based on latest available information.

Data compiled by Aerospace Industries Association.

The tremendous investment in research, engineering, plant and equipment, in manpower, services and management, even granting government support, are such that small concerns cannot compete for the major contracts. The difficulties encountered by General Dynamics, in the early 1960's, and by Douglas, more recently,[3] emphasize the managerial and investment problems inherent in the industry.

The governmental interest in the industry is shown by the data in Figure 1. Almost three-fifths of the industry's sales were absorbed by

3. The Convair Division of General Dynamics lost so much money on the 880 and 990 planes that the Corporation reported in successive years, the two greatest losses in American corporate history. There resulted a thorough reorganization and management upheaval. Douglas ran out of funds, probably as a result of poor estimating and poorer management controls in 1966-67, despite an excellent order backlog, and was forced to merge with McDonnell, which now is in control of the joint operation.

TABLE 3. *The Ten Largest Aerospace Companies, 1968*

Company and 1968 Rank Among Industrial Corporations	Headquarters	Sales	Assets	Net Income	Invested Capital	Number of Employees	Net Income as Percent of	
		(Thousands of dollars)					Sales	Invested Capital
McDonnell Douglas[a] (14)	St. Louis	3,609,295	1,335,099	94,724	459,306	124,740	2.6	20.6
Boeing (18)	Seattle	3,273,980	2,186,119	82,972	810,361	142,400	2.5	10.2
Ling-Temco-Vought[b] (25)	Dallas	2,769,737	2,648,150	36,332	175,453	114,579	1.3	20.7
General Dynamics[c] (27)	New York	2,662,238	865,932	38,683	335,756	101,400	1.5	11.5
North American Rockwell[d] (29)	El Segundo, California	2,639,784	1,361,594	73,750	687,945	114,430	2.8	10.7
United Aircraft (33)	East Hartford, Conn.	2,408,251	1,357,759	61,394	503,328	76,377	2.5	12.2
Lockheed Aircraft (35)	Burbank, California	2,217,366	936,783	44,476	370,688	95,404	2.0	12.0
TRW[c] (57)	Cleveland	1,487,547	881,622	72,193	472,742	80,314	4.9	15.3
Avco[c] (78)	New York	1,183,373	1,824,598	57,022	354,427	50,000	4.8	16.1
Gruman Aircraft Engineering (80)	Bethpage, New York	1,152,571	354,346	19,037	143,034	36,400	1.7	13.3

Source: *Fortune*, Vol. LXXIX (May 15, 1969), pp. 168-171.

a. Merger of two large aerospace firms, McDonnell and Douglas.

b. Includes Jones & Laughlin Steel and Wilson Co., among other nonaerospace concerns.

c. Includes several large nonaerospace divisions.

d. Merger of North American and Rockwell. Later largely nonaerospace.

the Department of Defense, about another fifth by the National Aeronautical and Space Agency, with the balance divided between nongovernmental customers, and customers for nonaerospace products and services produced in aerospace plants. Obviously, the industry must give careful heed to governmental policies and programs, including racial employment policies which are part and parcel of every government contract.

The industry-government relationship is further emphasized by Table 4 which lists the fifty largest defense contractors in 1969. Of the first dozen, only three—General Electric, American Telephone and Telegraph, and General Motors—are not primarily aerospace concerns. As already noted, General Electric has large aerospace divisions,

FIGURE 1. *Sales of the Aerospace Industry by Customer*

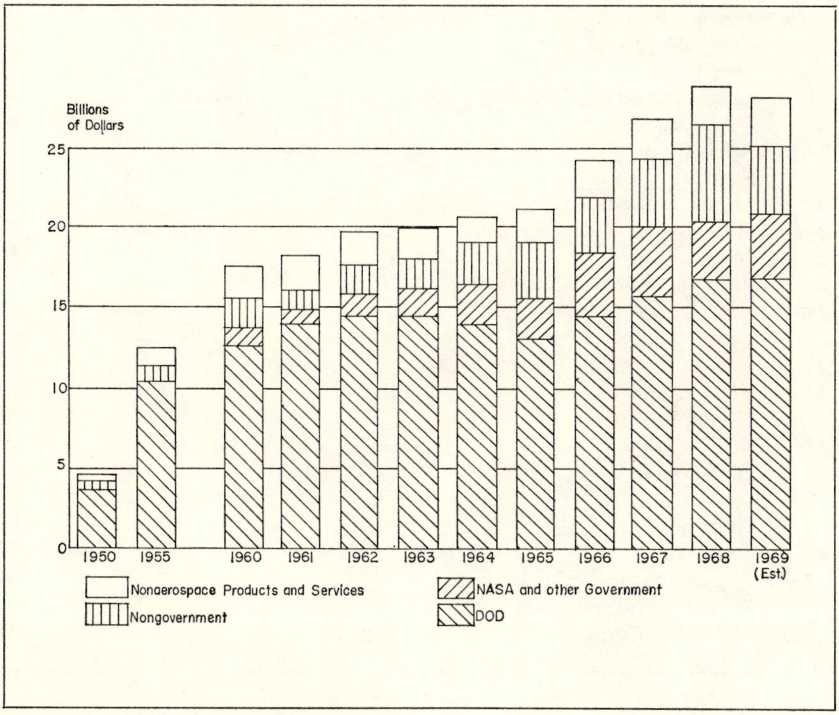

Source: Aerospace Industries Association.

TABLE 4. *The Fifty Largest Defense Contractors, 1969*

Rank in fiscal 1969	Company	Contract volume Millions of dollars	Rank in fiscal 1968
1.	Lockheed Aircraft Corp.	2,040	2
2.	General Electric Co.	1,620	3
3.	General Dynamics Corp.	1,243	1
4.	McDonnell Douglas Corp.	1,069	5
5.	United Aircraft Corp.	997	4
6.	American Telephone & Telegraph Co.	915	6
7.	Ling-Temco-Vought, Inc.	914	8
8.	North American Rockwell Corp.	674	9
9.	Boeing Co.	654	7
10.	General Motors Corp.	584	10
11.	Raytheon Co.	547	15
12.	Sperry Rand Corp.	468	16
13.	Avco Corp.	456	12
14.	Hughes Aircraft Co.	439	24
15.	Westinghouse Electric Corp.	430	27
16.	Textron, Inc.	428	13
17.	Grumman Corp.	417	11
18.	Honeywell, Inc.	406	20
19.	Ford Motor Co.	396	19
20.	Olin Corp.	354	21
21.	Litton Industries, Inc.	317	14
22.	Teledyne, Inc.	308	67
23.	RCA Corp.	299	26
24.	Standard Oil Co. [N. J.]	291	25
25.	Martin Marietta Corp.	264	17
26.	General Tire & Rubber Co.	264	28
27.	International Business Machines Corp.	257	30
28.	Raymond-Morrison-Knudsen*	254	35
29.	International Telephone & Telegraph Corp.	238	29
30.	Tenneco., Inc.**	237	—
31.	E. I. du Pont de Nemours & Co.	212	38
32.	FMC Corp.	196	33
33.	Norris Industries, Inc.	188	45
34.	Bendix Corp.	184	31
35.	Hercules, Inc.	180	37
36.	Northrop Corp.	179	22
37.	Uniroyal, Inc.	174	42
38.	TRW, Inc.	170	52
39.	Pan American World Airways, Inc.	167	32
40.	Asiatic Petroleum Corp.	156	49
41.	Mobil Oil Corp.	152	51

TABLE 4. *The Fifty Largest Defense Contractors, 1969* (*continued*)

Rank in fiscal 1969	Company	Contract volume Millions of dollars	Rank in fiscal 1968
42.	Standard Oil Co. [Calif.]	149	44
43.	Fairchild Hiller Corp.	149	56
44.	Collins Radio Co.	146	47
45.	Kaiser Industries Corp.	142	18
46.	General Telephone & Electronics Corp.	140	41
47.	Day & Zimmerman, Inc.	138	40
48.	Texas Instruments, Inc.	132	39
49.	Federal Cartridge Corp.	132	82
50.	Magnavox Co.	130	55

Source: Business Week, November 8, 1969.

Data: Defense Dept.

* Joint venture of Raymond International, Inc., Morrison-Knudsen, Inc., Brown & Root, Inc., J. A. Jones Construction Co.

** Merged with Newport News Shipbuilding & Dry Dock Co. which ranked 34th in fiscal 1968.

and General Motors is also active in the field. American Telephone and Telegraph is a large producer and servicer of aerospace communications. Textron's divisions (No. 16) include Bell Helicopter and Bell Aerosystems.

The product breakdown of the industry's sales is shown in Figure 2. The industry was once almost totally concerned with aircraft, but recently about 50 percent of its product sales dollars are in missiles or space vehicles—products which did not exist before 1950. In addition, of course, the modern turbojet, subsonic and supersonic aircraft are far more complicated and sophisticated than the piston engine planes which dominated military and civilian aviation until recently. The heavy input of a small number of numerous types of missiles, space vehicles, and high-speed manned aircraft, as compared with building a smaller variety of less complicated aircraft in large numbers, profoundly affects the labor force requirements of the industry. As we shall note, this adds problems for Negro employment by requiring even higher skills in the face of the fact that such skills are disproportionately absent from the Negro community.

MANPOWER

Employment and payrolls in the industry reflect these gigantic sales data. In 1968, the industry reported an average employee force of 1,418,000 and average annual payrolls of 13.8 billion dollars. Employment in the industry was respectively 7.2 percent of all manufacturing employment and 9.5 percent of all manufacturing payroll.[4] Today, one out of every 15 employees in manufacturing is employed in the aerospace industry. Table 5 summarizes employment and payroll data, 1959-1968.

The data in Table 5 also reveal another characteristic of the industry—the large percentage of salaried employees. Since 1960, the salaried payroll has consistently exceeded the hourly one, and the numbers of salaried employees have been almost equal to, or in some

TABLE 5. *Aerospace Industry Employment and Payrolls, 1959-1968*

	Employment (Annual Average in Thousands)			Payroll (Annual Average in Millions of Dollars)			Aerospace as Percent of Total	
Year Ending December 31	Total	Salaried	Production workers	Total	Salaried	Production workers	Manufacturing employment	Manufacturing payroll
1959	1,128	455	673	7,427	3,692	3,735	6.8	8.5
1960	1,074	467	607	7,317	3,835	3,482	6.1	8.2
1961	1,096	499	597	7,809	4,257	3,552	6.7	8.7
1962	1,177	558	619	8,889	5,045	3,844	7.0	9.2
1963	1,174	594	580	9,102	5,421	3,681	6.9	9.0
1964	1,117	565	552	8,897	5,326	3,571	6.5	8.3
1965	1,133	562	571	9,502	5,429	4,073	6.3	8.2
1966	1,298	612	686	11,394	6,220	5,174	6.8	8.9
1967	1,392	645	747	12,659	6,860	5,779	7.2	9.4
1968	1,418	664	754	13,759	7,728	6,031	7.2	9.5

Sources: Manufacturing Employment: U. S. Bureau of Labor Statistics, *Employment and Earnings.*

Manufacturing Payroll: U. S. Bureau of Employment Security—Office of Business Economics estimates.

Aerospace Employment and Payroll: Aerospace Industries Association, based on latest available information.

Data compiled by Aerospace Industries Association.

Note: Data for 1968 include estimates by Aerospace Industries Association.

4. See note 2, above.

TABLE 6. *Scientists and Engineers in Research and Development Total and Aerospace Industry, 1957-1968*

As of January	Total	Aircraft and Missiles	Aerospace as a Percent of Total
1957	229,400	58,700	25.6
1958	243,800	58,600	24.0
1959	268,400	65,900	24.6
1960	292,000	72,400	24.8
1961	312,100	78,500	25.2
1962	312,000	79,400	25.4
1963	327,300	90,700	27.7
1964	340,200	99,400	29.2
1965	343,600	97,400	28.3
1966	353,200	97,200	27.5
1967	367,200	98,800	26.8
1968	387,900	106,300	27.4

Source: National Science Foundation.
Data compiled by Aerospace Industries Association.
Note: Scientists and engineers working less than full time have been included in terms of their full-time-equivalent number.

years in excess of, the number of production workers. One reason for this is the tremendous research and development effort in the industry. Table 6 shows that the number of scientists and engineers employed in the industry have averaged about one-fourth of those in the country since 1957.

In addition to scientists and engineers in research and development, the aerospace industry requires huge clerical, accounting, finance, personnel, systems and computer and data processing staffs to operate and to control its manufacturing, research, and testing facilities. The significance of clerical, technical, engineering and scientific personnel in the industry has, of course, a distinct impact on the industry's capacity to employ Negroes, since Negroes are disproportionately unrepresented among these groups in our society.

The changing importance of missiles and space vehicles in the industry's employment picture is shown in Table 7. In 1963-1964, employment in this branch of the aerospace industry exceeded that in the traditional aircraft industry. This is significant for Negro labor trends because aircraft manufacturing requires a much higher percentage of production work. For example, in 1966, about two-thirds

TABLE 7. *Aerospace Industry*
Estimated Sales by Product Group, 1948-1969
(Millions of Dollars)

Year Ending December 31	Total Sales	Product Group: Aircraft	Missiles	Space Vehicles	Non-aerospace
1948	1,493	1,359	—	—	134
1949	2,232	2,032	—	—	200
1950	3,116	2,731	105	—	280
1951	6,264	5,067	633	—	564
1952	10,130	8,442	776	—	912
1953	12,459	10,420	918	—	1,121
1954	12,807	10,460	1,194	—	1,153
1955	12,411	9,781	1,513	—	1,117
1956	13,946	10,485	2,206	—	1,255
1957	15,858	11,398	3,033	—	1,427
1958	16,065	10,582	4,036	1	1,446
1959	16,640	9,714	5,042	386	1,498
1960	17,326	9,126	5,762	878	1,559
1961	17,997	8,847	6,266	1,264	1,620
1962	19,162	8,944	6,311	2,182	1,725
1963	20,134	8,527	6,003	3,774	1,830
1964	20,594	8,911	5,242	4,720	1,721
1965	20,670	9,747	3,626	5,329	1,968
1966	24,610	11,951	4,053	5,969	2,637
1967	27,267	14,981	4,417	5,290	2,579
1968	29,502	17,088	4,706	5,150	2,558
1969[E]	28,690	15,700	5,400	4,890	2,700

Source: Aerospace Industries Association.

Note: Includes military and nonmilitary sales and research, development, test and evaluation. Because of changes in source material, individual years are not always strictly comparable.

Nonaerospace figures exclude nonaerospace establishments owned and operated by aerospace companies.

[E] Estimate.

of those employed in aircraft were production workers, whereas only one-half of those in missile and space employment were so classified. Again because of the disproportionately lower educational attainment of Negroes, their opportunities of employment in production work are greater than in salaried employment. The high precision job shop nature of missile work and its heavy engineering and research content require skills and technical knowledge which greatly limit opportunities for those lacking in education or experience.

In 1967, the product mix of aerospace showed the full impact of the Vietnam war and the boom in commercial aviation. Figure 2 reflects the leveling off of the space program, a slight increase in missiles, and a decided increase in aircraft sales; the latter results from a 52 percent increase in Defense Department procurement of aircraft, including helicopters, between 1965 and 1967, and an increase in commercial airplane sales of more than 100 percent in the same period, with the trend continuing in 1968. The outlook for Negro employment is enhanced by these developments since they involve a trend toward mass production and consequent relatively greater need of semiskilled labor for which the inexperienced and disadvantaged can be more easily trained and utilized.

FIGURE 2. *Changing Pattern of Aerospace Sales*

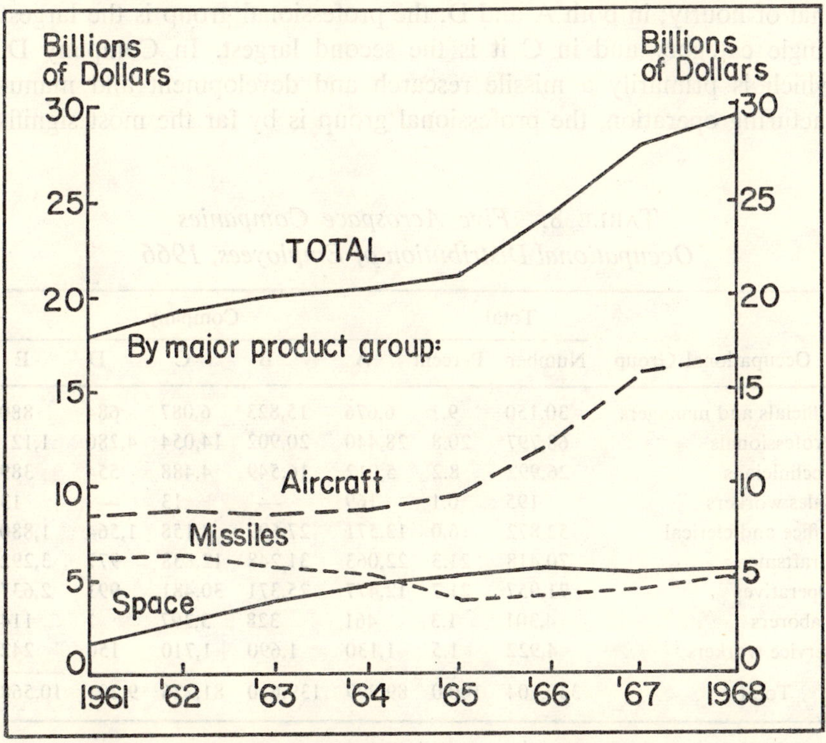

Source: Aerospace Industries Association for data and estimates. Chart by National Industrial Conference Board.

For 1969-1970, however, the character of production and the trend of employment should have unfavorable consequences for Negro workers. Table 7 shows that aerospace sales are expected to decline in 1969, and the decline will undoubtedly continue in the following year, with the brunt of unemployment occurring in aircraft plants. This is the result of declining sales of commercial planes and a diminution of purchases of planes and helicopters by the Department of Defense. A sizable proportion of the Negroes in the industry are likely to be affected because of their lack of seniority and their concentration in the aircraft and aircraft engine plants.

Occupational Distribution

We have already noted that the aerospace industry utilizes a high percentage of salaried and professional employees relative to total employment. Table 8 gives the broad occupational grouping for five key representative companies. In Companies A, B, and D, and for the five companies as a group, the number of salaried workers exceeds that of hourly; in both A and D, the professional group is the largest single category and in C it is the second largest. In Company D, which is primarily a missile research and development and manufacturing operation, the professional group is by far the most signifi-

TABLE 8. *Five Aerospace Companies*
Occupational Distribution of Employees, 1966

	Total		Company				
Occupational Group	Number	Percent	A	B	C	D	E
Officials and managers	30,150	9.1	6,676	15,823	6,087	684	880
Professionals	68,797	20.8	28,440	20,902	14,054	4,280	1,121
Technicians	26,992	8.2	5,012	16,549	4,488	554	389
Sales workers	195	0.1	169	—	13	—	13
Office and clerical	52,872	16.0	13,571	27,699	8,158	1,564	1,880
Craftsmen	70,418	21.3	22,063	31,248	12,838	977	3,292
Operatives	71,957	21.7	12,477	25,371	30,481	991	2,637
Laborers	4,301	1.3	461	328	3,397	1	114
Service workers	4,922	1.5	1,130	1,690	1,710	150	242
Total	330,604	100.0	89,999	139,610	81,226	9,201	10,568

Source: Data in author's possession.

cant one. This preponderance of salaried personnel exists despite the absence of large sales staffs. Selling to the government is a managerial, technical, or professional job.

Among the production workers, craftsmen is the largest occupational group in three of the five companies, and in Company B the largest in the entire work force. The high precision content of the work, its job shop characteristics and the lack of repetitive operations in many of the work situations, and above all the absolute need for high quality and zero defects in workmanship in order to assure human safety, all increase the demand for skilled craftsmen rather than semiskilled operatives or unskilled laborers. Indeed the five companies had a total of only 4,301 laborers, 3,397 in one company. The three lowest classifications were only 24.5 percent of the total number of employees. In contrast, more than one-half of all employees of the Big Three automobile companies—General Motors, Ford, and Chrysler—are classified as operatives. In automobiles,

TABLE 9. *Aerospace Industry*
Occupational Distribution of Employees
21 Companies, 127 Establishments, 1966

Occupational Group	Number of Employees	Percent of Total
Officials and managers	71,328	9.1
Professionals	179,436	22.8
Technicians	63,999	8.1
Sales workers	720	0.1
Office and clerical	130,261	16.5
Total white collar	445,744	56.6
Craftsmen	164,991	20.9
Operatives	155,167	19.7
Laborers	8,065	1.0
Service workers	14,055	1.8
Total blue collar	342,278	43.4
Total	788,022	100.0

Source: Data in author's possession.

operatives, laborers, and service workers comprise nearly two-thirds of the work force.

The occupational distribution for the industry is further explored in Table 9, which contains data covering 21 companies with 788,022 employees in 127 establishments. This represents about two-thirds of the total labor force in the aerospace industry.

The data in Table 9 show that professionals are the largest occupational group with craftsmen second, and operatives third. Salaried employees, including office and clerical, are a clear majority of the labor force in this large sample, with the employees who are semi-skilled (operatives) and unskilled (laborers and service workers) accounting for less than 25 percent of the total.

The significance of the aerospace industry's occupational distribution for Negroes is, again, that Negroes are concentrated in those classifications for which the industry has the least demand; and Negroes are most underrepresented in jobs for which the industry has the most pressing needs.

EARNINGS AND UNIONIZATION

The aerospace industry, with its emphasis on high skills, is a well-paying industry. In 1968, for example, production employees in "aircraft and parts" averaged $3.62 per hour and $152.04 per week. This placed them slightly below such industries as "motor vehicles and equipment" and "blast furnaces and basic steel products," but substantially above the 1968 average for manufacturing ($122.51 per week and $3.01 per hour), or durable goods manufacturing ($132.07 per week and $3.19 per hour).[5]

The aerospace industry generally pays the same wage rates regardless of location. In the lower wage areas, this places workers in the industry close to the top of the industrial scale. Benefits are also usually paid on a national basis, with widespread acceptance of generous pension, health and welfare, and other fringes provided at employer expense.

Most aerospace plants are unionized, with the International Association of Machinists and Aerospace Workers having the largest number of employees under contract, and the United Automobile,

5. Data from U. S. Bureau of Labor Statistics.

Aerospace and Agricultural Implement Workers (UAW) a close second. Both unions added "Aerospace" to their names after being founded by workers in other industries. In addition, a large number of craft unions, organizations of guards, and even unions of professional and technical employees have contracts with aerospace companies. Unionization occurred for the most part during the World War II period. A few companies—Northrop in Southern California, Grumman on Long Island, New York, and General Electric's missile and space operations in the Philadelphia area—are nonunion, and some plants are unionized by other than the IAM or UAW. Union racial policies will be analyzed in ensuing sections of the study in so far as they bear on company policies.

INDUSTRIAL LOCATION

Plants of the aerospace industry are located in all parts of the country, but Southern California has by far the heaviest concentration of the industry. As of October 1967, the data in Table 10 show that three Southern California labor market areas accounted for 23.8 percent of the employment in the industry. A total of 34.1 percent of the industry's employment is found in major West Coast centers, with Seattle, home of Boeing, having the second largest concentration of workers.

No area outside the West Coast could boast more than 4 percent of the industry's employment, but fourteen areas had over half the industry's workers. In most cities outside of Southern California, one aerospace company accounts for most of the employment: Boeing in Seattle, Lockheed in Atlanta, United Aircraft in Hartford, and McDonnell in St. Louis. Employment in the industry in such an area is thus almost completely dependent upon the ability of one company to maintain its sales position. In aerospace, this, of course, usually means success in obtaining and holding the employment-generating government contracts.

Superficially, the location of the industry would seem advantageous to Negro employment, for, despite the heavy West Coast concentration, the industry is found in many areas in which Negroes are a significant portion of the total population. As we shall note later in the study, however, testing and product requirements lead most aerospace companies to locate away from center city and thus away from the Negro population concentrations. This aggravates the Negro's search for work problems and is a factor in the low percentage of Negroes in the industry.

TABLE 10. *Aerospace Industry Employment in the Fourteen Largest Labor Market Areas October 1967*

Location	Aerospace Employment (in thousands)	Percent of Total Aerospace Employment
Total U. S. Aerospace Employment	1,393.4	100.0
Total fourteen largest labor market areas	833.9	59.9
Total West Coast labor market areas	475.4	34.1
Total major Southern California labor market areas	332.3	23.8
Los Angeles - Long Beach, California	247.2	17.7
Seattle, Washington	101.3	7.3
New York, New York	55.8	4.0
Anaheim - Santa Ana - Garden Grove, California	54.0	3.9
Hartford, Connecticut	51.0	3.7
Philadelphia, Pennsylvania	45.7	3.3
St. Louis, Missouri	43.0	3.1
Boston, Massachusetts	41.8	3.0
San Jose, California	41.8	3.0
Fort Worth, Texas	37.5	2.7
Wichita, Kansas	36.6	2.6
San Diego, California	31.1	2.2
Atlanta, Georgia	25.0	1.8
Minneapolis - St. Paul, Minnesota	22.1	1.6

Source: Aerospace Industries Association and data in author's possession.

CHAPTER III.

World War II
From Exclusion to Utilization

The pioneer manufacturers of flying machines sought to accomplish their tasks with the aid of an almost wholly white labor force. As a fledgling industry with modest labor requirements during World War I, the aircraft manufacturers, unlike their counterparts in automobiles or steel, were not required to import southern Negro labor to keep their factories manned. Moreover, the manufacture of planes, aircraft engines, and components remained, up to World War II, largely on a job basis. The product sales volume did not justify elaborate work division or mass production techniques. Hence there was little demand for unskilled labor, and in the 1920's and 1930's, very few Negroes had the training or skill to work as aircraft mechanics. In 1940, for example, only 186 nonwhite employees, 0.2 percent of the labor force, were found in the "aircraft and parts" industry by the census of that year. (See Table 11.) The few Negroes in the industry were nearly all janitors, porters, or outside laborers.

The virtual exclusion of Negroes from the aircraft industry prior to World War II was certainly consistent with conscious owner-managerial policies. *Fortune* magazine reported in the spring of 1940 that the aircraft industry had "an almost universal prejudice against Negroes . . . you almost never see Negroes in aircraft factories . . . there is little concealment about the anti-Negro policy. . . ."[6]

Company presidents both before and immediately after the Japanese attack on Pearl Harbor, were very frank indeed about the industry's racial policies. The president of Vultee (now a division of General Dynamics) told a Negro organization that "it is not the policy of this company to employ people other than of the Caucasian

6. *Fortune,* "Half a Million Workers," XXIII (March 1943), pp. 98, 163.

TABLE 11. *Aircraft and Parts Manufacturing Industry*[a]
Total Employed Persons by Color and Sex, 1940-1960

Year	All Employees			Male			Female		
	Total	Nonwhite	Percent Nonwhite	Total	Nonwhite	Percent Nonwhite	Total	Nonwhite	Percent Nonwhite
1940	107,131	186	0.2	102,526	182	0.2	4,605	4	0.1
1950	257,310	4,230	1.6	224,310	4,050	1.8	33,000	180	0.5
1960	644,390	23,480	3.6	541,680	20,588	3.8	102,710	2,892	2.8

Source: *U. S. Census of Population:*
1940: Vol. III, *The Labor Force,* Table 76.
1950: P-E No. 1D, *Industrial Characteristics,* Table 2.
1960: PC (2) 7F, *Industrial Characteristics,* Table 3.

[a] SIC, 372; Census, 268.

race. . . ."[7] When plans were announced by North American Aviation, Inc., to build a major bomber plant near Kansas City, Kansas, in March 1941, a group of Negro civic leaders inquired about the prospects for employment of members of their race. The president of the Company was quoted as follows:

> "We will receive applications from both white and Negro workers. However, the Negroes will be considered only as janitors and in other similar capacities. . . .
>
> "While we are in complete sympathy with the Negro, it is against the company policy to employ them as mechanics or aircraft workers.
>
> "We use none except white workers in the plant . . . at Inglewood [Cal.] and the plant in Dallas and we intend to maintain the same policy in Kansas City. . . ."[8]

Likewise, Glenn L. Martin, founder of the Baltimore company of the same name, told a Congressional committee in March 1942, that segregation practices in the state, plus fear of walkouts by white workers who would object to Negro employment, made it impractical to employ Negroes.[9] And a recruiter of the Boeing Company told a Negro applicant that there was "no place for Negro workers. . . ."[10]

There were some exceptions to the industry's initial negative approach to Negro employment. Lockheed in Southern California recruited Negro employees in the early forties without waiting for government prodding, as did United Aircraft in New England, and Bell in Buffalo, New York.[11] Moreover, companies like North American, Boeing, and Martin completely altered their policies in the face of all-out war, the need to utilize all available manpower, government pressure, and obvious morality and decency. The labor force in "aircraft and parts" rose to a high of 1,345,600 in 1943. Plants and companies which had lily-white labor complements before the war, trained and took on Negroes in a variety of jobs. The same North American president who said Negroes could work only as janitors at the Kansas City plant, was pictured talking to skilled Negro metal workers one year later by the Negro newspaper which

7. *Ibid.*
8. *The Call,* Kansas City, March 21, 1941.
9. *Norfolk Journal & Guide,* January 10, 1942.
10. Associated Negro Press report, *Louisiana Weekly,* December 13, 1941.
11. The information herein is based on the author's field notes of this period. See also, Herbert R. Northrup, *Organized Labor and the Negro* (New York: Harper & Brothers, 1944), pp. 205-209.

quoted his early statement.[12] Negroes made up about 5 percent of this plant's 17,000 workers and were found in nearly all blue collar departments and occupations.

In most northern plants, Negroes thus not only gained entrance to the industry, but also to skilled production jobs. In the South progress was much slower. New plants built in Texas, Louisiana, Georgia, and even in border areas like St. Louis hired few Negroes and operated with segregated facilities. The Fairchild Aircraft Company established an all-Negro plant at its Hagerstown, Maryland, works. The Douglas plant at Tulsa, Oklahoma, however, did employ a large number of Negroes without such segregation. On the other hand, the Vultee plant at Nashville, Tennessee, added few Negroes, even after a directive to do so by the President's Committee on Fair Employment Practice.

Negro women also were introduced into aircraft factories for the first time during the war. This was primarily in the North, although in St. Louis and the Cincinnati areas, where segregation was still practiced, Negro women were also employed.

There were a great many obstacles which thwarted Negroes, who wanted aircraft jobs in this period. Their lack of training has already been noted. In many areas, including but not confined to the South, Negro groups had to apply great pressure to gain entrance to training opportunities, including those which were taxpayer financed. Sometimes, the training for Negroes was segregated, and inferior. In many cases, valuable time and jobs were lost because of the procrastination in making training available to Negroes. In other cases, training for Negroes omitted preparation for certain key jobs.

Plant location was also a bar to Negro employment. Huge new plants had to be constructed in outlying areas. Public transportation was often poorest from Negro neighborhoods and since fewer Negroes had automobiles, car pools were more difficult to arrange.

On the other hand, the existence of aircraft and other war industries drew Negroes, as well as whites, to new areas. Farm-city migration was accelerated. Negro communities grew up or were greatly enlarged in the West Coast cities of San Diego, Seattle, and especially Oakland and Los Angeles. The labor force of these areas, as well as of the industry, was changed dramatically.

---

12. *The Call,* Kansas City, March 20 and April 10, 1942.

Union policies played a minor role in racial policies of the aircraft industry during World War II, although many of the plants became unionized by either the International Association of Machinists or the United Automobile Workers. At this time, the IAM had a provision in its initiation ritual which pledged members to recommend membership only to "qualified white mechanics." This provision was ignored by some of its locals, particularly the one at Lockheed's southern California operations. In some cases, IAM officials or local unions strongly opposed Negro employment. Generally, however, since few of its aircraft contracts then provided for the union shop, it did not take a position on Negro employment, although certainly at best, this union then was no supporter of fair employment practice, and in some cases supported or institutionalized the opposition of white workers to upgrading or employment of Negroes.

The UAW had an avowed equalitarian policy which in one case led it to fire an organizer who called a strike against Negro upgrading in a Curtiss-Wright plant, and to order the men back to work.[13] The UAW also actively solicited Negro members. It too, however, had few union shop agreements and left hiring and upgrading policies largely to management, within the general framework of the collective agreements of that period.

Negroes' greatest gains in the aircraft industry occurred in the automotive plants which were converted to war production. Here the Negro was no stranger, and here there would be jobs when the war was over. In the aircraft industry proper, Negro employment at the peak probably did not exceed 50,000—somewhat less than 4 percent of the industry's employment.[14]

From a peak of 1,345,600 in 1943, employment in aircraft and parts declined to 788,100 in 1945 and to 237,300 in 1946.[15] Most Negro employees were laid off with the mass of white workers who lost their jobs as plants closed at the end of the war. But not all gains disappeared. Those Negroes who were trained were better capable of finding new jobs. And the lily-white caste of the industry was forever ended, although in varying degrees among different companies. The 1950 decennial census found 4,230 Negroes in the aircraft and parts industry—1.6 percent of those employed (see Table 11).

13. *New York Times*, December 3, 1943.
14. See Northrup, *Organized Labor and the Negro, loc. cit.*
15. Data from U. S. Bureau of Labor Statistics.

CHAPTER IV.

From Aircraft to Aerospace, 1945-1960

The aircraft industry regrouped and recovered very slowly after the great cutbacks which followed the end of World War II hostilities. Single companies, at the receipt of telegrams from the Pentagon, laid workers off 10,000 or even 50,000 at a time. Whole huge plants were abandoned in locations throughout the country. Demands for civilian aircraft revived, but required only a small fraction of the wartime factory or worker demands, and the government was very slow to develop a significant interest in missile and space vehicles despite their demonstrated effectiveness by Germany. Employment in the industry remained fairly constant at about 250,000 until the outbreak of the Korean War.

NEGRO EMPLOYMENT, 1945-1950

Negro employees were hard hit by the postwar layoffs. As a newly hired group, they had little seniority. Many new plants where they had made impressive gains were completely shut down: Curtiss-Wright in St. Louis and Cincinnati (Evendale), Douglas at Tulsa, and North American at Kansas City, are examples. In addition, a number of companies, such as Northrop and Lockheed, shut down facilities in heavily populated areas of Los Angeles and moved their remaining operations to plants located in suburban or outlying areas. Such moves were motivated by sound business considerations, because of the need for space for testing products and the obvious dangers caused by aircraft maneuvering in populated areas. Nevertheless, the impact on Negroes was severe, because it left plants concentrated in areas where Negroes could not obtain housing.

The location of the major plants of the industry posed even greater obstacles for Negro workers as the post-World War II years passed because of the increasing substitution of private automobile transportation for the public urban systems. This has tended to increase Negro isolation in center cities and restrict their search for work: people need jobs to buy automobiles, but need automobiles to reach jobs. Negroes are disproportionately caught in this circle, as a result of discrimination in housing and in credit opportunities, their concentration in the cities, and their relative lack of education and knowledge of the labor market.[16]

There were also a few positive factors which contributed to Negro employment in the postwar era. Facilities abandoned by one company were taken over by others after some period, and in a number of cases without some of the less favorable characteristics for Negroes which had featured wartime operations. For example, although Curtiss-Wright was a significant employer of Negroes during the war, it did conform to segregation practices where they existed. In late 1945, McDonnell Aircraft Corporation took over the abandoned facility at Lambert Field, St. Louis. McDonnell's first act after acquiring the plant, " . . . prior to moving its personnel into the buildings, was to desegregate rest rooms, dressing rooms, locker areas, drinking fountains, rest areas and cafeterias."[17] In so doing, McDonnell followed a policy inaugurated in 1943, when it acquired a former garage in downtown St. Louis as its first major plant. Despite the fact that St. Louis was then a segregated city, this plant was operated without segregation. About 3 percent of McDonnell's employees were then colored.[18]

Other facilities which were desegregated when put back in operation by new owners or operators were the former Curtiss-Wright plant at Evandale, a Cincinnati, Ohio, suburb, which General Electric converted into a major jet engine facility; the former North American

16. On these problems see, in general, *The Negroes in the United States: Their Economic and Social Situation,* Bulletin No. 1511, U. S. Bureau of Labor Statistics, Washington, 1966; *Social and Economic Conditions in the United States,* U. S. Bureau of Labor Statistics Report No. 332 and U. S. Bureau of the Census, Current Population Reports, Series P-23, No. 24, 1967; Karl E. and Alma F. Tauber, *Negroes in Cities* (Chicago: Aldine Publishing Company, 1965); and especially J. R. Meyer, J. F. Kain, and M. Wohl, *The Urban Transportation Problem* (Cambridge, Mass.: Harvard University Press, 1965), pp. 144-170.

17. R. C. Krone, "The Civil Rights Act and its Effect in Missouri," address before the 64th Annual Conference, Missouri Association for Social Welfare, October 29, 1964. Mr. Krone is Vice-President—Personnel, McDonnell Aircraft Corporation.

18. *Ibid.*

plant in Grand Prairie, near Dallas, Texas, which was reactivated by Chance-Vought, then a division of United Aircraft, but now of Ling-Temco-Vought; and the former Bell Aircraft complex at Marietta, near Atlanta, Georgia, which Lockheed now operates. These three facilities were not reactivated until the Korean War period. Both General Electric and Chance-Vought immediately desegregated their plants, but Lockheed followed local practices for a time before doing so.[19] Neither Chance-Vought, nor later Bell Helicopter, which opened new facilities near Fort Worth in the early 1950's, employed Negroes to any degree in other than menial jobs during this period.

Despite some favorable aspects, the period 1945-1950 was hardly one of progress for Negro employment in the aircraft industry. By 1950, the decennial census found that only 1.6 percent of the approximately 250,000 persons employed in the industry were Negroes. (See Table 11.) To be sure, this was a far better showing than reported by the 1940 census. In the interim, however, the percentage of Negro employment in the industry had risen to 3 or 4 percent of the industry's labor force at the peak of wartime employment, and then declined by 50 percent as a result of the postwar layoffs.

THE KOREAN WAR TO 1960

The demands of the Korean War pushed up employment substantially in the aircraft industry and the commitment of the United States thereafter to maintain air supremacy kept employment on an upward trend until 1958. From the post-World War II level of approximately 250,000, employment in the aircraft and parts industry rose to 467,800 in 1951, 795,500 in 1953, and peaked at 895,800 in 1957.[20] As already noted, huge plants which were abandoned in 1944 and 1945 were reopened, and new facilities built. Vast sums were committed to research and development as manned aircraft entered the turbojet age, and new metals, electronic controls, and technology were needed to handle the new speeds, distances, and heights which could be flown.

---

19. On Lockheed's policy, see E. G. Mattison, "Integrating the Work Force in Southern Industry," in Herbert R. Northrup and Richard L. Rowan (eds.), *The Negro and Employment Opportunity* (Ann Arbor, Mich.: Bureau of Industrial Relations, University of Michigan, 1965), pp. 147-154.
20. Data from Aerospace Industries Association, based upon U. S. Bureau of Labor Statistics figures.

TABLE 12. *Aircraft and Parts Manufacturing Industry Occupational Distribution by Color and Sex, 1960*

	All Employees			Male			Female		
Occupational Group	Total	Nonwhite	Percent Nonwhite	Total	Nonwhite	Percent Nonwhite	Total	Nonwhite	Percent Nonwhite
Managers, officials, and proprietors	19,215	22	0.1	18,238	22	0.1	977	—	—
Professional, technical, and kindred workers	143,933	2,816	2.0	137,560	2,715	2.0	6,373	101	1.6
Clerical and kindred workers	108,742	1,501	1.4	48,370	1,030	2.1	60,372	471	0.8
Sales workers	3,030	—	—	2,971	—	—	59	—	—
Craftsmen, foremen, and kindred workers	167,173	4,338	2.6	162,775	4,217	2.6	4,398	121	2.8
Operatives and kindred workers	175,461	10,731	6.1	148,193	8,993	6.1	27,268	1,738	6.4
Laborers	5,219	981	18.8	5,038	961	19.1	181	20	11.0
Service workers	10,855	2,395	22.1	9,314	2,055	22.1	1,541	340	22.1
Occupation not reported	10,762	675	6.3	9,221	574	6.2	1,541	101	6.6
Total	644,390	23,459	3.6	541,680	20,567	3.8	102,710	2,892	2.8

Source: *U. S. Census of Population 1960*, PC(2) 7A, *Occupational Characteristics*, Table 36.

The Korean War boom helped to generate the lowest unemployment level in the post-World War II era. Negroes profited, as they have in boom times, by gaining a share of the work opportunities in war industries. Severe cutbacks, however, occurred from 1958 to 1961 and employment in the aircraft and parts industry fell to 619,200 in the latter year. One must presume that large numbers of Negro aircraft workers became unemployed as a result of these declines. Yet over the decade, as the data in Table 11 show, nonwhite employment (which is overwhelmingly Negro) rose from 1.6 percent to 3.6 percent of the total "aircraft and parts" work force.

The skill distribution shown by the 1960 census reveals the usual heavy concentration in the unskilled and semiskilled jobs and the under-representation of nonwhites in the higher classifications[21] (Table 12). Thus in 1960, 22.1 percent of the service workers, 18.8 percent of the laborers, and 6.1 percent of the operatives in the aircraft and parts industry were nonwhite; but beyond that, nonwhite participation varied from 2.6 percent of the craftsmen and foremen to no sales personnel and virtually no managers. Most sales personnel, as already noted, selling to the government are classified as professional or managerial by the companies. Few if any Negroes were in such jobs in 1960, but recruitment of some Negro engineers and technicians for inside work was not by then novel.

The aircraft industry in 1960 was more advanced than many others in the utilization of nonwhite women, both in the factory and in the office. As in the case of men, the largest number of nonwhite women in blue collar jobs were classified as semiskilled operatives; in the offices, nonwhite women held various clerical jobs. Negro female employment in aircraft plants was most common around 1960 in Southern California, and least common (as it is today) in the South.

Tables 13 and 14 explore Negro employment in the aircraft and parts industries on state and regional bases for the principal areas of aircraft production. Negro employment by state in 1960 was highest in Georgia, a temporary phenomenon that did not last after the major plant in the state greatly expanded production in the more skilled areas. Southern California, Ohio, New York, and Missouri

21. These data include nonwhites other than Negroes. This causes a slight distortion for Southern California data, where a number of Orientals are employed, but even there the numbers of nonwhite, non-Negroes are small.

TABLE 13. *Aircraft and Parts Manufacturing Industry*
Total Employed Persons by Race, Selected States, 1940-1960

State	1960 All Employees	1960 Negroes	1960 Percent Negro	1950 All Employees	1950 Negroes	1950 Percent Negro	1940 All Employees	1940 Negroes	1940 Percent Negro
California	182,826	6,665	3.6	82,534	1,301	1.6	37,719	10	*
Connecticut	57,743	782	1.4	18,234	120	0.7	10,817	3	*
Washington	54,118	1,034	1.9	17,254	155	0.9	5,449	—	—
New York	51,415	1,681	3.3	26,513	378	1.4	13,791	18	0.1
Ohio	49,500	2,023	4.1	16,078	682	4.2	4,299	14	0.3
Texas	40,178	838	2.1	23,116	339	1.5	118	4	3.4
Kansas	32,141	547	1.7	12,960	104	0.8	1,582	—	—
Missouri	22,841	861	3.8	5,979	104	1.7	806	8	1.0
New Jersey	22,452	523	2.3	15,762	211	1.3	10,993	11	0.1
Indiana	21,425	477	2.2	9,545	209	2.2	2,835	7	0.2
Georgia	12,973	814	6.3	66	7	10.6	11	—	—
Pennsylvania	11,921	158	1.3	4,917	61	1.2	3,773	19	0.5
Massachusetts	11,252	110	1.0	2,540	8	0.3	—	—	—
Oklahoma	6,346	108	1.7	818	24	2.9	137	—	—
Florida	3,833	107	2.8	209	5	2.4	54	—	—

Sources: U. S. *Census of Population:*
1940: Vol. III, *The Labor Force,* parts 2-5, Table 18.
1950: Vol. II, *Characteristics of the Population,* State volumes, Table 83.
1960: PC(1)D, *Detailed Characteristics,* State volumes, Table 129.

* Less than 0.05 percent.

TABLE 14. *Aircraft and Parts Manufacturing Industry*
Total Employed Persons by Race
Seven Standard Metropolitan Statistical Areas, 1950 and 1960

Standard Metropolitan Statistical Area	1960 All Employees	1960 Negro	1960 Percent Negro	1950 All Employees	1950 Negro	1950 Percent Negro
Los Angeles-Long Beach	153,337	6,283	4.1	70,209	1,183	1.7
Seattle, Washington	50,276	967	1.9	16,274	152	0.9
New York	37,826	1,558	4.1	19,643	358	1.8
Wichita, Kansas	26,254	520	2.0	11,681	97	0.8
Fort Worth, Texas	22,690	342	1.5	15,028	237	1.6
St. Louis, Mo.-Ill.	20,366	874	4.3	5,165	103	2.0
Philadelphia, Pa.-N.J.	4,221	136	3.2	2,366	67	2.8

Source: *U. S. Census of Population:*
1950: Vol. II, *Characteristics of the Population,* State volumes, Table 83.
1960: PC(1)D, *Detailed Characteristics,* State volumes, Table 129.

were the leading areas in the percentage of Negro employment at this time, and New York and California showed the greatest gains over the two decades. The substantial improvement of Negro representation in the industry in the two decades reported in Table 13 occurred throughout the country. Yet in no state with substantial employment in the industry did the proportion of Negroes exceed 4.2 percent.

Table 14 provides the same data for seven Standard Metropolitan Statistical Areas—that is, cities and suburbs comprising overall labor markets. These were in 1960 among the largest centers of aircraft and parts production. The superior position of Negroes in the Los Angeles, New York, and St. Louis areas and the relatively poor showing in Fort Worth and Seattle are emphasized by these data. When, however, one compares the employment data in Table 14 with 1960 population statistics, it is apparent that Negroes in the Los Angeles SMSA had the greatest opportunities for jobs in aircraft plants and those in Fort Worth, the least. Fort Worth with a city population that was about 16 percent Negro in 1960 had no higher a percentage of Negro aircraft employment than did Seattle, the population of which was 5 percent Negro. St. Louis had twice the proportion of Negro population as did New York and Los Angeles, but all three had about the same proportion of Negro aircraft workers. Yet no other area had more than a 4.3 percent proportion of Negro aircraft employees.

NIXON COMMITTEE FINDINGS

The extent and character of progress made by Negroes in the aircraft industry during the 1950's is corroborated by studies made for the President's Committee on Government Contracts from 1957 to 1960. Known as the Nixon Committee, because it was chaired by the then Vice-President, this Committee was charged with discouraging discrimination by government contractors. Data gathered by it relating to seventeen plants of thirteen aerospace companies for 1959 are summarized in Table 15. These data show about the same over all percentage of Negro employment as do the census data, and the same concentration of Negroes in lower-rated jobs.

The data in Table 15 are primarily for aircraft and aircraft parts manufacturing enterprises, rather than for missile and space production. This accounts for the relatively heavy concentration of semiskilled and unskilled jobs and the relatively small number of professional and other salaried groups. As missile and space vehicle production increased and aircraft production declined in the early 1960's, Negro employment was initially adversely affected.

TABLE 15. *Aerospace Industry, Total and Negro Employment by Major Occupational Group, 13 Companies, 17 Plants, 1959*

Occupational Group	All Employees	Negro	Percent Negro
Professional and technical	42,274	187	0.4
Supervisory	14,774	44	0.3
Clerical and stenographic	26,458	329	1.2
Skilled	63,443	2,301	3.6
Semiskilled	33,699	2,450	7.3
Unskilled	11,901	1,037	8.7
Other	5,099	188	3.7
Total	197,648	6,536	3.3

Source: President's Committee on Government Contracts (Nixon Committee) files.

DEVELOPMENTS IN THE SOUTH

By 1960, the major aircraft companies in the Dallas-Fort Worth area had made little progress in employing and upgrading Negroes. In fact, very few Negroes were employed in these plants except in laboring and service jobs. Moreover, the facilities of at least two of the major plants there remained segregated. Progress toward elimination of segregation and toward upgrading of Negro personnel had been started under the prodding of the Nixon Committee. Before, however, any real progress could be made, employment in Southwest aerospace plants suffered sharp declines. General Dynamics dropped from 27,000 in 1956 to 6,000 in 1960 and Chance-Vought from 16,800 in 1957 to 7,253 in 1960. Bell Helicopter remained at about 2,500. The lack of progress in Negro employment in the 1950's and the slow revival during the next decade were to have profoundly adverse effects on Negro employment in the area in the 1960's.

The principal plant in the Southeast aerospace industry is the huge facility at Marietta, Georgia, near Atlanta, which was built during World War II, and taken over and expanded by Lockheed during the Korean War. Lockheed hired substantially more Negroes than did the Southwest plants, but it too operated on a segregated basis in this period. Negroes were used on production lines, which were segregated, but the company resisted demands of the local affiliate of the International Association of Machinists to establish a segregated seniority system. When layoffs occurred in the late 1950's, white workers were faced with a choice of integrating the seniority lines or suffering further layoffs. In this way, Lockheed moved toward integration and then to the affirmative action which has figured so prominently in the leadership of the Southeast in aerospace employment in the 1960's that is described in the next chapter.

CHAPTER V.

Employment Expansion and Affirmative Action, 1960-1966

The 1960's did not commence auspiciously for Negro employment in the aerospace industry. The decline in employment in the aircraft industry which began in 1957 continued through 1964. Missile and space vehicle employment rose to offset or nearly offset that decline, but the character of the work in the two main segments of aerospace is quite different.

Missile and space vehicle work is, as has been noted, essentially of a job shop character, with much greater proportionate need for skilled craftsmen, technicians, and professionals than aircraft. Given the relative scarcity of Negroes with these skills, it was not till late 1963 and 1964, when civilian aircraft production, military procurement, and the space program all boomed in concert with increased emphasis on civil rights, that Negro employment in the aerospace industry began to show both qualitative and quantitative advances over the late 1950's.

THE EARLY MISSILE AND SPACE PERIOD, 1960-1964

Table 16 shows employment in 21 aerospace companies and 140 plants by race and sex for the total country and for various regions, based on data collected during the author's field studies. These data, of course, are not strictly comparable to those collected either by the Bureau of the Census or by the Nixon Committee. They do demonstrate, however, that Negro employment did not gain in the 1960-1963 period and probably even declined. The principal reason appears to be the changing product mix from aircraft to missiles and space vehicles, which offset company "affirmative

TABLE 16. *Aerospace Industry, Employment by Race, Sex, and Region 21 Companies, 140 Establishments, 1963*

Region	All Employees Total	All Employees Negro	All Employees Percent Negro	Male Total	Male Negro	Male Percent Negro	Female Total	Female Negro	Female Percent Negro
Northeast	147,395	3,598	2.4	128,764	3,258	2.5	18,631	340	1.8
New England	69,823	1,048	1.5	60,094	975	1.6	9,729	73	0.8
Middle Atlantic	77,572	2,550	3.3	68,670	2,283	3.3	8,902	267	3.0
South	60,175	1,095	1.8	52,152	945	1.8	8,023	150	1.9
Southeast	29,314	506	1.7	25,224	394	1.6	4,090	112	2.7
Southwest	30,861	589	1.9	26,928	551	2.0	3,933	38	1.0
Midwest	87,858	3,310	3.8	77,566	3,015	3.9	10,292	295	2.9
West Coast	352,547	10,284	2.9	284,025	8,293	2.9	68,522	1,991	2.9
Southern California	234,144	8,303	3.5	184,679	6,660	3.6	49,465	1,643	3.3
Other West Coast	118,403	1,981	1.7	99,346	1,633	1.6	19,057	348	1.8
Total United States	647,975	18,287	2.8	542,507	15,511	2.9	105,468	2,776	2.6

Source: Data in author's possession.

Note: Geographic definitions are as follows:

New England: Maine, Vermont, New Hampshire, Massachusetts, Connecticut, and Rhode Island.
Middle Atlantic: New York, Pennsylvania, New Jersey, Maryland, and Delaware.
Southeast: Virginia, West Virginia, North Carolina, South Carolina, Georgia, Florida, Alabama, Mississippi, Louisiana, Tennessee, and Kentucky.
Southwest: Texas, Oklahoma, New Mexico, and Arizona.
West Coast: Washington, Oregon, California, Idaho, and Nevada.
Midwest: All Midwest and Rocky Mountain States. Actual plants only in Colorado and Midwest except for small military installations.

action" programs, joint industry-government activities, such as the Plans for Progress program, and government pressure exerted through procurement policies designed to expand Negro employment. In addition, employment in the South continued to lag and meaningful integration had not gone far by then.

In 1963, *Business Week* magazine made a study of what this changed product mix meant to the labor force requirements at Douglas Aircraft Company. Figure 3 summarizes these changes. The *Business Week* survey found that the hourly worker was not only declining in importance in aerospace, "but where he survives . . . [is] both more skilled and more versatile. The rigid tolerances and quality control

Figure 3. *How Douglas' Labor Needs Have Changed*

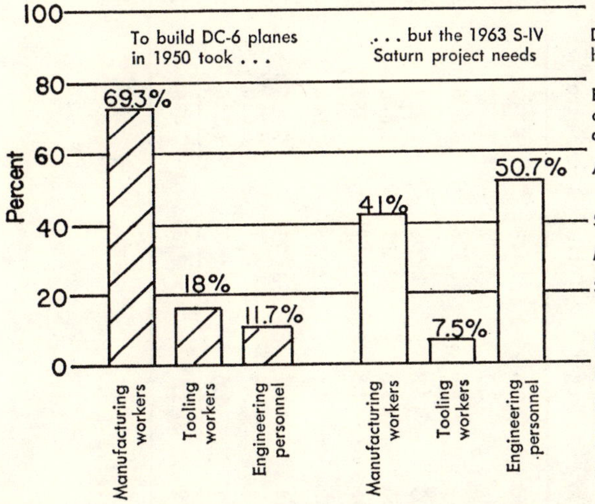

Douglas' engineering jobs have changed, too.

Engineering and scientific assignments:	Percent of work force 1953	1963
Aerodynamics and astrodynamics	8%	18%
Structural	29	10
Mechanical	17	11
Structural-mechanical	13	2
Propulsion	6	6
Electronics	20	31
Computing	5	16
Life sciences	2	2
Nuclear	0	2

Source: *Business Week,* June 22, 1963, by permission of McGraw-Hill Company.

requirements of spacecraft demand the first characteristic, its 'custom-made' nature the second. . . ."[22] The changing product mix of the industry during this period drastically reduced demands for such lower-skilled jobs as riveters, assemblers, fabricators, and foundry workers and greatly increased jobs for engineers and electronic technicians.[23]

In all the areas of job increase, proportionately fewer Negroes had the background even to qualify them for training. The results, of course, are clear in Table 16. Negro employment at best barely

22. *Business Week,* June 22, 1963, p. 44.
23. *Ibid.,* p. 46.

TABLE 17. *Aerospace Industry, Employment by Race, Sex, and Region 23 Companies, 179 Establishments, 1964*

Region	All Employees			Male			Female		
	Total	Negro	Percent Negro	Total	Negro	Percent Negro	Total	Negro	Percent Negro
Northeast	145,535	3,660	2.5	127,448	3,339	2.6	18,087	321	1.8
New England	77,373	1,648	2.1	66,912	1,533	2.3	10,461	115	1.1
Middle Atlantic	68,162	2,012	3.0	60,536	1,806	3.0	7,626	206	2.7
South	103,827	2,903	2.8	90,598	2,627	2.9	13,229	276	2.1
Southeast	57,764	2,068	3.6	50,521	1,846	3.7	7,243	222	3.1
Southwest	46,063	835	1.8	40,077	781	1.9	5,986	54	0.9
Midwest	93,414	3,862	4.1	82,596	3,604	4.4	10,818	258	2.4
West Coast	311,772	9,634	3.1	253,673	7,906	3.1	58,099	1,728	3.0
Southern California	216,474	8,108	3.7	173,011	6,650	3.8	43,463	1,458	3.4
Other West Coast	95,298	1,526	1.6	80,662	1,256	1.6	14,636	270	1.8
Total United States	654,548	20,059	3.1	554,315	17,476	3.2	100,233	2,583	2.6

Source: Data in author's possession.

Note: For geographic definitions, see Table 16.

TABLE 18. *Aerospace Industry*
Employment by Race, Sex, and Occupational Group
23 Companies, 179 Establishments
Total United States, 1964

Occupational Group	All Employees Total	All Employees Negro	All Employees Percent Negro	Male Total	Male Negro	Male Percent Negro	Female Total	Female Negro	Female Percent Negro
Officials and managers	60,541	172	0.3	59,895	169	0.3	646	3	0.5
Professionals	162,706	1,130	0.7	159,529	1,094	0.7	3,177	36	1.1
Technicians	56,363	929	1.6	51,658	876	1.7	4,705	53	1.1
Sales workers	887	1	0.1	852	1	0.1	35	—	—
Office and clerical	111,239	1,923	1.7	44,286	1,077	2.4	66,953	846	1.3
Total white collar	391,736	4,155	1.1	316,220	3,217	1.0	75,516	938	1.2
Craftsmen	132,402	3,826	2.9	128,571	3,674	2.9	3,831	152	4.0
Operatives	112,394	8,761	7.8	94,037	7,521	8.0	18,357	1,240	6.8
Laborers	5,772	837	14.5	4,487	806	18.0	1,285	31	2.4
Service workers	12,244	2,480	20.3	11,000	2,258	20.5	1,244	222	17.8
Total blue collar	262,812	15,904	6.1	238,095	14,259	6.0	24,717	1,645	6.7
Total	654,548	20,059	3.1	554,315	17,476	3.2	100,233	2,583	2.6

Source: Data in author's possession.

held its own in this period despite special government and company efforts to open up new opportunities for minorities, and despite an overall increase of 100,000 in total aerospace employment from 1960 to 1963.

On a regional basis the 1963 data show Southern California, the Mid-Atlantic area (mostly New York and Philadelphia), and the Midwest continuing to have the highest percentage of Negro employment. The South continued to demonstrate a poor record in this regard.

In 1964, some improvement occurred in the Negro employment picture. The data in Table 17 include some plants which were not covered by the 1963 survey summarized in Table 16, but these differences do not account for the dramatic improvement in the Southeast and West Coast, which accounted for the bulk of the improvement. The most important action which contributed to the upturn in Negro employment was undoubtedly the heightened pressure to improve the Negro's position in industry. The major aircraft producers made notable progress in developing special programs to increase Negro employment. Aspects of these programs will be discussed in detail after the 1966 data are examined. The Southwest, still with a heavy backlog of layoffs, showed little progress in 1964.

The distribution of Negroes within broad occupational groups in 1964 is shown in Table 18. The usual concentration in the less skilled categories is again apparent. The relatively high proportion of craftsmen (skilled employees) does, however, indicate that upward movement in at least the factory was under way by this date.

THE GENERAL PICTURE AND "AFFIRMATIVE ACTION" SINCE 1966

Tables 19 and 20 show employment in the aerospace industry by occupational group, race, and sex for 21 companies and 127 establishments located in all regions of the country. The sample includes all major aerospace corporations and about 60 percent of the industry's labor force. It includes all major facilities covered by the data in Tables 16-18, omitting only some of the smaller plants reported therein.

The first significant fact revealed by the data in Tables 19 and 20 is the continued expansion of Negro employment—more than 5 percent of total aerospace employees in 1968 and nearly twice the percentage revealed by the similar, but not completely comparable, data in

TABLE 19. *Aerospace Industry*
Employment by Race, Sex, and Occupational Group
21 Companies, 127 Establishments
Total United States, 1966

Occupational Group	All Employees			Male			Female		
	Total	Negro	Percent Negro	Total	Negro	Percent Negro	Total	Negro	Percent Negro
Officials and managers	71,328	292	0.4	70,638	289	0.4	690	3	0.4
Professionals	179,436	1,435	0.8	175,513	1,375	0.8	3,923	60	1.5
Technicians	63,999	1,209	1.9	57,284	1,128	2.0	6,715	81	1.2
Sales workers	720	2	0.3	673	2	0.3	47	—	—
Office and clerical	130,261	3,692	2.8	51,289	1,986	3.9	78,972	1,706	2.2
Total white collar	445,744	6,630	1.5	355,397	4,780	1.3	90,347	1,850	2.0
Craftsmen	164,991	7,595	4.6	158,623	7,050	4.4	6,368	545	8.6
Operatives	155,167	18,417	11.9	122,869	13,566	11.0	32,298	4,851	15.0
Laborers	8,065	1,804	22.4	6,344	1,619	25.5	1,721	185	10.7
Service workers	14,055	3,124	22.2	12,015	2,792	23.2	2,040	332	16.3
Total blue collar	342,278	30,940	9.0	299,851	25,027	8.3	42,427	5,913	13.9
Total	788,022	37,570	4.8	655,248	29,807	4.5	132,774	7,763	5.8

Source: Data in author's possession.

TABLE 20. *Aerospace Industry*
Employment by Race, Sex, and Occupational Group
21 Companies, 127 Establishments
Total United States, 1968

Occupational Group	All Employees			Male			Female		
	Total	Negro	Percent Negro	Total	Negro	Percent Negro	Total	Negro	Percent Negro
Officials and managers	74,803	447	0.6	74,026	438	0.6	777	9	1.2
Professionals	179,041	1,598	0.9	174,586	1,544	0.9	4,455	54	1.2
Technicians	62,253	1,308	2.1	54,945	1,198	2.2	7,308	110	1.5
Sales workers	694	4	0.6	673	4	0.6	21	—	—
Office and clerical	130,888	4,422	3.4	51,743	2,546	4.9	79,145	1,876	2.4
Total white collar	447,679	7,779	1.7	355,973	5,730	1.6	91,706	2,049	2.2
Craftsmen	175,538	9,566	5.4	167,377	8,706	5.2	8,161	860	10.5
Operatives	151,096	20,337	13.5	117,949	14,702	12.5	33,147	5,635	17.0
Laborers	9,991	2,071	20.7	7,013	1,703	24.3	2,978	368	12.4
Service workers	13,334	3,097	23.2	11,708	2,750	23.5	1,626	347	21.3
Total blue collar	349,959	35,071	10.0	304,047	27,861	9.2	45,912	7,210	15.7
Total	797,638	42,850	5.4	660,020	33,591	5.1	137,618	9,259	6.7

Source: Data in author's possession.

Table 16. This is the highest percentage of Negroes found in any analysis of the industry's racial data heretofore. Whether there has been any substantial improvement of the Negro ratio since early 1968 is not certain. On the one hand the industry has continued its affirmative action policies and has actively sought—often even given preference to—Negroes in employment. Aerospace firms have been extremely active in special training for the disadvantaged. As early as the first months of 1967 about 8,000 on-the-job trainees were enrolled in Southern California aerospace firms under provisions of the federal Manpower Development and Training Act. Nearly all these trainees were classified as disadvantaged, and virtually all were Negroes or Mexicans.[24] In more recent months, aerospace concerns have been active in the National Association of Businessmen's "JOBS" program, accepting and training the disadvantaged on a wide scale. In addition, several companies, such as Aerojet-General, Avco, North American Rockwell, and Lockheed have established, or assisted to establish, Negro run businesses in Negro neighborhoods.

Other special programs have also been pursued. United Aircraft's Pratt & Whitney division in Connecticut has made notable strides in rescuing dropouts and converting them through an elaborate training program into semiskilled or even skilled personnel. Pratt & Whitney has over 200 men and women in the training section of the personnel department, and had 7,000 persons in formal training in 1967 plus another 5,000 in a special short course.[25]

Boeing's Vertol division in Philadelphia has developed a careful, elaborate training program which has put many persons, including large numbers from the heavily Negro Chester, Pennsylvania, area into useful jobs, especially in its machine shop. McDonnell in St. Louis has among the highest proportion of Negroes in the industry in part because of its willingness to train those who might ordinarily be considered unemployable. Many other examples could be given of aerospace industry training and of special efforts to enroll Negroes in training courses.

Also in Philadelphia, General Electric's missile and space division has been a leading supporter of the Opportunities Industrialization

24. Letter to the author from Hugh C. Murphy, Administrator, Bureau of Apprenticeship and Training, U. S. Department of Labor, October 10, 1967.
25. See Edward R. Cowles, "Rx for Shop Skills," United Aircraft, *Bee-Hive*, Vol. XXXXIII (January 1968), pp. 25-29, for the details of the Pratt & Whitney training program.

Center, the much publicized self-help motivational and training institute, which has now been set up in over thirty other localities. Avco has built a plant in a Boston slum which will be operated and manned entirely by Negroes. General Dynamics, which is building the F-111 plane in Fort Worth, Texas, has established a satellite plant at San Antonio to train and to provide jobs for persons considered heretofore to be unemployable. Both the Avco facility which will employ 250 at full production, and that of General Dynamics which expects to have 200 jobs, are being established in collaboration with federal programs seeking to reduce hard-core, inner city unemployment. Ling-Temco-Vought and North American Rockwell are other aerospace companies which have set up special firms and/or similar activities for the disadvantaged.

All major aerospace firms are members of the National Alliance of Businessmen and Plans for Progress, with Lockheed being the first company enrolled in the latter. Originally Plans for Progress companies, but now almost all major government contractors are, in effect, committed to go beyond nondiscrimination and to develop programs and activities designed to further the employment of Negroes and other minorities. This has involved such already noted programs as hiring and training hard-core unemployed, establishing work areas or plants in Negro slum areas, special recruitment drives at Negro schools and colleges, and a host of other programs.

As the leading and largest government contractors, aerospace concerns are constantly being inspected by representatives of the various government procurement agencies, the Office of Federal Contract Compliance which now coordinates enforcement of the various Presidential Executive Orders relating to nondiscrimination by government contractors, the Equal Employment Opportunity Commission, and in many cases by state agencies as well. The obligations to take "affirmative action" are constantly before the aerospace companies, and they are usually the first to be "invited" to take part in new programs.

Pressure by the government has also resulted in companies literally giving preference to Negro applicants. Many leading aerospace concerns have told their employment interviewers that every effort should be made to hire Negroes who come even close to meeting minimum qualifications. Some have adopted an unwritten policy of outright preference: give the job to the Negro if he is available. One midwestern plant, where Negro employment was "disappointingly low" to the company's headquarters officials and to the government inspectors, hired 13.4 percent of its Negro applicants in the first seven months of 1967 as compared with 11.4 percent of its total applicants. Moreover, although total employment in this plant declined during this period, Negro employment increased even beyond the percentage increase resulting from the higher proportion of Negro recruits. This probably indicates some selection in layoffs to improve the percentage of Negroes on the payroll.

In one Southern California plant, which is located in a community where very few Negroes or Mexican-Americans dwell, the company moved to better its minority group employment (Mexican-Americans as well as Negroes) even though 10 percent of its 21,000 employees were from these groups. From November 1966 to August 1967, minority groups comprised 16.3 percent of all hires and were involved in 11.5 percent of all upgradings and promotions. Sixty percent of Negroes who applied were employed, but only 6 percent of the white persons who sought work were employed![26]

Numerous other examples could be cited of various types of "affirmative action." It is, for example, not uncommon for personnel executives to counsel with Negroes who have poor attendance or excessive tardiness records; or to approve several in-plant transfers for those who do not seem to be able to "get adjusted" to a supervisor; or otherwise to attempt to understand and to meet the problems of new Negro employees who seem unable to conform to the rules, regulations, or mores of the factory.

The executives of some companies have, of course, a greater commitment to equal employment opportunity than do those of others. For some it is a necessary order of business, to others, it is that plus a moral commitment. Within this framework, the author has not found any company of the twenty-one surveyed which was not making a real effort to expand Negro employment. Yet total Negro employment was less than 6 percent in 1968. This is approximately one-third of the proportion in the automobile industry and considerably less than that in many other industries. The reasons for this seeming paradox will be made clear after the ensuing discussion of occupa-

26. Data cited herein are from a variety of confidential sources, and have been carefully checked for accuracy.

tional differences and intraplant mobility of workers. First, however, it is necessary to explain why Negroes have probably not continued to increase their proportion of aerospace jobs since early 1968.

The Situation Since Mid-1968

In mid-1968, the aerospace industry, which had enjoyed continued employment expansion since the early 1960's, began a series of layoffs. Until this period, the remarkable boom in commercial aviation and the needs of the armed forces in Vietnam contributed to the increase in aircraft production and to increased employment therein. The fact that aircraft production utilizes large numbers of semiskilled personnel whereas missile and space vehicle production requires a much higher complement of skilled workers and technical and professional personnel has been reiterated earlier. The production shift to aircraft and the tight labor market which existed from 1965 to 1968 combined both to enhance Negro employment opportunities, and to give aerospace (as well as other) employers added incentive to find ways and means of utilizing Negroes and others whose training and background are below what was available in the looser labor markets of the late 1950's and early 1960's. Government and public policy to enhance employment opportunities for Negroes were thus operating in a favorable climate for success.

With the commercial aircraft boom at least pausing and the apparent phasing out of American participation in the Vietnam war, aircraft production began a decline in late 1968 that continued throughout 1969. A combination of low seniority based upon being the traditional last hired and the probable concentration in the sectors of the industry that are most directly feeling the turndown in aerospace employment has probably halted the increase in the ratio of Negro employment in the industry.

On the other hand, it should be emphasized that the turndown in aerospace is not a massive one. The industry expects total employment to be about 4.5 percent lower by the end of 1969 than it was one year previously, but production employment to be down 6.4 percent.[27] Much of this employment can be handled by attrition. In many cases, Negroes laid off will have acquired a sufficient amount of skill

27. Data from Aerospace Industries Association data published in the *Daily Labor Report,* May 20, 1969, pp. B-1 - B-13.

and experience to be able to obtain other jobs. Nevertheless, it would be unrealistic to believe that the proportion of Negro aerospace workers has continued to increase since 1968.

OFFICIALS AND MANAGERS

A feature of the present affirmative action campaign in the aerospace industry is the search for Negro managerial talent. The great bulk of the 292 Negroes listed as "officials and managers" in Tables 19 and 20 are first-line supervisors. Aerospace companies have diligently searched their ranks for supervisory talent, and continue to do so. Some Negro supervisors preside over all Negro labor or janitorial gangs, but most are out on the line managing mixed crews. Despite their small number and percentage, there have been a sufficient number of breakthroughs so that Negroes deserving of promotion out of the ranks now obtain full and fair consideration, or occasionally even preference, for supervisory appointments.

Few Negroes now have middle or top management jobs in the aerospace industry—or in industry generally. Traditionally Negroes with talent, education, and motivation have not sought careers in business. The doors have been much more open in certain professions, particularly teaching, and to a lesser degree, medicine and the law. Now the barriers are lowered. The potential Negro executive is today assiduously pursued by business recruiters, and the aerospace companies are in the forefront of the pursuers. But the availability is very small. The prestigious business schools, conscious of their need to attract and to interest Negroes in graduate business study, have developed several programs to do so, but the success is limited. The number of Negroes trained, or training for, executive positions continues to remain very small. It will be many years before the Negro manager is a common occurrence in aerospace or in any other major industry. Few today are found above middle management; this author knows of none in the top ranks of the aerospace industry. Several are in the personnel function; some in the engineering middle management. The fact that the Negro middle manager is becoming more common, if still relatively rare, presages a continued upward movement, qualitatively and quantitatively, albeit slowly.

PROFESSIONALS, TECHNICIANS, AND SALES WORKERS

The professional group is the largest occupational category in the industry. Aerospace companies have scoured the country looking for professional and technical employees. Unfortunately, Negroes seeking professional education and attainment have only recently been welcomed into engineering work, and consequently few Negroes even today seek engineering degrees. Moreover, the engineering taught at many of the traditionally Negro colleges is often substandard in general, but particularly inferior for the aerospace industry whose professionals are so often asked to develop products never heretofore made.

Nevertheless, most aerospace companies have their Negro engineer success stories (usually shown in pictures in the annual report!). Aerospace may well have as large, if not the largest, supply of Negro engineers of any industry, as it has of white engineers. Many companies in the industry have been recruiting Negro engineers for a long period, some as far back as World War II. A number do indeed have Negroes who are key members of their professional group. A Negro engineer who is available today can count on attractive job offers, both in terms of money and of the character of the work, from almost every major aerospace concern that learns of his availability. The unfortunate effect, of course, of years of discrimination is that so few Negroes can qualify as engineers.

Technicians are somewhat similarly situated in so far as Negro employment is concerned. Their technical training is the result either of school work somewhat below the engineering level, or they have advanced by experience and/or special training up from the ranks of shop craftsmen. In either case, they have backgrounds of work or training from which few Negroes were once admitted and for which few Negroes are now trained. Nevertheless, real progress has been made in this area. There are quite a few first-rate Negro technicians in aerospace plants, some of whom came up through the ranks over the years. But here again, future prospects are good only if the Negro population can become convinced of the potential which technical education promises. The jobs are there, but the obstacles to achieve the jobs remain formidable, as our discussion of the craftsmen situation, below, will again emphasize.

As has already been noted, few employees in the aerospace industry are classified as sales personnel, and those few are usually private plane salesmen or other specialty marketing personnel. A major distributor of one of the largest private plane manufacturing companies is a Negro. His salesmen and sales agencies are largely white and he is reputed to be very successful. Selling to the government, or to the major airlines, is a job calling for the designation of an executive, manager, or professional in so far as the aerospace industry is concerned. Whatever the designation, few Negroes are so employed. This is the practice throughout American industry, a practice that must change with the times. It will be instructive indeed, as the aerospace industry moves with the times, as it must, and utilizes Negroes in sales, marketing, sales engineering, and customer contact work, to observe how such changes are accepted by the industry's prime contractor, the government.

OFFICE AND CLERICAL

Despite some major progress, Negroes comprised only 3.4 percent of the clerical employees for 1968 in the Table 20 data. This reflects, among other aspects, the late start at which Negroes were accepted as office workers in the industry. The office and clerical group is the fourth largest in the industry, comprising 16.4 percent of the total work force. It not only offers a multitude of jobs, but includes many such as purchasing clerks, bookkeepers, personnel assistants, etc., from which promotion into lower-management ranks is customary.

In recent years, aerospace companies have made strenuous efforts to expand their Negro clerical work forces. They have sponsored special training programs, visited and recruited at predominantly Negro high schools, and taken graduates of special training groups, such as those sponsored by community human relations commissions, Urban Leagues, or the Opportunities Industrialization Centers. Two prime reasons for their inability to expand their Negro clerical percentage are lack of training and background and the locational factor.

Just as the segregated schools of the South and those in the inner city core are relatively deficient in their mathematics training, so they are in English grammar, punctuation, and spelling. The girl who graduates from such an institution and is told that she is a typist receives a rude shock when she is tested in an industrial setting. Her speed is likely to be substandard, but practice can overcome that. What is more serious is that she is likely to be a poor speller, have little idea of proper punctuation, and have had inferior training in how to set up a memorandum or business letter.

Aerospace industry officials—and most others—would often prefer to train high school graduates initially, rather than have to retrain them. The girl who thinks that she has learned stenography often resents being retaught and feels discriminated against because she is unaware how lacking in skills she actually is. As one personnel officer told the author: "When we suggest that we are willing to train a girl at our expense, she is sometimes outraged and files a case of discrimination with the state or the federal Equal Opportunity Commission. Inevitably, the record of her typing and English test exonerates us. But in the meantime, we have spent hours proving that we did not discriminate, lost a potential employee whom we need, and hurt our image with the friends and neighbors of the girl."[28]

The locational problem is a serious one which will be discussed in greater detail below. Suffice it here to point out that most aerospace facilities are located on the outskirts of cities and cannot be reached except by private car. Even, however, where public transportation exists, the travel problem remains a significant factor in reducing Negro participation in the industry and especially, the participation of Negro women. Studies of the author in other industries have confirmed the fact that, even where men are willing to travel long distances to work, women seeking work in an office are not.[29] Neighborhoods in which Negroes are concentrated are usually long distances from aerospace facilities. As a result, qualified Negro women tend to gravitate toward office and clerical work in the nearby center cities. Until Negroes can or do find housing in the outer city and suburbs, the aerospace industry's search for more Negro office and clerical employees will have only limited success.

THE CRAFTSMEN PROBLEM

Craftsmen is a broad designation in the aerospace industry. It includes maintenance and machine setup men, tool and die workers,

28. Interview, Los Angeles, January 1967.

29. See the discussion in the automobile industry sector, *supra*, part two.

machinists, electricians, millwrights, and others typically found in this category. It also includes some persons engaged in what is essentially assembly work. And it includes mechanics with great capability and versatility in electro-mechanical, hydraulics, pneumatics, or combinations of all three, as well as many other highly or even uniquely skilled workers.

During the past two decades, there has been a tremendous upgrading of skills in the industry. According to the Vice-President of Industrial Relations of Lockheed, "an amazing upward . . . shift in job skills occurred. . . . In 1944, what might be called the 'normal labor market' could fill more than 80 percent of the work force needs (operatives and low-skilled). Today less than half these jobs can be filled from that market. Even more critical is the sharp cutback of low-skilled jobs—those that might normally be filled by 'almost anyone.' A generation ago more than half the jobs were in this category. Today less than one-quarter are, and the number of workers at the craft level has about tripled."[30]

If this change in skill composition is critical for labor and management, it is even more so for Negro labor. Obtaining skilled blue collar work has always been difficult for Negroes in all industry. The craft unions in the building and metal trades have been historically, continually, and almost universally antagonistic to acceptance of Negroes as apprentices in areas of work under their control.[31] Small businessmen in these trades are frequently former craftsmen who share the racial outlook of their onetime colleagues, but who, in any case, are in no position to oppose the unions on such questions oı often, even to train many apprentices.

Negroes desirous of seeking employment leading to skilled blue collar work also cannot as easily short-circuit formal training as can many white workers. The latter often have the opportunity to work as aids or helpers to friends, neighbors, or relatives who work at a trade. Except in the southern trowel trades (bricklaying, plastering, or cement finishing), where a tradition of Negro participation has existed since slavery days, the Negro aspiring to skilled work finds

30. J. D. Hodgson, "The No-Longer-So-Blue-Collar Worker," address at the IRC Management Course, Williamsburg, Va., November 8, 1967, p. 3. Mr. Hodgson has since been appointed Under Secretary of Labor by President Nixon.

31. For background on this problem, see Herbert R. Northrup, *Organized Labor and the Negro* (New York: Harper & Brothers, 1944), Chapter 2.

few members of his race already in the trade and therefore able to aid him, and few whites willing to do so.

As a result, Negroes aiming at craftsmen's work find their best opportunities with those large employers, who have the need and financial resources to train and to upgrade their work force and who are expected as a social obligation, and now as a matter of law or public policy, to make certain that Negroes participate in that training and upgrading. Of course, the aerospace industry fits this description as well as, if not better than, most others. Moreover, the aerospace industry has probably done as good a job, if not a better one, than most industries in recruiting, training, and upgrading Negroes to the craftsmen level. The percentage of Negro craftsmen shown in Table 20 is exactly equal to the percentage of Negroes in the industry—5.4 percent. The author knows of no other major industry where Negro representation at the skilled level equals total representation.

Of course one may look at these data in an adverse way—that the overall recruitment level of Negroes is poor. The thrust of this analysis, however, is that the relatively low participation of Negroes in the aerospace industry is, above all, a function of the skill requirements of the industry. The rate of Negro participation in the industry is substantially reduced by the low percentage of Negroes in the salaried areas. In this aerospace is not unique, but rather typical of American industry. Since, however, professionals are the largest occupational category in the industry, comprising 22.4 percent of the total industry labor force, and since white collar and salaried employees make up 56.1 percent of the industry labor force, total Negro participation in the industry is affected in a major way by the lack of Negro representation in these occupational groups. Under the circumstances, Negro participation in the craftsmen group is relatively high, although certainly less than one-half the Negro population ratio in the country.

Among the other factors which keep Negro participation in aerospace craftsmen work from rising at a more rapid rate are of course educational deficiencies among Negro youth. Segregated southern schools and those in the inner city slums of northern cities provide inferior educational backgrounds particularly in communication skills and mathematics than do the white southern, or outer city or suburban schools which few Negroes attend. The large school drop-out rates of

Negroes accelerate this problem. The lack of Negro family industrial background in industry and skilled craft work, the demoralized Negro family structure with its missing father, and until recently, the predominant feeling that aspiration to skilled industrial work was not a practical hope, have all reduced the availability of Negroes for skilled work.

To offset these problems, the aerospace companies have made special efforts to recruit Negro apprenticeship candidates. The results have not been encouraging. Close contacts with high schools have uncovered far too few Negroes with the interest and mathematics background or capability. Those on the margin of mathematics competence have been offered special courses or tutoring by several companies, with very limited success in either enrollment or course completion. The Negro who qualifies in mathematics is now firmly college-oriented and is likely also to be uninterested in an apprentice course.

As a result of the historical problems of discrimination, the Negro aerospace craftsman, like his professional counterpart, is disproportionately found in the lower echelons of his group. Proportionately many fewer Negroes are tool and die workers, top-rated machinists, electromechanical, hydraulic, or pneumatic mechanics than are whites. Negro craftsmen are more heavily concentrated in less sophisticated sheet metal, pipe, millwright, or bench mechanic operations. Many of the latter have worked up from semiskilled operatives.

Such upgrading is the prime source of Negro craftsmen today. Many have come into the industry as unskilled employees and now are craftsmen with high-rated jobs. The aerospace industry is probably the most training conscious industry in America. Given the fantastically changing technology which underlies its products, it can do little without continous training. Most companies post training notices throughout plants and personnel departments and constantly urge employees to take training courses, and thereby help companies solve the skill shortages. In recent years, special efforts have been made to encourage Negroes to take advantage of training programs. What can happen when they do is set forth in three case histories in Table 21.

Unfortunately, Negro participation in training is almost universally below the proportion of Negroes in a plant. Motivational factors appear very important. Willingness to contribute one's time to

TABLE 21. *Aerospace Industry, Three Case Histories of Training and Results*

1 *John R - - - -*	2 *Porter P - - - -*	3 *Robert H - - - -*
John R is a Negro. He applied in 1960 and at the time was 28 years old, married and had been working as a garage mechanic "on commission." He was a high school graduate (South Carolina) and had been a mechanic in military service.	Porter P is a Negro. He applied in 1955. At the time he was 22 years old, married and had been working locally as a farm laborer. He had attended high school for two years in Alabama.	Robert H is a Negro. He was 28 and single in 1961 when he applied. He was a high school graduate (Norwich, Conn.). He had resigned as a "pilot and mechanic" from a Groton, Connecticut flight organization.
He was hired as a 3-week machine operator trainee at $2.00 per hour.	He was employed as a parts washer in October 1955. This job was the division's second lowest labor grade —yet it paid 27c per hour more than he had been earning.	He was hired in 1961 as an Engine Assembly Inspector "B" at $2.37 per hour. He was promoted that same year and his rate increased to $2.44 per hour.
Three years later, in 1963, he was accepted into the 26-week Production Machining course. Upon graduation in January of 1964, he was paid $2.57 per hour.	In 1959 he was enrolled in the 26-week Production Machining course and graduated in May of 1960 at $2.29 per hour.	In 1962 he was selected to attend the Jet Engine Familiarization course—a less than 8 hour course. Later in 1962 he was again promoted and his rate had risen to $2.93 per hour.
He received promotions in 1964 and 1965. The 1965 promotion was to Leadman and his rate of pay had risen to $2.84 per hour.	In 1961 he received a two grade promotion with a rate of $2.42 per hour.	In 1964 he was demoted one grade as a consequence of a work force reduction—but regained the lost grade by the end of the year.
Currently he is paid $3.33 per hour. (1966)	In 1966 he received a two grade promotion and his hourly rate was $3.10.	

2 *Porter P - - - -*	3 *Robert H - - - -*
In July, 1967, he was again promoted two labor grades to the second highest labor grade for nonsupervisory employees. His rate was $3.52 per hour in 1967.	In 1965 he attended the following Training School courses: Magnaflux Inspection 30 hours X-Ray Inspection 30 hours Quality Assurance Changes 20 hours Basic Layout Inspection 400 hours In 1966 he was promoted one grade and his base rate reached $3.43 per hour. In 1966 he also attended the following Training School courses: Alloy Type Testing 14 hours Visual Inspection 12 hours Foreman Candidate Training 120 hours In 1966 he was promoted to Foreman. His salary was the equivalent of $3.83 per hour. This year, 1967, as a foreman he has attended the following Training School courses: Statistical Quality Control for Supervisors 20 hours Fluorescent Penetrant Inspection 16 hours His current salary is the equivalent of $4.43 per hour. (1967)

Source: Company files.

train for a better future depends on background, expectations, and genuine belief in opportunity. That all three are lacking to some degree in the Negro community is not difficult to understand. There is also undoubtedly some reluctance on the part of Negroes in plants to do anything which would transfer them from a job situation which appears acceptable to white fellow workers to one which may not be. Some Negroes (and of course whites, too) are making more money than they ever expected. They see no need to spend time learning new skills, especially in a volatile industry where the end of a contract, or of hostilities in Vietnam, could bring a layoff. Yet until training opportunities are fully grasped, Negro upgrading will not achieve its great potential in the aerospace industry.

OPERATIVES

The operative jobs vary widely from some rather close tolerance assembly work to essentially entry jobs. The operative group was traditionally the largest occupational category in the aircraft and parts industry, and still is in the manufacture of engines and aircraft. In the overall aerospace industry, however, the number of craftsmen now exceeds the number of operatives. In missile and space work, the number of craftsmen greatly exceeds that of operatives.

Negroes hold a slightly higher proportion of operatives jobs in the aerospace industry than their proportion to the general population. Their operative representation is also more than twice that of their representation in the industry as a whole. Again, within the operative group, there is a tendency for Negroes to be disproportionately concentrated in the lower-rated sectors.

The aerospace companies which have both missile and space and aircraft work have a much higher percentage of Negroes in the latter. Aircraft engine factories also usually feature a higher proportion of Negroes than do missile and space facilities operating in the same area or region. The reasons, of course, are the character of work and the training and educational backgrounds of Negro applicants.

Assembly line work exists in aircraft factories, but it is far different than automobile assembly line operations. An aircraft company that produces one plane per day for a year or two is operating volume production by the standards of its industry. Automobile assembly plants are geared to produce up to sixty vehicles per hour. The aircraft jobs are not nearly as broken down as are those in the automobile industry. The latter industry can take unskilled persons off the street, and with little or no training start them on the assembly line. This cannot be done in aerospace. The assembly line work is much more complicated, and the cost of mistakes is too great to risk inadequate training. Before new applicants are put onto the line, they must have careful training, varying from a few weeks to several months. Life is involved, and the quality of workmanship cannot be compromised.

All major companies which have lower-rated semiskilled work have elaborate introductory or vestibule training programs. Some now even teach shop mores and manners—how to dress, use sanitary facilities, and live under shop regimentation—as well as the basic fundamentals of workmanship before taking up the rudimentary components of work to be done. From such programs, there is usually a high initial drop-out rate, but those that remain often become useful workers, and many advance up the occupational ladder.

The future of Negroes in the aerospace operative category is largely tied to the expansion of aircraft production. A combination of tremendous commercial expansion and the needs of the Vietnam war for combat aircraft and helicopters created a tight labor market. Companies then had to train workers for entry jobs in most areas in order to obtain any labor, and Negroes profited immensely from this situation. Layoffs tend to hit them hard as their seniority is less as a group than whites. Then, however, aircraft production slowed down. This has probably ended the expansion of Negro representation among aerospace industry operatives.

LABORERS AND SERVICE WORKERS

Not many employees in aerospace are found in the "laborer" category—about 1 percent of the total labor force. They are low-rated employees who do odd jobs around the plants and offices, but do not work in production. Negroes make up a far disproportionate share of this small group in aerospace as they do in all industry. For the Negro (or white) with little education, ability, or indeed prospects, these jobs offer a livelihood. Their insignificant number in aerospace, however, attests both to the nature of work in the industry, and the declining opportunity for those with little skills or potential. The unskilled person with reasonable potential and motivation today in aerospace need not even start as a laborer, but in most cases, can move directly into training for work in the operative category. The decline in Negro ratio of laborers between 1966 and 1968 undoubtedly is the result of upgrading such employees.

Service workers entail a wider occupational grouping and make up about 2 percent of the labor force in the industry, with Negroes again highly disproportionately represented. They include porters, messengers, cafeteria workers, and if not classified as laborers, groundskeepers and janitors—all jobs traditionally open to Negroes, and usually dead-end jobs. Also included in this grouping are plant guards, a larger group in aerospace than in most industries because of classified work and security problems. In many areas, Negroes were denied the opportunity to work as plant guards until very recently. The rationale seems to have been that Negro guards would have difficulty handling problems affecting white personnel. This reasoning was maintained long after Negro police officers and officers in the armed services lost their novelty. There is still underrepresentation of Negroes among plant guards, but no longer are they denied opportunities in this classification as a matter of course.

NEGRO WOMEN IN AEROSPACE

The aerospace industry became a large employer of Negro women during World War II, and the tradition has continued, especially in Southern California. Substantial gains have been made in the utilization of Negro women in the shop in recent years. They comprise in the Table 20 sample 10.5 percent of the 8,161 women classified as craftsmen and 17 percent of the 33,147 female operatives.

One reason for the increased use of women, and therefore also of Negro women, is the large amount of electrical and electronic assembly work in modern aerospace technology. Thousands of wires and circuits wend their way through the structures of aircraft, missiles, and space vehicles. Women are especially adept at such small assembly work and are extensively used for it. As the labor market tightened and civil rights pressures increased, Negro women increased their share of such work.

Recent years have also seen an increased utilization of Negro women in sheet metal assembly in aircraft plants and as grinders, welders, and small machine tool operators in engine plants. Several companies have had better experience with Negro women than Negro men in these jobs, particularly women with families. The tradition of female family support seems to generate a strong determination to take advantage of opportunities in the Negro women employed by these aerospace firms. In one such case, a plant manager bitterly opposed using Negro women until forced to do so by the company president. Later he was so pleased with the results that he had to be stopped from issuing an order requesting preference for Negro women.

There is still some reluctance to use Negro women in the shop—indeed a few plants have no women. Perhaps since shop work is not available in the inner city, as is office work, Negro women who work in blue collar jobs are apparently more willing to travel than are female office workers. It is nevertheless quite likely that the distance of most aerospace plants from Negro communities tends to reduce considerably the availability of Negro women for the industry's plant labor force.

INTRAPLANT MOVEMENT AND SENIORITY

The seniority systems in aerospace are quite varied, but in general do not seem to restrict Negro intraplant movement. There are some dead-end jobs. In a few companies, not necessarily in the South, laborers and janitors are outside any normal progression. Employees with any considered potential are hired in as operatives, usually in the light electronic or sheet metal assembly. Because job bidding is so prevalent, however, a laborer with qualification or potential can move out of his classification.

Most seniority districts tend to be broad with families of jobs clustered in one district. There are occasional plant-wide applications, and in some situations, transfers among plants of one company are part of the collective agreement. In a few cases, seniority lines are long and narrow, making it difficult to break into a job category, but these are not as common as the job cluster type in which a large group of job families provide the potential for movement on a broad front without transferring out of a seniority district, and therefore suffering loss of existing job seniority, in order to obtain a better job.

It should be emphasized that in the aerospace industry, the dynamic technology makes seniority far more important in layoffs than in promotions. Qualification is so important that training and ability are far more significant than length of service. The failure of Negroes to take full advantage of training opportunities hurts their progress. In an industry in which qualification cannot be shaded, and one in which the opportunities for training are almost endless, these opportunities must be grasped if equal opportunity is to be assured.

In general, the wider the seniority district, the greater the opportunity for Negroes for upgrading and advancement. As the most recently hired and the group which has the fewest skills, Negroes profit substantially from broad opportunities for movement. But, of course, a wide seniority progression system has its corollary disadvantages, too. When employment turns downward, it provides the broadest opportunities for bumping. With Negroes both relatively new and still overly concentrated in the semiskilled and relatively unskilled jobs, they are then especially vulnerable.

Job bidding is widely used in the industry to fill higher jobs. Company officials have repeatedly complained to the author that Negroes appear more reluctant to bid on jobs than do whites, and that Negroes often require great encouragement if they are to bid. The situation is similar to the already noted disproportionate reluctance of Negroes to take advantage of training opportunities. Again the reasons appear to be lack of experience in industrial practices, fear of moving from a job situation which is acceptable to white fellow workers to one which is not, or lack of motivation.

Attempts to promote Negroes to supervisory ranks also sometimes run into unexpected opposition. Refusal to accept such promotion is, of course, not unique in industrial experience. Many white workers prefer the more placid existence of an hourly employee to the responsibilities, frustrations, and pressures of the supervisor. Companies have, however, reported to the author in a number of cases that promotion was declined because it carried an "Uncle Tom" connotation, or because it meant a break with "Black Power" psychology. Apparently, in such instances a supervisory job was considered by the man's peers to be synonymous with going over to the white enemy. In one case, it was all quite puzzling to the employer who had been charged previously with discrimination for not elevating a Negro to supervisor.

In general, intraplant movement is affected by the same factors which affect Negro job opportunities generally. Basic, of course, is an expanding economy. Unless jobs are available, upward movement is difficult, and jobs held by Negroes can be lost. The supply side of Negro labor is, however, deeply disadvantaged by inferior education, training, and experience. The aerospace industry must require skill and educational attainments that disproportionately few Negroes possess, and there cannot be legitimate compromise with these requirements. Acquiring skills and education is a time-consuming process. Upward job movement of Negroes in this industry is, therefore, likely to continue to lag as long as the Negro educational and skill gap endures, even though the industry may offset the lag somewhat by its massive training program.

Negro job movement up the occupational ladder is also adversely affected by the locational factors, discussed in the next section, and directly affected by government policies which are examined in the last sector of this chapter. Union policies, as we shall point out, are relatively passive in the aerospace industry.

Discrimination and motivation go hand in hand. Because of the former, the latter is often lacking. Opportunities for promotion, for training, or for improvement are not grasped. The promotion process is thus slowed and discrimination often charged. Inexperience in industry, lack of help in setting goals, and the difficulty of breaking with the past all combine to resist upward job movement.

LOCATIONAL FACTORS

Although the aerospace industry is located in all regions of the country and near virtually every major center of Negro population, the nature of the industry requires plant site locations that are unfavorable to Negro employment. This is the result of a combination of circumstances: aerospace products are likely to need ample space for testing, which is not available within cities; but Negroes are more and more concentrated in center city inner cores and have difficulty finding housing in suburbs or towns near aircraft plants; and public transportation is not usually adequate to offset these factors.

Consider, for example, the situation in St. Louis. Since 1950, a quarter of a million whites have moved out of the city proper and an even greater number of Negroes have taken their place, so that now almost 40 percent of the city's population is Negro. The Negroes are concentrated on the so-called North Side. As in most cities, manufacturing employment has declined, many industries having moved to the predominantly white, fast growing suburbs.[32] A recent article in *Fortune* commented:

> The decline of industry in the city has been a bitter development for the North Side, where a survey found unemployment running above 12 percent late in 1966. Expanding employment in the county has provided relatively few jobs for city dwellers. At its huge plant seventeen miles from the North Side, McDonnell Douglas, by far the biggest employer in the metropolitan area, has actively recruited and trained St. Louis Negroes. But though McDonnell's work force has swelled from 22,000 to 42,000 since 1960, the company still employs fewer than 5,000 St. Louisans. The proportion of city residents on the payroll has actually slumped since 1960, from 17 to 12 percent.
>
> One employment obstacle for North Side people is the lack of direct public transportation to where the suburban jobs are. It takes as much as two hours, and three buses, to get from the North Side to the McDonnell plant. Later this year, with the help of a federal grant, the city will be starting a direct bus service, probably from the North Side to the McDonnell area. But the number of industrial jobs out there for unskilled and semiskilled city people is much smaller than the number of unemployed North Siders. Scattered around in the suburbs are quite a few service jobs that North Siders could fill, but the wages are generally not high enough to make up for the long trip.[33]

The situation described here is typical of the locational problem of the industry. In Southern California, for example, where the greatest concentration of aerospace work is found, there are many towns in which Negroes are unable to obtain housing. Transportation is almost impossible from the heavily populated Negro areas of Los Angeles to some of the major aerospace facilities located in these towns or in the counties outside of Los Angeles. The plants located either close to the areas in Los Angeles, such as Watts, where Negroes are concentrated, or on the few direct public transportation

32. "The St. Louis Economic Blues," *Fortune,* Vol. LXXVII (January 1968), pp. 210-211.
33. *Ibid.*, p. 210.

routes from these areas, generally have two or three times the proportion of Negroes that those plants have which are located in the outer county areas, even though the same companies and the same policies are involved. Despite intensive recruiting of Negroes, attempts to aid in the establishment of car pools, and even subsidizing of public transport, the outlying plants find that turnover of Negroes who have long distances to commute is very high.

The public transportation situation is unlikely to improve. Buses serving slum areas have become so much a target for violence that it is difficult both to obtain bus drivers and to provide a service. Employees of the company serving the Watts area of Los Angeles threatened to strike until they received more police protection, and union officials throughout the county have been concerned about the problem.[34]

Self-help Negro groups have tried operating buses in both Los Angeles and New York to carry people to work.[35] It is too early to assess the results of their work, but it is unlikely that these efforts can succeed without subsidy. Companies are often willing to provide that subsidy, and have in many cities. Usually, however, the buses do not attract many riders. Those who remain at work obtain automobiles; others drop out because of a long commuting distance or for other reasons; only a few both stay at work and ride the bus.

As was noted early, long commutes are an almost insuperable barrier for female office workers. It is very difficult for aerospace plants to attract Negro office workers, and will remain so until the American housing pattern is changed, and suburban living is more accessible to Negroes.

Even if open housing legislation materially reduces discrimination against Negroes seeking housing, Negro movement to the suburbs and therefore closer to aerospace plants is not likely to be rapid. Suburban housing frequently requires an income that Negroes are much less able than whites to possess. Given the facts of education and background, the Negro income gap will not easily or quickly be closed. Moreover, most Negroes are, like all groups in society, likely to desire to migrate to, and to reside near, their own kind rather

34. See, e.g., the Victor Riesel syndicated column of December 18, 1967; and *New York Times,* November 26, 28, and 29, 1967. Such crimes have been checked recently by use of the exact fare system in most large cities.

35. *New York Times,* November 26, 1967, and January 3-4, 1968.

than to risk social rebuffs or isolation in locations where few of their race reside.

Interestingly enough, in the Southern California area particularly, many of the outlying plants which have much fewer Negroes than those closer to areas of Los Angeles where Negroes are concentrated, also have a much less skewed in-plant distribution of Negroes. These outlying plants are, with some significant exceptions like the Lockheed major facilities at Burbank, either new or newly integrated. In such plants, the practice of confining Negroes to low-skilled jobs never existed, and was easier to avoid than it was to overcome where it had become institutionalized. In addition, Negroes who do find a home in the suburbs or outer county areas, or who are willing to commute long distances, are usually both well qualified for their jobs and highly motivated. They are, therefore, capable both of finding work and of gaining promotion and upgrading opportunities.

Nevertheless, despite some exceptions, the farther from center city is the aerospace plant, the fewer Negroes are found on its employment rolls. Workers who have had little experience, motivation, or assistance do not know enough to look for work at a great distance. The expense of long commutes cuts deep into the income from low-skilled and entry jobs, and the frustrations of getting to work that is far from home easily discourage the inexperienced or uninitiated commuter. Moreover, superior workers can often find work closer to home. Consequently, both employment and upward job movement in the industry are restricted by the necessities of plant location, and its typical distance from the central city where Negroes are more and more concentrated.

REGIONAL DIFFERENCES — GENERAL

Tables 22-33 show Negro employment in the aerospace industry by occupational groups for all major regions of the country in 1966 and 1968 except for the South, which is discussed in the following section. These tables utilize the same data which are summarized in Tables 19 and 20, but divide them on a regional basis by establishment. Many companies are thus represented by plants in several regions.

The first thing to note is that, almost without exception, the ratio of Negroes rose in all classifications above that of laborer in each

TABLE 22. *Aerospace Industry, Employment by Race, Sex, and Occupational Group, Northeast Region, 1966*

	All Employees			Male			Female		
Occupational Group	Total	Negro	Percent Negro	Total	Negro	Percent Negro	Total	Negro	Percent Negro
Officials and managers	13,740	50	0.4	13,605	49	0.4	135	1	0.7
Professionals	34,604	247	0.7	34,027	242	0.7	577	5	0.9
Technicians	13,287	255	1.9	12,121	234	1.9	1,166	21	1.8
Sales workers	174	—	—	172	—	—	2	—	—
Office and clerical	21,575	571	2.6	8,193	245	3.0	13,382	326	2.4
Total white collar	83,380	1,123	1.3	68,118	770	1.1	15,262	353	2.3
Craftsmen	35,073	1,165	3.3	34,592	1,079	3.1	481	86	17.9
Operatives	42,188	4,554	10.8	35,626	3,312	9.3	6,562	1,242	18.9
Laborers	3,988	563	14.1	2,958	474	16.0	1,030	89	8.6
Service workers	4,174	791	19.0	3,656	727	19.9	518	64	12.4
Total blue collar	85,423	7,073	8.3	76,832	5,592	7.3	8,591	1,481	17.2
Total	168,803	8,196	4.9	144,950	6,362	4.4	23,853	1,834	7.7

Source: Data in author's possession.

TABLE 23. *Aerospace Industry, Employment by Race, Sex, and Occupational Group, Northeast Region, 1968*

Occupational Group	All Employees Total	All Employees Negro	All Employees Percent Negro	Male Total	Male Negro	Male Percent Negro	Female Total	Female Negro	Female Percent Negro
Officials and managers	13,973	80	0.6	13,831	79	0.6	142	1	0.7
Professionals	34,640	282	0.8	34,100	274	0.8	540	8	1.5
Technicians	13,472	297	2.2	12,344	270	2.2	1,128	27	2.4
Sales workers	129	—	—	127	—	—	2	—	—
Office and clerical	21,600	720	3.3	8,090	306	3.8	13,510	414	3.1
Total white collar	83,814	1,379	1.6	68,492	929	1.4	15,322	450	2.9
Craftsmen	35,722	1,602	4.5	35,179	1,474	4.2	543	128	23.6
Operatives	41,034	4,815	11.7	34,677	3,578	10.3	6,357	1,237	19.5
Laborers	5,355	847	15.8	3,095	558	18.0	2,260	289	12.8
Service workers	3,961	809	20.4	3,486	750	21.5	475	59	12.4
Total blue collar	86,072	8,073	9.4	76,437	6,360	8.3	9,635	1,713	17.8
Total	169,886	9,452	5.6	144,929	7,289	5.0	24,957	2,163	8.7

Source: Data in author's possession.

TABLE 24. *Aerospace Industry, Employment by Race, Sex, and Occupational Group, New England Region, 1966*

Occupational Group	All Employees			Male			Female		
	Total	Negro	Percent Negro	Total	Negro	Percent Negro	Total	Negro	Percent Negro
Officials and managers	8,121	29	0.4	8,052	29	0.4	69	—	—
Professionals	17,689	54	0.3	17,420	53	0.3	269	1	0.4
Technicians	6,098	53	0.9	5,259	40	0.8	839	13	1.5
Sales workers	170	—	—	168	—	—	2	—	—
Office and clerical	11,177	192	1.7	3,491	65	1.9	7,686	127	1.7
Total white collar	43,255	328	0.8	34,390	187	0.5	8,865	141	1.6
Craftsmen	18,366	357	1.9	18,301	341	1.9	65	16	24.6
Operatives	34,681	3,946	11.4	28,622	2,761	9.6	6,059	1,185	19.6
Laborers	3,329	382	11.5	2,422	310	12.8	907	72	7.9
Service workers	2,001	198	9.9	1,689	159	9.4	312	39	12.5
Total blue collar	58,377	4,883	8.4	51,034	3,571	7.0	7,343	1,312	17.9
Total	101,632	5,211	5.1	85,424	3,758	4.4	16,208	1,453	9.0

Source: Data in author's possession.

region. This is especially significant in that it indicates progress through 1968 was on a broad national scale.

Turning first to the Northeast (Tables 22 and 23),[36] we find Negro employment ratios and in-plant distributions fairly close to national averages throughout the entire occupational hierarchy. In this region, Negro females have a higher ratio of jobs than the industry's national average, and Negroes are somewhat less concentrated in the bottom two categories. They are, however, also less well represented in the craftsmen category, but hold almost an identical share of the salaried positions as they do nationally.

The Northeast region is divided into two areas, New England (Tables 24 and 25) and Middle Atlantic (Tables 26 and 27). The high proportion of operatives in New England is attributable to the location there of major engine plants of United Aircraft, Avco, and General Electric, which utilize a much higher proportion of such labor than do many other aerospace plants. The Negro representation here is very similar to the national average, but the high proportion of operatives offsets the lag of Negroes in the craftsmen classification and raises the overall Negro percentage to slightly above 5 percent. Negro women make up an even larger percentage of female employment in New England than they do in the total Northeast area. A heavy migration of Negroes from both the South and from New York City particularly to cities in Connecticut has been a strong factor in the increased representation of Negroes in New England aerospace plants. In addition, United Aircraft, the region's major aerospace employer, has long had a deserved reputation for practicing equal employment, a factor which, with opportunities of good jobs at high wages, has attracted many Negroes to jobs in the area.

The Middle Atlantic data likewise hold close to the national average in all categories. Female employment of Negroes is considerably less than in New England, but the type of work which predominates does not offer the same opportunities. In the Middle Atlantic Region, craftsmen outnumber operatives, two to one; in New England, the ratios are almost reversed. Large missile and space operations and considerable job and machine work are found in this area. The once great aircraft production facilities of Martin-Marietta near Baltimore have been greatly reduced, and with them,

36. For regional definitions used throughout this study and for all tables, see Table 16, p. 160.

TABLE 25. *Aerospace Industry, Employment by Race, Sex, and Occupational Group, New England Region, 1968*

Occupational Group	All Employees			Male			Female		
	Total	Negro	Percent Negro	Total	Negro	Percent Negro	Total	Negro	Percent Negro
Officials and managers	8,331	35	0.4	8,261	35	0.4	70	—	—
Professionals	16,755	65	0.4	16,521	65	0.4	234	—	—
Technicians	6,188	90	1.5	5,382	70	1.3	806	20	2.5
Sales workers	129	—	—	127	—	—	2	—	—
Office and clerical	11,332	256	2.3	3,525	77	2.2	7,807	179	2.3
Total white collar	42,735	446	1.0	33,816	247	0.7	8,919	199	2.2
Craftsmen	17,403	480	2.8	17,265	437	2.5	138	43	31.2
Operatives	34,597	4,068	11.8	28,714	2,897	10.1	5,883	1,171	19.9
Laborers	4,883	682	14.0	2,630	393	14.9	2,253	289	12.8
Service workers	1,952	236	12.1	1,687	200	11.9	265	36	13.6
Total blue collar	58,835	5,466	9.3	50,296	3,927	7.8	8,539	1,539	18.0
Total	101,570	5,912	5.8	84,112	4,174	5.0	17,458	1,738	10.0

Source: Data in author's possession.

TABLE 26. *Aerospace Industry, Employment by Race, Sex, and Occupational Group, Middle Atlantic Region, 1966*

Occupational Group	All Employees			Male			Female		
	Total	Negro	Percent Negro	Total	Negro	Percent Negro	Total	Negro	Percent Negro
Officials and managers	5,619	21	0.4	5,553	20	0.4	66	1	1.5
Professionals	16,915	193	1.1	16,607	189	1.1	308	4	1.3
Technicians	7,189	202	2.8	6,862	194	2.8	327	8	2.4
Sales workers	4	—	—	4	—	—	—	—	—
Office and clerical	10,398	379	3.6	4,702	180	3.8	5,696	199	3.5
Total white collar	40,125	795	2.0	33,728	583	1.7	6,397	212	3.3
Craftsmen	16,707	808	4.8	16,291	738	4.5	416	70	16.8
Operatives	7,507	608	8.1	7,004	551	7.9	503	57	11.3
Laborers	659	181	27.5	536	164	30.6	123	17	13.8
Service workers	2,173	593	27.3	1,967	568	28.9	206	25	12.1
Total blue collar	27,046	2,190	8.1	25,798	2,021	7.8	1,248	169	13.5
Total	67,171	2,985	4.4	59,526	2,604	4.4	7,645	381	5.0

Source: Data in author's possession.

TABLE 27. *Aerospace Industry, Employment by Race, Sex, and Occupational Group, Middle Atlantic Region, 1968*

	All Employees			Male			Female		
Occupational Group	Total	Negro	Percent Negro	Total	Negro	Percent Negro	Total	Negro	Percent Negro
Officials and managers	5,642	45	0.8	5,570	44	0.8	72	1	1.4
Professionals	17,885	217	1.2	17,579	209	1.2	306	8	2.6
Technicians	7,284	207	2.8	6,962	200	2.9	322	7	2.2
Sales workers	—	—	—	—	—	—	—	—	—
Office and clerical	10,268	464	4.5	4,565	229	5.0	5,703	235	4.1
Total white collar	41,079	933	2.3	34,676	682	2.0	6,403	251	3.9
Craftsmen	18,319	1,122	6.1	17,914	1,037	5.8	405	85	21.0
Operatives	6,437	747	11.6	5,963	681	11.4	474	66	13.9
Laborers	472	165	35.0	465	165	35.5	7	—	—
Service workers	2,009	573	28.5	1,799	550	30.6	210	23	11.0
Total blue collar	27,237	2,607	9.6	26,141	2,433	9.3	1,096	174	15.9
Total	68,316	3,540	5.2	60,817	3,115	5.1	7,499	425	5.7

Source: Data in author's possession.

have gone numerous semiskilled jobs of which Negroes once held a good share. Boeing's Vertol Division near Philadelphia employs a large number of both craftsmen and operatives, and has done a very capable job of training and upgrading Negroes in the machining skills. The higher than average craftsmen representation of Negroes in this area testifies to the results of such programs.

The Midwest (Tables 28 and 29) has the highest percentage of Negroes of any area—7.2 as compared with 5.4 nationwide. Since the data also include the few installations in the Rocky Mountain and Northern Plains areas, where few Negroes live, the data in the tables, if anything, understate Negro representation in the traditional Midwest area.

The three great aerospace employment locations in the Midwest are Evendale, near Cincinnati, Ohio, where General Electric has its large jet engine facility; St. Louis, the home of McDonnell; and Wichita, Kansas, which contains a large facility of Boeing, and the manufacturing facilities of Cessna, Beech, and Lear-Jet. The heaviest Negro concentrations are found in the McDonnell and General Electric plants.

McDonnell, as noted earlier in this study, has long been a practicer of equal employment opportunity. Located near a center of Negro population, although a long commute from the St. Louis North Side, it has made strenuous efforts to recruit Negro employees. The great success of its Phantom jet fighter has enabled it to break down jobs into semiskilled components and has thus enabled it to develop entry jobs that have attracted large numbers of Negro men and women who have previously not worked in industry. McDonnell has also been quite successful in upgrading Negroes. Its long record of Negro employment has facilitated this, for Negroes employed many years ago have been able to work up, or to train for higher jobs. McDonnell's ratio of Negro employees is more than twice that of the industry, with a higher than average percentage in the skilled category.

General Electric likewise has a forceful program of equal opportunity, and has applied it at Evandale where many Negroes are migrants from the South. The result today is that the Evendale plant has a relatively high proportion of Negroes in the skilled categories.

At Wichita, Negro representation in the major plants has lagged, although both Boeing and Beech have made very strenuous efforts to improve minority group work participation. Beech has been quite

TABLE 28. *Aerospace Industry, Employment by Race, Sex, and Occupational Group, Midwest Region, 1966*

Occupational Group	All Employees			Male			Female		
	Total	Negro	Percent Negro	Total	Negro	Percent Negro	Total	Negro	Percent Negro
Officials and managers	11,231	73	0.6	11,148	73	0.7	83	—	—
Professionals	18,318	146	0.8	17,941	140	0.8	377	6	1.6
Technicians	8,160	129	1.6	7,528	123	1.6	632	6	0.9
Sales workers	120	2	1.7	117	2	1.7	3	—	—
Office and clerical	18,723	639	3.4	9,690	464	4.8	9,033	175	1.9
Total white collar	56,552	989	1.7	46,424	802	1.7	10,128	187	1.8
Craftsmen	32,697	2,043	6.2	31,454	1,929	6.1	1,243	114	9.2
Operatives	23,893	3,637	15.2	18,595	2,373	12.8	5,298	1,264	23.9
Laborers	1,825	660	36.2	1,438	589	41.0	387	71	18.3
Service workers	2,066	637	30.8	1,563	529	33.8	503	108	21.5
Total blue collar	60,481	6,977	11.5	53,050	5,420	10.2	7,431	1,557	21.0
Total	117,033	7,966	6.8	99,474	6,222	6.3	17,559	1,744	9.9

Source: Data in author's possession.

TABLE 29. *Aerospace Industry, Employment by Race, Sex, and Occupational Group, Midwest Region, 1968*

Occupational Group	All Employees			Male			Female		
	Total	Negro	Percent Negro	Total	Negro	Percent Negro	Total	Negro	Percent Negro
Officials and managers	11,192	81	0.7	11,115	80	0.7	77	1	1.3
Professionals	16,116	140	0.9	15,738	135	0.9	378	5	1.3
Technicians	6,846	115	1.7	6,314	109	1.7	532	6	1.1
Sales workers	140	3	2.1	135	3	2.2	5	—	—
Office and clerical	17,261	651	3.8	9,152	492	5.4	8,109	159	2.0
Total white collar	51,555	990	1.9	42,454	819	1.9	9,101	171	1.9
Craftsmen	34,332	2,277	6.6	32,731	2,117	6.5	1,601	160	10.0
Operatives	21,400	3,579	16.7	15,982	2,345	14.7	5,418	1,234	22.8
Laborers	1,572	512	32.6	1,331	461	34.6	241	51	21.2
Service workers	2,151	617	28.7	1,717	522	30.4	434	95	21.9
Total blue collar	59,455	6,985	11.7	51,761	5,445	10.5	7,694	1,540	20.0
Total	111,010	7,975	7.2	94,215	6,264	6.6	16,795	1,711	10.2

Source: Data in author's possession.

successful over the years in integrating its minority work force throughout its light plane manufacturing facility. The Negro population of Wichita, 8 percent in 1960, and estimated at about 12 percent today, is of course considerably less than that in the St. Louis or Cincinnati areas.

The most significant aspects of the favorable attitudes and programs in the major Midwest facilities is the high Negro representation in the craftsmen and office and clerical occupational groups. In the former, the Negro 1968 ratio in the Midwest region is 6.6, as compared with the 5.4 national average; in the office and clerical group, the Midwest percentage is 3.8; the national, 3.4. Negro females also are much better represented in the Midwest than in the country as a whole. A combination of favorable employer attitudes and policies of long standing, character of work and work mix, and the heavy Negro migration to the area have combined to make the Midwest aerospace centers among the most favorable in the industry to Negro employment.

The West Coast, and particularly Southern California, ranks above the Midwest as the area giving Negroes the best employment opportunities qualitatively, and second to the Midwest quantitatively. Total West Coast (Tables 30 and 31) includes, besides Southern California, the great Boeing plants in the Seattle area and the various installations near San Jose, south of San Francisco. At Seattle, where only about 5 percent of the population is Negro, Boeing has done extensive recruiting and upgrading and has many Negro engineers and technicians as well as lower-rated personnel. Both Lockheed and United Aircraft in Northern California have extensively recruited and trained Negroes, especially those from the Oakland area. In blue collar employment, Southern California (Tables 32 and 33) is clearly the leader, having a ratio of 13.1 percent in 1968, a figure in excess of Negroes in the population in the total aerospace employment area of the region and of the country and above the national Negro aerospace ratio of 10 percent and that of the Midwest ratio of 11.7 percent, the next highest in the industry. Within the blue collar occupations, the Southern California area has a black craftsmen ratio of 7.8 percent and one for operatives of 17.6 percent, both highs for the industry. The craftsmen ratio is especially notable, being one of the highest found in American industry anywhere. It attests to the long experience of Negroes in the industry in this region and to the training and upgrading which the companies have done particularly since 1964.

TABLE 30. *Aerospace Industry, Employment by Race, Sex, and Occupational Group, West Coast Region, 1966*

	All Employees			Male			Female		
Occupational Group	Total	Negro	Percent Negro	Total	Negro	Percent Negro	Total	Negro	Percent Negro
Officials and managers	35,016	134	0.4	34,615	132	0.4	401	2	0.5
Professionals	96,055	858	0.9	93,561	817	0.9	2,494	41	1.6
Technicians	32,115	679	2.1	27,856	638	2.3	4,259	41	1.0
Sales workers	284	—	—	242	—	—	42	—	—
Office and clerical	68,319	1,824	2.7	23,547	888	3.8	44,772	936	2.1
Total white collar	231,789	3,495	1.5	179,821	2,475	1.4	51,968	1,020	2.0
Craftsmen	73,318	3,831	5.2	69,099	3,490	5.1	4,219	341	8.1
Operatives	62,630	8,031	12.8	45,292	5,882	13.0	17,338	2,149	12.4
Laborers	1,711	353	20.6	1,467	335	22.8	244	18	7.4
Service workers	5,917	1,022	17.3	4,969	896	18.0	948	126	13.3
Total blue collar	143,576	13,237	9.2	120,827	10,603	8.8	22,749	2,634	11.6
Total	375,365	16,732	4.5	300,648	13,078	4.3	74,717	3,654	4.9

Source: Data in author's possession.

TABLE 31. *Aerospace Industry, Employment by Race, Sex, and Occupational Group, West Coast Region, 1968*

Occupational Group	All Employees			Male			Female		
	Total	Negro	Percent Negro	Total	Negro	Percent Negro	Total	Negro	Percent Negro
Officials and managers	37,369	228	0.6	36,877	222	0.6	492	6	1.2
Professionals	98,585	961	1.0	95,639	931	1.0	2,946	30	1.0
Technicians	32,313	721	2.2	27,334	662	2.4	4,979	59	1.2
Sales workers	239	—	—	225	—	—	14	—	—
Office and clerical	69,775	2,195	3.1	24,044	1,215	5.1	45,731	980	2.1
Total white collar	238,281	4,105	1.7	184,119	3,030	1.6	54,162	1,075	2.0
Craftsmen	77,018	4,775	6.2	71,618	4,214	5.9	5,400	561	10.4
Operatives	62,564	9,345	14.9	43,977	6,414	14.6	18,587	2,931	15.3
Laborers	2,197	396	18.0	1,853	381	20.6	344	15	4.4
Service workers	5,596	1,053	18.8	4,952	894	18.1	644	159	24.7
Total blue collar	147,375	15,569	10.6	122,400	11,903	9.7	24,975	3,666	14.7
Total	385,656	19,674	5.1	306,519	14,933	4.9	79,137	4,741	6.0

Source: Data in author's possession.

TABLE 32. *Aerospace Industry, Employment by Race, Sex, and Occupational Group, Southern California Region, 1966*

Occupational Group	All Employees			Male			Female		
	Total	Negro	Percent Negro	Total	Negro	Percent Negro	Total	Negro	Percent Negro
Officials and managers	21,056	99	0.5	20,748	97	0.5	308	2	0.6
Professionals	64,600	648	1.0	62,839	612	1.0	1,761	36	2.0
Technicians	18,336	496	2.7	16,067	470	2.9	2,269	26	1.1
Sales workers	271	—	—	236	—	—	35	—	—
Office and clerical	44,284	1,336	3.0	14,744	620	4.2	29,540	716	2.4
Total white collar	148,547	2,579	1.7	114,634	1,799	1.6	33,913	780	2.3
Craftsmen	48,342	3,035	6.3	45,412	2,771	6.1	2,930	264	9.0
Operatives	43,241	6,557	15.2	29,521	4,788	16.2	13,720	1,769	12.9
Laborers	1,462	331	22.6	1,235	313	25.3	227	18	7.9
Service workers	4,244	873	20.6	3,517	780	22.2	727	93	12.8
Total blue collar	97,289	10,796	11.1	79,685	8,652	10.9	17,604	2,144	12.2
Total	245,836	13,375	5.4	194,319	10,451	5.4	51,517	2,924	5.7

Source: Data in author's possession.

TABLE 33. *Aerospace Industry, Employment by Race, Sex, and Occupational Group, Southern California Region, 1968*

Occupational Group	All Employees			Male			Female		
	Total	Negro	Percent Negro	Total	Negro	Percent Negro	Total	Negro	Percent Negro
Officials and managers	21,894	175	0.8	21,517	170	0.8	377	5	1.3
Professionals	64,913	714	1.1	62,848	687	1.1	2,065	27	1.3
Technicians	16,990	510	3.0	14,713	482	3.3	2,277	28	1.2
Sales workers	229	—	—	218	—	—	11	—	—
Office and clerical	43,804	1,516	3.5	14,215	844	5.9	29,589	672	2.3
Total white collar	147,830	2,915	2.0	113,511	2,183	1.9	34,319	732	2.1
Craftsmen	48,258	3,787	7.8	44,522	3,336	7.5	3,736	451	12.1
Operatives	44,989	7,898	17.6	30,603	5,468	17.9	14,386	2,430	16.9
Laborers	1,939	364	18.8	1,608	349	21.7	331	15	4.5
Service workers	3,839	886	23.1	3,431	764	22.3	408	122	29.9
Total blue collar	99,025	12,935	13.1	80,164	9,917	12.4	18,861	3,018	16.0
Total	246,855	15,850	6.4	193,675	12,100	6.2	53,180	3,750	7.1

Source: Data in author's possession.

In the white collar ratio, Southern California ranks slightly above the Midwest but, interestingly, below the Southeast (which is discussed in the ensuing section). Qualitatively, however, Southern California ranks with the Middle Atlantic as having the highest percentage and largest number of Negro officials and managers, professionals, and technicians in the industry. Like their white counterparts, Negroes in these preferred positions like the challenges of the industry and the balmy Southern California weather. Perhaps more important, however, has been the fact that aerospace companies in this area have recruited Negro professionals since World War II, and have greatly extended their efforts in all key job areas since the early 1960's.

Southern California aerospace companies would probably lead all other areas in total white collar Negro representation but for their inability to overcome travel problems. Their office and clerical black female ratio is only 2.3 percent, and compared with a male ratio of 5.9 percent. The already noted commuting problems of Southern California Negroes to aerospace plant locations seems effectively to reduce Negro female office employment potential substantially despite the fact that they would be very well received, and are indeed much sought after.

Southern California is the headquarters and has many facilities of Lockheed, North American Rockwell, Hughes, Northrop, Ryan, the Convair Division of General Dynamics, the Douglas operations of McDonnell Douglas, Aerojet-General, and many smaller aerospace concerns. All are now making, and have been for several years, strenuous efforts to employ large numbers of minorities and to extend the great capabilities developed over the years to train and to upgrade minority employees on their payrolls. Whether Negroes will continue to progress in this most favorable climate will depend upon the extent to which the industry can offset the current job decline and resume its expansion.

SOUTHERN DEVELOPMENTS IN THE 1960's

In the South, one finds the usual concentration of Negroes in the common labor and service jobs that one associates with traditional patterns in this region, but beyond that, our data show that progress of Negroes in the southern aerospace industry has been most heartening. To be sure, Tables 34 and 35 do show also some underrepresentation of Negroes in craftsmen and operatives jobs as compared with the national picture, but in the office and clerical group Negro representation exceeds that nationally, and in the other white collar positions the ratio in the South is just below that nationally.

A clearer analysis of what has been accomplished in integration of southern aerospace plants can be gained by dividing the South into two areas—the Southeast (Tables 36 and 37) and the Southwest (Tables 38 and 39). It is immediately clear that great progress has been made in the Southeast. To be sure, concentrations of Negroes remain in the bottom two occupational groups. But Negro representation in all of the salaried occupational groups in the Southeast is equal to, or exceeds, that for the national sample! The author knows of no other industry where this is the case. Moreover, in the office and clerical group, the Negro ratio is 5.4 percent in the Southeast, the highest of any of our regions. Finally, in the key craftsmen occupations and in the operatives group, the ratio in the Southeast is approximately equal to that of the national sample.

What has happened in the Southeast is that a number of major aerospace companies have opened facilities, and partially because they have practiced equal employment, and partially under federal government prodding, they have changed employment practices of a region in a major manner. Despite the high skill content of their work, they have done much more in this regard than many other industries, for example, automobiles, which have tended much more to maintain the status quo. Many of these companies have installations at space centers like Huntsville, Alabama, Cape Kennedy, Florida, Bay St. Louis, Mississippi, or Michaud, Louisiana. Others, such as Martin-Marietta or United Aircraft established facilities near these. A third group, Lockheed at Marietta, Georgia, or Avco at Nashville, Tennessee, operated plants which had their genesis in World War II. All of them have brought with them a new urgency for equal opportunity and are constantly pushed farther into affirmative action by governmental presence and prodding.

In space center areas, for example, special councils of the major employers conduct training, recruit at Negro schools, scour the areas for potential employees, and otherwise do what they can to increase Negro representation in the plant. Moreover, their programs to

TABLE 34. *Aerospace Industry, Employment by Race, Sex, and Occupational Group, South Region, 1966*

Occupational Group	All Employees			Male			Female		
	Total	Negro	Percent Negro	Total	Negro	Percent Negro	Total	Negro	Percent Negro
Officials and managers	11,341	35	0.3	11,270	35	0.3	71	—	—
Professionals	30,459	184	0.6	29,984	176	0.6	475	8	1.7
Technicians	10,437	146	1.4	9,779	133	1.4	658	13	2.0
Sales workers	142	—	—	142	—	—	—	—	—
Office and clerical	21,644	658	3.0	9,859	389	3.9	11,785	269	2.3
Total white collar	74,023	1,023	1.4	61,034	733	1.2	12,989	290	2.2
Craftsmen	23,903	556	2.3	23,478	552	2.4	425	4	0.9
Operatives	26,456	2,195	8.3	23,356	1,999	8.6	3,100	196	6.3
Laborers	541	228	42.1	481	221	45.9	60	7	11.7
Service workers	1,898	674	35.5	1,827	640	35.0	71	34	47.9
Total blue collar	52,798	3,653	6.9	49,142	3,412	6.9	3,656	241	6.6
Total	126,821	4,676	3.7	110,176	4,145	3.8	16,645	531	3.2

Source: Data in author's possession.

TABLE 35. *Aerospace Industry, Employment by Race, Sex, and Occupational Group, South Region, 1968*

Occupational Group	All Employees			Male			Female		
	Total	Negro	Percent Negro	Total	Negro	Percent Negro	Total	Negro	Percent Negro
Officials and managers	12,269	58	0.5	12,203	57	0.5	66	1	1.5
Professionals	29,700	215	0.7	29,109	204	0.7	591	11	1.9
Technicians	9,622	175	1.8	8,953	157	1.8	669	18	2.7
Sales workers	186	1	0.5	186	1	0.5	—	—	—
Office and clerical	22,252	856	3.8	10,457	533	5.1	11,795	323	2.7
Total white collar	74,029	1,305	1.8	60,908	952	1.6	13,121	353	2.7
Craftsmen	28,466	912	3.2	27,849	901	3.2	617	11	1.8
Operatives	26,098	2,598	10.0	23,313	2,365	10.1	2,785	233	8.4
Laborers	867	316	36.4	734	303	41.3	133	13	9.8
Service workers	1,626	618	38.0	1,553	584	37.6	73	34	46.6
Total blue collar	57,057	4,444	7.8	53,449	4,153	7.8	3,608	291	8.1
Total	131,086	5,749	4.4	114,357	5,105	4.5	16,729	644	3.3

Source: Data in author's possession.

TABLE 36. *Aerospace Industry, Employment by Race, Sex, and Occupational Group, Southeast Region, 1966*

Occupational Group	All Employees			Male			Female		
	Total	Negro	Percent Negro	Total	Negro	Percent Negro	Total	Negro	Percent Negro
Officials and managers	6,158	24	0.4	6,126	24	0.4	32	—	—
Professionals	18,221	147	0.8	17,952	141	0.8	269	6	2.2
Technicians	6,669	116	1.7	6,288	106	1.7	381	10	2.6
Sales workers	115	—	—	115	—	—	—	—	—
Office and clerical	12,022	501	4.2	5,259	298	5.7	6,763	203	3.0
Total white collar	43,185	788	1.8	35,740	569	1.6	7,445	219	2.9
Craftsmen	11,441	468	4.1	11,263	465	4.1	178	3	1.7
Operatives	11,857	1,383	11.7	10,541	1,253	11.9	1,316	130	9.9
Laborers	292	92	31.5	236	85	36.0	56	7	12.5
Service workers	722	261	36.1	671	244	36.4	51	17	33.3
Total blue collar	24,312	2,204	9.1	22,711	2,047	9.0	1,601	157	9.8
Total	67,497	2,992	4.4	58,451	2,616	4.5	9,046	376	4.2

Source: Data in author's possession.

TABLE 37. *Aerospace Industry, Employment by Race, Sex, and Occupational Group, Southeast Region, 1968*

Occupational Group	All Employees			Male			Female		
	Total	Negro	Percent Negro	Total	Negro	Percent Negro	Total	Negro	Percent Negro
Officials and managers	6,801	39	0.6	6,764	38	0.6	37	1	2.7
Professionals	17,911	174	1.0	17,528	165	0.9	383	9	2.3
Technicians	6,792	155	2.3	6,339	141	2.2	453	14	3.1
Sales workers	160	1	0.6	160	1	0.6	—	—	—
Office and clerical	12,036	653	5.4	5,222	396	7.6	6,814	257	3.8
Total white collar	43,700	1,022	2.3	36,013	741	2.1	7,687	281	3.7
Craftsmen	11,741	622	5.3	11,506	615	5.3	235	7	3.0
Operatives	10,240	1,411	13.8	8,943	1,260	14.1	1,297	151	11.6
Laborers	533	178	33.4	442	173	39.1	91	5	5.5
Service workers	751	271	36.1	688	247	35.9	63	24	38.1
Total blue collar	23,265	2,482	10.7	21,579	2,295	10.6	1,686	187	11.1
Total	66,965	3,504	5.2	57,592	3,036	5.3	9,373	468	5.0

Source: Data in author's possession.

upgrade and to train persons have had great success—as the percentage of Negro craftsmen demonstrates.

Special mention needs to be made of the work of Lockheed since 1961. When it took over the huge facility at Marietta, Georgia, near Atlanta, in 1951, it did not eliminate the segregation practices. Then, Lockheed became the first company to join Plans for Progress, and embarked on a vigorous affirmative action program which soon obtained for it the reputation as the region's most active and interested employer of Negroes. Lockheed, already operating the largest facility in the area, has been aided by an expanding business. Its recruiting, training, and upgrading of Negroes are strongly reflected in the data in Tables 36 and 37, because Lockheed is by far the largest employer in the Southeast.[37]

The aerospace companies have had an impact in the Southeast on more than jobs. Thus when Boeing found that local real estate interests or home owners would not sell houses to Negro engineers in Huntsville, Alabama, the company purchased homes and re-sold them to its black personnel, thus integrating residential areas and assuring itself the talents which it required.

These facts take on added significance in view of the oft-expressed view that the money spent on the moon landing was doing nothing to solve the country's domestic problems. Yet in the Southeast, where the largest concentration of Negroes still dwell, and where segregation and discrimination have been most entrenched, it has been the aerospace concerns, performing work for the Department of Defense and for the National Aeronautical and Space Agency, that have done the most significant integration of high talent personnel and the most effective training and upgrading of Negro personnel that has been accomplished in that area. As expenditures diminish on space exploration and as airplane production declines, key southern Negro personnel are likely to see some of these gains regress.

The Southeast also exceeds the national average in the utilization of Negro female office and clerical employees. Here again active recruiting and training by aerospace companies in this region have produced commendable results. On the other hand, the overall utilization of Negro women in the Southeast is below the national average.

37. For studies of Lockheed's policies, see the article by E. G. Mattison, note 19, *supra;* and Gilbert Burck, "A New Business for Business: Reclaiming Human Resources," *Fortune,* Vol. LXXVII (January 1968), pp. 198-199.

Inexperience of black women in applying for work, their lack of industrial background and education in the South, and opposition of line supervision which has been considerably but not wholly overcome, are all factors, but progress has been steady even for this group since 1964.

Unfortunately, the data for the Southwest, despite real improvement between 1966 and 1968, are almost as disappointing as are those for the Southeast heartening. Tables 38 and 39 show that in both 1966 and 1968 Negroes were most heavily overconcentrated in the bottom two occupational groups; that they had only about one-half the representation among the semiskilled operatives that they hold nationally (in 1968, 7.5 percent to 13.5 percent); that their share of craftsmen's work was only 1.7 percent compared with 5.4 percent nationally and 5.3 percent in the Southeast; and that in the top three salaried categories, the Southwest also lagged somewhat. Finally Negro females had a smaller percentage of jobs in the Southwest than in any other region.

There are several reasons for this situation. A few of the southwest plants are located in places like Tucson, Arizona, or White Sands, New Mexico, where few Negroes dwell. These, however, are ralatively small, and the major plants of the area are in the Dallas-Fort Worth area of Texas. These plants are now all committed to equal employment opportunity, but they have been slow both to run short of labor and to adopt affirmative action programs. The General Dynamics plant at Fort Worth, which is building the F-111, was not working at capacity prior to 1967. In 1967, it added more than 8,000 persons to its payroll. Similarly, employment at the former Chance-Vought plant (now a Ling-Temco-Vought facility) rose 6,000 in 1967 and that at Bell Helicopter by a sizable amount also. Particularly General Dynamics and L-T-V began the 1960's with a very low labor force and a huge number of employees with recall rights. The fact that little integration occurred prior to the mid-1960's was thus a joint product of lack of progress in the 1950's combined with a slow build-up in the 1960's.

There are other reasons for the lack of progress in the Southwest prior to 1967. Some of the southwest plants did little training; one until 1967 required six months experience in entry jobs above laborer and service worker, which obviously meant some other company had to do its training and few Negroes would qualify. Until prodded by

TABLE 38. *Aerospace Industry, Employment by Race, Sex, and Occupational Group, Southwest Region, 1966*

	All Employees			Male			Female		
Occupational Group	Total	Negro	Percent Negro	Total	Negro	Percent Negro	Total	Negro	Percent Negro
Officials and managers	5,183	11	0.2	5,144	11	0.2	39	—	—
Professionals	12,238	37	0.3	12,032	35	0.3	206	2	1.0
Technicians	3,768	30	0.8	3,491	27	0.8	277	3	1.1
Sales workers	27	—	—	27	—	—	—	—	—
Office and clerical	9,622	157	1.6	4,600	91	2.0	5,022	66	1.3
Total white collar	30,838	235	0.8	25,294	164	0.6	5,544	71	1.3
Craftsmen	12,462	88	0.7	12,215	87	0.7	247	1	0.4
Operatives	14,599	812	5.6	12,815	746	5.8	1,784	66	3.7
Laborers	249	136	54.6	245	136	55.5	4	—	—
Service workers	1,176	413	35.1	1,156	396	34.3	20	17	85.0
Total blue collar	28,486	1,449	5.1	26,431	1,365	5.2	2,055	84	4.1
Total	59,324	1,684	2.8	51,725	1,529	3.0	7,599	155	2.0

Source: Data in author's possession.

TABLE 39. *Aerospace Industry, Employment by Race, Sex, and Occupational Group, Southwest Region, 1968*

Occupational Group	All Employees			Male			Female		
	Total	Negro	Percent Negro	Total	Negro	Percent Negro	Total	Negro	Percent Negro
Officials and managers	5,468	19	0.3	5,439	19	0.3	29	—	—
Professionals	11,789	41	0.3	11,581	39	0.3	208	2	1.0
Technicians	2,830	20	0.7	2,614	16	0.6	216	4	1.9
Sales workers	26	—	—	26	—	—	—	—	—
Office and clerical	10,216	203	2.0	5,235	137	2.6	4,981	66	1.3
Total white collar	30,329	283	0.9	24,895	211	0.8	5,434	72	1.3
Craftsmen	16,725	290	1.7	16,343	286	1.7	382	4	1.0
Operatives	15,858	1,187	7.5	14,370	1,105	7.7	1,488	82	5.5
Laborers	334	138	41.3	292	130	44.5	42	8	19.0
Service workers	875	347	39.7	865	337	39.0	10	10	100.0
Total blue collar	33,792	1,962	5.8	31,870	1,858	5.8	1,922	104	5.4
Total	64,121	2,245	3.5	56,765	2,069	3.6	7,356	176	2.4

Source: Data in author's possession.

the aerospace companies, the schools in the Fort Worth area, especially, do not seem to have provided much incentive or training for Negroes to enter into industry. Unlike the Atlanta, Georgia, area, where a sizable Negro middle class exists and housing is available for Negro professional, business, and other middle-class personnel, the Dallas-Fort Worth area lags in both such a middle class and in proper or even adequate housing. One company in particular believes housing has been a major block in recruiting Negro engineers for its Fort Worth facility. The major concerns in this area have worked with realtors to open housing to Negroes, but have not made either heavy inroads nor a frontal attack on the problem such as Boeing accomplished in Huntsville.

By early 1968, it appeared that the major aerospace employers in the Dallas-Fort Worth area were moving forcefully to increase their Negro employment. The improvements from 1966 to 1968 were the product of these efforts. Since then, however, the three major employers have been reducing their work forces. The cutbacks in the controversial F-111 fighter-bomber has curtailed employment at the Fort Worth plant of General Dynamics; the slowdown in Vietnam has reduced production and employment at the nearby Bell Helicopter plants; and Ling-Temco-Vought's deliveries and work force have also been reduced. With Negroes the last hired and the lowest on the seniority lists, the outlook for any improvement in representation or occupational status in southwestern aerospace plants remains rather bleak.

UNION IMPACT ON RACIAL POLICIES

Union influence has in general not been the significant factor in aerospace racial policies that it has been on the positive side in such industries as automobiles or meatpacking, or on the negative side, as in such industries as building construction, railroads, or pulp and paper. The two dominant unions in the industry, the International Association of Machinists and Aerospace Workers (IAM) and the United Automobile, Aerospace and Agricultural Implement Workers (UAW) originally avowed very different policies. The IAM, founded in the railroad shops of Atlanta during the latter half of the nineteenth century, at first limited membership to white workers by constitutional provision, and later accomplished the same thing by a secret ritual which pledged members to admit only competent white mechanics.[38]

In the 1930's, the IAM expanded into the aircraft industry. During World War II, its anti-Negro ritual became a source of embarrassment to its top officials, but not till the late 1940's was it repealed. In some cases, IAM union policies proved a bar to Negro employment in the industry during World War II, but in most cases the IAM did not have a compulsory union membership contract and therefore could not adversely affect Negro employment.

In recent years, the IAM attitude on race is basically a passive one. Locals of the IAM are very independent, with the international exercising only limited interference. As a result, there is little or no affirmative action in support of Negro employment and no national union interference when local unions either drag their feet, or oppose affirmative action programs.[39]

The UAW has had a militant program of equal opportunity for many years. In aerospace, it has supported company programs, but at the local union level, this support varies considerably. Unlike the situation in both automobiles and agricultural implements, Negroes comprise only a small part of the membership in the aerospace industry, and have not been able to exert influences in local unions as they have in these other industries. Consequently, although most managements feel that the UAW has given sound support to programs aimed at Negro advancement, it is also true that Negroes play a very minor role in local unions, have few offices above shop steward, and seem generally to the author to be much more inactive than in the automobile industry.

There have been some rank-and-file Negro rumblings against union lack of leadership in the industry. A CORE (Congress of Racial Equality) led group picketed the UAW and North American in the Los Angeles area in 1966, claiming inadequate promotions for Negroes. Generally, however, such demonstrations have been rare, especially since in recent years there has been a great upward movement of Negroes.

In aerospace, the dynamics of racial policies do not seem to be radically influenced by unions. The companies have taken the lead,

38. For background on the IAM, and its racial policies, see Northrup, *Organized Labor and the Negro,* pp. 8, 206-208.
39. See Burck, *op. cit.,* p. 198.

as they have in employee relations generally,[40] and the unions, although occasionally challenging, supporting, or encouraging, have been the followers. Neither the official indifference of the IAM, nor the loud affirmance of the UAW, seem to have had any decisive effects. Union-management seniority clauses are not aimed at hindering Negro upgrading, and as in the case of Lockheed in Georgia, attempts of local unions to obtain discriminatory seniority provisions have not been successful. Hence seniority clauses do not seem to have hindered Negro job movement. Moreover, job bidding, which is widely used, permits considerable movement within the plant.

GOVERNMENT POLICIES

The government is the aerospace industry's big customer, and government pressure is always a factor that aerospace companies must consider. There can be no doubt that the affirmative action plans which are so prominent in the industry stem from heavy (often heavy-handed) government pressure which motivates employers and keeps the problem in the forefront and constantly pushes the industry to take further affirmative action. But the government is not a single dimensioned pressure force. The government is also the customer, and it is the policeman. As customer, it demands, as it should, zero defect work. Life is involved and quality of workmanship cannot be compromised. The industry has to certify the capability of workmen on many jobs. Social programs are admirable, but there is no substitute for experience and ability. Affirmative action can go only so far, and educational, cultural, attitudinal deficiencies cannot be either glossed over or overcome quickly. The unfortunate plain fact is that the higher the qualifications which are required, the fewer Negroes are qualified and the more difficult it is to gain qualifications by short-run training or educational programs.

Much of the aerospace work is under tight security. Jail or arrest records at one time automatically meant clearance denials. Given the facts of city slums and Negro-police relations, this was a powerful bar to Negro advancement, or even employment, in the industry.

Now a more sophisticated approach is the rule. Arrest records are scrutinized and the minor infractions discounted. It appears govern-

---

40. On this point, see Harold M. Levinson, *Determining Forces in Collective Wage Bargaining* (New York: John Wiley & Sons, Inc., 1966), Chapter 2.

ment security and equal opportunity pressures are today more synchronized in approach than formerly.

There is now the danger that the government may push companies too far in liberalizing employment policies. Some in the industry are quite concerned about sabotage and poor workmanship. The pressures on both sides are great, but it should be reiterated that overly zealous minority group employment programs should certainly not be allowed to compromise workmanship standards in this industry. Yet the fact remains that government pressure has historically been a prime motivating force in obtaining increased employment opportunities for Negroes, and it is likely to continue. The results must be considered salutary.

A significant result of government pressure also is the aid which it gives to managers who greatly desire to increase minority employment. The result has been continued social engineering in developing training and motivational programs and a resultant increase in employment and upgrading of Negroes. The aerospace companies now have considerable experience in training those once considered too unskilled to apply—certainly a gain in itself. Of course, only when jobs are broken down by relatively large-scale production can employees so limited be utilized. Fortuitously, the drive for equal employment opportunity coincided not only with a tremendous expansion of employment in the industry—but an expansion which was concentrated during the 1965-1967 period in the manned aircraft portion of the industry which can utilize much less skilled labor than can missile or space vehicle development and manufacturing. The downturn in this segment of the industry could have a most adverse impact on Negro aerospace employment.

CHAPTER VI.

Some Problems of Equal Opportunity

The recruitment of large numbers of Negroes into aerospace plants has not been without its problems of adjustment and other difficulties. Excessive absenteeism, tardiness, turnover, learning to live under factory discipline, and slum habits brought into the plant have all been problems, and are discussed with other issues in this section.

IMPACT ON WHITE EMPLOYEES

Unlike the automobile industry in which Negroes comprise either a majority, or a very significant minority of many plants, Negroes remain a small minority in nearly all aerospace facilities. Consequently, there seems to have been little impact on the white labor market. In some industries or plants, where a sizeable portion of Negroes has been employed, whites no longer seek employment there, but no instance of this has been found in aerospace. There are jobs in the South, janitor, for example, in which it has been customary for generations to employ only Negroes. It is difficult there still today to find a white man who will accept such employment, or if he does, remain on the job.

Recent attempts to encourage the building of plants in the slums have led Avco and Aerojet-General to establish facilities in such areas which are entirely manned by Negroes. Although this is segregation, it has been both welcomed by Negro leaders and encouraged by the federal government. Time will tell where such approaches to Negro employment problems are viable while at the same time the federal government and Negro leaders attack all vestiges of segregation in other industrial facilities. Moreover, slum-located plants have yet to prove their economic viability. Such plans do, however, reach Negroes who might otherwise not receive any opportunity or training.

The combination of many new Negro employees and large numbers of females in aerospace plants has not been without its problems. Mixed dating or companionship seems to aggravate relations between the races about as much as anything. Alleged passes at white women, or mash notes directed to them, by Negro men have elicited a much larger number and proportion of complaints on the part of women employees than the aerospace companies usually have as a result of men and women being in the same plant. Whether this is because Negroes are more direct in their propositioning, or whether white women are more apt to complain because the approach is made by a Negro, is not clear from the evidence. It has, however, been a problem, and does concern many personnel executives because of its implications for trouble.

EFFICIENCY AND TURNOVER

Of one thing, every aerospace management contacted agrees—the rate of absenteeism, tardiness, and turnover of Negro employees is substantially higher than that of whites. Few detailed studies are available to support these assertions, but the unanimity of opinion and the little evidence available all point in that direction. In one company, 4,052 Negroes were hired in one year, but only 1,509 remained at the end of the twelve months. This turnover was more than three times that of whites for the same period. In a second concern over a six-month period, 11.3 percent of the hires and 10 percent of the terminations were Negroes.

Many other companies cited data for short periods, but nearly always they pointed in the direction of turnover two or three times as high for Negroes. Several reasons were adduced for these facts. The highest turnover group were younger Negroes without any industrial experience. Industrial discipline was a new phenomenon to them. "Man," said one, to a Midwest concern, "you mean 8 to 5 *every* day!" Used to picking up odd jobs for a while, hustling numbers, or doing other facets of slum area income-producing activity, steady work is a radical change and not one to which some could easily adapt.

The great exception to this rule was the mature Negro woman, 25 to 35 years of age, often with a family to support. Repeatedly, white supervisors, including often those who originally opposed hiring

Negro women, sang their praises as diligent, hard-working people who could be counted upon to work hard and stay on the job. The strong role that Negro women play in family life, and often as breadwinner, and the great responsibility thrust upon them, seem to have conditioned them to accept the rigors of factory work and to apply themselves diligently to it.

Even here there are sad exceptions. Training for entry jobs in aerospace is usually at wages in the neighborhood of $1.75 per hour. Progression beyond that is rapid, but one has to believe that progress is both possible and worthwhile. One major company found it was losing Negro women trainees after the first paycheck. Investigation showed that take-home pay of the trainees and welfare payments to women with several children were not too different in amount. The fact that the wage progression would go steadily upward was not enough to offset the debilitating effect of our self-defeating aid to dependent children program.

The same factors which contribute to the high turnover rate of Negroes also contribute to their higher rate of tardiness and absenteeism. Inexperience in industry, poor educational backgrounds, lack of motivation as a result of lack of belief in or experience with equal opportunity, are all factors. In addition, the long distances which many Negroes have to commute undoubtedly add to their problems in getting to work on time and regularly.

EFFICIENCY AND GOVERNMENT PRESSURE

Government policy must be credited with a large role in motivating employers and in keeping the significance of the problem to the forefront. As already noted, however, there is a fundamental conflict between social programs to aid the downtrodden and the need for zero defect work. Many companies feel that they are being pushed dangerously far to hire marginal employees. The line between hourly qualifying employees and those whose utilization could prove disastrous is a fine one. A number of concerns have greatly added to their inspection staffs in order to offset the utilization of increasing numbers of marginal employees, many of whom are Negroes.

In some areas, the state of the labor market is such that only marginal employees of either race are available. The satisfaction of several employers with Negro women represents, in part, the pleasant surprise to many operating personnel that there remained a relatively untouched group in the labor market who worked above the marginal level. The industry, however, is caught between the pressures for social progress and the need for zero defects. That the latter must prevail seems obvious. But the line is not always clear where conflict between the two programs exists, or whether the problem is really a basic labor shortage and the availability only of marginal workers, many of whom are Negroes.

One other aspect of government pressure should be noted. The availability of appeal to the government for Negro workers who feel aggrieved is not unknown to many. As in the case of labor relations, where the employee may file a grievance because he was disciplined, or not promoted, or for other reasons, so the Negro may do likewise, but he is more likely, if he believes race a factor, to file his case with a state or federal agency like the Equal Employment Opportunity Commission rather than to utilize the white employee controlled grievance procedure. Often as in the case of labor grievances, the grievant has a good case. More often, however, the real cause is something else—inefficiency, poor workmanship, or bad behavior, with the worst offender the most likely to file a case. That this causes employer anguish and white employee resentment is obvious. It takes time, effort, and great patience, and will be a factor in employee relations for years to come. But it has developed considerable resentment in some plants where white employees feel that some supervisors are afraid to discipline Negroes lest they have to defend themselves in investigations by government agencies. Charges of double standards because of race are not new, but now the charge is that Negroes in some plants are favored.

SOME PERSPECTIVES

Despite the great problems of adjustment, thousands of Negroes are learning valuable skills in the aerospace industry. They are now better prepared as workers to maintain their economic well-being and as citizens to care for themselves and their families. A substantial bank of skills has been added to the human capital in America by increased Negro employment in the aerospace industry. The difficulties, tribulations, and failures are relatively minor compared to this all-important accomplishment. Hopefully, the longer the plant tenure of the new Negro aerospace employees, the less will be the problems.

CHAPTER VII.

Determinants of Industry Policy

In the course of this study, a number of factors have been pointed out which have contributed to the racial employment policies of the aerospace industry. These and others should be noted again in the following concluding remarks.

THE DEMAND FOR LABOR

As in most industries, Negroes have made their greatest gains in the aerospace industry in times of full employment, and by the very nature of the industry, this means in times of war. The barriers were broken during World War II; serious upgrading occurred during the Korean War; and now the impetus of Vietnam, on top of the space program, has further expanded opportunities for development and promotion. But this has not been a smooth transition. Huge layoffs occurred after World War II, after the Korean armistice, and again in 1958, affecting the whole industry. Depending on the ebb and flow of government procurement, one company expands, another contracts, a plant may be abandoned or opened up.

As the last hired and the most recently upgraded, Negroes have found that their gains were washed out time and again. Yet, each time, as a result of the gains of the previous cycle, further gains were made in both numbers and in terms of occupational advancement; today's have been the greatest, and tomorrow's may be greater still, with again progress uneven, and many setbacks as the industry or some companies ebb and flow.

THE JOB STRUCTURE

Of fundamental importance in the industry is the job structure and the high professional content thereof. With professionals and skilled craftsmen the largest two occupational groups, and with Negroes disproportionately unrepresented in both groups, Negro advancement in the industry is certain to be retarded for many years. The unfortunate fact is that the higher the qualifications which are required, the fewer Negroes are qualified and the more difficult it is to gain qualification by short-run training or educational programs. As has been stressed, the aerospace industry must require skill and educational attainments that few Negroes possess, and there cannot be legitimate compromise with these requirements. Acquiring skills and education is a time-consuming process, so that upward job movement in this industry will continue to lag as long as the Negro educational and skill gap endures. Moreover, because of inexperience in industry, lack of help in setting goals, and the difficulty of breaking with the past, progress and upward job movement are made more difficult.

Past discrimination is difficult to overcome. Where Negroes are employed only for laboring jobs, they often lack background, capacity, and motivation to grasp new opportunities. It is expecting too much for a man who knew that he would always be a laborer ever to believe that he may be promoted if he takes training. Forty acres and a mule can be promised once too often to be taken seriously.

Opportunities appear greater in new plants. Rigidities are not set, custom can be violated without resistance of existing personnel, and past mistakes avoided. New plants may, however, be farther from cities, the new centers of Negro population, and here lack of public transportation and housing discrimination curtail Negro job and job advancement opportunities.

GOVERNMENT PRESSURE

Government pressure has been, and remains, a strong motivational force. With the government so large a customer, the industry cannot afford not to cooperate in all affirmative action programs. The government has not only opened up jobs, but has in effect in many cases pushed for what is close to outright preference for Negroes, and the industry has not only gone along, but often, first under pressure, endorsed the programs and activities and followed through diligently, and then having been committed, developed newer and more far-reaching affirmative action programs.

Yet even the most affirmative of actions cannot create jobs where there are none or fill skills that do not exist. The work must be there or the job openings are not. Layoffs will, as noted, have a profound effect on Negro employment in the industry.

Government pressure, moreover, is multidimensional as was discussed in detail on pages 216-217, and the needs of zero defects and security cannot be ignored.

SENIORITY AND UNIONISM

Because of the significance of skill and training in the industry, seniority has not been as significant as in some industries for promotion. Generally, seniority districts are broad enough so as not to interfere with opportunities for Negroes, and widespread use of job bidding further opens up potential advancement opportunities.

Unionism in the industry has not been a strong negative or positive factor in Negro job advancement. The UAW is more positive than the IAM, which originally was avowedly discriminatory, but is no more, yet is at best, passive. The UAW has not had the strong positive influence in this industry that it has had in the automobile industry where its position in all employee relations matters is much more powerful.

LOCATIONAL AND REGIONAL FACTORS

The location of aerospace companies in suburban or outer county areas, combined with the concentration of Negroes in cities, lack of good public urban transportation, and housing discrimination all tend to make getting to work in aerospace for Negroes a difficult problem and one which reduces Negro participation in the industry.

On a regional basis, the existence of large aerospace plants throughout the country has been generally salutary. Aerospace led the way in opening up new jobs to Negroes in the Far West during World War II, and in the Southeast in recent years. Its recent progress in the Southwest is especially noteworthy on a qualitative basis. The Southwest area lags considerably behind the Southeast in the utilization of Negro labor in this industry. Plants in this area are behind the trends in the industry despite diligent, but late efforts to improve Negro employment patterns there.

MANAGERIAL POLICY

Management is now committed to the full use of Negro labor in the industry. The needs and pressures are such that this policy will certainly not be turned back. From an industry which was once known for its extreme antagonism to Negro employment it has become as active as any in affirmative action programs. The reasons are an amalgam of what has been written above.

Of course, within the industry there exists a wide range of views and opinions among companies on questions of equal opportunity and affirmative action. It is fair to say, however, that most managements have a strong moral commitment to equal opportunity, but varying degrees of belief or support of the different affirmative action programs. Dealing as they do, primarily with government officials and air transport concerns, they do not feel the direct impact of the consuming public. Yet they are, and must be, very sensitive to public opinion and to their public image. For even the few who may be dubious about equal employment have a clear understanding of the necessity of proceeding to get the job accomplished as well as they can. The progress made, and the commitment which governmental and company policies have brought about augur well for the future of Negroes in the industry.

Part Four

THE NEGRO IN THE STEEL INDUSTRY

by

Richard L. Rowan

PART FOUR: LIST OF TABLES

CHART

APPENDIX A

CHAPTER I.

Introduction

The Steel Age actually began in the United States during the last half of the nineteenth century with the development of the Bessemer process and the open hearth furnace. Progress was slow, however, since steel producing was dependent in large measure on growth in the railroad and automobile industries. Expansion of rail lines, Henry Ford's Model T in 1908, and the first automobile assembly line in 1913, were healthy signs for the steel industry which was to become a major supplier of raw materials. Most American steel companies began to develop at the turn of the twentieth century to meet the demand for steel and steel products. Total steel production in the United States increased from 11.4 million tons in 1900 to 47.9 million tons in 1916.[1] Growth in the industry continued as the country developed and steel mills became significant employers of all types of labor. Even though United States Steel, Bethlehem, and Republic have become the three giants in the industry, a number of smaller firms have provided substantial employment opportunities for labor in many areas.

The past decade in the basic steel industry has been a troublesome one with the following factors of paramount importance: (1) heavy capital expenditures for new technology such as oxygen furnaces, (2) small return on sales, (3) large imports of steel from foreign markets, and (4) declining total employment. The great thrust of the civil rights movement occurred at a time when the industry was suffering some of its worst economic ills.

The 1969 net profit rankings of 500 companies by *Forbes* showed two steel companies in the top 50; United States Steel ranked 18, Bethlehem Steel 25, Armco Steel 76, Republic Steel 80, and National Steel 89.[2]

1. Douglas A. Fisher, *The Epic of Steel* (New York: Harper and Row, 1963), pp. 304-305.
2. "Dimensions of American Business," *Forbes*, May 15, 1969, p. 119.

The prospects are that the economic health of the industry will improve in the next decade but it requires a great deal of time and capital investment to make substantial changes in the steel industry.

The foregoing conditions make the industry an interesting one to study in terms of the Negro employment problem. The essential general question posed is: How has an industry that is declining in terms of employment and beset by financial, production, and marketing problems adjusted to a contemporary problem of employing and upgrading the Negro sector of the labor force?

DEFINITION OF THE INDUSTRY

For purposes of the study, the basic steel industry is defined as closely as possible in terms of the Standard Industrial Classification (SIC) system. The specific industry classification with which the study is concerned is SIC 3312 and Census 237, and the framework is as follows:

> Major Group 33—Primary Metal Industries
>
> Group No. 331—Blast Furnaces, Steel Works, and Rolling and Finishing Mills
>
> Industry No. 3312—Blast furnaces (including coke ovens), steel works, and rolling mills
>
> Establishments primarily engaged in manufacturing hot metal, pig iron, silvery pig iron, and ferroalloys from iron ore and iron and steel scrap; converting pig iron, scrap iron and scrap steel into steel; and in hot rolling iron and steel into basic shapes such as plates, sheets, strips, rods, bars, and tubing. Merchant blast furnaces and byproduct or beehive coke ovens are also included in this industry. Establishments primarily engaged in manufacturing ferro and nonferrous additive alloys by electrometallurgical processes are classified in Industry 3313.[3]

Table 1 gives an idea of the magnitude of the employment situation in SIC 3312 for the years 1958-1968. It can be seen readily that this has not been a significant growth industry in terms of employment for the years stated. Volatile activity has occurred, but there has been a steady decline in employment since 1965. This trend is expected to continue into the future.

3. Executive Office of the President, Bureau of the Budget, *Standard Industrial Classification Manual,* 1967, p. 128.

TABLE 1. *Employment in Blast Furnaces and Steel Mills*
SIC 3312
1958-1968

Year	Employees (in Thousands)	
	Total	Production Workers
1958	531.4	432.2
1959	515.3	414.7
1960	577.1	470.5
1961	526.5	424.7
1962	522.3	421.4
1963	520.0	424.6
1964	556.7	458.4
1965	580.2	477.4
1966	571.4	467.2
1967	555.5	447.7
1968	553.4	443.5

Source: U.S. Bureau of Labor Statistics, *Employment and Earnings Statistics for the United States, 1909-68,* Bulletin No. 1312-6, p. 154 and *Employment and Earnings,* March 1969, p. 57.

When one is working with both census and company data, it is difficult to follow completely a precise definition of the industry and arbitrary decisions must be made for inclusion and/or exclusion purposes. A careful attempt, however, has been made to reflect changes in the basic steel producing industry and, particularly, in analyzing current employment figures gathered on a company basis. Some of the background census data are available only for the primary iron and steel industry with no separate treatment for blast furnaces, steel works, and rolling mills. The cases are noted where more aggregate data are used.

RESEARCH METHODOLOGY

This study relies heavily on the techniques of survey and questionnaire. The limitations of such approaches are well known and need not be explored here. Despite the shortcomings involved, it is felt that the method is adequate for collecting data in an emotionally charged area of Negro employment in American industry.

Some of the major questions for which answers are sought are as follows:

1. What is the general background of the company or companies under consideration in terms of location and age? Do Negroes find employment more accessible in new plants or in old plants, in northern plants or in southern plants?
2. What is the total employment picture in terms of blue collar and white collar and job categories? How have Negroes fared in employment?
3. How intensive does the company or industry engage in manpower planning? How far into the future are employee requirements projected?
4. How does the company "declare" its policy in regard to nondiscrimination in employment? How is the policy implemented? Are Negroes better represented in companies where definite and firm policy in regard to their employment is made than in cases where the policy is only implicit?
5. How are employees recruited, selected, and trained? What special efforts are made in regard to Negroes?
6. What is the upgrading procedure for employees and for Negroes in particular? Do seniority systems handicap a Negro's progress?
7. What effect does new technology have on employment? Will the introduction of laborsaving equipment affect the Negro disproportionately?
8. What influence has the union had in regard to utilization of the Negro in the plant?
9. In terms of job opportunities for Negroes, how effective does the employer think equal employment opportunity legislation has been? What is the general relationship between the government and the employer in regard to civil rights matters?
10. What can be expected realistically in the future in terms of jobs for Negroes in the industry?

The general approach in collecting data in the study that sheds light on these and other questions involved (1) a survey of the literature, (2) a search of census material for 1940, 1950, and 1960, and (3) a questionnaire-interview process to gather current employment information.

Company data. A total of 23 companies, representing approximately 90 percent of the industry's employment and production, were selected for study. The selection included the eight largest companies in the industry (over 25,000 employees), ten middle-sized companies (5,000 to 25,000 employees), and five small companies (under 5,000 employees). Employer response was excellent with 21 of the 23 companies (91 percent) agreeing to cooperate through personal interviews and/or answering questions pertaining to racial employment practices. The following companies make up the sample used:

Large Companies (over 25,000 Employees)	*Middle-sized Companies (5,000 to 25,000 Employees)*	*Small Companies (under 5,000 Employees)*
United States Steel Corporation	Kaiser Steel Corporation	Alan Wood Steel Company
Bethlehem Steel Corporation	Wheeling Steel Corporation	Laclede Steel Company
Republic Steel Corporation	McLouth Steel Corporation	Carpenter Steel Company
National Steel Corporation	Colorado Fuel & Iron Corporation	Latrobe Steel Company
Jones & Laughlin Steel Corporation	Granite City Steel Company	Jessop Steel Company
Armco Steel Corporation	Pittsburgh Steel Company	
Inland Steel Company	Sharon Steel Corporation	
Youngstown Sheet & Tube Company	Interlake Steel Corporation	
	Lukens Steel Company	
	Allegheny Ludlum Steel Corporation	

Subsequent to the employer's statement of willingness to cooperate in the study, in response to a letter specifying details of the project, a questionnaire was sent and followed up by a personal interview shortly thereafter at company headquarters. The person interviewed was generally the vice-president of industrial relations or the personnel manager and, in some instances, additional industrial relations staff people were interviewed. Ample time was provided in every case to cover the topics in the questionnaire which included: general company background, general and racial employment data, manpower planning and policy in regard to minority groups, recruitment, selection and training, adjustments to technological change, the union response to company policy, and the government-employer relationship in equal employment opportunity. The cooperation of the companies in allowing open discussion relevant to Negro employment and in making available data that have been handled on a confidential basis has made it possible to present a truly representative picture of racial employment in the steel industry.

Government data. The government data used are of two major types: (1) census material for 1940, 1950, and 1960 and special reports of the Bureau of Labor Statistics, and (2) reports of the agencies responsible for implementing civil rights legislation and executive orders.

The census data are used primarily for background information and to indicate trends in employment. It is not always possible to obtain data that are strictly comparable for several time periods. As noted earlier, an effort has been made to present as detailed information as possible in conjunction with SIC 3312, but in some instances more aggregate data only have been available. Research in the area of Negro employment would have been facilitated greatly if the government had continued the "Negro in Industry" series after 1940.[4]

Two principal agencies, whose work deals exclusively with civil rights matters, assisted in the study. The Equal Employment Opportunity Commission (EEOC) and the Office of Federal Contract Compliance (OFCC) have furnished valuable data within the confines of confidentiality requirements. Discussions with staff members of these agencies have enabled us to gain perspective on certain problems.

The EEOC, in cooperation with the OFCC, collects each year employer reports, EEO-1, showing total employment, male and female, and employment of Negro, Oriental, American Indian, and Spanish American persons, male and female, in nine standard occupational categories. Additional information covering apprentices and on-the-job trainees is also collected.

The data gathered by EEOC are used for analytical purposes by OFCC and a voluntary agency, Plans for Progress.[5] Use of the data by private researchers is governed by agency rules and law in order to protect the anonymity of an individual employer or establishment. This means that the information is available for private use only in an aggregate form where no single employer can be identified.

4. Published in the *Monthly Labor Review* prior to 1941.

5. Plans for Progress, a voluntary effort by American businessmen, was conceived in 1961 as an adjunct to the President's Committee on Equal Employment Opportunity. When this Committee was dissolved in 1965, Plans for Progress was reorganized as a separate entity by President Johnson's Executive Order 11246.

Even though this restricts the usefulness of the data, it is helpful in making regional or area comparisons.

Civil rights organizations. The Urban League, NAACP, and various human relations commissions have provided insight into employment problems on a local level. These organizations have not been able financially to support research programs and little is available from them in a published form. Some attention is being given currently to the necessity for research activity and, particularly, in the national headquarters of the respective organization. A wealth of information is many times available, however, from an official of one of these organizations who has worked closely with the Negro and white business community in a given location.

CHAPTER II.

The Structure of the Basic Steel Industry

An examination of the summary statistics for the steel industry for the period 1957-1968 (Table 2) reflects volatile activity in almost any area of concern. The following sections analyze this activity in terms of employment and earnings, revenue and the return on revenue, investment and the return on investment, capital expenditures, and production.[6]

A GENERAL OVERVIEW OF THE STEEL INDUSTRY

Employment and earnings. Employment in the basic steel industry has varied over the past decade but, in general, the trend has been downward. The average number of employees in 1968 was 551,557 compared to 623,834 in 1957, an overall decline of 72,277 or 11.6 percent. The periods of decline and growth in employment between 1957 and 1968 can be specified as follows:

Period	*Decline*	*Growth*
1957-1959	x	
1959-1960		x
1960-1963	x	
1963-1964		x
1964-1965		x
1965-1966	x	
1966-1967	x	
1967-1968	x	

6. The statistical analysis in these sections draws heavily on the following basic sources: American Iron and Steel Institute, *Annual Statistical Report 1968,* and *Charting Steel's Progress During 1966.* Also consulted was: National Iudustrial Conference Board, Statistics of Manufacturing Industries, *Primary Metals: I, General Iron and Steel,* 1963.

TABLE 2. *Steel Industry, Summary Statistics*

1957-1968

Year	Average Number of Employ-ees†	Average Number of Salaried Employ-ees†	Average Number of Wage Employ-ees†	Average Hourly Earn-ings in Steel (BLS)	Average Payroll Cost per Hour	Produc-tion of Raw Steel (Millions of Net Tons)	Revenue (Billions of Dollars)	Net Income (Billions of Dollars)	Percent Return on Revenue	Invest-ment (Billions of Dollars)	Percent Return on Invest-ment	Capital Expendi-tures (Billions of Dollars)
1968	551,557	130,873	420,684	3.82	4.58	131.5	18.7	1.0	5.3	n. a.	n. a.	2.4
1967	555,143	130,990	424,153	3.62	4.32	127.2	16.9	0.8	4.9	n. a.	n. a.	2.1
1966	575,547	128,835	446,712	3.58	4.25	134.1	18.3	1.1	5.9	16.5	6.7	2.0
1965	583,851	125,312	458,539	3.46	4.14	131.5	18.0	1.1	5.9	15.8	6.9	1.8
1964	553,555	118,901	434,654	3.41	4.01	127.1	16.4	1.0	6.1	14.9	6.8	1.6
1963	520,289	114,753	405,536	3.36	3.93	109.3	14.6	0.8	5.4	14.4	5.5	1.0
1962	520,538	117,876	402,662	3.29	3.87	98.3	14.0	0.6	4.1	14.1	4.0	0.9
1961	523,305	117,381	405,924	3.20	3.75	98.0	13.3	0.7	5.2	14.2	5.0	1.0
1960	571,552	121,664	449,888	3.08	3.58	99.3	14.2	0.8	5.7	13.6	6.1	1.5
1959	515,057	115,319	399,738	3.10	3.66	93.4	14.2	0.8	5.8	13.1	6.5	0.9
1958	523,451	111,886	411,565	2.91	3.43	85.3	12.6	0.8	6.3	12.6	6.5	1.1
1957	623,834	115,400	508,434	2.73	3.13	112.7	15.6	1.1	7.3	11.7	10.1	1.7

Source: American Iron and Steel Institute.

† Average of the monthly number of employees receiving pay after adjustment for turnover.

n.a.: Comparable data not available.

The average number of wage employees (blue collar) declined from 508,434 in 1957 to 420,684 in 1968 (17.3 percent) whereas the average number of salaried employees (white collar) increased from 115,400 in 1957 to 130,873 in 1968 (13.4 percent). This shift in employment is very important in terms of the minority problem, since Negroes have been employed traditionally in the blue collar areas. The downward trend in wage employees probably reflects the changing technology in the steel industry exemplified in part by the move away from the open hearth furnace to the basic oxygen process and automation in the rolling mills. In 1957, some 611,000 tons of raw steel were produced by the basic oxygen process compared to 48,812,000 tons in 1968, an increase of 7,888.9 percent. During the same time period, the production of raw steel by the open hearth process (including basic and acid) declined from 101,658,000 tons in 1957 to 65,836,000 tons in 1968, a decline of 35.2 percent. The increase in salaried employees (white collar) can be explained in large measure by the research and development activities in the industry, computer technology, and allied office and clerical functions.

Employment is probably the most difficult statistic to analyze in the steel industry. An examination of employment trends in the industry can be misleading in terms of new hires. Turnover rates would have to be examined carefully in order to show an accurate picture of new employment in the industry. Apparently, it is almost impossible to know at a given time the exact number of employees in a basic steel plant. The important thing to be noted here is that even though the trend in employment has been downward, there could have been considerable employment at various intervals as the result of turnover.

Among the few industry statistics that reflect a consistent increase over the past decade are average hourly earnings and average payroll cost per hour. Average hourly earnings have risen from $2.73 in 1957 to $3.82 in 1968 while average payroll cost per hour has risen from $3.13 in 1957 to $4.58 in 1968. Average hourly earnings in steel compare quite favorably with the average for all manufacturing as noted below:

	Average Hourly Earnings		
Industry	*1940*	*1950*	*1968*
Steel SIC 3312	$.84	$1.69	$3.82
All Manufacturing	$.66	$1.44	$3.01

The figures above indicate that average hourly earnings in steel rose by about 355 percent between 1940 and 1968. Of course, the BLS data do not show full employment costs for the industry since such items as paid holidays and vacations and pension plans are excluded. Steelworkers have consistently exceeded the average for all manufacturing. The advantage for steelworkers in 1968 was $.81 per hour compared to $.18 in 1940 and $.25 in 1950.

Revenue and its return. Revenue in the steel industry has not grown significantly over the period 1957-1968, nor has the percent return on revenue. In 1957 total revenue was 15.6 billions of dollars compared to 18.7 billions of dollars in 1968. The percent return on revenue (a ratio of profits to sales measured in dollars of similar value) in 1957 was 7.3 whereas in 1968 it was down to 5.3. Net income has remained at about one billion dollars over the entire period. Profits in the industry have been affected seriously by increases in employment costs, higher prices for purchased goods and services, start-up costs of new equipment, and interest and expense on a growing long-term debt. The financial picture in the steel industry is not a bright one, and it has been observed that "the U. S. steel industry finds it easier to make steel than money." [7]

Investment and its return. The steel industry's investment (total assets less current liabilities) has increased almost every year since 1957. In 1957, the investment was 11.7 billions of dollars compared to 16.5 billions of dollars in 1966, an increase of 4.8 billion or 41 percent. The rate of return on investment in the industry, however, has fallen from 10.1 percent in 1957 to 6.7 percent in 1966. In recent years, the rate of return on investment has not shown a tendency to move much above the 6.5 percent level. This performance reflects the growth of long-term debt as the industry continues to borrow for plant renewal and expansion.

Capital expenditures. Over the past decade the steel industry spent approximately fifteen billion dollars for property additions and improvements. About one to two billion dollars have been spent on capital improvements each year since 1957. The heaviest capital outlay was in 1968 with over two billion dollars invested to improve the range and quality of steel products and to enhance efficiency. Large investments are being made in such areas as the basic oxygen

7. 42nd Financial Analysis of the Steel Industry, Supplement to *Steel,* April 3, 1967, p. 56a.

process, continuous casting equipment, wide hot strip mills, vacuum degassing, and improved annealing equipment. As new seniority units are created to accommodate the technological changes, additional opportunities for Negroes should develop.

Production. Production of raw steel increased each year between 1958 and 1966, but declined from 1966 to 1968. In 1957, 112.7 millions of tons of steel were produced compared to 131.5 millions of tons in 1968, an increase of 16.7 percent. The most significant increase in tonnage produced occurred between 1962 and 1964 when net tons produced increased from 98.3 million to 127.1 million.

Table 3 presents a comparison between the older and newer processes in steel production. It is obvious that the basic oxygen process and the electric furnace are becoming much more important in the production of steel than the open hearth or Bessemer processes. This trend will have a decided impact on the employment picture of the industry. A larger number of skilled jobs will be available in the future, and unskilled positions will decline. The interesting thing about this prospect is that even though the number of skilled jobs will increase, they will not be rated as highly as before. The top

TABLE 3. *Steel Industry, Production of Raw Steel by Process*
1957-1968
(Thousands of net tons)

Years	Open Hearth	Bessemer	Basic Oxygen	Electric	Total
1957	101,658	2,475	611	7,971	112,715
1958	75,880	1,396	1,323	6,656	85,255
1959	81,669	1,380	1,864	8,533	93,446
1960	86,368	1,189	3,346	8,379	99,282
1961	84,502	881	3,967	8,664	98,014
1962	82,957	805	5,553	9,013	98,328
1963	88,834	963	8,544	10,920	109,261
1964	98,098	858	15,442	12,678	127,076
1965	94,193	586	22,879	13,804	131,462
1966	85,025	278	33,928	14,870	134,101
1967	70,690	‡	41,434	15,089	127,213
1968	65,836	‡	48,812	16,814	131,462

Source: American Iron and Steel Institute.
‡ Included with open hearth.

position in the basic oxygen process is rated currently at about 18, whereas the highest job in the open hearth operation may be rated 32. This discrepancy will require collective bargaining modifications in making job assignments in the future. Steel management will have an opportunity to further implement equal employment programs as the new technology goes into operation.

Some care must be exercised in making comparisons on a year-by-year basis for steel production, since over time steel can be made with a higher strength-to-weight ratio, and a specific job may require less steel today than five or ten years ago.

The Raw Steel Production Index, charted below and adopted by the American Iron and Steel Institute, provides a convenient means of comparing steel output during different years.

CHART 1. *Steel Industry Index of Raw Steel Production*

1957-1959 = 100

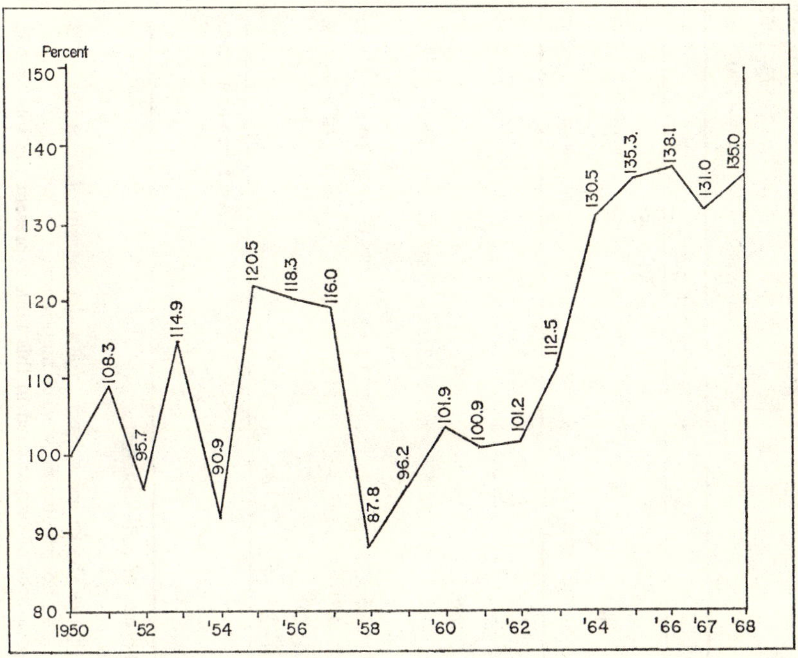

Source: American Iron and Steel Institute.

TABLE 4. *Steel Industry, Indexes of Output per Man-hour*
1957 – 1965
(Indexes, 1957-1959 = 100; average annual rates in percent)

	Output per						Related Data			
Year	All employee	All employee man-hour	Production worker	Production worker man-hour	Nonproduction worker	Nonproduction worker man-hour[2]	Output[3]	All employee man-hours	Production worker man-hours	Nonproduction worker man-hours[2]
1957	101.4	101.1	99.3	98.8	112.0	112.0	114.8	113.6	116.2	102.5
1958	90.8	93.5	91.6	95.0	87.6	87.6	85.8	91.8	90.3	98.0
1959	107.6	105.0	109.5	106.2	99.8	99.8	99.3	94.6	93.5	99.5
1960	97.2	98.6	97.7	99.6	94.6	94.8	99.5	100.9	99.9	105.0
1961	101.7	101.7	103.4	103.3	95.0	95.5	95.2	93.6	92.2	99.7
1962	107.5	106.9	109.3	108.4	100.5	101.2	100.2	93.7	92.4	99.0
1963	114.7	111.8	115.2	111.5	112.1	112.8	106.3	95.1	95.3	94.2
1964	122.0	116.5	121.6	114.7	124.2	125.1	120.7	103.6	105.2	96.5
1965[1]	126.4	120.8	125.9	118.9	128.5	129.3	131.2	108.6	110.3	101.5
	Average annual rates									
1957-1965	3.4	2.7	3.4	2.5	3.2	3.3	2.9	–0.2	0.4	–0.4

Source: Bureau of Labor Statistics.

1. Preliminary.
2. The figures shown are subject to a wider margin of error than are other measures for this industry because of the method for estimating nonproduction worker man-hours.
3. The measures of output used in this table represent the total production of the industry resulting from all employees and do not represent the specific output of any single group of employees.

The Index is based on annual average raw steel production (97.1 million net tons) for the years 1957 to 1959 inclusive, considered as 100. Production data for other years are translated to a percentage of this 1957-1959 average. The years 1952, 1954, and 1958 stand out as low points in production compared to the high points of 1955, 1965, 1966, and 1968.

Indexes of output per man-hour for the steel industry are shown in Table 4.

Output per man-hour in the industry has fluctuated during the period 1957-1965, but the general trend has been upward. Over this period, nonproduction worker man-hours have remained relatively stable, while production worker man-hours have tended to fluctuate with changes in output. With an upward trend in output, nonproduction worker man-hours have diminished in relative importance, and indexes of output per production worker man-hour show a smaller increase than those of output per all employee man-hour. Output per production worker man-hour increased 2.5 percent while output per all employee man-hour increased 2.7 percent over the 1957-1965 period.[8]

SIZE

The steel industry consists of over 200 companies with more than 100 producing raw steel. Large-scale plants, employing over 1,000 people, are characteristic of the blast furnaces and steel mills industry. In fact, 28 producers represented approximately 90 percent of steel production in the United States in 1968.

The dominant firms in the basic steel industry are: United States Steel Corporation, Bethlehem Steel Corporation, and Republic Steel Corporation. These three companies together produced 62,472,888 net tons of steel in 1968; the tonnage figure represents 52.2 percent of all steel produced in that year by the 28 companies. The same companies employed 382,093 people or 55.2 percent of the employees in the 28 basic steel companies in 1968. Fifteen companies produced more than one million tons of raw steel in 1968. The merger movement has not seriously affected the steel industry in recent years. A merger between Wheeling Steel Corporation and Pittsburgh Steel Company, did not significantly change the relative position of

8. U. S. Bureau of Labor Statistics, *Indexes of Output Per Man-Hour, Steel Industry, 1947-1965*. BLS Report No. 306, June 1966.

TABLE 5. *Steel Industry, Production and Employment Selected Companies*
1968

Company	Ingot Production Net Tons	Number Employed Average
United States Steel Corporation	32,352,200	201,017
Bethlehem Steel Corporation	20,372,000	131,000
Republic Steel Corporation	9,748,688	50,076
National Steel Corporation	8,462,500	30,053
Armco Steel Corporation	7,700,000	45,427
Jones & Laughlin Steel Corporation	7,688,000	41,610
Inland Steel Corporation	7,015,000	30,552
Youngstown Sheet & Tube Company	5,633,500	25,800
Wheeling-Pittsburgh Steel Corporation	3,570,000	17,554
Kaiser Steel Corporation	2,925,000	13,470
Colorado Fuel & Iron Corporation	1,639,000	11,681
Sharon Steel Corporation	1,490,212	7,309
McLouth Steel Corporation	1,452,000	4,440
Northwestern Steel & Wire Company	1,090,869	3,643
Interlake Steel Corporation	1,074,495	9,162
Granite City Steel Company	974,335	5,249
Lukens Steel Company	878,000	5,253
Detroit Steel Corporation	845,000	3,827
Alan Wood Steel Company	839,408	3,308
Cyclops Corporation	837,217	7,331
Allegheny Ludlum Steel Corporation	692,316	17,148
Laclede Steel Company	632,082	4,281
Keystone Consolidated Industries, Inc.	606,554	8,200
Continental Steel Corporation	390,424	2,693
Phoenix Steel Corporation	361,231	2,366
Atlantic Steel Company	310,033	1,923
Carpenter Technology Corporation	149,024	5,258
Latrobe Steel Company	33,741	2,246
Total—28 Companies	119,762,829	691,877

Source: *44th Annual Financial Analysis of the Steel Industry,* Supplement to *Steel,* April 7, 1969.

the combined company in the industry. It became the ninth largest employer and producer of steel in the industry whereas Wheeling was tenth and Pittsburgh was fourteenth. In the spring of 1968, several mergers and diversification plans were announced in the industry including the following: United States Steel and Burlington Industries plan a venture into the executive air travel and aircraft leasing business; Ling-Temco-Vought and Jones and Laughlin are considering a merger as are National Steel and Southwire, Carpenter

Steel and Cryogenics, and Allegheny Ludlum and Goddard. Inland Steel Company has established a staff unit to study diversification. These and similar activities are likely to continue into the future as the industry attempts to make inroads into new markets.[9]

The size of the large companies mentioned above should not overshadow the importance of some of the middle-sized and small companies in terms of employment in particular locations. Armco Steel Corporation in Middletown, Ohio, Kaiser Steel in Fontana, California, Granite City Steel in Granite City, Illinois, Sharon Steel in Farrell, Pennsylvania, Lukens Steel in Coatesville, Pennsylvania, Laclede Steel in Alton, Illinois, and Carpenter Steel in Reading, Pennsylvania, in addition to others, provide major sources of employment in their respective communities.

PROCESS AND ORGANIZATION INTEGRATION

Since the turn of the century, the basic steel industry has moved toward a greater degree of vertical integration. Fisher notes that in the late nineteenth century "Processes in the iron industry were disconnected. One company mined the ore, another smelted it, a third puddled it into wrought iron, and a fourth operated rolling mills. In the 1890s, some steel companies began to integrate their operations to include several stages of the process." [10] Perlman and Taft observe that "In 1882, Carnegie, Phipps and Company took the first step towards industrial integration." [11]

By 1958 a Census report indicated that of the total value added by manufacture in the blast furnaces and steel mills industry, 56 percent was accounted for by 37 fully integrated establishments and 29 percent was accounted for by 93 semi-integrated establishments.[12] Vertical integration in the iron and steel industry continues to characterize the business organization and the production processes in the industry.

9. See *Wall Street Journal,* June 7 and 10, May 9 and 17, and April 19 and 30, 1968.
10. Douglas A. Fisher, *The Epic of Steel* (New York: Harper and Row, 1963), p. 129.
11. Selig Perlman and Philip Taft, *History of Labor in the United States, 1896-1932* (New York: The Macmillan Company, 1935), p. 98.
12. National Industrial Conference Board, Statistics of Manufacturing Industries, *Primary Metals: I, General Iron and Steel Industry, 1963,* p. 9.

GEOGRAPHIC FACTORS

Steel is produced in 31 states but the bulk of steelmaking is conducted in seven states: Pennsylvania, Ohio, Indiana, Illinois, Maryland, Michigan, and New York as shown in Table 6. About 80 percent of the country's steelmaking capacity is located in these states. Pennsylvania and Ohio are the most important steel producing states. These two states produced approximately 41 percent of all steel (over 53 million tons) in 1968.

The major factors determining the location of steel plants are proximity to coal and iron ore as raw materials, costs of assembling raw materials, transportation, and nearness to steel consuming markets. The basic raw materials, coal and iron ore, are concentrated geographically in the United States. Even though iron ore deposits are found in a large number of states, the Great Lakes area has been the principal source of iron ore in this country. The Mesabi Range in Minnesota, from which the first shipments of ore came in 1892,[13] has the greatest deposits and in 1968 the Great Lakes area supplied

TABLE 6. *Steel Industry, Raw Steel Production by States, 1968*

(Thousands of net tons)

States	Total	Percent of Total
New York	7,228	5.5
Pennsylvania	31,018	23.6
R.I., Conn., N.J., Del., Md.	8,025	6.1
Va., W. Va., Ga., Fla., N.C.	4,453	3.4
Kentucky	2,478	1.9
Ala., Tenn., Miss.	4,611	3.5
Ohio	22,606	17.2
Indiana	17,911	13.6
Illinois	10,510	8.0
Michigan	9,218	7.0
Minn., Mo., Okla., Texas	4,810	3.7
Ariz., Colo., Utah, Wash., Ore., Hawaii	4,383	3.3
California	4,210	3.2
Total	131,461	100.0

Source: American Iron & Steel Institute.

13. Fisher, *op. cit.,* p. 129.

over one-half of the ore consumed by the steel industry. In the past, steel mills were located nearer the source of coal than the source of iron ore since it was considered more economical to transport iron ore to the coal fields. Approximately 25 states have coal deposits suitable for coking; however, 90 percent of the country's coal mines are located in Pennsylvania, Ohio, Indiana, Illinois, Virginia, West Virginia, and Kentucky. Almost three-fourths of the coking coal mined in the United States in 1968 was accounted for by West Virginia, Kentucky, Pennsylvania, and Illinois. The steel industry used about 88 million tons of coal in 1968.

The geographic structure of the steel industry has changed somewhat since World War II toward greater geographic decentralization and market orientation. Table 7 indicates that in the postwar years of expansion of the steel industry's capacity, all regions, except Pennsylvania and Ohio, either raised or maintained their percentage of the country's capacity. Industrial growth and the development of markets in the Midwest, Southwest, and Pacific regions has led to the building of steel making facilities in those areas in the past two decades.

TABLE 7. *Steel Industry, Regional Changes in Steel Capacity* 1948 – 1960

Region	Percent of Total Capacity 1/1/48	Percent of Total Capacity 1/1/60
Mass., R.I., Conn., N.Y., N.J.	5.4	5.3
Del., Md., Va.	5.5	6.0
Pa., Ohio	49.7	45.3
W. Va., Ky.	3.8	3.5
Ga., Fla., Ala., Miss., Tenn.	4.0	4.0
Indiana	11.8	12.4
Illinois	8.8	8.6
Michigan	3.7	5.4
Minn., Mo.	1.2	1.2
Okla., Texas	0.7	1.8
Colo., Utah, Ariz.	2.7	2.8
Wash., Ore., Calif.	2.6	3.6

Source: American Iron and Steel Institute.

TABLE 8. *Steel Industry, Shipments of Finished Steel by Major Market Classifications*
1965 and 1968

Market	Percent of Total* Net Shipments	
	1968	1965
Automotive Industry	21.0	21.7
Steel Service Centers and Distributors (Excluding oil and gas)	15.4	16.0
Construction and Contractors' Products (Excluding oil and gas)	15.5	15.7
Machinery (Including electrical and farm)	10.3	10.8
Containers	8.6	7.9
Converting and Processing Forgings; Bolts; Nuts; etc.	5.7	6.9
Appliances: Other Domestic and Commercial Equipment	4.7	4.8
Oil and Gas	5.7	4.6
Rail Transportation	3.3	4.1
Shipbuilding	1.1	1.1
Export and All Other	8.7	6.4
	100.0	100.0

Source: American Iron and Steel Institute.

* Finished steel shipments including exports but excluding shipments to reporting members of the industry for conversion into further finished products and for resale.

MAJOR MARKETS FOR STEEL

A total of 92 million tons of steel were shipped to all markets in 1968 compared to 92.7 million tons in 1965. The five basic domestic markets in 1968, as noted in Table 8, were: automotive industry, steel service centers and distributors, construction and contractors' products, machinery, and the container industry. These five markets took 71 percent of all steel shipments. The automotive industry alone received 21 percent of steel shipments in 1968.

The market position of United States steel producers has been seriously threatened in recent years by imports from abroad. Foreign steel producers have made considerable headway in American markets, particularly when labor-management contracts are about to expire and there is any uncertainty about continued production. Table 9 indicates that imports rose from 1.2 million tons in 1957 to

TABLE 9. *Steel Industry, Foreign Trade in Steel Mill Products*
1957–1968
(Thousands of net tons)

Years	Exports	Imports
1957	5,348	1,155
1958	2,823	1,707
1959	1,677	4,396
1960	2,977	3,359
1961	1,990	3,163
1962	2,013	4,100
1963	2,224	5,446
1964	3,442	6,440
1965	2,496	10,383
1966	1,724	10,753
1967	1,685	11,455
1968	2,170	17,960

Source: American Iron and Steel Institute.

18.0 million tons in 1968.[14] Exports have fallen from 5.3 million tons in 1957 to 2.2 million tons in 1968.

The situation reflected in Table 9 led to a study of the import problem by the Committee on Finance of the United States Senate. A summary of the conclusions of that study led to the following observations:

> If the trends . . . persist, the Nation must be prepared to see steel imports ultimately reach such high percentages of the markets for certain steel products as to render them unprofitable for the domestic industry to make.
>
> U. S. steel production has fallen from 61 percent of world output in 1945 to 26 percent in 1966, and will probably drop to 21 percent in 1975. Between 1947 and 1966 Japan's share of world steel output has increased tenfold, Italy's tripled, the U.S.S.R.'s doubled, and Red China produced more steel in 1966 than any country had in 1947, with the exception of the United States and the U.S.S.R.
>
> . . .
>
> Hourly steel labor costs in 1966 were $4.63 in this country compared with $1.87 in West Germany, $1.76 in Italy, $1.53 in France, and $1.10 in Japan.[15]

---

14. See *Business Week,* July 6, 1968, p. 85, for a discussion of the import problem.
15. American Iron and Steel Institute, *Steel Imports,* Summary of the Staff Study of the Committee on Finance, United States Senate, March 1968, pp. 3, 11.

In particular regard to the employment problem, it was observed that:

> Seven domestic steel facilities have been dismantled or idled as a result of rising imports. The impact on employment is difficult to gage, however, because during the years 1964-66 the United States experienced increased domestic production of steel despite sharply rising imports.[16]

As a solution to the import problem, the industry has been forced into the peculiar position of asking Congress for assistance in restricting entry of foreign steel, and a cut in prices has been sought to protect some markets. Not all companies, however, have accepted these approaches as satisfactory to an amelioration of the problem. For example, U. S. Steel announced a price decrease in May 1968 to meet competition from foreign steel, but Armco, Inland, Jones and Laughlin, and Bethlehem refused to follow.[17] As the industry continues to find an answer to the basic import problem, there will be adjustments in the employment area even though the impact is difficult to measure.

UNIONIZATION

The consistent record of high earnings in the basic steel industry reflects, in large measure, the strength of the union—the United Steelworkers of America, now led by I. W. Abel. This union has played an important role in the development of the American labor movement. Organized as the Amalgamated Association of Iron, Steel and Tin Workers in 1876, it was absorbed by the Steel Workers' Organizing Committee in 1936 and shortly thereafter the United Steelworkers of America emerged as the dominant union in the industry.[18] Membership in the Union stood at approximately 1,200,000 in 1967.

Almost all plants in the steel industry have been organized by the United Steelworkers of America. It has been one of the few unions to make a substantial impact on southern labor. Local 1013, USW, formed in Birmingham, Alabama in 1944 is today one of the largest local unions in the South with a membership of nearly 6,000 covering

16. *Ibid.*, p. 11.
17. *Wall Street Journal,* May 13, 1968.
18. Philip Taft, *Organized Labor in American History* (New York: Harper and Row, 1964).

a portion of the employees of United States Steel's Fairfield operation. Interestingly enough the union and management usually have taken the same point of view in regard to Negro employment in the steel industry. The master contract with local plant amendments constitutes an agreement concerning the utilization of labor. There is some indication that the situation is changing with Negro members demanding a more effective voice in the union. A recent report states:

> USW Negro unionists, disenchanted after what they describe as years of "beautiful words but little action," threaten a political revolt unless President I. W. Abel and other USW leaders respond to demands for a louder voice—and more jobs—in the steel union.
>
> . . .
>
> The black staffmen attacked USW's "lack of action" on Negro issues since 1965, and emerged with a commitment . . . on mill jobs, according to one participant [in a meeting of 48 black staff representatives with the USW vice-president]. The union will demand a strong plant-wide seniority clause. This would open new jobs in promotional sequences now closed to Negroes because some local unions and plant managements have ignored a 1962 "enabling" clause on plant-wide seniority.[19]

The union and management in the industry have agreed, in the past, that rigid departmental seniority rules would govern upgrading and intraplant transfers. If the statements above are indicative of things to come, major changes will have to be made and agreement will be difficult to reach.

Despite general organization in the industry by the USW, there are several plants covered by independent unions and a few nonunion plants. Generally, in a heavily unionized industry such as steel the existence of an independent union, or no union, does not yield a basically different approach to Negro employment by management. The relevance of union policy in regard to Negro employment in the industry will be discussed in later sections of this study.

---

19. *Business Week,* June 29, 1968, p. 126.

CHAPTER III.

Pre-World War II Negro Employment Profile

This chapter is concerned with the employment of Negroes in the iron and steel industry during the pre-World War II period. Prior to World War II, the Bureau of Labor Statistics prepared excellent articles on the Negro in industry. Since that time, however, very few comparable studies have been done to report information on the basis of race. This has the unfortunate consequence of handicapping those who would like to analyze racial employment trends. A part of the reluctance of the government to report racial data in various forms has been the response to the civil right movement which feared such data would be misused. Apparently, thinking in regard to this matter has moved full circle as the former Secretary of Labor stated:

> . . . the policy and the practice, as of today, is that in all situations subject to the control in this respect of the Secretary of Labor, employment records will include racial identification *wherever this is necessary or helpful in assuring against racial discrimination and in promoting affirmative action programs to eliminate racial disadvantage.*[20]

There is still confusion in industry today concerning the legal aspects of racial identification in employment records. It is ironical that employers are required to report detailed information pertaining to minority employment when it is not clear that the law permits them to maintain data that would allow this to be done in an efficient manner. It appears that the point has been reached where employment records should contain racial information in order to further implement nondiscriminatory programs. Research activities would be greatly facilitated also if the government would reinstate its Negro in industry series begun in the 1930's.

---

20. See statement of former Secretary Willard Wirtz to NAACP in Bureau of National Affairs, *Daily Labor Report,* May 18, 1966, No. 97, G-2.

The analysis that follows is based on two Bureau of Labor Statistics wage surveys for the periods March 1935 and April 1938.[21] These surveys contain important employment data on a racial basis. The 1935 survey covers a sample of 90,484 wage earners in the steel industry, and the 1938 survey is based on a sample of 80,711 workers. These figures are not strictly comparable, but they do provide a means of making a rough estimate of the Negro's progress in the industry in the pre-World War II period.

DISTRIBUTION OF NEGROES WITHIN THE INDUSTRY

Negroes always have been an important factor in employment in the iron and steel industry; however, their numerical strength was not increased significantly until World War I. The shortage of labor, in addition to reduced immigration, prompted the hiring of Negroes at that time. The 1930 Census of Population indicated that 12.8 percent (one out of eight) of all workers in the industry was Negro.[22] It is interesting to note by comparison that the 1960 Census reported 11.2 percent Negro employees in the blast furnaces, steel works, and rolling and finishing mills (SIC 3312) industry (12.7 percent Negro in the basic iron and steel industry), and the 1966 EEO-1 figures show 12.8 percent Negro employees in the basic steel industry (SIC 3312). (See Tables 17, 20, and 25.)

Wage surveys made by the Bureau of Labor Statistics in 1935 and 1938 found a downward movement in the employment of Negroes in the industry. In 1935, 10.0 percent of those wage earners studied were Negro while in 1938, 9.7 percent were Negro. Obviously, the depression affected Negro labor more seriously than whites in terms of layoff. Despite these circumstances, the Bureau reported in 1937 that "the iron and steel industry is of outstanding importance as a field of employment for Negroes, since it is one of the few manufacturing industries in which Negro employment equals approximately the proportion of Negroes in the total population."[23]

---

21. U. S. Bureau of Labor Statistics, *Monthly Labor Review*, Vol. 44, No. 3, March 1937, pp. 564-579, and Vol. 51, No. 5, November 1940, pp. 1139-1149.
22. The 1930 Census of Population shows 48,867 Negro workers among a total of 377,556 employees in the iron and steel industry.
23. U. S. Bureau of Labor Statistics, *Monthly Labor Review*, Vol. 44, No. 3, March 1937, p. 565.

TABLE 10. *Iron and Steel Industry*
Distribution of White and Negro Wage Earners
by Division of Industry and District, March 1935

Division of Industry and District	Total Wage Earners	Whites		Negroes	
		Number	Percent	Number	Percent
All divisions	90,484	81,420[1]	90.0	9,064	10.0
Eastern district	11,713	10,047	85.8	1,666	14.2
Pittsburgh district	37,758	35,117	93.0	2,641	7.0
Great Lakes and Middle West district	32,328	30,237	93.5	2,091	6.5
Southern district	8,685	6,019	69.3	2,666	30.7
Blast furnaces	6,706	5,663[2]	84.4	1,043	15.6
Eastern district	841	619	73.6	222	26.4
Pittsburgh district	2,277	2,144	94.2	133	5.8
Great Lakes and Middle West district	2,555	2,258	88.4	297	11.6
Southern district	1,033	642	62.1	391	37.9
Steelworks	15,474	14,121[3]	91.3	1,353	8.7
Eastern district	1,727	1,381	80.0	346	20.0
Pittsburgh district	7,272	6,716	92.4	556	7.6
Great Lakes and Middle West district	5,188	5,037	97.1	151	2.9
Southern district	1,287	987	76.7	300	23.3
Rolling mills	68,304	61,636[4]	90.2	6,668	9.8
Eastern district	9,145	8,047	88.0	1,098	12.0
Pittsburgh district	28,209	26,257	93.1	1,952	6.9
Great Lakes and Middle West district	24,585	22,942	93.3	1,643	6.7
Southern district	6,365	4,390	69.0	1,975	31.0

Source: Bureau of Labor Statistics.

1. Includes 607 Mexicans.
2. Includes 54 Mexicans.
3. Includes 277 Mexicans.
4. Includes 276 Mexicans.

Tables 10 and 11 present interesting comparisons for March 1935 and April 1938 in terms of Negro employment by division of the industry and region. Several observations are significant from these statistics: (1) in the three major branches of the industry, Negroes have been more heavily concentrated at blast furnaces than in rolling mills or steel works. In the 1935 survey, 15.6 percent of all workers at blast furnaces were Negro compared to 20.8 percent in 1938. During the same periods, the percentage of Negroes in steel works remained at about 8.7 whereas in rolling mills the percentage dropped from 9.8 to 8.8; (2) on a regional basis, Negro representation has varied widely. In both 1935 and 1938, the highest percentage of Negroes in the industry was found in the South with the lowest percentage found in the West and Great Lakes and Middle West districts. The significant increase in Negro employment in the Great Lakes and Middle West district since this time is discussed in later sections of this study. In the 1935 survey, Negroes represented 30.7 percent of all wage earners in the iron and steel industry in the South, and in the 1938 survey Negroes represented 44.7 percent of all male workers

TABLE 11. *Iron and Steel Industry Distribution of Male Workers by Branch of Industry, Region, and Race, April 1938*

Branch of Industry and Region	All Workers			Percentage Distribution		
	Total	Whites[1]	Negroes	Total	Whites[1]	Negroes
All branches	80,711	72,909	7,802	100.0	90.3	9.7
North	73,819	67,972	5,847	100.0	92.1	7.9
West	2,632	2,580	52	100.0	98.0	2.0
South	4,260	2,357	1,903	100.0	55.3	44.7
Blast furnaces	5,996	4,747	1,249	100.0	79.2	20.8
Steel works	11,457	10,464	993	100.0	91.3	8.7
Rolling mills	63,258	57,698	5,560	100.0	91.2	8.8
North	58,720	54,486	4,234	100.0	92.8	7.2
West	1,599	1,588	11	100.0	99.3	0.7
South	2,939	1,624	1,315	100.0	55.3	44.7

Source: Bureau of Labor Statistics.
1. Includes 944 Mexicans.

in the industry in the South. In contrast the Negro in the Great Lakes and Middle West district constituted 6.5 percent of all wage earners in the industry in 1935 and in 1938 Negroes constituted 2.0 percent of all male workers in the industry in the West.

It is not surprising that the Negro was highly represented in the blast furnace area of the industry. This part of the industry contains a great deal of the hot, dirty, heavy work that Negroes were thought to be eminently qualified to perform. In some respects, this provided opportunities for Negroes to move up into skilled positions. For example, Negro bricklayers were used in the building and repair of blast furnaces.

In the two periods covered, average hourly earnings for Negroes were substantially less than those for white workers. In the 1935 study, earnings for all males were 68.1 cents, whereas for whites alone, the average was 69.5 cents and Negroes it was 54.6 cents. In contrast, the 1938 survey revealed that male workers earned an average of 84.1 cents, while the earnings of male whites was 85.7 cents, and those of male Negroes were 68.7 cents. There did not seem to be any wage discrimination between Negro and white workers in the same occupation. The difference in average hourly earnings reflects restricted occupational opportunities for Negroes in the industry. Negroes were found in the less skilled and lower-paid occupations as shown later. It is interesting to note that regardless of the alleged restriction of Negroes in some occupations the Bureau found that "the presence of some Negroes in the highly skilled occupations is important as indicating opportunity for advancement out of the ranks of the unskilled wage earners."[24] This observation can be evaluated against the record now available and analyzed for the 1960's in later sections of this study.

SKILL DISTRIBUTION

Tables 12 and 13 provide data on the distribution of male workers and wage earners in the iron and steel industry by division, skill, and race for March 1935 and April 1938. The skill distribution in the industry reveals the basic cause for lower earnings for Negroes compared to white employees.

In March 1935, Negroes as a percent of total wage earners in the skilled, semiskilled, and unskilled classifications were 4.5 percent, 8.8

24. *Ibid.*, p. 564.

percent, and 18.6 percent, respectively. In April 1938, Negroes as a percent of total workers in each skill group were 3.6 percent, 9.2 percent, and 18.5 percent, respectively. A comparison of these statistics and the skill composition of each racial group reveals that Negroes have been heavily concentrated in the unskilled occupations with relatively little representation in the skilled areas. Writing in 1944, Professor Northrup indicates that "Probably there is only one other skilled category in American manufacturing industry [iron molding] where Negroes have been able to secure a percentage of the work any-

TABLE 12. *Iron and Steel Industry Distribution of Wage Earners by Division of Industry, Skill, and Race, March 1935*

Division of Industry and Skill Class	Total Wage Earners		Whites			Negroes		
	Number	Percent	Number	Percent	Percent of total wage earners in class	Number	Percent	Percent of total wage earners in class
All divisions	83,951	100.0	74,969	100.0	89.3	8,982	100.0	10.7
Skilled	29,941	35.7	28,595	38.1	95.5	1,346	15.0	4.5
Semiskilled	24,504	29.2	22,354	29.8	91.2	2,150	23.9	8.8
Unskilled	29,506	35.1	24,020	32.1	81.4	5,486	61.1	18.6
Blast furnaces	6,180	100.0	5,149	100.0	83.3	1,031	100.0	16.7
Skilled	1,700	27.5	1,608	31.2	94.6	92	8.9	5.4
Semiskilled	1,928	31.2	1,724	33.5	89.4	204	19.8	10.6
Unskilled	2,552	41.3	1,817	35.3	71.2	735	71.3	28.8
Steel works	14,418	100.0	13,077	100.0	90.7	1,341	100.0	9.3
Skilled	5,995	41.6	5,858	44.8	97.7	137	10.2	2.3
Semiskilled	2,867	19.9	2,548	19.5	88.9	319	23.8	11.1
Unskilled	5,556	38.5	4,671	35.7	84.1	885	66.0	15.9
Rolling mills	63,353	100.0	56,743	100.0	89.6	6.610	100.0	10.4
Skilled	22,246	35.1	21,129	37.2	95.0	1,117	16.9	5.0
Semiskilled	19,709	31.1	18,082	31.9	91.7	1,627	24.6	8.3
Unskilled	21,398	33.8	17,532	30.9	81.9	3,866	58.5	18.1

Source: Bureau of Labor Statistics.

TABLE 13. *Iron and Steel Industry, Distribution of Male Workers by Branch of Industry, Skill, and Race, April 1938*

Branch of Industry and Skill Group	All Workers		Whites[1]			Negroes		
	Number	Percent	Number	Percent	Percent of total workers in group	Number	Percent	Percent of total workers in group
All branches	80,711	100.0	72,909	100.0	90.3	7,802	100.0	9.7
Skilled	27,320	33.8	26,345	36.1	96.4	975	12.5	3.6
Semiskilled	32,594	40.4	29,609	40.6	90.8	2,985	38.3	9.2
Unskilled	20,797	25.8	16,955	23.3	81.5	3,842	49.2	18.5
Blast furnaces	5,996	100.0	4,747	100.0	79.2	1,249	100.0	20.8
Skilled	2,045	34.1	1,907	40.1	93.3	138	11.0	6.7
Semiskilled	2,403	40.1	1,854	39.1	77.2	549	44.0	22.8
Unskilled	1,548	25.8	986	20.8	63.7	562	45.0	36.3
Steel works	11,457	100.0	10,464	100.0	91.3	993	100.0	8.7
Skilled	4,667	40.7	4,552	43.5	97.5	115	11.6	2.5
Semiskilled	3,368	29.4	3,070	29.3	91.2	298	30.0	8.8
Unskilled	3,422	29.9	2,842	27.2	83.1	580	58.4	16.9
Rolling mills	63,258	100.0	57,698	100.0	91.2	5,560	100.0	8.8
Skilled	20,608	32.6	19,886	34.4	96.5	722	13.0	3.5
Semiskilled	26,823	42.4	24,685	42.8	92.0	2,138	38.5	8.0
Unskilled	15,827	25.0	13,127	22.8	82.9	2,700	48.5	17.1

Source: Bureau of Labor Statistics.

1. Includes 944 Mexicans.

where near to their normal proportion of jobs—that is, the proportion which all Negroes comprise of all workers in the industry."[25] About two-thirds of the Negroes (61.1 percent) in contrast to less than one-third (32.1 percent) of the whites were found in unskilled occupations in March 1935. In April 1938, 49.2 percent of the Negroes and 23.3 percent of the whites were in the unskilled class. On the other hand, in March 1935, 15.0 percent of the Negroes and 38.1 percent of the whites were in skilled occupations whereas in April 1938, 12.5 percent of the Negroes and 36.1 percent of the whites were in the skilled

25. Herbert R. Northrup, *Organized Labor and the Negro* (New York: Harper and Brothers, 1944), p. 176.

group. For both time periods, and for both Negroes and whites, the representation in semiskilled occupations was relatively the same.

In the specific branches of the industry, the relative position of Negroes was better at blast furnaces than in steel works or in rolling mills in both March 1935 and April 1938. Negroes accounted for a major part of the unskilled workers in each branch of the industry and, in the skilled class, Negroes were poorly represented. The Bureau reported that for April 1938 the skill make-up of the Negro group for the whole industry was almost the same in both the North and the South: Approximately one-eighth of the Negroes were skilled, two-fifths were semiskilled, and one-half were unskilled. A comparison of the Negro and white ratios shows the less favorable position of Negroes in the industry. White workers accounted for about two-fifths of the skilled and semiskilled and one-fourth of the unskilled group in the North; in the South, whites accounted for over two-fifths of the skilled and semiskilled groups and over one-tenth of the unskilled group. The above emphasizes the fact that Negroes have been confined to the unskilled positions in the industry even though there has been some representation in the skilled jobs.

OCCUPATIONAL DISTRIBUTION

An examination of the occupational distribution of Negroes in the industry, as shown in Table 14, provides additional evidence of the opportunities for Negroes in skilled and semiskilled jobs. In both time periods, Negro representation in the important crafts was practically nonexistent. Discrimination and lack of qualifications probably explain this situation, but it is difficult to determine the relative importance of each in the 1930's. It is fairly clear, however, that employers did favor white employees for certain positions, and Negroes were assigned generally to laborer jobs.

In both of the Bureau studies, there were no Negroes among the carpenters and roll turners, and out of a total of approximately 1,200 machinists, there was only one Negro. In highly skilled crafts such as blacksmiths, boilermakers, bricklayers, and millwrights, the percentage of Negroes varied from 0.3 for bricklayers to 5.5 for boilermakers (there were no boilermakers in 1938). The only crafts that included a significant percentage of Negroes in either period were welders, boilermakers in 1935, and riggers. Even though Negroes held a limited

TABLE 14. *Iron and Steel Industry, Distribution of Workers in Selected Occupations by Race, March 1935 and April 1938*

Occupation	March 1935					April 1938				
	Total Wage Earners	Whites		Negroes		All workers	Whites		Negroes	
		Number	Per cent	Number	Per cent		Number	Per cent	Number	Per cent
Blacksmiths	194	192[1]	99.0	2	1.0	198	194	98.0	4	2.0
Blacksmiths' helpers	149	143[2]	96.0	6	4.0	143	130	90.9	13	9.1
Boilermakers	73	69	94.5	4	5.5	96	96	100.0	—	—
Bricklayers	550	541[3]	98.4	9	1.6	302	301	99.7	1	0.3
Bricklayers' helpers	286	221[4]	77.3	65	22.7	172	141	82.0	31	18.0
Carpenters	227	227	100.0	—	—	192	192	100.0	—	—
Clerical, plant	n.a.	n.a.	n.a.	n.a.	n.a.	2,611	2,599	99.5	12	0.5
Cranemen, misc.	3,121	3,026[1]	97.0	95	3.0	3,279	3,190	97.3	89	2.7
Crane followers	1,656	1,479[4]	89.3	177	10.7	1,801	1,627	90.3	174	9.7
Electricians	698	695	99.6	3	0.4	918	916	99.8	2	0.2
Electricians' helpers	135	135	100.0	—	—	140	138	98.6	2	1.4
Engineers, locomotive	538	504	93.7	34	6.3	447	421	94.2	26	5.8
Engineers, power	176	176	100.0	—	—	250	249	99.6	1	0.4
Firemen, locomotive	102	93	91.2	9	8.8	62	59	95.2	3	4.8
Inspectors and repairmen, motors	582	577	99.1	5	0.9	607	607	100.0	—	—

Machinists	1,195	1,194	99.9	1	0.1	1,256	1,255	99.9	1	0.1
Machinists' helpers	253	248	98.0	5	2.0	292	281	96.2	11	3.8
Millwrights	1,175	1,159[2]	98.6	16	1.4	1,333	1,323	99.2	10	0.8
Millwrights' helpers	709	668[1]	94.2	41	5.8	518	514	99.2	4	0.8
Pipe fitters	500	494	98.8	6	1.2	543	535	98.5	8	1.5
Pipe fitters' helpers	207	200	96.6	7	3.4	160	145	90.6	15	9.4
Pumpers	142	139[2]	97.9	3	2.1	153	152	99.3	1	0.7
Riggers	224	218	97.3	6	2.7	235	221	94.0	14	6.0
Roll turners	330	330	100.0	—	—	462	462	100.0	—	—
Welders	446	426	95.5	20	4.5	409	392	95.8	17	4.2

Source: Bureau of Labor Statistics.

1. Includes 2 Mexicans.
2. Includes 1 Mexican.
3. Includes 3 Mexicans.
4. Includes 7 Mexicans.

number of craft jobs, they were well represented compared to other industries in the 1930's.

The helper occupations, which provide an opportunity to learn a skilled job, contained a moderate number of Negroes in either March 1935 or April 1938; however, the bricklayers' helpers was an exception with 22.7 percent Negro in 1935 and 18.0 percent Negro in 1938. There were no Negro electricians' helpers in 1935 and only 2 (1.4 percent) in 1938. In the other helper occupations, there were 41 millwrights' helpers (5.8 percent) in 1935 and 4 (0.8 percent) in 1938; 7 pipe fitters' helpers (3.4 percent) in 1935 and 15 (9.4 percent) in 1938; and 6 (4.0 percent) blacksmiths' helpers in 1935 and 13 (9.1 percent) in 1938.

TABLE 15. *Iron and Steel Industry Distribution of Common Laborers by Division of Industry, District, and Race, March 1935*

Division and District	Total Common Laborers	Whites		Negroes	
		Number	Percent	Number	Percent
All divisions	6,113	4,918[1]	80.5	1,195	19.5
Eastern district	867	588[2]	67.8	279	32.2
Pittsburgh district	2,478	2,205	89.0	273	11.0
Great Lakes and Middle West district	2,137	1,948[3]	91.2	189	8.8
Southern district	631	177	28.1	454	71.9
Blast furnaces	546	386[4]	70.7	160	29.3
Steel works	1,638	1,323	80.8	315	19.2
Rolling mills	3,929	3,209	81.7	720	18.3
Eastern district	701	465	66.3	236	33.7
Pittsburgh district	1,510	1,381	91.5	129	8.5
Great Lakes and Middle West district	1,398	1,250[5]	89.4	148	10.6
Southern district	320	113	35.3	207	64.7

Source: Bureau of Labor Statistics.

1. Includes 193 Mexicans.
2. Includes 3 Mexicans.
3. Includes 190 Mexicans.
4. Includes 9 Mexicans.
5. Includes 57 Mexicans.

TABLE 16. *Iron and Steel Industry Distribution of Common Laborers by Branch of Industry, Region, and Race, April 1938*

Branch and Region	Total Common Laborers	Whites		Negroes	
		Number	Percent	Number	Percent
All branches	4,517	3,628	80.3	889	19.7
North	4,043	3,461	85.6	582	14.4
West	95	93	97.9	2	2.1
South	379	74	19.5	305	80.5
Blast furnaces	584	367	62.8	217	37.2
Steel works	911	766	84.1	145	15.9
Rolling mills	3,022	2,495	82.6	527	17.4
North	2,793	2,414	86.4	379	13.6
West	43	42	97.7	1	2.3
South	186	39	21.0	147	79.0

Source: Bureau of Labor Statistics.

The common laborer situation has been quite different for the Negro than that of the skilled or semiskilled position. In the two wage surveys of 1935 and 1938, the Bureau found Negroes accounted for 19.5 and 19.7 percent of total common laborers in the sample for the two periods respectively. Tables 15 and 16 show that Negroes made up about one-third of the common laborers at blast furnaces and slightly less than one-fifth of the common laborers in steel works and rolling mills for the time periods covered. Indeed, in the April 1938 survey, it was found that Negroes accounted for 80.5 percent of all common laborers in the industry in the South and 14.4 percent of the same occupations in the North. These statistics indicate that differences in average hourly earnings between Negroes and whites in the industry are due primarily to limited occupational opportunities and not to wage discrimination.

The limited number of Negroes in the skilled or craft areas reflects a union, as well as a management, problem in restricting job and advancement opportunities. Craft unions, and to some extent industrial unions, have discriminated against Negroes who wished to gain entry into particular occupations. Apprentice programs have been barred to Negroes in some instances under joint union-management control. In the South, management decisions to adopt the morés of the community led to employment and upgrading practices that confined the Negro to the common laborer occupations. The Negro generally has played an important role in the development of the iron and steel industry, but his participation has been in the lower-paying job categories. Discrimination against the Negro has occurred usually after employment through barriers to advancement.

In concluding some observations on the decade of the 1930's and preparing to examine the period 1940-1960 in the next chapter, one can gain insight from the following excerpt from an early study of the Negro in iron and steel:

> . . . the decrease in the proportion of Negro steel workers during the thirties seems to have been the result primarily of employer personnel policies which were adopted at a time when unionism was at most only a future threat to unrestricted management control. After a comprehensive study of labor conditions in the industry during the NRA period, Professor C. R. Daugherty stated that there was "general agreement that Negro workers had been laid off in disproportionate numbers. . . ." This was partly the consequence of the fact that Negroes are concentrated in the least skilled, and hence, least indispensable jobs, and partly of favoritism of white workers in layoffs.[26]

The speculation that "there has been some increase in the proportion of Negroes in iron and steel production since this country entered the war" was borne out in the 1950 Census which is discussed in the following chapter.

---

26. *Ibid.*, pp. 174-175.

CHAPTER IV.

Negro Employment, 1940-1960

This chapter is concerned with Negro employment in the primary iron and steel industry during the period 1940-1960. The basic data sources are the censuses for 1940, 1950, and 1960. Particular emphasis is placed on the following areas: total employed persons by race and sex, employment in selected states and standard metropolitan statistical areas by race and sex, and total employed persons by occupation, race, and sex. A review of this early employment experience provides a background for analyzing the current period in a later chapter.

THE NATIONAL SCENE, 1940-1960

World War II had a decided impact on employment in almost all industries in the United States, and the iron and steel industry was influenced considerably. The ground lost by Negroes in the decade of the 1930's was regained in the 1940's as the industry turned to any available labor supply. Negro employment in the war industry categories, such as metals, chemicals, and rubber, almost tripled during the war years. The shift of Negroes from the farm to the factory in this period was dramatic with the proportion of the employed male Negro labor force on farms declining from 47 percent in April 1940 to 28 percent in April 1944. In addition, the number of Negro men employed as skilled craftsmen, foremen, and operatives doubled.

The Department of Labor saw the following prospects for Negro employment in the postwar period:

> (1) the Negro has made his greatest employment gains in those occupations (especially semiskilled factory jobs) which will suffer the severest cutbacks during the post-war period, (2) further, he has made his biggest advances in those industries (especially the "metals, chemicals, and rubber" group) which will experience the greatest post-war declines.[27]

27. U. S. Bureau of Labor Statistics, "War and Postwar Trends in the Employment of Negroes," *Monthly Labor Review,* Vol. 60, No. 1, January 1945, pp. 1-5.

TABLE 17. *Primary Iron and Steel Industry*
Total Employed Persons by Race and Sex
1940 – 1960

Year	All Employees: Total	All Employees: Nonwhite Total[c]	All Employees: Nonwhite Negro	All Employees: Percent Negro	Male: Total	Male: Nonwhite Total	Male: Nonwhite Negro	Male: Percent Negro	Female: Total	Female: Nonwhite Total	Female: Nonwhite Negro	Female: Percent Negro
Blast Furnaces, Steel Works, and Rolling and Finishing Mills[a]												
1940	543,319	35,982	35,856	6.6	524,917	35,728	35,602	6.8	18,402	254	254	1.4
1950	660,180	72,450	72,390	11.0	624,720	70,620	70,560	11.3	35,460	1,830	1,830	5.2
1960	620,394	69,865	69,312	11.2	589,246	68,935	68,464	11.6	31,148	930	848	2.7
Total Basic Iron and Steel[b]												
1940	1,263,215	69,737	69,453	5.5	1,169,623	68,968	68,690	5.9	93,592	769	763	0.8
1950	950,741	121,004	120,444	12.7	897,793	118,533	117,998	13.1	52,948	2,471	2,446	4.6
1960	918,535	117,469	116,482	12.7	869,421	115,784	114,921	13.2	49,114	1,685	1,561	3.2

Source: *U. S. Census of Population:*
1940: Vol. III, *The Labor Force,* Part 1, Table 76.
1950: PE No. 1D, *Industrial Characteristics,* Table 2.
Vol. II, *Characteristics of the Population,* Table 133.
1960: PC (2) 7F, *Industrial Characteristics,* Table 3.

a. SIC, 3312; Census, 237
b. SIC, 331; Census, 237, 238.
c. Includes 99 percent Negro for each year.

It was noted further that the Negro was generally the last to be hired, and therefore faced the possibility of being the first laid off, in those industries where he had made the most gains. These predictions were not completely accurate for the steel industry. Certain employment adjustments did occur in the iron and steel industry after the war, but the Negroes' advances in large measure were carried over into the decade of the 1950's.

Table 17 presents data on total employed persons by race and sex for the blast furnaces, steel works, and rolling and finishing mills and total iron and steel industries. The increase in Negro employment, in both absolute and relative terms, between 1940 and 1950 is striking. Overall employment in blast furnaces, steel works, and rolling and finishing mills advanced by 116,861 of which 36,534 or 31.3 percent was Negro. Negroes as a percent of all employees increased from 6.6 to 11.0 during 1940-1950. Examination of the statistics for the total basic iron and steel industry reflects the same trend. Apparently much of the improvement in Negro employment experienced during World War II was able to be maintained into 1950.

A comparison of the data for 1950 and 1960 reveals a decline in employment in the blast furnaces, steel works, and rolling and finishing mills industry of 39,786 of which 3,078 were Negroes. Even though there was a decline in the number of Negroes, their relative position remained almost the same as that of 1950. In 1960, 11.2 percent of all employees was Negro compared to 11.0 percent in 1950. The decade of the 1950's brought unsettling activities such as the Korean conflict, a recession in 1957-1958, and the 116-day steel strike in 1959. In addition to these events, the industry began to give serious consideration around 1955 to major technological changes such as the basic oxygen furnace developed in 1952 at Linz and Donawitz in Austria.[28] The varied foregoing circumstances weighed heavily on the employment scene; however, on balance the Negro was able to hold a position established by 1950.

NEGRO EMPLOYMENT IN SELECTED STATES, 1940-1960

Chapter 2 indicates that steel is produced in some 37 states but about 75 percent of all steel is produced in seven states. Table 18

28. *Business Week,* Special Report, "The World Steel Race," no date, circa 1965.

TABLE 18. *Primary Iron and Steel Industry*
Employment for Selected States by Sex and Race, 1940-1960

State	Year	All Employees			Male			Female		
		Total	Negro	Percent Negro	Total	Negro	Percent Negro	Total	Negro	Percent Negro
Alabama	1940	34,406	12,978	37.7	33,519	12,881	38.4	887	97	10.9
	1950	42,268	15,442	36.5	40,658	15,296	37.6	1,610	146	9.1
	1960	40,734	12,468	30.6	39,295	12,343	31.4	1,439	125	8.7
California	1940	34,442	324	0.9	32,264	319	1.0	2,178	5	0.2
	1950	27,736	2,466	8.9	25,957	2,416	9.3	1,779	50	2.8
	1960	33,391	2,541	7.6	30,822	2,493	8.1	2,569	48	1.9
Colorado	1940	6,934	123	1.8	6,745	123	1.8	189	—	—
	1950	8,681	230	2.6	8,261	224	2.7	420	6	1.4
	1960	9,149	249	2.7	8,709	249	2.9	440	—	—
Connecticut	1940	50,115	497	1.0	40,064	487	1.2	10,051	10	0.1
	1950	8,691	706	8.1	7,794	697	8.9	897	9	1.0
	1960	7,367	677	9.2	6,579	677	10.3	788	—	—
Illinois	1940	136,362	5,009	3.7	122,467	4,844	4.0	13,895	165	1.2
	1950	86,600	14,063	16.2	80,351	13,639	17.0	6,249	424	6.8
	1960	73,604	11,561	15.7	68,749	11,345	16.5	4,855	216	4.4
Indiana	1940	72,223	5,653	7.8	68,948	5,575	8.1	3,275	78	2.4
	1950	69,502	11,289	16.2	65,199	10,937	16.8	4,303	352	8.2
	1960	74,864	11,995	16.0	70,535	11,802	16.7	4,329	193	4.5
Kentucky	1940	11,838	829	7.0	11,008	821	7.5	830	8	1.0
	1950	6,270	427	6.8	6,018	423	7.0	252	4	1.6
	1960	8,172	218	2.7	7,893	215	2.7	279	3	1.1

Maryland	1940	34,273	5,575	16.3	31,801	5,501	17.3	2,472	74	3.0
	1950	29,533	8,131	27.5	28,304	8,029	28.4	1,229	102	8.3
	1960	35,785	9,827	27.5	34,236	9,732	28.4	1,549	95	6.1
Massachusetts	1940	41,770	148	0.4	37,274	144	0.4	4,496	4	0.1
	1950	14,402	257	1.8	13,247	253	1.9	1,155	4	0.3
	1960	9,901	305	3.1	9,114	301	3.3	787	4	0.5
Michigan	1940	63,086	2,638	4.2	56,325	2,618	4.6	6,761	20	0.3
	1950	47,173	8,448	17.9	44,199	8,209	18.6	2,974	239	8.0
	1960	51,912	9,601	18.5	48,900	9,392	19.2	3,012	209	6.9
Minnesota	1940	9,644	17	0.2	8,624	17	0.2	1,020	—	—
	1950	6,614	80	1.2	6,318	78	1.2	296	2	0.7
	1960	4,749	25	0.5	4,532	25	0.6	217	—	—
Missouri	1940	20,349	1,832	9.0	18,905	1,820	9.6	1,444	12	0.8
	1950	13,433	3,058	22.8	12,589	3,020	24.0	844	38	4.5
	1960	10,182	2,238	22.0	9,616	2,227	23.2	566	11	1.9
New Jersey	1940	43,392	1,739	4.0	38,702	1,722	4.4	4,690	17	0.4
	1950	20,383	2,513	12.3	18,728	2,453	13.1	1,655	60	3.6
	1960	16,818	2,567	15.3	15,612	2,529	16.2	1,206	38	3.2
New York	1940	85,811	2,131	2.5	78,241	2,096	2.7	7,570	35	0.5
	1950	52,106	5,339	10.2	49,170	5,156	10.5	2,936	183	6.2
	1960	50,401	5,935	11.8	47,459	5,822	12.3	2,942	113	3.8
Ohio	1940	205,517	9,884	4.8	193,501	9,822	5.1	12,016	62	0.5
	1950	167,863	20,535	12.2	159,153	20,149	12.7	8,710	386	4.4
	1960	154,941	18,967	12.2	147,093	18,724	12.7	7,848	243	3.1
Oklahoma	1940	2,750	63	2.3	2,651	63	2.4	99	—	—
	1950	2,266	151	6.7	2,133	148	6.9	133	3	2.3
	1960	1,784	194	10.9	1,652	194	11.7	132	—	—

TABLE 18. *Primary Iron and Steel Industry*
Employment for Selected States by Sex and Race, 1940-1960
(*Continued*)

State	Year	All Employees Total	All Employees Negro	All Employees Percent Negro	Male Total	Male Negro	Male Percent Negro	Female Total	Female Negro	Female Percent Negro
Pennsylvania	1940	274,829	9,911	3.6	262,385	9,855	3.8	12,444	56	0.5
	1950	257,880	15,595	6.0	245,325	15,349	6.3	12,555	246	2.0
	1960	238,647	14,601	6.1	226,298	14,460	6.4	12,349	141	1.1
Texas	1940	8,465	1,069	12.6	7,934	1,057	13.3	531	12	2.3
	1950	10,771	2,657	24.7	10,259	2,626	25.6	512	31	6.1
	1960	17,160	4,313	25.1	16,494	4,291	26.0	666	22	3.3
Utah	1940	1,149	1	0.1	1,100	1	0.1	49	—	—
	1950	5,475	9	0.2	5,259	8	0.2	216	1	0.5
	1960	6,876	—	—	6,592	—	—	284	—	—
Washington	1940	5,120	30	0.6	4,842	29	0.6	278	1	0.4
	1950	3,525	158	4.5	3,348	158	4.7	177	—	—
	1960	3,418	230	6.7	3,291	227	6.9	127	3	2.4
West Virginia	1940	18,644	361	1.9	17,000	360	2.1	1,644	1	0.1
	1950	17,452	397	2.3	16,432	389	2.4	1,020	8	0.8
	1960	17,078	358	2.1	16,277	335	2.1	801	23	2.9
Wisconsin	1940	30,085	274	0.9	27,779	273	1.0	2,306	1	*
	1950	18,376	1,417	7.7	17,133	1,368	8.0	1,243	49	3.9
	1960	19,424	1,781	9.2	17,966	1,757	9.8	1,458	24	1.6

Source: *U. S. Census of Population:*
1940, Vol. III, *The Labor Force,* State volumes, Table 18.
1950, Vol. II, *Characteristics of the Population,* State volumes, Table 83.
1960, PC (1) D, *Detailed Characteristics,* State volumes, Table 129.

* Less than 0.05 percent.

shows the total employed persons in 22 states by sex and race in the primary iron and steel industry for 1940, 1950, and 1960.

Pennsylvania and Ohio have been the most important states, in terms of employment, in the industry even though the actual number of employees in each state declined over the period 1940-1960. Negroes as a percent of all employees increased considerably in both states between 1940 and 1950; however, the percentage Negro remained almost exactly the same in 1950 and 1960.

Indiana, Illinois, Michigan, and New York have continued to be important steel producing states with each employing over 50,000 iron and steel employees between 1940 and 1960. Alabama, California, and Maryland also have been major steel areas with about 30,000-40,000 employees each. Negro employment has been significant in each of the states named above with the largest relative gains occurring between 1940 and 1950 and very little change in the relative position of Negroes between 1950 and 1960. The following figures are illustrative of the relative changes in Negro employment in the principal steel producing states between these years:

	Percent Negro			Change	
State	1940	1950	1960	1940-1950	1950-1960
Alabama	37.7	36.5	30.6	− 1.2	− 5.9
California	0.9	8.9	7.6	+ 8.0	− 1.3
Illinois	3.7	16.2	15.7	+12.5	− 0.5
Indiana	7.8	16.2	16.0	+ 8.4	− 0.2
Maryland	16.3	27.5	27.5	+11.2	0.0
Michigan	4.2	17.9	18.5	+13.7	+ 0.6
New York	2.5	10.2	11.8	+ 7.7	+ 1.6
Ohio	4.8	12.2	12.2	+ 7.4	0.0
Pennsylvania	3.6	6.0	6.1	+ 2.4	+ 0.1

An examination of the state data indicates that, on a percentage basis, Alabama and Maryland have been the most prominent in the employment of Negroes in the iron and steel industry. The reason for this can be explained in part by the heavy concentration of Negroes in and around such cities as Birmingham (Fairfield operations of U.S. Steel), Gadsden, Alabama (Republic Steel), and Baltimore (Sparrows Point plant of Bethlehem Steel). Employers have had a large body of Negro labor to draw upon in these areas, and there has been little reluctance to hire Negroes for the basic unskilled jobs in the industry.

In absolute terms, Pennsylvania and Ohio have been the leading states in the employment of Negroes in the United States.

Table 18 reveals that Negro females have never been a substantial part of the iron and steel employment picture, and the same would be true for white women. Negro women constituted 125 of 1,439 total females (8.7 percent) in 1960 in Alabama and 141 of 12,349 (1.1 percent) in Pennsylvania in the same year. Female labor in the steel plants has been looked upon with disfavor by employers and unions except in emergency situations when there was a scarcity of males in the labor market. One employer explained in an interview that "since World War II, we have tried to rid our plants of female labor."[29] Apparently, it is difficult and expensive to provide personal services for females working in steel plants and, as a rule, they do not make good union members. Production hazards in steel producing may also discourage employers from using women workers, and certain state laws are restrictive.

NEGRO EMPLOYMENT IN SELECTED SMSA'S, 1950-1960

Negro employment in the basic iron and steel industry has varied according to standard metropolitan statistical area. Table 19 presents industry racial data for selected SMSA's for 1950 and 1960.

In the areas selected, the number of Negroes in iron and steel reached a high of 20,197 in Chicago in 1950 and 19,181 in 1960 (a combination of Chicago and Gary-Hammond-East Chicago areas); on the other extreme, Negroes accounted for a low of 158 in 1950 and 168 in 1960 in the Allentown-Bethlehem-Easton area. This comparison is made only to indicate the low and high points in Table 19. The two SMSA'S, quite obviously, are not strictly comparable for analytical purposes.

The data indicate that, in terms of total employment in the area, the following were the four most important iron and steel centers in 1960: Pittsburgh, Chicago-Gary-Hammond-East Chicago, Youngstown-Warren, and Baltimore. In absolute terms, however, the four most important areas in 1960 for Negro employment in the industry were: Chicago, Baltimore, Birmingham, and Pittsburgh. On a percentage basis, Negroes were well represented in the following areas: Birmingham, Baltimore, St. Louis, and Cleveland. Of course, the data in Table

29. Personal Interviews, 1967.

19 do not reflect the skill and/or occupational distribution of Negroes in the various areas selected.

Even though Negroes may have been employed in larger numbers in areas such as Birmingham and Baltimore, their skill distribution may be quite different than in areas with fewer Negroes employed such as Youngstown-Warren or Buffalo. In the past, entrance into the industry in an area like Birmingham was relatively easy for Negroes who generally were not tested and with whom there was an implicit (if not explicit) understanding that they would remain on unskilled or less desirable jobs and separate line-of-progression ladders. Changes have occurred since President Kennedy's Executive Order 10925 in 1961 to integrate steel plants in the South, and one might expect to find fewer Negroes in the industry in the 1970 census as a result of employment standards being used with all applicants. On the other hand, one may expect to see more upgrading of Negroes who have been hired than at any time in the past. The sacrifice of some jobs for better jobs in the future may be a harsh fact of reality.

Between 1950 and 1960 changes have occurred in the SMSA's with increases and decreases in employment. The following denotes the changes as shown in Table 19 for 1950-1960 in the industry:

Increases in Total and Negro Employment	*Decreases in Total and Negro Employment*	*Percentage Increase in Negro Employment*	*Percentage Decrease in Negro Employment*
Baltimore	Birmingham	Allentown-Bethlehem-Easton	Birmingham
Buffalo	Chicago	Baltimore	Cleveland
Los Angeles-Long Beach	Cleveland	Buffalo	St. Louis
Philadelphia	Pittsburgh	Chicago	San Francisco-Oakland
	St. Louis	Los Angeles-Long Beach	
	San Francisco-Oakland	Philadelphia	
	Youngstown-Warren	Pittsburgh	
		Youngstown-Warren	

It is interesting to note that between 1950 and 1960 actual Negro and total employment declined in the Chicago, Pittsburgh, and Youngstown-Warren areas, but Negroes as a percentage of employment in iron and steel increased for these large steel producing centers. Declines were registered for Negroes, both in absolute and relative

TABLE 19. *Primary Iron and Steel Industry*
Employment for Selected Standard Metropolitan Statistical Areas by Sex and Race, 1950 and 1960

Standard Metropolitan Statistical Area	Year	All Employees			Male			Female			Percent Negro in SMSA	Percent Negro Employed All Ind. SMSA
		Total	Negro	Percent Negro	Total	Negro	Percent Negro	Total	Negro	Percent Negro		
Allentown-Bethehem-Easton												
	1950	21,405	158	0.7	20,104	156	0.8	1,301	2	0.2	0.6	0.5
	1960	21,060	168	0.8	19,373	159	0.8	1,687	9	0.5	0.8	0.7
Baltimore												
	1950	28,959	8,069	27.9	27,757	7,968	28.7	1,202	101	8.4	19.8	19.4
	1960	35,028	9,800	28.0	33,492	9,705	29.0	1,536	95	6.2	21.9	20.0
Birmingham												
	1950	28,448	10,988	38.6	27,100	10,884	40.2	1,348	104	7.7	37.3	34.7
	1960	26,820	9,039	33.7	25,623	8,958	35.0	1,197	81	6.8	34.6	29.4
Buffalo												
	1950	30,762	3,800	12.4	29,517	3,703	12.5	1,245	97	7.8	4.1	3.6
	1960	32,033	4,511	14.1	30,751	4,446	14.5	1,282	65	5.1	6.3	5.1
Chicago												
	1950	115,809	20,197	17.4	107,485	19,556	18.2	8,324	641	7.7	10.7	9.6
	1960[a]	50,929	9,254	18.2	47,262	9,096	19.2	3,667	158	4.3	14.3	11.8
Cleveland												
	1950	31,957	6,546	20.5	29,549	6,423	21.7	2,408	123	5.1	10.4	9.6
	1960	29,434	5,862	19.9	27,185	5,792	21.3	2,249	70	3.1	14.3	12.6
Gary-Hammond-East Chicago												
	1960[a]	56,528	9,927	17.6	53,523	9,751	18.2	3,005	176	5.9	15.2	12.6
Los Angeles-Long Beach												
	1950	11,578	1,273	11.0	10,863	1,256	11.6	715	17	2.4	5.0	5.2
	1960	11,892	1,369	11.5	11,036	1,357	12.3	856	12	1.4	6.9	6.4

Philadelphia												
	1950	29,227	3,927	13.4	26,905	3,851	14.3	2,322	76	3.3	13.1	11.9
	1960	29,337	3,978	13.6	27,494	3,930	14.3	1,843	48	2.6	15.4	14.6
Pittsburgh												
	1950	141,536	9,239	6.5	134,494	9,104	6.8	7,042	135	1.9	6.2	5.3
	1960	123,651	8,231	6.7	116,620	8,162	7.0	7,031	69	1.0	6.7	5.7
St. Louis												
	1950	16,091	3,947	24.5	15,263	3,892	25.5	828	55	6.6	12.8	11.2
	1960	13,277	2,987	22.5	12,471	2,946	23.6	806	41	5.1	14.3	11.8
San Francisco-Oakland												
	1950	10,142	964	9.5	9,392	934	9.9	750	30	4.0	6.6	5.8
	1960	9,992	928	9.3	8,955	900	10.1	1,037	28	2.7	8.5	7.0
Steubenville-Weirton												
	1960[b]										4.3	N.A.
Wheeling-Steubenville												
	1960[b]	27,834	910	3.3	26,274	899	3.4	1,560	11	0.7	3.3	3.2
Wheeling												
	1960[b]										2.4	N.A.
Youngstown-Warren												
	1950	53,793	5,909	11.0	51,707	5,861	11.3	2,086	48	2.3	6.6	5.9
	1960	40,513	5,015	12.4	38,963	4,976	12.8	1,550	39	2.5	9.1	7.6

Source: *U. S. Census of Population:*
1950: Vol. II, *Characteristics of the Population,* State volumes, Tables 83, 34.
1960: PC (1) D, *Detailed Characteristics,* State volumes, Tables 129, 96.

a. Lake County deleted and added to Porter County in 1950 to form Gary-Hammond East Chicago area.

b. Jefferson County, Ohio and Brooke and Hancock Counties in W. Va. deleted in 1959; added to Weirton to form new area.

terms, in the Birmingham, Cleveland, St. Louis, and San Francisco-Oakland areas.

OCCUPATIONAL DISTRIBUTION, 1960

Table 20 shows an occupational distribution by color and sex for total employed persons in the primary iron and steel industry in 1960. Comparable census data giving occupation by color for the years 1940 and 1950 are not available. The statistics do not tell the whole story in regard to Negro utilization; however, some upgrading is evident.

In absolute terms, the Negro held more jobs in the operatives, semi-skilled, group (46,997) than in any other occupational category in 1960. On a relative basis, Negroes constituted a greater percentage (27.7 percent) of the laborers, unskilled, jobs. Most of the advances of the Negro have taken place within the blue collar areas designated as craftsmen and foremen, operatives, laborers, and service workers. In 1960, 114,796 of 117,469 jobs, including occupations not reported (97.7 percent), held by Negroes were in the blue collar areas. The white collar occupations, managers and officials, professional and technical workers, clerical and sales workers, had a Negro representation ranging from 0.3 percent in sales to 2.4 percent in clerical work. Negroes shared white collar jobs to a larger degree with white employees in the clerical occupations with 2,182 of 90,665 places, however, this amounted to scarcely no representation; for example, Negro females constituted only 120 of 32,783 clerical employees in 1960. In the sales area, there were 21 Negro males and no Negro females in a total of 7,464 sales workers.

The lack of Negroes in various occupations in 1960 can be explained in a number of ways. Discrimination based on race, lack of education and training, inadequate personnel policies, union seniority systems, and general trends in the economy apparently have all played a part in preventing Negroes from being hired into certain jobs. It is difficult to isolate only one factor as the controlling one in the employment of Negroes in the industry. Later analysis will explore in depth some of the causes of Negro exclusion or restriction in certain occupational categories.

POPULATION AND EMPLOYMENT RATIOS

The last two columns in Table 19 show the percent Negro in selected SMSA's and the percent Negro employed in all industries in the

TABLE 20. *Primary Iron and Steel Industry*
Total Employed Persons by Occupational Group, Sex, and Color, 1960

	All Employees			Male			Female		
Occupational Group	Total	Nonwhite[a]	Percent Nonwhite	Total	Nonwhite	Percent Nonwhite	Total	Nonwhite	Percent Nonwhite
Managers and officials	21,010	163	0.8	20,428	143	0.7	582	20	3.4
Professional and technical workers	46,035	307	0.7	43,793	287	0.7	2,242	20	0.9
Clerical workers	90,665	2,182	2.4	57,882	2,062	3.6	32,783	120	0.4
Sales workers	7,464	21	0.3	7,383	21	0.3	81	—	—
Craftsmen and foremen	290,495	20,299	7.0	288,835	20,098	7.0	1,660	201	12.1
Operatives	281,890	46,997	16.7	274,329	46,487	16.9	7,561	510	6.7
Laborers	146,132	40,546	27.7	144,890	40,204	27.7	1,242	342	27.5
Service workers	17,978	3,542	19.7	15,813	3,110	19.7	2,165	432	20.0
Occupation not reported	16,866	3,412	20.2	16,068	3,372	21.0	798	40	5.0
All Occupations	918,535	117,469	12.8	869,421	115,784	13.3	49,114	1,685	3.4

Source: *U. S. Census of Population,* 1960, PC (2) 7A, *Occupational Characteristics,* Table 36.

a. Nonwhite includes about 99 percent Negro and the analysis of the data treats Nonwhite and Negro as synonymous.

SMSA's. These figures must be used with caution, since they may be easily misinterpreted and misused. The difficulty arises when one tends to generalize on the percentages with what may appear to be a quota system in mind. There may be a tendency to use the percentages in the following ways:

(1) When the percent Negro in the SMSA is greater than the percent Negro in the industry, some may conclude that discrimination exists and that Negroes have been excluded on such grounds alone; therefore, more Negroes should be hired on this basis.

(2) When the percent Negro in the SMSA is less than the percent Negro in the industry, employers may be prompted to use it as an excuse not to do very much about the Negro employment problem.

(3) A consideration of the percentages alone may lead some to think in terms of a quota system which is undesirable as a means of solving equal employment opportunity problems.

Population and/or employment ratios may be useful from an analytical viewpoint, but they should be used with care. The differences between Negro representation in a SMSA and in an industry may be explained in a variety of ways and discrimination may or may not be a factor.

Apparently, the percentages referred to have been used as a means to measure the progress under an affirmative action program. It is too easy to assume that a rise in either the absolute figures or percentages means a significant or effective program for employing Negroes. It may or *may not* mean much. In searching for a way to measure progress, one should not be too quick to make quantitative comparisons and hastily conclude that employer A, who has increased Negro employment by x amount and by x percent over the years, is complying with all aspects of a nondiscriminatory employment program whereas employer B, who shows no increase (and perhaps a decrease) in the number and percent of Negroes employed, is discriminating or doing nothing to implement an affirmative action program. Statistics do not tell the whole story. The quality of the employer's effort to employ, train, and upgrade Negroes is of paramount importance to the Negroes' future opportunities in American industry.

CHAPTER V.

Negro Employment in the 1960 Period

The decade of the 1850's has been referred to as the "fitful fifties" in analyzing the development of the American labor movement. One hundred years later this same characterization could be made in regard to the civil rights movement. The 1954 Supreme Court decision prohibiting segregation in the public schools and the 1955-1956 Montgomery, Alabama bus boycott marked the real beginning of the Negro's demand for a "rightful place" in the economic, social, and political activities of the country. Just to have a *particular place* was no longer sufficient; the Negro now asked to be integrated on an equal basis into all phases of American life. The demonstrations, begun at the lunch counters in the 1950's, were carried to the front offices of business firms in the 1960's. After achieving an opportunity to enjoy services in public places, the Negro asked businessmen to provide jobs on a nondiscriminatory basis.[30]

Several important trends in the composition of the labor force caused concern by the civil rights movement in the late 1950 and early 1960 period. In general, these were: (1) the number of young people in the work force was increasing at a rapid rate with a rise of about 600,000 per year in workers under 25 years of age expected during 1960; (2) an increase in the number of older workers, persons over 45 years of age; (3) a larger number of women entering the labor force with more women than men added to the work force in the decade of 1950; and a shift from goods producing to service industries as a source of employment. Manufacturing jobs continue to be the most important source of employment opportunities, but their number is declining steadily. The shift from goods producing to service industries has resulted in a shift in job opportunities from blue collar

30. See August Meier, "Civil Rights Strategies for Negro Employment," in A. M. Ross and H. Hill, *Employment, Race, and Poverty* (New York: Harcourt, Brace and World, 1967), pp. 175-204.

to white collar occupations.[31] As these trends were developing, the general unemployment rate was above 5 percent for most of the period 1955-1966. Negro unemployment was even more distressing during this time, since it was typically twice the general unemployment rate.

The trends mentioned above caused unrest and frustration in the Negro community. Teenagers, who dropped out of school, were limited in their employment opportunities as a high school diploma became an absolute minimum for most jobs; older workers were displaced by technological change; blue collar jobs, which had offered employment to Negroes, were disappearing; and white collar positions were difficult for Negroes to obtain since historically the white collar world was a white man's world. Against this general background, a basic dilemma evolved: the Negro saw that traditional sources of employment were declining or gone and the growth areas in jobs were either closed or severely restricted to him. This meant, in simple terms, that the Negro's chance to earn a living was being curtailed significantly by forces outside his control. Hope was being abolished and therein lay the crux of the conflict between white and black. It has been observed by civil rights leaders that the Negro can sustain hardship and difficulties, but he cannot accept hopelessness. The existence of human nature causes one to reject this condition regardless of skin color.

Within the general setting described, the Negro in the basic steel industry has been met with additional employment and upgrading problems. The particular factors influencing the job situation in the industry over the past decade were: (1) declining employment in the years 1955-1968, (2) poor profit position of almost all companies in the industry, (3) large advances in technology resulting in adjustments in the work force and some displacement, and (4) significant imports of foreign steel which have threatened the competitive position of United States firms. The statistical data that follow for the period 1963-1968, must be examined against the conditions stated for the general economy and those for the industry as a whole if one is to be able to make a realistic appraisal of the future.

It should be borne in mind that the work force in the steel industry is a mature one. Steelworkers average 16 years of service in the same company, and the average steelworker is 43 years of age.[32]

31. Gordon Bloom and H. R. Northrup, *Economics of Labor Relations,* 5th ed. (Homewood, Illinois: R. D. Irwin, Inc., 1965), pp. 9-26.

32. American Iron and Steel Institute, *Charting Steel's Progress During 1966,* p. 43.

TABLE 21. *Basic Steel Industry*
Percent Negro Employment by Occupational Group and Sex, 1963-1968

	All Employees[a]					Male					Female				
Occupational Group	1963	1964	1965	1966	1968	1963	1964	1965	1966	1968	1963	1964	1965	1966	1968
Officials and managers	0.7	0.8	n.a.	1.0	1.3	0.7	0.8	n.a.	1.0	1.3	—	—	n.a.	—	0.8
Professionals	0.1	0.2	n.a.	0.2	0.5	0.1	0.2	n.a.	0.2	0.5	—	—	n.a.	—	0.6
Technicians	0.5	1.0	n.a.	1.4	2.2	0.5	1.0	n.a.	1.5	2.3	0.3	0.6	n.a.	0.9	1.1
Sales workers	0.2	0.3	n.a.	0.3	0.3	0.1	0.1	n.a.	0.1	0.1	0.5	0.6	n.a.	0.7	0.6
Office and clerical	1.2	1.5	n.a.	2.3	2.9	1.2	1.7	n.a.	2.4	3.0	1.0	1.2	n.a.	2.1	2.8
Total white collar	0.8	1.0	1.2	1.4	1.9	0.8	1.0	1.2	1.4	1.8	0.9	1.1	1.5	1.9	2.5
Craftsmen (Skilled)	5.3	5.7	n.a.	5.9	6.3	5.3	5.7	n.a.	5.9	6.3	3.4	4.3	n.a.	6.0	7.8
Operatives (Semiskilled)	17.1	17.7	n.a.	17.8	18.7	17.2	17.8	n.a.	17.9	18.8	3.8	4.4	n.a.	5.2	5.6
Laborers (Unskilled)	27.0	26.5	n.a.	27.7	28.7	27.2	26.6	n.a.	27.7	28.7	10.3	11.0	n.a.	27.4	26.0
Service workers	18.6	18.2	n.a.	19.1	20.0	19.3	18.7	n.a.	19.5	20.4	12.5	13.9	n.a.	15.6	16.0
Total blue collar	15.5	15.8	15.6	16.1	16.7	15.5	15.9	15.6	16.1	16.7	7.0	8.0	9.0	13.5	13.7
Total	12.5	12.7	12.3	12.8	13.3	12.8	13.1	12.7	13.2	13.6	2.1	2.4	2.6	3.9	4.3

Source: Data in possession of the author.

a. 21 companies, 94 plants for 1964; 1965; 1966; 1968; 21 companies, 93 plants for 1963.

THE NATIONAL SCENE

Table 21 shows the percent Negro employment by occupation, sex, and race for 1963-1968 in the basic steel industry. The data cover 21 companies and 94 plants for 1964, 1965, 1966, and 1968, and 21 companies and 93 plants for 1963. The same companies and plants are represented for the period 1963-1968 so that meaningful comparisons can be made in examining the relative position of Negroes in various periods.

A general hypothesis was made at the outset of the study that as a result of government and private civil rights activity since 1960 the Negro's position in the steel industry would have improved significantly. The data presented in the following tables do not support this hypothesis. From the standpoint of quantification alone, it is easy to reach the general conclusion that the Negro's relative occupational status in the basic steel industry has improved very little—if at all—over the years 1963-1968. The Negro appears to have been locked into job positions by 1963 and very little change has occurred. Of course, progress in the area of equal employment opportunity can be measured in ways other than in the use of statistics. The figures do not reflect adequately the important changes that may be taking place in terms of such factors as employee and employer attitudes, recruitment, and general employment policies and practices of a firm. Despite the statistics, these things may be changing in a way that will lead to the long-run betterment of the Negro's position. Difficulties do arise, however, because of short-run considerations and demands that situations change immediately. The nonquantitative aspects of employer activities are discussed in a following chapter. The statistical materials presented and analyzed herein are important and necessary for an understanding of the Negro's position in the industry, but they are not sufficient for a complete evaluation of the minority employment problem.

As noted in Tables 22-26, total and Negro employment in the basic steel industry increased from 1963 to 1964, and 1965 to 1966, and decreased from 1964 to 1965 and from 1966 to 1968. Employment increased slightly over the entire period 1963-1968 from 453,895 to 462,509 of which 56,526 were Negro in 1963 and 61,401 in 1968. As would be expected, male employment increased more significantly than female employment. Total males employed rose from 437,207

TABLE 22. *Basic Steel Industry, Employment by Occupational Group, Sex, and Race, United States, 1963*

Occupational Group	All Employees[a]			Male			Female		
	Total	Negro	Per-cent Negro	Total	Negro	Per-cent Negro	Total	Negro	Per-cent Negro
Officials and managers	33,407	244	0.7	33,273	244	0.7	134	—	—
Professionals	9,562	13	0.1	9,403	13	0.1	159	—	—
Technicians	10,345	51	0.5	9,762	49	0.5	583	2	0.3
Sales workers	2,808	6	0.2	1,960	2	0.1	848	4	0.5
Office and clerical	36,802	424	1.2	25,026	304	1.2	11,776	120	1.0
Total white collar	92,924	738	0.8	79,424	612	0.8	13,500	126	0.9
Craftsmen (Skilled)	110,403	5,874	5.3	110,315	5,871	5.3	88	3	3.4
Operatives (Semiskilled)	172,088	29,357	17.1	170,285	29,289	17.2	1,803	68	3.8
Laborers (Unskilled)	70,589	19,093	27.0	70,121	19,045	27.2	468	48	10.3
Service workers	7,891	1,464	18.6	7,062	1,360	19.3	829	104	12.5
Total blue collar	360,971	55,788	15.5	357,783	55,565	15.5	3,188	223	7.0
Total	453,895	56,526	12.5	437,207	56,177	12.8	16,688	349	2.1

Source: Data in possession of the author.

a. 21 companies, 93 plants.

TABLE 23. *Basic Steel Industry, Employment by Occupational Group, Sex, and Race, United States, 1964*

Occupational Group	All Employees[a]			Male			Female		
	Total	Negro	Per-cent Negro	Total	Negro	Per-cent Negro	Total	Negro	Per-cent Negro
Officials and managers	37,616	301	0.8	37,465	301	0.8	151	—	—
Professionals	10,316	16	0.2	10,141	16	0.2	175	—	—
Technicians	10,833	107	1.0	10,204	103	1.0	629	4	0.6
Sales workers	2,936	8	0.3	2,071	3	0.1	865	5	0.6
Office and clerical	40,333	618	1.5	28,203	467	1.7	12,130	151	1.2
Total white collar	102,034	1,050	1.0	88,084	890	1.0	13,950	160	1.1
Craftsmen (Skilled)	115,751	6,614	5.7	115,659	6,610	5.7	92	4	4.3
Operatives (Semiskilled)	181,042	31,986	17.7	179,370	31,913	17.8	1,672	73	4.4
Laborers (Unskilled)	75,979	20,114	26.5	75,516	20,063	26.6	463	51	11.0
Service workers	8,386	1,527	18.2	7,515	1,406	18.7	871	121	13.9
Total blue collar	381,158	60,241	15.8	378,060	59,992	15.9	3,098	249	8.0
Total	483,192	61,291	12.7	466,144	60,882	13.1	17,048	409	2.4

Source: Data in possession of the author.

a. 21 companies, 94 plants.

TABLE 24. *Basic Steel Industry, Employment of White Collar and Blue Collar Workers by Sex and Race, United States, 1965*

Occupational Group	All Employees[a]			Male			Female		
	Total	Negro	Percent Negro	Total	Negro	Percent Negro	Total	Negro	Percent Negro
White collar	103,808	1,255	1.2	89,577	1,047	1.2	14,231	208	1.5
Blue collar	350,332	54,563	15.6	347,732	54,330	15.6	2,600	233	9.0
Total	454,140	55,818	12.3	437,309	55,377	12.7	16,831	441	2.6

Source: Data in possession of the author.

a. 21 companies, 94 plants.

TABLE 25. *Basic Steel Industry, Employment by Occupational Group, Sex, and Race, United States, 1966*

Occupational Group	All Employees[a]			Male			Female		
	Total	Negro	Percent Negro	Total	Negro	Percent Negro	Total	Negro	Percent Negro
Officials and managers	38,628	371	1.0	38,494	371	1.0	134	—	—
Professionals	11,327	23	0.2	11,075	23	0.2	252	—	—
Technicians	10,912	156	1.4	10,355	151	1.5	557	5	0.9
Sales workers	2,633	8	0.3	1,711	2	0.1	922	6	0.7
Office and clerical	39,775	918	2.3	27,067	657	2.4	12,708	261	2.1
Total white collar	103,275	1,476	1.4	88,702	1,204	1.4	14,573	272	1.9
Craftsmen (Skilled)	111,047	6,586	5.9	110,997	6,583	5.9	50	3	6.0
Operatives(Semiskilled)	172,683	30,719	17.8	171,328	30,648	17.9	1,355	71	5.2
Laborers (Unskilled)	69,807	19,356	27.7	69,109	19,165	27.7	698	191	27.4
Service workers	8,458	1,612	19.1	7,536	1,468	19.5	922	144	15.6
Total blue collar	361,995	58,273	16.1	358,970	57,864	16.1	3,025	409	13.5
Total	465,270	59,749	12.8	447,672	59,068	13.2	17,598	681	3.9

Source: Data in possession of the author.

a. 21 companies, 94 plants.

TABLE 26. *Basic Steel Industry, Employment by Occupational Group, Sex, and Race, United States, 1968*

Occupational Group	All Employees[a]			Male			Female		
	Total	Negro	Percent Negro	Total	Negro	Percent Negro	Total	Negro	Percent Negro
Officials and managers	39,606	509	1.3	39,475	508	1.3	131	1	0.8
Professionals	11,625	57	0.5	11,310	55	0.5	315	2	0.6
Technicians	11,731	261	2.2	11,163	255	2.3	568	6	1.1
Sales workers	2,680	8	0.3	1,756	2	0.1	924	6	0.6
Office and clerical	40,579	1,186	2.9	27,268	816	3.0	13,311	370	2.8
Total white collar	106,221	2,021	1.9	90,972	1,636	1.8	15,249	385	2.5
Craftsmen (Skilled)	112,486	7,113	6.3	112,384	7,105	6.3	102	8	7.8
Operatives (Semiskilled)	169,828	31,836	18.7	168,611	31,768	18.8	1,217	68	5.6
Laborers (Unskilled)	65,164	18,673	28.7	64,496	18,499	28.7	668	174	26.0
Service workers	8,810	1,758	20.0	7,871	1,608	20.4	939	150	16.0
Total blue collar	356,288	59,380	16.7	353,362	58,980	16.7	2,926	400	13.7
Total	462,509	61,401	13.3	444,334	60,616	13.6	18,175	785	4.3

Source: Data in possession of the author.

a. 21 companies, 94 plants.

in 1963 to 444,334 in 1968, whereas females employed rose from 16,688 to 18,175 over the same period. Negro males employed increased from 56,177 to 60,616 and Negro females employed increased from 349 to 785 in the period 1963-1968. Compared to growth industries, such as aerospace and electronics, employment advances in the basic steel industry have been insignificant. A few positions have been made available as a result of retirements, quits, and research and development but the numbers have been small.

According to the statistics presented in Tables 21-26, the relative overall position of the Negro in the industry has not changed between 1963 and 1968. The percent Negro of all employees in the industry during these years is amazingly the same: 1963—12.5 percent, 1964—12.7 percent, 1965—12.3 percent, 1966—12.8 percent, and 1968—13.3 percent. These figures suggest that the Negro's position in the industry has been frozen. If improvements are made for the Negro in the industry, they will likely come in the form of promotion and upgrading. There is little reason to believe that the total employment picture will change drastically for either Negroes or whites in the near future. This situation, of course, explains in part why civil rights enforcement agencies presently are concerned chiefly with altering long standing seniority systems and work rules rather than actual hiring practices in the industry. While most employers have removed restrictive barriers to employment, there are still problems in integrating the existing work force and particularly at the plant level.

OCCUPATIONAL DISTRIBUTION

For reporting purposes, the equal employment opportunity agencies require employers to submit information by job categories using the following classification of occupations:

White Collar Occupations	*Blue Collar Occupations*
Officials and managers	Craftsmen (Skilled)
Professionals	Operatives (Semiskilled)
Technicians	Laborers (Unskilled)
Sales workers	Service workers
Office and clerical	

Employment in the white collar occupations is generally direct. A person may be hired as a professional, salesman, technician, or office and clerical employee, and, if a movement upward is made, it likely would be into an official or managerial position. On the other hand, in the blue collar occupations an employee may begin as a laborer with the expectation of moving up the blue collar ladder to a craftsman's position. The progression in the blue collar jobs would be from unskilled to semiskilled to skilled positions.

The employment problems for Negroes are somewhat different in the white collar areas than in the blue collar ones. In the white collar field, the basic problem is gaining access to the job, whereas in the blue collar areas the difficulty lies in upgrading and the opportunity to advance after employment. One of the crucial questions in examining the data on white collar jobs is: how many Negroes have been employed? In regard to blue collar workers, the same question is asked but, in addition, it is appropriate to ask: what change has occurred in the relative position of the Negro in the semiskilled and skilled jobs? The latter would indicate upgrading and promotion activities in the industry.

The analysis which follows is based on Tables 22-26 which present employment by occupation, sex, and race for the basic steel industry for the years 1963-1968. In the steel industry, no standard procedure is used to differentiate among occupations for reporting Negro employment; however, the following may be useful as a guide:

The White Collar Occupations

Officials and managers. This category includes the managerial jobs and those people who have the major responsibility of organizing and directing the work force. The corporate officials and plant managers and supervisory people would be included in this category. It is the top of the white collar hierarchy.

The total number of people employed as officials and managers has increased each year since 1963. Between 1963 and 1968, the number increased from 33,407 to 39,606. Negroes constituted 244 (0.7 percent) of the total in this category in 1963 and 509 (1.3 percent) of the total in 1968. All Negroes employed as officials and managers for these periods were male except for one Negro female in 1968. In absolute terms, the total employees in this category increased by 6,199 of which 265 were Negroes. On a relative basis, the total increased by 18.6 percent, whites by 17.9 percent, and Negroes by 108.6 percent. Even though some progress has been made in hiring Negroes in this category, it has not been significant on a quantitative basis. It should be noted that the relative gain for Negroes was greater than that for whites.

Professionals. Professional jobs in steel would include accountants, writers, personnel specialists, economists, lawyers, purchasing agents, and metallurgists. These are people who generally possess an advanced degree in a specialized field such as a doctorate in engineering or a master in business administration.

The professional group in the industry has increased by 21.6 percent since 1963. Negro representation in this job category has been practically nonexistent. The distribution of Negroes as professionals has been as follows: 13 in 1963, 16 in 1964, 23 in 1966, and 57 in 1968. In other words, Negroes constituted only 0.1 percent of all professionals in 1963, 0.2 percent in both 1964 and 1966, and 0.5 percent in 1968. The total number of employees in the professional category was 9,562 in 1963, 10,316 in 1964, 11,327 in 1966, and 11,625 in 1968.

The requirement of advanced degrees and specialized training for entry into professional occupations in the industry explains in part the poor Negro representation. Very few Negroes are enrolled in a master in business administration (MBA) program or a doctorate in engineering (Ph.D.) program in the United States at the present time. Efforts are being made to encourage Negroes to participate more widely in these programs, and it is hoped that the future will reflect success in these endeavors with more Negroes prepared for the professional job category.

Technicians. Technicians are employed in many departments in steel mills and, in particular, they may be located in a laboratory or drafting room. Personnel such as laboratory testers (physical or chemical) where the quality and chemical specifications of steel are measured, draftsmen who prepare layout and detail drawings of machine parts, machines, special instruments, and structures, and metallurgical observers who serve as the liaison between the quality control department and the open hearth department that makes steel, are included in the technician classification.

The number of technicians in the iron and steel industry has risen gradually between 1963 and 1968. There were 10,345 in 1963, 10,833 in 1964, 10,912 in 1966, and 11,731 in 1968. Negro employment in this category has increased by 412 percent since 1963. Negro technicians were distributed as follows in the years 1963-1968: 51 in 1963,

107 in 1964, 156 in 1966, and 261 in 1968. On a relative basis, Negroes were 0.5 percent of all technicians in 1963, 1.0 percent in 1964, 1.4 percent in 1966, and 2.2 percent in 1968. In contrast to the professional and officials and managers categories, the technicians group has included a few Negro females in every year—2 in 1963, 4 in 1964, 5 in 1966, and 6 in 1968.

It is expected that the employment of technical personnel will increase in the future because of the industry's expanding research and development programs. Negro employees undoubtedly will continue to increase in this job category. Improvements in educational facilities to prepare people to fill vacancies and the industry's general willingness to hire Negroes in technical jobs will be reflected in a better representation of Negroes in future years.

Sales workers. This category is self-explanatory and includes both inside and outside personnel who sell steel to varied customers.

Among the occupations in the steel industry, the Negro has fared the worst in the sales area. Discrimination against the Negro is more clearly demonstrated in regard to sales positions than in any other job category. At the present time, there are no Negro outside salesmen in the basic steel industry, and there are relatively few inside Negro salesmen. In 1963, there were 6 Negro sales workers and 8 in 1964, 1966, and 1968. This is a small representation compared to almost 3,000 white persons employed as sales workers in those years.

Employers are very direct in discussing what they consider to be problems in hiring Negroes into sales positions. More often than not an employer maintains that the company cannot afford to lose business which may result from sending a Negro out to contact a customer. The sales area also is looked upon as one where certain social arrangements away from a business place are important. For example, a salesman may be expected to take his client to dinner or discuss a contract over cocktails at a private club. Many employers do not think the time has come where these social arrangements, necessary to a business deal, can be handled without difficulty and the loss of income. Whether these fears on the part of the industry are real or imaginary is hard to determine, but, nevertheless, they have been responsible for restricting opportunities to Negroes.

There is concern in the industry about the absence of Negro salesmen. Almost all employers recognize that the barriers will have to be removed, but no one seems willing to make the first move. An executive in a middlesized company has indicated that he would like to be the first to make a breakthrough, and several managers in small companies have shown an interest in following such action. However, these companies appear to be waiting for the giants in the industry to lead the way. If this is the case, the future does not look particularly bright for Negroes who wish to enter sales positions. If the fear of losing profit is a real deterrent of hiring Negroes as salesmen, the largest companies in the industry may be the last to move since they have been among the least profitable in recent years.

Office and clerical. This category consists of those who work as stenographers and clerical office workers in all phases of steel operations. Clerical jobs are important in production and maintenance, metallurgical control, inspection, and in all types of planning and development work in the industry. Computer programming, key punch operator, typist, and stenographer are a few of the specific jobs included herein.

The Negro has made more progress in entering office and clerical positions than in any other white collar job. Negroes constituted 1.2 percent of all office and clerical employees in 1963 and 2.9 percent in 1968. In absolute terms, however, these percentages represented only 424 Negro office and clerical employees in a total of 36,802 in 1963 and 1,186 Negroes in a total of 40,579 in 1968. Female Negro employees were about one-fourth of the total Negro employment in this job category.

There appears to be no discrimination against Negro female employees in the industry today despite the fact that there are very few women represented in the employment figures. There is a combination of factors that seems to explain this phenomenon. Negro girls are not participating widely in high school curricula that prepare a person for office and clerical jobs. This may result from poor student counseling, or the message of available job opportunities requiring clerical skills may not have reached effectively into the Negro community. Prior discrimination against Negro female workers in the industry may cause women to seek employment elsewhere. Every employer interviewed in this study indicated a willingness to hire Negro office and clerical help. At the same time, most employers were discouraged by the relatively few Negro girls who applied for jobs with typing, stenographic, or general clerical skills. Apparently there is no guarantee that once a girl graduates from a high school typing or commercial course that she can type or file correspondence. The business community undoubtedly could provide a service if it would relate its own office and clerical needs to the high schools in a realistic manner.

Inadequate public transportation facilities to outlying areas where steel plants are located might also explain why few female employees, either Negro or white, are represented in the industry. Generally a woman would prefer to remain in the center of the city where abundant job opportunities exist than to travel to a remote location. The city is more accessible and also offers some diversion to the female employee who may enjoy shopping or leaving the office on a lunch break. Life within a steel plant revolves around a self-contained unit and normally once an employee enters the gates he or she does not leave the immediate work area until a shift is completed. Female employees are likely to prefer wider social contacts than ordinarily are found in a steel plant.

White collar occupations summary. On balance, the Negro worker, either male or female, has made little relative progress in gaining white collar jobs in the basic steel industry. The following figures based on Tables 22-26 reveals this in quantitative terms.

The percent Negro of all white collar employees and of male and female employees in white collar jobs has remained quite small for the years 1963 through 1968 even though there was an increase. In absolute terms, Negroes improved their position over the period under consideration; in fact, the number of both men and women in white collar positions more than doubled between 1963 and 1968. But when the number of Negro white collar workers is compared with the number of whites, the differences are significant. For example, in 1963, 738 Negroes compared to 92,186 whites were in white collar jobs; in 1968, 2,021 Negroes compared to 104,200 whites were in this category. A breakdown by sex would indicate the same pattern.

A percentage distribution of all Negroes among the job categories indicates that Negro men constitute only a small portion of white collar positions, whereas about one-half of Negro females in the industry hold white collar jobs. The number of females in the industry is so small, however, that it does not influence the relative position of the Negro when the aggregate data are examined.

Contrary to what the statistics may show, in terms of the lack of progress among Negro white collar workers, the companies in the industry may legitimately claim that affirmative action has been taken

TABLE 27. *Basic Steel Industry, White Collar Employment by Sex and Race, 1963-1968*

	1963	1964	1965	1966	1968
All white collar employees:					
Total	92,924	102,034	103,808	103,275	106,221
Negro	738	1,050	1,255	1,476	2,021
Percent Negro	0.8	1.0	1.2	1.4	1.9
Total Negro Employees	56,526	61,291	55,818	59,749	61,401
Percent of Negroes in white collar jobs	1.3	1.7	2.2	2.5	3.3
White collar employees:			Male		
Total	79,424	88,084	89,577	88,702	90,972
Negro	612	890	1,047	1,204	1,636
Percent Negro	0.8	1.0	1.2	1.4	1.8
Total Negro employees	56,177	60,882	55,377	59,068	60,616
Percent of Negroes in white collar jobs	1.1	1.5	1.9	2.0	2.7
White collar employees:			Female		
Total	13,500	13,950	14,231	14,573	15,249
Negro	126	160	208	272	385
Percent Negro	0.9	1.1	1.5	1.9	2.5
Total Negro employees	349	409	441	681	785
Percent of Negroes in white collar jobs	36.1	39.1	47.2	39.9	49.0

Source: Tables 22-26.

in some cases. Government agencies and civil rights groups may assert that the action taken is unsatisfactory because it did not result in larger increases in the numbers, but this is only one point of view. It appears to be part of the job of the enforcement agencies and civil rights groups to be unhappy about what private industry is doing in regard to the employment problem. Samuel Gompers, as a spokesman for the labor movement, asked for "more and more" and there is no reason to believe that spokesmen for the civil rights movement will do otherwise. Employers will never satisfy the pressure groups, but this fact should not lead to the erroneous belief that private industry is doing nothing.

With the exception of the sales area, employers in the steel industry appear to be making an effort to place Negroes in white collar positions. Discussion of hiring practices is presented in a later chapter, but it can be indicated here that some attempt has been made by many employers in recruiting at Negro colleges and local high schools for people to fill white collar vacancies. There is a general lack of clerical skills available, and those who do possess these skills have many job opportunities. In a given location, four or five employers may be competing for two or three qualified Negroes. The scarcity of Negroes in business undergraduate and graduate programs is well known. Many employers in the steel industry have become discouraged in recruiting graduates of these programs, since the competition among industries for the available talent is quite keen. As far as this research has been able to determine, there is no company in the basic steel industry that will not hire and provide equal employment opportunities to Negro technical, professional, and managerial people in the white collar job categories.

The Blue Collar Occupations

Craftsmen. Craftsmen include the skilled workers in the production and maintenance departments of a steel plant. Craftsmen positions are usually those rated in job class 10 and above in a job rating system that ranges from job class 1 through job class 32. Most of the maintenance jobs in a steel mill such as millwright, motor inspector, and bricklayer, are rated as skilled or craft work. On the production side, a roller in a rolling mill or a melter at an open hearth would be classified as a craftsman. Craftsmen jobs are among the best of the blue collar occupations in terms of working conditions and earnings. The hourly rates for a selected number of craftsmen positions are stated below:[33]

Job Class 11	$3.12
Job Class 13	$3.27
Job Class 20	$3.80
Job Class 23	$4.02
Job Class 32	$4.70

A craftsman in the steel industry normally has arrived at his position as a result of completing an apprenticeship program leading to a maintenance job or by moving up through a line of progression based on seniority in a production unit.

33. Labor-Management Agreement between a major company and the United Steelworkers of America, rates effective August 1, 1967.

Total employment in the craftsmen positions increased from 1963 to 1964 and decreased from 1964 to 1968, following the general employment trends in the industry. In a similar manner, Negro craftsmen followed the same pattern, but their relative position improved slightly in each year. The number of craftsmen employed in the basic steel industry in 1963, 1964, 1966, and 1968 was exceeded only by the number of operatives. The actual numbers were: 110,403 in 1963; 115,751 in 1964; 111,047 in 1966; and 112,486 in 1968. Negroes were represented as follows: 5,874 in 1963; 6,614 in 1964; 6,586 in 1966; and 7,113 in 1968. It should be noted here that even while total craftsmen declined between 1964 and 1968, the number of Negro craftsmen increased. On a relative basis, the Negro position was: 5.3 percent in 1963; 5.7 percent in 1964; 5.9 percent in 1966; and 6.3 percent in 1968. It is significant that the Negro's relative position did not deteriorate as a result of employment declines between 1964 and 1968. Gradual progress has been made in the craftsmen's position for each period studied.

The proportion of skilled craftsmen in all blue collar jobs has remained about 30 percent during 1963-1968. It is expected, however, that among skilled plant personnel, larger numbers of maintenance employees such as instrument repairmen will be needed. The increasingly complex machinery, instruments, and equipment used in the industry will stimulate the demand for more highly trained employees.[34] These people will be provided by two principal sources: apprenticeship training and upgrading of existing personnel and new hires. Negroes will participate in the skilled areas in the future to the extent that seniority systems and local upgrading arrangements will permit and also to the extent they may be found in the labor market as prospective employees. The problems that Negroes face as craftsmen in the basic steel industry are related directly to a plant's seniority system. The Negro's struggle to gain equal employment opportunities as craftsmen is discussed in detail in a later part of this study.

Operatives. This category includes the semiskilled workers who are rated generally in job classes 5 through 9 in a steel plant. Operatives may be classified as a tuyerman or stove tender at a blast furnace, 3rd helper at an open hearth, 2nd furnaceman at a basic oxygen furnace,

34. U. S. Bureau of Labor Statistics, *Occupational Outlook Handbook,* Bulletin No. 1450, 1966-67 edition, pp. 698-708.

or shearman at a rolling mill. The large majority of production jobs in a steel mill are semiskilled or operative jobs. The basic hourly rates for some of the semiskilled jobs are:

Job Class 6	$2.75
Job Class 7	$2.82
Job Class 8	$2.90

General Employment in the 1960 Period

The operatives classification includes the largest proportion of employees found in any single job category in the industry; for example, in 1968, 36.7 percent of all employees were classified as operatives, and approximately the same situation existed for other years. In absolute terms, the number of operatives was: 172,088 in 1963, 181,042 in 1964, 172,683 in 1966, and 169,828 in 1968. Negro representation was: 29,357 in 1963, 31,986 in 1964, 30,719 in 1966, and 31,836 in 1968. On a relative basis, the Negro held 17.1 percent of the semiskilled jobs in 1963, 17.7 percent in 1964, 17.8 percent in 1966, and 18.7 percent in 1968. The change in these percentages has been small in this job category for Negroes, an increase between 1963 and 1968 of 1.6.

An examination of the absolute changes in the number of male and female operatives for 1963 and 1968 reveals some interesting employment patterns. Total employment in the job category decreased by 2,260 between 1963 and 1968; this decrease included a decline in the number of males by 1,674 and a decline in females by 586. Total Negro male employment in the same period increased by 2,479, while females remained constant. The figures indicate that Negro males gained in employment as semiskilled workers and the number of Negro females did not change while both males and females, other than Negroes, lost ground in the industry. These results are not surprising particularly since operative positions in the basic steel industry are more adaptable to male rather than female labor.

It is expected that the number of operative jobs in the industry will increase in the future. The same set of conditions that influence the access to skilled positions determines the opening of semiskilled positions to Negroes. These factors are discussed later in reference to employer policies and seniority systems.

Laborers. The laborers group consists of the unskilled workers who hold jobs in classes 1-4 in a production department. The labor pool in most departments in basic steel producing includes unskilled workers who are beginning employees expected to move into vacancies on more advanced jobs at an early date. In the labor pool, the employee can observe general plant practices and operating procedures in the department where he starts to work. A dustman at a blast furnace and a cinderman at a rolling mill are examples of unskilled labor in a steel plant. The standard hourly wage scale for some of the unskilled jobs is as follows:

Job Class 1-2	$2.45
Job Class 3	$2.52
Job Class 4	$2.60

There were fewer laborers than either craftsmen or operatives in the basic steel industry in 1963, 1964, 1966, and 1968. In each of these years, there were approximately 70,000 laborers, or unskilled workers. Negro representation was 19,093 (27.0 percent) in 1963, 20,114 (26.5 percent) in 1964, 19,356 (27.7 percent) in 1966, and 18,673 (28.7 percent) in 1968. The total number of laborers, both white and black, decreased between 1963 and 1968, but Negroes or a percentage of total employment in the category increased.

The general decline in the number of unskilled workers in the industry reflects the reduced hiring as a result of laborsaving devices and the upgrading of skill requirements. Increased numbers of craftsmen and operatives indicate some upward movement of laborers, but it further suggests that new employees may be hired directly into positions above the unskilled classification. The number of Negro unskilled employees increased while the total number of workers in this category declined during 1963-1966, but both total and Negro employment in laborers jobs declined between 1966 and 1968.

In contrast to the skilled and semiskilled positions, the number of unskilled jobs is not likely to increase in the next decade. The increasing use of high pressure in blast furnaces; basic oxygen furnaces; oxygen in open hearth and electric furnaces; and continuous casting equipment will result in greater operating efficiency and slackening in the demand for unskilled employees. The Negro's position in the industry will be determined by his ability to move out of the laborers' category in a nondiscriminatory line of progression, transfer to semiskilled or skilled positions between departments, enter apprenticeship programs, and to be hired directly into jobs above the laborers' class.

Service workers. Service workers include janitors, guards, watchmen, and those normally in nonproduction jobs and responsible for cleaning and protection of plant property. The number of service workers has increased gradually over the years between 1963 and 1968, and Negro employees in this category have increased slightly. The total number of service workers was 7,891 in 1963, 8,386 in 1964, 8,458 in 1966, and 8,810 in 1968. Negro representation was 1,464 (18.6 percent) in 1963, 1,527 (18.2 percent) in 1964, 1,612 (19.1 percent) in 1966, and 1,758 (20.0 percent) in 1968. The service worker group does not constitute a very important part of the employment picture in the industry. It appears that Negro workers have been well represented in this job category on both an absolute and relative basis. The jobs in this classification usually are terminal positions, and they are not in a line of progression unit such as those classified as laborers. Future employment of service workers will remain about the same with slight improvements as the industry expands. Negroes will continue to hold jobs in this area of employment; however, no significant deviation from the trend of the past is expected.

Blue collar occupations summary. Table 28 presents the change in blue collar employment between 1963 and 1968. The statistics show that total blue collar employment has decreased by 4,683 workers or a decrease of 1.3 percent. Total Negro blue collar employees increased by 3,592 (6.4 percent) while total white blue collar employees decreased by 8,275 (2.7 percent) between 1963 and 1968.

The statistics in Table 28 reveal some important changes in Negro employment in blue collar jobs in the steel industry. Between 1963 and 1968, Negroes made improvement in both the craftsmen and operatives categories which indicates some movement up the seniority ladders into better jobs. These changes occurred when the total number of operatives in the industry declined and the number of whites in the category also declined. The improvement in the Negro's position may reflect employer activity in implementing nondiscriminatory programs in the industry.

The gains noted have not been large enough to change the relative position of the Negro in the industry during 1963-1968. Negro employment has remained about 12 to 13 percent of total employment over this period of time. The fact remains, however, that slow progress is being made.

TABLE 28. *Basic Steel Industry,*
Change in Blue Collar Employment by Race, 1963-1968

Occupational Group	Change 1963-1968 Number	Percent
Total all employees	+8,614	+ 1.9
Total Negro employees	+4,875	+ 8.6
Total all blue collar employees	−4,683	− 1.3
Total Negro blue collar employees	+3,592	+ 6.4
Total white* blue collar employees	−8,275	− 2.7
Craftsmen	+2,083	+ 1.9
Negro	+1,239	+21.1
White*	+ 844	+ 0.8
Operatives	−2,260	− 1.3
Negro	+2,479	+ 8.4
White*	−4,739	− 3.3
Laborers	−5,425	− 7.7
Negro	− 420	− 2.2
White*	−5,005	− 9.7
Service workers	+ 919	+11.6
Negro	+ 294	+20.1
White*	+ 625	+ 9.7

Source: Tables 22-26.
* "White" includes all employees other than those classified as Negro.

It is encouraging to note that the most significant advances made by Negro workers have been among operatives and craftsmen. The greatest relative change of any group was registered among Negro craftsmen with an increase of 21.1 percent. This indicates that some upgrading of Negroes has been made and that new opportunities are being made available. Table 29 puts the above in clearer perspective. It can be seen that of all Negro employees, the heaviest concentration has been in the operatives category, and there has been a gradual increase in the percentage distribution of Negroes in the craftsmen group. Negroes in the steel industry remain almost entirely in blue collar jobs, but the trend has been toward better utilization of Negroes in the more skilled positions. The degree of change reported in Table 29 can be interpreted in several ways. The percentage changes are

TABLE 29. *Basic Steel Industry Percentage Distribution of Negroes in Blue Collar Occupations, 1963-1968*

Occupational Group	1963	1964	1966	1968	Change 1963-1968
Craftsmen (Skilled)	10.4	10.8	11.0	11.6	+1.2
Operatives (Semiskilled)	51.9	52.2	51.4	51.8	−0.1
Laborers (Unskilled)	33.8	32.8	32.4	30.4	−3.4
Service workers	2.6	2.5	2.7	2.9	+0.3
Total blue collar	98.7	98.3	97.5	96.7	−2.0
Total employment	100.0	100.0	100.0	100.0	—

Source: Tables 22-26.

not large, and one may have expected to see much more progress as a result of private, public, and civil rights pressures. Most would agree that more can and should be done, but the crucial question is what can be expected realistically? The changes indicated in the various skill positions are minor, but the trend provides some room for optimism.

Perhaps the most striking thing about the statistics in Tables 28 and 29 is the general lack of growth in employment in the blue collar jobs. Certainly the future is not a bright one in terms of abundant job opportunities. Craftsmen positions will become increasingly more important as the nature of technology changes at an accelerated rate, but the number of jobs is not likely to increase significantly. Changes in the position of the Negro in blue collar jobs in the industry will have to take place to a large extent among those already hired. Training and apprenticeship programs are crucial toward elevating the Negro in this industry in addition to a modification of work rules to allow the Negro to progress up a line of promotion. It would be unwise, however, to expect to see large changes in the number of Negroes (or whites) in the blue collar occupations in the steel industry. There will continue to be some movement out of these job categories, and there will be upward movements within the skill areas, but the differences will not be highly noticeable in the immediate future. The trend does seem to indicate a breakthrough for Negroes into positions not held in the past, and there is hope that this will provide for equal employment opportunities on a wider scale.

CHAPTER VI.

Regional and Selected Plant Comparisons

The previous chapter was concerned with the general employment of Negroes in the steel industry in the period 1963-1968. For each of the years studied, it was found that Negroes consisted of about 12.5 percent of all employees in the industry. This figure includes approximately 1 to 2 percent Negro white collar workers and between 15 and 17 percent Negro blue collar workers for 1963-1968.

The present chapter breaks the aggregate data into regional components in order to make comparisons within the country. Employment data for the following five regions are presented:

Eastern:	Connecticut, Maryland, Massachusetts, New Jersey, New York, eastern Pennsylvania.
Southern:	Alabama, Kentucky, Oklahoma, and Texas.
Pittsburgh:	Western Pennsylvania, eastern Ohio, and the northernmost corner of West Virginia.
Great Lakes and Midwest:	Illinois, Indiana, Michigan, Minnesota, and Missouri, as well as the western portion of New York and Lake Counties of Ohio. The district has been extended to include the plants located in inland Ohio and distant Colorado and Utah.
West Coast:	Washington and California.

In addition to the regional comparisons, several large and small plants have been selected to show employment differences by plant size.

TABLE 30. *Basic Steel Industry, Percent Negro Employment by District and Sex, 1963-1968*

District	All Employees					Male					Female				
	1963	1964	1965	1966	1968	1963	1964	1965	1966	1968	1963	1964	1965	1966	1968
Eastern	15.8	16.1	14.7	15.2	15.6	16.3	16.6	15.1	15.7	16.1	0.9	1.0	1.5	1.8	2.1
Southern	22.4	21.9	21.9	22.5	21.3	22.8	22.4	22.5	23.0	21.7	0.7	0.6	0.9	1.3	2.5
Pittsburgh	7.0	7.2	6.8	6.8	6.9	7.3	7.5	7.1	7.0	7.1	0.9	1.3	1.5	1.5	1.8
Great Lakes and Midwest	14.7	15.0	15.0	15.7	16.6	15.1	15.4	15.3	16.0	16.9	3.8	4.2	4.4	7.1	7.7
West Coast	6.4	6.8	7.0	7.0	7.7	6.6	7.0	7.2	7.2	8.0	2.4	2.2	2.2	2.3	2.3
Total All Districts	12.5	12.7	12.3	12.8	13.3	12.8	13.1	12.7	13.2	13.6	2.1	2.4	2.6	3.9	4.3

Source: Tables in Statistical Appendix.

REGIONAL COMPARISONS

Table 30 shows percent Negro employment by district, sex, and race for the industry for 1963-1968. The percentages shown are based on absolute figures in Table A-1 through A-26 in the statistical appendix. The change in the relative position of the Negro in any of the regions has not been dramatic over the period 1963-1968. Some advancement was made by Negroes in the Great Lakes and Midwest and West Coast districts, but their overall position deteriorated in the Eastern, Southern and Pittsburgh districts. The foregoing is consistent with the earlier finding that growth in the steel industry appears to be shifting from the East and South to the Midwest and West Coast. A large amount of plant expansion in the industry has occurred in recent years in Indiana where Bethlehem, Jones and Laughlin, and United States Steel have built new facilities.

Among the regions studied, Pittsburgh and the West Coast have the smallest representation of Negro workers in the industry. In the Pittsburgh district, the relative position of the Negro has remained almost the same between 1963-1968 whereas some progress has been made by Negroes in the West Coast steel industry. The poor showing in the Pittsburgh district can be explained in part by the general lack of Negroes in the population. For example, the 1960 census shows 6.7 percent Negro population in the Pittsburgh SMSA; the central city figure was 16.7 percent Negro while outside the central city Negroes constituted only 3.4 percent of the population. Steel plants are located, obviously, outside of the central city. Another factor that contributes to the Pittsburgh situation is the lack of plant expansion among the leading steel producers in the area.

In order to evaluate the importance of the districts for Negro employment opportunities, it is necessary to examine the occupational distribution of Negroes by regions. The following sections present a comparative analysis of regional differences for 1968 based on occupations.

Occupational Distribution

White collar occupations. Negroes have not had a significant representation in white collar occupations in most industries, and this is particularly true for steel. Regardless of the region of the country where steel plants are located, Negroes do not constitute more than

4.3 percent of total employees in any white collar occupation. This is made clear in Table 31 which shows the percent Negro white collar employment by occupation and district for 1968.

The data in Table 31 indicate that steel plants in the Great Lakes and Midwest region, which includes the important Gary-Chicago complex, have led the country in their efforts to integrate white collar occupations. It appears that the greatest improvement has been in hiring Negro technicians and office and clerical workers. The foregoing occupations do not require that Negroes come into contact with customers, the supervisory problem does not arise, and a great deal of training and experience are not required for their performance. Employers are reluctant to move fast on integrating the officials and managers positions, where foremen and supervisors would be found, for fear of disturbing morale in the plant, and they have refused to employ Negro salesmen for fear of losing sales. The general absence of progress in the professionals category for Negroes can be explained in part by the job requirements that oftentimes include the necessity for advanced degrees such as a Ph.D. in engineering or an M.B.A. in an applied field of business.

Steel plants in the Pittsburgh district seem to have done the least in terms of integrating the white collar occupations. These plants lag behind the Southern district, which includes Birmingham, in all white

TABLE 31. *Basic Steel Industry*
Percent Negro White Collar Employment by
Occupational Group and District, 1968

Occupational Group	National Average	Districts: Eastern	Southern	Pittsburgh	Great Lakes and Midwest	West Coast
Officials and managers	1.3	1.6	0.3	0.6	1.8	0.9
Professionals	0.5	0.5	1.3	0.2	0.6	1.7
Technicians	2.2	1.5	4.2	0.7	3.1	1.9
Sales workers	0.3	—	—	0.4	—	—
Office and clerical	2.9	2.3	2.5	1.8	4.3	2.2
Total white collar	1.9	1.7	1.8	1.0	2.8	1.6

Source: Tables in Statistical Appendix.

TABLE 32. *Basic Steel Industry*
Percent Negro Blue Collar Employment by Occupational Group and District
1968

Occupational Group	National Average	Districts				
		Eastern	Southern	Pittsburgh	Great Lakes and Midwest	West Coast
Craftsmen (Skilled)	6.3	5.0	7.8	3.4	9.0	4.4
Operatives (Semiskilled)	18.7	19.8	35.8	10.0	23.3	11.6
Laborers (Unskilled)	28.7	39.7	50.8	15.2	31.2	16.3
Service workers	20.0	28.8	26.5	12.3	21.5	12.2
Total blue collar	16.7	19.6	26.6	8.9	20.4	9.7

Source: Tables in Statistical Appendix.

collar jobs except officials and managers. A general lack of expansion in the steel industry in the Pittsburgh district may account for the region's poor showing; however, the policies and practices of some of the large firms in the area would also have to be examined for a complete explanation. It will be interesting to observe whether the opening of the new United States Steel Corporation building in Pittsburgh will result in a significant change in the number of Negro office and clerical personnel in the future.

Blue collar occupations. It has been shown earlier that Negroes have been hired in large numbers in blue collar positions in the steel industry. Many of the more unpleasant jobs have been performed almost exclusively by Negroes since they entered the industry in the late nineteenth century. A current view of the Negro's relative position in blue collar employment in steel is presented in Table 32.

The laborers (unskilled) occupation is the one in which Negroes have the largest representation in all sections of the country. In the Southern district, Negroes held 50.8 percent of the laborers jobs in 1968. This high percentage probably represents the availability of a large supply of unskilled Negro labor and employment practices that allowed Negroes to enter the industry with limited expectations of moving into skilled jobs except in all black departments. Many Negroes have remained in unskilled jobs over the years. In districts other than the South, Negro representation in the unskilled occupations has ranged from 15.2 percent in Pittsburgh to 39.7 percent in the Eastern area. These figures are high and indicate much of the problem that the steel industry faces today in terms of alleged discrimination that has frozen Negroes into low positions in the job hierarchy. Contemporary efforts on the part of the courts to remove present effects of past discrimination in the industry may result in some significant movement of Negroes out of the unskilled jobs and into more advanced positions.

In the operatives category, plants in the Southern district led the rest of the country in Negro representation (35.8 percent). This interesting phenomenon can be explained in part by the large number of semiskilled jobs in the blast furnace and coke oven operations where almost all black departments are found. Negroes have had no difficulty in moving up seniority ladders in departments where they constituted a majority or all of the employees. The major problem that the Negro operative in steel is faced with today is the general lack of realistic opportunities to transfer to more desirable departments in the plant. This is an industrywide problem and not peculiar to the South.

Negro representation in the craftsmen (skilled) occupations in the industry has varied from 9.0 percent in the Great Lakes and Midwest district to 3.4 percent in the Pittsburgh district. There is a significant difference in the Negro's position in the skilled occupations compared to the unskilled and semiskilled jobs in all districts. Many of the skilled jobs in steel are located in the maintenance (craft) departments where Negroes have been excluded traditionally. The representation of Negroes in skilled occupations that does exist occurs mainly in production departments with heavy Negro concentration. Major improvement in the Negro's relative position in the top blue collar jobs is not likely to be achieved until rigid collective bargaining provisions restricting intraplant mobility are relaxed.

The total blue collar position of the Negro was notably better than the white collar position in 1968. The national average of 16.7 percent Negro in blue collar jobs was exceeded by the Southern, Great Lakes and Midwest, and Eastern districts but, again, the Pittsburgh and West Coast districts were below the average. In fact, both of the latter two districts were only about one-half of the national average with 8.9 and 9.7 percent Negro.

CHANGES IN NEGRO EMPLOYMENT, 1963-1968

Table A-27 in the statistical appendix presents a detailed picture of the change in employment between 1963 and 1968 for both Negro and white employees by district and occupation. The data in this table have been reduced in the following tabulations to show the absolute change in Negro employment. Percentage changes are almost meaningless, in regard to these figures, since they are based on such small numbers. For example, in the West Coast district, Negro representation among officials and managers increased by 1,200 percent between 1963 and 1968, but the actual increase was only from 1 to 12 Negroes in that category.

Table 33 gives the change in Negro employment by occupations between 1963 and 1968. In general, the signs of change are positive, but the actual accomplishments in Negro employment have been relatively insignificant.

Among the white collar occupations, the most important changes occurred in the Great Lakes and Midwest district where Negro officials and managers increased by 206 and office and clerical employees increased by 480 between 1963 and 1968. The increases in these two occupations in this one district account for more than one-half of the total increase in Negro white collar jobs in the period covered. Other than the Great Lakes and Midwest, only the Pittsburgh district had a change greater than 100 Negroes in any of the white collar occupations (office and clerical, 135). Decreases were noted for Negro sales workers in the Eastern district, and officials and managers in the Southern district.

On the whole, the industry cannot—and should not—find much consolation in the changes noted in Table 33. To be sure, certain affirmative action programs have been entered into and a diligent search has been made by some to find qualified Negro white collar workers. But the record speaks for itself; and, unfortunately, it seems to say that the industry has moved mainly by outside pressure and that not much can be expected from voluntary activity. The sad corollary to the above, of course, is that the supply of Negro labor qualified for white collar positions is quite small. As pointed out earlier, qualified Negro college graduates to fill professional and technical jobs in the steel industry are difficult to find and, if found, they have attractive offers in many industries. Negro, as well as white, girls are not likely to

TABLE 33. *Basic Steel Industry*
Change in Negro Employment by
Occupational Group and District, 1963-1968

	Districts				
Occupational Group	Eastern	Southern	Pittsburgh	Great Lakes and Midwest	West Coast
Officials and managers	+ 63	− 34	+ 18	+ 206	+ 12
Professionals	+ 7	+ 8	+ 2	+ 19	+ 8
Technicians	+ 20	+ 37	+ 21	+ 128	+ 4
Sales workers	− 1	—	+ 3	—	—
Office and clerical	+ 96	+ 24	+135	+ 480	+ 27
Total white collar	+185	+ 35	+179	+ 833	+ 51
Craftsmen (Skilled)	+272	+201	+112	+ 599	+ 55
Operatives (Semiskilled)	+851	+365	−726	+1902	+ 87
Laborers (Unskilled)	−563	−750	−163	+1022	+ 34
Service workers	+156	− 37	+ 3	+ 159	+ 13
Total blue collar	+716	−221	−774	+3682	+189
Total	+901	−186	−595	+4515	+240

Source: Table A-27, Statistical Appendix.

find an office and clerical position appealing in a steel plant located in a remote part of a metropolitan area. Competition is keen among downtown offices for Negro girls to fill office and clerical jobs. These conditions are not stated as an excuse for the industry to relax its efforts, but they must be taken into account if a realistic appraisal of Negro employment is to be made.

The story of change in the Negro blue collar occupations is similar to that for white collar jobs. Positive changes have been registered for all blue collar occupations in the districts except for declines as follows: laborers in the Eastern district, laborers and service workers in the Southern district, and operatives and laborers in the Pittsburgh district. The declines occurred principally as a result of new technology and/or a cutback in production.

The general changes in the Negro craftsmen group is somewhat encouraging with increases in all districts. The significant thing to note here is that some upgrading of Negroes into skilled positions appears to be happening. Even in the Southern district, the number of Negro craftsmen increased by 201.

In the operatives area, the most notable changes have occurred in the Pittsburgh district, where a decline of 726 Negroes was registered, and in the Great Lakes and Midwest district, where an increase of 1,902 Negro operatives was made. In the other districts, the number of Negro operatives increased by 851 in the Eastern district, 365 in the Southern district, and 87 in the West Coast district. Changes in actual Negro employment in the laborers and service workers categories have not been great between 1963 and 1968 except for the large decline of Negro laborers in the Eastern and Southern Districts and the large increase in the number of Negro laborers in the Great Lakes and Midwest district.

In the important craftsmen and operative occupations, the Negro is making gains in most parts of the country except in the operative category in the Pittsburgh district where the industry seems to be declining generally. On balance, the gains for the Negro in the blue collar jobs in the industry have been the best in the Great Lakes and Midwest district and the worst in the Pittsburgh district. The above reflects basically two things: (1) growth and expansion of the steel industry in the Great Lakes and Midwest district with the availability of Negro labor principally in the Gary-Hammond-Chicago area, and (2) a decline of the industry in the Pittsburgh district where Negro labor has never been abundant in certain parts of the Pennsylvania-Ohio-West Virginia complex.

The record of Negro blue collar employment in the Southern district is an interesting one. As pointed out earlier, Negroes always have been hired in large numbers in the steel industry in the South, particularly in the large steel centers such as Gadsden and Birmingham, Alabama. The difficulty faced there usually has not been in a Negro finding employment but in gaining access to training, upgrading, and promotion. A reverse trend now seems to be taking place in the Southern district. The statistics indicate that the number of Negro laborers has decreased significantly, but they have moved into craftsmen and operative positions about on a par with other parts of the country with the possible exception of the Great Lakes and Midwest. What this means, in part, is that with a standardization of employment tests and requirements for employees in the Southern steel industry the uneducated Negro may find it increasingly more difficult to become employed. Prior to 1962 separate seniority rosters were maintained for Negroes and whites in Southern steel plants. Many Negroes were hired for positions requiring little or no education or ability, since it generally was assumed that a Negro would not move up a line of promotion into skilled jobs. Of course, under a nondiscriminatory system, once a Negro is hired it is expected that he can move to the top of the promotion ladder. The change in the South could be the result of outside pressures from government and civil rights groups which have directed their interests more toward the South than to any other section of the country.[35]

The comparisons between white collar and blue collar Negro employment presented above indicate the general problems facing the Negro in the labor force today. A recent study observes that the unskilled and semiskilled positions in American industry are declining while white collar jobs are increasing at a rapid rate. It concludes further that "Manpower experts find the trend ominous. If Negroes continue to hold only the type of jobs they generally occupy now, their unemployment rate by 1975 would be around 20%, . . . A much faster Negro breakthrough into white-collar and skilled craftsmen's ranks is necessary. . . ." [36] Later sections of this paper provide some rationale for judging just how rapid such changes may occur in the basic steel industry.

NEGRO EMPLOYMENT IN SELECTED LARGE AND SMALL PLANTS, 1968

Table 34 presents Negro employment data for fifteen selected large plants where total employment exceeds 10,000. Every district is represented except the West Coast which does not have a plant in the study with over 10,000 employees.

The percent Negro column in Table 34 reflects significant differences among plants of comparable size. For example, the extreme case is that of two plants in the Eastern district; one plant has 17,278 employees and 106 Negroes (0.6 percent), and the other one has 26,668 employees and 8,288 Negroes (31.1 percent). This rather

35. See the author's, "Negro Employment in Birmingham: Three Cases," in A. M. Ross and H. Hill, *Employment, Race, and Poverty* (New York: Harcourt, Brace and World, 1967), pp. 308-336.

36. *Wall Street Journal,* June 4, 1968.

TABLE 34. *Basic Steel Industry*
Negro Employment in Selected Large Plants (over 10,000), 1968

Plant	Total Employment	Total Negro	Percent Negro	District
1	11,810	2,603	22.0	Great Lakes and Midwest
2	19,025	2,732	14.4	Great Lakes and Midwest
3	11,048	2,318	21.0	Great Lakes and Midwest
4	21,261	3,819	18.0	Great Lakes and Midwest
5	17,532	5,544	31.6	Great Lakes and Midwest
6	10,428	1,234	11.8	Pittsburgh
7	11,837	175	1.5	Pittsburgh
8	11,715	346	3.0	Pittsburgh
9	12,530	325	2.6	Pittsburgh
10	10,749	1,580	14.7	Pittsburgh
11	11,100	1,143	10.3	Pittsburgh
12	13,232	1,191	9.0	Pittsburgh
13	17,278	106	0.6	Eastern
14	26,668	8,288	31.1	Eastern
15	13,374	3,947	29.5	Southern

Source: Data in author's possession.

unusual case indicates that large plant size is not necessarily a primary determining factor in the employment of Negroes in the steel industry. The plant with very few Negroes is located in an area that has less than 1 percent Negro population, whereas the plant with a large number of Negroes (31.1 percent) is located in an area with approximately 28.0 percent Negro population. This suggests that the availability of Negro labor in an area is more important than plant size in determining Negro representation in this industry. Comparisons of other large plants bear out the above observations. Whenever a plant is located near a large Negro population, the Negro representation in the industry generally is quite high and vice versa.

Table 35 presents Negro employment data for 21 selected small plants (under 5,000 employees) for 1968. A study of the percent Negro in the small plants leads to the same conclusions as set forth above in connection with the large plants. Geography and plant location appear to influence the employment of Negroes more than plant size.

By comparison, a plant with 4,029 employees and 314 Negroes (7.8 percent) is located in the Great Lakes and Midwest district (Missouri) and a plant of similar size with 4,317 employees and 1,248 Negroes (28.9 percent) is located in the Southern district (Alabama). A further comparison would be plant number 6 with 2,288 employees and 21 Negroes (0.9 percent) in Minnesota to plant number 20 with 1,930 employees and 401 Negroes (20.8 percent) in Los Angeles. Variations appear within and between districts depending on the location of the plant.

It should not be inferred from the above that plant size and Negro population are the only variables that influence Negro employment in the steel industry. The figures do suggest rather strongly, however, that when examined together plant size is much less important in ex-

TABLE 35. *Basic Steel Industry*
Negro Employment in Selected Small Plants (under 5,000), 1968

Plant	Total Employment	Total Negro	Percent Negro	District
1	4,029	314	7.8	Great Lakes and Midwest
2	3,099	527	17.0	Great Lakes and Midwest
3	3,659	185	5.1	Great Lakes and Midwest
4	4,978	1,144	23.0	Great Lakes and Midwest
5	1,578	129	8.2	Great Lakes and Midwest
6	2,288	21	0.9	Great Lakes and Midwest
7	1,668	2	0.1	Pittsburgh
8	4,339	535	12.3	Pittsburgh
9	4,369	29	0.7	Pittsburgh
10	4,073	11	0.3	Pittsburgh
11	880	11	1.2	Pittsburgh
12	3,041	418	13.7	Eastern
13	4,239	458	10.8	Eastern
14	3,359	40	1.2	Eastern
15	1,826	372	20.4	Eastern
16	4,754	73	1.5	Southern
17	4,317	1,248	28.9	Southern
18	4,616	682	14.8	Southern
19	1,081	130	12.0	West Coast
20	1,930	401	20.8	West Coast
21	2,768	258	9.3	West Coast

Source: Data in author's possession.

plaining the employment of Negroes than the supply of Negro labor. Employment policy in a firm is important in assessing the Negro's role in the industry, and this will be discussed in a following chapter.

Some stress already has been given to the fact that Negroes seem to have been hired in the steel industry wherever they are represented in the population and, particularly, in blue collar production jobs. Further evidence of this is found in the material just presented. Apparently, then, in order to understand the qualitative position of the Negro in the industry, it is necessary to know the way in which management policy is developed and executed toward giving the employed Negro an opportunity to elevate himself.

CHAPTER VII.

Racial Employment Policy in the Steel Industry

The previous chapters emphasize the quantitative aspects of Negro employment in the basic steel industry. Statistical data are important and necessary to reflect the Negro's position in the industry but, as already noted, they do not provide a complete picture of employment activity. Employment policy must be evaluated in order to gain a more thorough understanding of the Negro's job position and future prospects for his utilization in the industry. This chapter discusses several aspects of racial employment policy including manpower planning, recruiting, selection, training, and upgrading. The analysis is based on responses by industry officials to questions asked in personal interviews.

EMPLOYMENT POLICY

Employee relations, industrial relations, and personnel are related terms for a functional area of business that deals with human resources and competes with others such as production, marketing, and finance for recognition and budget. In general, the industrial relations function has not been as well developed in American industry as perhaps production or finance, and this appears to be particularly true for the steel industry. In some respects, this complicates the problem of achieving goals of equal employment opportunity. If the firm considers a minority employment program in an industrial relations department from the point of view of costs alone, it is likely to restrict it before long-run benefits can accrue. On the other hand, if the company views a minority employment program as an investment, it will pursue it with adequate support to the personnel people, to insure a satisfactory return. Activity among employers varies, but there seems to be too much emphasis on the costs, and not enough on the benefits, of operating a sound equal employment opportunity program.

The thrust of the current civil rights movement, with its emphasis on jobs and upgrading, brings additional pressures on the industrial relations function. There is a need for a clear statement of racial employment policy at all levels of a company and adequate resources should be employed for its implementation.[37]

DECLARATION OF COMPANY POLICY

In 1942, the American Management Association conducted a study titled *The Negro Worker.* It reported:

> The first requisite in the program of Negro integration is a firm declaration of company policy,
>
> * * *
>
> The interpretation of management's policy of non-discrimination to labor is the responsibility of supervisors and foremen. . . . Supervision must be "sold" on the idea.[38]

In 1969, company racial employment policy was being "declared" in the following ways: Plans for Progress statements, plant newspapers, printed handouts to employees, company magazines, bulletin boards, labor-management agreements, management policy manual, newspaper ads, and discussions with supervisors.

Most of the companies interviewed in the study indicated that membership in Plans for Progress[39] meant that steps had been taken to develop effective policies in regard to equal employment opportunity. In June 1964, eleven steel companies, including Armco, Bethlehem, Colorado Fuel and Iron, Great Lakes Steel, Inland, Jones and Laughlin, Pittsburgh, Republic, United States Steel, Wheeling, and Youngstown Sheet and Tube, entered Plans for Progress together.

---

37. See George Strauss, "How Management Views Its Race Relations Responsibilities," in A. M. Ross and H. Hill, *Employment, Race, and Poverty* (New York: Harcourt, Brace & World, 1967), pp. 261-289, for a discussion of "some of the problems management faces as it deals with civil rights pressures in the middle 1960's."
38. American Management Association, *The Negro Worker, An Analysis of Experience and Opinion on the Employment and Integration of the Negro in Industry* (New York: The Association, 1942), p. 2.
39. Plans for Progress, a voluntary effort by American businessmen, was conceived in 1961 as an adjunct to the President's Committee on Equal Employment Opportunity. When this Committee was dissolved in 1965, Plans for Progress was reorganized as a separate entity by President Johnson's Executive Order 11246.

Policy statements of the companies differ slightly, but the gist of them is contained in the United States Steel Corporation's policy as follows:

> It is the policy of the Corporation to seek and employ the best qualified personnel in all its facilities and at all of its working locations; to provide equal opportunities for the advancement of employees including upgrading, promotion, and training; and to conduct these activities in a manner which will not discriminate against any person because of race, color, creed, or national origin.[40]

The above statement generally is followed by a set of plans to enable objectives to be met. These plans cover undertakings such as dissemination of policy, responsibility for implementation of policy, recruitment, placement, and training. Most company plans are similar except for Granite City Steel which believes in the concept of merit employment and no special search being made for Negro employees. All of the companies interviewed, except Carpenter Steel and Latrobe Steel, are members of the Plans for Progress organization. The latter two companies have stated nondiscrimination policy in newspaper ads, discussions with supervisors, and in written communications.

It is not sufficient, obviously, for a firm only to announce a policy and a plan of action. These things are not self-effectuating. Communication of company policy, formulated at corporate headquarters, should be carried out in an efficient manner.[41] Line personnel need counseling and advice to put racial policy into practice. Existing staffs in some companies have not had time to do the job in addition to a myriad of other duties, and there seems to be a reluctance to seek outside assistance in regard to minority group problems. It is not enough for corporate headquarters to instruct a distant plant to integrate by a certain date under stated policy of the company. The local plant manager and personnel officers may have difficulty in understanding and implementing such directives when they do not appreciate the significance of the problem on a national level.

There has been too much made of the assertion that local plants have sufficient know-how to solve all of their problems. This is borne out, in part, by the industry response to the question, "how do supervisory people interpret the policy (in regard to nondiscrimination) for labor?" In almost every case, the respondent either avoided the ques-

40. *U. S. Steel News,* July 1964.
41. See Theodore V. Purcell, "Break Down Your Employment Barriers," *Harvard Business Review,* Vol. LXVI (July-August 1968), pp. 65-76.

tion or indicated that supervisors are expected to meet with employees and convey the message that nondiscrimination in employment practices is to prevail. The job of the plant supervisor or foreman is not an easy one. Bonus systems and continuous pressure to "get the production out" can overshadow what a supervisor hears at a monthly meeting or reads in the house organ about an equal employment opportunity program. The gap between policy and practice can be bridged if modifications are made in the organizational structure to allow a more direct liaison between corporate headquarters and line personnel.

Various aspects of personnel policy in the steel industry are discussed in the following sections with emphasis on recruiting, selecting, and training minority group employees.

RECRUITMENT PROGRAMS

Firms attempt to locate and hire qualified personnel in a variety of ways. Labor market conditions have a significant influence over a company's recruiting activity. When the market is tight, the employer cannot afford to be as particular as usual in hiring new employees. Even though the Negro's employment status may be enhanced by a tight labor market, this economic condition is not sufficient alone to improve greatly the Negro's relative job position in the industry.[42] Unless special programs are developed and implemented, the Negro's position in the industry is not likely to change much.

Some of the routine avenues used in the search for black employees include colleges, high schools, public and private employment services, newspaper ads, civil rights organizations, referrals by employees, and walk-in applicants. In general, the results have not justified the extensive recruitment activities conducted through the above channels. This has caused some employers to move outside the normal procedures in seeking black employees.[43]

A college recruitment program to meet company-wide needs for entry level management personnel is used by a majority of the firms interviewed. The predominantly Negro colleges, located mainly in the South, have been visited regularly by company recruiters in recent years. A majority of the steel companies interviewed indicated dis-

42. For another interesting point of view, see: James Tobin, "On Improving the Economic Status of the Negro," *Daedalus,* Fall 1965, pp. 878-898.
43. See Ulric Haynes, Jr., "Equal Job Opportunity: The Credibility Gap," *Harvard Business Review, Vol. LXVI* (May-June 1968), pp. 113-120.

appointment in their experiences at the Negro schools. Much of the disappointment probably arises from unrealistic expectations. Southern Negro colleges, in general, are not prepared to educate adequately for industry. Obviously, all Negro colleges are not inferior.[44] Employers in the steel industry have found, for example, that Tennessee A & I is an excellent source for employing engineering talent, but given the demand the supply of qualified students is quite inadequate. The competition for a few good Negro students at any one college is keen, and the steel industry has not been as attractive to these graduates as some other industries. For example, an employer in a small steel company near Philadelphia noted that he has attempted to hire Negro college graduates, but he has been unsuccessful because other companies in the area pay higher wages and are more appealing in terms of general working conditions. Another company in Detroit indicated that, if given a choice, a Negro would rather work in an automobile firm than a steel company.

Hourly workers are recruited on an informal basis in most instances, and the industry depends heavily on the walk-in applicant and referrals for these employees. In locations where the Negro population is large, such as Birmingham, Chicago, and Baltimore, this may result in many Negro applicants; however, in several places where steel plants are located, such as Bethlehem and Latrobe, Pennsylvania, the Negro population is small and, consequently, few Negro walk-ins or referrals would be expected.

Special programs designed to bring Negroes into the plant have been utilized in some cases. Interestingly enough, most of these programs have been engaged in by the smaller or middle-sized company. This may be explained in part by the fact that the employment manager in such a company usually feels more closely identified with community problems than his counterpart in a large company. One industrial relations director in the Great Lakes and Midwest district commented on his company's program as follows: "Special recruiting efforts directed toward increasing minority group employment including summer and permanent job listings with local community organizations which provide employment referral services to minority group members, partici-

44. See Earl J. McGrath, *The Predominantly Negro Colleges and Universities in Transition* (New York: Teachers College, Columbia University, 1965); and Nathan Hare and Stephen J. Wright, "Black Students and Negro Colleges," *Saturday Review*, July 20, 1968, pp. 44-46, 58.

pation in the Jobs Now Program and the Vice President's Summer Employment Youth Motivation Program" have all been used.[45] Another particular program conducted by a firm in this same district provides some insight into recruiting in difficult areas.

A small company in the Midwest decided in 1967 to launch a hard-core jobless plan to overcome potential racial conflict in the small town in which it operates. The company has a total employment of about 7,000 with approximately 700 Negroes, and it resides in an area that contains about 6 percent Negro population. In cooperation with the NAACP and a private training organization, the company decided to hire and train thirty-five hard-core unemployed persons. Recruiting stations were operated four hours a day in various depressed areas to accept applications from the unemployed and underemployed. The NAACP assisted in processing the applications. From 67 applicants, 23 (20 Negroes and 3 whites) were initially chosen and 8 later joined the group, bringing the total recruited to 31. Ages ranged from 18 to 51, the median education attainment was seventh grade; 19 had been arrested and 13 convicted, and some had dishonorable discharges from the service. After the recruits spent one week in training with the private organization, they were employed on a half-day basis while attending classes with the training group the remainder of the day. This lasted about two months and then the trainees went into the company full time in unskilled and semiskilled jobs where the minimum pay was $2.41 per hour.

The company succeeded in having 26 of the 31 complete the program. Certain unexpected dividends developed from the program: (1) the probation period turnover results have been better among this group than those who were walk-ins, (2) the recruits blended into the existing work force without noticeable differences, (3) a large number were found to have considerable advancement potential, and (4) a rapport was established with those who can provide a valuable employee referral source among minority groups in the future. The company's special recruiting efforts made them aware of shortcomings in the routine hiring practices. A major lesson from this experiment appears to be that a special program, enthusiastically supported and entered into as an investment in human resources, can work and pay dividends to the firm and to the community it serves.

45. Personal interviews, 1967.

Not all companies agree that special programs should be conducted to recruit Negroes. These companies usually base their employment on merit, and they object "to the idea of going out and finding qualified Negroes, because this approach, they feel, is giving preferential treatment to the Negro population."[46] One company official states the case as follows:

> The American public has been badly misled; employers have been duped; and our obligations under the Plans for Progress program is to employ . . . as we have for many years . . . on the basis of merit only. Currently, many of the people responsible for administering the progress under Title VII and Plans for Progress are interested in statistical improvement in the percentages of Negroes on their payrolls. I must say that, in my opinion, the percentage of Negroes on our payroll will probably be reduced and not increased as a result of the necessity of upgrading our employment standards to keep abreast of technological changes occurring within our industry. If we were hiring Negroes for the first time, obviously our statistics would improve, but I resent the following and predict that there will be substantial opposition to these points:
>
> (1) Paying a premium salary to Negro college graduates just for the sake of getting a Negro on the payroll.
>
> (2) Seeking out Negroes by recruiting at all-Negro colleges.
>
> (3) Seeking out, exclusively, Negro employment sources just for the purpose of getting Negroes on the payroll.
>
> (4) The emphasis on culturally deprived being applicable only to Negroes, because it is equally applicable to culturally deprived whites.
>
> (5) The lack of intestinal fortitude on the part of businessmen to make the merit employment concept a reality and not use it for the purpose of preference to Negroes.[47]

This position is extreme, but it indicates the lack of unanimity concerning the various programs used in recruiting Negroes in industry today.

SELECTION PROCEDURES

In general, the companies interviewed stated that a high school diploma or equivalency is a preferred educational requirement for entry level jobs. This requirement has been relaxed under tight labor market conditions, and employers have learned that valuable employees can be

46. The Bureau of National Affairs, Inc., *The Negro and Title VII,* Survey No. 77, Washington, D. C., July 1965, p. 5.
47. *Ibid.,* pp. 5-6.

selected without a high school education. For example, one plant of a middle-sized company in Chicago has 8,000 employees distributed in all job classifications without a high school education, and it has been determined that less than 1 percent are illiterate. The following statement from another company summarizes the overall industry attitude toward the high school requirement:

> The nature of entry level jobs in the white collar and blue collar groups differ with consequent differences in entry requirements. A high school education is a general but not an absolute requirement in the white collar work force. Specific entry level white collar jobs such as Typist or Stenographer obviously require applicants who possess skills sufficient to enable them to perform the work. . . .
>
> . . . We have departed from the requirement that all applicants for [blue collar work] be high school graduates. Instead, evidence of functional literacy is the important substitute standard. . . . We are faced with the problem of trying to maintain entrance requirements which are not unrealistically high for entry level work, but will at the same time provide our operations with employees who have an immediate or potential ability to perform the semi-skilled or skilled work to which they can advance.[48]

The foregoing places emphasis on a potential employee, who is not a high school graduate, being able to demonstrate ability to perform and to be upgraded. There is a certain amount of risk involved in hiring an employee into blue collar entry jobs if he cannot be expected to progress up the long, narrow ladder in the steel industry. One of the difficulties in southern steel plants today arises from the large number of Negro employees who were hired without a high school education or a determination of potential ability to be promoted. The pressures are to promote and upgrade these people, and employers are caught in a dilemma. It was unfair, of course, to hire certain employees with the implied (if not explicit) understanding that they would not be promoted beyond a certain position and, therefore, avoiding the need to establish potential before hiring. The situation has changed and plants in all parts of the country are attempting to evaluate an employee's growth potential before employment. A high school education is only one of several factors that are being studied in the evaluation and selection process. The personnel interview, references, and work experience are being analyzed as crucial elements in the employment decision.

48. Personal interviews, 1968.

Various tests are used in the screening process for new employees in the industry. Most of the companies interviewed indicated that testing needs to be re-examined in order to make it more useful in selecting personnel.[49] In many cases, it was admitted that test scores alone could not be used to determine employability. In regard to Negroes, one company stated that ". . . Our own experience has indicated that comparatively low test scores of minority group members, particularly on mental ability tests, significantly underestimate their potential."[50] Given these conditions, the company has not established an arbitrary cutoff score to determine employment eligibility.

There is concern in the industry about the use and validation of tests. One employer noted: "We are aware of the growing evidence that cultural factors adversely affect the test performance of minority group members. For this reason, we have advised all of our employee relations functions which use tests for pre-employment screening to bear constantly in mind that tests are only one element in the selection process."[51] Considerable government pressure, of course, has been responsible largely for the employer's interest in improving the selection process through testing. The Equal Employment Opportunity Commission has issued "Guidelines on Employment Testing Procedures" but it is not clear how useful they have been in the industry.[52] There is reason to believe that unless the industry continues to move in the direction of being able to validate tests, their future use is in jeopardy since they are likely to be challenged by civil rights and equal employment opportunity agencies.

APPRENTICESHIP PROGRAMS

Most of the skilled maintenance jobs in the steel industry, including crafts such as bricklayer, electrician, machinist, roll turner, and tool and diemaker, are filled through apprenticeship training.[53] In order to be admitted to an apprenticeship program, that may run for four years with 144 hours of related training each year, an employee generally

49. See Richard S. Barrett, "Gray Areas in Black and White Testing," *Harvard Business Review,* Vol. LXVI (January-February 1968), pp. 92-95.
50. Personal interviews, 1967.
51. *Ibid.*
52. Equal Employment Opportunity Commission, *Guidelines on Employment Testing Procedures,* August 24, 1966.
53. For a general discussion of the Negro and apprenticeship programs, see F. Ray Marshall and Vernon M. Briggs, Jr., *The Negro and Apprenticeship* (Baltimore: The Johns Hopkins Press, 1967).

must be a high school graduate, pass certain pysical and mental tests and, in some instances, demonstrate in writing reasons for wanting to enter the program. It is significant that apprenticeship training covers areas where Negroes have been excluded traditionally in the work force. Few Negroes are found in the skilled building trades as a result of past discrimination, and it has been difficult for them to gain entry into the industrial crafts where similar jobs are found.

The companies interviewed in this study had a total of 3,348 employees in apprenticeship training with Negroes accounting for only 168 places or 5.0 percent. Several factors seem to explain the small representation of Negroes: (1) lack of motivation on the part of Negroes in applying for apprenticeship training as a result of past work history, (2) inability of Negroes to meet rigid admission requirements, and (3) discrimination. In regard to discrimination, it appears that employers are making an effort to remove bars against Negroes; however, no Negroes were found in apprenticeship programs in three companies representing a total of 94 apprentices. It is clear that special programs directed to Negroes and other disadvantaged groups need to be developed and implemented if they are to share in the increasing number of skilled positions in the industry.

One pilot program to ". . . lift the workers' educational levels to enable them to qualify for training and job opportunities when available" is now under way.[54] This program for 1,600 steelworkers in nine steel plants in the Gary-Chicago and Baltimore areas is being conducted by the Board for Fundamental Education of Indianapolis under a Manpower Development and Training Act contract with the U. S. Office of Education. Seven steel companies — Inland, National, Republic, Youngstown Sheet and Tube, and United States Steel in the Chicago area, and Armco and Bethlehem in the Baltimore area—and the United Steelworkers of America, in cooperation with the federal government, are participating in the project. The groups to which the effort is directed are:

> . . . unemployed persons who might be hired for job openings available in the steel industry, but . . . do not meet the current educational or, perhaps, the physical standards for acceptance that have been established by the companies.

54. U. S. Department of Health, Education, and Welfare, Office of Education, Bureau of Adult, Vocational, and Library Programs, Division of Manpower Development and Training, Washington, D. C., *The Cooperative Steel Industry Adult Basic Education Program* (no date, circa 1967), p. 1.

> The second group are those who are already employed but who appear to be 'locked-in' at a certain level of educational development. Many of these individuals have voluntarily passed up job promotions when such were offered, or have been promoted to a better job only to find that they could not perform it because they could not read, or write well enough or do required arithmetic. Others have found occupational progression impossible because they speak a language other than English.[55]

As stated above, the program places emphasis on the fundamentals of reading and arithmetic. Upon completion of the first level of instruction, the trainee should have:

(1) A sight vocabulary of 3,000 basic words.
(2) The ability to add, subtract, multiply and divide.
(3) An acceptable form of English usage which permits the individual to write a communicative letter.

At the end of the second level of instruction, each participant should have:

(1) A 7,000 to 10,000 sight vocabulary.
(2) A degree of competency in comprehension.
(3) An insight into reasoning and logical thought.
(4) A good degree of vocabulary satisfaction.
(5) A functional use of fractions, decimals, weight measures, and graphs.
(6) A knowledge of acceptable English usage.
(7) An understanding of scientific terminology.
(8) An awareness of basic United States history.[56]

If the employee completes both levels of instruction, he should have an improved opportunity to move into better positions in the industry. Since the program has not been completed, it is too early to determine the results. A preliminary report indicates a fair degree of response among steelworkers in the places selected for participation. The highest percentage of attendance experienced was at U. S. Steel's South Chicago Works where employees attended 83.8 percent of the time, and the poorest attendance record was at Inland's East Chicago plant where employees attended 67.6 percent of the time. The percent of instruc-

55. *Ibid.*, p. 2.
56. *Ibid.*, p. 5.

tional hours attended for total participants in all plants was 73.5.[57] The reports covering activities under the program are not broken down by race, and this makes it difficult to analyze the Negro's position or experience. Interviews with employers suggest that a major proportion of those participating are Negroes, but the actual figures are not available.

It would be unfair to prejudge the success of this venture, but employer outlook provides little reason to expect outstanding results. One employer in a large company, where attendance by participants was better than in most, stated that he did not think the results would be significant; he felt that absenteeism was too great to accomplish the objectives of the program. Perhaps the most important thing is that it represents a voluntary effort and, hopefully, this means that the industry will continue to experiment until workable solutions can be found to the problems of employing, training, and upgrading the disadvantaged worker.

SENIORITY SYSTEMS AND UPGRADING

Seniority systems, established under collective bargaining agreements, generally determine the upgrading of hourly employees in the basic steel industry. Even in the few cases where the union does not represent employees, seniority appears to be the acceptable mechanism for promotion and job security. In most instances, the union has institutionalized a system that was in effect before it entered. As a rule, the seniority systems are complex, and the local supplements to the basic agreement govern their implementation. The systems reflect peculiarities of the plant and the relative bargaining strengths of the local union and plant management. Despite the general complexity of the problem, there are some obvious facts in regard to the Negro's situation and seniority systems.

Overt discriminatory systems are few; instead, the subtle manipulation of transfer rights, promotion criteria, and type of seniority unit result in observable inequalities. Nondiscrimination clauses are found in almost all labor-management agreements since 1962, and at least one

57. Report Number 2, *Cooperative Steel Project,* submitted to Division of Manpower Development and Training, United States Office of Education, by Board for Fundamental Education, Indianapolis, Indiana, January 8, 1968. (See also Report No. 1.)

was included as early as 1954. These clauses usually read as follows:

> It is the continuing policy of the Company and the Union that the provisions of this Agreement shall be applied to all Employees without regard to race, color, religious creed, national origin, or sex. The representatives of the Union and the Company in all steps of the grievance procedure and in all dealings between the parties shall comply with these provisions.[58]

There has been a difference between policy and practice and differences continue to exist in some cases even though both parties agree to the principle of nondiscrimination. For example, contract language notwithstanding, separate seniority lists by race were maintained prior to 1962 in southern steel plants. Interviews with employers and local union officials indicate a willingness to admit prior discrimination and an interest in overcoming this conditon.

The following factors impinge on the contemporary problems of seniority and integrating a steel plant:

(1) As a producer of raw materials for other industries, the steel industry has not been a leading advocate of social reform in the communities in which it operates. In Birmingham, for example, steel companies and unions did not accept as their role the changing of local customs in regard to the white community's behavior toward Negroes. The company maintained segregated facilities and discriminatory employment practices toward Negroes, because the community was built on a segregated system. This built-in thinking is not easy to overcome; however, some changes are occurring. Separate facilities have disappeared gradually since 1962, and the more recalcitrant attitudes have begun to mellow. The president of a large steelworkers' local interviewed in Birmingham, spoke of the necessity to change in order to survive.[59]

(2) When discrimination has been found in the industry, it has occurred usually *after* employment. Entrance of Negroes into the steel industry in blue collar jobs has been easy historically. In fact, the steel industry was a leader in this country in hiring Negroes. On the other

58. Labor-Management Agreement, Company and United Steelworkers of America, 1965.

59. See the author's, "Negro Employment in Birmingham: Three Cases," in A. M. Ross and H. Hill (eds.), *Employment, Race, and Poverty* (New York: Harcourt, Brace and World, 1967), pp. 308-336.

hand, the employment experience in terms of upgrading reveals discriminatory practices.

(3) Many Negroes entered the industry without any expectation of moving up a promotion ladder. In some cases, they were hired with no established qualifications—i.e., scores on mental tests and high school education—and they have worked in unskilled positions for many years.

(4) Most white employees entered the industry with the expectation of being promoted as rapidly as their seniority would allow. These people were tested and required to meet other qualifying conditions for employment, since it was hoped that they would not become stuck in the middle of a line of progression.

(5) The companies and the union have allowed rigid departmental structures to be established in most plants, and departmental seniority is the major criterion for upgrading and promotion. Departmental seniority has become so highly institutionalized in the industry that any suggested modification is looked upon with dismay by companies and the union.

(6) Negroes have been assigned more frequently to some departments than to others, and there remain some predominantly Negro and all white departments.

(7) Negroes (and whites) have an opportunity to make intraplant transfers, but the moves mean (a) that the employee relinquishes seniority (after a certain time period) in the unit from which he transfers, and (b) he becomes a "new" employee in the department to which he transfers in that his seniority for upgrading purposes begins on the day he enters the new department.

The factors stated above make the current efforts to upgrade Negroes difficult. Consider two examples:

Example 1. Employee A, a Negro, has 20 years' service in department A; he is now in job class 5, the top position he could achieve prior to an integration of promotion rosters in 1962.

Employee B, a white person, has 15 years' service in Department A; he is now in job class 9 and expects to be promoted to job class 10 shortly.

The seniority system, prior to 1962, did not mean much to Employee A; he was discriminated against in that a ceiling was placed on his promotion opportunities. When the lines of promotion were integrated in 1962, Employee A was provided a chance to move up, but the relevant question becomes: what is Employee A's "place" in the revised system? Should Employee A be required to live with the "status quo" until he retires? Should he be given special training and moved to his "rightful place" in job class 11 upon an opening? Should he be trained and moved into job class 11 immediately, given "freedom now," even if it means displacing a white employee? The "status quo" and "freedom now" solutions appear to be extreme and clearly unacceptable and indefensible under Title VII of the Civil Rights Act, and employers are not completely satisfied with the "rightful place approach."[60] Arguments will be made, no doubt, for each of these approaches by various groups, but they likely will be discounted by employers for something that appears more rational and operational.

It is possible that in the steel industry, without particular attention to overcoming the loss suffered by the incumbent Negro as a result of past discrimination, progress in the future will be slow. Most employees in the industry have long service records, turnover is low, and new positions are being created only in the skilled classifications.

Example 2. Employee C, a Negro, has twenty years' seniority in Department C; he is now in job class 7 in this predominantly Negro department.

Employee D, a white person, has fifteen years' service in Department D; he is in job class 7 in this all white department.

Given the conditions stated above, can Employee C transfer to Department D to assume a position vacated by a white employee? The answer is yes, providing certain rules governing intraplant movement are adhered to, but when C transfers, he loses seniority in the department from which he moves, and he goes to the bottom of the seniority ladder in the department he enters. The rules regulating intraplant movements between departments are rigid, and they apply to both Negro and white transfers. The difficulty is that a Negro (or white) would be reluctant to move to a new department, even if it were attractive, when he must give up seniority for promotion purposes. Unless changes are made in the labor-management agreement to make the

60. For discussion of these points, see: Notes, "Title VII, Seniority Discrimination and the Incumbent Negro," *Harvard Law Review,* Vol. 80, No. 6, 1260-1283, 1967. Also see: Peter Deeringer, "Promotion Systems and Equal Employment Opportunity," in Industrial Relations Research Association, *Proceedings of the 19th Annual Meeting,* 1967.

rules governing intraplant movements more flexible, this route is not likely to achieve favorable results for long service Negroes in particular departments of a plant.

The foregoing, while focusing on the steel industry, suggests the need in American industry generally to place additional emphasis on equal employment policy and its more effective implementation. The industrial relations function should be re-evaluated in the firm in light of the tremendous pressures that are being brought by government agencies and society as a whole to provide job opportunities and to upgrade minority employees. A company can no longer look upon equal employment programs solely from the cost point of view and expect meaningful change to occur in its personnel profile. There is need for an investment approach in human resources in most companies today. The latter can lead to more constructive action in integrating the country's work force.

Once equal employment policy has been established and communicated, special programs of recruiting, selecting, and training minority employees should be devised. Such efforts are not likely to succeed unless the firm commits necessary funds and management talent to them. This may be difficult in a low profit industry such as steel which is experiencing declining employment in the blue collar areas, but the challenge remains.

CHAPTER VIII.

Concluding Remarks

Employment in the steel industry has been volatile over the past decade, however, the general trend has been downward. There are fewer employees in the industry today than there were in 1960. The increase in white collar employees has been offset by the decrease in blue collar workers over this period. The Negro has played an important part in the labor force of the steel industry for many years. Large numbers of unskilled and semiskilled positions, not found in other more highly skilled industries, provided many opportunities for Negroes.

Even though the Negro has been employed by the industry, he has not always shared in the most advanced positions. Discriminatory systems in plants located in many sections of the country have denied Negroes their proper advancement opportunities. It is agreed generally, however, that ". . . despite the continuing necessity for efforts to eliminate racial discrimination, there appears to be a reasonable basis for doubting that this factor is the principal *present* source of economic disadvantage for the Negro."[61] The current situation, in which employers are willing to operate nondiscriminatory programs, is a complicated one as a result of the following factors: (1) There is declining employment in the blue collar positions in the industry today, (2) most workers in the industry are long-term employees with continuous service under a collective bargaining agreement recognizing departmental seniority as a basic factor in promotion, (3) Negroes have been hired into the industry in large numbers in the past, (4) they were hired in many instances without established qualifications, since it was assumed that they would not be promoted beyond a certain level, and (5) many Negroes have worked only in all Negro departments or in unskilled positions within an integrated department. These

61. Charles C. Killingsworth, *Jobs and Income for Negroes,* A Joint Publication of the Institute of Labor and Industrial Relations, The University of Michigan-Wayne State University and the National Manpower Policy Task Force, Washington, D. C., May 1968, pp. 31-32.

factors mean that the Negro more or less is locked into position in the industry in the areas where he has always worked. Changes are occurring and they will continue to occur, as is evident from the statistics produced in this volume pertaining to craftsmen and operative positions; but, realistically, the industry is not one where abundant blue collar opportunities for Negroes or whites await the future. The forces of technology, moving at a rapid rate in the industry, imports of foreign steel, removing a substantial amount of business away from United States firms, and industry adjustments to low rates of return, will not produce strong incentives to hire additional labor in the years ahead.

It is clear that management desires to implement equal employment opportunity programs in the industry today. Government pressure, backed by court decisions, has caused an awareness on the part of the employer to the necessity of operating nondiscriminatory employment systems. In some cases, progress will be slow because employers simply do not know how to overcome the basic problems of integrating departments and/or lines of promotion. Considerations of efficiency and the white incumbents cause employers to look upon government proposals to remedy present effects of past discrimination as extreme and impractical. The steel industry has not been a profitable one in recent years, and this stark reality bears heavily on decisions related to changing work rules and practices that could result in loss of production, low employee morale, and strife at the workplace. The crucial question, of course, is what price should the firm or industry pay for efficiency? Certainly, it would be inappropriate to argue that discriminatory systems should be allowed as the price of improving the profit position of the industry; it would be just as naive, on the other hand, to suggest that given the poor economic position of the industry changes will occur as quickly as might otherwise be the case. The significant finding here is that employers have accepted the mandate for change, and there is considerable activity under way to find solutions to the problems of Negro utilization.

There is reason for some optimism concerning the prospects of employees in white collar positions in the industry. The Negro's share of most white collar occupations increased between 1963 and 1968 in all districts. This trend is likely to continue into the future. White collar positions are not covered by collective bargaining agreements and discriminatory barriers have not become institutionalized in most cases. Particular problems have arisen in the sales area, and there are practically no Negroes in this occupational category. The industry recognizes this as an undesirable situation, and some companies are making an effort to place Negroes in the sales field. Marked percentage increases for Negroes in the officials and managers, technicians, and office and clerical occupations occurred between 1963 and 1968. Even though the absolute changes have been small, the trend is in an encouraging direction.

It is hoped that an accommodation between the public and private sectors can be reached in order that problems of minority employment can be solved efficiently. Government agencies and employers in the industry appear to agree that discrimination in employment should be eliminated, but there remain the difficult questions as to how this can be done and when shall it be done? As the slow, tedious processes of conciliation and voluntary compliance fail to yield satisfactory returns, the unfortunate consequence of court-intervention begins to appear in the picture.

When the Office of Federal Contract Compliance and the Equal Employment Opportunity Commission become exasperated in their attempts to bring about change, the Attorney General enters in what is being described currently as pattern or practice of discrimination cases.[62] This reflects the fact that the parties could not resolve their problems through voluntary, private agreement making mechanisms, or that there was not enough time to do so. The bothersome thing about the court, of course, is that constructive agreement is not likely to be reached there. Vested interest positions will be defended, and the court's decision will favor that side that presents the better case. This is a win-lose situation. The losing side is supposed to live with a condition that it found intolerable in the first place. There must be a better way of doing things.

On balance, the position of the Negro in the industry appears to be improving at a slow pace. If the improvements are permanent, and there is reason to believe that they will be, an acceleration of progress can occur in the future. Warren Bennis has summarized the challenge very effectively as follows:

> Man before Darwin, was elevated as the "darling of the gods." This Victorian fiction has been dissolved by too many wars, too much poverty, and too many diseased. But we remain a moral and ethical animal; our survival and security depend on the exploitation of moral and ethical systems.[63]

How true and how difficult!

62. See Section 707, Civil Rights Act of 1964.
63. Warren G. Bennis, *Changing Organizations* (New York: McGraw-Hill, 1966), p. 2.

Appendix A
STATISTICAL DATA

TABLE A-1. *Basic Steel Industry*
Employment by District, Sex, and Race
1963 - 1968

District[a]	All Employees Total	All Employees Negro	All Employees Percent Negro	Male Total	Male Negro	Male Percent Negro	Female Total	Female Negro	Female Percent Negro
				1963					
Eastern	67,278	10,627	15.8	65,065	10,606	16.3	2,213	21	0.9
Southern	28,547	6,382	22.4	27,974	6,378	22.8	573	4	0.7
Pittsburgh	155,681	10,975	7.0	149,023	10,916	7.3	6,658	59	0.9
Great Lakes and Midwest	187,827	27,613	14.7	181,296	27,365	15.1	6,531	248	3.8
West Coast	14,562	929	6.4	13,849	912	6.6	713	17	2.4
Total All Districts	453,895	56,526	12.5	437,207	56,177	12.8	16,688	349	2.1
				1964					
Eastern	75,330	12,128	16.1	73,131	12,107	16.6	2,199	21	1.0
Southern	29,215	6,406	21.9	28,597	6,402	22.4	618	4	0.6
Pittsburgh	163,063	11,762	7.2	156,277	11,676	7.5	6,786	86	1.3
Great Lakes and Midwest	199,382	29,894	15.0	192,700	29,613	15.4	6,682	281	4.2
West Coast	16,202	1,101	6.8	15,439	1,084	7.0	763	17	2.2
Total All Districts	483,192	61,291	12.7	466,144	60,882	13.1	17,048	409	2.4

				1965					
Eastern	70,993	10,409	14.7	68,853	10,377	15.1	2,140	32	1.5
Southern	26,812	5,882	21.9	26,151	5,876	22.5	661	6	0.9
Pittsburgh	153,974	10,515	6.8	147,149	10,414	7.1	6,825	101	1.5
Great Lakes and Midwest	186,683	27,920	15.0	180,217	27,634	15.3	6,466	286	4.4
West Coast	15,678	1,092	7.0	14,939	1,076	7.2	739	16	2.2
Total All Districts	454,140	55,818	12.3	437,309	55,377	12.7	16,831	441	2.6
				1966					
Eastern	74,702	11,389	15.2	72,477	11,348	15.7	2,225	41	1.8
Southern	28,667	6,451	22.5	28,040	6,443	23.0	627	8	1.3
Pittsburgh	151,626	10,314	6.8	144,849	10,209	7.0	6,777	105	1.5
Great Lakes and Midwest	193,905	30,454	15.7	186,732	29,945	16.0	7,173	509	7.1
West Coast	16,370	1,141	7.0	15,574	1,123	7.2	796	18	2.3
Total All Districts	465,270	59,749	12.8	447,672	59,068	13.2	17,598	681	3.9
				1968					
Eastern	73,821	11,528	15.6	71,435	11,477	16.1	2,386	51	2.1
Southern	29,031	6,196	21.3	28,427	6,181	21.7	604	15	2.5
Pittsburgh	150,518	10,380	6.9	143,455	10,252	7.1	7,063	128	1.8
Great Lakes and Midwest	194,041	32,128	16.6	186,614	31,553	16.9	7,427	575	7.7
West Coast	15,098	1,169	7.7	14,403	1,153	8.0	695	16	2.3
Total All Districts	462,509	61,401	13.3	444,334	60,616	13.6	18,175	785	4.3

Source: Data in author's possession.

a. Note: Geographic definitions are as follows:

Eastern: Connecticut, Maryland, Massachusetts, New Jersey, New York, eastern Pennsylvania.
Southern: Alabama, Kentucky, Oklahoma, and Texas.
Pittsburgh: Western Pennsylvania, eastern Ohio, and the northernmost corner of West Virginia.
Great Lakes and Midwest: Illinois, Indiana, Michigan, Minnesota, and Missouri, as well as the western portion of New York and the Lake Counties of Ohio. The district has been extended to include the plants located in inland Ohio and distant Colorado and Utah.
West Coast: Washington and California.

Table A-2. *Basic Steel Industry*
Employment by Occupational Group, Sex, and Race
Eastern District, 1963

Occupational Group	All Employees[a]			Male			Female		
	Total	Negro	Percent Negro	Total	Negro	Percent Negro	Total	Negro	Percent Negro
Officials and managers	5,327	39	0.7	5,283	39	0.7	44	—	—
Professionals	1,425	2	0.1	1,423	2	0.1	2	—	—
Technicians	1,275	2	0.2	1,221	2	0.2	54	—	—
Sales workers	200	1	0.5	194	—	—	6	1	16.7
Office and clerical	5,751	50	0.9	4,073	37	0.9	1,678	13	0.8
Total white collar	13,978	94	0.7	12,194	80	0.7	1,784	14	0.8
Craftsmen (Skilled)	15,317	573	3.7	15,312	573	3.7	5	—	—
Operatives (Semiskilled)	25,355	4,618	18.2	25,004	4,617	18.5	351	1	0.3
Laborers (Unskilled)	11,343	5,036	44.4	11,320	5,034	44.5	23	2	8.7
Service workers	1,285	306	23.8	1,235	302	24.5	50	4	8.0
Total blue collar	53,300	10,533	19.8	52,871	10,526	19.9	429	7	1.6
Total	67,278	10,627	15.8	65,065	10,606	16.3	2,213	21	0.9

a. 9 companies, 13 plants.

TABLE A-3. *Basic Steel Industry*
Employment by Occupational Group, Sex, and Race
Eastern District, 1964

Occupational Group	All Employees[a]			Male			Female		
	Total	Negro	Percent Negro	Total	Negro	Percent Negro	Total	Negro	Percent Negro
Officials and managers	5,554	54	1.0	5,515	54	1.0	39	—	—
Professionals	1,453	2	0.1	1,450	2	0.1	3	—	—
Technicians	1,358	2	0.1	1,296	2	0.2	62	—	—
Sales workers	198	1	0.5	192	—	—	6	1	16.7
Office and clerical	5,969	58	1.0	4,253	45	1.1	1,716	13	0.8
Total white collar	14,532	117	0.8	12,706	103	0.8	1,826	14	0.8
Craftsmen (Skilled)	17,316	796	4.6	17,295	796	4.6	21	—	—
Operatives (Semiskilled)	28,999	5,654	19.5	28,724	5,653	19.7	275	1	0.4
Laborers (Unskilled)	12,990	5,207	40.1	12,965	5,206	40.2	25	1	4.0
Service workers	1,493	354	23.7	1,441	349	24.2	52	5	9.6
Total blue collar	60,798	12,011	19.8	60,425	12,004	19.9	373	7	1.9
Total	75,330	12,128	16.1	73,131	12,107	16.6	2,199	21	1.0

a. 9 companies, 13 plants.

TABLE A-4. *Basic Steel Industry*
Employment of White Collar and Blue Collar Workers by Sex and Race
Eastern District, 1965

Occupation Classification	All Employees[a]			Male			Female		
	Total	Negro	Percent Negro	Total	Negro	Percent Negro	Total	Negro	Percent Negro
White collar	16,614	159	1.0	14,703	136	0.9	1,911	23	1.2
Blue collar	54,379	10,250	18.8	54,150	10,241	18.9	229	9	3.9
Total	70,993	10,409	14.7	68,853	10,377	15.1	2,140	32	1.5

a. 9 companies, 13 plants.

TABLE A-5. *Basic Steel Industry*
Employment by Occupational Group, Sex, and Race
Eastern District, 1966

Occupational Group	All Employees[a]			Male			Female		
	Total	Negro	Percent Negro	Total	Negro	Percent Negro	Total	Negro	Percent Negro
Officials and managers	6,329	84	1.3	6,286	84	1.3	43	—	—
Professionals	1,556	3	0.2	1,552	3	0.2	4	—	—
Technicians	1,363	8	0.6	1,308	8	0.6	55	—	—
Sales workers	176	—	—	175	—	—	1	—	—
Office and clerical	6,469	106	1.6	4,643	75	1.6	1,826	31	1.7
Total white collar	15,893	201	1.3	13,964	170	1.2	1,929	31	1.6
Craftsmen (Skilled)	17,069	753	4.4	17,064	753	4.4	5	—	—
Operatives (Semiskilled)	27,918	5,244	18.8	27,738	5,243	18.9	180	1	0.6
Laborers (Unskilled)	12,303	4,816	39.1	12,246	4,816	39.3	57	—	—
Service workers	1,519	375	24.7	1,465	366	25.0	54	9	16.7
Total blue collar	58,809	11,188	19.0	58,513	11,178	19.1	296	10	3.4
Total	74,702	11,389	15.2	72,477	11,348	15.7	2,225	41	1.8

a. 9 companies, 13 plants.

TABLE A-6. *Basic Steel Industry*
Employment by Occupational Group, Sex, and Race
Eastern District, 1968

Occupational Group	All Employees[a]			Male			Female		
	Total	Negro	Percent Negro	Total	Negro	Percent Negro	Total	Negro	Percent Negro
Officials and managers	6,549	102	1.6	6,511	102	1.6	38	—	—
Professionals	1,671	9	0.5	1,666	9	0.5	5	—	—
Technicians	1,425	22	1.5	1,376	22	1.6	49	—	—
Sales workers	188	—	—	188	—	—	—	—	—
Office and clerical	6,480	146	2.3	4,594	104	2.3	1,886	42	2.2
Total white collar	16,313	279	1.7	14,335	237	1.7	1,978	42	2.1
Craftsmen (Skilled)	16,962	845	5.0	16,948	845	5.0	14	—	—
Operatives (Semiskilled)	27,681	5,469	19.8	27,411	5,468	19.9	270	1	0.4
Laborers (Unskilled)	11,263	4,473	39.7	11,203	4,473	39.9	60	—	—
Service workers	1,602	462	28.8	1,538	454	29.5	64	8	12.5
Total blue collar	57,508	11,249	19.6	57,100	11,240	19.7	408	9	2.2
Total	73,821	11,528	15.6	71,435	11,477	16.1	2,386	51	2.1

a. 9 companies 13 plants.

TABLE A-7. *Basic Steel Industry*
Employment by Occupational Group, Sex, and Race
Southern District, 1963

Occupational Group	All Employees[a]			Male			Female		
	Total	Negro	Percent Negro	Total	Negro	Percent Negro	Total	Negro	Percent Negro
Officials and managers	2,404	41	1.7	2,401	41	1.7	3	—	—
Professionals	517	—	—	517	—	—	—	—	—
Technicians	1,069	4	0.4	1,036	4	0.4	33	—	—
Sales workers	32	—	—	31	—	—	1	—	—
Office and clerical	2,145	28	1.3	1,691	28	1.7	454	—	—
Total white collar	6,167	73	1.2	5,676	73	1.3	491	—	—
Craftsmen (Skilled)	9,431	555	5.9	9,428	555	5.9	3	—	—
Operatives (Semiskilled)	8,331	2,651	31.8	8,291	2,651	32.0	40	—	—
Laborers (Unskilled)	4,163	2,947	70.8	4,133	2,947	71.3	30	—	—
Service workers	455	156	34.3	446	152	34.1	9	4	44.4
Total blue collar	22,380	6,309	28.2	22,298	6,305	28.3	82	4	4.9
Total	28,547	6,382	22.4	27,974	6,378	22.8	573	4	0.7

a. 4 companies, 7 plants.

TABLE A-8. *Basic Steel Industry*
Employment by Occupational Group, Sex, and Race
Southern District, 1964

Occupational Group	All Employees[a]			Male			Female		
	Total	Negro	Percent Negro	Total	Negro	Percent Negro	Total	Negro	Percent Negro
Officials and managers	2,452	26	1.1	2,449	26	1.1	3	—	—
Professionals	482	—	—	482	—	—	—	—	—
Technicians	1,054	4	0.4	1,021	4	0.4	33	—	—
Sales workers	40	—	—	39	—	—	1	—	—
Office and clerical	2,144	18	0.8	1,646	18	1.1	498	—	—
Total white collar	6,172	48	0.8	5,637	48	0.9	535	—	—
Craftsmen (Skilled)	9,723	613	6.3	9,720	613	6.3	3	—	—
Operatives (Semiskilled)	8,553	2,715	31.7	8,513	2,715	31.9	40	—	—
Laborers (Unskilled)	4,299	2,882	67.0	4,268	2,882	67.5	31	—	—
Service workers	468	148	31.6	459	144	31.4	9	4	44.4
Total blue collar	23,043	6,358	27.6	22,960	6,354	27.7	83	4	4.8
Total	29,215	6,406	21.9	28,597	6,402	22.4	618	4	0.6

a. 4 companies, 7 plants.

TABLE A-9. *Basic Steel Industry*
Employment of White Collar and Blue Collar Workers by Sex and Race
Southern District, 1965

Occupation Classification	All Employees[a]			Male			Female		
	Total	Negro	Percent Negro	Total	Negro	Percent Negro	Total	Negro	Percent Negro
White collar	5,869	40	0.7	5,392	40	0.7	477	—	—
Blue collar	20,943	5,842	27.9	20,759	5,836	28.1	184	6	3.3
Total	26,812	5,882	21.9	26,151	5,876	22.5	661	6	0.9

a. 4 companies, 7 plants.

TABLE A-10. *Basic Steel Industry*
Employment by Occupational Group, Sex, and Race
Southern District, 1966

Occupational Group	All Employees[a]			Male			Female		
	Total	Negro	Percent Negro	Total	Negro	Percent Negro	Total	Negro	Percent Negro
Officials and managers	2,399	6	0.3	2,397	6	0.3	2	—	—
Professionals	610	2	0.3	595	2	0.3	15	—	—
Technicians	958	8	0.8	940	8	0.9	18	—	—
Sales workers	16	—	—	16	—	—	—	—	—
Office and clerical	2,102	26	1.2	1,607	22	1.4	495	4	0.8
Total white collar	6,085	42	0.7	5,555	38	0.7	530	4	0.8
Craftsmen (Skilled)	8,991	664	7.4	8,991	664	7.4	—	—	—
Operatives (Semiskilled)	8,475	2,705	31.9	8,435	2,705	32.1	40	—	—
Laborers (Unskilled)	4,620	2,900	62.8	4,585	2,900	63.2	35	—	—
Service workers	496	140	28.2	474	136	28.7	22	4	18.2
Total blue collar	22,582	6,409	28.4	22,485	6,405	28.5	97	4	4.1
Total	28,667	6,451	22.5	28,040	6,443	23.0	627	8	1.3

a. 4 companies, 7 plants.

TABLE A-11. *Basic Steel Industry*
Employment by Occupational Group, Sex, and Race
Southern District, 1968

Occupational Group	All Employees[a]			Male			Female		
	Total	Negro	Percent Negro	Total	Negro	Percent Negro	Total	Negro	Percent Negro
Officials and managers	2,399	7	0.3	2,397	7	0.3	2	—	—
Professionals	639	8	1.3	621	8	1.3	18	—	—
Technicians	976	41	4.2	952	40	4.2	24	1	4.2
Sales workers	25	—	—	19	—	—	6	—	—
Office and clerical	2,104	52	2.5	1,613	40	2.5	491	12	2.4
Total white collar	6,143	108	1.8	5,602	95	1.7	541	13	2.4
Craftsmen (Skilled)	9,687	756	7.8	9,681	756	7.8	6	—	—
Operatives (Semiskilled)	8,431	3,016	35.8	8,407	3,016	35.9	24	—	—
Laborers (Unskilled)	4,321	2,197	50.8	4,295	2,197	51.2	26	—	—
Service workers	449	119	26.5	442	117	26.5	7	2	28.6
Total blue collar	22,888	6,088	26.6	22,825	6,086	26.7	63	2	3.2
Total	29,031	6,196	21.3	28,427	6,181	21.7	604	15	2.5

a. 4 companies, 7 plants.

TABLE A-12. *Basic Steel Industry*
Employment by Occupational Group, Sex, and Race
Pittsburgh District, 1963

Occupational Group	All Employees[a]			Male			Female		
	Total	Negro	Percent Negro	Total	Negro	Percent Negro	Total	Negro	Percent Negro
Officials and managers	10,349	50	0.5	10,299	50	0.5	50	—	—
Professionals	4,658	8	0.2	4,531	8	0.2	127	—	—
Technicians	3,407	7	0.2	3,179	7	0.2	228	—	—
Sales workers	2,241	5	0.2	1,417	2	0.1	824	3	0.4
Office and clerical	13,795	126	0.9	9,350	85	0.9	4,445	41	0.9
Total white collar	34,450	196	0.6	28,776	152	0.5	5,674	44	0.8
Craftsmen (Skilled)	35,528	1,115	3.1	35,507	1,115	3.1	21	—	—
Operatives (Semiskilled)	58,973	6,130	10.4	58,531	6,128	10.5	442	2	0.5
Laborers (Unskilled)	24,004	3,215	13.4	23,818	3,215	13.5	186	—	—
Service workers	2,726	319	11.7	2,391	306	12.8	335	13	3.9
Total blue collar	121,231	10,779	8.9	120,247	10,764	9.0	984	15	1.5
Total	155,681	10,975	7.0	149,023	10,916	7.3	6,658	59	0.9

a. 12 companies, 31 plants.

TABLE A-13. *Basic Steel Industry*
Employment by Occupational Group, Sex, and Race
Pittsburgh District, 1964

Occupational Group	All Employees[a]			Male			Female		
	Total	Negro	Percent Negro	Total	Negro	Percent Negro	Total	Negro	Percent Negro
Officials and managers	11,778	52	0.4	11,730	52	0.4	48	—	—
Professionals	5,039	6	0.1	4,906	6	0.1	133	—	—
Technicians	3,525	13	0.4	3,274	12	0.4	251	1	0.4
Sales workers	2,347	7	0.3	1,508	3	0.2	839	4	0.5
Office and clerical	15,444	147	1.0	10,875	86	0.8	4,569	61	1.3
Total white collar	38,133	225	0.6	32,293	159	0.5	5,840	66	1.1
Craftsmen (Skilled)	37,631	1,283	3.4	37,611	1,283	3.4	20	—	—
Operatives (Semiskilled)	59,428	6,462	10.9	59,023	6,461	10.9	405	1	0.2
Laborers (Unskilled)	25,084	3,472	13.8	24,908	3,472	13.9	176	—	—
Service workers	2,787	320	11.5	2,442	301	12.3	345	19	5.5
Total blue collar	124,930	11,537	9.2	123,984	11,517	9.3	946	20	2.1
Total	163,063	11,762	7.2	156,277	11,676	7.5	6,786	86	1.3

a. 12 companies, 31 plants.

TABLE A-14. *Basic Steel Industry*
Employment of White Collar and Blue Collar Workers by Sex and Race
Pittsburgh District, 1965

Occupation Classification	All Employees[a]			Male			Female		
	Total	Negro	Percent Negro	Total	Negro	Percent Negro	Total	Negro	Percent Negro
White collar	37,810	256	0.7	31,729	173	0.5	6,081	83	1.4
Blue collar	116,164	10,259	8.8	115,420	10,241	8.9	744	18	2.4
Total	153,974	10,515	6.8	147,149	10,414	7.1	6,825	101	1.5

a. 12 companies, 31 plants.

TABLE A-15. *Basic Steel Industry*
Employment by Occupational Group, Sex, and Race
Pittsburgh District, 1966

Occupational Group	All Employees[a]			Male			Female		
	Total	Negro	Percent Negro	Total	Negro	Percent Negro	Total	Negro	Percent Negro
Officials and managers	11,617	57	0.5	11,561	57	0.5	56	—	—
Professionals	5,477	8	0.1	5,305	8	0.2	172	—	—
Technicians	3,543	15	0.4	3,322	14	0.4	221	1	0.5
Sales workers	2,280	8	0.4	1,374	2	0.1	906	6	0.7
Office and clerical	13,766	192	1.4	9,137	113	1.2	4,629	79	1.7
Total white collar	36,683	280	0.8	30,699	194	0.6	5,984	86	1.4
Craftsmen (Skilled)	34,464	1,063	3.1	34,462	1,063	3.1	2	—	—
Operatives (Semiskilled)	54,810	5,292	9.7	54,462	5,291	9.7	348	1	0.3
Laborers (Unskilled)	23,196	3,386	14.6	23,083	3,386	14.7	113	—	—
Service workers	2,473	293	11.8	2,143	275	12.8	330	18	5.5
Total blue collar	114,943	10,034	8.7	114,150	10,015	8.8	793	19	2.4
Total	151,626	10,314	6.8	144,849	10,209	7.0	6,777	105	1.5

a. 12 companies, 31 plants.

TABLE A-16. *Basic Steel Industry*
Employment by Occupational Group, Sex, and Race
Pittsburgh District, 1968

Occupational Group	All Employees[a]			Male			Female		
	Total	Negro	Percent Negro	Total	Negro	Percent Negro	Total	Negro	Percent Negro
Officials and managers	11,969	68	0.6	11,913	68	0.6	56	—	—
Professionals	5,399	10	0.2	5,210	9	0.2	189	1	0.5
Technicians	3,811	28	0.7	3,615	26	0.7	196	2	1.0
Sales workers	2,283	8	0.4	1,377	2	0.1	906	6	0.7
Office and clerical	14,405	261	1.8	9,508	166	1.7	4,897	95	1.9
Total white collar	37,867	375	1.0	31,623	271	0.9	6,244	104	1.7
Craftsmen (Skilled)	35,892	1,227	3.4	35,860	1,227	3.4	32	—	—
Operatives (Semiskilled)	54,096	5,404	10.0	53,759	5,403	10.1	337	1	0.3
Laborers (Unskilled)	20,037	3,052	15.2	19,938	3,051	15.3	99	1	1.0
Service workers	2,626	322	12.3	2,275	300	13.2	351	22	6.3
Total blue collar	112,651	10,005	8.9	111,832	9,981	8.9	819	24	2.9
Total	150,518	10,380	6.9	143,455	10,252	7.1	7,063	128	1.8

a. 12 companies, 31 plants.

TABLE A-17. *Basic Steel Industry*
Employment by Occupational Group, Sex, and Race
Great Lakes and Midwest District, 1963

Occupational Group	All Employees[a]			Male			Female		
	Total	Negro	Percent Negro	Total	Negro	Percent Negro	Total	Negro	Percent Negro
Officials and managers	13,960	113	0.8	13,926	113	0.8	34	—	—
Professionals	2,638	3	0.1	2,608	3	0.1	30	—	—
Technicians	4,413	38	0.9	4,170	36	0.9	243	2	0.8
Sales workers	332	—	—	315	—	—	17	—	—
Office and clerical	13,586	213	1.6	8,863	148	1.7	4,723	65	1.4
Total white collar	34,929	367	1.1	29,882	300	1.0	5,047	67	1.3
Craftsmen (Skilled)	46,063	3,503	7.6	46,005	3,500	7.6	58	3	5.2
Operatives (Semiskilled)	74,571	15,454	20.7	73,754	15,394	20.9	817	60	7.3
Laborers (Unskilled)	29,121	7,635	26.2	28,894	7,589	26.3	227	46	20.3
Service workers	3,143	654	20.8	2,761	582	21.1	382	72	18.8
Total blue collar	152,898	27,246	17.8	151,414	27,065	17.9	1,484	181	12.2
Total	187,827	27,613	14.7	181,296	27,365	15.1	6,531	248	3.8

a. 13 companies, 36 plants.

TABLE A-18. *Basic Steel Industry*
Employment by Occupational Group, Sex, and Race
Great Lakes and Midwest District, 1964

Occupational Group	All Employees[a]			Male			Female		
	Total	Negro	Percent Negro	Total	Negro	Percent Negro	Total	Negro	Percent Negro
Officials and managers	16,452	168	1.0	16,394	168	1.0	58	—	—
Professionals	3,006	8	0.3	2,967	8	0.3	39	—	—
Technicians	4,712	88	1.9	4,457	85	1.9	255	3	1.2
Sales workers	348	—	—	329	—	—	19	—	—
Office and clerical	15,226	380	2.5	10,381	305	2.9	4,845	75	1.5
Total white collar	39,744	644	1.6	34,528	566	1.6	5,216	78	1.5
Craftsmen (Skilled)	46,473	3,765	8.1	46,426	3,761	8.1	47	4	8.5
Operatives (Semiskilled)	78,452	16,511	21.0	77,671	16,445	21.2	781	66	8.5
Laborers (Unskilled)	31,386	8,299	26.4	31,157	8,249	26.5	229	50	21.8
Service workers	3,327	675	20.3	2,918	592	20.3	409	83	20.3
Total blue collar	159,638	29,250	18.3	158,172	29,047	18.4	1,466	203	13.8
Total	199,382	29,894	15.0	192,700	29,613	15.4	6,682	281	4.2

a. 13 companies, 37 plants.

Table A-19. *Basic Steel Industry*
Employment of White Collar and Blue Collar Workers by Sex and Race
Great Lakes and Midwest District, 1965

Occupation Classification	All Employees[a]			Male			Female		
	Total	Negro	Percent Negro	Total	Negro	Percent Negro	Total	Negro	Percent Negro
White collar	40,035	781	2.0	34,809	682	2.0	5,226	99	1.9
Blue collar	146,648	27,139	18.5	145,408	26,952	18.5	1,240	187	15.1
Total	186,683	27,920	15.0	180,217	27,634	15.3	6,466	286	4.4

a. 13 companies, 37 plants.

TABLE A-20. *Basic Steel Industry*
Employment by Occupational Group, Sex, and Race
Great Lakes and Midwest District, 1966

Occupational Group	All Employees[a]			Male			Female		
	Total	Negro	Percent Negro	Total	Negro	Percent Negro	Total	Negro	Percent Negro
Officials and managers	16,890	219	1.3	16,860	219	1.3	30	—	—
Professionals	3,316	9	0.3	3,255	9	0.3	61	—	—
Technicians	4,816	125	2.6	4,583	121	2.6	233	4	1.7
Sales workers	161	—	—	146	—	—	15	—	—
Office and clerical	15,847	577	3.6	10,616	432	4.1	5,231	145	2.8
Total white collar	41,030	930	2.3	35,460	781	2.2	5,570	149	2.7
Craftsmen (Skilled)	45,821	3,903	8.5	45,778	3,900	8.5	43	3	7.0
Operatives (Semiskilled)	75,934	16,873	22.2	75,326	16,810	22.3	608	63	10.4
Laborers (Unskilled)	27,473	7,984	29.1	26,982	7,793	28.9	491	191	38.9
Service workers	3,647	764	20.9	3,186	661	20.7	461	103	22.3
Total blue collar	152,875	29,524	19.3	151,272	29,164	19.3	1,603	360	22.5
Total	193,905	30,454	15.7	186,732	29,945	16.0	7,173	509	7.1

a. 13 companies, 37 plants.

TABLE A-21. *Basic Steel Industry*
Employment by Occupational Group, Sex, and Race
Great Lakes and Midwest District, 1968

Occupational Group	All Employees[a]			Male			Female		
	Total	Negro	Percent Negro	Total	Negro	Percent Negro	Total	Negro	Percent Negro
Officials and managers	17,263	319	1.8	17,229	318	1.8	34	1	2.9
Professionals	3,433	22	0.6	3,332	21	0.6	101	1	1.0
Technicians	5,304	166	3.1	5,026	163	3.2	278	3	1.1
Sales workers	184	—	—	172	—	—	12	—	—
Office and clerical	16,039	693	4.3	10,505	478	4.6	5,534	215	3.9
Total white collar	42,223	1,200	2.8	36,264	980	2.7	5,959	220	3.7
Craftsmen (Skilled)	45,789	4,102	9.0	45,740	4,094	9.0	49	8	16.3
Operatives (Semiskilled)	74,507	17,356	23.3	73,990	17,292	23.4	517	64	12.4
Laborers (Unskilled)	27,734	8,657	31.2	27,295	8,485	31.1	439	172	39.2
Service workers	3,788	813	21.5	3,325	702	21.1	463	111	24.0
Total blue collar	151,818	30,928	20.4	150,350	30,573	20.3	1,468	355	24.2
Total	194,041	32,128	16.6	186,614	31,553	16.9	7,427	575	7.7

a. 13 companis, 37 plants.

TABLE A-22. *Basic Steel Industry*
Employment by Occupational Group, Sex, and Race
West Coast District, 1963

Occupational Group	All Employees[a]			Male			Female		
	Total	Negro	Percent Negro	Total	Negro	Percent Negro	Total	Negro	Percent Negro
Officials and managers	1,367	1	0.1	1,364	1	0.1	3	—	—
Professionals	324	—	—	324	—	—	—	—	—
Technicians	181	—	—	156	—	—	25	—	—
Sales workers	3	—	—	3	—	—	—	—	—
Office and clerical	1,525	7	0.5	1,049	6	0.6	476	1	0.2
Total white collar	3,400	8	0.2	2,896	7	0.2	504	1	0.2
Craftsmen (Skilled)	4,064	128	3.1	4,063	128	3.2	1	—	—
Operatives (Semiskilled)	4,858	504	10.4	4,705	499	10.6	153	5	3.3
Laborers (Unskilled)	1,958	260	13.3	1,956	260	13.3	2	—	—
Service workers	282	29	10.3	229	18	7.9	53	11	20.8
Total blue collar	11,162	921	8.3	10,953	905	8.3	209	16	7.7
Total	14,562	929	6.4	13,849	912	6.6	713	17	2.4

a. 3 companies, 6 plants.

TABLE A-23. *Basic Steel Industry*
Employment by Occupational Group, Sex, and Race
West Coast District, 1964

Occupational Group	All Employees[a]			Male			Female		
	Total	Negro	Percent Negro	Total	Negro	Percent Negro	Total	Negro	Percent Negro
Officials and managers	1,380	1	0.1	1,377	1	0.1	3	—	—
Professionals	336	—	—	336	—	—	—	—	—
Technicians	184	—	—	156	—	—	28	—	—
Sales workers	3	—	—	3	—	—	—	—	—
Office and clerical	1,550	15	1.0	1,048	13	1.2	502	2	0.4
Total white collar	3,453	16	0.5	2,920	14	0.5	533	2	0.4
Craftsmen (Skilled)	4,608	157	3.4	4,607	157	3.4	1	—	—
Operatives (Semiskilled)	5,610	644	11.5	5,439	639	11.7	171	5	2.9
Laborers (Unskilled)	2,220	254	11.4	2,218	254	11.5	2	—	—
Service workers	311	30	9.6	255	20	7.8	56	10	17.9
Total blue collar	12,749	1,085	8.5	12,519	1,070	8.5	230	15	6.5
Total	16,202	1,101	6.8	15,439	1,084	7.0	763	17	2.2

a. 3 companies, 6 plants.

TABLE A-24. *Basic Steel Industry*
Employment of White Collar and Blue Collar Workers by Sex and Race
West Coast District, 1965

Occupation Classification	All Employees[a]			Male			Female		
	Total	Negro	Percent Negro	Total	Negro	Percent Negro	Total	Negro	Percent Negro
White collar	3,480	19	0.5	2,944	16	0.5	536	3	0.6
Blue collar	12,198	1,073	8.8	11,995	1,060	8.8	203	13	6.4
Total	15,678	1,092	7.0	14,939	1,076	7.2	739	16	2.2

a. 3 companies, 6 plants.

TABLE A-25. *Basic Steel Industry*
Employment by Occupational Group, Sex, and Race
West Coast District, 1966

Occupational Group	All Employees[a]			Male			Female		
	Total	Negro	Percent Negro	Total	Negro	Percent Negro	Total	Negro	Percent Negro
Officials and managers	1,393	5	0.4	1,390	5	0.4	3	—	—
Professionals	368	1	0.3	368	1	0.3	—	—	—
Technicians	232	—	—	202	—	—	30	—	—
Sales workers	—	—	—	—	—	—	—	—	—
Office and clerical	1,591	17	1.1	1,064	15	1.4	527	2	0.4
Total white collar	3,584	23	0.6	3,024	21	0.7	560	2	0.4
Craftsmen (Skilled)	4,702	203	4.3	4,702	203	4.3	—	—	—
Operatives (Semiskilled)	5,546	605	10.9	5,367	599	11.2	179	6	3.4
Laborers (Unskilled)	2,215	270	12.2	2,213	270	12.2	2	—	—
Service workers	323	40	12.4	268	30	11.2	55	10	18.2
Total blue collar	12,786	1,118	8.7	12,550	1,102	8.8	236	16	6.8
Total	16,370	1,141	7.0	15,574	1,123	7.2	796	18	2.3

a. 3 companies, 6 plants.

TABLE A-26. *Basic Steel Industry*
Employment by Occupational Group, Sex, and Race
West Coast District, 1968

Occupational Group	All Employees[a]			Male			Female		
	Total	Negro	Percent Negro	Total	Negro	Percent Negro	Total	Negro	Percent Negro
Officials and managers	1,426	13	0.9	1,425	13	0.9	1	—	—
Professionals	483	8	1.7	481	8	1.7	2	—	—
Technicians	215	4	1.9	194	4	2.1	21	—	—
Sales workers	—	—	—	—	—	—	—	—	—
Office and clerical	1,551	34	2.2	1,048	28	2.7	503	6	1.2
Total white collar	3,675	59	1.6	3,148	53	1.7	527	6	1.1
Craftsmen (Skilled)	4,156	183	4.4	4,155	183	4.4	1	—	—
Operatives (Semiskilled)	5,113	591	11.6	5,044	589	11.7	69	2	2.9
Laborers (Unskilled)	1,809	294	16.3	1,765	293	16.6	44	1	2.3
Service workers	345	42	12.2	291	35	12.0	54	7	13.0
Total blue collar	11,423	1,110	9.7	11,255	1,100	9.8	168	10	6.0
Total	15,098	1,169	7.7	14,403	1,153	8.0	695	16	2.3

a. 3 companies, 6 plants.

TABLE A-27. *Basic Steel Industry*
Change in Employment by District, Occupational Group, and Race
1963-1968

Occupational Group	Eastern		Southern		Pittsburgh		Great Lakes and Midwest		West Coast	
	Number	Percent	Number	Percent	Number	Percent	Number	Percent	Number	Percent
Officials and managers	+1,222	+ 22.9	− 5	− 0.2	+1,620	+ 15.7	+3,303	+ 23.7	+ 59	+ 4.3
Negro	+ 63	+ 161.5	− 34	− 82.9	+ 18	+ 36.0	+ 206	+182.3	+ 12	+1,200.0
White	+1,159	+ 21.9	+ 29	+ 1.2	+1,602	+ 15.6	+3,097	+ 22.4	+ 47	+ 3.4
Professionals	+ 246	+ 17.3	+122	+ 23.6	+ 741	+ 15.9	+ 795	+ 30.1	+159	+ 49.1
Negro	+ 7	+ 350.0	+ 8	*	+ 2	+ 25.0	+ 19	+633.3	+ 8	*
White	+ 239	+ 16.8	+114	+ 22.1	+ 739	+ 15.9	+ 776	+ 29.4	+151	+ 46.6
Technicians	+ 150	+ 11.8	− 93	− 8.7	+ 404	+ 11.9	+ 891	+ 20.2	+ 34	+ 18.8
Negro	+ 20	+1,000.0	+ 37	+925.0	+ 21	+ 300.0	+ 128	+336.8	+ 4	+ *
White	+ 130	+ 10.2	−130	− 12.2	+ 383	+ 11.3	+ 763	+ 17.4	+ 30	+ 16.6
Sales workers	− 12	− 6.0	− 7	− 21.9	+ 42	+ 1.9	− 148	− 44.6	− 3	*
Negro	− 1	*	—	—	+ 3	+ 60.0	—	—	—	—
White	− 11	− 5.5	− 7	− 21.9	+ 39	+ 1.7	− 148	− 44.6	− 3	*
Office and clerical	+ 729	+ 12.7	− 41	− 1.9	+ 610	+ 4.4	+2,453	+ 18.1	+ 26	+ 1.7
Negro	+ 96	+ 192.0	+ 24	+ 85.7	+ 135	+ 107.1	+ 480	+225.4	+ 27	+ 385.7
White	+ 633	+ 11.1	− 65	− 3.1	+ 475	+ 3.5	+1,973	+ 14.8	− 1	− 0.1
Total white collar	+2,335	+ 16.7	− 24	− 0.4	+3,417	+ 9.9	+7,294	+ 20.9	+275	+ 8.1
Negro	+ 185	+ 196.8	+ 35	+ 47.9	+ 179	+ 91.3	+ 833	+227.0	+ 51	+ 637.5
White	+2,150	+ 15.5	− 59	− 1.0	+3,238	+ 9.5	+6,461	+ 18.7	+224	+ 6.6

TABLE A-27. *Basic Steel Industry*
Change in Employment by District, Occupational Group, and Race
1963-1968
(Continued)

Occupational Group	Eastern Number	Eastern Percent	Southern Number	Southern Percent	Pittsburgh Number	Pittsburgh Percent	Great Lakes and Midwest Number	Great Lakes and Midwest Percent	West Coast Number	West Coast Percent
Craftsmen (Skilled)	+1,645	+ 10.7	+256	+ 2.7	+ 364	+ 1.0	− 274	− 0.6	+ 92	+ 2.3
Negro	+ 272	+ 47.5	+201	+ 36.2	+ 112	+ 10.0	+ 599	+ 17.1	+ 55	+ 43.0
White	+1,373	+ 9.3	+ 55	+ 0.6	+ 252	+ 0.7	− 873	− 2.1	+ 37	+ 0.9
Operatives (Semiskilled)	+2,326	+ 9.2	+100	+ 1.2	−4,877	− 8.3	− 64	− 0.1	+255	+ 5.2
Negro	+ 851	+ 18.4	+365	+ 13.8	− 726	− 11.8	+1,902	+ 12.3	+ 87	+ 17.3
White	+1,475	+ 7.1	−265	− 4.7	−4,151	− 7.9	−1,966	− 3.3	+168	+ 3.9
Laborers (Unskilled)	− 80	− 0.7	+158	+ 3.8	−3,967	− 16.5	−1,387	− 4.8	−149	− 7.6
Negro	− 563	− 11.2	−750	− 25.4	− 163	− 5.1	+1,022	+ 13.4	+ 34	+ 13.1
White	+ 483	+ 7.7	+908	+ 74.7	−3,804	− 18.3	−2,409	− 11.2	−183	− 10.8
Service workers	+ 317	+ 24.7	− 6	− 1.3	− 100	− 3.7	+ 645	+ 20.5	+ 63	+ 22.3
Negro	+ 156	+ 51.0	− 37	− 23.7	+ 3	+ 0.9	+ 159	+ 24.3	+ 13	+ 44.8
White	+ 161	+ 16.4	+ 31	+ 10.4	− 103	− 4.3	+ 486	+ 19.5	+ 50	+ 19.8
Total blue collar	+4,208	+ 7.9	+508	+ 2.3	−8,580	− 7.1	−1,080	− 0.7	+261	+ 2.3
Negro	+ 716	+ 6.8	−221	− 3.5	− 774	− 7.2	+3,682	+ 13.5	+189	+ 20.5
White	+3,492	+ 8.2	+729	+ 4.5	−7,806	− 7.1	−4,762	− 3.8	+ 72	+ 0.7
Total	+6,543	+ 9.7	+484	+ 1.7	−5,163	− 3.3	+6,214	+ 3.3	+536	+ 3.7
Negro	+ 901	+ 8.5	−186	− 2.9	− 595	− 5.4	+4,515	+ 16.4	+240	+ 25.8
White	+5,642	+ 10.0	+ 670	+ 3.0	−4,568	− 3.2	+1,699	+ 1.1	+296	+ 2.2

Source: Tables A-2 through A-26.
* Unable to calculate percentage.

Part Five

THE NEGRO IN THE RUBBER TIRE INDUSTRY

by

Herbert R. Northrup

LIST OF TABLES

CHAPTER I.

Introduction

Although the rubber tire industry owes its growth and prosperity to the rise of the automobile, it has never been nearly as significant an employer of Negroes, in terms either of numbers or proportion, as has the automobile industry.[1] The reasons for this are many—rates and times of employment expansion in rubber tire manufacturing, employer hiring and upgrading policies, seniority plans which restricted wide plant movement, high wages and benefits which permitted concomitant high hiring standards for which relatively few Negroes qualify, expansion in the South where Negro opportunities and educational attainments are less, and until recently, managerial and union policies which did not challenge the status quo. The rubber tire industry even today is an excellent example of how the narrow educational and social background of the average Negro handicaps him when he competes for opportunities that pay well but are sought also by whites.

This study is concerned with the development, status, and problems involved in racial employment policies in the rubber tire industry and in the principal companies therein. Basic to an understanding of these policies is the nature of the industry which is the subject of the next chapter.

1. For an analysis of the automobile industry's racial policies, see Part Two.

CHAPTER II.

The Rubber Tire Industry

According to legend, Columbus, after watching Indian boys playing with a rubber ball, brought a sample back to Europe; but for more than 340 years, no one could find commercial uses for the product of the rubber tree of the tropics, except as a means to rub out pencil marks because articles made of rubber would melt and run in hot weather and would congeal and crack in cold weather. In 1839, the temperature problem was finally overcome when Charles Goodyear found that a mixture of rubber and sulphur heated together would "vulcanize," as he termed it, yielding a material largely indifferent to heat and cold.[2]

Following Goodyear's discovery, the rubber industry in the United States grew slowly. In 1870, the year in which Benjamin Franklin Goodrich began commercial production in the first rubber factory in Akron, Ohio, only 4,000 tons of rubber were imported into the United States. In the early years of the industry, rubber manufacturing companies made a variety of products: fire hoses, wringer rollers, bottle stoppers, washers, surgeon's gloves, and drug sundries. Some rubber tires were made for horse-drawn buggies and bicycles, but most rubber went into other products.

The first tires were made of solid rubber, but after 1890, the pneumatic tire gradually replaced the solid tire, first on bicycles and buggies, then on automobiles, and somewhat later on trucks and other heavy vehicles. Until World War I, the tire remained only one of many rubber products; but as auto production accelerated during the war, tire output quadrupled. By 1918, the automobile tire became the single most important rubber product, and today accounts for about two-thirds of the industry's raw material consumption.[3]

During World War II, the Japanese invasion of Southeast Asia and what is now Indonesia cut off the area that had become the lead-

2. Hugh Allen, *Rubber's Home Town* (New York: Stratford House, 1949), p. 112.
3. Rubber Manufacturers Association, *The Rubber Industry in the U. S. A.* (New York: The Association, 1967 ed.), p. 19.

ing source of natural rubber. Synthetic rubber was promptly developed and now accounts for more than 75 percent of the raw material used. The United States industry in 1966 consumed 554,000 long tons of natural rubber and 1,666,000 long tons of the synthetic product.[4]

The Tire Segment of the Rubber Industry

Table 1 shows the four segments of the rubber industry by the industrial subgrouping used by the federal government for data gathering purposes—the Standard Industrial Classification system (SIC). This Table also compares these subgroups in terms of employment, payrolls, value added by manufacture, cost of materials, value of shipments, and capital expenditures for the year 1965.

Tires and inner tubes employed only 88,659 persons in 1965, 34.1 percent of the total in the four standard industrial classifications. Payrolls, however, were 41.6 percent of the industry's total, indicating a high wage industry. Value added by manufacture, cost of materials, value of shipments, and capital expenditures all were highest for tires and tubes of the industry, and were 46.2, 54.5, 50.1, and 62.2 percent of the industry's totals, respectively. Obviously rubber tire is a capital intensive industry, requiring high expenditures for raw materials and equipment, and paying high wages.

These data also demonstrate that the rubber tire industry (tubes account for less than 4 percent of employment) is an industry with quite different characteristics than the manufacturing in the other three rubber standard industrial classifications. Whereas it is high wage, and capital intensive, the others are both lower paying and less capital intensive. As a matter of fact, rubber footwear manufacturing is similar to garment production in terms of its labor force and methods of production; and fabricated rubber manufacturing is an industry of varied product and methods, but in general much more akin to footwear than to rubber tire. The reclaimed rubber industry is, of course, small and labor rather than capital intensive.[5]

4. *Ibid.*, p. 18.
5. SIC 3079, plastic products, n.e.c., is combined with rubber manufacturing in much government data. Plastic is now used in many applications where rubber once was (for example, wire insulation), and the processes and products are similar to those of SIC 3069, fabricated rubber products, n.e.c. The manufacturing and labor force of SIC 3079 is, however, quite different from rubber tires, the main focus of this monograph.

TABLE 1. *The Rubber Manufacturing Industry Employment, Payrolls, Sales, and Other Data by Standard Industrial Classifications, 1965*

	Total	Tires and Inner Tubes (SIC 3011)	Rubber Footwear (SIC 3021)	Reclaimed Rubber (SIC 3031)	Fabricated Rubber Products, N.E.C. (SIC 3069)	Tires and Inner Tubes as Percent of Total
Total Employees	259,821	88,659	29,965	1,981	139,216	34.1
			(000$)			
Payrolls	1,726,947	719,181	139,852	13,977	853,937	41.6
Value added by manufacture	3,468,404	1,601,514	246,578	26,608	1,593,704	46.2
Cost of materials	3,337,853	1,817,586	161,448	25,488	1,333,331	54.5
Value of shipments	6,749,324	3,380,209	398,011	52,462	2,918,642	50.1
Capital expenditures	250,151	155,666	9,815	1,723	82,947	62.2

Source: *Compendium of Manufacturing Production Statistics for the United States* (Washington: Georgetown Economic Data Library, Department of Economics, Georgetown University, 1967), pp. 101-102.

Note: Employment data used in this table are from Census of Manufactures. They are not comparable to Bureau of Labor Statistics used in later tables.

The labor and civil rights issues in the various branches of the industry are similar in that the key companies and union in rubber tires are also involved in other branches of the industry; and that rubber tires, by dollar and sales volume, clearly sets the outlook, the policies, the program, and the pace for the rest of the industry. The problems are different among segments of the industry, however, in terms of the character of work, the opportunities, and the intensities of the issues. It is the rubber tire industry which commands the best jobs, in terms of wages, and conditions of work, and therefore opportunity. Our analysis, therefore, will concentrate on SIC 3011, tires and inner tubes, but in many cases will include, or pertain to, the three other SIC's (and even to other industries) since the principal rubber tire companies, described below, not only make tires, but in most cases manufacture a variety of other rubber products and are in many other businesses as well.

Industrial Structure

More than 300 companies have been organized to produce rubber tires.[6] In 1921, 178 establishments were manufacturing rubber tires, but by 1933 only 44 remained.[7] During 1967, 14 American companies built rubber tires, although the corporate identity and/or brand names of some other companies acquired by the Big Four continue to be maintained.[8] Table 2 lists the tire companies in the United States in 1967.

From the early decades of tire manufacturing, the American industry has been dominated by the Big Four: B. F. Goodrich, founded in 1870; United States Rubber (Uniroyal since March 1967), founded in 1892; Goodyear, founded in 1898; and Firestone, founded in 1900.[9] The extent of Big Four dominance has fluctuated little over the past 50 years. In almost every year since 1920, the rubber tire "concentration ratio" (the percentage of total market sales accounted for by an industry's four largest sellers) has varied between 70 and

---

6. Allen, *op. cit.*, p. 162.
7. *U. S. Census of Manufactures 1921* (Washington: Government Printing Office, 1922); and *ibid., 1933*.
8. For example, Uniroyal still produces the Fisk and Gillette lines, Firestone those of Seiberling and Dayton, and Goodyear, Kelly-Springfield and Lee.
9. "50-Year-Old Rubber Goods Producers," *Rubber Age,* May 1967, pp. 111-130.

TABLE 2. *Rubber Tire Companies in the United States, 1968*

Armstrong Rubber Company
Cooper Tire & Rubber Company
Dayton Tire & Rubber Company*
Derman Rubber Manufacturing Company
Dunlop Tire & Rubber Corporation
Firestone Tire & Rubber Company
Gates Rubber Company
General Tire & Rubber Company
B. F. Goodrich Company
Goodyear Tire and Rubber Company
Kelly-Springfield Tire Company**
Lee Tire & Rubber Company**
Mansfield Tire & Rubber Company
McCreary Tire & Rubber Company
Mohawk Rubber Company
Schenuit Industries, Inc.
Seiberling Tire & Rubber Company*
Uniroyal, Inc.

Source: Rubber Manufacturers Association.
* Owned by Firestone.
** Owned by Goodyear.

75 percent.[10] General Tire, founded in 1915,[11] is a trailing fifth in rubber tire production, but it too is very big business. In 1967, each of the Big Four had total sales in all product lines in excess of one billion dollars, and General, which exceeded the billion mark in 1966, fell just below it the following year.

Table 3 shows basic business data for the six largest rubber tire companies, as well as their rank among the 500 largest industrial corporations. The sales, assets, income, invested capital, and employees are their totals in all businesses. The five largest rubber companies are "conglomerates," operating not only in the rubber tire business, but in many others as well. Thus Goodyear makes, besides tires, a wide variety of rubber and automobile products, and is in

10. Leonard W. Weiss, *Case Studies in American Industry* (New York: John Wiley & Sons, 1967), p. 325; Harold S. Roberts, *The Rubber Workers* (New York: Harper & Bros., 1944), p. 15; and John D. Gaffey, *The Productivity of Labor in the Rubber Tire Manufacturing Industry* (New York: Columbia University Press, 1940), p. 60.
11. "50-Year-Old Rubber Goods Producers," *op. cit.*, pp. 162-164.

TABLE 3. *The Six Largest Rubber Tire Companies, 1968 Statistics*

Company and 1968 Rank Among Industrial Corporations		Headquarters	Sales ($000)	Assets ($000)	Net Income ($000)	Invested Capital ($000)	Number of Employees	Net Income as Percent of Sales	Net Income as Percent of Invested capital
Goodyear Tire & Rubber	(22)	Akron	2,925,745	2,377,054	148,262	1,162,638	119,744	5.1	12.8
Firestone Tire & Rubber	(36)	Akron	2,131,444	1,882,646	127,035	1,010,479	102,400	6.0	12.6
Uniroyal	(60)	New York	1,429,156	1,121,372	56,946	493,671	67,595	4.0	11.5
B. F. Goodrich	(82)	Akron	1,139,710	1,035,010	44,842	552,111	47,660	3.9	8.1
General Tire & Rubber[a]	(97)	Akron	1,039,072	812,661	43,326	385,002	45,800	4.2	11.3
Armstrong Rubber[b]	(423)	West Haven, Conn.	174,998	177,689	7,129	66,610	5,454	4.1	10.7

Source: *Fortune,* Vol. LXXIX (May 15, 1969), pp. 168-183.

a. Figures for fiscal year ending November 30, 1968.

b. Figures for fiscal year ending September 30, 1968.

addition, very active in aerospace products, manufacturing airplane, missile, and space parts and products. Firestone, besides a variety of rubber products, makes automobile parts and other products. Uniroyal and Goodrich are major factors in the footwear and plastics businesses and each has very large chemical divisions. All the Big Four make tire cord through what are, in effect, textile divisions. Goodyear and Firestone, and to a lesser extent Goodrich and Uniroyal, operate chains of retail stores which sell a wide variety of goods, such as appliances, radios, and televisions besides tires.

General is even more of a conglomerate, having entered a number of businesses which have not even an indirect relation to the tires or other rubber products. Thus it controls Aerojet-General, a major aerospace concern, a motion picture making enterprise, a radio and television network, and other diverse enterprises.

The sixth largest company, Armstrong Rubber (no relation to Armstrong Cork), is much smaller corporate-wise, but is affiliated with Sears, Roebuck, the country's number one merchandiser. Armstrong is now apparently approaching General as the number five tire producer, largely as a result of the tremendous tire volume done by Sears stores which it supplies. Armstrong is primarily a tire manufacturer.

Tire production figures by company are not readily available, but it is no secret in the industry that the order of tire sales by company is precisely the same as the order of company size set forth in Table 3. The top three maintain their position in part by large original equipment business—that is, sales to automobile manufacturers—Goodyear to Chrysler, Firestone to Ford, Uniroyal to General Motors, and each plus Goodrich, often additional business to other of the Big Three automobile producers besides its chief customer. In addition, the major tire companies vie with the smaller ones for the private brand businesses of mail order, department and specialty stores, and of petroleum companies. Tire replacement business is also competed for by major companies, often through their own retail outlets, as well as by the smaller concerns. The major companies offer several brands in the replacement tire market.

The Character of the Work

To understand the pattern of Negro employment in rubber tire manufacturing, one must know something about the kinds of work men and women do in rubber tire factories. The machines and processes used are of course best understood by visiting and observing a tire plant in operation. For those unable to take such a tour, the following brief description will provide the basis for a general understanding of the kinds of jobs Negro Americans have held in the past and are obtaining today in the nation's tire plants. This description will follow the manufacturing process from the arrival of bales of rubber at a plant to the shipment of finished tires.

Both natural and synthetic rubber arrive at a tire plant in baled lumps. The rubber needed for each kind of tire must be made up in batches according to a particular recipe by blending natural and synthetic rubber and mixing that blend with other materials. This mixing is done in the "compounding room." Batch recipes come from the laboratory, and workmen follow them in mixing together the prescribed combination of synthetic rubber, natural rubber (in a ratio averaging about 3 to 1), sulphur and other vulcanizing chemicals, and carbon black. Much of the mixing is done in a "roll mill" consisting of two horizontal parallel smooth steel rolls geared to operate at different speeds to create a wiping action heating and mixing the materials passing between them. In the old days, mixing was a pretty rough and ready process (one company's engineer tested the mix by biting it and judging its quality by its feel—through his false teeth); the heavy materials were lifted by hand, the machines heated the air, carbon black floated in the air, and the straining, sweating men obviously justified the mixing room's nickname, "the black room." Today, most initial mixing in tire plants is done in a Banbury mixer, a massive and enormously expensive machine that can mix a very large batch much faster than can roll mills, although they are often used to complete the processing of material first mixed in a Banbury.

Within the rubber tire industry, one speaks of a rubber tire being "built." So it is by a man called a "tire builder" who constructs the tire of plies (lengths of cotton, nylon, rayon, or other fabric impregnated with rubber), of a heavy strip of solid rubber forming the tread, and of "beads" (rubber-wrapped wires shaping the tire lip that fits over the wheel's metal rim). The plies are made by a calender that exerts great pressure to force warmed rubber around each thread in the fabric. The calenders, like the Banburies, are electronically controlled through a counsel bedecked with gauges and buttons. The operators must be responsible and well trained; their work is prestigious and well paid; in most tire plants only a few craftsmen are paid more than the operator of the plant's largest calender. (New processes are now in development to make tires on assembly lines rather than to "build" them.)

The solid rubber strip forming the tire tread is produced by a "tubing machine" in which warmed rubber is forced through a die giving it the correct width and thickness. Tuber operators are paid about as well as Banbury operators.

The beads are made by wrapping calendered rubber fabric strips around wire hoops. The fabric sticks out several inches all around the hoop, and this projecting fabric is bound into the plies making up the body of each tire.

In the "cutting room," fabric and tread strips are cut to length. Fabric cutting is especially significant because diagonal cuts prepare the strips for assembly on the bias, that is, so the threads of alternate calendered fabric strips run perpendicular to one another within the body of the tire.

Each tire builder works with a revolving horizontal drum on which he builds each tire out of a number of calendered fabric plies, a tread strip, and two beads fed to him from supplier machines. Each segment is cemented to every other segment it touches. Each tire builder must be strong and agile. He is paid on an incentive basis and is expected to work very quickly and efficiently to maximize returns on the expensive machinery under his hands.

The tire builders who work on truck, airplane, and off-the-road vehicle tires rank in pay with Banbury and cement mixer operators and operators of small calenders and are paid rates just below the large calender operators, millwrights, pipefitters, and other craftsmen. The automobile tire builders rank in pay just behind the truck tire builders.

When the tire builder finishes his work and takes the tire off the drum, it is several feet wide and looks like a large floppy barrel with holes in top and bottom. This rubber barrel is given its proper shape and is cured in a high temperature mold. The tire-to-be is put in the mold, and an air bag, in effect, a very heavy duty innertube, is placed inside the tire. The mold is then closed around the tire. Heated, the air bag inflates and forces the outer surface of the tire into the tread pattern cut into the surrounding metal mold. The tire is kept in the mold until the heat has vulcanized the rubber imparting permanence to its molded shape.

Between steps in the tire manufacturing process, the raw rubber, the mixed rubber, plies, tread strips, beads, raw tires, and finished tires must be moved about. The material handling jobs, stock handler, conveyor tender, tread hauler, palletizing trucker, floorman, yardman, porter, and other simple jobs such as equipment cleaner, white side wall painter, tire wrapper, buffer, and janitor require little in education or training. In recent years, much of the material-handling work has been taken over by automated equipment, and many laboring jobs have disappeared.

Between these low-level jobs and the tire builder jobs there are a variety of positions calling for literacy and some days or even a few weeks of on-the-job training. Examples of such positions are assistant operator, or operator's helper on the more demanding machines, millman, lift truck operator, bead machine and bias cutter operatives, mold changers, and shippers.

The top blue collar jobs in rubber tire plants are in their large maintenance departments (these jobs offer the highest hourly wages, but calender operators and some tire builders paid incentive rates are sometimes able to earn more). Some 10 to 15 percent of tire plant production employees are maintenance department skilled workers. These men must complete apprenticeships before qualifying as journeymen for such jobs as machinists, welders, millwrights, mechanics, pipefitters, and electricians.

Employment and Productivity Trends

According to the Census of Manufactures, rubber tire employment reached an early peak of 96,244 in 1929, declined to almost 61,000 in the Great Depression and then rose steadily during World War II.[12] Data published by the U. S. Bureau of Labor Statistics corroborate the World War II trend. As set forth in Table 4, the Bureau of Labor Statistics data show average annual rubber tire employment reaching an all time peak of 143,400 in the postwar year of 1946, and then downtrending to a low of 97,300 in 1963. After two years of only slight employment gains, employment jumped to 107,100 in 1966,

12. Data from U. S. Census of Manufactures are not comparable to those of the U. S. Bureau of Labor Statistics. Both however, show the same trends.

TABLE 4. *Rubber Tire and Inner Tube Industry (SIC 301) Total and Production Worker Average Annual Employment 1940-1967*

	All Employees	Production Workers	Production Workers as Percent of All Employees
	(000)		
1940	70.8	57.5	81.2
1941	82.8	67.3	81.3
1942	84.4	68.6	81.3
1943	113.3	92.0	81.2
1944	126.6	102.1	80.6
1945	128.2	102.5	80.0
1946	143.4	114.4	79.8
1947	135.9	108.0	79.5
1948	123.5	97.6	79.0
1949	107.5	83.9	78.0
1950	110.2	86.8	78.8
1951	114.8	89.8	78.2
1952	121.9	94.9	77.9
1953	122.7	94.7	77.2
1954	108.9	81.4	74.7
1955	118.5	90.5	76.4
1956	114.5	87.0	76.0
1957	112.9	85.1	75.4
1958	104.1	76.6	73.6
1959	104.5	77.0	73.7
1960	104.8	76.8	73.3
1961	97.7	70.6	72.3
1962	99.4	72.2	72.6
1963	97.3	69.9	71.8
1964	99.0	70.9	71.6
1965	101.8	72.7	71.4
1966	107.1	75.9	70.9
1967	101.2	69.0	68.2

Source: U. S. Bureau of Labor Statistics, *Employment and Earnings Statistics for the United States, 1909-68*, Bulletin No. 1312-6, pp. 690-691.

only to fall back in 1967 to 101,200, a figure slightly below that of 1965.

Production worker employment followed the same trend, but more sharply, reaching a peak in 1946 of 114,400, and declining to a low of 69,900 in 1963. After rising to 75,900 in 1966, production worker employment fell to 69,000 in 1967, the lowest figure since 1942. Production workers thus bore the brunt of the industry's declining employment. Table 4 shows that in 1941 and 1942 production workers comprise 81.3 percent of all rubber tire and tube workers; by 1967, that percentage had declined to 68.2. Since nearly all Negroes in the industry were employed as production workers prior to 1960, the downward trend of employment has been of great significance to them.

Even more severe has been the trend of employment in Ohio, and especially in Akron, the "rubber tire capital" of the world. Table 5 shows that trend of employment in that state since 1949, and in its rubber tire center since 1958. In Ohio, rubber tire and tube employment rose from 54,100 in 1949 to 64,200 in 1953, and then declined to 42,100 in 1967. Akron data show a drop from 42,800 in 1958 to 35,700 in 1967. Anyone who visits Akron is quickly aware that the bulk of this last employment is attributable to a decline in the number of production employees. The conversion of old factory buildings to offices is a familiar sight in Akron. Were it not for the expansion in salaried employment, the Akron decline would be much more severe. Thus it is the production workers, and particularly those in the Akron area who have borne the brunt of the downward employment trend—a trend which would appear much more drastic if, over this period, the industry had not staffed many new plants. Since, as we shall point out, Negroes, for a variety of reasons, experienced greater difficulty in obtaining employment in plants opening in the 1945-1963 period than they did in older plants, these trends are of direct pertinence for this study.

While employment was declining in the years since World War II, rubber tire sales were expanding. Table 6 compares trends in employment and production from 1940 to 1967. As these data demonstrate, the rubber tire industry energetically sought to offset its high labor costs (which will be discussed below) by an intense mechanization, automation, and methods improvement program. The impact is shown, in part, in Table 6. While employment during this 28-year period rose 42.9 percent, output rose 175.5 percent. From 1946, the peak employment year to 1967, output rose 98.1 percent, but employment *declined* 29.4 percent. Improvement of old plant operations and movement of production from inefficient high-cost

TABLE 5. *Rubber Tire and Inner Tube Industry Average Annual Employment in State of Ohio and in Akron 1949-1967*

	Ohio	Akron
	(000)	
1949	54.1	
1950	56.3	
1951	61.0	
1952	63.6	
1953	64.2	
1954	54.0	
1955	57.8	
1956	55.9	
1957	54.3	
1958	49.9	42.8
1959	50.4	42.8
1960	49.2	42.5
1961	44.0	38.4
1962	43.7	38.0
1963	43.7	37.6
1964	42.2	37.1
1965	42.8	37.5
1966	43.6	37.7
1967	42.1	35.7

Source: U. S. Bureau of Labor Statistics, *Employment and Earnings Statistics for States and Areas, 1939-67*, Bulletin No. 1370-5, pp. 343, 347.

old plants to efficient, low-cost new ones continue and are projected for the future.

The net effect of this employment-productivity picture is that, at the time of high prosperity and maximum civil rights interest and pressure, the rubber tire industry, unlike such industries as automobiles or aerospace, has had few new jobs to offer and therefore considerable difficulty in offsetting past employment policies and practices.

Occupational Distribution

Although production workers have declined as a percentage of all rubber tire employees, they continue to be the dominant group in the industry. From observation and data in our possession, we

TABLE 6. *Rubber Tire Industry*
Employment and Production, 1940-1967

	Total Employment Tires and Inner Tubes (Average for year) (000)	Tire Production (Auto, truck, and bus) (000 Units)
1940	70.8	59,186
1941	82.8	61,540
1942	84.4	15,351
1943	113.3	20,423
1944	126.6	33,446
1945	128.2	44,524
1946	143.4	82,298
1947	135.9	95,550
1948	123.5	81,314
1949	107.5	76,368
1950	110.2	92,754
1951	114.8	83,405
1952	121.9	90,411
1953	122.7	96,121
1954	108.9	89,141
1955	118.5	112,119
1956	114.5	100,365
1957	112.9	106,906
1958	104.1	96,536
1959	104.5	117,916
1960	104.8	119,757
1961	97.7	116,734
1962	99.4	133,812
1963	97.3	139,026
1964	99.0	158,044
1965	101.8	167,743
1966	107.1	177,388
1967	101.2	163,061[a]

Percentage Change		Percentage Change	
1940-1967	+42.9	1940-1967	+175.5
1946-1967	−29.4	1946-1967	+ 98.1

Source: Employment, see Table 4; production, Rubber Manufacturers Association, *Rubber Industry Facts*, 1968 edition, p. 22.

[a] Output reduced by long strike at three major companies.

estimate that the production workers in tire plants may be subdivided as follows:

Unskilled material handlers, janitors, etc.	20 percent
Millmen, operators' assistants, helpers, etc.	40 percent
Tire builders, Banbury, calender, cement mixer operators, etc.	25 percent
Skilled maintenance craftsmen	15 percent

Within the broad category of production worker, considerable variation of skill is required. The estimated skill subdivision just set forth points up the fact that about 20 percent of the plant jobs require little skill, background, or education, a factor of great importance to Negroes, in view of their relative disadvantaged educational background and their inexperience in industry.

On the other hand, as we shall examine below, seniority arrangements generally provide upgrading opportunities which are predicated upon in-plant training by movement from lower to higher jobs. Those who lack requisite education or potential for upgrading pose a serious problem for management and unions not only as a result of their own frustration at being bypassed, but also because they block training opportunities for those who must advance around them to higher-rated jobs. Hence, standards have historically been set on the basis of where the employee is expected to move, rather than for what he is being hired. This fact, as we shall note, has hindered Negro employment in the rubber tire industry.

Table 7 provides a more detailed occupational breakdown based upon data in the authors' possession from 12 tire companies for the year 1966. On a plant-by-plant basis, the data which are combined in Table 7, show some variation. For example, one tire plant reported 41 percent of all male employees as operatives; another reported 62 percent as operatives. Again, one tire plant reported 1 percent of all male employees as technicians; another reported 4 percent.

These figures differ from plant to plant, first, because of differences in fact in the occupational cross-section; and, second, because of differences among plants in the way in which some jobs are classified. If, for example, a plant contains a company division or sales headquarters, the white collar categories will have a larger representation

TABLE 7. *Rubber Tire Industry*
Occupational Distribution of Employees
12 Companies, 50 Plants, 1966

Occupation	Number of Employees	Percent of Total
Officials and managers	8,537	8.5
Professionals	5,135	5.1
Technicians	3,027	3.0
Sales workers	2,121	2.1
Office and clerical	9,482	9.5
Total white collar	28,302	28.2
Craftsmen	14,868	14.8
Operatives	49,730	49.7
Laborers	4,120	4.1
Service workers	3,207	3.2
Total blue collar	71,925	71.8
Total	100,227	100.0

Source: Data in authors' possession.

than if the plant is strictly a manufacturing operation. Likewise, the extent of automation will have a distinct impact on the number and proportion of operatives and laborers.

Insofar as interplant differences in classification of particular jobs are concerned, the biggest variations occur in regard to jobs which some managements designate as skilled, but which others term semiskilled. As shown in Table 7 about one-half of the personnel in the industry is classified as "operatives," which means "semiskilled workers." Yet, based on our previous discussion of the character of work performed in a rubber tire factory, the category "operatives" covers an exceptionally broad range of jobs in tire manufacturing. On the one hand, some material handling jobs can be mastered in a few days by a semiliterate; on the other hand, auto, truck, or airplane tire building requires two to six months of on-the-job training for men able to read, to calculate, and to follow detailed written specifications. More demanding still, calender operators must be literate, must receive months of training, and must be able to carry the heavy responsibility of carefully observed control of million dollar machines.

All of these jobs in some rubber tire factories are classified as "operatives'" work. Other plants classify calender operatives, for example, as skilled craftsmen. In terms of income, as well as skill, which "operative" position one holds in some plants makes a great deal of difference.

Rubber tire plants classify very, very few employees as laborers, and less than 5 percent are classified as service workers. The laborers', service workers', and, as was discussed above, many operatives' jobs—some one-third of all tire factory production jobs—can be performed adequately by people with less than high school educations after less than a month's on-the-job training. For such jobs, the factories can hire people with limited education and with little or no previous industrial experience (the lot of a disproportionately large number of American Negroes). If, however, as was already noted, employment qualifications are based on the higher jobs in the progression rung, the disadvantaged are not aided by the fact that they are qualified to perform the lower-rated work.

The second largest occupational group in the rubber tire industry is that of craftsmen—some 14.8 percent of the total employment. As in most industries, Negroes have fared poorly in trying to win representation in this group, with its tradition of restrictive entry rules for training and general antagonism to Negro participation. Moreover, as we shall note below, the high wages in the industry and the lack of employment expansion have insured many tire companies, at least until recently, of an adequate supply of craftsmen without special efforts on their part.

In the white collar areas, the largest group is the office and clerical, followed by officials and managers (including supervisors). The fact that only 28.2 percent of the employees in the industry are salaried emphasizes the blue collar or manufacturing orientation. In this it is similar to the automobile industry, its principal customer, but quite different from an industry like aerospace, in which the salaried personnel predominate and professionals are the largest occupational group.[13] Yet our data will show that Negro employment in the rubber tire industry is proportionately closer to aerospace than to automobiles.

---

13. See Parts Two and Three.

Wages, Fringe Benefits, and Hours

Rubber tire plants have always paid relatively high wages. Following a strike in 1914, the late William Green, then an Ohio state senator, and later a long time president of the American Federation of Labor, headed a legislative committee investigation which reported that Akron rubber workers averaged $2.60 a day versus a $1.50 national average in manufacturing. That report also noted that industry working conditions were "improving."[14] Like most factory jobs then, there was plenty of room for improvement: the pace was fast, many jobs were extremely dirty, and so much heavy lifting was required in the early tire plants that companies hired few men weighing less than 175 pounds. But the pay was very good even then.

Over the years, tire manufacturing wage rates have remained relatively high. Table 8 compares average hourly and weekly earnings in selected manufacturing industries for 1967. The tire industry leads all others. Wage rates are higher in the tire plants in Akron, Eau Claire, Wisconsin, and Detroit than anywhere else, but even in Los Angeles and in the tire plants of the South, the nearly invariable rule is that production workers in rubber tire plants receive higher wages than do those in comparable jobs in other local industries. Employees in other rubber products industries earn very substantially less.

Fringe benefits of rubber tire workers are also high, including generous pensions, health and welfare plans, and a supplemental unemployment insurance program that almost guarantees an annual wage to employees after a few years' service. The last benefit was included in a large wage and fringe benefit package that ended a three-month strike in 1967.

Since the early 1930's, several rubber tire plants of Akron have adhered to an unique six-hour day, six-day week with time and one-half paid only after four hours of overtime, or forty hours. At one time, rubber tire plants throughout the country were on this schedule. During World War II, the industry went to a forty-hour week, and most plants outside of Akron remained on that schedule.

In recent years, the Goodrich plant at Akron and the Uniroyal plant at Detroit have joined most of the industry on the eight-hour day. Employers found the six-hour schedule relatively inefficient and new employees found it reduced their earnings. Many older em-

14. *Journal of the Ohio State Senate*, Vol. CIII (1913). Appendix, pp. 213-214.

TABLE 8. *Gross Weekly and Hourly Earnings Production Workers, United States, Selected Industries, 1967*

Industry	Average Weekly Earnings	Average Hourly Earnings
All manufacturing	$114.90	$2.83
Durable goods manufacturing	123.60	3.00
Tires and tubes	168.59	3.78
Other rubber products	109.61	2.68
Aircraft and parts	146.54	3.44
Primary metal industries	136.94	3.34
Motor vehicles and equipment	144.84	3.55

Source: *Monthly Labor Review*, Vol. XCI, No. 5 (May 1968), Table C-1.

ployees prefer the shorter workweek, however, because they developed second jobs or other "moonlighting" interests, which they could not keep up if they were required to work an eight-hour day in their primary job. Indeed, Akron is known as the moonlighting capital of the country, so frequent has the custom of a second job become.[15]

Because of the overriding importance of rubber company employment in Akron, the short workweek has probably not been a factor in Negro employment there. In the Detroit area, however, it reduced the weekly take-home pay of beginning employees below that of the automobile industry although wage rates in the tire plants there exceed those in the automobile industry. Company officials believe that it hurt their recruiting efforts until it was negotiated out of existence in 1968.[16]

The Impact of High Wages and Fringe Benefits

The high wages and fringe benefits, regardless of hours, make rubber tire plants attractive places to work. Technological changes have eliminated most of the hard and dirty work from tire plants. Employment has been relatively steady over time, except for the severe cutbacks of the late 1940's and 1950's. The pay structure and good

15. On this point see, Sebastian de Grazia, *Of Time, Work and Leisure* (New York: Twentieth Century Fund, Inc., 1962), p. 71; and John C. Deiter, *Multiplejob-holding and the Short Workweek Issue* (Ann Arbor, Mich.: University Microfilms, Inc., 1965), p. 81.
16. Interviews, Detroit, November 1967.

working conditions attract so many applicants that even in the tight labor markets of the 1960's most rubber tire plants in the South, two in Akron, and several elsewhere were able to maintain very high employment standards. They continued to require a high school education and a high score on a general aptitude test battery administered by state employment service offices until late 1967. Yet, for the most part, they still obtained as many workers as they needed to fill their production jobs. These tire plants have even required high school diplomas for jobs that could easily be efficiently filled by men with less education. The high school requirement has assured these plants that most new employees would be promotable and has provided a rough ("rough" because some high school nongraduates can make the grade and some graduates cannot) but generally convenient method of selecting the very best among their surplus number of job applicants. The high school diploma requirement has now generally been eliminated in order to further Negro employment, not in most cases because a labor supply with high school diplomas was not available.

The relatively favorable wages and benefits of rubber tire production workers seem likely to continue for some time. Unless tires can be compressed for economical shipment, foreign competition will not be a serious factor. The dominant union in the field, as will be discussed below, militantly pushes for ever higher wages and fringes, the industry is strike vulnerable and can apparently find the means to meet such demands. To the Negro in the industry, and to all workers, this brings the benefits of what top industrial wages can buy. But to those on the outside and desiring jobs in the industry, it means keen competition for much sought-after work. With disadvantaged educational, training, and industrial backgrounds, this does not augur well for Negroes competing to win employment in the rubber tire plants.

Unionization

Virtually all rubber tire plants are unionized by one union—the United Rubber, Cork, Linoleum and Plastic Workers of America (URW). An early affiliate of John L. Lewis' Committee for Industrial Organization, the United Rubber Workers, as it was originally called, won recognition from most of the major producers after a series of sitdown strikes in Akron in the early 1930's. The failure of the American Federation of labor to grant the URW an industrial union charter, and the AFL's insistence that craftsmen in the industry must be represented by craft unions instead of the URW, led the latter to leave the AFL and to join the CIO. Later URW expanded its jurisdiction to include employees in related industries, but it has never been a large organization.[17] In 1967, URW claimed 210,000 members.

Although URW is not large compared with other unions, its bargaining power is substantial. It represents employees in all tire plants except one small operation in Pennsylvania where District 50, formerly United Mine Workers, is recognized, plus one or two newly opened facilities. Usually, URW has won bargaining rights in new plants within the first two years of their opening. Plants in the South have unionized about as quickly as new ones elsewhere. URW organizers have been greatly aided by reporting Akron wages and fringes and promising unorganized workers that they would push toward that goal for them.

The bargaining power of the rubber workers' union is also enhanced by fierce oligopolistic competition in the industry and the interchangeability of one company's products for another. The customer who wants tires is not likely to wait for them until a strike is over; instead he will buy them from another supplier. If the customer is General Motors, or a private brand purchaser of the magnitude of Montgomery Ward & Company or Standard Oil of New Jersey, a strike can have disastrous effects. URW officials and members soon realized this, and strikes, or threats thereof, were used to push up benefits, to loosen incentives, and to weaken production standards, in addition to maximizing wages and benefits in contract renewals. In 1967, the Big Five adopted a strike insurance plan as a means of offsetting the URW's whipsawing policies. Nevertheless, aided by a loan of several million from Walter Reuther's automobile workers, the URW struck three companies in the industry for three months.

A feature of the URW organization is the high degree of local autonomy and factionalism. The international union's control over local affiliates is decidedly weaker than that exercised by many other internationals. Moreover, a large number of contests and factional

---

17. The early years of unionism in the rubber industry are described by Roberts, *loc. cit.*; and by Donald Anthony, in Twentieth Century Fund, *How Collective Bargaining Works* (New York: The Fund, 1942), pp. 631-681.

fights have occurred in recent years with considerable turnover in local officers and a number of bitter contests for national union offices as well.

These aspects of industrial relations and union government are significant for Negro employment in several ways. The fact that the industry is unionized on an industrial rather than craft basis assures greater internal fluidity and mobility than would be the case if a craft type of organization prevailed, for there are no barriers among jobs which are created or strengthened by the necessity of transferring from one union to another. Moreover, the philosophy and organizational vitality of an industrial union requires it to take into membership all employees regardless of race.

The high degree of local autonomy, however, limits the ability of the international union to commit the organization fully to equal employment opportunity, and especially to any affirmative action program. Factionalism and insecurity of elected officials also inhibit their taking any strong stand against the wishes of the dominant white membership, especially in view of the relatively small number of Negroes who would be favored by such action. We shall note below that the URW international union has always opened its doors to Negroes and stood for fair employment, but that in practice these policies have neither been emphasized nor effectively carried out where local unions and membership have been recalcitrant.

Industrial Location

The American rubber industry began in New England where America's first rubber factory, the Roxbury India Rubber Company of Massachusetts, opened in 1832.[18] In 1870, when Benjamin Franklin Goodrich began building the first rubber factory in Akron, Ohio, the American rubber industry, in which tires were a very minor factor, was scattered among many cities, mostly in New England.

The rubber tire industry, building first for horse-drawn carriages and bicycles, then for automobiles, concentrated in Akron where external economies accumulated and aided the growth of many Akron area companies. That growth was sometimes interrupted, spectacularly so in the post-World War I panic of 1920-1921, and not all

18. R. R. Ormsby, "The Rubber Industry" in John G. Glover and R. L. Lagai (eds.), *The Development of American Industry* (New York: Simmons-Boardman Publishing Co., Inc., 1959), pp. 394-416.

Akron rubber companies succeeded, and others sold to larger firms.[19] The freewheeling entrepreneur, Ohio Columbus Barber, for example, created the Diamond Match Company in the 1890's. He subsequently moved this operation to Barberton, just south of Akron. The vacated building became the home of the Diamond Rubber Company which in 1912 was sold to Goodrich for $40,000,000.[20] Frank A. Seiberling lost control of Goodyear in the panic of 1921 to Dillon, Read and Co. Although he left behind tens of millions of dollars in debt, within a few years he had begun a new and highly successful tire plant in O. C. Barber's town of Barberton and built the Seiberling Rubber Company.[21] In 1929, because of the many Akron success stories, two-thirds of all value added by tire and tube manufacturers was added in Akron.[22]

Other tire plants of 1929 were in Barberton (Seiberling), which was purchased by Firestone in 1965; Dayton (Dayton Tire), purchased by Firestone in 1961; Mansfield (Mansfield Tire), as well as in other Ohio cities; in Chicopee Falls, Massachusetts (Fisk), purchased by U. S. Rubber in 1939; Detroit (U. S. Rubber [Uniroyal]), with a plant that in both 1929 and 1967 was producing more tires than any other plant in the world; Cumberland, Maryland (Kelly-Springfield), purchased by Goodyear Tire in the depths of the depression; and in the West Coast's tire center, Los Angeles. Goodyear had opened a tire plant in Los Angeles in 1920 to be within the West Coast market, and by 1929, Firestone, Goodrich, and Uniroyal had all built or bought plants in Los Angeles.

Tire shipping costs and high wages and restrictive shop practices in Akron have contributed to the industry's dispersal of plant facilities in recent years. Tires are very expensive to ship. A boxcar filled with tires contains much more air than tires by volume. Although the air-to-rubber ratio has been halved by the new system of "banding" whereby steel banks hold tires in bundles compressed to one-half their normal width, shipping costs remain high.[23]

19. Harvey S. Firestone and Samuel Crowther, *Men and Rubber* (New York: Doubleday, Page and Company, 1926), elaborate upon the winnowing effects of that period. See also Glenn D. Babcock, *History of the United States Rubber Company* (Bloomington, Indiana: University of Indiana Press, 1966) and Alfred Lief, *The Firestone Story* (New York: Whittlesey House, 1951).
20. Allen, *op. cit.*, pp. 134-138.
21. *Ibid.*, pp. 139-169.
22. Gaffey, *op. cit.*, p. 153.
23. *Ibid.*, pp. 171 ff.

In 1938, average hourly earnings for tire production workers were $1.04 in Akron, and $.74 outside of Akron.[24] Despite some equalization and the payment of Akron rates in at least two major plants of Uniroyal (U. S. Rubber), the major producer which has never had an Akron area plant, Akron wages and earnings are still the highest in the industry. In addition, the equipment and plant layouts in Akron are among the oldest in the industry, despite tremendous expenditures on modernization. Moreover, union restrictions on output and the most efficient use of manpower are more stringent in Akron than in most other areas.

In 1935, 53 percent of all tires were built in Akron.[25] Since then shipping and labor costs have moved the industry to concentrate expansion away from Ohio's tire headquarters. Prior to the mid-1930's, of course, as already noted, some dispersal had occurred, especially in the Los Angeles area in order to save shipping costs to the West. In 1929, Goodyear entered the South, building a plant at Gadsden, Alabama, which in volume rivals Unroyal's Detroit facility. The Goodyear Gadsden plant was constructed to meet the needs of Sears Roebuck to minimize shipping costs for Sears tires then produced by Goodyear for retailing in the South. Firestone also established a southern plant, in Memphis, Tennessee, before World War II, as did Armstrong in Natchez, Mississippi.

Since World War II, plant dispersal has continued. Today about 66 percent of all tires, including one-half the production of Goodyear, Firestone, Goodrich, and General, and all of Uniroyal's and Armstrong's (now the Sears supplier) are manufactured outside of Akron. Nevertheless, Akron still produces one-third of the nation's tires, including about 40 percent of that of its four largest companies,[26] but Akron's percentage continues to decline.

The post-World War II expansion in the industry has seen plants built in other areas of the Midwest and West, in a few areas of the East, but especially in the South. Table 9 lists tire manufacturing facilities by company, region, and plant location. Not only are tire plants now located throughout the South, but today expansion in the industry is being concentrated there.

---

24. *Ibid.*, p. 172.
25. *U. S. Census of Manufactures, 1935* (Washington: Government Printing Office, 1937).
26. Authors' estimates, based upon company data.

TABLE 9. *Rubber Tire Plants in the United States Company, Region, and Plant Location, 1968*

State	Company	Location
Northeast:		
Mass.	Uniroyal	—Chicopee Falls
Conn.	Armstrong	—West Haven
N. Y.	Dunlop	—Buffalo
Pa.	Firestone	—Pottstown
	Goodrich	—Oaks
	Lee (Goodyear)	—Conshohocken
	McCreary	—Indiana
Md.	Kelly-Springfield (Goodyear)	—Cumberland
	Schenuit	—Baltimore
South:		
Va.	Goodyear	—Danville
	Mohawk	—Salem
N. C.	General	—Charlotte
Ky.	General	—Mayfield
Tenn.	Firestone	—Memphis
	Goodyear	—Union City
	Gates	—Nashville
Ga.	Firestone	—Albany
Ala.	Goodyear	—Gadsden
	Goodrich	—Tuscaloosa
	Uniroyal	—Opelika
Miss.	Armstrong	—Natchez
	Mansfield	—Tupelo
Ark.	Armstrong	—Little Rock
	Cooper	—Texarkana
	Mohawk	—West Helena
Okla.	Goodrich	—Miami
	Uniroyal	—Ardmore
Texas	General	—Waco
	Kelly-Springfield (Goodyear)	—Tyler

State	Company	Location
Midwest except Ohio:		
Mich.	Goodyear	—Jackson
	Uniroyal	—Detroit
Ill.	Firestone	—Bloomington Decatur
	Kelly-Springfield (Goodyear)	—Freeport
Ind.	Goodrich	—Ft. Wayne
Wis.	Uniroyal	—Eau Claire
Iowa	Armstrong	—Des Moines
	Firestone	—Des Moines
Kansas	Goodyear	—Topeka
Colorado	Gates	—Denver
Ohio:		
	Cooper	—Findlay
	Dayton (Firestone)	—Dayton
	Denman	—Warren
	Firestone	—Akron
	General	—Akron Brian
	Goodrich	—Akron
	Goodyear	—Akron
	Mansfield	—Mansfield
	Mohawk	—Akron
	Seiberling (Firestone)	—Barberton
California:		
	Armstrong	—Hanford
	Firestone	—Los Angeles Salinas
	Goodrich	—Los Angeles
	Goodyear	—Los Angeles
	Uniroyal	—Los Angeles

Source: Rubber Manufacturers Association.

In December 1967, General Tire opened a new plant in Charlotte, North Carolina, and scheduled production of 8,500 per day for 1968. Late in 1968, Mohawk opened a plant with a capacity of 2,400 tires per day in Salem, Virginia. Also in 1968, Goodrich added radial tire capacity to its Tuscaloosa, Alabama, plant and Uniroyal commenced doubling the capacity of its Opelika, Alabama, facility. Southern expansion of the industry in 1968 also saw Firestone expand the capacity of its Memphis plant and build a new facility at Albany, Georgia, with a capacity of 25,000 tires per day; Armstrong announced a new production facility at Little Rock, Arkansas; Goodyear began construction of a new plant at Union City, Tennessee, with a capacity of 17,500 tires per day scheduled for early 1969, and 20,000 tires per day by late that year; and Uniroyal announced a new facility for Ardmore, Oklahoma.[27]

Rubber tire expansion of manufacturing facilities is thus being concentrated in the area where approximately 50 percent of all Negroes dwell. On the other hand, it is also the area where a labor pool of whites exists. These workers have had the advantage of an education superior to that traditionally available to Negroes. It is an area where prejudice and discrimination on the job have been most frequently practiced and most strongly held.

Post-World War II expansion in the Midwest and Far West has also moved facilities away from the larger metropolitan areas where Negroes are concentrated. New plants in the Far West have been in Salinas and Hanford, California, rather than in Los Angeles; and in the Midwest in Iowa and Kansas or in smaller communities of Illinois, again with less Negro representation in the population. Plant dispersal of this character has a direct impact on Negro employment, as we shall discuss below, although its motives have been lower labor, production, and shipping costs, not lower Negro employment.

---

27. *Rubber Age* carries announcements of these various plant expansion plans.

CHAPTER III.

Negro Rubber Tire Employment, The Years Before World War II

Akron was a town of 10,000 when Goodrich, Tew, and Company opened a plant there in 1871 with rubber hose its chief product.[28] The growth of the city paralleled the growth of its rubber companies: Goodrich, Goodyear, Firestone, Mohawk, General, and (in adjacent Barberton) Seiberling. By 1930, Akron had a population of 255,000 and 54 percent of the city's manufacturing employees worked for rubber companies. In 1935, most of Akron's labor force still worked in rubber tire plants, and most of the rubber tire manufacturing labor force still worked in Akron.[29] After World War II the industry began to build more new plants outside of Ohio's rubber tire capital to improve its labor and transportation costs.

EARLY NEGRO EMPLOYMENT

When Akron rubber companies expanded their employment in the years before World War I, they hired from a labor force that was 99 percent white. As a result only a few Negroes were employed in the industry prior to then. On the other hand, most plants did have a few Negroes, usually in laborer or janitorial jobs.[30]

World War I saw a rapid increase in demand for rubber tire labor, as occurred in automobiles, steel, and other industries. Like other industries, the Akron tire concerns recruited extensively in the South, but the heaviest recruiting was done in the largely white areas of nearby West Virginia's Appalachia. So extensive was the migration

28. See, e.g., Hugh Allen, *Rubber's Home Town* (New York: Stratford House, 1949), pp. 116-121.
29. *U. S. Census of Population, 1930,* Vol. I, p. 27; and Roberts, *op. cit.,* pp. 8-9.
30. Based on interviews with company officials, 1966-1967.

from West Virginia into Akron, that wags termed the tire city "the capital of West Virginia."[31]

Actually the migration of other southern whites into Akron was also very heavy before and after World War I, and the term "West Virginians" was seemingly applied to all such migrants. For example, by 1929, 29 percent of Goodyear's Akron employees had been born in Ohio; but 43 percent had been born in West Virginia, Tennessee, Kentucky, Georgia, or North Carolina.[32] In 1930, one-third of Akron's population was West Virginian or southern born. Nearly all of those people were white, with Negroes comprising only 3.6 percent of the population.[33] Akron's white population contrasted with that of other northern industrial centers in that native American in-migrants made up a much larger percentage of the total than did foreign-born immigrants. For example, in 1930, nearby Cleveland was typical of most American industrial cities of the East and Midwest in that 65 percent of its residents were either foreign born or the children of foreign-born parents. Akron's first and second generation foreign-born population comprised only 32 percent of the city's 1930 population.[34]

Whereas large numbers of Negroes entered the automobile and steel industries during this early period, it was reported that "A considerable sprinkling of Negroes also was recruited from the South and brought into the [tire] industry chiefly during the [first World] war period."[35] According to an unpublished study of Akron's first Negro social agency, "Negroes were given their first opportunity to work in the [tire] industry, at the Firestone Tire and Rubber Company."[36] Like his friend Henry Ford, Harvey Firestone, Sr., founder of the company that bears his name, became deeply committed to giving Negroes a share of employment. Firestone not only was the first to employ Negroes, but throughout most of the industry's history, has consistently had the highest percentage of Negroes of any Akron

31. Alfred W. Jones, *Life, Liberty, and Property* (Philadelphia: J. B. Lippincott & Co., 1941), p. 61.
32. Hugh Allen, *The House of Goodyear* (Cleveland: The Corday & Gross Co.), p. 348.
33. Jones, *op. cit.*, pp. 59, 66.
34. *Ibid.*
35. John D. Gaffey, *The Productivity of Labor in the Rubber Tire Manufacturing Industry* (New York: Columbia University Press, 1940), p. 65.
36. "History of the Association for Colored Community Work," unpublished study in possession of authors, probably written in 1943. The Association was the predecessor of the Urban League of Akron.

plant, and in its Memphis, Tennessee plant, the highest percentage in any plant in the country.

The Firestone interest in Negro employment was also furthered by Harvey Firestone, Jr., for many years chief executive of the Company. The latter was greatly interested in the Liberia, Africa, holdings of the Company, which have apparently been a factor in maintaining the Company's continued concern for Negro employment over the years. In the pre-World War II period, Negroes in Firestone, as in the rest of the industry, were almost always confined to janitorial and laboring jobs, and in the hot, dirty work in the then nonmechanized compounding room, which in some plants was known as the "Black Department." Only an occasional Negro succeeded in working into a few of the better blue collar jobs, and none were found in white collar employment.

Census data do not distinguish the rubber tire industry from other branches of rubber products. Table 10, which shows the number and percentage of Negroes in rubber products, by sex, for the census years 1920-1940, does, however, point up the paucity of Negroes in the industry. In 1920, for example, when the data report only laborers and operatives, which undoubtedly include all Negroes, but no salaried workers who were then all white, Negroes comprised 2 percent of the total. Twenty years later, Negro representation among all rubber workers had grown by less than one thousand and the proportion hardly at all. Moreover, since these data include rubber products other than tires, the number and proportion of Negroes in tire plants may well have been less in each of these three census years because nontire rubber plants have a larger percentage of easy-to-learn unskilled jobs than do tire plants and were located in many areas with larger Negro populations than Akron had during this era.

The data in Table 10 also reveal that rubber was a man's industry. Few women, white or colored, worked in rubber products factories prior to World War II, and fewer still in the rubber tire plants where strength was an important prerequisite.

The poor representation of Negroes in the rubber products industry of the 1920-1940 era may be contrasted with the situation in automobiles. In 1930, for example, the census reported that nearly 30,000, or about 5 percent of the 640,500 employees in automobile factories "were nonwhite."[37]

---

37. See Part Two.

TABLE 10. *Rubber Products Industry*
Total Employed Persons by Race and Sex, United States, 1920-1940

Year	All Employees			Male			Female		
	Total	Negro	Percent Negro	Total	Negro	Percent Negro	Total	Negro	Percent Negro
1920[a]	137,671	2,685	2.0	114,885	2,541	2.2	22,786	144	0.6
1930[b]	166,391	3,492	2.1	130,784	3,403	2.6	35,607	89	0.2
1940	159,021	3,343	2.1	122,219	3,241	2.7	36,802	102	0.3

Sources: *U. S. Census of Population:*
1920: Vol. IV, *Occupations*, Tables 6, 10.
1930: Vol. V, *Occupations—General Report*, Table 1.
1940: Vol. III, *The Labor Force*, Part 1, Table 76.

[a] Laborers and operatives only (10 years old and over).

[b] Gainful workers (10 years old and over).

Northern Areas Outside of Akron

Outside of Akron, Negro employment was generally sparse except in two areas—Detroit and the South. In Detroit, the United States Rubber Company (now Uniroyal, Inc.) and Henry Ford led in employing Negroes. The former plant, located in the heart of the city, took advantage of a labor supply attracted by the automobile industry. Mr. Ford built a rubber tire plant for his River Rouge complex in the late 1930's and put his then unique philosophy of integration into practice. In 1940, the census reported that 5.1 percent of the employees in Michigan's rubber products industry were Negro.[38]

For California, the census of 1940 reported only 21, or 0.3 percent, of the 7,243 "rubber products" workers were Negroes.[39] It is doubtful if rubber tire plants in the East or in Midwest areas outside of Akron or Detroit had a much larger ratio at this time.

Early Southern Practice

By 1940, three plants had been established in the South: the huge Goodyear plant, Gadsden, Alabama; Firestone, Memphis, Tennessee; and Armstrong, Natchez, Mississippi. These plants adopted southern practices, which following unionization during and after World War II, remained intact until the 1960's. As one company expressed it:

> . . . the company did not attempt, as a stranger in the community, to impose what it deemed to be socially desirable concepts upon the local citizens where such concepts were contrary to their traditions and practices. As a result, the . . . plant, as well as all plants of other companies in the South, was built with racial segregation as a consideration. The concept of "separate but equal" was the foundation of this concept. Thus separate but identical facilities, in terms of quality and relative size, were constructed and labeled "colored" and "white." Included were showers, lockers, toilets, smoking areas, cafeterias and drinking fountains. *There were, moreover, separate lines of progression in the plant, based upon racial considerations alone, for purposes of seniority and job bidding. There was virtually no department in which members of both races worked.* As we all know, this environment was the product of attitudes inherited by the company. . . .[40] (Emphasis supplied)

38. *Ibid.*, pp. 12-15; Northrup field notes, Detroit, 1940 and 1943; and *U. S. Census of Population, 1940*, Vol. III, *The Labor Force*, Part 3, Table 18.
39. *U. S. Census of Population, 1940*, *ibid.*, Part 2, Table 18.
40. Unpublished memorandum in possession of authors.

The separate departments and lines of progression in the South, as elsewhere in the industry, were, in fact, anything but "separate *and* equal." Negroes were confined to the lower end of the job spectrum and to the dirty, hot compounding room. On the other hand, southern plants employed substantially more Negroes than did those in the North. In 1940, for example, Firestone officials in Memphis estimated their Negro work force comprised 30-40 percent of the approximately 2,000 employees then employed.[41] The Negro labor force at the other two southern plants comprised a smaller proportion, but was considerably larger than the typical northern plant.

Thus the situation in the rubber tire industry as of 1940, provided an interesting contrast to that in the industry for which its product was manufactured. Because of the pioneering and determination of Henry Ford, Negroes were employed in jobs throughout his great River Rouge works. No comparable situation existed in rubber tire plants (except at the new River Rouge tire plant), nor were Negroes employed in as large numbers in northern tire plants as they were in the automotive foundries and paint shops.

On the other hand, even Henry Ford made no effort to breach southern mores. The only automobile plants in the South were assembly facilities, and they used a lily-white force except for janitors and porters. Southern tire plants of the pre-World War II period had a heavy need for unskilled laborers and those who would accept the tough, unpleasant work of the compounding room. Hence they hired a much larger force of Negroes than did the northern plants, and certainly hired a larger percentage of Negroes than did the southern automobile assembly plants.[42] Firestone, however, because of the interest of the founder-president and his family, went beyond other companies in giving southern Negroes opportunities for factory work. Although at the Memphis plant, Negroes worked only in the compounding room and in other unskilled jobs. Their representation in the plant was twice or three times that in the other southern tire factories. In addition, Negroes did the unskilled work in all departments, rather than only in certain ones. Later, when integration on skilled jobs occurred, the longtime presence of Negroes within each

41. From Northrup field notes, Memphis, June 22, 1940.
42. For the automobile situation, see Part Two.

department and their large numbers made the transition more easily than it might otherwise have been.

Collective Bargaining and Departmental Segregation

During the 1930's at least two Akron companies made attempts to open up key jobs, such as tire building or calendering, to Negroes. In some cases, the Negroes chosen were not able to do the work assigned; in others, the Negroes put on the jobs were harassed by fellow employees or unfairly supervised by foremen. With great pressure on management not to permit anything to interfere with production or delivery of product to large key customers, these early experiments in industrial social progress and justice were abandoned, and collective bargaining allowed to build additional walls against progress.[43]

Collective bargaining prior to World War II brought Negroes, as well as whites, the benefits accruing from such relationships, but it also institutionalized the *status quo* insofar as employment opportunities were concerned. The general seniority rule of this period limited bumping and promotion rights to departments only. When a job opening occurred, the men in the department (a) with most seniority, (b) wanting the job, and (c) capable of doing the work, would get the job. If no person with the requisite ability in the department desired the job, then the company would hire someone from outside or could, at the discretion of management, transfer someone able and willing from another department. As a rule, management avoided transferring someone from another department, because that person's job change would leave an opening in the other department. The first person transferred would have to be trained for his new job and *his* replacement would have to be trained—and perhaps the replacement's replacement would have to be trained. Management usually avoided interdepartmental transfers because of the extra training and dislocation costs involved.

When the United Rubber Workers and the companies agreed to departmental seniority, they were merely accepting preunion practice. The racial implications were not considered. Nevertheless, departmental seniority had the effect of institutionalizing racial employment discrimination. The general policy, as noted, was to hire Negroes

43. Interviews, Akron, October 1967.

only for laboring jobs, custodial service, and for the compounding room. Since departmental seniority kept Negroes from moving between departments on their own seniority, ability, and initiative, and since management did not move Negroes out of the departments into which they were hired, employment discrimination persisted in the rubber tire plants. Union contracts held Negroes, once hired, within the discriminatory pattern established by the hiring policies of the plants.

Dispersal and Mechanization

Besides affecting Negro job opportunities through seniority, unionization in the rubber tire industry also encouraged plant dispersal and mechanization. The full effect of both would await the end of World War II. The location of plants away from metropolitan areas and the substitution of equipment for manpower, however, meant that the industry would eventually locate plants away from Negro population concentration and eliminate most of the worst characteristics of jobs traditionally assigned to Negroes. In the long run, this meant that fewer Negroes would apply for jobs; that white workers would compete for jobs once considered too unpleasant for them; and that the high wages would permit the industry to set job qualifications for which proportionately few Negroes could, by reason of educational and training disabilities, successfully compete. These trends, however, did not become fully apparent until the post-World War II decade.

CHAPTER IV.

Negro Rubber Tire Employment, World War II to 1960

Few industries were more decisively affected by World War II than was rubber manufacturing. The major sources of raw materials were quickly captured by the enemy. Huge synthetic rubber plants were built with government support. Nonessential civilian rubber tire needs were suspended for the war's duration. Products such as barrage balloons, pontoons, inflatable rubber boats, self-sealing fuel tanks, and many other war uses of rubber were added to the industry's production mix.

Yet despite these great changes, the rubber tire industry continued to produce its primary product, tires, in war as well as in peace. The military economy, like the civilian one, was geared to rubber-borne transport. Tires were essential for military vehicles. An expanded labor force was required to fill these military production needs. After a temporary decline in employment resulting from the elimination of nonessential civilian tire requirements, the military and essential civilian employment in rubber tire plants rose by more than 35 percent in late 1942 over such employment in 1939. A survey by the U. S. Bureau of Labor Statistics in August of that year, which covered approximately 98 percent of the labor force in rubber tire plants, reported that approximately 67,000 workers were employed in rubber tire factories at that time.[44]

NEGRO EMPLOYMENT DURING WORLD WAR II

During World War II, Negroes made a considerable net gain in total employment in the industry. According to the U. S. Bureau of Labor Statistics survey:

44. Harry M. Douty, "Wages in Rubber Tire and Tube Plants, August 1942," *Monthly Labor Review*, Vol. LVI (February 1943), pp. 233-254.

> Negroes constituted about 5 percent of the total labor force of the industry in August 1942. The proportion of Negro employment was less than 5 percent in other Midwest, Far West, and East, and approximately 5 percent in the Akron-Detroit area. In the South, Negroes formed 20 percent of the labor force. Negroes were employed principally in compounding and milling occupations, and as janitors and general plant laborers.[45]

The Bureau of Labor Statistics data summarized in Table 11 indicate that Negroes sharply increased their representation in the industry during the war in all sections of the country except the South. In the Akron plants, in the huge Uniroyal (then United States Rubber) facility in Detroit, the proportion of Negroes rose rapidly, and in the Los Angeles operations of the Big Four, a sizable percentage of Negroes was employed for the first time.

In the South, the proportion of Negroes in the three tire plants located there was already high prior to the war. The numbers of Negroes in these plants rose about proportionately to the total em-

TABLE 11. *Rubber Tire Industry*
Number of Plants and Factory Workers, by Region and Race, 1942

Region	Number of Plants	Number of Workers	Percentage of Plants	Percentage of Workers	Percentage of Negroes in Labor Force
All Regions	32	66,721	100	100	5
Akron and Detroit[a]	8	45,367	25	68	5
Other Midwest[b]	9	4,486	28	7	> 5
Far West[c]	5	7,764	16	12	> 5
East[d]	7	4,940	22	7	> 5
South[e]	3	4,164	9	6	20

Source: *Monthly Labor Review*, Vol. LVI (February 1943), pp. 240-241 (U. S. Bureau of Labor Statistics Survey, August 1942).

[a] 6 plants in Akron, 2 in Detroit.

[b] 6 plants in Ohio, 1 each in Indiana, Michigan, and Illinois.

[c] 5 plants in California, one Far Western plant, which produced few tires, not included.

[d] 3 plants in Pennsylvania, 1 in New York, 2 in Connecticut, and 1 in Massachusetts.

[e] 1 plant each in Tennessee, Alabama, and Mississippi.

45. *Ibid.*, p. 240.

ployment increase. The ratio was, however, four times as great as the national average, with Firestone's Memphis operation continuing to have the highest percentage of Negroes in any plant in the country.[46]

Quantity and Quality

Although Negro proportional representation in the rubber tire industry increased substantially during the war, the numbers of Negroes involved was not great nor was there significant quantitative change in the jobs available to them. Compared to such industries as automobiles or aircraft, which employed well over a million workers during the wartime peak, rubber tire's wartime employment was not large. Negro employment in both the aircraft and rubber tire industries comprised about 5 percent of the total. In the former industry, which employed 1,345,600 persons in 1943, that meant 67,250 jobs for Negroes;[47] in rubber tires, which employed 128,200 in 1945, it meant only about 6,410 jobs.

Moreover, in sharp contrast to such industries as automobiles and aircraft, the occupational *status quo* in the rubber tire plants survived the war very much undisturbed. Negroes generally did not break out of the traditional areas of work, only a few Negroes making their way into the all-white departments. One industrial relations director recounted this experience:

> Once during the War, a personnel man led a half dozen Negroes into a busy—and lily-white—cutting room of one large Akron tire plant. Within minutes every machine in the department was silent. The personnel man led the Negroes out, the machines were turned on, and that department remained lily-white.[48]

The situation was similar elsewhere. Neither industry, union, nor government mounted an effective campaign for change, and the need for Negro workers in this industry, unlike many others, was insufficient either to cause or to effect radical alteration of the pre-existing policies or practices of departmental segregation.

Within the compounding departments, however, Negroes did make progress. The Banbury mixer was developed prior to World War I, and was in general use soon thereafter. When Negroes first were

46. Northrup field notes of that period.
47. See Part Three, p. 149.
48. Interview, Akron, October 1967.

brought into the processing departments, they were confined largely to material handling, rough weighing, and other laboring jobs, but not permitted to work on the Banbury machines. During World War II, Negroes made use of departmental seniority to gain jobs as Banbury operators. As noted earlier, this is one of the higher-paid jobs in a rubber tire factory. At the Firestone facilities in Akron, this upgrading was met by a threat of white workers that they would strike if it occurred. Firestone management declined to be intimidated and no walkout ensued.

Female Employment

As already noted, the rubber tire industry traditionally has been a man's industry. Prior to World War II less than 1 percent of the plant labor force was female. War conditions did not result "to any appreciable extent" in the use of female labor in tasks performed traditionally by men, but "a large influx of female workers . . . occurred . . . for fabrication work on special war products."[49] In August 1942, women comprised 27 percent of the employment in the industry, ranging from a high of nearly 40 percent in Los Angeles, to a low of 16 percent in the South.[50] Negro women were probably represented in about the same proportion as men.[51] The office, however, remained lily-white. The Negro secretary, like the male salaried worker, was not yet to be found in this industry, nor in many others as well.

THE POST-WORLD WAR II PERIOD

The rubber tire industry's post-World War II adjustments were remarkably mild at first, but more difficult later. Employment, which reached a wartime peak in 1945 of 128,200, rose to an all time high of 143,400 in 1946 as tire production increased from 44.5 to 82.3 million. (See Table 6.) The following year, production rose by more than 13 million units, but employment fell by more than 7,000. For the next two years both employment and output declined, with the former in 1949 at the lowest between 1942 and 1958, and the latter in that year at the lowest ever reached since World War II.

49. Douty, *op. cit.*, p. 239.
50. *Ibid.*, p. 240.
51. No data are available. Based upon Northrup's field notes of the period, plus interviews in 1967 with various personnel executives in the industry.

A study by the United States Employment Service for the first six months of 1947 found Negroes holding 7 percent of the "rubber products" industry jobs, which, of course, include those in nontire rubber plants.[52] Although this ratio exceeds that of prewar Negro employment, it would appear likely that Negroes lost substantially in the layoffs of 1947-1949, most of which came after this study was made. As a group, they held the least seniority and were, therefore, the first laid off. Moreover, they were concentrated in the laboring and material handling jobs which are the easiest and first to be mechanized.

Fragmentary data from this period, supplied by two Akron companies support the premise that Negro employment declined sharply in the late 1940's. In December 1946, one company had 10.4 percent Negro employment in its factory and no Negro white collar employees with a net percentage of 7.8 percent Negro—up from 1.5 percent Negro in 1942. Compilation of these data were discontinued by this company in January 1947, but companies' officials confirm that the layoffs which followed had a disproportionate impact on Negroes and substantially reduced their proportions.[53]

A second company employed 2,072 persons, 15.6 percent of whom were Negro, in factory employment between 1941 and 1947, but only 21 persons, 19 percent of whom were Negro the following two years. This company hired 507 factory employees in 1951 and 1952, 20 percent of whom were Negro, but only 163 factory employees, 14 percent of whom were Negro, during the remainder of the 1950's. Unlike the previous company, this latter one continued to employ a sizable proportion of Negroes, but its total Akron employment consistently declined, and many Negroes laid off in 1948 or 1949, never regained their jobs.[54]

Separate data by race for the rubber tire industry in the late forties are not available, but census figures on the rubber products industry do indicate general racial employment trends. Table 12 shows employment by race and sex for the census years 1940-1960 for the

52. Quoted by Charles S. Johnson and Preston Valien, "The Status of Negro Labor," in Colston E. Warne, *et al.* (eds.), *Labor in Postwar America* (Brooklyn, N. Y.: Remsen Press, 1949), p. 557.
53. Based on data supplied by company officials and interviews, October 1967 and December 1968.
54. *Ibid.*, December 1968.

United States. Between 1940 and 1950, Negro employment quadrupled and the percentage of Negroes in the industry almost tripled. Although Negro employment rose faster than total employment during this decade, it is unlikely, for the reasons already noted, that Negro employment in 1950 was as large a percentage as that which prevailed at the end of World War II.

Tables 13 and 14 show the same data for the principal rubber tire plant areas of the period. By 1950, Negroes comprised 4.7 percent of Ohio's rubber products employees and 6 percent in the Akron standard metropolitan statistical area (SMSA). In California, Negroes comprised 6.9 percent of the work force in 1950 as compared with 0.3 percent in 1940. And in Michigan, the number of Negro employees tripled over the ten-year period, increasing the Negro share of jobs by two and one-half times.

Although the data for Ohio show, and for Akron, undoubtedly indicate, that Negroes substantially increased their numbers and ratio of jobs in rubber products plants there, between 1940 and 1950, it is very unlikely that either Negro employment or their labor force ratio in 1950 were equal to the World War II period record. Akron, because of its high wages and union restrictions on productivity, was by 1950 already experiencing the decline in production jobs which has gone on almost continually since 1947. For the reasons already noted—low seniority and concentration in jobs which were relatively easily mechanized—Negro rubber workers suffered disproportionately in these production and employment shifts.

The gains of Negroes in Michigan reflected the fact that the United States Rubber plant in Detroit was on its way to rival the Firestone Memphis, Tennessee, plant as the industry's employer of the highest percentage of Negroes. Henry Ford's successors, however, had given up producing their own tires. The Ford plant was dismantled and shipped to Russia under the federal lend-lease program of foreign aid immediately after World War II hostilities ended.

The South continued to have the highest percentage of Negroes in the rubber products industry. Moreover, in 1950 Firestone's Memphis plant remained the plant with the largest Negro ratio. By this time, Goodrich had joined Goodyear with an Alabama plant, having taken over a wartime government constructed facility in Tuscaloosa, and General was producing tires at Waco, Texas, another government built plant.

TABLE 12. *Rubber Products Industry*
Total Employed Persons by Race and Sex
United States, 1940-1960

	All Employees			Male			Female		
Year	Total	Negro	Percent Negro	Total	Negro	Percent Negro	Total	Negro	Percent Negro
1940	159,021	3,343	2.1	122,219	3,241	2.7	36,802	102	0.3
1950	237,525	13,624	5.7	177,322	11,570	6.5	60,203	2,054	3.4
1960[a]	267,830	17,520	6.5	203,943	15,401	7.6	63,887	2,119	3.3

Sources: *U. S. Census of Population:*
1940: Vol. III, *The Labor Force*, Part 1, Table 76.
1950: Vol. II, *Characteristics of the Population*, Table 133.
1960: PC(2) 7F, *Industrial Characteristics*, Table 3.

[a] Includes miscellaneous plastic products.

TABLE 13. *Rubber Products Industry*
Total Employed Persons by Race and Sex
Ohio, 1940-1960 and Akron SMSA, 1950-1960

Year	All Employees			Male			Female		
	Total	Negro	Percent Negro	Total	Negro	Percent Negro	Total	Negro	Percent Negro
				Ohio					
1940	50,061	817	1.6	40,494	807	2.0	9,567	10	0.1
1950	71,584	3,369	4.7	55,625	2,939	5.3	15,959	430	2.7
1960[a]	86,767	4,282	4.9	66,310	3,992	6.0	20,457	290	1.4
				Akron (Standard Metropolitan Statistical Area)					
1950	49,429	2,975	6.0	39,627	2,582	6.5	9,802	393	4.0
1960[a]	44,261	3,201	7.2	36,598	3,016	8.2	7,663	185	2.4

Sources: *U. S. Census of Population:*
1940: Vol. III, *The Labor Force*, Part 4, Table 18.
1950: Vol. II, *Characteristics of the Population*, State volume, Table 83.
1960: PC(1) D, *Detailed Characteristics*, State volume, Table 129.

[a] Includes miscellaneous plastic products.

TABLE 14. *Rubber Products Industry*
Total Employed Persons by Race and Sex
California, Michigan, and Three Southern States, 1940-1960

Year	All Employees			Male			Female		
	Total	Negro	Percent Negro	Total	Negro	Percent Negro	Total	Negro	Percent Negro
				California					
1940	7,243	21	0.3	6,483	21	0.3	760	—	—
1950	13,539	932	6.9	10,316	834	8.1	3,223	98	3.0
1960[a]	28,673	2,112	7.4	20,936	1,695	8.1	7,737	417	5.4
				Michigan					
1940	9,476	487	5.1	7,789	484	6.2	1,687	3	0.2
1950	11,751	1,458	12.4	9,408	1,294	13.8	2,343	164	7.0
1960[a]	17,363	1,503	8.7	13,034	1,337	10.3	4,329	166	3.8
				Three Southern States[b]					
1940	4,690	755	16.1	4,249	749	17.6	441	6	1.4
1950	10,673	1,917	18.0	8,753	1,835	21.0	1,920	82	4.3
1960[a]	13,633	2,035	14.9	11,866	1,994	16.8	1,767	41	2.3

Sources: *U. S. Census of Population:*
1940: Vol. III, *The Labor Force*, Part 2-5, Table 18.
1950: Vol. II, *Characteristics of the Population*, State volumes, Table 83.
1960: PC(1) D, *Detailed Characteristics*, State volumes, Table 129.

[a] Includes miscellaneous plastic products.
[b] Alabama, Mississippi, Tennessee.

In all areas, women increased their role in the rubber products plants, and Negro women shared in these gains. Most women have, however, been employed in sectors of the rubber industry other than tires. Although post-World War II employment of Negro women has remained considerably in excess of the prewar figure, tire plants still do not employ many females, except in offices, and those still in the plants were almost all hired during World War II.

The data in Tables 12, 13, and 14 are not, as already noted, definitive indicators of Negro rubber tire employment. They do, however, tend to confirm the observations of industry personnel concerning Negro employment trends in this period.[55]

TECHNOLOGICAL CHANGE AND PLANT DISPERSION, 1947-1960

As already noted, employment in the rubber tire industry reached a peak of 143,400 in 1946. It then declined sharply to 107,500 in 1949, rose unevenly to 122,700 in 1953, and then began a general downward trend that was not reversed until 1964. Meanwhile, production of tires almost doubled.[56] Few industries have enjoyed such dramatic increases in productivity.

Besides being a period of enormous technological change, the period 1947-1960 saw tremendous investment in new plants outside of Akron, particularly in the South which may soon rival Ohio's rubber city as a center of the industry, as well as in other sections of the country. The impact on Negro employment varied, but it appeared in 1950 that Negroes would be greatly disadvantaged by those developments.

The great advances in technology and productivity were the result not only of tremendous investment in new equipment in older plants, but also represented openings of new plants in which was installed the most modern automated equipment. The backbreaking jobs in the industry were replaced by machinery, and the need for a large unskilled labor force disappeared. This meant fewer jobs for Negroes. The reasons were the following:

In the first place, the jobs automated out of existence included

55. Interviews, fall 1967 and December 1968.
56. See Tables 5 and 6.

many of those for which Negro labor was hired: laborers, material handlers, mixers, and many in the compounding room. Second, the industry began in this period to seek, and because of its high wages, was easily able to find, an educated, well qualified work force for jobs in new plants and the few available open jobs in the older plants. Since Negroes are disproportionately more poorly educated than whites, and have considerably less background and experience in industry, they were (and are) at a distinct disadvantage in competing for such jobs.[57]

In new southern plants, companies were able to choose a labor supply from an abundance of applicants. Few Negroes could meet the specifications. Moreover, the general practice was to use state employment offices for testing and screening. These state offices were segregated until the early 1960's, often accepting Negroes only for laboring jobs.[58] The companies moving South in the 1950's and even in the early 1960's made no special effort to employ Negroes, and in fact, employed very few. Those already in the South, particularly again Firestone in Memphis, maintained a much larger percentage of Negroes, but segregation still continued to be the general rule. As a result, in some of the older southern plants, notably the largest, Goodyear's Gadsden, Alabama, facility, Negro employment declined disproportionately because jobs in which Negroes were concentrated were eliminated and the displaced Negroes were not permitted to bid into or to exercise their seniority in all-white departments.

In the early 1950's the rubber tire industry in Akron largely maintained the racial-occupational *status quo*, but some changes were brewing. In 1952, a study of Akron's Negro situation reported as follows:

> Rubber does employ Negroes. About 4,000 or ⅓ of the 12,000 Negroes in Akron's work force are employed in the rubber industry. Practically all are employed by the four largest companies where their ratio in the company work force ranges from 5% to 10%.

57. Data on old and newer plants in the South are presented in Tables 31-33, in the following chapter.

58. For a discussion of the practices of state employment offices in the South, prior to the enactment of the Civil Rights Act of 1964, see Paul H. Norgren and Samuel E. Hill, *Toward Fair Employment* (New York: Columbia University Press, 1964), pp. 36-39. Federal tax money supports these offices, and did so even while obvious discriminatory practices were extant. Such practices were outlawed by Title VII of the Civil Rights Act of 1964. That such practices continue, not only in the South, is indicated by recent indictments of both the Louisiana and Ohio State Employment Services by the U. S. Department of Justice for "a pattern of discrimination."

When we look at the types of work Negroes perform, we find a basic pattern. Most Negroes are unskilled workers, laborers or janitors. Half or more of the janitors in the four major rubber firms are Negroes. They are also concentrated in hot and heavy jobs in the mill rooms. No Negroes in the industry, other than janitor-supervisors have ever become a part of management. Of the more than 10,000 regular white collar workers employed by the big four rubber companies, not one is a Negro.

Why this pattern? First, it reflects hiring policy. Negroes are not hired for white collar jobs. Negroes are generally not hired in certain departments such as maintenance or the tire division where they can work towards more desirable and better paying jobs.

In recent years there has been some opportunity for Negroes to work at so-called "white jobs" and if this trend increases, the pattern of Negro employment in the rubber industry will change considerably.

For example, two Akron firms have had Negroes upgraded to tire-building jobs in the last two years. There are now approximately a dozen tire-builders in the rubber industry in Akron. Several years ago there were none. However, there are approximately 2,000 tire-builders in the city, so there is obviously room for improvement.

Another job which is rated high in prestige and pay is the calender operator. This has been traditionally a "white" job. One plant now has several Negroes working on calenders and all indications point to more opportunities for Negroes on these jobs in many of the other plants.

Of the many hundreds of skilled maintenance workers in the rubber factories, only two are Negroes. These have been hired recently by one of the smaller companies.

What are the factors behind this trend toward the improvement of job opportunities for Negroes? Hiring policy has not changed (except in isolated cases) since Negroes were first hired as production workers during World War II. Negroes have not recently been hired on "white" jobs. *Plant-wide seniority* seems to be the key to the change for all of the firms where noticeable upgrading of Negro workers has taken place have a system of plant-wide seniority written into their union agreements with the United Rubber Workers.

Plant-wide seniority has allowed Negroes to bid for jobs outside the divisions and departments where they have been concentrated and contained. In two major firms without plant-wide seniority, Negroes have not departed from their traditional jobs. The integration of Negroes on new jobs does not work without management and union firmness in dealing with opposition among white workers who may resist the change. Union initiative seems to have been an important factor not only in establishing the plant-wide seniority system, but in the processing of grievances resulting from race discrimination that have cropped up as Negroes have tried to expand their job opportunities. The rising pressure of the Negro group in the plants, on a sometimes complacent union leadership and a resisting company management, has helped the gradual movement of Negroes to better jobs.

> Since movement into office employment and management are outside union jurisdiction, we must expect that the main drive for integration here will have to come from management. There is some evidence that such changes will soon take place.[59]

The Change in Seniority Rules

The change in seniority rules, referred to in the quotation above, was not to benefit Negro rubber tire workers especially, but in fact did just that. The sharp drop in employment after 1947 resulted in a growing concern among employees for security. One result of this was a strong push on the part of the rubber workers' union for plant-wide, rather than departmental, seniority. Essentially the union wanted employees to have the contractual right to bid on open jobs outside of their department so that a job opening in one department could be taken by an able man with seniority in *any* other department and the vacancy created by that man could be filled by an able man with seniority in *any* other department and so on and so on. At first management stoutly resisted this proposal because of the relatively high costs in training and dislocation incurred by a string of inter-departmental transfers. Then in 1952, two Akron tire plants gave in and granted plant-wide seniority. In time, plant-wide bidding rights became common in the industry, although in most plants, the number of bids outside of a department, or the number of successful bids by an individual outside his department, during a given time period, for example one year, is limited in order to reduce the upset and expense involved.

Plant-wide seniority was not instituted to benefit Negroes. In fact, there seems to have been little weight given during the 1952 labor contract negotiations to the racial implications of plant-wide seniority. The contracts were changed because white senior union members wanted to widen their range of job opportunities, and because layoffs had made security an urgent issue. The companies resisted the change because of the added costs that they would have to bear.

Nevertheless, plant-wide seniority did in fact bring immediate and eventually significant benefits to Negro employees in the rubber tire plants, for the new contracts gave every Negro employee his first access to all production jobs for which his seniority and ability could

59. Akron Committee for a Community Audit, *The Akron Community Audit* (Akron: The Committee, 1952), pp. 32-33.

qualify him. Two of the major companies granted plant-wide seniority in 1952, and within months Negroes with seniority became tire builders and calender operators. For two years, Negro employment in these two rubber tire plants could be sharply contrasted with Negro employment in the other rubber tire plants in Akron because of Negro upward movement. Then in 1954, other plants also granted plant-wide seniority, and their Negro employees moved into departments from which they had been totally excluded.

The plant-wide seniority provisions proved of major significance to Negroes in the late 1950's when large automated Banbury machines were introduced in Akron and other locations. These huge Banburys each eliminated several smaller hand fed machines and their employee complements, a large portion of whom were Negroes. Those displaced, however, were able to exercise seniority throughout a plant location. The net effect was to scatter Negroes throughout several plants where they had been heretofore highly concentrated in a few departments.

Outside of Akron (except in the South) the racial-departmental segregation pattern was also broken as plant-wide seniority rights were negotiated. Most top jobs in the plants continued to be held by whites because of their longer service, and most Negroes continued to be found in the traditional laboring, janitorial, and compounding room jobs. But now a sprinkling of Negro tire builders, calender operators, and operatives in heavy service departments became common to most nonsouthern plants in which Negroes had acquired sufficient seniority to bid successfully for the better jobs.

Southern Plants, 1950-1960

Some of the labor contracts negotiated in the rubber industry cover all tire plants of a company, usually with local supplements to care for matters peculiar to the local situation. When the contracts provided for bidding out of departments, they were at first either ignored, or the contracts were not applied by mutual consent of company and union insofar as southern plants were concerned.

At the huge Goodyear facility in Gadsden, Alabama, for example, racially segregated seniority rosters continued to be maintained throughout the 1950's (as well as racial segregation in dining, locker room, water fountain, and recreational facilities). Despite the clear rights set forth in their union contract, Local No. 12 of the rubber workers' union and the Goodyear management continued to interpret the agreement to bar Negroes from bidding into white departments. Where Negroes filed a grievance, the local union refused to process it. This situation continued until altered by legal action in the mid-1960's.[60]

In the Tuscaloosa, Alabama, plant of Goodrich, segregated departmental seniority was maintained until the mid-1960's, with Negroes confined to service and preparation, as was the historical pattern. Similarly, in the Natchez, Mississippi, plant of Armstrong Rubber, there was no department in which members of both races worked and Negroes were confined to the traditional areas, and departmental seniority was retained throughout this period. In the Waco, Texas, plant of General Tire, which was also built during World War II, the proportion of Negroes was never large, but again declined after World War II and during the 1950's. In the late 1950's, the company began once more attempting to employ Negroes, but in the traditional jobs.[61] In the West Helena, Arkansas, plant of the Mohawk Rubber Company, which was built in the 1950's, departmental seniority and segregation of Negroes followed traditional practices. The Company hired on a discriminatory basis and the predominantly white local union insisted on departmental seniority.[62]

Firestone's Memphis plant again stood out as the most progressive in industrial race relations of the rubber tire plants in the South. It had been the first southern plant to use Negroes as Banbury operators, and it continued throughout this period to employ the largest percentage of Negroes. In 1958, for example, approximately 30 percent of the plant's nearly 3,000 employees were Negro.[63] Moreover, an inspector from the President's Committee on Government Contracts, chaired by the then Vice-President and known as the Nixon Com-

60. It will be further discussed in the following chapter. The facts recounted are based upon those set forth in *Local Union No. 12, United Rubber, Cork, Linoleum and Plastic Workers,* 150 NLRB 312 (1964); 57 LRRM 1535.

61. These situations were verified by interviews and field investigations. See also *Wall Street Journal,* November 9, 1966.

62. See testimony before the Arkansas Advisory Committee on Civil Rights, Forest City, Arkansas, April 23, 1966, pp. 6-71. Typescript in files of United States Civil Rights Commission, Washington, D. C.

63. Data from an unpublished report to President's Committee on Government Contracts, covering 1957 and 1958 investigations of Firestone's Memphis plant.

mittee, which handled racial employees' problems in firms with government contracts during the Eisenhower Administration, reported in that year that:

> Both white and Negro employees were working on several types of tires and tube making machinery in several classifications. White women and male Negro employees were working together on the same benches and the same machines. White and colored employees were sweeping floors, operating tractors, and working in the Shipping Department. There were no Negroes observed among the office employees.[64]

Firestone, as the above quotation indicates, moved in the 1950's to open up jobs to Negroes that had previously been all white. Implementation of the plant-wide seniority provisions began in 1955 when a number of Negroes on layoff protested the hiring of whites while they were denied work. Unlike other concerns in the South, the Company was sympathetic, and the Negroes, being nearly one-third of the local union membership, and already working in all departments, although in unskilled jobs, had leverage not possessed by their counterparts in other southern locals of the United Rubber Workers, most of which are less than 10 percent Negro. Nevertheless, integration did not come easily.

Unlike the Goodyear, Gadsden, situation, the Company and the local union at Firestone's Memphis plant permitted the case to go to arbitration. The arbitrator, however, ruled that the parties had an oral supplement to the agreement, and an acceptance practice, to maintain segregated departments. Accordingly, he ruled that the contract had not been violated.

Four Negro employees then took the matter to court. While the court case was pending, negotiations began on a new contract. The Company during negotiations sent the union a letter advising it that henceforth it would observe the contract without racial distinction. The new agreement was signed in January 1957, and within a few months all laid-off Negroes were re-employed on jobs formerly limited to white employees. Occasional sabotage occurred on machines, formerly reserved for white operators, but a strong stand by management and the local union's lack of support for troublemakers quickly brought matters under control.

64. *Ibid.*

Supervisory Employment

The first Negro supervisors in the industry were put on the job by Firestone at Akron in 1955. Just prior to then, the Company developed a new presupervisory training program which was required for all supervisory candidates and for which top management carefully selected candidates. Among the earliest graduates was the industry initial black foreman, exclusive of straw bosses over yard or janitorial crews.

The Situation in 1960

By 1960, Negro employees in rubber tire plants had witnessed a decade of great change, with some gains and some losses. Unfortunately, definitive data are not available. The census data in Tables 12, 13, and 14 not only included all rubber products' industrial classifications, but in 1960, miscellaneous plastic products as well. These data show that the number and percentage of Negroes increased in this overall classification, with increases especially in Akron and California. In Michigan and in the three southern states of Alabama, Mississippi, and Tennessee, Negroes added to their total number of jobs, but in proportion, suffered sharp declines.

Overall, employment in the rubber tire industry, which had fallen from 143,400 in 1946 to 110,200 in 1950, peaked for the decade of the 1950's in 1953 at 122,700, and then fell unevenly to 104,800 in 1960. (See Table 4.) It is very unlikely that Negro employment in the tire industry rose while total employment fell. On the contrary, it is likely that Negro employment actually fell disproportionately. During this period, much of the expansion of the industry occurred in the Midwest where few Negroes dwell, or in the South. The higher employment standards set by companies opening new southern facilities and the automating of laboring and material handling jobs reduced the number and proportion of Negroes hired. In addition, the failure of all but Firestone to end departmental segregation in the South reduced the proportion of Negroes in older southern facilities since Negroes displaced by technological changes or other factors could not exercise seniority on the bulk of the available jobs.

On the bright side of the ledger, the 1950's saw the end of departmental segregation in northern plants and in Firestone's Memphis facility, and the first Negro supervisors in Akron. Negroes were thus better represented throughout the work force and in addition, a precedent had been set to apply against the practices in the South which would remain until the mid-1960's.

Two key areas still remained largely out of the reach of Negroes in 1960—the whole range of white collar jobs and the skilled crafts. A few Negroes were hired for office and professional work prior to 1960, but only a few. For reasons which will be analyzed in the following chapter, the craft area continued in this industry, as in most others, to be a white man's preserve.

CHAPTER V.

Negro Employment in the 1960's

The 1960's did not begin auspiciously for Negro rubber tire workers. Employment in the industry fell from 118,500 in 1955 to 104,100 in 1958; then rose to 104,800 in 1960, before commencing another decline that was not arrested until a low point of 97,300 was reached in 1963.[65] To be sure, most plants in Akron and Los Angeles continued to upgrade Negroes into the better blue collar jobs and to maintain Negro employment at an 8-10 percent ratio. Moreover, Negro employment at the Uniroyal plant in Detroit remained at 20 percent and that of the same company in Los Angeles climbed to about the same ratio, while the Firestone plant in Memphis continued to have the highest percentage, about 30 percent of the workers there being Negro at this time.

In general, Negroes in the South continued to lose ground and this has been the area of most new plant expansion in recent years. Only Firestone opened up all blue collar departments in the South to Negroes in any numbers prior to the Civil Rights Act of 1964. Under the prodding of the federal government, General Tire also opened up a few top jobs to Negroes in the early 1960's. When the first Negro was promoted to tire builder at Waco, an illegal strike occurred. General kept the plant open and had the Negro tire builder's foreman bring him to work every day for two weeks till the strike was defeated and ended.

In most cases, however, union-management agreements for plant-wide seniority rights usually either exempted other southern plants or were ignored by tacit consent. New plants were established in some cases in areas where few Negroes live—Miami, Oklahoma, and Mayfield, Kentucky. Other new plants were opened with the latest automated equipment and rigid, high employment standards which few Negroes could meet. Although the major tire companies were

65. See Table 4.

early adherents to the "Plans for Progress" organization, there is little evidence that affirmative action was practiced in new southern plants. Three plants established in the late 1950's or early 1960's in areas of the South where a substantial Negro population dwells, employed, as late as 1966, only 44 Negroes in a total employment of 1,380, a ratio of about 3 percent Negro. Moreover nearly all of the Negroes in these plants were found in the lower-rated blue collar jobs.[66]

NEGRO EMPLOYMENT IN 1964

Table 15 shows Negro rubber tire employment for 1964, by occupational group, for a sample of ten companies and thirty-nine plants employing more than 90 percent of the total industry work force. These data reveal that the industry's proportion of Negro workers increased somewhat since 1942 (see Table 11), and probably remained relatively stable since the mid-1950's. Negroes in 1964 continued to be highly concentrated in the lower blue collar occupations. They were still largely excluded from all white collar and craftsmen jobs at this date. There were, however, a few who by this time had overcome the barriers.

Regional Differences

Turning next to a regional breakdown in 1964, and utilizing the same data, we find a shift in job opportunities from the South to Ohio, other midwestern states, and California (Table 16). To be sure the highest proportion of Negroes in the industry was still found in southern plants in 1964, but the ratio was 12 percent as compared with 20 percent in 1942 (Table 11). The already noted automating of labor and material handling work, the denial of opportunities for Negroes in key departments in most southern plants, the staffing of new plants with an overwhelming white work force, and the location of some plants in areas of sparse Negro population, were the factors responsible for the declining proportion of Negroes in the South.

Actually the data in Table 16 underestimate the disadvantaged position of Negroes in southern rubber tire plants. More than 60 percent of all Negro rubber tire workers were then employed in one facility—Firestone's Memphis plant. Without this one plant, the pro-

66. Data in authors' possession.

TABLE 15. *Rubber Tire Industry*
Employment by Race, Sex, and Occupational Group
Total United States, 10 Companies, 39 Plants, 1964

Occupational Group	All Employees			Male			Female		
	Total	Negro	Percent Negro	Total	Negro	Percent Negro	Total	Negro	Percent Negro
Officials and managers	7,165	23	0.3	7,123	23	0.3	42	—	—
Professionals	3,134	3	0.1	3,074	3	0.1	60	—	—
Technicians	1,995	22	1.1	1,878	19	1.0	117	3	2.6
Sales workers	886	31	3.5	827	30	3.6	59	1	1.7
Office and clerical	6,393	79	1.2	2,105	43	2.0	4,288	36	0.8
Total white collar	19,573	158	0.8	15,007	118	0.8	4,566	40	0.9
Craftsmen	11,516	172	1.5	11,491	171	1.5	25	1	4.0
Operatives	42,081	4,905	11.7	38,842	4,659	12.0	3,239	246	7.6
Laborers	3,960	749	18.9	3,619	741	20.5	341	8	2.3
Service workers	2,924	914	31.3	2,676	873	32.6	248	41	16.5
Total blue collar	60,481	6,740	11.1	56,628	6,444	11.4	3,853	296	7.7
Total	80,054	6,898	8.6	71,635	6,562	9.2	8,419	336	4.0

Source: Data in authors' possession.

TABLE 16. *Rubber Tire Industry*
Employment by Race, Sex, and Region
10 Companies, 39 Plants, 1964

	All Employees			Male			Female		
Region	Total	Negro	Percent Negro	Total	Negro	Percent Negro	Total	Negro	Percent Negro
East	13,444	626	4.7	12,125	565	4.7	1,319	61	4.6
Ohio	29,963	2,523	8.4	25,858	2,427	9.4	4,105	96	2.3
Midwest except Ohio	16,607	1,387	8.4	15,229	1,270	8.3	1,378	117	8.5
South	13,276	1,589	12.0	12,356	1,563	12.6	920	26	2.8
California	6,764	773	11.4	6,067	737	12.1	697	36	5.2
Total	80,054	6,898	8.6	71,635	6,562	9.2	8,419	336	4.0

Source: Data in authors' possession.
Note: Geographic definitions are as follows:
East: Connecticut, Maryland, Massachusetts, New Jersey, New York, and Pennsylvania.
Other Midwest: Colorado, Illinois, Indiana, Iowa, Kansas, Michigan, and Wisconsin.
South: Alabama, Arkansas, Georgia, Kentucky, Mississippi, Oklahoma, Tennessee, Texas, and Virginia.

portion of Negroes in southern tire plants in 1964 would have been only 5.9 percent!

The Ohio data indicate that Akron, still the center of the industry, seems after 1950 to have remained stable in so far as the Negro employment ratio is concerned. In the East, few tire plants are located close to centers of the Negro population except the relatively small Schenuit Company plant in Baltimore. This undoubtedly contributed to the relatively small percentage of Negroes in plants in this area in 1964.

In the Midwest, the relatively high Negro percentage of rubber tire workers is misleading. Many of the non-Ohio midwestern plants are new, and opened with hiring standards that few Negroes could meet. Others, such as the Uniroyal plant in Eau Claire, Wisconsin, are in areas where few Negroes dwell. In most of these plants little effort, at least prior to 1964, was made to employ Negroes.

There is in the Midwest, as in the South, one facility which employs most of the Negroes who work in the industry in this region. Here it is the Uniroyal plant in Detroit in which in 1964, 72 percent of the Negroes in the non-Ohio Midwest, were working. If the totals of this plant were excluded from the 1964 data, the proportion of Negroes would be only 3.3 percent, the lowest of any region in the country.

The sharp increase in Negro employment in California rubber tire plants by 1964 reflects several factors. First was the tremendous population growth of the West in general, and southern California in particular. This has resulted in expansion in the West Coast tire plants. At the same time, the ratio of the Negro population of Los Angeles, where the four oldest West Coast tire plants are located, rose from 9 percent in 1950 to double that percentage in 1965.[67] In the Los Angeles area, rubber tire work, despite its higher wages, is a less attractive and glamorous source of employment than is aerospace. The tendency of white workers to prefer the latter gives Negroes a greater opportunity in rubber tire plants. Finally, the rubber tire plants in Los Angeles are much more accessible to the centers of Negro population there than are many aerospace facilities.[68] This

67. The Center for Research in Marketing, Inc., *The Negro Population: 1965 Estimates and 1970 Projections* (Peekskill, N. Y.: The Center, 1966).

68. For an analysis of the locational problems affecting Negro employment in the southern California aerospace industry, see Part Two.

has encouraged Negroes to seek work in the former plants rather than in many of the latter.

By 1964, three of the four older plants in Los Angeles all had about a 10 percent complement of Negroes, whereas the two newer California plants, located away from the metropolitan area and the centers of Negro population had only about a 3 percent Negro ratio. Again, however, one plant dominated the Negro-white ratio and again it was the Uniroyal plant, where the percentage of Negroes was about double that of the area total. If the Uniroyal totals for California in 1964 were subtracted from those of the area, the ratio of Negroes would have been only 9 percent instead of 11.4 percent.

AN OVERALL LOOK—1966 AND 1968

By 1966, employment in the rubber tire industry had been on the upgrade for two years. Plant expansion and new plant construction, both of which were to increase in ensuing years, were commencing throughout the industry. Title VII of the Civil Rights Act of 1964 became effective in mid-1965. The Office of Federal Contract Compliance, which polices minority employment for government contractors, was demanding "affirmative action" in southern as well as northern tire plants, and Negro rubber tire workers in the South were appealing to a variety of government bodies to seek redress of their grievances. Changes were occurring, and the climate was propitious for change.

The Rubber Products Industry, 1966

Before turning specifically to the tire segment of the rubber industry, which is the basic concern of this study, an examination of data in the total rubber products industry is helpful because of the significance of rubber tire companies in the various branches of industry in addition to tires. Table 17 shows data for 927 establishments in Standard Industrial Classification 30 (rubber and plastic products not otherwise classified) for 1966 based upon reports made to the Equal Employment Opportunity Commission. The data are for whites, nonwhites (about 95 percent of whom are Negro), and by occupational group. They include 343,692 employees about one-fourth of whom are actually in the rubber tire industry.

TABLE 17. *Rubber Products Industry (SIC 30)*
Employment by Color and Occupational Group
927 Establishments, 1966

Occupational Group	All Employees	Nonwhite	Percent Nonwhite
Officials and managers	28,719	356	1.2
Professionals	13,325	161	1.2
Technicians	8,828	284	3.2
Sales workers	8,840	183	2.1
Office and clerical	32,132	735	2.3
Total white collar	91,844	1,719	1.9
Craftsmen	36,830	1,789	4.9
Operatives	159,964	20,301	12.7
Laborers	7,819	2,062	26.4
Service workers	47,235	8,190	17.3
Total blue collar	251,848	32,342	12.8
Total	343,692	34,061	9.9

Source: Data in authors' possession, computer compiled from reports to the Equal Employment Opportunity Commission.

These data may, with caution, be only roughly compared with those of the 1960 census (Table 12, p. 42). The census data are based on household interviews; those in Table 17 on reports from companies. Given the potential for noncomparability resulting from this and related factors, the sharp increase in the percentage of Negroes, 6.5 percent to 9.9 percent, still indicates improvement in the Negro position. On the other hand, the tiny representation of Negroes in white collar jobs, their overrepresentation among unskilled, and underrepresentation among skilled, indicate that Negroes in the rubber products industry in 1966, like most others, had much progress to make.

Major Tire Company Data, 1966 and 1968

Another approach to an overall look is provided by Table 18, which summarizes the data by race, sex, and occupational group for the 1966 consolidated reports of twelve tire companies. Since the five largest companies are also major factors in chemicals, textiles, and automobile parts in addition to rubber products other than tires, these data include about twice the number of employees that work in rubber tire establishments.

TABLE 18. *Twelve Rubber Tire Companies*
Consolidated Report Data by Race, Sex, and Occupational Group, 1966

Occupational Group	All Employees			Male			Female		
	Total	Negro	Percent Negro	Total	Negro	Percent Negro	Total	Negro	Percent Negro
Officials and managers	26,201	139	0.5	25,856	135	0.5	345	4	1.2
Professionals	13,190	51	0.4	12,934	51	0.4	256	—	—
Technicians	7,095	122	1.7	6,122	83	1.4	973	39	4.0
Sales workers	11,404	605	5.3	10,894	594	5.5	510	11	2.2
Office and clerical	26,984	335	1.2	10,307	161	1.5	16,677	174	1.0
Total white collar	84,874	1,252	1.5	66,113	1,024	1.6	18,761	228	1.2
Craftsmen	27,968	700	2.5	27,063	665	2.5	905	35	3.9
Operatives	94,771	10,674	11.3	76,439	8,906	11.7	18,332	1,768	9.6
Laborers	17,044	3,186	18.7	14,215	2,950	20.8	2,829	236	8.3
Service workers	6,963	1,892	27.2	6,118	1,774	29.0	845	118	14.0
Total blue collar	146,746	16,452	11.2	123,835	14,295	11.5	22,911	2,157	9.4
Total	231,620	17,704	7.6	189,948	15,319	8.1	41,672	2,385	5.7

Source: Data in authors' possession.

TABLE 19. *Eleven Rubber Tire Companies*
Consolidated Report Data by Race, Sex, and Occupational Group, 1968

Occupational Group	All Employees			Male			Female		
	Total	Negro	Percent Negro	Total	Negro	Percent Negro	Total	Negro	Percent Negro
Officials and managers	30,312	289	1.0	29,885	286	1.0	427	3	0.7
Professionals	13,761	91	0.7	13,311	85	0.6	450	6	1.3
Technicians	8,720	210	2.4	7,613	165	2.2	1,107	45	4.1
Sales workers	15,006	697	4.6	14,503	690	4.8	503	7	1.4
Office and clerical	26,723	479	1.8	7,577	189	2.5	19,146	290	1.5
Total white collar	94,522	1,766	1.9	72,889	1,415	1.9	21,633	351	1.6
Craftsmen	29,280	943	3.2	28,550	917	3.2	730	26	3.6
Operatives	103,542	12,757	12.3	82,935	10,439	12.6	20,607	2,318	11.2
Laborers	17,133	3,656	21.3	15,048	3,462	23.0	2,085	194	9.3
Service workers	6,628	1,704	25.7	5,645	1,562	27.7	983	142	14.4
Total blue collar	156,583	19,060	12.2	132,178	16,380	12.4	24,405	2,680	11.0
Total	251,105	20,826	8.3	205,067	17,795	8.7	46,038	3,031	6.6

Source: Data in authors' possession.

These data show a smaller percentage of Negroes in toto and in nearly all key areas except sales workers as compared with the data in Table 17. Undoubtedly, a higher percentage of Negroes in nonrubber tire company plastic, footwear, and miscellaneous rubber products concerns, where the pay and working conditions are relatively poor, is a key reason for the higher percentage of Negroes shown in Table 17.

The lower representation of all white collar groups except sales in Table 18 is difficult to understand. It may be that the tire companies were not providing employment opportunities for minorities as well as nontire rubber companies. On the other hand, since the data in Table 17 include all nonwhites, and those in Table 18 only Negroes, this may account for some of the differences.

The relatively high percentage of sales workers among Negroes in Table 18 deserves comment since it is not as significant as might be thought. The sales area is one in which Negroes are very much underrepresented throughout the country, and a 5.3 percentage of salesmen would be indeed high. Actually, many of those classified as sales are in fact service employees in sales establishments. Some progress has been made, as will be discussed below, but far fewer than 5 percent of those engaged in marketing are Negroes.

Table 19 shows consolidated company report data for 1968. Data for two small companies which were included in Table 18 were not available for 1968, while one small company not used in 1966 was added to the data in Table 19. Nevertheless, the net differences are so inconsequential that comparison of the two years is appropriate.

The 1968 consolidated report data show continued but slow progress in Negro employment. The number and percentage of Negroes rose in all categories except service and sales, and in the latter, the number of Negro jobs increased but not at as fast a rate as total sales employees. A combination of civil rights pressure and concern and a continuing tight labor market contributed to the progress which occurred with a very small total employment increase.

THE RUBBER TIRE INDUSTRY—1966 AND BEYOND

Turning now to the subject of our principal focus, the tire branch of the rubber products industry, a general look is provided by Tables 20 and 21, which show respectively, employment by race, sex, and occupational group for twelve companies and fifty establishments in 1966, and for eleven companies and fifty-one establishments in 1968. Again two small companies are represented in the 1966 data, but not in those for 1968, and one found in 1968 is not in Table 20, but the loss of comparability is too slight to distort the overall picture. Both tables include about 98 percent of total rubber tire industry employment. Because central office and research center facilities of the major companies include employees not concerned with the rubber tire industry, the data may contain some nontire groups among the white collar occupations.

The 1966 and 1968 data in Tables 20 and 21 are also generally comparable with the 1964 sample in Table 15. The later data include one or two more companies and several more establishments, but these additions are relatively small and do not materially alter the data. It is therefore instructive to ascertain what changes have occurred, first in the overall picture, then within the various occupational groups.

The first observation that must be made is that very little, if any, change occurred overall between 1964 and 1966. In the 1964 sample, Negro employment was 8.6 percent of the total work force, white collar employment 0.8 percent, and blue collar employment 11.1 percent. The comparable figures for 1966 were for total employment 8.1 percent, for white collar, 1.4 percent, and for blue collar, 10.8 percent. The reductions in blue collar and total ratios may be partially or even wholly attributable to differences in the 1964 and 1966 samples; or they may indicate that the industry continued to find it easier to employ whites than Negroes to meet its rigorous employment standards.

In the white collar area, general improvement, if slight, is found in all occupational groups, with the total percentage of Negroes still very low in 1966 (1.4 percent), but almost double that two years earlier. The data are affected by a jump in the percentage of sales employees from 3.5 to 7.5, a figure which, as noted, must be handled with caution, and will be analyzed in greater detail below. Nevertheless, the white collar data do indicate that the industry made some effort to respond to the civil rights movement and to affirmative action.

Table 21 shows continued, but slight progress in 1968. The drop in the Negro sales ratio indicates that the 1966 figure may have been a statistical observation. In 1968, it probably continues to include

TABLE 20. *Rubber Tire Industry*
Employment by Race, Sex, and Occupational Group
Total United States, 12 Companies, 50 Establishments, 1966

	All Employees			Male			Female		
Occupational Group	Total	Negro	Percent Negro	Total	Negro	Percent Negro	Total	Negro	Percent Negro
Officials and managers	8,537	47	0.6	8,490	47	0.6	47	—	—
Professionals	5,135	15	0.3	5,025	15	0.3	110	—	—
Technicians	3,027	39	1.3	2,814	37	1.3	213	2	0.9
Sales workers	2,121	159	7.5	1,992	149	7.5	129	10	7.8
Office and clerical	9,482	129	1.4	2,940	61	2.1	6,542	68	1.0
Total white collar	28,302	389	1.4	21,261	309	1.5	7,041	80	1.1
Craftsmen	14,868	338	2.3	14,817	334	2.3	51	4	7.8
Operatives	49,730	5,745	11.6	45,589	5,364	11.8	4,141	381	9.2
Laborers	4,120	703	17.1	3,787	682	18.0	333	21	6.3
Service workers	3,207	976	30.4	2,906	945	32.5	301	31	10.3
Total blue collar	71,925	7,762	10.8	67,099	7,325	10.9	4,826	437	9.1
Total	100,227	8,151	8.1	88,360	7,634	8.6	11,867	517	4.4

Source: Data in authors' possession.

TABLE 21. *Rubber Tire Industry*
Employment by Race, Sex, and Occupational Group
Total United States, 11 Companies, 51 Establishments, 1968

Occupational Group	All Employees Total	All Employees Negro	All Employees Percent Negro	Male Total	Male Negro	Male Percent Negro	Female Total	Female Negro	Female Percent Negro
Officials and managers	11,284	96	0.9	11,197	96	0.9	87	—	—
Professionals	7,155	54	0.8	6,923	50	0.7	232	4	1.7
Technicians	4,001	83	2.1	3,806	79	2.1	195	4	2.1
Sales workers	3,096	154	5.0	2,832	151	5.3	264	3	1.1
Office and clerical	11,772	219	1.9	3,510	79	2.3	8,262	140	1.7
Total white collar	37,308	606	1.6	28,268	455	1.6	9,040	151	1.7
Craftsmen	15,383	438	2.8	15,266	434	2.8	117	4	3.4
Operatives	53,560	6,869	12.8	49,278	6,423	13.0	4,282	446	10.4
Laborers	1,914	436	22.8	1,899	436	23.0	15	—	—
Service workers	3,152	919	29.2	2,899	887	30.6	253	32	12.6
Total blue collar	74,009	8,662	11.7	69,342	8,180	11.8	4,667	482	10.3
Total	111,317	9,268	8.3	97,610	8,635	8.8	13,707	633	4.6

Source: Data in authors' possession.

some service personnel. Except for sales and service, the number and proportion of Negroes in 1968 was slightly higher in all categories. The decline in Negro service personnel may have resulted from conscious efforts to upgrade such employees, which the authors know have occurred in the industry.

The small changes which occurred in the industry by 1967 reflect the basic problem which has beset the industry's civil rights posture. It is an industry which has only a limited number of new employment opportunities. After fifteen years of declining employment, it enjoyed three years of slightly increasing employment from 1963 to 1966, and then employment again turned down. The industry's high wage and benefit pattern assures it not only of an adequate labor supply to meet its needs, but in most areas, except for Detroit and Los Angeles, a supply of labor that permits it to pick and choose the cream of those available. Unfortunately, years of discrimination in education and industrial opportunity result in Negroes being substantially underrepresented among the best prepared applicants.

New plants opened between World War II and 1964, were purposely located in areas that meet not only the marketing requirements of the industry, but the labor supply needs as well. The new plants have been staffed mostly with high school graduates and those with requisite training and experience. Relatively few Negroes have been able to compete with this pool of labor. By the time that the Civil Rights Act of 1964 became effective, the employment pattern in the industry was too well established and ingrained to be affected promptly by new attitudes and affirmative action commitments, especially in view of the trend in employment.

Of course improvement occurred by 1968. Although some companies have maintained their rigid employment standards, most have taken on high school dropouts, employed hard-core slum residents, and consciously sought Negro applicants. In some cases without being pushed by government, companies have re-examined the Negroes in their work force and upgraded those who appeared to have the background or potential to take on new responsibilities. In other cases, companies worked with government agencies to assure Negro representation in their work force. One such event occurred in California in 1963. The report of the state Fair Employment Practice Commission (which mentions no names but refers to what seems to be Armstrong Rubber plant in Hanford, California), describes the situation:

> In July 1963 [the California] FEPC learned of the plans of a large rubber company to open a new plant in the "X" Valley, and immediately arranged a meeting with the industrial relations director of that company for a discussion of recruitment and hiring policy.
>
> The company, it was found, would employ 400 production workers for this factory. About 90 had already been hired, none of whom was Negro. Another 100 persons were to be employed in the office, and the 65 office people already hired included no Negroes.
>
> The company was most willing to implement a broad, equal opportunity policy, and to have FEPC advice to this end. Recruitment was being conducted entirely through the Department of Employment at "X," so FEPC staff met with the manager of that office to discuss methods of including larger minority representation in referrals to the plant. It was decided that it would be desirable also to recruit through the "X" office of the Department of Employment in order to include in the pool of possible employees the large population of Negroes in that area, and to reach Mexican Americans living there as well. These minority communities were then informed of the new opportunities in this situation and encouraged to look into them.
>
> Contact was maintained by Commissioner Brombacher and staff. By September 1964 the company had hired 466 employees, of whom 26 percent were Mexican American, 5 percent Filipino, and almost 4 percent Negro. Negro workers included front office personnel and the important position of plant nurse. Supervisory staff included two Mexican Americans and one Oriental.
>
> Of special interest here is the fact that as the company actively extended its employment recruiting to the full range of potential applicants, it happened that the levels of minority representation in the work force became approximately those which obtain in the population generally in that labor market area. In any event, the firm was able to maximize the pool of recruitment prospects from which to select qualified workers.[69]

Intervention by other government agencies occurred on a broad front in the South, and will be discussed as part of the analysis by regions below. The fact that all major rubber companies are not only covered by Title VII of the Civil Rights Act but, in addition, are government contractors and therefore subject to the affirmative action policies of the Office of Federal Contract Compliance has forced many to reassess their policies. Some, by reason of accident of location, complaints, or inadequate response, have been pushed

69. Fair Employment Practice Commission, State of California, *Affirmative Actions in Employment. A Special FEPC Report* (San Francisco: The Commission, 1965), pp. 5-6.

harder than others; some have attempted to do a constructive reappraisal of their policies and programs before they were targets of government compliance; and a few maintain a detached neutrality. Thus the labor relations manager of one of the smaller companies stated in regard to affirmative action:

> The McCreary Tire and Rubber Company, Indiana, Pennsylvania, is located in an area with a very low Negro population. Thus, we do not employ a large percentage of Negroes. Our company policy is to give equal opportunity for employment and success to all persons regardless of race, color, creed, nationality, or sex. No special preference is given to members of minority groups; but, at the same time, they are not discriminated against.[70]

On the other side are companies which, under government pressure, have actually given preference to Negroes in order to improve their ratios or to better their statistics in some of the traditionally white jobs. Unlike the situation in aerospace, for example, where affirmative action and some preference resulting in substantial increase in Negro employment and upgrading[71] (although percentagewise, in total below that of tires), the rate of change in rubber tires was, and will probably continue to remain, slow. The reason, of course, is the relative stability of employment. An examination of the situation, first by occupational groups, then by regions, will emphasize the difficulties of change.

Officials and Managers

In 1966, only 47 of 8,537, or 0.6 percent, of the officials and managers were Negroes. By 1968, the number had slightly more than doubled, but the ratio was only 0.9 percent. Most were foremen, or first-line supervisors in areas such as compounding rooms, where large numbers of Negroes are concentrated. Except in a few situations of all-Negro janitorial forces, most Negro foremen supervise mixed crews.

The paucity of Negro officials and managers reflects the precivil rights era mores of industry generally, not merely that of the rubber tire industry. In 1966, rubber tire companies had only one-half the

---

70. *A Current Look at: (1) The Negro and Title VII, (2) Sex and Title VII* (Washington: Bureau of National Affairs, Inc., 1967), Personnel Policies Forum. Survey No. 82, p. 3.
71. The data on aerospace and automobiles referred to here and hereafter are from the studies in this volume.

percentage in this category as did automobile companies, but twice the percentage of the aerospace industry. But the differences which we are here discussing are between 1.2 and 0.4 percent—not significant numbers indeed.

The rubber tire industry, like most others, has virtually no Negroes in its upper or middle management ranks. Traditionally Negroes with talent, education, and motivation have not sought carriers in business. Their acceptance has been much greater in certain professions, particularly teaching, and more recently in government. Today, the barriers are lowered, and the potential Negro executive is assiduously pursued by business recruiters. The rubber tire companies, however, have neither an especially attractive location, a glamorous industry, nor a noted history of equal employment. Since the availability of Negro recruits for top jobs remains small, the recruiting efforts of the tire companies have not met with substantial success.

Professionals and Technicians

The rubber tire industry is not a technically-oriented industry like aerospace or electronics. Slightly more than 5 percent of the rubber tire work force are professionals and only about 3 percent are in the technical class. This compares very closely with the automobile industry, but is in sharp contrast to the aerospace industry in which nearly one-third of the employment is classified as professional and technical. The data in Tables 20 and 21 show only 15 Negro professionals and 39 technicians, respectively 0.3 and 1.3 percent of the total in 1966; and 54 Negro professionals and 83 technicians, 0.8 and 2.1 percent respectively, in 1968. These percentages are both less than those in automobiles and aerospace, but again the totals in no industry are large.

The attempts by rubber companies to recruit in these occupations are subject to the same disabilities as in the official and manager group. There are very few Negro engineers being trained. The same is true of chemists. The rubber tire industry has had difficulty competing with industries like aerospace for the reasons noted, and does not have the breadth of job opportunities, nor a large number of new job opportunities. There is no reason to expect the racial mix in these key job categories to change substantially for years to come. Progress in the future, as it has been since 1964, is likely to be slow.

Sales Workers

As noted above, the rubber tire industry shows a higher proportion of sales workers than is generally found in industry. Indeed this is an occupational group in which Negroes are usually even less well represented than in the officials and managers category. Yet the data in Table 20 show almost as large a percentage of Negroes in the sales as the proportion of Negroes in the industry—7.5 percent Negro for sales, and 8.1 percent for total employment. In 1968, the sales ratio stood at 5 percent. The reason, as already noted, for the above average Negro representation, is the inclusion of service employees working in retail and wholesale establishments operated by the major tire companies.

Data for one major company are available which distinguish sales and service employees. This company in 1966 had 3,295 sales employees, of whom 1,584, or 48 percent were in service; it had 359 Negro sales employees of whom 355, or 99 percent were in service![72] In the rubber tire industry, as in American industry generally, there are few Negro salesmen.

Although most service employees in sales change tires and perform similar jobs, it must be noted also that not all sales-service employees work at low-rated jobs. The large rubber tire companies have developed programs to train Negroes as store clerks and managers for their retail outlets. Many of these stores employing Negroes are in predominantly Negro areas, but by no means all are. The manager of the Goodyear store and service garage on Philadelphia's Main Line is a Negro, for example.

The retail operations of the tire companies offer an opportunity for Negro employment in an area of expansion and one of widespread location. Many outlets are franchises over which the companies do not exert direct supervision of personnel policies. Many others are, however, company owned. In the former, the major companies can provide direction and assistance; in the latter, they have direct control. Several have recognized that the retail outlets offer one of their best potential areas for equal opportunity activity and are moving to recruit and to train heavily for such jobs. It can be expected that there will be continued effort in this direction.

72. Data in authors' possession.

On the other hand, much of the selling is done through dealers. Successful store managers are in line for promotion as sales representatives, but here company success in integrating Negroes is at best mixed. Some dealers have told companies not to permit Negro representatives to call on them. Selling has a strong social side and here objections to Negro sales representatives has been strongest. Retail store managers do not seem to counter these problms.

Office and Clerical

The largest white collar group, and the third largest occupational category in the rubber tire industry, is that of office and clerical. Neither Negro males or females are well represented in this group. Moreover, the rubber tire industry's progress by 1968 was very slow. It is behind both aerospace and automobiles in terms of percentage of Negro office and clerical employees. The reasons appear to be the late start of most rubber tire companies to open their offices to Negroes. By the time policies were changed, the companies had few openings, little turnover, and competition from all other American employers who belatedly sought to reverse past practices.

Another factor affecting the Negro office employee potential is that new plants, and therefore, plant offices, are usually located on the outskirts of small communities. Many of these communities have few Negroes, but even if the Negro population is substantial, it does not usually dwell, or is not able to find homes, close by the plant. Studies of other industries have demonstrated that Negro female office workers will not commute long distances to work.[73] They usually can find work close by and long travel seriously retards their duties at home. In this, of course, they are undoubtedly no different from their white co-workers.

The Craftsmen Problem

The second largest occupational group in the industry, comprising about 15 percent of the total employment, is craftsmen. Yet Negroes comprised only 2.3 percent of this important, high-paid group in 1966 and only 2.8 percent in 1968. Throughout American industry, Negro craftsmen are underrepresented, but the rubber tire industry has had an even lower representation than comparable industries. The reasons are both those common to industry generally, but are

73. See Parts Two and Three.

also related to the ability of the industry to employ its craftsmen without training them.

Traditionally, industry obtains its craftsmen from three sources: company apprentice programs; employment of those who learn their skills elsewhere, including immigrants; and upgraders or learners trained on the job after production experience. In the rubber tire industry, company training has not loomed as large as a source of craft job recruitment as it has, for example, in the automobile industry. The high wages of the industry have attracted sufficient trained personnel so that the same rubber tire companies have not spent a great deal of money and effort in training. In view of the fact that few Negroes have been trained in the crafts, except in the southern trowel trades (bricklaying, cement work, and plastering),[74] the labor force from which the industry hired for craft work was almost lily white. Few, if any, Negro craftsmen were found in the industry prior to 1955.

Goodyear Tire which has long had an apprentice training program has, like most other companies, found it difficult to recruit Negroes for the program; or if it did find interested Negroes, they did not usually do well enough in the competitive examinations to win a place in the program. In April 1968, Goodyear arranged with the Akron Urban League and the school board there to underwrite at a cost of $50,000, a five months course to prepare twenty Negro youths for its apprenticeship program. All but one passed the tests and were placed as apprentices.[75]

Goodyear's apprenticeship program is governed by an agreement with Local No. 2 of the rubber workers' union. Goodyear notified the local of its plan and publicized it in the company paper, but it did not seek union concurrence beforehand. The union has filed a grievance as a result of the company's unilateral departure from the usual method of choosing apprentices. If union consent had been sought, the membership may not have approved the action even if the local leadership was willing to support the move. *Fortune* magazine quoted "one rubber worker's wife" who was criticizing "a program that prepared the hard-core unemployed for pre-apprenticeship train-

74. The background on employment discrimination in the crafts is found in Herbert R. Northrup, *Organized Labor and the Negro* (New York: Harper & Bros., 1944), especially Chapter 2.
75. Field interviews, December 1968.

ing in the rubber plants." She stated: "A lot of white guys want to get apprenticeships too and they don't like this reverse discrimination."[76]

It remains to be seen whether companies caught between union and white employee pressure on the one side, and government and civil rights pressure on the other, will, or even can, continue such affirmative actions.

Negroes already in the work force of a company who show aptitude may be placed in a maintenance department as a helper and then upgraded to a craft job over time. Given the difficulties of gaining apprentice appointments in the tradtional manner, this is by far the easier route for Negroes to become craftsmen. Unfortunately, many Negro production workers lack the educational background, particularly in basic arithmetic, to qualify as draftsmen. Others prefer to remain on production jobs where they are because often they can earn more than they would make in maintenance at least until they qualified as craftsmen. An additional problem is that since so few Negroes are in skilled crafts, many of them prefer not to attempt to qualify. It is more compatible to be where fellow members of one's race are clearly accepted and are already found in large numbers.

The number of Negroes in craftsmen's jobs in the rubber tire industry is, therefore, likely to continue to be small. The craftsmen hired from the outside are certainly most likely to be almost all white. Unless such special arrangements as Goodyear developed can be utilized, opportunities for in-company apprentice and upgrader training are unlikely to attract many Negroes. The following paragraphs taken from our automobile study, apply equally well to rubber tire.

> Opportunities for training which require sacrifice for eventual improvement are not grasped. Inexperience in industry, lack of family help in setting goals, the absence of similar opportunities in previous generations, and the difficulty of breaking with the past all continue to reduce the number of Negroes who grasp the opportunities for skilled trades training.
>
> It is expecting much to believe that Negroes will take advantage of such training opportunities without special effort. If the number of Negro apprentices applying from existing employees is to be increased, it appears obvious that special motivational and training

76. Peter M. Swerdloff, "Hopes and Fears of Blue Collar Youth: A Report from Akron," *Fortune*, Vol. LXXIX (January 1959), p. 152.

efforts will have to be made. Educational and motivational deficiencies must be overcome if qualifications are to be raised and if the desire is to be created to acquire the skills which both pay very well and provide a trade that will likely always be useful. There have been efforts to encourage Negro employees to go into the apprentice programs, but they have been neither massive nor particularly successful thus far. Whether with greater effort on the part of the companies, greater success would result cannot be predicted, but such efforts would at least provide the answer for the industry and its critics.[77]

Operatives

Nearly one-half of all rubber tire workers are classified as operatives. As was noted early in the study, this classification includes relatively low-skill entry jobs and others in which considerable skill and high pay are involved, as well as many gradations of skill in between. In 1966 Negroes comprised 11.6 percent of all operatives, in 1968, the ratio was 12.8 percent. This is a substantially smaller Negro representation than in the automobile industry where 20.2 percent were Negro, but about equal to the aerospace ratio. It is the operative category in which most new employees are hired.

Within the operatives classification Negroes continue to be concentrated in the compounding room, but represented in nearly all other departments and jobs, except in some southern plants. (Regional differences are discussed below.) Most companies now have Negro tire builders and calender operators, and Negroes have recently accumulated sufficient seniority to bid successfully on jobs in heavy tire service. Another high-paying job, Banbury operator, has a heavy Negro representation because it is the key position in the compounding room where Negroes historically came into the industry.

The overconcentration in the compounding room is likely to continue for some years for a number of reasons. In the first place, Negroes were confined to this department until the mid-1950's generally, and well into the 1960's in most southern plants. With low turnover and little employment growth, movement into other departments is not rapid.

A second reason for the continued concentration of Negroes in the compounding room is, because of tradition, employment officials often assign Negroes to such work as a matter of course. Although most companies have a policy against such placement, it undoubtedly

77. See Part Two.

still occurs. Finally, many Negroes who have worked in compounding rooms for many years are reluctant to bid out. The pay is relatively good and they seem to prefer to work with fellow members of their own race rather than in a group where they are such a distinct minority, and where hostility might not be absent.

Laborers and Service Workers

Only 7 percent of the work force is classified as laborers or service workers. Many of the former jobs have been eliminated by technological advancement; others have been reclassified as semiskilled under union pressure. The rubber industry has the usual overconcentration of Negroes in such jobs—17.1 percent of the laborers and 30.4 percent of the service workers in 1966; and 22.8 percent and 29.2 percent in 1968. Such overconcentration is the pattern in industry generally.

Female Employment

The nature of work in the rubber tire industry is not very conducive to encouraging female employment. About 12 percent of the employees were women in 1966 and 1968, and more than half of these were office and clerical workers. Negroes comprise only one-half the percent of the female labor force that they are of male employment. The fact that only 68—1 percent—of the female office and clerical employees were Negro in 1966 and 140, or 1.7 percent in 1968, is the prime reason for the poor representation of Negro women. This statistic again emphasizes the paucity of colored white collar personnel in the industry, and the industry's shortcomings in this regard.

INTRAPLANT MOVEMENT AND SENIORITY

As pointed out in previous chapters, the seniority systems in the industry, when combined with racially restrictive employment policies, resulted in a racial-departmental segregation pattern in the industry. This pattern still remains visible, even though new seniority provisions developed in the 1950's in the industry greatly facilitate movement among departments. The Negro concentration in the compounding department also remains because in the South, only Firestone's Memphis plant provided, in practice, for interdepartmental bidding before the 1960's. Negro tire workers in the South, except at Firestone, were thereby denied the right to bid on jobs outside of their traditional areas of work for at least a decade after such rights had been generally negotiated.

At present nearly all plants in the industry permit some method of bidding on jobs outside of one department. Usually, there are restrictions on the number of bids within a given time in order to limit the upset and expense of excessive intraplant movement which can be very costly and interfere with efficient production. Such limits on movement that do exist are not racially contrived. Of course, neither the original departmental seniority rules, nor the later changes which permitted interdepartmental movement, were negotiated with the race situation involved, although the refusal to enforce the new rules in the South was certainly completely discriminatory in origin and practice. The current rules for interdepartmental transfer do not, however, appear to preclude Negro intraplant movement, nor to discriminate against Negroes. Of course, in individual cases it is possible that they are so applied. But the slow moves of Negroes out of the traditional areas of work appear today to be the results of three factors.

The first of these is, of course, the declining employment in the industry. The substantial number of openings required to alter the racial composition of the work force rapidly simply do not exist. In the second place, as already noted, Negroes often appear reluctant to bid on jobs outside of departments where large numbers of members of their race are working. Lack of experience in industrial practice, distrust of local unions which have not protected their rights vigorously, fear of the reaction of white workers, and lack of motivation, all are involved. Finally, of course, the industry has been able to attract an extremely well qualified labor force. Negroes who have been employed with the idea that they would never be promoted are frequently at a distinct disadvantage in competing with the white labor force. This is especially true in an industry that has not been required to do extensive in-plant training and generally confines its training to that done on the job. Those who do not have the prerequisite prejob background or training have great difficulty competing—and Negroes are disproportionately concentrated in this group.

Negro movement to better paying jobs within, as well as without, departments of their employment and to supervisory jobs is hindered by the same factors. Refusal to accept opportunities, and especially refusal to accept promotion to first-line supervision, is not, of course, unique in industrial experience. Many white workers have declined especially to take on the often frustrating pressures of the foreman. When a Negro refuses for whatever reason, however, opportunities for integration and leadership are missed.

Besides these general factors, Negro intraplant movement is also affected by locational, regional, government, union, and management factors. All these are discussed in ensuing sections of this study.

LOCATIONAL FACTORS

Where a plant is located—both within an area in relation to the centers of Negro population and in what region—has an effect on employment opportunities for Negroes. This section discusses the locational factors, that is, the impact of plant location within areas generally. The following one deals with regional differences and impacts.

The older rubber tire plants—those in Akron, Detroit, Memphis, and Los Angeles, particularly—are located in areas in which Negroes have no special problem of accessibility. These plants are in locations that are close to the concentrations of Negro population. Even where they are not accessible to public transportation, they do not require long commutes from Negro dwelling areas.

New plants, however, like those in industry generally, are more likely to be situated in suburban or outlying areas. Transportation to them from the center cities where Negroes are concentrated is usually wholly dependent on private cars. Many of these plants are also in towns where few Negroes live. In California, for example, new plants are in Salinas and Hanford, where far fewer Negroes live than in Los Angeles. In the East, such locations as Oaks or Pottstown, Pennsylvania, or in the South and Midwest, Bloomington or Freeport, Illinois, Des Moines, Iowa, Mayfield, Kentucky, or Miami, Oklahoma, are all areas of small Negro population. Moreover, these plants, like new ones in the South, are usually outside the towns and accessible only by private car. To the disadvantaged, this adds another barrier to employment.

REGIONAL DIFFERENCES—GENERAL

Tables 22-29 show employment by race, sex, and occupational group in 1966 and 1968 for major regions of the country, except the South, as defined in Table 16 (p. 429). The discussion of the South is reserved for the next section. Tables 22-29 utilize the same data which are summarized in Tables 20-21, but divide them on a regional basis by establishment. Thus in most regions, all major companies are represented.

Turning first to the East, (Tables 22 and 23), we find that the overall percentage of Negroes has climbed from 4.7 percent in 1964 (Table 16) to 5.5 percent in 1966 and 6 percent in 1968. The national average, however, was over 8 percent in both 1966 and 1968. (Tables 20 and 21.)

The East falls below the national average because of its lower blue collar concentration—in 1968, 8 percent as compared with 11.7 percent. In the white collar area, however, the Negro ratio in the East is double that of the national average. A significant factor, however, is the sales group which may include a heavy service employee representation.

In the East, there is wide variation in Negro employment from plant to plant, partially because of locational factors. A number of plants are found in areas where few Negroes dwell, but also are well located for Negro employment. Thus, there are a number of plants which have a Negro complement ratio equal to, or better than, the national average. This accounts for the fact that the Negro employment ratio is as high as it is. The regional average is, however , reduced by other plants where Negro employment in 1966 varied from 0.7 percent to 5.3 percent, as compared with five plants in the region with ratios from 9.3 to 15.4. percent. It is very likely, therefore, that managerial policy, as well as population concentrations, is a factor in these racial distributions and consequent regional ratio.

Ohio, and Akron especially continue to dominate the rubber tire industry, having over one-third of the employees in the 1966 and 1968 samples. Tables 24 and 25 show that more Negroes (as well as more whites) work in Ohio rubber plants than in any other state or region. The ratio of Negro rubber tire workers in Ohio is equal to that nationally. If the non-Akron plants were eliminated from the Ohio sample, the ratio there would be slightly higher. This ratio

TABLE 22. *Rubber Tire Industry*
Employment by Race, Sex, and Occupational Group
East Region, 1966

Occupational Group	All Employees			Male			Female		
	Total	Negro	Percent Negro	Total	Negro	Percent Negro	Total	Negro	Percent Negro
Officials and managers	1,566	5	0.3	1,560	5	0.3	6	—	—
Professionals	947	3	0.3	933	3	0.3	14	—	—
Technicians	519	8	1.5	482	7	1.5	37	1	2.7
Sales workers	1,437	157	10.9	1,311	147	11.2	126	10	7.9
Office and clerical	1,682	30	1.8	493	15	3.0	1,189	15	1.3
Total white collar	6,151	203	3.3	4,779	177	3.7	1,372	26	1.9
Craftsmen	2,261	48	2.1	2,245	46	2.0	16	2	12.5
Operatives	7,704	568	7.4	7,242	506	7.0	462	62	13.4
Laborers	238	46	19.3	226	44	19.5	12	2	16.7
Service workers	423	66	15.6	414	63	15.2	9	3	33.3
Total blue collar	10,626	728	6.9	10,127	659	6.5	499	69	13.8
Total	16,777	931	5.5	14,906	836	5.6	1,871	95	5.1

Source: Data in authors' possession.
Note: For geographic definitions, see Table 16, p. 429.

TABLE 23. *Rubber Tire Industry*
Employment by Race, Sex, and Occupational Group
East Region, 1968

Occupational Group	All Employees			Male			Female		
	Total	Negro	Percent Negro	Total	Negro	Percent Negro	Total	Negro	Percent Negro
Officials and managers	1,729	11	0.6	1,723	11	0.6	6	—	—
Professionals	1,011	5	0.5	987	5	0.5	24	—	—
Technicians	602	18	3.0	568	15	2.6	34	3	8.8
Sales workers	2,201	154	7.0	1,951	151	7.7	250	3	1.2
Office and clerical	1,672	25	1.5	452	10	2.2	1,220	15	1.2
Total white collar	7,215	213	3.0	5,681	192	3.4	1,534	21	1.4
Craftsmen	2,104	28	1.3	2,089	27	1.3	15	1	6.7
Operatives	8,637	738	8.5	8,152	671	8.2	485	67	13.8
Laborers	327	85	26.0	323	85	26.3	4	—	—
Service workers	408	66	16.2	399	64	16.0	9	2	22.2
Total blue collar	11,476	917	8.0	10,963	847	7.7	513	70	13.6
Total	18,691	1,130	6.0	16,644	1,039	6.2	2,047	91	4.4

Source: Data in authors' possession.

TABLE 24. *Rubber Tire Industry*
Employment by Race, Sex, and Occupational Group
Ohio Region, 1966

Occupational Group	All Employees			Male			Female		
	Total	Negro	Percent Negro	Total	Negro	Percent Negro	Total	Negro	Percent Negro
Officials and managers	3,472	27	0.8	3,443	27	0.8	29	—	—
Professionals	2,541	11	0.4	2,478	11	0.4	63	—	—
Technicians	1,380	11	0.8	1,295	10	0.8	85	1	1.2
Sales workers	527	2	0.4	527	2	0.4	—	—	—
Office and clerical	4,350	53	1.2	1,250	26	2.1	3,100	27	0.9
Total white collar	12,270	104	0.8	8,993	76	0.8	3,277	28	0.9
Craftsmen	6,317	185	2.9	6,308	185	2.9	9	—	—
Operatives	15,951	2,051	12.9	14,377	1,941	13.5	1,574	110	7.0
Laborers	1,786	238	13.3	1,536	224	14.6	250	14	5.6
Service workers	1,486	433	29.1	1,277	421	33.0	209	12	5.7
Total blue collar	25,540	2,907	11.4	23,498	2,771	11.8	2,042	136	6.7
Total	37,810	3,011	8.0	32,491	2,847	8.8	5,319	164	3.1

Source: Data in authors' possession.

TABLE 25. *Rubber Tire Industry*
Employment by Race, Sex, and Occupational Group
Ohio Region, 1968

Occupational Group	All Employees			Male			Female		
	Total	Negro	Percent Negro	Total	Negro	Percent Negro	Total	Negro	Percent Negro
Officials and managers	5,520	53	1.0	5,470	53	1.0	50	—	—
Professionals	4,400	44	1.0	4,265	41	1.0	135	3	2.2
Technicians	2,187	33	1.5	2,092	32	1.5	95	1	1.1
Sales workers	652	—	—	645	—	—	7	—	—
Office and clerical	6,254	112	1.8	1,726	33	1.9	4,528	79	1.7
Total white collar	19,013	242	1.3	14,198	159	1.1	4,815	83	1.7
Craftsmen	6,160	241	3.9	6,142	241	3.9	18	—	—
Operatives	16,785	2,591	15.4	15,075	2,424	16.1	1,710	167	9.8
Laborers	563	135	24.0	563	135	24.0	—	—	—
Service workers	1,504	407	27.1	1,305	391	30.0	199	16	8.0
Total blue collar	25,012	3,374	13.5	23,085	3,191	13.8	1,927	183	9.5
Total	44,025	3,616	8.2	37,283	3,350	9.0	6,742	266	3.9

Source: Data in authors' possession.

declined slightly between 1964 and 1966, and rose slightly in 1968, but the differences are very slight. Certainly, however, no great gains were registered in this period.

Within occupational groups, Ohio lagged somewhat in most white collar groups in 1966, but one year later was ahead in officials and managers (the result of upgrading Negroes to foremen) and in professionals—the result of extensive recruiting). Negroes in Ohio are better represented than the national average in the two key blue collar areas—craftsmen and operatives.

Ohio, although still the dominant area in the industry, is not a growing one. The plants are old, although well kept up and modernized, and employment practices of the past tend to endure. With most plant expansion occurring elsewhere, opportunities for change in the Ohio area are slow to make themselves felt. Within the state, the Negro plant ratio ranged in 1966 from a high of 10 percent to a low of 0.9 percent, the latter being a plant outside of Akron. Akron's Negro rubber plant ratio low was 6.9 percent.

Within the city of Akron, the variation in Negro representation, plant to plant, is significant, not only in terms of total ratios, but by occupation as well. Although the four largest tire plants there are within a few miles of one another, one plant had 3.4 percent Negro white collar workers in 1966, whereas the other three ranged from 0.4 percent to 1.1 percent. The company with the largest white collar representation of Negroes had the *lowest* blue collar ratio—9.8 percent—compared to a range from 12.3 to 17.8 percent for the other three. One company had 5.4 percent Negro craftsmen; the others ranged from 0.2 to 3.7 percent. And the operatives' rates ranged from 25.2 percent to 10.5 percent.

Akron rubber tire plants share a common labor market. Obviously the variations are the product of managerial decision making and/or happenstance which have their roots in events of yesteryear. Firestone employs the highest percentage of Negroes in Akron, the result of its long years of leadership in this regard. On the other hand, General Tire hired Akron's earliest Negro office workers and now Goodyear leads in Negro white collar employment. One of the first companies to join Plans for Progress, Goodyear thereafter put great emphasis on recruitment of Negro salaried employees and has maintained this concern ever since.

Attempts to improve Negro representation among salaried employees in Akron have been thwarted by lack of decent housing. Many of the city's areas are lily-white and apparently determined so to remain. Much Negro housing has been destroyed by urban renewal and not replaced while too few of the better dwelling units have been open to Negroes capable of paying higher rents or prices. Perhaps, as open housing legislation begins to be felt, this will change. Until it does, Negro salaried and professional employees are likely to pass Akron by. The Akron tire companies have not taken a public position on this problem insofar as the authors can determine.

In the Midwest outside of Ohio, the data in Tables 24 and 25 show a decline between 1966 and 1964 from 8.4 percent to 6.9 percent where it remained in 1968. This decline is probably the result of the inclusion of two additional plants with very small Negro percentages in the later data. Between the two years, there would have been virtually no change in Negro ratios if these plant totals were omitted from the 1966 data.

In the white collar area, the non-Ohio Midwest lags behind the national average, as it also does substantially in the key craftsmen group and also for operatives. Actually, this region is the most laggard in the country in all key areas. The fact that this area is the second largest in the industry, now exceeded only by Ohio, makes this situation the more serious.

Moreover, as our discussion of the 1964 data emphasized, the non-Ohio Midwest ratios are inflated by just one plant—Uniroyal's huge Detroit facility which in 1968 has 50.1 percent of the region's Negro employees, but only 19 percent of the total employees. If Uniroyal's Detroit plant were subtracted from the region's data, the percentage of Negros would be only 4!

There are many reasons for the poor showing of Negroes in many Midwest area plants. Several plants are located in areas where the Negro population is small—Denver, Colorado, Des Moines, Iowa, Eau Claire, Wisconsin—are examples. Other plants are new, and started up with stringent employment standards which few Negroes could successfully meet in competition with a large supply of available whites with better education and backgrounds. Moreover, most of these plants were put into production between World War II and 1960, when affirmative action was not generally practiced in the

Table 26. Rubber Tire Industry
Employment by Race, Sex, and Occupational Group
Midwest Region (except Ohio), 1966

Occupational Group	All Employees			Male			Female		
	Total	Negro	Percent Negro	Total	Negro	Percent Negro	Total	Negro	Percent Negro
Officials and managers	1853	6	0.3	1,843	6	0.3	10	—	—
Professionals	1,048	1	0.1	1,031	1	0.1	17	—	—
Technicians	586	12	2.0	530	12	2.3	56	—	—
Sales workers	125	—	—	122	—	—	3	—	—
Office and clerical	2,091	33	1.6	703	12	1.7	1,388	21	1.5
Total white collar	5,703	52	0.9	4,229	31	0.7	1,474	21	1.4
Craftsmen	3,214	30	0.9	3,188	28	0.9	26	2	7.7
Operatives	13,617	1,328	9.8	12,210	1,173	9.6	1,407	155	11.0
Laborers	871	123	14.1	835	118	14.1	36	5	13.9
Service workers	680	131	19.3	617	125	20.3	63	6	9.5
Total blue collar	18,382	1,612	8.8	16,850	1,444	8.6	1,532	168	11.0
Total	24,085	1,664	6.9	21,079	1,475	7.0	3,006	189	6.3

Source: Data in authors' possession.

TABLE 27. *Rubber Tire Industry*
Employment by Race, Sex, and Occupational Group
Midwest Region (except Ohio), 1968

Occupational Group	All Employees			Male			Female		
	Total	Negro	Percent Negro	Total	Negro	Percent Negro	Total	Negro	Percent Negro
Officials and managers	2,128	14	0.7	2,107	14	0.7	21	—	—
Professionals	1,146	4	0.3	1,094	4	0.4	52	—	—
Technicians	648	16	2.5	620	16	2.6	28	—	—
Sales workers	208	—	—	201	—	—	7	—	—
Office and clerical	2,273	48	2.1	761	20	2.6	1,512	28	1.9
Total white collar	6,403	82	1.3	4,783	54	1.1	1,620	28	1.7
Craftsmen	3,774	53	1.4	3,690	50	1.4	84	3	3.6
Operatives	13,981	1,430	10.2	12,605	1,279	10.1	1,376	151	11.0
Laborers	630	64	10.2	623	64	10.3	7	—	—
Service workers	630	129	20.5	604	126	20.9	26	3	11.5
Total blue collar	19,015	1,676	8.8	17,522	1,519	8.7	1,493	157	10.5
Total	25,418	1,758	6.9	22,305	1,573	7.1	3,113	185	5.9

Source: Data in authors' possession.

TABLE 28. *Rubber Tire Industry*
Employment by Race, Sex, and Occupational Group
California, 1966

Occupational Group	All Employees			Male			Female		
	Total	Negro	Percent Negro	Total	Negro	Percent Negro	Total	Negro	Percent Negro
Officials and managers	620	6	1.0	619	6	1.0	1	—	—
Professionals	262	—	—	254	—	—	8	—	—
Technicians	210	5	2.4	198	5	2.5	12	—	—
Sales workers	31	—	—	31	—	—	—	—	—
Office and clerical	653	5	0.8	235	3	1.3	418	2	0.5
Total white collar	1,776	16	0.9	1,337	14	1.0	439	2	0.5
Craftsmen	1,102	34	3.1	1,102	34	3.1	—	—	—
Operatives	3,018	610	20.2	2,854	566	19.8	164	44	26.8
Laborers	957	187	19.5	922	187	20.3	35	—	—
Service workers	168	45	26.8	161	43	26.7	7	2	28.6
Total blue collar	5,245	876	16.7	5,039	830	16.5	206	46	22.3
Total	7,021	892	12.7	6,376	844	13.2	645	48	7.4

Source: Data in authors' possession.

TABLE 29. *Rubber Tire Industry*
Employment by Race, Sex, and Occupational Group
California, 1968

Occupational Group	All Employees			Male			Female		
	Total	Negro	Percent Negro	Total	Negro	Percent Negro	Total	Negro	Percent Negro
Officials and managers	711	11	1.5	703	11	1.6	8	—	—
Professionals	248	1	0.4	238	—	—	10	1	10.0
Technicians	239	6	2.5	225	6	2.7	14	—	—
Sales workers	35	—	—	35	—	—	—	—	—
Office and clerical	818	22	2.7	309	12	3.9	509	10	2.0
Total white collar	2,051	40	2.0	1,510	29	1.9	541	11	2.0
Craftsmen	1,099	39	3.5	1,099	39	3.5	—	—	—
Operatives	3,834	779	20.3	3,667	727	19.8	167	52	31.1
Laborers	182	45	24.7	180	45	25.0	2	—	—
Service workers	154	40	26.0	148	37	25.0	6	3	50.0
Total blue collar	5,269	903	17.1	5,094	848	16.6	175	55	31.4
Total	7,320	943	12.9	6,604	877	13.3	716	66	9.2

Source: Data in authors' possession.

industry, and no special efforts were made to insure a reasonable share of employment for Negroes. Once these patterns were established, they can be only slowly altered, again because of the stability and low turnover in the work force.

There are, however, some plants in the non-Ohio Midwest whose low Negro representation can be attributed only to managerial policy, be it overt or indifferent. These plants are moderately close to concentrations of Negro population and are branches of companies which have had reasonably satisfactory experience with Negro labor in Akron or elsewhere. The low Negro employee ratio in this region, outside of the Uniroyal Detroit plant, in many ways reflects the historic problem of Negroes in the rubber tire industry: the ability of the industry to attract the best in the labor market, the educational and training disabilities of Negroes which make it difficult for them to compete at the top rung of the labor force, either white collar or blue collar, and until recently, the lack of concern on the part of most of the rubber tire industry in substantial action to assist Negroes to remedy their disadvantaged position.

At Uniroyal's Detroit plant, the situation has been different. The plant is located in the heart of Detroit, and in an area of heavy Negro population concentration. Because of the sixday week, which was in effect in this plant before 1968, the company's weekly wage rate was below that of the automobile concerns, although the hourly rate was higher. The practical needs of a labor force made this plant a large employer of Negroes since World War II. In 1966, it was one of the three plants in the industry having a Negro labor force of approximately 25 percent or more. The others, of course, are the Los Angeles plant of this same company, and Firestone's Memphis facility.

California—Tables 28 and 29—by 1966 led all other areas in the percentage of Negro employees. This has been the result of a very substantial increase of Negroes in blue collar jobs, particularly operatives. Among white collar employees the average in California in 1968 was superior to that nationally, in the officials and managers, technical, and office and clerical groups. Among blue collar groups, the Negro ratio was over 50 percent higher in California than nationally. The California craftsmen ratio was somewhat higher than the national average—3.5 to 2.8 percent—but operatives' ratio, 20.3 percent in California as compared with 12.8 percent nationally—is where the main difference lies.

The growth in the Negro ratio in California rubber tire plants is wholly attributable to the Los Angeles situation. Over 90 percent of the Negroes in the industry in California work in the four major plants in this city. Negroes comprise over 15 percent of the Los Angeles rubber tire labor force. As already noted, Uniroyal's plant has the largest ratio, nearly 25 percent.

The prime reasons for the fast increase in the Negro ratio in Los Angeles plants have already been noted. The population explosion in southern California has led to an increased demand for tires there, and a consequent West Coast expansion in the industry. At the same time, the aerospace industry, with its more pleasant and glamorous jobs, has been expanding also, thereby eliminating a large source of labor that might otherwise seek jobs in tire plants. Moreover, many aerospace plants are either inaccessible except by private car or require a long, arduous commute from the Los Angeles centers of Negro population. The high pay of the rubber plants is most attractive to Negroes, and their availability under these conditions, important for the industry which here, perhaps uniquely except in Detroit, does not attract the cream of the labor market. As long as these conditions prevail, Negroes will continue to increase their share in California's blue collar labor force.

SOUTHERN DEVELOPMENTS

Developments in the South in recent years are significant in revealing both industry policy and problems of Negro rubber tire workers. The 1966 data mark the first time in which the South did not lead other regions in the industry in the ratio of Negro rubber tire workers. The reasons have already been noted, but require elaboration. They are first, the historic exclusion of Negroes from white collar jobs in the South prior to the Civil Rights Act of 1964; second, the failure of most southern plants built between 1950 and 1964 to utilize a sizable proportion of Negroes; and finally, the failure of some older plants to provide jobs for Negroes who were displaced by technological advancement.

A glance at Tables 30 and 31 shows a Negro white collar complement of 0.6 percent in 1966 and 1.1 in 1968—low for an industry which has not, in any region, made great strides in employing Negro white collar workers. In the South, the aerospace industry in 1966 employed Negroes in 3 percent of its office and clerical jobs; the rubber industry's ratio was 1.1 percent. Of course, the rubber tire industry does not have the large and expanding offices which are found in many southern aerospace facilities. Nevertheless, a record of only eight Negro office and clerical workers, the lowest white collar skilled job, in twelve plants in 1966 and of twelve in eleven plants in 1968, is indicative of the lack of progress in employing white collar personnel in southern tire plants. In the other white collar areas, in 1966, there were just three officials and managers (all supervisors in one plant) and three technical personnel—14 Negro white collar personnel out of a total of 2,402. The record for 1968 was not much better. No Negro professional was in any of these plants in either year.

We have already noted that most new plants established between World War II and 1964 have not employed Negroes to the same degree as did older ones. There are, of course, exceptions. The Cooper Tire & Rubber Company plant in Texarkana, and the Mohawk Rubber Company plant in West Helena, both in Arkansas, are relatively new but rank second only to the Firestone Memphis facility in the ratio of Negro employment in the South.

No other new southern plant known to the authors had as much as a 5 percent Negro complement in 1966. One of these plants—Goodrich, Miami, Oklahoma—is located where virtually no Negroes reside. In at least one other plant area the Negro population is very small. The basic reason for the low utilization of Negroes, however, has first of all been the ability of these plants to establish and to maintain high employment standards and to select the most qualified from those who met these standards. Negroes, as the products of poor education and inadequate industrial training or experience, were immediately disproportionately eliminated from consideration by these standards, and no special efforts, until very recently, were made to qualify them.

The newer southern plants have also been highly automated. Material handling labor and other unskilled jobs have been virtually eliminated. The compounding rooms no longer have the unpleasant working conditions that once were typical. Negroes who were formerly favored for such jobs are no longer needed, or must compete with better trained whites.

The differences in Negro utilization between the older and newer southern plants are clearly illustrated by examining Tables 32 and 33, and 34 and 35, which compare data both for 1966 and 1968 for the four oldest plants, all established by 1946, with four newer plants built since that date but prior to 1964. To make the comparison between the two groups very clear, all plants are located in areas of substantial Negro population.

The Negro ratio in the older plant group in 1966 was more than three times that of the newer one—16.4 percent to 5.8 percent. The big differences were found in the blue collar area. The new plants had no Negro craftsmen and only 6.0 percent Negro operatives; the older plants, a few, 2.7 percent, Negro craftsmen and 19.8 percent Negro operatives. The older plants also had a higher complement of Negro laborers and service workers.

Some of the newer plants which employed few Negroes in 1966 nevertheless did use Negroes on top skilled jobs (but not as craftsmen). One plant located in the deep South, for example, had eighteen Negro employees, less than 4 percent of its total. Five of these were janitors, some were mixers in the compounding room, but the remainder held a variety of jobs including that of tire builder. Likewise, the four new plants had two Negro technicians and four office and clerical employees, whereas the four oldest ones had no Negro technicians and one office worker. On the other hand, the only three Negroes in the managerial classification were three supervisors (including one departmental foreman) in Firestone's Memphis plant.

By 1968, the differences between the two groups had narrowed, but the ratio in the older four was still substantially higher than that of the newer group. Substantial efforts on the part of one newer plant—Uniroyal's Opelika, Alabama, facility, account for some of this change. Nevertheless, the employment pattern established by the rubber tire industry in the South will continue to reflect adversely on the industry record for many years.

Among the newer plants, two smaller ones in Arkansas, as already noted, had a high ratio of Negroes. One older plant had a very low ratio. Firestone's Memphis plant continued to have the highest Negro ratio in the industry. Indeed Firestone in 1966 employed 57 percent of the 1,653 Negro rubber tire workers in the total South (Table 30), and 67 percent of those in the four oldest plants there (Table

TABLE 30. *Rubber Tire Industry*
Employment by Race, Sex, and Occupational Group
South Region, 1966

Occupational Group	All Employees			Male			Female		
	Total	Negro	Percent Negro	Total	Negro	Percent Negro	Total	Negro	Percent Negro
Officials and managers	1,026	3	0.3	1,025	3	0.3	1	—	—
Professionals	337	—	—	329	—	—	8	—	—
Technicians	332	3	0.9	309	3	1.0	23	—	—
Sales workers	1	—	—	1	—	—	—	—	—
Office and clerical	706	8	1.1	259	5	1.9	447	3	0.7
Total white collar	2,402	14	0.6	1,923	11	0.6	479	3	0.6
Craftsmen	1,974	41	2.1	1,974	41	2.1	—	—	—
Operatives	9,440	1,188	12.6	8,906	1,178	13.2	534	10	1.9
Laborers	268	109	40.7	268	109	40.7	—	—	—
Service workers	450	301	66.9	437	293	67.0	13	8	61.5
Total blue collar	12,132	1,639	13.5	11,585	1,621	14.0	547	18	3.3
Total	14,534	1,653	11.4	13,508	1,632	12.1	1,026	21	2.0

Source: Data in authors' possession.

TABLE 31. *Rubber Tire Industry*
Employment by Race, Sex, and Occupational Group
South Region, 1968

Occupational Group	All Employees			Male			Female		
	Total	Negro	Percent Negro	Total	Negro	Percent Negro	Total	Negro	Percent Negro
Officials and managers	1,196	7	0.6	1,194	7	0.6	2	—	—
Professionals	350	—	—	339	—	—	11	—	—
Technicians	325	10	3.1	301	10	3.3	24	—	—
Sales workers	—	—	—	—	—	—	—	—	—
Office and clerical	755	12	1.6	262	4	1.5	493	8	1.6
Total white collar	2,626	29	1.1	2,096	21	1.0	530	8	1.5
Craftsmen	2,246	77	3.4	2,246	77	3.4	—	—	—
Operatives	10,323	1,331	12.9	9,779	1,322	13.5	544	9	1.7
Laborers	212	107	50.5	210	107	51.0	2	—	—
Service workers	456	277	60.7	443	269	60.7	13	8	61.5
Total blue collar	13,237	1,792	13.5	12,678	1,775	14.0	559	17	3.0
Total	15,863	1,821	11.5	14,774	1,796	12.2	1,089	25	2.3

Source: Data in authors' possession.

TABLE 32. *Rubber Tire Industry*
Employment by Race, Sex, and Occupational Group
South Region, Four Oldest Plants, 1966

Occupational Group	All Employees			Male			Female		
	Total	Negro	Percent Negro	Total	Negro	Percent Negro	Total	Negro	Percent Negro
Officials and managers	644	3	0.5	643	3	0.5	1	—	—
Professionals	215	—	—	210	—	—	5	—	—
Technicians	184	—	—	171	—	—	13	—	—
Sales workers	—	—	—	—	—	—	—	—	—
Office and clerical	396	1	0.3	144	—	—	252	1	0.4
Total white collar	1,439	4	0.3	1,168	3	0.3	271	1	0.4
Craftsmen	1,451	39	2.7	1,451	39	2.7	—	—	—
Operatives	5,296	1,047	19.8	4,850	1,037	21.4	446	10	2.2
Laborers	119	70	58.8	119	70	58.8	—	—	—
Service workers	318	251	78.9	306	243	79.4	12	8	66.7
Total blue collar	7,184	1,407	19.6	6,726	1,389	20.7	458	18	3.9
Total	8,623	1,411	16.4	7,894	1,392	17.6	729	19	2.6

Source: Data in authors' possession.

TABLE 33. *Rubber Tire Industry*
Employment by Race, Sex, and Occupational Group
South Region, Four Oldest Plants, 1968

Occupational Group	All Employees			Male			Female		
	Total	Negro	Percent Negro	Total	Negro	Percent Negro	Total	Negro	Percent Negro
Officials and managers	756	6	0.8	755	6	0.8	1	—	—
Professionals	218	—	—	213	—	—	5	—	—
Technicians	176	5	2.8	162	5	3.1	14	—	—
Sales workers	—	—	—	—	—	—	—	—	—
Office and clerical	437	3	0.7	159	—	—	278	3	1.1
Total white collar	1,587	14	0.9	1,289	11	0.9	298	3	1.0
Craftsmen	1,642	75	4.6	1,642	75	4.6	—	—	—
Operatives	5,687	1,098	19.3	5,222	1,089	20.9	465	9	1.9
Laborers	149	84	56.4	149	84	56.4	—	—	—
Service workers	325	235	72.3	312	227	72.8	13	8	61.5
Total blue collar	7,803	1,492	19.1	7,325	1,475	20.1	478	17	3.6
Total	9,390	1,506	16.0	8,614	1,486	17.3	776	20	2.6

Source: Data in authors' possession.

TABLE 34. *Rubber Tire Industry*
Employment by Race, Sex, and Occupational Group
South Region, Four Plants Built between 1950 and 1964, 1966

Occupational Group	All Employees			Male			Female		
	Total	Negro	Percent Negro	Total	Negro	Percent Negro	Total	Negro	Percent Negro
Officials and managers	148	—	—	148	—	—	—	—	—
Professionals	40	—	—	39	—	—	1	—	—
Technicians	62	2	3.2	60	2	3.3	2	—	—
Sales workers	—	—	—	—	—	—	—	—	—
Office and clerical	120	4	3.3	60	4	6.7	60	—	—
Total white collar	370	6	1.6	307	6	2.0	63	—	—
Craftsmen	140	—	—	140	—	—	—	—	—
Operatives	1,175	71	6.0	1,175	71	6.0	—	—	—
Laborers	74	16	21.6	74	16	21.6	—	—	—
Service workers	17	10	58.8	16	10	62.5	1	—	—
Total blue collar	1,406	97	6.9	1,405	97	6.9	1	—	—
Total	1,776	103	5.8	1,712	103	6.0	64	—	—

Source: Data in authors' possession.

TABLE 35. *Rubber Tire Industry*
Employment by Race, Sex, and Occupational Group
South Region, Four Plants Built between 1950 and 1964, 1968

Occupational Group	All Employees			Male			Female		
	Total	Negro	Percent Negro	Total	Negro	Percent Negro	Total	Negro	Percent Negro
Officials and managers	218	1	0.5	218	1	0.5	—	—	—
Professionals	39	—	—	35	—	—	4	—	—
Technicians	58	1	1.7	58	1	1.7	—	—	—
Sales workers	—	—	—	—	—	—	—	—	—
Office and clerical	142	6	4.2	57	3	5.3	85	3	3.5
Total white collar	457	8	1.8	368	5	1.4	89	3	3.4
Craftsmen	169	2	1.2	169	2	1.2	—	—	—
Operatives	1,643	175	10.7	1,643	175	10.7	—	—	—
Laborers	47	19	40.4	47	19	40.4	—	—	—
Service workers	17	7	41.2	17	7	41.2	—	—	—
Total blue collar	1,876	203	10.8	1,876	203	10.8	—	—	—
Total	2,333	211	9.0	2,244	208	9.3	89	3	3.4

Source: Data in authors' possession.

32). If the Firestone totals were deducted from those in Tables 30 and 32, the 1966 ratio of Negroes would fall from 11.4 to 6.2 percent for the total South; and for the four oldest plant groups, it would decline from 16.4 to 8.5 percent.

The Firestone Record at Memphis

Firestone had thus by 1966 for thirty years consistently maintained the highest Negro ratio in the industry at its Memphis plant. There are several reasons why it has been able to do this. It is located in a city which has a large Negro population (35-40 percent in 1965). Its top wages and deserved reputation for employing Negroes assure it of a continuing supply of Negro applicants, many of whom are high school graduates. But most important, Firestone at Memphis has attempted to maintain Negro employment at, or near, the ratio of Negroes in the population there. And Firestone, and Firestone alone, of all rubber tire companies in the South, both integrated its seniority rosters, opening up all blue collar jobs to Negroes, *and* at the same time maintained its leadership by far in the utilization of Negroes. Moreover, the integration occurred in the 1950's before the Civil Rights Act made it mandatory.

By 1966, Firestone alone had Negro foremen in the South; of the mere 41 Negroes classified as craftsmen in southern tire plants in 1966, 39 worked for Firestone. The Memphis plant had by then made only very modest strides in expanding white collar opportunities for Negroes. This is the only area where the plant did not clearly lead all other southern facilities in the industry, but it began an upgrading and recruiting program in 1967 aimed at remedying this lag.

Goodrich, Tuscaloosa

The Goodrich plant at Tuscaloosa, Alabama, did not open up certain production departments to Negroes until 1964. Prior to then, the plant was divided into three seniority areas; maintenance, white departments, and Negro departments. After the 1964 contract was signed, these three areas were merged. A few Negroes and whites now work in departments formerly reserved for members of one race. One Negro has been upgraded to tire builder, and one Negro salary worker employed as of late 1968. As in the case of Firestone's experience, several years before, there was no overt opposition, but a few incidents did occur and then ended when management promptly threatened discharge for those caught fomenting racial trouble. As of late 1968, some segregation in facilities still existed, and white worker opposition to change was apparently quite strong, with rumors of widespread Ku Klux Klan membership among white plant workers.

Goodrich's Tuscaloosa plant has had relatively stable employment and Negro employment has remained at about a 10 percent level. Future employment prospects will depend, of course, on many factors—the ability of Negroes to compete for the high-paying jobs, the company's concern with civil rights, and possible plant expansion—but given the national stress on civil rights and the awareness of the company to that stress, one may be cautiously optimistic about future Negro job representation.

Litigation at Goodyear, Gadsden

The oldest southern plant, and the largest in terms of employment, is Goodyear's Gadsden, Alabama, facility. It is also the plant having the smallest percentage of Negroes of those in the four oldest plants group. The reasons are not unrelated to the fact that Negro employees in this plant were forced to resort to extensive litigation in order to secure their rights.

The litigation had its roots in the discriminatory seniority system which had been in effect at the plant since 1943 when Local No. 12, United Rubber, Cork, Linoleum and Plastic Workers, AFL-CIO (URW) was certified by the National Labor Relations Board as exclusive bargaining agent for the plant's blue collar workers. According to the United States Court of Appeals, Fifth Circuit:

> . . . Until March 1962, three separate seniority rolls—white male, Negro male, and female—were maintained, although the bargaining contract between Goodyear and Local 12 appeared to provide for plantwide seniority without regard to race or sex. As a matter of custom and interpretation during this period, Negro employees with greater seniority had no rights over white employees with less seniority, and vice versa, with respect to promotions, transfers, layoffs, and recalls. Also as a matter of custom, racially separate plant facilities such as lunchrooms, restrooms and showers were maintained, although no provision in the bargaining contract dealt with such matters.
>
> The eight complainants were laid off in August or September 1960, and were recalled approximately one year later. In October 1961, Buckner, one of the eight complainants, having been notified that he

was to be again laid off, inquired why a white employee with less seniority continued to remain employed. He was informed by the assistant manager of Goodyear's labor department that the posted job was a "white job." Thereupon, Buckner and the other complainants, who were also in layoff status, executed affidavits that during their period of layoff subsequent to August or September 1960, new workers had been hired in violation of plant seniority rules. These affidavits were forwarded to the President of Local 12, requesting that Local 12 investigate the alleged grievances and take remedial action. The complainants appeared before the grievance committee on December 8, 1961, and presented a more complete "Statement of Complaint" which charged (1) that the original layoff and recall had not been in accordance with contract-stated seniority and that complainants demanded reinstatement with back wages, (2) that upon recall complainants wanted all transfer privileges as set forth in the contract, and (3) that complainants demanded the right to all plant privileges without color barriers. The committee concluded that "no contract violation exists, therefore, the Union has no ground on which to base a complaint against the company." Subsequent appeals to the union executive board and the full union membership were likewise denied. In March 1962, complainants appealed the action of Local 12 to George Burdon, the union's International President. In light of the information requested by Burdon, and provided by the complainants and Local 12, he concluded that the decision refusing to process the grievances should be reversed.[78]

Local No. 12 chose to ignore the International Union and continued to refuse to process the grievances of its Negro members. The Negroes then appealed to the President's Committee on Equal Employment Opportunity, established by the Kennedy Administration to handle minority employment related to government contractors (PCEEO was the successor of the President's Committee on Government Contracts [Nixon Committee] which operated during the Eisenhower Administration and it in turn was later succeeded by the Office of Federal Contract Compliance established by the Johnson Administration). PCEEO succeeded in working out an agreement between Local No. 12 and Goodyear, which had recently joined Plans for Progress, to discontinue confining Negro and white employees to segregated departments and to cease restricting opportunities of Negroes for upgrading, recall, or job transfers. Furthermore this agreement resulted in the reinstatement of those Negroes who instituted the case.

78. *Local No. 12, United Rubber, Cork, Linoleum and Plastic Workers of America, AFL-CIO vs. National Labor Relations Board,* 368 F. 2d 12 (CA5, 1966); 63 LRRM 2395.

Again according to the Court of Appeals, Fifth Circuit:

> . . . there is no evidence that any racially discriminatory practices with regard to job opportunities, transfer, promotion, layoff, or participation in Goodyear's training program existed after March 1962. It is further clear from the record, however, that Local 12 continued to refuse to process the grievances concerning back wages for the period of layoff occasioned by application of the seniority system in effect prior to March 1962, as well as those concerning the continued segregated nature of plant facilities.[79]

On October 22, 1962, the Negro rubber workers then filed charges before the National Labor Relations Board against Local No. 12, charging the local with failure to bargain in good faith on their behalf. On December 18, 1964, the NLRB, in a divided decision, concluded that Local No. 12

> . . . by refusing to process the grievances concerning back wages and segregated plant facilities, had thereby, (1) restrained or coerced complainants in their section 7 right to be represented without invidious discrimination, (2) caused or attempted to cause Goodyear to discriminate against complainants, and (3) refused to bargain in complainants' behalf, thus violating sections 8(b) (1) (A), 8(b) (2), and 8(b) (3) of the act. Petitioner was accordingly ordered to process the grievances through arbitration and to propose to Goodyear specific contractual provisions prohibiting racial discrimination in terms and conditions of employment pursuant to the oral agreement of March 1962.[80]

Local No. 12 appealed the NLRB's decision to the Court of Appeals, Fifth Circuit which unanimously upheld the NLRB.[81] Local No. 12 then asked the United States Supreme Court to review the case, but the Supreme Court declined, thereby leaving the Court of Appeals' decision in effect.[82]

The fast pace of mechanization in the industry, the high wages paid rubber workers, the consequent competition for jobs, and the lack of a strong company determination to prevent the erosion of Negro participation in jobs as Gadsden had affected Negro job representation there with the already noted result that the oldest and largest southern plant had the smallest ratio of Negroes of any of the older plants. In all fairness, however, it must be emphasized that the ratio

79. *Ibid.*
80. *Ibid.* The NLRB case is found at 150 NLRB 312 (1964); 57 LRRM 1535.
81. Note 78, *supra.*
82. 389 U. S. 837 (1967); 66 LRRM 2306.

of the Gadsden facility in 1966 was higher than in all new plants in our sample save two.

Mohawk—Segregation in One Plant, Affirmative Action in Another

Mohawk Rubber Company, a relatively small Akron concern, established a second plant in West Helena, Arkansas, a small community near the Mississippi River in the mid-1950's. About 600 persons were employed in the plant. Strict departmental and facility segregation was followed. Negroes were employed as janitors, and in the cement and the processing departments. Local No. 539 of the URW strongly supported the segregation policy and voted to oppose plantwide bidding for jobs whenever Negroes requested it. All white collar employees and craftsmen were white.

After Title VII of the Civil Rights Act became effective, a few Negroes were employed in other departments. As of April 1966, however, the racial composition of the plant was largely unaltered, the white collar force and craftsmen were still all white, and although signs were removed, facilities were still largely *de facto* segregated. At this time 96 of 619 employees, or 15.5 percent of the labor force were colored. Thus despite the limitation on Negro employment opportunities, Mohawk had one of the largest ratios of Negro workers in the South.[83]

In late 1968, Mohawk opened a new plant in Salem, Virginia. All facilities were planned on an integrated basis, with the company making obvious efforts to employ and to train Negroes.

Armstrong—Violence at Natchez

Just prior to World War II, the Armstrong Rubber Company built a plant at Natchez, Mississippi. Complete segregation of seniority lines, departments, and facilities was followed and remained in effect until the 1960's, when the company was threatened with sanctions, including loss of government contracts, by the President's Committee on Equal Employment Opportunity, and its successor, the Office of Federal Contract Compliance. A heavy Ku Klux Klan influence in the area which undoubtedly infiltrated into the local rubber workers union, contributed to violence as the 10 percent Negro complement

83. Information based on testimony before the Arkansas Advisory Committee on Civil Rights, Forest City, Arkansas, April 23, 1966, pp. 6-76. Typescript in files of United States Civil Rights Commission, Washington, D. C.

of workers in the plant began to receive a measure of equal opportunity. Armstrong operated its Natchez plant on a decentralized basis, with little corporate direction or leadership in the personnel area.

Pursuant to orders from the PCEEO and later the OFCC, the company began to move toward elimination of separate facilities and seniority rosters in the early 1960's. Progress was slow, and hindered by militant white union opposition and alleged intimidation. As a result few Negroes took advantage of the opportunities which they were officially afforded. By March 1966, Negroes were still not employed in the offices, in maintenance, or in the tire divisions. Facilities remained at least *de facto* segregated.

Threatened by a loss of government contracts, the company in late 1966 employed skilled Negro maintenance personnel, office and clerical help, promoted Negroes to the tire division, and started training at least one Negro for a supervisory job. Facility integration was also speeded in late 1966, but *de facto* segregation was largely maintained by efforts of the militant white group in the work force. Integration efforts were met with forceful resistance. Such actions were typical of Natchez, generally, and did not merely involve Armstrong employees. Klan infiltration of the local unions at International Paper Company and Johns-Manville Corporation, other major Natchez employers was an equal reality. A bomb placed under the hood of the car of the local president of the National Association for the Advancement of Colored People, an Armstrong employee, resulted in his severe injury. Other assaults outside the plant occurred.

On November 9, 1966, the *Wall Street Journal*, in a feature article, quoted the Director of the OFCC that Armstrong's efforts at compliance were not "good enough," and that the company "failed to give Negroes a fair crack at available jobs" at Natchez. This article also quoted the company as "trying to comply."[84] Above all, it had the effect of convincing the local union leadership that the government would impose sanctions if further progress toward elimination of discrimination was not forthcoming. The article also gave the company stronger support in the community for its actions. It did not, however, convince the most avid racists.

On February 27, 1967, Wharlest Jackson, treasurer of the local

84. Monroe W. Karmin, "Job-Bias Showdown," *Wall Street Journal*, November 9, 1966, pp. 1, 14.

NAACP, and an Armstrong employee who had recently been promoted to a former all-white job, was murdered by a bomb attached under the hood of his truck. He was driving home from work. This second bombing of an Armstrong employee brought in the police, the FBI, heavy rewards from city and company, and no arrest nor conviction.[85]

This tragedy, however, seems to have been the last violent gasp of the Klan. The company proceeding in its government spurred and approved upgrading and integration program, altering its organization and approach to personnel problems in general and to equal employment opportunity in particular. As described by the Corporate Manager of Labor Relations:

> In assessing the progress of the company's Natchez facility, it is significant to note that, until 1964, there was little central control or direction of plant operations in areas such as equal employment opportunity and, as late as 1966, the functions of the Corporate Personnel Department were handled by a single individual. A rapid transition to a centralized operation and more adequate corporate staffing have permitted more corporate control and assistance to the local plant, particularly in connection with equal employment opportunity.
>
> Since March, 1967, there have been extensive changes in the racial composition of the company's Natchez plant. The percentage of Negroes employed in the total work force has risen from 16.4 to 21.9 at present. As late as February, 1967, Negroes represented less than 1% of the employees in skilled, professional, technical, clerical, and managerial positions. At the present time, 5% of the employees in such classifications are Negro. It is significant to note that, during this period, total employment in these classifications decreased from 625 to 596, while Negro employment rose from 18 to 35. This gain was accomplished in spite of the fact that ten applications for these jobs during this period were from whites to every one from a Negro. An example of the company's aggressive efforts to expand employment opportunities for Negroes is furnished by reference to a distribution center recently opened in Jackson, Mississippi. In this facility 3 of 6 clerical employees are Negroes and slightly over one half of the warehouse employees are Negroes. This employment is almost in exact correlation to the percentage of Negroes in the Jackson area.
>
> Prior to the summer of 1963, Negroes were restricted to 25 job classifications. They are now found in 80 different job classifications, including 19 employed as tire builders. In 1963, there were 22 segregated departments. At the present time, there are only 9 departments which do not have a bi-racial composition. These are all either

85. *Washington Evening Star*, February 28, 1967; *New York Times*, March 1, 1967.

skilled craft departments or departments employing fewer than 3 people. During 1968, Negroes represented 45% of employees hired. Net employment of whites has been increased by only 3 this year, while net employment of Negroes has been increased by 53. The number of Negro job applicants, also, has substantially increased. From representing slightly less than one fourth of all applicants in 1963, Negro applicants have increased to total over 50% of all applicants in 1968.

The foregoing achievements have been made by utilizing imaginative and aggressive management efforts. The company recruits heavily at predominantly Negro schools, advertises for help in newspapers of predominantly Negro distribution, uses the Urban League and M.D.T.A. schools as a source of referrals, as well as recognized leaders in the Negro community, publicizes promotions of Negroes in the company newspaper, sponsors tours of the plant for predominately Negro schools, hires employees qualified to perform entry level jobs without regard to potential for being upgraded, and maintains an active communications program with its employees concerning equal opportunity. The company has eliminated all forms of pre-employment tests for factory employees, as well as formal education and residency requirements.

The company's collective bargaining agreement with the union, prior to September, 1967, severely limited interdepartmental transfers. While the company, in 1966, placed greater stress upon encouraging such transfers as were permitted under the agreement, it did not change the interpretation given to the agreement even since separate lines of progress were eliminated in 1966. In September, 1967, the company negotiated a plant-wide seniority clause in its uniform agreement with the United Rubber Workers covering all four of the company's tire plants.[86]

The Southern Plants—Final Comment

These case histories indicate the problems which are inherent in overcoming past practice in the South, and the difficulties involved in integrating previously segregated plants. Firestone, which moved the earliest, had the best results and the least difficulties. Its large complement of Negro employees provided a helpful pressure group which prevented the local union from militantly espousing segregation. To its great credit, Firestone integrated its blue collar work force before government compulsion required the move.

Goodrich moved slowly and only after 1964. The fact that relatively few transfers have as yet occurred has undoubtedly muted opposition, but so far the company has nipped any possible trouble before it became difficult to handle.

86. Letter to authors, November 18, 1968.

Goodyear agreed to integration in 1962, after intervention by the government; considerable further litigation was necessary to bring the union in line. In general, however, it does not seem that Goodyear moved to protect Negro employment until direct government pressure was brought to bear, and by then, Negro employment at Gadsden had probably substantially diminished.

Mohawk's Arkansas plant has one of the highest Negro ratios in the industry, but it began operations in the mid-1950's on a segregated basis, while Firestone was eliminating segregation. With departmental seniority still practiced, *de facto* job segregation, with some change, is likely to feature this plant for many years to come. At Salem, Virginia, Mohawk integrated its facility from the start.

Faced with militant and violent opposition to change, Armstrong has, under intense government pressure, made widespread change at Natchez. Despite social pressures and violence, slight turnover and inadequate Negro background, education, and experience, improvement has been significant.

General also moved slowly at Waco, Texas, but was not deterred by white worker opposition and a strike. Later General opened a plant at Charlotte, North Carolina, which was integrated from the start.

In perspective, these case studies involve the companies with the *better* record of employing Negroes in southern rubber tire plants. Most plants, which were established between 1955 and 1964, concentrated on employing the cream of the labor market, and did not concern themselves with employing Negroes. One facility opened in 1960 and did not employ Negroes till 1963. Another company, which began operations a few years later, concentrated on employing young men with high school educations. Its Negro complement, in an area heavily populated by Negroes, was less than 5 percent in 1966. Companies such as Uniroyal, Goodyear, and Gates—whatever their records elsewhere—simply did not take any affirmative action, nor deem it a major concern to employ more than the few Negroes who managed either to obtain jobs as janitors or to qualify for the better jobs until the mid-1960's. Unlike most older plants, they had not only an upgrading task, but also the job of increasing their Negro representation generally, in order to meet the minimum affirmative action regulations of the federal government.

Beginning in 1967, the policies which inhibited Negro employment were altered by most tire companies building new plants or expanding those in the South. Careful affirmative active plans at such new facilities, as Mohawk, Salem, Virginia; General, Charlotte, North Carolina; Firestone, Albany, Georgia; and Goodyear, Union City, Tennessee; preclude the type of hiring which was done between 1948 and 1962. Uniroyal is doubling the size of Opelika, Alabama, plant, and at the same time is expanding its minority employment at a much faster rate. Reliance on tests and the high school diploma, hiring prerequisite, have been eliminated or modified to facilitate Negro employment opportunity. The newest plants may some day rival some of the oldest ones in terms of Negro employment if plans in effect at the end of 1968 are carried to fruition. Many of those which were built between 1950 and 1964, however, will continue to lag because of the policies adopted at their inception and the small turnover and employment change.

UNION IMPACT ON RACIAL POLICIES

It is a proud boast of the United Rubber, Cork, Linoleum and Plastic Workers that its ranks have always been open to all workers regardless of race, color, creed, or national origin. This is correct. Moreover, the URW maintains an internal union fair employment practice committee, headed by a Negro staff member, which conducts educational activities on minority rights and provides a procedure whereby Negroes or other minorities may seek redress if their rights have not been respected. The union newspaper gives regular publicity to the URW support of fair employment activities with pictures, speeches of officials, and other communications. URW presidents, throughout the years, have repeatedly committed themselves and the international union to support of the union's posture.

In organizing, the URW has always shunned separate Jim Crow locals in the South. This policy cost it a loss to a then rival union in 1941 in an election at Firestone's Memphis plant, but the following year, with strong Negro support in a second NLRB election, it gained the bargaining rights there which it has maintained ever since.[87] Gen-

87. F. Ray Marshall, *Labor in the South* (Cambridge: Harvard University Press, 1967), pp. 190-191.

erally, URW organizing on an equal basis has won it strong Negro support.

In actual fact, however, the URW's fair practices committee's work, like those of other unions, is largely educational. Such committees have little power, and perhaps even less in the URW, for the local rubber workers' unions have traditionally zealously guarded their independence and the international has rarely been strong enough to override a determined and large local union. Moreover, the international officials have often been sufficiently disunited so that they have not interfered with local union prerogatives.

Within local unions, Negroes hold a variety of offices. Because of their concentration in the compounding departments, they are usually able to select departmental or division stewards in these areas. This position often carries with it a position on the local union executive board and/or negotiating committee. Negroes are not, however, generally found above this rank in the local union hierarchy. There are, however, some Negro local union officials. The Detroit local, composed of Uniroyal employees, has usually had a Negro vice-president. In 1967, he succeeded to the presidency when the white president resigned; but in 1968 he was defeated by a white unionist in a local election in which voting apparently followed racial lines quite consistently.

It is in matters of upgrading of Negroes that the URW has generally failed to practice what it preaches despite good faith and apparent honest intentions. We have already noted that initially the URW followed industry practice by agreeing to departmental seniority. When combined with discriminatory hiring practices, this effectively barred Negroes from a significant portion of job opportunities, including most of the better blue collar jobs. In the 1950's, these contracts were revised, as before without consideration of their racial impact but in response to the desires of the white majority. The impact, however, was to open up a significant number of jobs to Negroes in all regions except the South.

In the South, the URW has, like most other industrial unions, had the most difficult time practicing what it preaches. After the national contract provided for bidding out into all departments, Negroes in southern plants continued to be denied their contractual rights to do so. Firestone broke the bar at Memphis in 1956-1957. With the largest Negro plant work force in the industry, and hence a Negro membership capable of exerting considerable pressure within the local union, the local union officials, who included Negroes, cooperated with the Firestone move, but did not overtly support the company. The biracial slate of local union officers was defeated by an all-white group in the next local union election, but by 1959 Negroes had again won representation on this local's officer group.[88]

Without specifying its nature, Professor F. Ray Marshall reports that the international union also "had trouble" with its Tuscaloosa, Alabama, local.[89] There at the Goodrich plant, a token number of previously all-white jobs have been opened to Negroes since 1964. The local union has "gone along" but given no support to integration. At West Helena, Arkansas, the local representing Mohawk company employees has opposed attempts to open up previously all-white departments to Negroes.

Local unions at Gadsden, Alabama, and Natchez, Mississippi, have been the most adamant opponents of integration. At the former plant, it will be recalled that the intervention in 1962 of the President's Committee on Equal Employment Opportunity (now the Office of Federal Contract Compliance) was required to open up previously all-white departments at Goodyear's Gadsden plant; and the Negro union members were compelled to pursue litigation that went all the way to the United States Supreme Court before the local union at Gadsden would process their grievances. Moreover, the Gadsden local's discriminatory conduct and court defense continued in spite of the clear statement of the international president that its refusal to process the grievances of the Negro members was wrong and violated the URW's policy. This was a clear example of the impotency of the international union in such matters, as well as the discriminatory intransigence of the local union.[90]

The events which transpired at the Armstrong Rubber plant in Natchez involve literally, the most violent opposition of white workers and their local union to civil rights pressures. The local union was in the forefront of the opposition, and did not cease its overt attempts to prevent change until the publication of the *Wall Street Journal* article indicating that the company faced loss of its government busi-

88. F. Ray Marshall, *The Negro and Organized Labor* (New York: John Wiley & Sons, Inc., (1965), pp. 188-189.
89. *Ibid.*, p. 188.
90. See above, pp. 473-476.

ness.[91] As already noted, Negroes who accepted promotions into previously all-white departments were assaulted. One was severely injured by a bomb and another was murdered. When separate drinking fountains were removed, a two-day strike resulted and when the cafeteria was integrated, it was boycotted by whites. Only the real threat of serious job loss caused the local union officials to understand that they must at least accept change.

In the southern tire plants built between 1950 and 1964, in which the percentage of Negroes is usually below 5 percent, there has been little overt opposition to Negro employment on the part of white employees and neither opposition to, nor support of, integration on the part of the local unions. Such a small Negro labor force has not evoked the emotional opposition to change that occurred in Gadsden or Natchez. In these plants, as in most throughout the country, the URW has played little direct role in the plants' racial composition or in the racial-occupational distribution.

Basically the URW has accepted the *status quo*. Seniority rules which once institutionalized discrimination, later were changed and furthered integration. In the South, the URW has played mostly a passive role in integration, but several of its local unions have taken leadership in opposing integration or improved Negro job opportunities. In such cases, the international union has reaffirmed its nondiscrimination policy and supported the rights of Negroes, but it has never extended such support to the extent of forcing a local union to comply with equal opportunity or treatment. The basic reason is the political impotence of the international union to enforce its policies and the lack of enough Negro members to provide counter political weight to overcome such impotence.

Those who might defend the URW's policies could emphasize the democratic nature of a union with an unusually high degree of local union autonomy and the continuing respect of such autonomy by the international union. Democracy, however, involves not only local autonomy and majority rule, but also the safeguarding of minority rights and equal treatment of all. The URW has fallen short here. Negro rights have not been safeguarded in several situations, and Negroes have not been treated equally under contracts until government intervention compelled change. In one sense, union racial poli-

91. See note 84, p. 477.

cies have been passive. They have not purposefully instituted change. True, the international union has advocated equality. On the other hand, several local unions have fought for segregation and discrimination.

In another sense, however, URW policy has fostered change that had adversely affected Negro employment opportunities. The union's tremendous leverage at the bargaining table, and the industry's relative weakness when faced with a potential strike which diverts business of large key customers to competitors have resulted in vigorous industry concentration on methods to offset high labor costs. The tremendous increases in productivity and consequent labor displacement have eliminated jobs and potential jobs of Negroes. Moreover, the high union wages have attracted an abundance of exceptionally qualified personnel from which the companies may choose their labor force. Union policies have been the dynamic factor which has altered production methods and labor requirements, and which for many years led the industry to adopt employment policies that made it extremely difficult for Negroes to compete for jobs.

GOVERNMENT POLICIES

Undoubtedly, government policy has had considerable effect on the racial policies of the industry. This is especially true of plants in the South. Without government pressure, there would probably have been little or no progress in Natchez or even Tuscaloosa; the Negro rubber workers at Gadsden required assistance both from executive and judicial branches to achieve their rights in Gadsden. Only in Memphis did real progress come without direct federal intervention or the passage of legislation.

Throughout the country, it required the civil rights revolution before the industry ceased contenting itself with "skimming the cream" of the labor market in filling jobs without considering the impact of its policies on the racial composition of its work force. The plants established between 1950 and 1964 are for the most part those with the smallest Negro ratio. To man these plants, the principal, if not the sole, consideration was to employ those with the best education, best test score, and best potential, and to ignore all other considerations. Now such a policy insures both a low Negro ratio and a direct conflict with policies of the federal government which demand that government contractors "affirmatively" move to expand employment opportunities for Negroes.

Likewise, few Negroes are employed in salaried positions in the industry and fewer still were so employed prior to the passage of the Civil Rights Act of 1964. Again the government was the spur, and now nearly every company in the industry is searching for Negro salaried personnel, or otherwise attempting to improve their low ratios in these occupational groups.

One aspect of government policy in this and other industries continues to cause widespread dismay in industry circles and results in a vast waste of time, money, and manpower. That is the lack of coordination among government agencies supervising enforcement of equal opportunity provisions of the Civil Rights Act or the Presidential Executive Orders relating to government contractors. A single rubber tire plant, for example, may be inspected by a procurement agency (for example, General Services Administration or the Defense Supply Administration of the Defense Department), by the Office of Federal Contract Compliance, and by the Equal Employment Opportunity Commission. If it is located in a city or state, which has a local or state human relations agency, it may also be inspected by one or both of these agencies. No agency will accept the reports of the other; each desires to perform an elaborate inspection *de novo*. One may find the plant in noncompliance after all others have given it a clean bill, or even praise for its efforts. In any case, the amount of time demanded of industry, and taken by government, for inspections is greatly expanded and results more hindered than helped by this uncoordinated activity.

The government push to improve Negro job opportunities, as already noted, runs counter to the industry's long-held policy of utilizing its high wages to select only the top job candidates. Many in industry feel that lowered standards will adversely affect the ability of the industry to increase productivity enough to offset the high labor costs imposed under collective bargaining. It is too early to predict such a result, but obviously lower employment standards could have that result. It is also true, however, that tight labor markets in Detroit, Los Angeles, and even somewhat in Akron have forced companies to lower hiring standards just to obtain needed workers. Whatever the cost, the addition of new, inexperienced workers always involves problems. They are discussed in the next chapter.

CHAPTER VI.

Some Problems of Equal Opportunity

The recruitment of additional Negroes into the rubber tire plants has not been in such numbers as to cause great difficulties, but there have been problems of adjustment. In addition, the attack on segregation in the South has created a number of problems and reactions which require note, as do the methods of government investigation. These and other issues are discussed in this chapter.

IMPACT ON WHITE EMPLOYEES

Unlike the automobile industry in which Negroes comprise either a majority, or a very significant minority in many plants, Negroes remain a small minority in all except a few rubber tire plants. Consequently, except in Detroit, Los Angeles, and to some extent in Memphis, the impact on the white labor market has not been significant. In some industries or plants, where a sizable portion of the Negroes has been employed, whites no longer seek employment there, nor leave quickly after they do accept jobs. No plant in tire manufacturing as yet has reached this situation. In Detroit and, to a lesser extent, Los Angeles, however, the labor market has been such since late 1965 that a majority of new applicants have been Negroes. This has tended constantly to increase the Negro ratio. The high earnings, however, would seem to offset some of the reluctance exhibited by many white employees about being part of a work force that is heavily Negro.[92]

In the South, where the government has pushed integration on the job, white reaction has been varied. In some cases white employees have bid on, and won, jobs formerly reserved for Negroes just as Negroes have bid on formerly all-white jobs. This has caused con-

92. For some of the problems and reactions of white workers in such situations, see Part Two.

siderable bitterness among Negroes who feel that they can lose as many jobs as they gain. On the other hand, it is difficult to see how some jobs can be reserved for Negroes and all others opened to them with discrimination. Yet it is true, that if all jobs are available on a competitive basis, Negro educational and experience disadvantages make it difficult for them to win a proportionate share.

In the case of janitorial or certain all laboring or service jobs that have traditionally been associated with Negroes, integration attempts in the South have been generally quite unsuccessful. If whites are employed in such jobs, they do not remain long. The stigma of a "Negro job" is often an effective deterrent to the recruitment of whites. Of course, in times of high unemployment that deterrent could be less operative.

Facility Integration—Nature and Impact

Compulsory segregation of facilities is, in terms of economic theory, a method of distinguishing the Negro work force from the white, and thereby making it either more costly to employ Negroes, or if they are employed, to integrate Negroes throughout the plant. By hiring no Negroes in a segregated economy, the plant would need only one set of time clocks, drinking fountains, locker rooms, toilets, and eating facilities. If Negroes were employed, but confined to segregated departments, the number of duplicate facilities could be kept at a minimum. On the other hand, if a plant were totally mixed under the segregation laws, then the most expensive setup would be required, for facilities throughout the plant would have to be duplicated. The basic economics of segregation were thus carefully designed to limit the ability of Negroes to compete with whites for jobs by making it more costly to employ Negroes and most expensive to employ them on an integrated basis. These laws were, of course, designed by southern states between 1880 and World War I, at a time when the white lower, or nonplantation classes came to power. Segregation in education, transportation, housing, and political disenfranchisement, of course, added to the economic burden of Negroes by giving them inferior training, inferior location for and access to jobs, and impotency to alter the situation. The impact of decades of required segregation and inferior treatment still depreciates the ability of Negroes to compete for work on an even basis with whites.

The elimination of all segregated facilities has been a determined goal of the Office of Federal Contract Compliance, and it has firmly demanded that this occur promptly in all southern rubber tire plants, as well as in those of other plants. (The authors know of no segregated facilities in northern tire plants.) The response of the white rubber tire employees has been one of opposition, varying from violence to peaceful boycott. In Natchez, the white employees struck for two days over integrated drinking fountains and boycotted the integrated restaurant. Boycotts of newly integrated locker room facilities by whites have been a common reaction in this and other industries. Enforcement of *de facto* segregation of facilities, either by custom, fear, or harassment, is another.

The humorist-philosopher, Harry Golden, has often said that integration in the South would be furthered by the custom of "stand up eating." He proposed when the early lunch counter sitdowns occurred, to remove all seats, opining that whites did not seem to object to standing as they did to sitting with Negroes while eating. Faced with boycotted eating facilities and consequent financial losses, tire manufacturers and other employers have turned to this concept with the use of vending machines in southern plants. The impersonality of the machine seems to remove the heat from racial integration. Since people usually carry the products of machines to tables where their friends are, generally Negroes and white eat in the same room but not at the same tables, and the boycotts subside.

A similar gimmick satisfies the drinking fountain problem. Paper cups supplied seem to end fountain damage and sabotage. The individual cup apparently satisfies the segregation psychosis of the racists and permits all to drink from one set of fountains, which incidentally tap water from one supply.

Locker rooms are the last bastion of the boycott in all once segregated plants. Most whites, at least initially, refuse to use them and instead change and shower at home. In time perhaps, the sweaty odor of the unbathed husband will induce his wife and family to pressure him to discover that a shower and fresh clothes in an integrated environment are preferable to sweat, smell, and dirt in the segregation of the home.

Both the Equal Employment Opportunity Commission and the Office of Federal Contract Compliance have been criticized for concentrating too much of their efforts on integrating facilities. Insofar as such efforts might detract from those most directly concerned with opening new job opportunities, this is a valid point. On the other hand, the segregation laws were enacted in order to make it more costly to employ Negroes and they do in fact label Negroes as second-class citizens unfit to associate with whites. Moreover, segregated facilities frequently are built around segregated work locations. Maintaining such segregation places an added burden on Negroes desiring to advance to former all-white jobs. Elimination of segregated facilities is not as important as opening up new jobs, but it is undoubtedly a necessary concomitant of the same process.

EFFICIENCY AND TURNOVER

Some rubber tire employers who have hired a large number of Negroes in recent years all believe that the rate of absenteeism, tardiness, and turnover of Negro employees is higher than that of whites. The authors were unable to obtain any statistical studies to support these contentions, but these findings do concur with those in other industries.[93] On the other hand, it must be emphasized that employers found no significant difference in the absenteeism, tardiness, nor turnover of Negroes and whites where members of both races were employees with at least two years seniority.

Most of the evidence of excess problems with new Negroes comes from Akron, Detroit, and Los Angeles. Here the concern was with new employees, most of whom had never previously held a full-time job. For such employees, used to picking up part-time work, the factory social system is a new experience. Rubber tire companies have been slow to realize the need for special training and indoctrination for such employees who find the factory a strange and bewildering place. It is easy for such workers to become discouraged, to "blow their pay check" on one weekend and miss Monday because of a hangover, or to purchase an inadequate used car and break down on the way to work.

Inexperience in industry, poor educational backgrounds, lack of motivation as a result of lack of belief in or experience with equal opportunity, are all factors in absentee, tardiness, and turnover rates.

93. See, e.g., *ibid.*, pp. 106-108; and Part Three pp. 219-220.

It would be surprising if the new Negro employees did not fall behind in these measures. Those who survive six months or one year adapt to the requirements of industrial life, take advantage of their earnings, and move toward the stability of other experienced employees.

Efficiency and Government Pressure

We have already noted that government pressure may well force the industry to employ persons below the standards set by many plants if the Negro ratio in a number of facilities is to be increased. This involves a cost to industry, which may be passed on to the public. On the other hand, it is not possible to integrate Negroes into the work force without cost. It may well be far cheaper and infinitely better to lower standards somewhat to accomplish such integration. Plants in Detroit, Los Angeles, and Akron have had to do just that in order to obtain needed employees. It does seem reasonable that plants elsewhere are re-examining their standards to determine if their impact has been to exclude Negroes unnecessarily without adding substantially to productivity.

Since industry is being asked to lower its standards, government could well cooperate by reducing the costs and irritations of inspections and compliance activities. A little coordination and a reduction of duplication would achieve much.

A final aspect of government pressure is the tendency of some Negroes to appeal to the Equal Employment Opportunity Commission any disciplinary matter. This is understandable in view of the failure of local unions to seek adequate redress for Negro grievances, and the impotency of the URW fair practice committee. Moreover, charges are often valid and redress needed.

On the other hand, EEOC investigators seem often convinced that a charge has merit without sufficient basis or careful investigation, and where inefficiency, poor workmanship, or bad behavior might be the real cause of the problem. The result is employer anguish, white worker resentment, and the reluctance of supervisors to discipline Negroes for fear of "getting the government on my neck," as one foreman expressed it.[94] Charges of double standards formerly referred to the belief of Negroes that they were held to higher standards than whites. Now the charge is that Negroes are sometimes favored.

94. Interview, Los Angeles, January 1967.

SOME PERSPECTIVES

It would be surprising indeed if the overturning of past practices, the opening up of new jobs, and employment of Negroes with no previous experience in industry did not result in problems. Such problems, although violent in one southern location, have been comparatively minor, in some cases perhaps because changes in the racial-occupational representation of Negroes have been relatively small. The greatest problems outside of the South have been in Akron, Detroit, and Los Angeles where the bulk of Negroes are employed. Yet the difficulties in these areas have been relatively minor for tire employers, and the experience with Negro employees who are not new in industry lends hope that longer tenure will greatly lessen the problems of today's new black rubber workers.

CHAPTER VII.

Determinants of Industry Policy

A number of factors have been noted throughout this study which have contributed to the racial policies of the rubber tire industry. These and others are discussed in this concluding chapter.

THE DEMAND FOR LABOR

Throughout industry, Negroes have made their greatest gains in times of labor shortage. The rubber tire industry is no exception to this generalization. Negroes came into the industry during World War I, expanded their job opportunities during World War II, and increased their representation in many plants in the prosperous 1960's.

The demand for labor in the rubber tire industry has, however, been a special situation. Between 1947 and 1963, productivity rose dramatically while employment declined. Pushed by unrelenting union pressure to grant top wages, the industry replaced men by machines at a rapid rate. This not only reduced the demand for labor, but altered it substantially. Unskilled jobs disappeared, and the high wages enabled the industry to employ only the cream of the labor market to fill the few available new jobs.

Negroes were disproportionately affected. Previously concentrated in jobs which were eliminated, they later had to compete in a labor market where their disproportionate lack of education and experience left them at a distinct disadvantage. The contrast in Negro representation in old southern tire plants, with those built between 1950 and 1964, demonstrates the results, as does the lack of Negro participation in new midwestern plants. In view of the ability of the industry to pay the wages which it does, it is likely to continue to attract an abundance of well-qualified labor. Negroes will, therefore, continue to find the job competition severe except in areas experiencing a labor shortage, such as Detroit or Los Angeles in the mid-1960's.

THE JOB STRUCTURE

The job structure in the industry is favorable to Negro employment. More than one-half of the total number of employees are semiskilled, unskilled or service workers. A large portion of these jobs requires a very small amount of training. The industry can utilize persons with little or no experience and a minimum of education for a sizable number of jobs.

It is not industry policy, however, except where the local labor market permits no other choice, to employ persons with qualifications only for entry jobs. Rather the industry searches for, and usually can obtain, employees capable of progressing up the occupational hierarchy. This policy, taken together with the manner in which the wage structure attracts qualified people, negates to a considerable extent the advantages which the job structure would seem to provide in the employment of Negroes. As a result, companies in many locations have been compelled to take special measures if a sizable proportion of Negroes are to be employed.

GOVERNMENT PRESSURE

Government pressure has been a prime motivating force in altering industry policy and in moving it toward a more equalitarian and affirmative stance. Only one plant in the South ended racial-departmental employment segregation before the Civil Rights Act of 1964. It has required the threat of loss of government business to alter segregation and overt discrimination in some plants, and time-consuming litigation to achieve progress in others. As late as 1962, major installations were built and staffed without serious regard for the impact of policies on Negro employment. Certainly, there is little evidence that the industry as a whole, despite some clear exceptions, was moving very fast toward equal employment practices until the federal government became directly involved.

UNIONISM AND SENIORITY

The United Rubber, Cork, Linoleum and Plastic Workers has had an effect on Negro job opportunities more indirectly than purposefully. The URW's bargaining power and wage policy have been prime factors in the industry's stress on technological change and its emphasis and ability to employ the best in the labor force. This has, of course, had an adverse impact on Negro job opportunities.

Initially, the URW negotiated departmental seniority contracts which aided in confining Negroes to segregated (and less advantaged) jobs and departments. Later when the union, again without regard to the racial situation, won rights for plantwide bidding, Negroes profited especially by bidding into previously all-white departments.

In the South, however, only Firestone opened up all blue collar jobs before 1964. In other plants, local URW unions conspired with management to ignore the contractual rights of Negroes, or to write contracts that perpetuated segregation and discrimination. The organizational setup of the URW made it powerless to interfere, despite its avowed policies of nondiscrimination. Finally, when segregation and discrimination practices have been altered, URW local unions have at best been passive. At Gadsden a local resisted dealing fairly with Negroes until the United States Supreme Court refused to set aside a National Labor Relations Board order. At Natchez, the local union allied itself with violent opposition until the threat of business and job losses brought acquiescence. The most which the international union has done is to align itself with the forces of equal opportunity, to stress its commitment, and therefore, to give no aid or comfort to those opposing these precepts.

LOCATIONAL AND REGIONAL FACTORS

In general, the older plants are located advantageously for Negro employment, the newer ones disadvantageously. There are, of course, exceptions to this generalization, but it is largely true.

The older plants in Akron, Detroit, Los Angeles, and the South are in relatively easily accessible parts of areas having sizable concentrations of Negro population. Even in the East, plants in Chicopee Falls, Massachusetts, West Haven, Connecticut, and Baltimore, Maryland are relatively accessible to nearby Negro population concentrations.

In contrast, new plants are located in small towns in Indiana, Illinois, Pennsylvania, Oklahoma, and California where few Negroes live; and in these areas, and in the South, outside the cities or easily accessible towns where no public transportation is available. Thus the tendency is for plant location to increase the disabilities for Negroes in job competition in new plants although the impact on Negro employment is not purposeful.

Naturally, too, companies seek areas of ample labor supply when locating new plants. This means more competition for jobs and for Negroes, more difficulties than in the tight labor markets where some of the older plants are located.

MANAGERIAL POLICY

Managerial policy toward civil rights issues, as toward many other problems, is determined by a wide variety of institutional factors, but also by personalities, events, and times. Industrial management in the rubber tire industry is not heavily consumer- or personnel-oriented. This does not mean that retail customers or employees are either ignored or given inconsiderate treatment as a matter of policy. Rather it is a matter of emphasis. The major tire companies historically and by the nature of the business have emphasized their function as tire suppliers to the automobile industry and to large private brand customers. This orientation is natural not only because of the size of these customers, but also because tire replacement consumers tend to replace original equipment with the same brand. Given the fierce competition in the industry and the difficulties of differentiating the product of one company from another, sales to the major customers are certain to be foremost in the minds of the industry's managers.

One can, therefore, understand the industry's reluctance to tolerate work interruptions, and its willingness to pay very high wages in order to establish a *modus vivendi* with a strong union which understands all too well that the industry is willing to concede much to avoid strikes. The ability of the industry to offset labor costs by productivity, of course, increases its capacity, as well as willingness, to adopt such a policy.

Within this same context, the industry's racial policies become intelligible. In view of the pressures from large customers to avoid interruptions of sales and service and from the union to pay ever higher wages, it has concentrated its internal efforts on maximizing productive efficiency and minimizing labor costs. Negroes have been employed when the labor market made that employment wise or necessary, but prior to the 1960's few special efforts have been made to employ Negroes where their employment seemed not the most efficient action to take. Of course, there were exceptions, as we shall again note below. This, however, seems an accurate generalization. It accounts for the slowness of the industry to employ Negroes in white collar jobs, and for the small percentage of Negroes in new plants where the industry took advantage of its ability to attract a labor surplus and chose only the best of those available. The fear of work stoppages, and their costs, and the possible impact on efficiency also account for the reluctance of most of the industry to end southern segregation practices until required to do so by legal action or threat of loss of government business.

Personnel management in this environment is clearly secondary to sales and production. Personnel considerations become critical principally when they directly affect the two primary functions. The potential, for example, in recent years of Negro consumer reaction to a company's racial policies is undoubtedly of some concern. General Tire, which lacks sales to the major automobile firms, appears in some of its advertising to be directing its appeal to potential Negro customers. The realization of the existence of a Negro market may have affected this company's racial employment policies in recent years.

The Negro market is, however, small, and does not seem to have been a serious factor in consideration of most companies' racial policies. The government market is, however, large, and government muscle is indeed respected. In addition, however, international considerations, which include rubber plantations in Africa, and worldwide sales, have been mentioned by companies as factors in their racial policies. The potential for bad publicity abroad may have aided in greater stress of racial employment in recent years.

With its orientation, the rubber tire industry tends to move with, but not ahead of, the times. It does what is required to insure that its services are maintained. Today's times require special efforts to employ Negroes and that is being done. The major companies are all members of Plans for Progress and the National Alliance of Business. They are making special efforts to employ Negro white collar personnel, to add to their blue collar ratio, to train the hard core, and to promote Negroes to supervisory positions. They are searching for

Negro managerial candidates, professionals, and technicians, and they are providing special aid, scholarships, and other educational opportunities to the Negro community. They did little pioneering in these areas, but once they began their programs, they have earnestly pursued them. The small employment increase in the industry insures that change will occur slowly, but it is indeed occurring. The main reason is that these are the times to act on Negro employment, and the industry is, as usual, in tune with the times.

Managerial Differences

We have already noted that company differences within the industry are significant, and generalizations are inadequate to do them justice. Firestone, for example, was the first to employ Negroes in Akron and has long had the highest Negro ratio there. It has maintained the Negro ratio at Memphis at about one-third of the work force there, apparently as a matter of policy. It integrated the blue collar jobs there at least five years before any other company did so in the South, and well before it was required to act by government directive. The role of the company founder in opening up jobs to Negroes, the company interest in Liberia, the fact that members of the Firestone family have been active in interracial organizations and the long interest, like his father, of Harvey Firestone, Jr., and his brothers, in Negro job opportunities is undoubtedly a factor.

The variation of Negro employment policies in Akron can be attributable only to management policies. The leading employer of Negroes is not the leading employer of Negro white collar workers; another company has a relatively poor record both in Akron and elsewhere. Different managerial emphases at different times undoubtedly account for these variations which are difficult and slow to erase because of the stability of the work force.

The human factor affects managerial decisions, as it does others. The interest of some managers in the problem of race, the reactions of individual plant managers, and the degree of central control over racial policies have all played a role. Except in such situations as Firestone's Memphis plant, the industry has tended to leave racial policies to decentralized discretion. The result has been a failure to recognize the need for special action. Plant managers are paid to produce tires at the lowest possible cost. Unless central headquarters forces them to consider the racial implications of their actions, plant management cannot be expected to do so. The Armstrong Natchez experience provides a good example of why central direction and control is essential. For most companies, it is only within the last few years that such control and direction have been forthcoming, or at least stressed, as they are now.

CHAPTER VIII.

Concluding Remarks

Employment in the rubber tire industry is again declining. The tremendous investment in new southern plants in recent years seems certain to have an adverse impact on employment in older plants in Akron and elsewhere. This means that the current stress on Negro employment, particularly in the South, must continue. Higher wages and increased production through technical advancement, appear likely to feature this industry in the future, as in the past. One must therefore expect that the industry will, as in the past, be able to attract overall a very qualified labor force and that any increase in Negro participation in the industry will be small, and the result of affirmative action rather than the workings of the labor market.

Part Six

THE NEGRO IN THE PETROLEUM INDUSTRY

by

CARL B. KING

and

HOWARD W. RISHER, JR.

LIST OF TABLES

CHAPTER I.

Introduction

The highly intricate technology utilized throughout the petroleum industry has virtually eliminated any demand for poorly trained or for uneducated personnel. The processing operations, from the time crude oil is taken from the oil wells to the delivery of the refined product to the consumer, are among the manufacturing operations which can presently be subjected to the highest degree of automation. This is particularly true for operations within the modern refinery. Many refineries have pared employment in one or more operations to skeleton crews by utilization of closed loop, computer control systems. In fact, employment at most locations has now declined from the peak years of the 1950's. The nature of the petroleum industry employment situation thus illustrates both an accentuated example of the present Negro employment problem and also an example of possible problems which may arise for low-skill workers as other major industries develop similar levels of technology.

Although labor market factors in the industry have had a significant effect on Negro employment and upgrading, a number of other factors, such as industrial location and the pressures of government, have each had a bearing on racial employment policies. The petroleum industry does employ many workers in major urban areas with large Negro populations. The problem of Negro employment is complicated for the industry, however, by the attitudes prevailing in many southern towns, by the problems of urban transportation, and by the fact that a large number of operations are still carried on in rural areas. The use of government pressure to effectuate change is in turn burdened by the need for plant security, by the necessity of meeting delivery dates, and by labor force quality as it relates to product quality and plant safety. Finally, Negro employment has been affected at times by customer pressure, union sentiment, and historical social developments. As a result, each company must consider a number of highly interrelated factors in establishing its racial employment policies.

This study is concerned with the development, status, and problems involved in racial employment policies in the petroleum industry, with particular emphasis on Negro employment in the principal companies therein. Basic to an understanding of these policies is the nature of the industry which is the subject of the following chapter.

CHAPTER II.

The Petroleum Industry

The petroleum industry is a distinct grouping of companies performing operations related to two basic resources: crude petroleum and natural gas. Although several thousand companies are engaged in one or more aspects of the industry's operations, few of these companies have followed the recent trends toward product diversification. Most firms concentrate solely on providing the equipment and services necessary for the large concerns to bring petroleum products to market. The major business functions associated with the petroleum industry are outlined in Table 1.

TABLE 1. *Major Petroleum Functions*

1. Exploration and Production
   - A. Drilling
   - B. Recovery and Storage
2. Transportation
   - A. Crude
   - B. Refined Products
3. Manufacturing
   - A. Refining
   - B. Petrochemicals
4. Marketing
   - A. Wholesaling
   - B. Retailing

INDUSTRIAL SUBDIVISIONS

Exploration and production are important functions. Oil and gas have to be located beneath the ground and brought to the surface. Today these operations are still primarily carried on by small firms similar to those made famous during the early history of the industry. The risk has been diminished by the introduction of highly scientific exploration techniques, but the operation still maintains a great deal of the early "wildcatting" spirit. Although the obvious rewards of successful exploration and production still attract many small firms, this sector of the industry is dominated by the several major concerns analyzed in this study. These firms, in fact, have found that the supply of crude offered by small contractors to be highly satisfactory. It is often more economical for the large company to allow the specialty firm to assume the risks and costs of crude oil exploration. Although the importation of foreign crude from South America and the Middle East has grown in importance in recent years, 87 percent of the crude refined is produced domestically.[1] A post-World War II development has been the exploitation of the oil rich areas off the coasts of Louisiana, Texas, and California.

From the oil fields the crude must be transported to the refineries or petrochemical plants. This is done primarily by pipeline to inland plants and storage areas; there is, however, a significant volume of crude shipped along the Mississippi by barge, and along the eastern seaboard by tanker to refineries in the Northeast. Most of the pipeline networks and ships are owned or leased by one of the major petroleum corporations.

Today's refineries are huge, highly complex plants. They are typically located near the producing oil fields or centrally located in major marketing areas. The number of plants is gradually diminishing as new, often larger and more economical plants are put on stream. Refineries vary in number and amount of products produced, and in method of production. In 1966, consumption of products refined in the United States averaged 11,490,000 barrels daily.[2] Gasoline represented 50 percent of this output.[3]

During the postwar period most of the major petroleum corporations have also extended their activities to the production of a series of petrochemical products. These are produced typically in facilities built on or near existing refinery grounds. They have been constructed in close proximity to the refineries in order to utilize the stored crude stock and its transportation system, and to avoid dupli-

1. American Petroleum Institute, *Petroleum Facts and Figures, 1967* (New York: American Petroleum Institute, 1968), p. 87.
2. U. S. Bureau of Mines, *Minerals Yearbook: 1966* (Washington: U. S. Government Printing Office, 1967), p. 809.
3. American Petroleum Institute, *loc. cit.*

cation of costly processes. Petrochemical operations are the fastest growing sector of the petroleum industry. This has generally been conducive to improved employment opportunities for Negroes. This study, however, will analyze petrochemical operations only when those operations are an integral part of a major refinery. The diverse activities of the petrochemical sector will be studied in more depth in Part Seven which will deal with the chemical industry as such.

From the manufacturing sector of the industry the refined products must be transported to storage areas, wholesale distribution centers and finally, to the retail service station or other consumer. Transportation during this phase of the industry's operations is dominated by trucks. Pipeline transportation in this segment of the industry is now of lesser significance than both water and truck transportation. The means of transportation are often owned by small, independent distributors.

The petroleum bulk plants and terminals which serve as distribution centers for petroleum products are generally concentrated in highly populated, high consumption regions. The product distribution sector of the industry has grown slowly as the consumption of petroleum products has expanded. The major corporations operate both large marketing offices in most major cities and numerous distribution plants. Today 17 corporations market in at least 25 states.[4] Competition among the nationally known petroleum firms is particularly strong in this sector.

Retail sales operations are controlled almost exclusively by local proprietors. Approximately 220,000 service stations, 12,000 fuel oil dealers, and 7,000 liquefied petroleum gas dealers are now selling petroleum products throughout the nation.[5] Although the facilities may be leased from one of the large oil companies, the employment policies and practices are closely controlled by local management. This study does not attempt to analyze Negro employment for these establishments. Those employees of major firms retailing to government and industry have, however, been included.

The complexity of the industry as portrayed in the preceding paragraphs does not allow easy statistical analysis. Too many small firms play an integral part in bringing petroleum products to the consumer.

4. *Ibid.*, p. 156-158.
5. Estimates based on statistics from the *1963 Census of Business, Retail Trade.*

Moreover, there is no single source of annual industry employment data, although several government agencies report employment data for various sectors of the industry. Even among government agencies, however, there is less than complete agreement on industry definitions, data collection techniques, or resulting employment data. This study, therefore, attempts to cite any limitations which may apply to data used. Most of the employment statistics emphasized have been collected and compiled by the authors, and any resulting weaknesses are solely their responsibility.

The emphasis of this study will be on those major firms which dominate the refining sector of the industry. These firms control the petroleum industry, and the employment trends therein. These are the only firms which maintain significant work forces. Government interest and pressure has also thus far concentrated on these few firms. In view of their significance and precedent-setting policies, it is likely that any analysis of these firms will give a fair picture of the industry.

SALES AND STRUCTURE

The petroleum industry, as outlined in the preceding section, is one of the largest industrial groups in the United States today. Complete domestic sales data are impossible to compile. The inordinate number of small firms, the huge volume of intracompany transactions, and the difficulties encountered in definition have forced the cessation of such efforts. As an indication of the size of the industry, sales totals for the twenty largest petroleum corporations are provided in Table 2. The sales totals for most of these concerns include revenues from both foreign and domestic operations. In 1967 sales revenues for this grouping showed a record $53.5 billion total. This sales volume represented 6.8 percent of the gross national product, and 9.8 percent of manufacturing sales. With petroleum products such an integral part of the nation's consumption patterns, annual industry sales can be expected to continue growing at a rate similar to that of the national economy.

The Twenty Major Concerns Studied

Table 3 lists the twenty concerns which have been included in the Table 2 data. Each firm had sales revenues in 1967 in excess of $500 million. Each has the capacity to refine over 100,000 barrels of crude

TABLE 2. *Major Petroleum Company Sales and the National Economy 1960-1967*
(Dollar Figures in Billions)

		Sales of		Petroleum Sales as Percent of	
Year Ending December 31	Total Gross National Product	Manufacturing industries	20 largest Petroleum Companies[a]	GNP	Manufacturing industries
1960	$503.7[r]	$369.6	$30.9	6.1	8.4
1961	520.1[r]	370.6	32.2	6.2	8.7
1962	560.3[r]	399.7	34.9	6.2	8.7
1963	590.5[r]	417.5	37.5	6.4	9.0
1964	631.7[r]	445.6	38.6	6.1	8.7
1965	681.2[r]	483.3[r]	42.7	6.3	8.7
1966	747.6[r]	527.6[r]	47.0	6.3	8.9
1967	789.7	536.9[r]	53.4	6.8	9.8

Sources: Gross National Product and Manufacturing Industries: U. S. Department of Commerce, *Survey of Current Business.*
Petroleum Company Sales: *Fortune*, "The 500 Largest U. S. Industrial Corporations."

[a] Totals include both domestic and foreign sales.

[r] Revised

petroleum per day. These companies have retained similar positions within the industry for half a century. Today they hold 83 percent of the nation's domestic refining capacity.[6] They also own significant but smaller proportions of the producing oil wells, the pipelines, ship and truck transportation facilities, the wholesale bulk stations and terminals, and the retail outlets. This high degree of vertical integration has developed to insure a steady flow of crude to the refineries, and of high quality products to the product markets. The many remaining firms typically operate in one or at most two functional levels of the industry.

New firms seeking to initiate operations in the industry find the investment outlays prohibitive. A competitive refinery may cost $200 million to put on stream. Even if this hurdle can be reached, the major companies maintain such control over other industry sectors that success may still be unobtainable. Most of the small firms now

6. *Oil and Gas Journal,* April 1, 1968, p. 126.

TABLE 3. *Characteristics of 20 Petroleum Companies, 1968*

Company	Sales[a] (000,000)	Employees	Number of Refineries	Refining Capacity (Barrels/Day)
Standard Oil (N. J.)	$14,091.3	151,000	5	1,021,000
Mobil Oil	6,221.0	78,300	10	810,500
Texaco	5,459.8	78,475	12	925,000
Gulf Oil	4,558.5	60,300	7	653,600
Standard Oil of California	3,634.8	47,885	14	835,300
Shell Oil	3,317.1	39,080	8	875,800
Standard Oil (Ind.)	3,213.7	47,809	12	959,700
Continental Oil	2,251.6	34,384	8	265,040
Phillips Petroleum	2,106.9	35,359	6	389,500
Sun Oil[b]	1,778.2	29,446	5	454,000
Union Oil Co. of Calif.	1,536.0	17,250	8	436,800
Sinclair Oil	1,465.1	19,802	4	450,000
Cities Service	1,439.7	23,100	2	241,000
Atlantic Richfield	1,413.7	19,756	3	404,000
Signal Companies[c]	1,318.0	37,000		n.a.
Getty Oil	1,085.8	12,974	1	140,000
Ashland Oil & Refining[d]	1,068.4	17,000	6	217,500
Marathon Oil	797.4	8,026	3	159,100
Standard Oil (Ohio)	716.3	14,574	2	180,600
Hess Oil & Chemical	486.0	3,119	2	117,000

Sources: *Fortune*, "The 500 Largest Industrial Corporations," Vol. LXXIX (May 15, 1969), pp. 168-174; and *Oil and Gas Journal*, "Annual Refining Survey: 1968," Vol. LXVII (March 24, 1969), 1. 109.

[a] Sales figures here do not include excise taxes collected by the manufacturer and, therefore, may be lower than those published by the corporations themselves.
[b] Includes Sunray DX Oil which was merged into Sun Oil in July 1968.
[c] Name changed from Signal Oil & Gas in April 1968.
[d] Figures for fiscal year ending September 30, 1968.

operating in the industry, except at the retail level, depend on the major firms as important customers. Crude oil produced by small firms is sold to one of the large concerns for refining. Even the specialty products produced by small refineries are often sold to major corporations for further distribution. In fact competition within the industry is at two distinct levels: among the nationally known firms marketing products through retail service stations and other outlets, and among the small firms which struggle among themselves and with larger companies for survival.

The product mix of the industry has remained proportionately stable over the past decade. Gasoline remains the leading product, accounting for nearly half of the total output. Distillate fuel oils, residual fuel oils, and kerosene have maintained their same relative importance after gasoline. There has been, however, significant upgrading of product quality over the decade. There has also been a shift to jet fuels and aviation gasolines since World War II. The industry's output during the year fluctuates to meet product demand, with fuel oils increasing in importance during the winter and gasolines again being increased to meet summer driving demands. Recent changes in technology allow greater fluctuation in product output. Table 4 summarizes production input-output relationships for 1956 and 1966.

TABLE 4. *Production Changes, 1956-1966*
(Thousands of Barrels)

	1956	1966	Percent Change
Input			
Crude oil	2,905,106	3,447,193	+19
Foreign	341,451	446,404	+31
Domestic	2,563,655	3,000,789	+17
Natural gas	135,062	235,610	+74
Total Input	3,040,168	3,682,803	+21
Output			
Gasoline	1,393,556	1,813,334	+30
Distillate fuel oils	665,687	784,717	+18
Residual fuel oils	426,699	263,961	−38
Kerosene	123,480	226,822	+84
Other products[a]	430,746	593,969	+38
Total Output	3,040,168	3,682,803	+21

Source: American Petroleum Institute, *Petroleum Facts and Figures, 1967, 1959.*
[a] Other products include jet fuel, lubricating oils, wax coke, asphalt, still gas, road oil, and petrochemical feedstocks.

Government Sales

A small but significant share of this output is sold to federal and state government agencies. In 1967 only three petroleum companies were among the 50 largest defense contractors—Standard Oil (N. J.), 30th; Standard Oil of California, 43rd; and Texaco, 49th.[7] The Department of Defense alone signed contracts for 1968 for $305 million.[8] Total sales volume to government is estimated in excess of $550 million. This sales volume is not of great importance in light of industrial and household consumption, but it does provide leverage for enforcing government racial employment policy directives. Government pressure has been modified, however, to a great degree by the essential nature of petroleum products. Only a few firms have the capacity to produce the products necessary for continuing the Vietnam War and for other governmental operations.

EMPLOYMENT

The continued development and improvement of automatic equipment in each of the processing phases from the oil fields through refining have caused many changes in employment since World War II. Only the wholesaling and retailing sectors of the industry have steadily expanded employment during this period. Automation has had little effect in each of these sectors. Employment trends are summarized in Table 5.

Refinery Employment

The following employment statistics vividly portray the decrease in demand for manpower because of automation and improved methods. Refinery employment, for example, reached an employment peak in 1953, and although output has continued to expand, employment has been decreasing since that year. Refining, in fact, has the highest sales per employee of any industry: $71,941 per man in 1967.[9]

Most of this decline has occurred slowly. Large layoffs because of work force reductions or plant closings have been a major factor only during the period 1957-1958 when business generally was experiencing a major downturn. The decrease has come as a result of quits or retirements. Many plants continue to be overstaffed today. The industry has historically maintained paternalistic attitudes

7. *Business Week*, December 9, 1967, p. 152.
8. *Wall Street Journal*, December 4, 1967, p. 2.
9. *Fortune*, Vol. LXXVII (June 15, 1968), p. 206.

TABLE 5. *Employment in the Petroleum Industry Selected Years, 1940-1966*

Year	Crude Petroleum and Natural Gas Extraction	Petroleum Refining	Petroleum Pipelines	Petroleum Product Wholesaling	Gasoline Service Stations
1966	228,613	109,876	16,250	168,052	559,049
1965	232,192	114,654	16,653	161,815	553,455
1964	231,147	117,756	17,110	160,007	505,584
1962	254,760[a]	130,054[a]	23,692[a]	172,730[a]	483,916[a]
1960	252,984	252,714	20,821	171,812	635,100
1950	230,940	258,210	20,100	159,810	453,870
1940	181,860	178,980	17,420	N.A.	407,700

Sources: U. S. Bureau of the Census, *Census of Population:*
1960 Industrial Characteristics, Table 2.
1950 Industrial Characteristics, Table 2.
1940 Industrial Characteristics, Table 1.
U. S. Bureau of the Census, *County Business Patterns:*
1962 U. S. Summary Statistics
1964 U. S. Summary Statistics
1965 U. S. Summary Statistics
1966 U. S. Summary Statistics } Table 1B

[a] There is a discrepancy between the two data sources; trends in employment are still significant.

toward its employees, and this has carried into the declining employment period. Reductions are expected to continue during the coming decades, "but probably at a slower rate."[10]

Advances in technology and the resulting increases in production caused a rapid rise in worker productivity. From 1947 to 1957 productivity in refining rose at an average annual rate of 5.0 percent. Since that time output per man-hour has risen by 6.6 percent per year.[11]

OCCUPATIONAL DISTRIBUTION

Occupational distributions in the industry are significant because of the high degree of education or skills required and the concomitant relative supply of Negroes with such education and skill. There are,

10. U. S. Bureau of Labor Statistics, Division of Technological Studies, *Technological Trends in Major American Industries,* Bulletin No. 1474 (Washington: U. S. Government Printing Office, 1966), p. 182.
11. *Ibid.*

however, differences in the various sectors of the industry, which are examined below.

Exploration

Prospecting for oil is a highly specialized and scientific undertaking. Oil and gas are found by studying surface and subsurface characteristics. Professionally trained persons are needed to make estimates concerning the presence or absence of minerals. The most common are geologist, geophysicist, chemist, and electrical engineer.

Most exploration is done with the use of an instrument called a seismograph. This instrument is used, among several techniques, to record shock waves resulting from a blast beneath the surface. A seismograph crew is composed of a team of 10 to 18 persons and headed by a geophysicist. Others in the party include equipment operators, drillers, explosive handlers, and shooters.

Besides the prospecting employees, exploration work requires landmen, scouts, and draftsmen. Landmen negotiate for oil rights and keep deeds to oil and gas leases. Scouts keep track of drilling and exploration done by other firms in a particular area.

Many of these men are on salary and have received extensive formal and on-the-job training. Their work generally requires substantial travel. Few Negroes have had either the education, training, or at least until very recently, the access thereto. The occupational distribution in both exploration and production is set forth in Table 6.

Production

Production activities are considered in two parts. First the drilling for minerals, and second, the work required to bring the mineral to the surface and to storage tanks and/or crude pipelines are discussed.

Rotary drilling is the most common type. The process requires about six men. They are the rotary driller supervisor and four or five helpers. The supervisor must be able to meet a variety of emergencies and usually acquires his job only after many years of experience as a helper on a rig. The second man in charge is the derrickman. He works on a platform high up in the rig and oversees the selection of casings and drill stems to be drilled into the ground. On the floor of the rig there are two or three rotary floormen who handle pipe. Finally, a fireman operates the engines which provide drilling

TABLE 6. *Occupational Distribution in Crude Exploration and Production,*[a] *1960*

Occupation	Total Employment		Percent of Total
Professional, technical, and kindred workers	35,309		14.0
Accountants and auditors	4,923	1.9	
Engineers, technical	9,016	3.6	
Geologists and geophysicists	10,670	4.2	
Technicians, other engineering and physical sciences	3,649	1.5	
Other	7,051	2.8	
Managers, officials, and proprietors	22,986		9.1
Clerical and kindred workers	31,122		12.3
Sales workers	1,317		0.5
Craftsmen, foremen, and kindred workers	54,495		21.5
Foremen (n.e.c.)	12,969	5.1	
Mechanics and repairmen	8,763	3.4	
Stationary engineers	25,175	10.0	
Other	7,588	3.0	
Operatives and kindred workers	103,148		40.8
Mine operatives and laborers (n.e.c.)	90,490	35.8	
Truck drivers	7,764	3.1	
Other	4,894	1.9	
Service workers	1,498		0.6
Not reported	3,109		1.2
Total	252,984		100.0

Source: *U. S. Census of Population, 1960*, PC(2)7C, *Occupation by Industry*, Table 2.

[a] Crude Petroleum and Natural Gas Extraction (Census).

power. Besides the man on the rig, drilling often requires a few roustabouts who perform unskilled jobs.

Working conditions vary for drillers. Their work is where the oil is and this may be near populated areas or in the Gulf of Mexico. The work in either case is very dangerous. The men work in shifts as it is very expensive to shut down a rig. Most of the major petroleum companies contract out drilling work to independent contractors who have their own crews and who bid for this work. Drilling crews are generally either employed near the drilling site, or more usually, hired elsewhere and sent where needed. Few Negroes work as drillers except in odd laboring jobs.

Production work is less strenuous than drilling. The bulk of employment is made up of pumpers and switchers, who are generally employees of the major companies rather than contractors. These men maintain the flow of crude from the wells by inspecting and operating producing wells. They live near or in producing fields and collection tanks. Other employees are welders, carpenters, electricians, and machinists. Finally, there are production roustabouts who do the heavy physical work. Again, their jobs do not require high skill levels. (See Table 6.)

Working conditions for production men vary, depending on the location and type of equipment used. It is safer than drilling and there is very little travel for those who remain in a particular producing field.

A petroleum engineer and his staff of engineers are in charge of overall planning and supervision of drilling and production. They are professionally trained and recruited from colleges.

Pipeline

The major oil companies formerly had large numbers of hourly employees who built and maintained pipelines. Now almost all of this work is contracted out and much of it is done by machine. Nevertheless, there are a few craftsmen employed by the major oil companies. There is very little turnover. Professionally trained engineers who oversee planning and operation are in demand. Mechanics and operators are needed to run pumping stations which have large and complex equipment. Overall, however, the pipeline function is not one that employs a large number of people. (See Table 7.)

Refining and Petrochemical

Employment in refineries or petrochemical plants is highly concentrated in the operating departments—process or mechanical (maintenance) employees. Together these groups account for approximately 70 percent of the total employment. Only 25 percent of these employees are in supervisory, clerical, technical, or professional positions. The remaining 75 percent are production workers. There will very often be a large research staff working in the plant. The remaining employees will be distributed among the various staff groups necessary to operate a large industrial plant—employee relations, accounting, and plant security, to name a few.

TABLE 7. *Occupational Distribution in Petroleum and Gasoline Pipelines, 1960*

Occupation	Total Employment		Percent of Total
Professional, technical, and kindred workers	1,942		9.3
Engineers, technical	1,003	4.8	
Other	939	4.5	
Managers, officials, and proprietors	1,632		7.8
Clerical and kindred workers	3,237		15.6
Sales workers	80		0.4
Craftsmen, foremen, and kindred workers	6,802		32.7
Foremen (n.e.c.)	1,172	5.6	
Mechanics and repairmen	1,670	8.0	
Stationary engineers	2,715	13.1	
Other	1,245	6.0	
Operatives and kindred workers	5,272		25.3
Service workers	183		0.9
Laborers	1,153		5.5
Not reported	520		2.5
Total	20,821		100.0

Source: *U. S. Census of Population, 1960,* PC(2)7C, *Occupation by Industry,* Table 2.

There are a large number of engineers and scientists employed at a refinery or petrochemical plant. The majority are chemical engineers or chemists with advanced degrees. Other professions are mechanical engineering, electrical engineering, civil engineering, physics, and mathematics. Since the technology used in a refinery or petrochemical plant is highly complex and subject to rapid change and advancement, the plant manager and important line managers are usually engineers or scientists.

Production workers are either in the process, mechanical, sometimes referred to as maintenance, or labor departments. Process employment is relatively fixed according to the type of equipment and the kinds of products produced at a location. The number of mechanical employees varies according to the employment policies of the refinery. Some refineries have a "complete" mechanical department in that they have a sufficient number of workers to accomplish all of the ordinary mechanical and labor work. Others rely on private contractors to supply craftsmen and labor for varying amounts of construction and maintenance. A number of new refineries contract out all maintenance work to contractors who bring in members of building and mechanical trades unions to do this work. The well-known opposition of these unions to Negro employment seems certain to affect adversely Negro potential employment in such refineries.

Currently, most of the large refineries (150,000 plus barrels a day capacity) which do not contract out maintenance have sizeable mechanical departments. These refineries are staffed with about 60 percent of hourly mechanical employees and 40 percent of hourly process employees. (See Table 8.)

New production employees generally start in the labor department. Some of the jobs in that classification are: janitor, still cleaner, common laborer, yard labor, fork lift operator, and truck driver. Those members of the labor department who meet the qualifications of labor agreements and company policies move into the mechanical or process department.

New employees in the mechanical department progress from helper to trainee, trainee to craftsman 1st class, craftsman 1st class to sub-foreman or gang leader. Some of the most common mechanical jobs are: pipe fitter, boilermaker, brickmason, carpenter, insulator, instrument repairman, painter, machinist, electrician, special equipment operator, mechanic, welder, tinner, and rigger.

Employees in the process department start as helpers and then become assistant stillmen or assistant operators. The top jobs are stillmen and operators. The major divisions are: distillation, utility, grease, compounding, checking, and boilerhouse. These divisions may vary from firm to firm; the jobs performed are of course essentially similar.

Seniority and company promotion policy are the two most common determinants of progression. In some refineries and petrochemical plants, however, new employees enter in training programs and after a four-year period of classroom and on-the-job training become craftsmen 1st class or stillmen.

As already noted, the major oil companies that operate both refineries and petrochemical plants generally build the two operations next to one another. Production workers in both plants receive comparable wages, and usually belong to the same union. Petrochemical

TABLE 8. *Occupational Distribution in Refining, 1960*

Occupation	Total Employment		Percent of Total
Professional, technical, and kindred workers	40,335		16.0
Accountants and auditors	7,502	3.0	
Engineers, technical	11,179	4.4	
Chemists	2,892	1.2	
Other	18,762	7.4	
Managers, officials, and proprietors	14,829		5.9
Clerical and kindred workers	45,042		17.8
Sales workers	5,378		2.1
Craftsmen, foremen, and kindred workers	58,979		23.3
Foremen (n.e.c.)	13,252	5.2	
Mechanics and repairmen	12,907	4.8	
Stationary engineers	10,730	4.2	
Other	22,900	9.1	
Operatives and kindred workers	65,433		25.9
Service workers	4,297		1.7
Laborers	14,761		5.8
Not reported	3,660		1.5
Total	252,714		100.0

Source: *U. S. Census of Population, 1960*, PC(2)7C, *Occupations by Industry*, Table 2.

plants generally employ less than one-half the number of employees found in the adjoining refinery.

Approximately 30 percent of refinery employment is found in service operations related to the refining process. Almost 90 percent of these employees are in clerical, technical, or professional work.

Product Wholesaling

Product wholesaling includes two types of operations. The physical distribution of products takes place at bulk plants and terminals. Managerial control of wholesaling activities is maintained with large, regional office forces.

The work force at each distribution center is relatively small. The typical bulk plant work force will include only manual workers, a few supervisory personnel, and the necessary clerical help. The crew will vary in size with the importance of the marketing area which it supplies, with a minimum employee complement of ten or less and a maximum seldom higher than fifty workers. Possibly one-half of the jobs at the product storage area, the bulk plant, are in truck driving and delivery work. The remaining manual jobs include bulk plant operators, in some plants a few assistant operators, and automotive maintenance mechanics. (See Table 9.)

TABLE 9. *Occupational Distribution in Product Wholesaling, 1960*

Occupation	Total Employment	Percent of Total	
Professional, technical, and kindred workers	9,368		5.4
Accountants and auditors	3,982	2.3	
Engineers, technical	1,931	1.1	
Other	3,455	2.0	
Managers, officials, and proprietors	32,750		19.1
Clerical and kindred workers	39,573		23.0
Sales workers	20,020		11.7
Craftsmen, foremen, and kindred workers	12,293		7.1
Foremen (n.e.c.)	3,319	1.9	
Mechanics and repairmen	6,235	3.6	
Stationary engineers	1,575	0.9	
Other	1,164	0.7	
Operatives and kindred workers	48,192		28.1
Deliverymen	6,799	4.0	
Truck drivers	36,712	21.4	
Other	4,681	2.7	
Service workers	1,372		0.8
Laborers	6,056		3.5
Not reported	2,188		1.3
Total	171,812		100.0

Source: *U. S. Census of Population, 1960,* PC(2)7C, *Occupation by Industry,* Table 2.

Jobs which require certain skills are filled by previously trained workers. Most units are too small to warrant training programs. Generally this sector has the lowest skill requirements of any in the industry. Hiring is under the control of the local supervisory personnel.

This is one sector of the industry in which automation is not expected to have much effect although work crews on the loading rack may eventually experience slight employment reductions because of mechanical installations. The many workers driving trucks or working in the maintenance areas cannot, however, easily be replaced by mechanical equipment.

White collar employees working in product wholesaling have generally been consolidated into a small number of major offices. A few clerical employees may work out of the bulk stations, but the majority of the office and clerical employees work as members of large staffs processing paperwork for an entire marketing area. The employment explosion in data processing operations will be discussed in greater detail in a later chapter. Beyond clerical help, each sales office includes salesmen and various personnel planning marketing activities for the region. Most central marketing operations are located in large metropolitan areas.

The employment data provided for each sector indicate that the industry generally requires highly skilled personnel. This is true for both salaried and production workers. Those occupations for which Negroes are most often qualified are no longer expanding. Production workers now being hired have been selected with the expectation that they will be qualified for promotions as openings occur. No employees have been hired in recent years that are expected to remain as laborers. Too often Negroes, hired in the past as laborers, had few qualifications; these men are not now qualified to take advantage of new opportunities.

EARNINGS AND UNIONIZATION

Regardless of employment trends, the petroleum industry remains one of the highest-paying industries for the production worker. This is the result of each sector's emphasis on high skills, and also of the small proportion of total expenses represented by labor costs. In 1966, for example, production workers in "crude petroleum and natural gas production" averaged $122.26 per week and $2.87 per hour. Those employed in "petroleum refining" averaged $151.56 per week and $3.60 per hour. These wages are well above the 1966 average weekly earnings for manufacturing ($111.92), and comparable to those in such high-paying industries as contract construction ($145.51) and transportation equipment ($141.86).[12]

12. American Petroleum Institute, *op. cit.*, p. 302.

Added to the basic wage the petroleum industry offered 99.7¢ in fringe benefits; the all manufacturing average fringe benefits for the same year (1965) was 67.6¢. This represented for the petroleum industry 28 percent of the payroll costs.[13] The high costs of these benefits is founded historically in the company unions and paternalistic practices initiated by the industry in the 1920's.

Unionization

Unionization thus far in the petroleum industry, with the exception of the refining sector, has met with only limited success. The failure of the union movement to gain a strong position within the industry lies, not with the unions, but with the nature of the industry. Potentially, the vertical integration and high level of investment mean that reduced output at one level can cause great losses at all levels. In those operating areas other than refining—crude production, bulk crude transportation, and product distribution—the production units are small and widely scattered. Considerable effort and expense have been spent by national unions trying to organize them, but to no avail. These units continue largely to be unorganized or as a part of the many independent unions, often former company unions.

In the refining sector, labor-management agreements cover 90 percent of the production workers. Of this group, over 25 percent are members of small independent unions. The remaining 75 percent belong to national unions, predominantly the Oil, Chemical and Atomic Workers International Union (OCAW), the Teamster's, District 50 formerly of the United Mine Workers, and the International Union of Operating Engineers (IUOE). It is significant that the national union locals continue to bargain, with the exception of one company, Sinclair, on a plant basis. Recently, however, OCAW has won common contract termination dates in an endeavor to broaden the basis of bargaining. It remains to be seen whether union coverage can be increased as a result.

Even with the high degree of unionization in refining, the unions have been able to achieve few successes in bargaining. Although wages and benefits have remained high, this is in part attributable to the paternalistic practices which existed in the oil industry for many years. Today, management has chosen to maintain the highly

---

13. *Ibid.*, p. 304.

acceptable economic position of its employees. The rapid advances in refining technology over the past thirty years have both reduced the number of production workers and the importance of each man to the production process. Consequently, the strike as it is utilized in other industries is only of limited value. Even when the work force does vote to walk out, "the supervisory force . . . can operate the plant at 50 percent or more of capacity."[14] In those cases in which a strike might affect plant output significantly, the products of other refineries operated by the company can be diverted to the marketing area affected. Thus, no union group, regardless of size, can be expected to gain the prominence and power enjoyed by several of the national unions in other major industries. The exception might occur if a number of refineries can be struck simultaneously to increase union pressure, but even in this case supervisors can maintain considerable output. Similarly, the threat of the strike in other sectors of the industry is diminished by the ownership of alternate crude production fields and transportation facilities. Finally, the possibility of union or employee action is further diminished by a surprisingly high degree of loyalty expressed by the employees toward the various companies.

Although the industry has refused to bargain on other than a local basis, a general pattern is usually established by negotiations with Standard Oil (N. J.), American Oil (Standard of Indiana), or Sinclair. Generally, the rank-and-file members of the major unions have traditionally maintained more power in their hands and at the local level than most other national unions. In the last few years, new OCAW leadership and coalition attempts by other unions could result in a changed pattern.

In negotiating both independent and national unions commonly continue past the termination date of the contract. With independent contracts, a provision is usually included to provide for the automatic extension of the contract if both sides agree. Strikes to gain contract demands are now very infrequent; those strikes which do occur are typically over job security issues.

Union racial policies will be analyzed in ensuing sections of the study to ascertain their effect on industry employment policies. The

14. Floyd Brandt, *Independent and National Unionism in the Oil Refining Industry* (unpublished Ph.D. dissertation, Harvard University, 1960), p. 11.

high degree of local autonomy in both national and independent unions, however, obviously precludes any effective national control of local properties. As in similar cases in other industries, this, in effect, has meant little national union interference with discriminatory practices at the local level.

INDUSTRIAL LOCATION

The location of employment units in the petroleum industry, as in other industries, affects the number and nature of Negro employment. Location is significant in two ways: nearness to centers of Negro population; and accessibility in terms of local transportation to plants from areas of Negro residence concentration. Both play a role in determining Negro employment in the petroleum industry.

Exploration and Production

The exploration and production of crude oil has traditionally been a southwestern industry. In 1966 the three states of Texas, Louisiana, and Oklahoma produced 1,956,863,000 barrels of crude or 65 percent of the total. The other major production area, California, produced 345,295,000 barrels or 11 percent of the total. The remaining crude produced in 1966 came from 27 other states.[15] The relative importance of the four leading states has been increasing in recent years.

Within each of the states, oil wells may be found in almost any location, from within city limits to isolated desert regions. The oil must be produced where it is located. Important crude producing areas in southern Louisiana, the Gulf Coast areas of Texas, and the Los Angeles area of California have large Negro populations near them. The other important regions in western and northeastern Texas, Oklahoma, Kansas, Wyoming, and New Mexico have, however, few if any Negroes residing in neighboring areas. The possibility of increased Negro employment in crude exploration and production is therefore not great.

Transportation

Transportation facilities for either crude oil or petroleum products extend throughout the United States. Pipelines which carry the largest

15. American Petroleum Institute, *op. cit.*, p. 41.

tonnage of crude oil and products are located either in the oil fields or between inland towns. Water transportation is generally less costly but few towns and cities have access to river or ocean ports. Refineries in 1966 received 75 percent of their crude oil by pipelines.[16] Crude gathering pipelines (from oil fields) or crude trunk lines (to refineries) are located in 35 states. Leading states in crude oil pipeline mileage include Texas, Kansas, Oklahoma, Illinois, and Missouri. Product pipeline mileage is located in 44 states, with Texas, Pennsylvania, and Kansas as leading states. Generally states with high mileage are important crude producers, important refiners, or states lying between the oil fields and the refineries.

Few of the inland areas through which pipelines run have large Negro populations. Pipelines lie between areas that may be expected to have concentrations of Negroes.

Trucking is centered around product distribution centers, and will be discussed in that section.

Refining

Important refining locations have moved from the oil fields to consumption centers and seaport distribution centers. By shifting locations, management can better avoid the possibility of oil field depletion and also be more responsive to the consumer. Finally, the shipment cost of crude oil is significantly below that of refined products.

There are four main refining regions in the United States: the Philadelphia-New York corridor, the Chicago-Gary, Indiana, area, the Louisiana-Texas Gulf Coast area, and the areas of California near Los Angeles and San Francisco. Total state refining capacity for each of these areas accounted for 71 percent of United States capacity in 1966. (See Table 10.)

Nearly all large plants (50,000 barrels or more per day) are located within commuting distance (25 miles) of large Negro communities. A Department of Labor study made in December 1965 placed 82 percent of 73,318 refining production workers within Standard Metropolitan Statistical areas.[17] In view of the trend toward Negro concentration in the large cities, Negroes might be expected to repre-

16. *Ibid.*, p. 149.
17. U. S. Department of Labor, *Handbook of Labor Statistics, 1967*, Bulletin No. 1555 (Washington: Government Printing Office, 1968), p. 175.

TABLE 10. *Capacity of Operating Refineries, 1966*

State	Number of Refineries	Capacity	Percent of Total
California	31	1,407,400	13.5
Illinois-Indiana	24	1,185,815	11.4
Pennsylvania-New Jersey	19	1,104,100	10.6
Louisiana-Texas	62	3,693,882	35.5
32 Other States	124	3,021,250	29.0
Total	260	10,412,447	100.0

Source: American Petroleum Institute, *Petroleum Facts and Figures, 1967*, p. 77.

sent a high proportion of the work force in plants so located. This study will attempt to show why this has not been true. One reason is that transit facilities from Negro residence areas to refineries are often quite poor.

Product Wholesaling

Petroleum bulk stations and terminals are located where they can best meet the needs of service stations and other retailing outlets. Thus, these locations are closely related with population concentrations throughout the nation. Moreover, a high population means larger facilities and greater employment opportunities. Thus this sector of the industry may provide greater opportunities for Negro employment in the future.

Sales offices are located generally in the largest cities. A large, centrally located city is chosen by the company in each of its major marketing regions. Among other cities used by one or more companies are New York, Chicago, Atlanta, Houston, and Los Angeles —all centers of Negro population.

In general, then, industrial location poses some problems for Negro employment in the petroleum industry, but the industry's concentration is similar to that of the Negro population in a number of areas.

CHAPTER III.

Negro Employment Practices, 1940 and Before

Three major characteristics regarding Negro employment are found in 1940. First, there was an almost total lack of Negro employees in salaried jobs throughout the petroleum industry. Second, there was a large concentration of Negroes in the southern refining industry who were performing unskilled work. Third, in most cases where there were sizable numbers of Negroes employed, segregation and discriminatory practices were evident.

SALARIED EMPLOYMENT

Negroes held fewer than 1 percent of all refinery and production white collar, professional, and managerial positions in the South in 1940.[18] This is believed to be accurate for the remainder of the United States. At this time few companies had employment policies which promised nondiscrimination in petroleum or any other industry, and even those who made an effort to upgrade Negroes made no significant effort to employ them in salaried jobs. Furthermore, few Negroes aspired to these jobs or had the requisite education and skills which these jobs required. For example, in New York City male Negroes accounted for only 2 percent of all clerical and sales employment.[19] Generally, female Negroes were also not employed in white collar jobs. In Houston, Texas, female Negroes represented less than 1 percent of the female clerical work force.[20]

---

18. *U. S. Census of Population, 1940,* Vol. III, *The Labor Force,* Part 1, Table 83.
19. *Ibid.,* Part 4, Table 13.
20. *Ibid.,* Part 5, Table 13.

HOURLY EMPLOYMENT

Negro employment was substantially higher in the hourly classification. Refining provided the largest source of employment. (See Table 11.) Approximately 71 percent of the Negroes employed in refining worked in the South, where they accounted for 6 percent of the work force.[21] In the Northeast, Negroes represented only 2 percent of the work force. In the North Central and Western regions, they represented an almost negligible percentage of the refinery labor force.[22]

Negroes had a long history of working in the southern refining industry. The primary use of Negroes was to meet the refineries' demands for unskilled work caused by a scarcity of industrial labor in this region. By 1940, Negroes made up a substantial percentage of the unskilled work force. Approximately 77 percent of the nonwhite males were laborers, 12 percent operatives, 8 percent service, and 2 percent were craftsmen.[23] Undoubtedly these craftsmen were found in the trowel trades (bricklaying, masonry, cement, and plastering work) which Negroes have dominated in this area since slavery days. Negroes were similarly concentrated in the Northeast with 62 percent in labor and 4 percent in crafts.[24]

Fewer Negroes were employed in exploration and production work (see Table 12). Ninety-four percent of Negroes employed in this function were in the South; yet even here they represented less than 1 percent of the work force.[25] Negroes found employment difficult because there is less demand for unskilled labor in drilling and production work. For example, over 70 percent of the nonwhite males who were employed in this function were operatives.[26] Furthermore, the size of employment at drilling and production locations is much smaller than at refineries. Thus, Negroes were more likely to be excluded from the drilling crews where close personal relationships were likely to develop. Travel and public lodging were often required of drilling crews and this hindered Negro employment because many restaurants and lodging facilities refused to accommodate Negroes.

---

21. *Ibid.*, Part 1, Tables 76 and 77.
22. *Ibid.*, Table 77.
23. *Ibid.*, Table 83.
24. *Ibid.*, Parts 3-5, Table 20.
25. *Ibid.*, Part 1, Table 77.
26. *Ibid.*, Table 83.

TABLE 11. *Refining*
Total Employed Persons by Race and Sex, 1940-1960

	All Employees			Male			Female		
Year	Total	Negro	Percent Negro	Total	Negro	Percent Negro	Total	Negro	Percent Negro
1940	178,019	5,332	3.0	164,794	5,274	3.2	13,225	58	0.4
1950	258,210	10,140	3.9	229,380	9,960	4.3	28,830	180	0.6
1960	252,714	7,866	3.1	222,716	7,504	3.4	29,998	362	1.2

Sources: *U. S. Census of Population:*
1960: PC(2)7F, *Industrial Characteristics,* Table 3.
1950: PE No. 1D, *Industrial Characteristics,* Table 2.
1940: Vol. III, *The Labor Force,* Part 1, Table 76.

TABLE 12. *Crude Petroleum and Natural Gas Extraction*
Total Employed Persons by Race and Sex, 1940-1960

	All Employees			Male			Female		
Year	Total	Negro	Percent Negro	Total	Negro	Percent Negro	Total	Negro	Percent Negro
1940	183,619	909	0.5	178,522	891	0.5	5,097	18	0.4
1950	230,940	1,440	0.6	218,250	1,350	0.6	12,690	90	0.7
1960	252,984	1,722	0.7	231,563	1,561	0.7	21,421	161	0.8

Sources: *U. S. Census of Population:*
1960: PC(2)7F, *Industrial Characteristics,* Table 3.
1950: PE No. 1D, *Industrial Characteristics,* Table 2.
1940: Vol. III, *The Labor Force,* Part 1, Table 76.

Finally, much of the production work was done in areas where there were few Negroes (such as Oklahoma and Western Texas); and local labor was utilized.

Working Conditions

Negroes were hired below the standards set up for whites. Prior to World War II, white applicants generally were required to have better than a ninth grade education. Negroes had to be able only to do hard work. In some plants all new hires started in the same labor department. In others, there were white and Negro departments. In both cases, the results were the same: Negroes did not enter into lines of progression out of the labor department. In some plants, Negroes were precluded by labor contracts from moving out of the department, but in most cases, these contracts merely institutionalized the status quo which management had inaugurated. In others, there were gentlemen's agreements, backed by strong social pressures, that Negroes would not bid on traditional white jobs and whites would not bid on Negro jobs.

Negroes performed much of the heavy physical work required in constructing refineries and in repairing them. They worked with craftsmen but were not given formal training except occasionally in the trowel trades. Negroes also worked in the operating department where they cleaned stills and other equipment. The wages paid to members of the labor department were the lowest. Moreover, it was common for whites doing similar work to receive a higher rate than was paid Negroes.

Unions and Segregation

The large Texas Gulf Coast and Louisiana refineries were the target of several union organization drives during the 1930's. Negroes often helped the white members win elections because they represented a large segment of those eligible to vote. Following these elections, separate locals for white and Negro members were frequently established. The Negro union leaders apparently were often happy with this situation because it allowed them some control over their own matters. Segregated locals, certified under the Wagner Act, would elect joint bargaining committees. The white local was usually assured a majority vote on contract issues and the segregated locals added a further bar to movement for Negroes out of the unskilled jobs.

Other aspects of the work environment were also segregated. Shower-rooms, toilets, drinking fountains, cafeterias, and eating places were all segregated. Company-sponsored events, such as testimonials and athletic clubs were also segregated.

These characteristics persisted despite efforts by many parties to improve the conditions of Negro employment in the petroleum industry. When combined with declining employment and the more rigorous skill requirements of ever more automated equipment, they form the basis for present difficulties encountered in attempts to improve the conditions of Negroes in the petroleum industry.

CHAPTER IV.

Early Attempts to Upgrade Negro Employment, 1940–1960

Overall progress for Negroes in petroleum during the period 1940-1960 was small, but important breakthroughs were made. Almost entirely, these changes took place in refining and particularly in the southern plants. Negroes in hourly job classifications were most affected by these changes.

Three factors were primarily responsible for changes in the characteristics of Negro employment, which have been described in Chapter III. They were (1) the demand for employees; (2) company employment practices, both those in general and those specifically directed to Negroes; and (3) activity arising from Executive Orders of the President of the United States.

WORLD WAR II TO THE KOREAN WAR

World War II had two effects on Negro employment in petroleum. It created a labor shortage and it brought about federal recognition and response to discrimination practices in American industry. The latter developments are discussed first.

Early Federal Intervention

President Roosevelt was the first President to require private industries with defense contracts with the federal government to agree not to discriminate against Negroes in regard to employment opportunities. The President issued Executive Order No. 8802 in 1941 and another Executive Order No. 9346 in 1943. The latter order, as did the first, required federal contractors to agree: "not to discriminate against any employee or applicant for employment because of race, creed, color or national origin."[27] It went further, however, in its attempt to eliminate discrimination in all other aspects of the employment relationship. The second Order created a Committee on Fair Employment Practice which was to aid the federal agencies in methods of compliance with the nondiscrimination clause. Final disposition of noncompliance charges rested with the President.[28]

Negroes were the largest group to make use of the Order. Twenty complaints were filed against oil concerns holding government contracts. A particularly significant complaint was filed by an employee of the Shell Oil refinery at Houston, Texas.

The complaint alleged that management and Local 367, of the Oil Workers International Union, barred Negroes from rising above the levels of laborer, janitor, and gardener. The company and union agreed to change the contract and to submit the issue of wage rates, which were also allegedly discriminatory, to the War Labor Board. The company then attempted to upgrade seven qualified Negroes. The white craftsmen said no and the company backed down. A shake-up in union leadership resulted when the local officers who favored integration were ousted. Tensions rose and a strike followed. The men returned to work after voting to strike over the upgrading issue. Management made a wage offer to the Negroes but they felt it was insufficient. The war ended soon afterward; the committee, which President Truman extended, was abolished by Congress in 1946, and no results occurred at the refinery.[29]

This case illustrates the types of problems which were present in attempts to upgrade Negroes employed in the petroleum industry and often in industry generally. White employees, union and nonunion, were generally opposed to improving the job status of Negroes. Managements were not eager to implement changes which they thought would produce work stoppages. Furthermore, strong public opinion regarding enforcement of the nondiscrimination clause was lacking. In 1953, a presidential committee, established to study discrimination,

27. Executive Order No. 8802, 6 Fed. Reg. 13652 (1941).

28. The Committee had a salaried chairman. Regional offices were established to aid enforcement. The Committee had the power to hold hearings and to take "appropriate" steps to correct noncompliance.

29. See Fair Employment Practice Committee, Final Report, 1946 (Washington: U. S. Government Printing Office, 1947), p. 23.

found that the nondiscrimination clause, which had been required continuously since 1943, was "forgotten, dead and buried."[30]

Other efforts by the government during World War II to break down racial inequalities in the work environment were more limited but more practical and effective. The War Labor Board prohibited "colored laborer" and "white laborer" classifications where pay rates were unequal for the same work.[31] But the War Labor Board refused to condemn the practice of separate facilities and a seniority clause was not condemned unless it was exclusionary on its face.[32] Despite these problems, there was created an awareness by some that a problem existed. After World War II, several petroleum companies rewrote their employment policies expressly to prohibit discrimination because of race or color in order to move more easily toward a fairer employment posture.

The World War II Labor Shortage

Economics proved to be more effective than government action. The demand for refining employees rose during the war because of labor shortages and increased production. Construction of new and better equipment and demands for repair work meant large numbers of maintenance employees were needed. Negroes benefitted. For example, the labor shortage induced one major southern refinery to abandon its policy of employing no Negroes. By 1947, there were 400 Negroes employed at that plant.

Refining employment continued to rise after the war, reaching an all-time high in 1954. Negro employment rose in all regions of the country as a result.

The gains made in areas outside the South reflect in large part the increase in Negro population in those areas after the war. In the South, refineries continued to employ Negroes according to their requirements for unskilled labor. By 1950, at least five refineries in the Louisiana and Texas Gulf Coast area employed over 250 Negroes each. Nevertheless, as the data in Table 13 show, only in the West did Negroes increase their proportion of jobs as well as their number of jobs, between 1940 and 1950.

30. See 32 LRRM 81.

31. *In re Southport Petroleum Company*, 8 WLR 714 (1942).

32. *In re Western Electric Company*, 13 WLR 12 (1943).

TABLE 13. *Negro Male Employees in Refining*[a] *by Regions, 1940-1960*

	1940		1950		1960	
Region	Number	Percent	Number	Percent	Number	Percent
Northeast	2,045	26.1	3,351	24.2	2,095	19.6
North Central	784	10.0	1,803	13.1	1,475	13.8
South	4,936	63.0	8,206	59.4	6,697	62.7
West	66	0.9	454	3.3	415	3.9
Total	7,831	100.0	13,814	100.0	10,682	100.0

Sources: *U. S. Census of Population:*
1960: PC(1), DUS, *U. S. Summary: Detailed Characteristics*, Table 260.
1950: Vol. II, *Characteristics of the Population*, Part 1, Table 161.
1940: Vol. III, *The Labor Force*, Part 1, Table 77.

[a] Includes the manufacture of petroleum and coal products. Refining is approximately 90 percent of total.

Upgrading Experiences

Prior to 1954, few Negroes in refineries experienced upward job mobility. As before 1940, most Negroes were hired into the labor department and could expect to remain there performing manual and unskilled work. This pattern, however, was challenged to a degree by changing job requirements in the post war refineries. Machines began doing much of the work previously performed by labor gangs. Companies with large numbers of Negroes began looking for work for these Negroes. At least in the South, managements were presented with a problem because the job of machine operator was generally considered outside the Negroes' traditional work status. It "belonged" to whites.

Some interesting situations developed. For example, in many plants, Negroes were not permitted to operate motorized equipment. Nevertheless, Negroes working in warehouses would operate fork lift trucks while inside the building. When a load reached the loading platform a white worker would take over. No one protested this type of arrangement.

Attempts to broaden Negro work formally generally met with resistance. At one refinery in Louisiana management in an attempt to find work for Negroes moved a group from construction work to semiskilled work in a process department which was previously all white. There were segregated locals at this location and the white local contested the move in court, alleging breach of contract and custom. Management remained firm, the case was dismissed, and the change became permanent.

Some progress at other plants in the South was also accomplished. By 1950, Negroes in the operative classification had increased to approximately 5 percent and 7 percent in Texas and Louisiana, respectively.[33] This expanded job territory was, for the most part, still within the traditional labor departments. Thus the condition of Negroes employed in the refineries was not significantly different than in 1940, although there was some improvement.

The major change was the increase in total Negro employment in refining. Unfortunately, this proved a temporary boon for Negroes, as we shall discuss below.

FROM THE KOREAN WAR TO 1960

Refining employment, as did employment in the other functions in the petroleum industry, reached a peak in the early 1950's and then began to decline after 1953. The reasons are significant for any study of Negro labor.

Employment Decline

By 1960, there were 35,000 fewer refinery employees than in 1953.[34] There were several reasons for this decline. First, there was a net decrease of approximately 20 refineries during this period. The less efficient refineries which were not capable of producing large percentages of gasoline per barrel of crude by the use of cracking principles found it difficult to compete with those that did. The major oil refineries began shutting down smaller units and concentrating on further expansion of large refineries. These had provided the majority of wartime fuels and other substances and they possessed the latest technology. Second, payrolls of operating plants were cut. Refineries were caught in a cost-price squeeze during the late 1950's

33. *U. S. Census of Population, 1950*, Vol. II, *Characteristics of the Population*, Parts 18 and 43 (percentages estimated from Tables 73 and 77).
34. American Petroleum Institute, *Petroleum Facts and Figures, 1959* (New York: American Petroleum Institute, 1959), p. 88.

and early 1960's. Many refineries had excess employees, primarily in the maintenance functions, as a result of their historic disinclination to reduce staff under any condition. This attitude was altered by economic necessity after 1954 and substantial layoffs occurred. Moreover the trend toward larger distillation units had an impact on the total manpower needed in process departments. It is possible to operate a 100,000 barrel-per-day still with the same manpower as a 25,000 barrel-per-day still. Consequently new refineries did not create a compensating demand for process employees. Thus, the hiring of hourly workers virtually ceased in the refineries for more than a decade.

Finally, refineries began contracting out construction and maintenance work. The degree of contracting varies by company and by location. Most refineries contract for major maintenance work such as turnarounds, new construction, and major damage repair. Some contract all maintenance and unskilled labor. The trend toward contracting was also induced by rising labor costs. Labor costs for both skilled and unskilled work typically rise faster in refineries than outside. Moreover, many maintenance employees are not used 100 percent of the time. And the time between turnarounds has been widened so that they are necessary only every two or three years.

The cutback in new hires, the trend toward contracting maintenance work and the layoffs all adversely affected efforts to improve the condition of Negroes in the refining function. Negroes were hit hardest by the layoffs as they were concentrated in those jobs which were reduced and/or eliminated.

Between 1950 and 1960, the number of Negroes in petroleum refining fell from 10,140 to 7,866 and the proportion of Negroes in this sector of the industry declined from 3.9 to 3.1 percent. (See Table 11.) In 1960, the unemployment rate for all males in refining operations was 2.2 percent while it was 5.9 percent for nonwhites.[35]

Nixon Committee Activity and Pressures

Upon taking office, President Eisenhower issued Executive Order 10479 which launched the President's Committee on Government

35. *U. S. Census of Population, 1960*, Vol. I, *Characteristics of the Population*, Part 1, Table 213.

Contracts. The Committee, headed by the then Vice-President Richard M. Nixon, had authority to receive complaints, make investigations, and recommend action to the various government agencies. The Committee, hereafter referred to as the Nixon Committee, had no express enforcement power. As under earlier executive orders dealing with this problem, it was up to the agencies to threaten breach of contract for noncompliance or to withhold contracts for the same reason.

In 1955 the Committee received complaints against several Texas Gulf Coast and Louisiana refineries. Consequently, it began an investigation of Negro employment in this industry. The findings of its survey made in 1958 are shown in Table 14.

By far the majority of Negroes were in the South and Northeast. The Nixon Committee attempted to exert its influence to improve Negro employment in those areas where there were sizable Negro populations. Its efforts, however, were hindered because of the decline in refinery employment. The Committee then turned to the task of upgrading the positions of those Negroes who were already hired. The emphasis was in the southern refining industry.

TABLE 14. *Negro Employment in Refining by Regions, 1958*
28 Locations, 15 Companies

Region	Total	Negro	Percent Negro	White Collar	Negro	Percent Negro	Production	Negro	Percent Negro
Northeast	10,322	685	6.6	2,389	15	0.6	8,233	670	8.1
North Central	13,404	301	2.2	3,527	—	—	9,679	301	3.1
South	29,986	3,577	11.9	6,462	10	0.2	23,019	3,567	15.5
Far West	15,369	114	0.7	3,566	2	0.1	11,803	112	0.9

Source: "Oil Industry Study." Memorandum to Vice-President Richard M. Nixon, Chairman, President's Committee on Government Contracts, 1958.

Regional Definitions:

Northeast —New England and Mid-Atlantic.
North Central—Ohio, Indiana, Illinois, and adjacent areas.
South —Texas, Louisiana, and Southeast.
Far West —Pacific States.

Blue Collar Employment[36] *and Qualifications*

As stated above, it was the general practice in the South to hire Negroes for the labor department where they had their own segregated lines of seniority into traditional Negro jobs. Whites were hired as general helpers and they bid on jobs leading into the process or maintenance department. In some refineries this practice was part of the collective bargaining agreement while in others it was just customary. The practice of separate lines of seniority was formally terminated as a result of court action by Negroes and negotiations by the Nixon Committee during 1956-1960. Henceforth Negroes and whites would start in the same job classification and would work under the same rules governing seniority and other criteria for promotion.

At this point, however, past practices presented a difficult problem in regard to Negro employees who had previously been hired. Some of these Negroes wanted past practices corrected immediately. They felt that plant seniority should determine job assignments *outside* the labor department and that they should be promoted immediately.

Management, on the other hand, wanted a degree of control over entry jobs into the process and maintenance departments. They wanted to ensure that individuals with work assignments in these areas had the qualifications to perform their jobs safely and efficiently. This attitude was similar to managements' dealings with white employees hired after World War II. The modern cracking refinery is complicated and thermal units are very dangerous. The control of these units is handled from intricate instrument panels and requires an alert, responsible, and reasonably educated and experienced operator. Moreover, the men who repair this equipment need many of these same characteristics plus considerable skill training.

As a consequence, managements increased the qualification standards for operators and maintenance men after the war. Most refineries required white applicants to have a high school education. Negroes, however, were employed regardless of educational attainment, and indeed often with as little as possible, for at the time of

36. For a vivid discussion of Negro employment in the southern refining industry, see F. Ray Marshall, "Some Factors Influencing the Upgrading of Negroes in the Southern Petroleum Refining Industry," *Social Forces,* Vol. XLIII (December 1963), pp. 185-192.

their hire, it was understood that they would always be utilized in unskilled, labor work.

To insure qualifications, managements at this point proposed to use testing to determine which Negroes could meet previous standards established for whites. Some effort was made to induce Negroes to attend schools to upgrade their educational level. The tests were designed to demonstrate the employee's understanding of mathematics, ability to read and write, mechanical comprehension, and learning ability. Testing of whites was not widespread prior to 1955. Since then, the customary procedure has been to require all applicants to have a high school education and to pass these tests. Negroes were not tested at first because they were not considered candidates for jobs above the labor grades. When these jobs were opened up to Negroes, managements usually insisted that they be tested. Negroes objected because they were not job applicants, but rather employees with many years' seniority. In fact, as we shall note, Negroes fared poorly with tests not only because of educational deficiencies, lack of training and background, and other cultural heritages of discrimination, but because as a group they were employed for their fitness as laborers, not because of fitness for promotion.

Unionism and Seniority

Managements did not present a unified front on whether to retain departmental seniority or to provide plant seniority. The former is not discriminatory, *per se*, but when combined with discrimination, it can become a vehicle to perpetuate discrimination even after the overt discriminatory practices have been abolished. For example, a Negro with twenty years' plant seniority may have been confined to the labor department all these years. If after twenty years, he was allowed to bid on a job in the process department, but departmental seniority prevailed, he would be the least senior man in processing. Although his *plant* seniority might outrank all others in processing, he would be the first laid off. In some plants where one bids out of a department, he loses his seniority therein. Obviously Negroes who have been confined to a department by discrimination would use their plant seniority to bid on other jobs once they are permitted to bid outside "Negro jobs." Some managements favored this; most, however, preferred departmental seniority because it involves less plant movement either of whites or Negroes, and is therefore a less disruptive and costly system.

Generally, white employees and their locals were opposed to efforts to upgrade Negroes. At several refineries, near riot conditions existed when managements began recognizing the right of Negroes to fill previously white jobs. No strikes were, however, called for this reason during the period. The shortage of jobs and the existing layoffs perhaps acted as a restraining influence, but it also made the fight for jobs more bitter.

The Oil Workers International Union (later the Oil, Chemical and Atomic Workers) was in a difficult position with regard to the lawsuits and investigations by the Nixon Committee. The International Union supported the Negroes who filed suits against locals for discriminatory practices. It took, however, no direct action to enforce the International's nondiscriminatory policy. Obviously its weakness and the ability of the locals to defy it precluded any such action.

The Nixon Committee attempted to exert moral and economic pressure on managements, unions, and employees in regard to correcting discriminatory practices. The Committee took the position that hiring and promotion standards were management's and union's prerogative as long as the standards were applied equally to whites and Negroes. Consequently, the Committee did not take a position regarding seniority or testing. Most refineries continued to use departmental seniority rather than plant, and to test, both of which, in turn, supported the *status quo* for Negro employees.

The outcome of the abolishment of separate, discriminatory lines of seniority and the testing of Negroes to determine their eligibility to move out of labor departments varied from refinery to refinery. At one location, 78 Negroes out of 741 had moved into previously "white" jobs by 1959. At another, only 3 Negroes out of 250 moved into higher jobs. The majority of refineries in the Southwest had experiences similar to the latter location. By 1960, only approximately 7 percent of Negroes employed in this region had moved into higher job classifications.

Efforts to upgrade Negroes were also hampered by declining employment and the low turnover of personnel in refineries. A major obstacle, however, was the requirements for advancement set by managements and in some cases opposition by unions. Few Negroes could pass the tests. Moreover, Negroes at refineries which had departmental seniority rules could not progress as fast as those Negroes who could use plant seniority for the reasons already noted.

Little progress was made in the South regarding separate, segregated facilities. In other refining areas, however, several state equal employment laws which prohibited this practice, were either enacted or impending by 1960, and by then this practice was mostly nonexistent in refineries outside of the South.

White Collar Employment

White collar employment increased substantially between 1950-1960. In 1950, only approximately 20 percent of refining personnel were in white collar occupations while in 1960 the percentage had risen to about 40. The same pattern was occurring in the other functions. Companies were hiring in these occupations throughout the period 1955-1960. During the late 1950's, the Nixon Committee emphasized the need for equal employment opportunity in this sector.

The major growth and turnover in the industry was in the professional and clerical fields. Males continued to dominate the former and females comprised a majority of clerical jobs.

Despite the concern of the Nixon Committee, few Negroes were able to take advantage of employment opportunities in these two areas. (See Table 14.) Negroes were still not in a good position to compete for professional jobs in the petroleum industry. Few Negroes studied in the science and engineering fields. Those who did were reluctant to work for industries such as petroleum because they were, in general, not convinced that they would be given equal treatment. Finally, managements were skeptical, and perhaps justifiably so, of the Negro college graduate who matriculated at a Negro school. This feeling may have been strongest in the South. Some colleges in the South, such as the University of Texas, were integrated but there were not many Negro students, and few of those were in engineering or science.

The situation with clerical jobs was somewhat similar. Relatively few Negro females had clerical skills in 1960. Those that did were very reluctant to seek employment in traditionally white offices. And Negro females had to take a series of tests which were required for all applicants. The tests covered grammar, punctuation, capitalization, spelling, and vocabulary. Negro females generally scored lower than whites on these tests, thus their chances for employment were reduced. In 1960, only 1.4 percent of females employed by refineries were Negroes.[37]

CONCLUDING REMARKS

Prodded by the federal government, specific steps were being taken by the petroleum industry to improve the status of Negro employment during the period 1955 to 1960, but progress was slow. Action was concentrated in refining as this was the function with large concentrations of hourly employees and refineries were often near areas with many Negroes in the population. Declining employment was a serious detriment to progress here, and past discrimination was perpetuated by the backgrounds of Negro laborers, union discrimination, departmental seniority, and testing. In the white collar fields efforts were hampered by lack of communication between petroleum employer (and other industries) and the Negro community, and by a dearth of qualified Negro applicants.

---

37. Based on U. S. Census of Population data.

CHAPTER V.

Affirmative Action and Negro Employment, 1960–1968

The decade of the 1960's has witnessed a number of changes in racial employment policies in the petroleum industry. Prodded by the federal government, the industry began to re-examine its policies in the early 1960's, and to move toward upgrading of Negroes on its payrolls. Then, as prosperity continued, some employment expansion occurred which aided the institution of newly adopted affirmative action policies and commenced showing noticeable results.

DEVELOPMENT OF AFFIRMATIVE POLICIES, 1960-1964

The early part of the decade saw more policy and procedural changes than substantive changes in Negro employment. Table 15, which includes data for nine major companies, shows that in 1964 Negroes were still concentrated in the traditional blue collar jobs. Nevertheless, changes were occurring which were necessary preludes to substantive action later. Moreover, these changes were especially significant in the South.

For example, educational requirements for bidding on jobs were relaxed or abolished in several large refineries. Also, the tests which were used to determine employee eligibility to bid on jobs outside the labor department were simplified. Nevertheless, few Negroes entered previously white jobs. Table 16 shows that employment in all branches of the petroleum industry continued to fall sharply in the 1960-1964 period. In the face of these economic realities, there was little opportunity for management to employ additional Negroes (or whites). Moreover, any attempt to expand opportunities for Negroes was certain to run into opposition from existing white employees

TABLE 15. *Petroleum Industry*
Employment by Race, Sex, and Occupational Group
Total United States—9 Companies, 1964

Occupational Group	All Employees			Male			Female		
	Total	Negro	Percent Negro	Total	Negro	Percent Negro	Total	Negro	Percent Negro
Officials and managers	10,942	19	0.2	10,896	19	0.2	46	—	—
Professionals	16,464	36	0.2	16,222	35	0.2	242	1	0.4
Technicians	7,197	41	0.6	6,604	38	0.6	593	3	0.5
Sales workers	8,295	170	2.0	8,289	170	2.1	6	—	—
Office and clerical	24,165	324	1.3	10,845	133	1.2	13,320	191	1.4
Total white collar	67,063	590	0.9	52,856	395	0.7	14,207	195	1.4
Craftsmen	25,625	229	0.9	25,594	229	0.9	31	—	—
Operatives	19,893	873	4.4	19,258	871	4.5	635	2	0.3
Laborers	4,243	692	16.3	4,051	692	17.1	192	—	—
Service workers	5,058	399	7.9	4,339	373	8.6	719	26	3.6
Total blue collar	54,819	2,193	4.0	53,242	2,165	4.1	1,577	28	1.8
Total	121,882	2,783	2.3	106,098	2,560	2.4	15,784	223	1.4

Source: Data in authors' possession.

TABLE 16. *Total Employment for Major Petroleum Companies by Functions for United States, 1960 and 1964*

Functions	Number of Employees	
	1960	1964
Refining	125,356	93,516
Crude exploration and production	88,380	60,594
Pipeline transportation	21,810	13,073
Wholesaling and marketing	119,220	103,872
Research and engineering	9,566	14,163

Source: American Petroleum Institute, *Petroleum Facts and Figures, 1965*, p. 306.

who must surely have been concerned about their job security. This was a period when refineries were not hiring hourly personnel, layoffs were occurring at many locations, and possibilities for upward job mobility were greatly reduced.

White Collar Employment

White collar work in the 1960-1964 period offered the best possibilities for improved Negro job opportunities as hiring continued in these classifications. Companies began making determined efforts to hire Negroes for these jobs. Progress was made, albeit small. Because of inferior educational opportunities and accomplishments and past discriminatory practices, few Negroes had the qualifications to apply to petroleum companies; if they did, they also had great opportunities elsewhere and were difficult to recruit. Moreover, many Negroes probably did not believe that past practices were in fact abolished and hence were reluctant to apply for jobs with petroleum companies. As a result, the actual number of Negroes employed in white collar work during this period was not great. Nevertheless a number of breakthroughs did occur in that Negroes obtained jobs in several companies that had previously not employed them in salaried classifications.

Texas and Louisiana Refinery Developments

A final major development in this period occurred in key southern locations. Texas refineries began integrating facilities in 1963. Elimination of separate sanitary facilities, locker rooms, cafeterias, etc. was started by some companies and completed by others. Segregated white and colored local unions were also merged at this time.

In Louisiana, integration moved more slowly. The state vigorously defended its Jim Crow laws requiring separate sanitary and convenience facilities despite repeated judicial nullification of many such discriminatory practices. Until the passage of the Civil Rights Act of 1964, Louisiana refineries continued to operate under state legislation. In 1964, with state legislation clearly pre-empted by the new federal Act, Louisiana refineries finally began integrating facilities. The practice of separate white and colored local unions also ended at this time in Louisiana.

AFFIRMATIVE ACTION, 1965-1968

Beginning in 1965, three major factors have affected Negro employment in the industry. First, many refineries initiated their first hiring programs since the work-force reductions of the late 1950's. About this time, retirements were reducing employment totals below those necessary for efficient operations. In addition, prosperity brought increased consumer demand for petroleum products and this in turn was responsible for renewed hiring efforts. As a result, employment in most units either stabilized or actually increased in this period. Automation which has so often reduced employment in the petroleum industry had the opposite effect in one sector in this period. An especially sharp increase occurred in the number of data processing and computer-related employees. Several companies have more than doubled their staffs in these fields since 1963.

A second factor affecting Negro employment in this period was that the petroleum industry, as did other industries, came under stronger pressure from the federal government to implement equal employment opportunity practices. Federal policies relating to government contractors became more stringent. Moreover, Title VII of the Civil Rights Act went into effect. Investigations by federal contracting agencies and by the Office of Federal Contract Compliance and the new Equal Employment Opportunity Commission occurred with greater frequency and greater vigor. A final factor affecting Negro employment since 1965 has been the increase in the number of Negroes with educational backgrounds demanded by the petroleum industry, and the greater interest of Negroes who are qualified in seeking employment in that industry.

Tables 17 and 18 show the number and percentage of Negroes in the industry by occupational group, sex, and race for 1966 and 1968. The data include employment figures for seventeen major petroleum companies. This represents a significant increase in sample size over the 1964 totals presented in Table 15. Nevertheless, the employment trends among Negroes do confirm the authors' field observations, and are believed representative of the industry.

The data for 1966 and 1968 support a previous discussion on the recent reversal of the attrition in employment during the late 1950's and early 1960's. The total employment for the seventeen sample firms increased by 2.6 percent between 1966 and 1968, from 348,710 to 357,606. This slow growth can be expected to continue into the near future. It is important to note, however, that the occupations traditionally open to Negroes, the low-skill blue collar jobs, show a slight decline in the same period. The growth in job opportunities was concentrated among the professional, managerial, and clerical positions. Overall growth for white collar occupations in this period was 3.9 percent.

The data indicate that Negro employment in the industry has risen from 2.3 percent in 1964 to 3.7 and 3.9 percent in 1966 and 1968 respectively. From 1966 to 1968 Negro employment grew in the seventeen firm sample from 13,057 to 14,089, a 7.9 percent increase. This is an encouraging increase when the factors affecting employment are carefully considered. Moreover, the occupations in which Negroes have made the greatest relative gains are those same occupations which until recently were closed completely to Negroes in many plants. The most significant gains realized during this period were among male craftsmen, female clerical employees, and the white collar occupations generally. The meaning of these changes and expected future opportunities for Negro employees can best be understood after a detailed analysis of all factors involved, starting with the industry's recent affirmative action activities.

Affirmative Action Programs

Although the factors affecting Negro employment have in many companies become much more favorable, the changes in Negro employment patterns have thus far been less than companies, the government, or civil rights groups might have desired. Because of the industry's size and significance in our economy, each of the

TABLE 17. *Petroleum Industry*
Employment by Race, Sex, and Occupational Group
Total United States—17 Companies, 1966

Occupational Group	All Employees			Male			Female		
	Total	Negro	Percent Negro	Total	Negro	Percent Negro	Total	Negro	Percent Negro
Officials and managers	36,718	71	0.2	36,523	70	0.2	195	1	0.5
Professionals	46,536	260	0.6	45,394	240	0.5	1,142	20	1.8
Technicians	17,325	223	1.3	16,024	201	1.3	1,301	22	1.7
Sales workers	37,699	896	2.4	37,595	895	2.4	104	1	1.0
Office and clerical	67,782	2,628	3.9	27,940	900	3.2	39,842	1,728	4.3
Total white collar	206,060	4,078	2.0	163,476	2,306	1.4	42,584	1,772	4.2
Craftsmen	64,412	1,232	1.9	64,269	1,218	1.9	143	14	9.8
Operatives	60,928	4,116	6.8	59,777	4,083	6.8	1,151	33	2.9
Laborers	12,344	2,431	19.7	11,752	2,390	20.3	592	41	6.9
Service workers	4,966	1,200	24.2	4,210	1,063	25.2	756	137	18.1
Total blue collar	142,650	8,979	6.3	140,008	8,754	6.3	2,642	225	8.5
Total	348,710	13,057	3.7	303,484	11,060	3.6	45,226	1,997	4.4

Source: Data in authors' possession.

TABLE 18. *Petroleum Industry*
Employment by Race, Sex, and Occupational Group
Total United States—17 Companies, 1968

Occupational Group	All Employees			Male			Female		
	Total	Negro	Percent Negro	Total	Negro	Percent Negro	Total	Negro	Percent Negro
Officials and managers	39,186	117	0.3	38,904	109	0.3	282	8	2.8
Professionals	49,568	350	0.7	48,250	307	0.6	1,318	43	3.3
Technicians	17,884	298	1.7	16,508	261	1.6	1,376	37	2.7
Sales workers	36,732	1,000	2.7	36,542	983	2.7	190	17	8.9
Office and clerical	70,631	3,357	4.8	28,614	1,054	3.7	42,017	2,303	5.5
Total white collar	214,001	5,122	2.4	168,818	2,714	1.6	45,183	2,408	5.3
Craftsmen	65,311	1,414	2.2	64,961	1,400	2.2	350	14	4.0
Operatives	62,460	4,534	7.3	60,305	4,427	7.3	2,155	107	5.0
Laborers	10,903	1,961	18.0	10,240	1,925	18.8	663	36	5.4
Service workers	4,931	1,058	21.5	4,202	951	22.6	729	107	14.7
Total blue collar	143,605	8,967	6.2	139,708	8,703	6.2	3,897	264	6.8
Total	357,606	14,089	3.9	308,526	11,417	3.7	49,080	2,672	5.4

Source: Data in authors' possession.

major firms is constantly exposed to a myriad of pressures to initiate "affirmative action" programs. Each of the major firms has responded positively to this pressure in any of several ways.

The industry, for instance, is well represented in the "Plans for Progress" organization which is committed to go beyond nondiscrimination and provides programs to increase minority employment prospects. This has involved the firms in such activities as hiring and training unemployed and underemployed Negroes in skills needed by the industry, special recruitment drives in Negro communities and schools, cooperation with public and private Negro action groups, and other similar programs. The results of such activities have unfortunately been limited by the industry's still small new hire needs, its demand for employees with the skills necessary to handle petroleum operations, and an apparent and understandable reluctance of the various companies to inject huge sums into programs which will not directly benefit the firm involved.

Several leading petroleum concerns have recently begun literally to provide preference for Negro applicants. Records are kept of the race of each applicant and a glaring qualification deficiency must be evident to cause the rejection of any Negro applicant. This policy has been responsible for the hiring of several Negro college graduates whose educational backgrounds would not formerly have warranted employment in such a highly technical industry.

"Affirmative action" has also meant attempts by personnel executives to aid in the adjustment of new or young Negro hires to the work situation. Counseling programs are now not uncommon for minority employees who show early signs of tardiness or excessive absenteeism; "buddy" programs involving pairing of recruits with experienced workers have proved beneficial to both the newly hired worker in teaching him the social mores of the job, and to the older worker who perhaps for the first time really believes in the company's new civil rights policies. An added emphasis on providing complete understanding of all rules, responsibilities, and mores affecting the job has also proved beneficial to the successful employment of minorities. In fact, the recognition that minority cultural patterns often cause employment problems may prove to be one of the most beneficial developments of this period.

There has been, of course, a significant difference in the personal commitment of company executives to providing improved employment opportunities to Negroes. Many concerns have men dedicated to this concept both at work and in their private life. Regardless of the degree of personal commitment, however, each of the firms has now made most of the necessary changes in both policy and practice to assure equal opportunity to all applicants. If, however, we examine the data provided in Tables 17 and 18, it is evident that the results of the past few years have improved Negro representation in the industry, but as indicated, not substantially. The reasons for this apparent contradiction can best be understood by a thorough analysis of the industry's hiring methodology, an analysis of the problems involving the various occupational groups, and other factors affecting Negro employment in the middle 1960's.

CRITERIA FOR SELECTION AND PROMOTION

It has already been noted that the industry has generally required proof of high school graduation (or its equivalent) and the successful completion of a series of tests for entering most blue collar jobs. Test results are also used by many concerns to determine eligibility for promotion into the better process and maintenance positions. This section of the study will discuss in further detail the importance of this policy to the industry and the effect it has had on Negro employment therein.

The hiring situation in petroleum is rather unique in industry today. Despite the downward trend in employment, the industry has an excellent reputation for job security, turnover is relatively low, and starting pay is excellent. Applicants believe that the industry offers exceptional employment opportunities. Most firms have no difficulty finding highly qualified personnel to fill the few openings which occur. It also must be emphasized that new hires, particularly in refining, must be highly qualified. No one is employed without the expected qualifications and promise of advancement; each new hire is expected to progress with experience into the top jobs. As men are promoted, they soon acquire more responsibility than employees in most other industries. With the continuous flow of materials that is present from the time crude is produced until the product is delivered to the dealer, just a small error in the reading of a meter or in the adjustment of a valve may quickly cause the ruin of many thousands of dollars in crude stock or products, or even worse, in the loss of life and of millions of dollars in plant and equipment through fire or explosion.

Even though hiring standards must necessarily be kept high, the large supply of applicants has made the task of selection almost too easy. Typically, hiring officers need only interest themselves with the top 5 or 10 percent of the applicants. Therefore, the industry has not had to concern itself greatly with the efficiency or validity of its selection techniques, particularly with regard to the number of qualified applicants who were being rejected.

The results of these selection techniques have had an unintentional but "demonstrable racial effect." Samuel Jackson, former Director of the NAACP and former Commissioner of the EEOC, has called this "systemic" discrimination and argues that such a system is in violation of Title VII of the Civil Rights Act.[38] Although this concept of the law seems unsupported, concern for the effects of its hiring system has also developed recently in the petroleum industry. The industry continues to maintain the same highly selective requirement of all applicants. Yet the hiring procedure until the middle 1950's, as noted in earlier chapters, allowed many uneducated, often black applicants to take laboring positions which offered little opportunity for advancement. It was in these positions that most Negroes first began work in the petroleum industry. Many of these men are still working in the same positions today, with little hope of promotion. The repercussions of this practice are still being felt as government demands the upgrading of Negro personnel.

With the elimination of this practice of in effect hiring Negroes that were considered "nonpromotable," the industry went generally to a high school diploma as the initial requirement in the selection process. For many firms the lack of a diploma prevented the applicant even from submitting an application or having any contact with hiring officials. The small manpower requirements of the industry during the early 1960's and a still undeveloped public concern for fair employment practices allowed this policy to serve the industry effectively for several years.

There is, to be sure, a very obvious need for strong arithmetic and reading skills for all personnel eligible for promotion in the industry.

---

38. For a further discussion of this relatively new concept see: Samuel C. Jackson, "EEOC vs. Discrimination, Inc.," *The Crisis*, Vol. 75 (January 1968), pp. 16-19.

The high school diploma serves well as a quick and efficient technique of eliminating the poorly educated. There is little proof, however, that the available jobs can be done only by men with a twelfth grade education, nor is there evidence that high school graduation insures the attainment of any specific skills level. Unfortunately for the Negro, who must often endure cultural and institutional deficiencies in obtaining an adequate education, this requirement has produced highly discriminatory results. It was only in the mid-1960's that any of the petroleum concerns began to resolve this problem with more objective measures of ability and skill levels.

The types of tests customarily used have been: (1) learning ability, (2) shop arithmetic, (3) mechanical aptitude, (4) mental alertness, and (5) reading ability. Less popular but also used are personal stability tests (purportedly to eliminate panic during emergencies) and achievement tests in chemistry. Each of these tests has a degree of face validity but few firms have developed adequate proof of predictive validity. In fact, the results obtained from the use of such tests in the industry provide some evidence of an unintentional, "systemic" discrimination. For example, an analysis of test results for a major southern refinery during the first seven months of 1968 showed that of 708 white applicants tested, 72 percent passed, while for 167 Negro applicants, only 16 percent passed. Similar results were found in a second large southern refinery where 66 percent of 131 white applicants passed but only 9 percent of 69 Negro applicants were successful.

The industry has recognized this problem for several years. Attempts are being made to develop better testing programs through experimental validation studies. Unfortunately the low new hire rate and the slow advancement of new hires prolongs such efforts for an inordinate amount of time. To compensate for this problem, many refineries have simply lowered the cutoff scores for all applicants or, secretly, only for Negroes. Recently Sinclair entered into a consent decree (U.S. Dist. Ct., S.D. Texas, July 12, 1969) to validate tests to be responsive to the hiring requirements of jobs in the industry.

The employment standards of each sector, with a single exception, are expected to rise continually as technology changes. Jobs for the low skill applicant will be gradually eliminated as part of this upgrading. The lone exception will be in wholesale distribution of petroleum products. Most of the jobs in this sector are related to the operation and maintenance of delivery trucks, jobs which poorly educated applicants can be trained to perform. As validated hiring criteria are developed for these jobs, many now underemployed minority workers may be placed in better employment situations. The relatively few Negroes in this sector cannot be explained away by the nature of the work or the lack of current job opportunities.

The industry will also not be able to supply a significant number of jobs to youth or other hard-core unemployed. Hiring standards cannot be lowered if those employed are to be able to progress beyond laboring positions. The training programs that are necessary to make such workers into good employees are very costly when established for the few applicants who might be hired in any one plant. Nevertheless, management can continue to work toward improved hiring procedures. The industry at a minimum must provide a fair and accurate evaluation of each applicant's chances of success on the job. Thus far it has been able to "skim the cream," but its future and necessary civil rights posture requires it to do more with its hiring problem, that was once so simple, and is now so complicated.

ANALYSIS OF OCCUPATIONAL GROUPS

The data in Tables 17 and 18 show variation in Negro representation among the various occupational groups and between men and women. This section discusses the situation in each of the nine broad occupational categories.

Officials and Managers

The data in Tables 17 and 18 show 71 Negro officials and managers in 1966, and 117 in 1968—0.2 percent of the total in 1966 and 0.3 percent in 1968. Most of these are line supervisors, many in predominantly Negro work areas, such as labor gangs or packaging. Despite extensive recruiting efforts by petroleum companies involving both present employees and recent college graduates, few Negroes have been placed in any supervisory positions. Those Negro employees who have assumed supervisory responsibilities have seldom advanced beyond the first level of supervision.

Managers beyond the first level generally must have at least a Bachelor's degree in engineering or other related field; the number of Negroes majoring in subjects relevant to petroleum operations has been negligible. Because of the prevailing practice of strict departmental seniority and resulting narrow job knowledge, Negroes with the ability to assume a foreman's position have typically been limited to those departments in which they have worked, as a rule, departments into which most Negro employees were channeled. Therefore, while few Negro foremen will manage all black crews, the Negro foreman supervising a predominantly white crew will be quite rare.

Table 19 shows the number and percentage of Negro supervisors by industry sector. These data have severe limits because of the few companies involved. Moreover differences in company structure, data computation, and nomenclature can have an important impact on so small a sample. Nevertheless, these data are presented in order to illustrate the situation in each sector of the industry.

The data in Table 19 for refining show the same percentage as found for the industry as set forth in Table 17. No Negro managers or officials were found in the crude exploration or pipeline sectors, and only one in research. The largest number and ratio of Negro officials is found in wholesaling and marketing. Such persons may actually be managers of company-operated service stations, including some in predominantly Negro areas. Few Negroes have been promoted to sales managers, particularly since the use of Negro salesmen has only recently been initiated.

The petroleum industry has had great difficulty attracting promising Negro college graduates who might have managerial potential. The

TABLE 19. *Petroleum Industry*
Employment of Managers and Officials by
Industry Sector and Race, 1966

Industry Sector	Number of Companies	Total Employees	Negro Employees	Percent Negro
Crude exploration and production	6	1,958	—	—
Pipeline transportation	5	168	—	—
Refining	9	4,378	7	0.2
Wholesaling and marketing	6	2,729	14	0.5
Research	6	299	1	0.3

Source: Data in authors' possession.
Note: For limitations of data, see text.

demand is greatest in the industry for engineers, chemists, and geologists, preferably graduates with a Master of Science or Ph.D. degree. Recruiters routinely visit up to fifteen predominantly Negro colleges (few of which graduate people in these fields) and most of the major state universities and private colleges searching for applicants who meet the rigorous educational requirements, but to no avail. Even those Negroes who have chosen to study business find themselves limited in Negro colleges to accounting, secretarial, and a few other courses, most of which are taught by products of similar Negro colleges with little or no experience in business.

Until recently this deplorable system that has been imposed upon the black community served a very limited but useful purpose. Young Negroes chose to pursue careers in fields which would provide protection from discrimination and disappointment, particularly in teaching, the ministry, or government. Those graduates who did enter business were limited by the quality of their education and the employment practices of business to a low level clerical or similar position.

Now that industry is eagerly seeking the Negro graduate, relatively few are qualified, or being trained for, the highly technical positions open to them. The petroleum industry has attempted several special recruiting programs, and has established several financial aid programs for Negro students but success is slow and erratic. A few Negroes, to be sure, have been hired as engineers, chemists, and computer programmers but most of the recently hired Negro graduates have entered industry after brief periods in the more traditional Negro occupations. Several now work in the personnel function; some began in marketing; still others have entered accounting and finance. As these recent hires progress into higher positions, the industry may well find that more young Negro students will have realized that the barriers no longer exist. Recruitment of potential managers may then be somewhat easier.

Professionals and Technicians

Professional workers and technicians represent an especially important job classification to the petroleum industry. Most of the industry's managers come from these positions. Since the competitive position of each firm is so highly dependent on the size and quality of its product line, firms place great emphasis on recruiting and hiring particularly well qualified professional employees.

Although many of these men are engaged in routine quality control work, still others are engaged in original research, hoping to develop improved products. Our nation's educational system has not been designed, from grade school through college, to provide Negroes with the necessary education to compete for these jobs, especially where the bulk of Negroes dwell in center city or in the South.

Tables 17 and 18 show that Negro professionals in the industry comprised only 0.6 percent of the total in 1966 and 0.7 in 1968, and that Negro technicians in both years were between 1 and 2 percent of the total. Table 20 combines professionals and technicians by sectors. Again the reader should understand the limitations of these data, as set forth earlier. They do, however, confirm the picture set forth in Tables 17 and 18. Again, marketing leads in the utilization of Negro professionals and pipelines have the poorest record.

The demand for professional employees is such that firms have for many years been unable to afford discrimination in hiring them. Highly qualified graduates, regardless of race, attract excellent job offers from most key firms in this industry, as in others. The petroleum industry has Negroes holding many responsible, high-paying professional positions but the overall record remains very discouraging. Recently the industry has been able to attract several Negro programmers and systems analysts, occupations which more and more Negroes seem to be entering and for which there is a high and growing demand.

TABLE 20. *Petroleum Industry*
Employment of Professionals and Technicians by
Industry Sector and Race, 1966

Industry Sector	Number of Firms	Total Employees	Negro Employees	Percent Negro
Crude exploration and production	6	8,159	45	0.6
Pipeline transportation	5	562	1	0.2
Refining	9	6,405	54	0.8
Wholesaling and marketing	6	2,457	31	1.3
Research	6	2,627	25	1.0

Source: Data in authors' possession.
Note: For limitations of data, see text, p. 558.

The industry has a further problem in hiring Negro professionals. Since the industry is highly concentrated in southern states, Negroes have been reluctant to accept offers knowing that they may later be expected to move to a southern location. Several personnel managers have cited examples of Negroes who have left the firm rather than be exposed to the housing problems and racial attitude of the South. In the North, they can continue to enjoy benefits of their salary and position even though they may not yet be accepted by white society. The location of marketing and research facilities in the North explains in part why these sectors have the highest percentage of Negro professionals and technicians.

Technicians in the industry generally have had exceptional high school records or some college training. They are employed for tasks ranging from limited research to quality control. In refining they may be moved into these positions after a period spent as laborer or operative. Negroes have been offered only limited employment opportunities in these fields although the tasks may not require a high skill level or education beyond high school. Opportunities will remain limited but an effective effort by the industry may well cause significant changes in the Negro employment picture in this group.

Sales Workers

Industry generally has not employed Negroes in positions which required close contact with customers or the public. The petroleum industry until recently followed a similar policy. Those Negroes who were employed as sales workers dealt solely with the black community. Most firms were afraid that the industry's customers would not accept Negroes well. Recent experience shows that while exceptions persist this belief has certainly not been supported as a general rule. Negroes can be used successfully as Tables 17 and 18 show that over 2.0 percent of the industry's sales workers are Negroes. A six-company sample in 1966 found 323 of 10,000 employees, or 3.2 percent, in wholesaling and marketing to be Negro.[39] This is a better record than most industries. For example, the study of the steel industry found no Negro sales employees.[40]

The petroleum industry employs two types of sales personnel. A small number of men perform the customary duties associated with

39. Data in authors' possession.
40. See Part Four.

sales to industry and government. These men typically have technical degrees so that they may better assist their customers.

The second type of "salesman" is responsible for the operation of fifteen to thirty service stations. It is his duty to select, train, and motivate service station managers. He is responsible for protecting the company's investment and name at each location. In effect, he is second-line management for each station, with his pay directly affected by the profitability of his stations. It is in this job that the industry has been reluctant to place Negroes. They have been afraid, and occasionally justifiably, that station managers would not accept Negro representatives in this position. They have since discovered that carefully selected Negroes can perform these jobs admirably. The man chosen must be qualified to deal with, and win the respect of, often hostile managers. The results, thus far, have been both surprising and encouraging according to officials of several companies.

Office and Clerical Workers

Office and clerical occupations are among the few in the petroleum industry which have rapidly expanded in the last few years. Most of the growth has been in computer-related job categories. The initiation of widespread credit card sales at service stations, particularly, has been responsible for several thousand new job opportunities. This growth has allowed the industry to add many Negroes to industry payrolls. Most of the Negroes now working in "office and clerical" positions have been hired within the last five years. Tables 17 and 18 show that in 1966, 3.9 percent of the office and clerical group was Negro, while in 1968, the percentage was 4.8.

Negroes had historically enjoyed few opportunities in petroleum office and clerical occupations. Only the recent addition of Negro females as key punch and other clerical machine operators and other computer-related employees has allowed the industry to bolster its Negro office and clerical force to the figures already cited.

Relatively few Negroes are employed as stenographers or private secretaries. The low turnover in many clerical positions in the industry is not expected to provide many good opportunities in the more traditional occupations for the near future.

The industry has traditionally followed the practice of offering preference in clerical job openings to relatives of present employees. Clerical jobs in petroleum offices are generally among the better jobs of this character in the area. Plants and offices with openings are often able to fill them even before notices can be sent to newspapers and employment agencies simply because the grapevine has spread news of the job throughout the plant. Needless to say, this practice has limited the number of Negroes hired into these jobs. In many plants and towns, alleviation of this practice and a change toward better opportunities for Negro applicants has caused strong resentment among white employees.

Table 21 shows employment of office and clerical employees by sector for a small number of companies. (See page 54 for limits of data.) Here refining and wholesaling and marketing have the highest Negro representation, and pipeline transportation the least. The data processing employees are of course highly concentrated in these two groups.

Because it has so few jobs to offer, the petroleum industry has put forth special effort to hire Negroes into clerical jobs. Companies have developed their own training programs, visited at slum area high schools, and supported and hired graduates of special training programs, such as those sponsored by branches of the Urban League or the Opportunities Industrialization Center. These efforts have met with limited success because of two basic factors: poor educational opportunities and locations of many plants and offices.

Big city school systems have become the target of much justifiable criticism because of the poor education that is offered. Girls who graduate from these schools simply are not prepared to assume jobs

TABLE 21. *Petroleum Industry*
Employment of Office and Clerical Workers by
Industry Sector and Race, 1966

Industry Sector	Number of Firms	Total Employees	Negro Employees	Percent Negro
Crude exploration and production	6	3,855	94	2.4
Pipeline transportation	5	279	2	0.7
Refining	9	4,950	266	5.4
Wholesaling and marketing	6	5,732	268	4.7
Research	6	302	10	3.3

Source: Data in authors' possession.
Note: For limitations of data, see text, p. 558.

in industry. The basic language and clerical skills are often below those acceptable for the lowest entry jobs. In addition, basic office machine skills are often subpar, and her dress and personal habits may be different and less desirable than those demanded by superiors and co-workers. Many graduates of big city systems have become, with the needed training and coaching, acceptable and often distinguished employees but for some, the cultural differences and lack of satisfactory schooling have been too great.

The locational factor has presented problems in the hiring of both black and white clerical workers. The industry has purposely worked to maintain good salaries and working conditions for female workers. Turnover has been reduced through these efforts. Many plants, small offices, and other facilities, however, are in highly industrialized areas of big cities or in small towns and rural areas. Neither location is always attractive to highly qualified clerical workers. Moreover, many locations have few Negroes who live within commuting distance of the facility. As a result, qualified Negro applicants tend to seek work only in center city areas. The industry, thus far, has concentrated its efforts only in these areas.

Craftsmen

In both 1966 and 1968 (see Tables 17 and 18), Negroes comprised about 2 percent of the industry's craftsmen. Table 22 shows that most craftsmen, and most Negro craftsmen are found, as would be expected, in the refining sector of the industry. This is where most craftsmen work and where Negroes have had a history of employment. The second largest group of total craftsmen is in the wholesaling and marketing areas.

Although the number of refining craftsmen who are Negroes is increasing, few Negroes are presently performing the top jobs in this classification. Testing, departmental seniority systems, and low turnover have prevented Negroes from moving into the top paying jobs. At most refineries there are Negroes in positions near the top of their various departments.

If Negroes are to occupy these jobs in significant numbers, they will have to participate in training programs, both formal and on the job. The top jobs in refineries require a considerable degree of skill and responsibility. Training is an absolute necessity. In a recent

TABLE 22. *Petroleum Industry*
Employment of Craftsmen by Industry Sector and Race, 1966

Industry Sector	Number of Firms	Total Employees	Negro Employees	Percent Negro
Crude exploration and production	6	4,547	6	0.1
Pipeline transportation	5	924	9	1.0
Refining	9	16,188	279	1.7
Wholesaling and marketing	5	1,151	11	1.0
Research	5	198	1	0.5

Source: Data in authors' possession.
Note: For limitations of data, see text, p. 558.

survey of training programs in southern refineries, there were 25 Negroes in training programs out of 220 trainees—slightly more than 10 percent.[41]

New employees, including Negroes, will have the best chances to benefit from training. Some refineries hire employees into training programs that have automatic step progression. Normally, these programs last four years, after which time the employee is qualified to become a craftsman first class or head operator. This type of program should benefit Negroes, provided, of course, they participate in meaningful numbers. Negroes have difficulty with on-the-job training in some areas because white employees may be reluctant to work with Negroes. There is need for management in this (and other industries) to communicate to first-line supervisors and skilled employees the necessity to give Negroes equal job opportunity for all jobs, and to back up that communication with action to see that equal employment opportunities are enforced.

Most Negro foremen are in charge of employees in labor departments, i.e., they supervise Negro workers. Although it is not common, Negroes have supervised white employees in the South. Outside the South, there are a few Negro foremen in other departments. Until more Negroes have the chance to perform the skilled jobs, the number of Negro foremen will remain very small because these are the jobs from which promotion to supervision occurs.

41. Data in authors' possession.

TABLE 23. *Petroleum Industry*
Employment of Operatives by Industry Sector and Race, 1966

Industry Sector	Number of Firms	Total Employees	Negro Employees	Percent Negro
Crude exploration and production	6	2,703	32	1.2
Pipeline transportation	5	344	3	0.9
Refining	9	8,341	770	9.2
Wholesaling and marketing	6	5,236	133	2.5
Research	6	34	2	5.9

Source: Data in authors' possession.
Note: For limitations of data, see text, p. 558.

Operatives

Over 6.0 percent of the industry's operatives were Negro in 1966 and by 1968, the ratio had risen to over 7 percent. As one would expect, most Negro operatives are located in refining. The data in Table 23 show that 9.2 percent of the operatives in nine refineries are Negroes. The number of Negro operatives in all segments of the industry is insignificant.

Few Negroes have worked in crude exploration and production, as operatives or, as we have noted, in any other classifications. Most drilling work is contracted out and other production work is usually done by employees who are familiar with oil field work. There has been little new employment in this sector. Furthermore, production units are small, and, although concentrated in the South, are not always located near large Negro populations.

It is more difficult to explain the lack of Negroes in marketing distribution work. These units are typically located near large urban areas where there are sizable Negro populations. Furthermore, many of the employees are truck drivers, a job which does not require extensive training or experience. It is true, of course, that the standard of care required in the transportation of petroleum products on public highways should be very high. Careful screening of applicants is warranted, but, even so, one would expect to find a significant number of Negroes. Distribution centers typically employ mechanics and semiskilled labor. Very few Negroes are employed in these jobs also.

In refining, the situation is better. This is the result of upgrading efforts rather than new hiring, although the latter has helped. For the most part, Negroes in semiskilled jobs have passed tests and/or have met educational requirements established by managements for movement out of labor departments. Many are in positions which will lead to jobs in process and maintenance departments. And, many are in formerly "white" jobs. For example, in one southern refinery 200 Negroes out of 500 employees are now in jobs which were denied them ten years ago.

Conditions still merit improvement. Wider seniority districts would improve the upward movement potential of Negroes. This would enable older Negroes to move ahead of younger whites and thus remove some of the inequities which arose under earlier discriminatory practices. At one refinery, for example, which adopted plant seniority, Negroes bid and won over 60 percent of new job openings.

Now that there are sizable numbers of Negroes in semiskilled work, one would expect that shortly more Negroes will be moving into skilled job levels. A major obstacle for the older employees will continue to be test qualification procedures already discussed.

Laborers and Service Workers

Employees in labor positions are generally either new hires or old employees. New hires are promoted quickly because their ability to perform higher jobs is tested at the "gate," that is, before they are hired. Others remain behind because of lack of education or inability to pass the necessary tests. Negroes have traditionally performed laboring and service work, but the proportion of Negroes in these jobs is declining as the jobs are automated and Negroes promoted. Thus in 1966 (Table 17), 19.7 percent of the laborers and 24.2 percent of the service workers were Negroes; in 1968, these percentages stood at 18 and 21.5, respectively (see Table 18).

It is still not unusual in the South to have at one refinery seventy hourly job titles in the labor department and only six of these integrated. Fourteen other job titles are currently held only by Negroes. The high percentage of Negro laborers and service workers shown in refineries in Table 24 reflects the large concentration of Negroes in the refineries of Louisiana and especially Texas.

Upgrading older Negroes requires special effort on the part of management. Many of these Negroes have little or no education. They

TABLE 24. *Petroleum Industry*
Employment of Laborers and Service Workers by Industry Sector and Race, 1966

Industry Sector	Number of Firms	Total Employees	Negro Employees	Percent Negro
Crude exploration and production	6	1,496	32	2.1
Pipeline transportation	5	192	6	3.1
Refining	9	2,804	686	24.5
Wholesaling and marketing	6	445	52	11.7
Research	6	117	13	11.1

Source: Data in authors' possession.
Note: For limitations of data, see text, p. 558.

are not able to read, write, or do simple arithmetic. Most refineries are willing to pay all or part of an employee's expenses incurred in getting a high school degree. Some Negroes have taken advantage of these programs.

Unfortunately, a majority of Negroes have not taken advantage of these programs. Many have as little education as before. The years have curbed and blunted any latent desire for advancement. It is asking much of a man who was hired as a laborer, under conditions when both he and his employer *knew* that he would *never* be promoted, now to expect after ten or twenty years that he will grasp opportunities.

Some refineries, which have a small number of Negroes in this predicament, have nevertheless instituted special training programs for the purpose of qualifying older employees in laboring jobs for certain higher-paying work. These men are trained for jobs which do not require much formal education. This is true of the occupation "painter," for example.

Overall there is very little demand for unskilled employees in the petroleum industry. Thus, the industry is not in a good position to hire employees who do not have the potential to become highly skilled workers. Unfortunately, in this regard, is the fact that most companies in the petroleum industry do not operate their own service stations. This is an area that could potentially affect the high unemployment rates among urban Negro youths. The utilization of young hard-core unemployed youths as service station attendants may not be an adequate long-term solution to their problem. The job even with experience may offer low pay, which often will be below that available from welfare payments, and there is of course little opportunity for advancement.

Because this is an area where the industry can participate in efforts to improve Negro employment, some companies sponsor training programs in service station work. The programs are designed to find, train, and place Negro youths in filling stations. The pay is low but for many Negroes living in the city slums, it is their first opportunity to hold a steady job and to have the responsibilities that go with it. Furthermore, these companies hope that some of the trainees will later operate their own stations, with financial help from the companies. It is too early to determine the success of these efforts.

EMPLOYMENT OF NEGRO WOMEN

Women have never enjoyed significant job opportunities in the petroleum industry. Although this has been true for both black and white female workers, it was especially true for Negro women until the period following passage of the Civil Rights Act of 1964. The only jobs open to women have traditionally been among the office and clerical positions, which accounted in the 1968 employment sample for over 80 percent of the female employees. Table 18 shows that 5.5 percent of the 42,017 female office and clerical employees were Negroes. This represents a threefold increase over the percentage of Negro women holding similar jobs in 1964 (see Table 15).

Few women are presently working as production workers in any sector of the industry. The work is simply too physically demanding to expect women to perform effectively. Most jobs are executed outdoors, with a requirement occasionally for heavy physical exertion. There is also an important need for close cooperation among the small crews on each unit, and interchangeability of work which militates against assigning some jobs to women. Although there remain some job possibilities for women in product packaging and maintenance operations, few women are being utilized in these positions. Negro women are well represented among the few women holding production jobs.

The increase in civil rights pressure and a tightened labor market do seem to have opened new job opportunities for Negro secretaries and stenographers. Most of the long established office locations had few, if any, Negroes working in the better clerical jobs prior to the Civil Rights Act. This was particularly true of the offices located in the Southwest. Since then, however, many new job opportunities have been opened to qualified Negro applicants. There have been some difficult experiences with white employees but by remaining firm, management has been able to introduce these women to the work force. The changes that are occurring will continue at a slow pace because of a low turnover rate in such jobs.

As already indicated, since the late 1950's a new and very significant source of new job opportunities has developed around the increased usage of the computer. The petroleum industry has been forced to establish many entirely new office locations to house the employees related to these activities. The demand for qualified women in these occupations has been so great that the industry has begun several training programs, alone or in cooperation with other industries, to help fill the void. These programs may consist only of on-the-job training or they may mean several weeks at private or public business schools to which the firm has heavily contributed.

Negro women have enjoyed great success in obtaining jobs in these occupations. Most of the major offices needing these occupations are located in large cities and the industry has been quick to take advantage of these openings to improve its Negro employment image. A sample of women working in either "computer services," "data processing," or "credit card sales" for six firms in 1967 shows that 540 or 14.2 percent of the 3,799 total were Negroes.[42] Offices with 30 percent of the work force Negro are not uncommon in some computer-oriented facilities. This is significantly higher than the employment of Negroes in any other area of the industry's operations.

Where the firm has been willing to provide the necessary training for promising Negro women, the results have been quite encouraging. For many Negro women, particularly in the South, the opportunity to work in an office is completely new. There have been problems with improper dress or poor language skills, but with help, these problems can be alleviated. This is one area within the petroleum industry which holds promise for better minority employment opportunities.

42. *Ibid.*

REGIONAL AND LOCATIONAL FACTORS

Historically, the petroleum industry has been a southern industry. This has been true ever since 1901 when the mighty "Spindletop" oil field was discovered in Texas. The importance of southern states to the industry's operations was discussed in Chapter II. Although facilities have been dispersed gradually to more efficiently meet the nation's demand for petroleum products, many of the current industrial and union leaders continue to be recruited from southern towns and families. The racial employment policies which developed at southern locations during the early years of the industry still exert a strong detrimental effect on present efforts to improve Negro employment opportunities.

The crude production sector of the industry, of course, is highly concentrated in southwestern states. Many areas have small oil deposits, but only California of the nonsouthwestern states produces crude in significant quantity. Texas, Louisiana, and Oklahoma have been the dominant producers of domestic crude for several years. The Negro population in areas of each of the important crude producing states, with the exception of Louisiana, is often small. Segregation and discrimination in these areas have been a way of life. Moreover, crude oil is produced in these states in rural, isolated areas which have few if any educated Negro residents.

The nature of the work has also limited the employment of Negroes in this sector. The work crews, as discussed in Chapter II, are small, and necessarily cohesive groups. Frequent travel to new drilling sites is not uncommon. Many jobs require men to live away from family and friends. This is particularly true of those jobs on off-shore drilling rigs. Few white employees find such conditions acceptable. The industry has, thus far, found it very difficult to place Negroes into any of these tightly-knit work groups which exist in crude production. The already presented data on employment by industry sector attests to the lack of Negroes in crude production.

Those Negroes who are working in this sector remain in the lowest job classifications. The industry has had little success in upgrading Negroes into skilled occupations. A sample of employment in crude production for Louisiana, Oklahoma, and Texas (Table 25) found no Negroes employed as craftsmen and few with white collar positions. The sample data cited in Tables 19-24 indicate that Negroes nation-

TABLE 25. *Crude Oil Production*
Employment by Race and Occupational Group
Louisiana, Oklahoma, and Texas—Nine Firms, 1966

Occupational Group	All Employees	Negro	Percent Negro
White collar employees	9,818	34	0.3
Craftsmen	395	—	—
Operatives, laborers, and service employees	4,348	82	1.9
Total	14,561	116	0.8

Source: Data in authors' possession.

ally enjoy somewhat better opportunities in crude production than in the Southwest but that employment in all areas remains relatively small.

Few Negroes are also employed in pipeline shipment of crude and petroleum products. Again, pipeline facilities are important only in transporting crude oil and its products between production areas and consumption areas. Therefore, pipelines have been located and are controlled from units between metropolitan areas and are found in rural and suburban regions which often have few Negro residents. Moreover, the decreasing employment totals of this sector have effectively prevented the industry from attempting to improve Negro employment even in these areas.

The large refineries, however, have been built in or near major metropolitan areas. The Texas-Louisiana Gulf Coast region still dominates but important refining regions have developed also around New York, Philadelphia, Chicago, St. Louis, Los Angeles, and San Francisco. Each of these cities has a large Negro labor market. In fact, the odors produced by a large refinery are partially responsible for depressing the surrounding neighborhoods to the squalid conditions which have become acceptable only to the area's poorest residents. Needless to say, Negroes often represent a high proportion of the residents living near these refineries. Negroes in other sections of these cities may also live within easy commuting distance.

The extent of the utilization of Negro workers has varied, however, from region to region. Negroes have long been employed throughout this sector but the number and type of employment opportunities open to them have been affected by local custom. Sample employment statistics for each of the four major refining regions are summarized in Tables 26-29.

Negroes have not been employed extensively in white collar positions in any region. Employment of Negroes in these occupations has been especially low in southern plants. The problems of recruiting qualified Negro graduates for managerial, professional, and technical positions have been discussed previously.

Qualified Negro clerical and office workers have not been recruited until recently, as we have noted, but they now can be more readily attracted by firms which often have offices located in the more attractive areas of the cities.

The tradition of hiring Negroes only for unskilled and certain semiskilled positions has continued to limit Negro employment in the better jobs. Few Negroes have been upgraded to craftsmen positions anywhere in the refining sector. The sample data indicate that the East has had the best record of employing Negroes in these occupations. Again, the number of Negroes working as craftsmen in the South is especially low. the lack of qualifications among Negro applicants is partially responsible for the absence of Negroes from these jobs. On the other hand, until very recently, the industry made no effort to open any of these jobs to Negroes.

The job opportunities which Negroes have been afforded have been as laborers, service employees and, at times, as operatives. Southern refineries, particularly, have provided many high-paying but low-status jobs to Negroes. Many occupations in this area have traditionally been filled exclusively by Negro workers. In the East and the West, refineries also have employed many Negroes (relative to the population distribution) in these occupations. The patterns of Negro employment in each region are expected to improve gradually as openings occur now that equal opportunity and affirmative actions have been made industry policies.

In recent years small, obsolete refineries, located within metropolitan areas, have been shut down. Although only a few plants have been built in the past decade, there does appear to be some movement of operations to rural areas near metropolitan centers. Any movement away from urban sections has a negative effect on Negro employment, but the number of jobs that might be lost in the future will

TABLE 26. *Refining*
Employment by Race, Sex, and Occupational Group
Pennsylvania, New Jersey, and Delaware—11 Plants, 1966

Occupational Group	All Employees Total	All Employees Negro	All Employees Percent Negro	Male Total	Male Negro	Male Percent Negro	Female Total	Female Negro	Female Percent Negro
Officials and managers	1,147	4	0.3	1,145	4	0.3	2	—	—
Professionals	1,120	7	0.6	1,104	7	0.6	16	—	—
Technicians	988	6	0.6	952	5	0.5	36	1	2.8
Office and clerical	1,019	18	1.8	607	8	1.3	412	10	2.4
Total white collar	4,274	35	0.8	3,808	24	0.6	466	11	2.4
Craftsmen	5,445	259	4.8	5,430	259	4.8	15	—	—
Operatives	3,039	277	9.1	3,033	277	9.1	6	—	—
Laborers	404	180	44.6	404	180	44.6	—	—	—
Service workers	474	84	17.7	437	82	18.8	37	2	5.4
Total blue collar	9,362	800	8.5	9,304	798	8.6	58	2	3.4
Total	13,636	835	6.1	13,112	822	6.3	524	13	2.5

Source: Data in authors' possession.

TABLE 27. *Refining*
Employment by Race, Sex, and Occupational Group
Illinois and Indiana—9 Plants, 1966

Occupational Group	All Employees			Male			Female		
	Total	Negro	Percent Negro	Total	Negro	Percent Negro	Total	Negro	Percent Negro
Officials and managers	1,149	—	—	1,148	—	—	1	—	—
Professionals	631	3	0.5	630	3	0.5	1	—	—
Technicians	711	5	0.7	693	5	0.7	18	—	—
Office and clerical	598	16	2.7	287	5	1.7	311	11	3.5
Total white collar	3,089	24	0.8	2,758	13	0.5	331	11	3.3
Craftsmen	4,387	50	1.1	4,387	50	1.1	—	—	—
Operatives	2,043	21	1.0	2,043	21	1.0	—	—	—
Laborers	414	25	6.0	413	25	6.1	1	—	—
Service workers	248	14	5.6	225	14	6.2	23	—	—
Total blue collar	7,092	110	1.6	7,068	110	1.6	24	—	—
Total	10,181	134	1.3	9,826	123	1.3	355	11	3.1

Source: Data in authors' possession.

TABLE 28. *Refining*
Employment by Race, Sex, and Occupational Group
Louisiana and Texas—13 Plants, 1966

Occupational Group	All Employees			Male			Female		
	Total	Negro	Percent Negro	Total	Negro	Percent Negro	Total	Negro	Percent Negro
Officials and managers	2,280	2	0.1	2,276	2	0.1	4	—	—
Professionals	1,731	4	0.2	1,704	4	0.2	27	—	—
Technicians	1,190	7	0.6	1,113	6	0.5	77	1	1.3
Office and clerical	1,606	5	0.3	942	2	0.2	664	3	0.5
Total white collar	6,807	18	0.3	6,035	14	0.2	772	4	0.5
Craftsmen	11,886	208	1.7	11,803	208	1.8	83	—	—
Operatives	4,441	931	21.0	4,412	931	21.1	29	—	—
Laborers	1,126	883	78.4	1,118	882	78.9	8	1	12.5
Service workers	632	286	45.3	625	283	45.3	7	3	42.9
Total blue collar	18,085	2,308	12.8	17,958	2,304	12.8	127	4	3.1
Total	24,892	2,326	9.3	23,993	2,318	9.7	899	8	0.9

Source: Data in authors' possession.

TABLE 29. *Refining*
Employment by Race, Sex, and Occupational Group
California—12 Plants, 1966

Occupational Group	All Employees			Male			Female		
	Total	Negro	Percent Negro	Total	Negro	Percent Negro	Total	Negro	Percent Negro
Officials and managers	617	—	—	617	—	—	—	—	—
Professionals	1,221	6	0.5	1,218	6	0.5	3	—	—
Technicians	709	2	0.3	686	2	0.3	23	—	—
Office and clerical	789	8	1.0	509	5	1.0	280	3	1.1
Total white collar	3,336	16	0.5	3,030	13	0.4	306	3	1.0
Craftsmen	3,917	35	1.0	3,912	35	0.9	5	—	—
Operatives	2,401	115	4.8	2,398	115	4.8	3	—	—
Laborers	497	52	10.5	487	52	10.7	10	—	—
Service workers	235	10	4.3	229	10	4.4	6	—	—
Total blue collar	7,050	212	3.0	7,026	212	3.0	24	—	—
Total	10,386	228	2.2	10,056	225	2.2	330	3	0.9

Source: Data in authors' possession.

remain small. The investment in plant and equipment is too great to allow many firms to make this move.

Finally, there are several hundred small refineries which continue to operate near the oil fields. These plants employ work forces which often total less than 100 employees. These are generally marginal operations which are highly dependent on the availability of crude near the plant. Frequent closings and plant movements are common. Negro employment is undoubtedly similar to that in crude production, although no evidence has been collected to support this view.

Negro employment in the product wholesaling and distribution sector has also been affected by location although in this sector, the effect has not been consistent. Any town, transportation center, or industrial area will have a heavy demand for both gasoline and heating fuels. Distribution is performed by either the producer or by small wholesalers from one or more locations near the consumer. No generalities can be developed about the accessibility of these facilities to Negro applicants.

The preceding discussion by occupational classification shows that few Negroes have been able to obtain jobs in this sector, and the evidence indicates that there may be significant regional differences. This seems to be true of all firms dealing in wholesale distribution, regardless of size. The industry-wide practice of allowing personnel at the facility, usually first-level supervisors, to have complete control of the hiring process with little direction from the personnel staff may well be responsible for this poor record. Increased utilization is possible, and has been proven so by several firms, if management is willing to exert sufficient control over local supervisors.

UNION IMPACT ON RACIAL POLICIES

The impact of the union movement has generally not been an important factor, either positive or negative, in the establishment of racial employment policies in the petroleum industry. In Chapter II it was noted that union strength in the industry has never approached that common in so many of our other manufacturing industries. Membership is divided among three national unions, the Oil, Chemical and Atomic Workers Union (OCAW), the Operating Engineers (IUOE), and the Teamsters, and among numerous independent unions. The degree of unionization is highest in the refining sector of the industry with each of the remaining sectors having varying but insignificant union strength.

The strongest union in the industry, the OCAW, has actively advocated an equalitarian policy since 1943.[43] In 1950 at the union's national convention a resolution was passed by unanimous vote affirming a notably strong policy against discrimination. After a lengthy floor debate, it was resolved:

> . . . that the Oil Workers International Union, CIO [now OCAW] . . . take the following steps to end racial discrimination:
>
> 1. Insist that all labor contracts signed by the International and the locals guarantee equal rights for all employees, regardless of race, religion or sex.
> 2. Demand of candidates for public office that they commit themselves plainly as to whether they support fair employment practices . . . and that insofar as possible only such persons who favor civil rights legislation be supported.
> 3. Participate in all community, state and national programs intended to end racial discrimination.
> 4. That the Vice-President as Chairman of the Fair Employment Practice Committee of the Oil Workers International Union, proceed to establish functioning Fair Employment Practice Committees in the various locals of the Oil Workers International Union, which shall report to him quarterly.[44]

Despite this stated policy, few if any locals took the steps necessary to eliminate the discriminatory practices discussed previously. Segregated locals, separate seniority lines, and other instances of discrimination continued at many facilities for several years after this floor debate.

The International's apparent lack of control over the several locals originates in the governmental structure of the union. The OCAW has been historically an intensely democratic union, with each local retaining a large degree of its autonomy. Although the International leadership has conscientiously worked to eliminate discrimination, it

---

43. Melvin Rothbaum, *The Government of the Oil, Chemical and Atomic Workers Union* (New York: John Wiley & Sons, Inc., 1962), p. 20.
44. *Proceedings*, Oil Workers International Union, CIO, 20th Convention, August 14-20, 1950, p. 368.

does not possess the power to impose changes of such import. Despite the continuing practices of many locals, the OCAW was able to develop a "reputation for equalitarian racial treatment" among the Negro communities near petroleum facilities.[45] The necessary changes to insure equal opportunities to Negro employees ostensibly have been executed, and, in fact, limited evidence indicates that Negroes have received preferential treatment from several locals.

The other prominent national unions in the industry, the IUOE and the Teamsters, have apparently maintained a hands-off policy in recent years. The Operating Engineers have been cited as discriminatory in the past but no specific instances of such practices in the petroleum industry have been found.[46] The independent unions, in most cases, wield too little power to be of much consequence in formulating racial policies. Moreover, no union power has been found to supersede that of management in this now vital area. Management has retained the full power to impose the end to overt racial discrimination. As many firms have found, however, this control does not affect the union social structure.

Since Negroes represent such a small percentage of the work force throughout the industry, they cannot be expected to play an important part in local union activities. The Negro has, in fact, worked against the integration of separate locals, particularly in southern plants, because such actions tend to diminish the power of Negroes in collective bargaining. In integrated locals, both North and South, few Negroes have been able to obtain offices above shop steward.

The union-management departmental seniority clauses prevalent in the industry have forced workers into long, narrow progression lines. Although this system has prevented the rapid upgrading of Negroes in recent years, the highly specialized job knowledge necessary in each department prevents the use of any other system. Movement from department to department is impossible for most jobs without the experience gained during long years in grade. Movement between plants is possible only when similar jobs exist or when the worker is willing to start at the bottom of the seniority ladder. The seniority system has thus imposed many long years of waiting upon any aspiring Negro workers.

45. F. Ray Marshall, "Independent Unions in the Gulf Coast Refinery Industry," *Labor Law Journal*, Vol. LIII (September 1961), p. 840.

46. Garth L. Mangum, *The Operating Engineers* (Cambridge: Harvard University Press, 1964), p. 232.

GOVERNMENT ACTION AND MANAGEMENTS' RESPONSE

Government agencies, both federal and state, have been significant in bringing about an improvement in the condition of Negro employment in the petroleum industry. Two major agencies dealing with Negro employment are the Office of Federal Contract Compliance (OFCC), created pursuant to Presidential Executive Orders, and the Equal Employment Opportunity Commission (EEOC), which was established by Title VII of the Civil Rights Act of 1964.

The OFCC is the latest in the long line of agencies established since the Truman Administration to police equal opportunity among contractors doing business with the federal government. President Johnson renamed it, and assigned it to the Department of Labor.

The activities of the similar committee, the President's Committee on Government Contracts (PCGC, or Nixon Committee) during the late 1950's has already been noted. Substantial changes in employment practices resulted. That Committee's approach was basically to require contractors to be "color-blind" in selection, promotions, and other employment activities. Presidents Kennedy's and Johnson's Executive Orders went a step further and required contractors to take "affirmative action" to eliminate the effects of past discrimination. The orders did not require standards to be lowered, but did pressure contractors to seek out qualified Negroes for all job classifications.

Moreover, the new Committee directed contractors, in addition to those requirements established by the Nixon Committee to: (1) include the statement "Equal Opportunity Employer" in all employment advertising; (2) request unions to submit statements that workers of all races are eligible for membership; (3) desegregate facilities; and (4) file regular compliance reports with the Committee's staff. More recently, the OFCC has required employment units with contracts to submit in writing their own annual affirmative action programs. It is too soon to judge the effects of this last regulation.

No petroleum contracts have been cancelled or withheld because of alleged discriminatory practices or failure to fulfill a contracting agency's (usually the Department of Defense or Interior), or OFCC's regulations. Some locations have been found not in compliance with OFCC regulations and told to take steps to become compliant. Apparently, the threat of noncompliance has been a sufficient incentive to bring all the petroleum companies within the grounds of the agency's expectations concerning equal employment practices.

Title VII has not had the same initial effect as the executive orders. Because of the executive orders, most petroleum companies did not have to make sweeping changes to comply with Title VII. Thus far, the effects of the Act have been limited to correcting individual situations. In fact, most complaints have been settled satisfactorily at the local level. The recent case involving Sinclair which concerns testing programs, as discussed earlier, as well as seniority, is the most significant, and could have an effect on some rather common practices in the refining industry.

Of course, some petroleum companies had equal employment policies before the government began putting this pressure on the industry. During the 1950's and 1960's managements have restated many times their companies' equal employment policies. Most of the larger petroleum companies have joined the "Plans for Progress" organization, and are actively supporting its activities. The President of Standard Oil (Ohio), Mr. Charles E. Spahr, served as chairman of this organization for several years.

An equal employment policy is not, however, likely to be self-implementing. The past practices of the industry and the personal attitudes of management personnel cannot be corrected quickly. It is generally necessary for top management to impress lower management personnel, especially first-line supervisors, with the strong commitment of the firm to this policy and that progress is expected of them. Some companies have created the position of minority employment or merit employment officer working with the corporate staff. This officer's duty is to coordinate the work of his firm in EEO matters with the guide lines and demands of government agencies. He may conduct periodic reviews of matters related to minority employment at each plant and office; he may help to establish programs at company locations to improve minority employment opportunities; and he may be responsible for reporting to top management on such matters. Moreover, local management personnel are encouraged to participate in community programs and events related to employment problems of minority workers. For example, most oil concerns have chosen to support the National Alliance of Businessmen program which is designed in part to reduce hard-core unemployment.

The changes which have occurred in the employment practices of the industry may well have taken place without government pressure. Government pressure has helped, however, to hasten this process. The pressures exerted by government have been effective, not so much because of the possible loss of contracts but because of the fear of bad publicity. The demand for petroleum products, particularly since the expansion of the Vietnam conflict, and the political power of the petroleum industry nearly negate the possibility of contract cancellation. Moreover, many of the petroleum concerns would be satisfied to lose the small yearly income from government contracts if this would eliminate the complications which arise from doing business with the government. Petroleum concerns are, however, very conscious of their public images in this fiercely competitive industry. A possible boycott of any company's retail outlets by a racial or ethnic group could prove expensive. It is for this reason that government has been able to bring about the necessary changes.

CHAPTER VI.

Problems Arising from Equal Opportunity

The new emphasis on the employment and upgrading of Negroes in petroleum facilities has not occurred without the rash of minor problems which are to be expected with any change in a cultural system. The demands for rigorous skill performance and proper discipline placed upon heretofore untested young Negro employees have necessitated attempts at understanding by both sides. Excessive absenteeism, tardiness, turnover, learning to live under factory discipline, and slum habits brought into the plant or office have all been problems, and are discussed with other issues in this section.

IMPACT ON WHITE EMPLOYEES

In most plants or offices, Negroes represent either a very small minority of the work force, or have been employed in large numbers for many years. Only in data processing facilities, where all employees have been hired recently, have large numbers of Negroes been added to the payrolls. Therefore, the gradual addition of Negroes has not caused the serious problems experienced in other industries. There has been some resentment over the increased effort to recruit Negroes, and particularly so in those plants which have traditionally given special consideration to employee relatives; but for the most part, the white employees have accepted this step as inevitable. The actual impact on the white labor market has been insignificant.

An initial problem which arose largely in the South centered around the tradition of "white jobs" and "Negro jobs." The culture in southern plants and also but less obviously in other areas has always channeled Negro applicants into a restricted number of job categories.

This system was initially promulgated and largely condoned by management until the mid-1950's.

Today this practice has been largely, but not entirely, eliminated. Negroes have begun to progress into previously white occupations while black occupations are gradually being eliminated by automation. Resentment, which was strong at first, is being forgotten as Negro workers are accepted into their new positions. Undoubtedly the slow rate of progress necessitated by the low turnover has helped white employees to better accept this change.

Fortunately most petroleum facilities have employed Negroes for many years. The numbers have admittedly been small, but the resulting contacts have served to reduce the problems of increased Negro employment. This has not always been true of the many offices operated by the petroleum industry. Here the addition of Negro secretaries or file clerks may have first occurred only two or three years ago. Reports of managers refusing to accept Negro secretaries are not uncommon. Similar complaints have also been filed by long-term clerical employees who can no longer accept such change readily. Most situations have been remedied easily, however, by strong pressure exerted by management. Many management personnel who were at first apprehensive about such change have been surprised at the ease with which the Negro worker was accepted into the work force.

IMPACT ON EFFICIENCY

The pressure to hire additional Negro employees has inevitably meant the selection of a small number of applicants who previously, and perhaps more accurately, would have been judged unqualified. These men often develop into highly competent employees, but they may require close attention to overcome the educational and cultural deficiencies common to slum life.

Efficiency and Safety

The industry thus far has developed formal training programs in only a few selected occupations. Employees in process operations are expected to acquire the requisite skills through experience and the aid of senior employees. The success of this system is dependent on both the ability of the worker and on the cooperation of the instructor. If the new worker is to continue progressing to higher jobs as the industry expects, the system must work well at all levels, with each employee receiving adequate coaching.

The lack of effective, systematic training may well retard the learning process for poorly qualified employees. This retardation may affect not only the acquisition of skills and job knowledge, but also the development of the necessary mental attitudes to be a dependable employee. On the other hand, the pressures being exerted upon the petroleum companies make it important to upgrade Negro employees as quickly as possible. The result of this paradox has been the occasional, erroneous promotion of men who have yet to become completely competent.

There are, of course, jobs in the industry which can be performed by men attempting to gain the necessary skills. Errors by these employees can be discovered and corrected with proper control procedures. Many jobs in other industries are of this nature. On the other hand, there are numerous jobs in the oil industry which can be dangerous if held by incompetent personnel. Explosions, fires, loss of life, or lost production can be caused simply by the opening or closing of the wrong valve, or making an inaccurate adjustment to equipment. Therefore, the industry must be understandably highly selective and cautious in the employment of poorly qualified applicants.

A further safety concern may prove to be more fiction than fact. Sabotage possibilities during periods of military conflict have forced the industry to investigate closely the personal history of each applicant. Each company has conducted lengthy security investigations for each applicant considered. Jail or arrest records have meant automatic clearance denials. The effect of this policy on the employment of city slum residents is all too obvious. Now firms are being asked to analyze arrest records and possibly discount minor infractions.

Thus far the industry has not been very receptive to this shift in attitude. One firm has maintained the necessity of security clearance to gain positions as service station attendant trainees. These positions were originally established to provide job opportunities for unemployed Negro youths. They have expressed disappointment in the lack of success of recruitment efforts thus far!

Turnover, Absenteeism, and Tardiness

It is apparent from discussions with management personnel and the limited available data that the record of absenteeism, tardiness, and turnover among Negro employees is higher than that of white employees. This is not necessarily true for the older, mature black employees, most of whom have many years of dependable employment in the industry. It is directed rather toward the younger, recently hired Negroes with little work experience. The demands of steady, day-after-day employment may be a new experience not only to them but also to their entire family.

One manager cited an example of a highly recommended young Negro who was hired through a Negro community group. Monday through Thursday of each week the youth was consistently on time and worked diligently; Friday he never reported for work. After some investigation the manager discovered that the young man was taking home more money on Thursday night than he ever hoped to make and, therefore, had little reason to come Fridays. After spending several months or even years in the unregimented life of slum areas, it is not surprising that many Negroes have trouble adapting to industrial discipline. The problem of "unemployables" in our slums will not be solved simply by providing job opportunities.

To reduce the cost of this problem, several firms in the petroleum industry have adopted a "buddy" program to counsel all new hires. Mature employees are chosen for their skill and dependability to act as friends and confidants to help young workers to adjust to the work culture. Rather than have the new employee become discouraged because of minor difficulties, the "buddy" is there to aid in their solution. The industrial experience becomes less frightening to the new hire, and the "buddy" gains a great deal of satisfaction for his efforts. Both men become better employees and the firm has saved the money and time lost through turnover.

A rather interesting phenomenon has developed among Negro college graduates hired by the industry. The petroleum industry, as with other industries, has been pressured to hire increasing numbers of Negro college graduates. The highly technical nature of the industry imposes very selective hiring standards for applicants considered for most jobs. The number of Negro graduates qualified to meet these standards is small indeed. Those lucky few that have the necessary educational background today have virtually unlimited employment opportunities, often at a salary significantly higher than that paid to similarly qualified white employees. Several placement agencies have begun adroitly to take advantage of this situation by finding firms willing to pay increasingly higher salaries, and placing the Negro employee in a rapidly changing series of better-paying jobs. This system has become deleterious both to the industry's efforts to improve Negro employment and to the long-term career interests of the Negro worker. Industry, however, has little choice but to cooperate in the system.

A similar practice has developed among highly qualified Negro clerical employees. Here, also, the demand far exceeds the available supply. Negro girls quickly become cognizant of their new power in industry, and have begun to job hop, always looking for the better job. The petroleum industry has long enjoyed very low turnover among female employees simply because they have provided attractive opportunities. This has diminished the effect of this practice to the industry but, on the other hand, has made the history of short-term jobs that much more distasteful. The lack of qualified Negro college graduates and clerical employees will continue to cost industry money for many years.

GOVERNMENT PRESSURE

The task of enforcing government policy on equal employment opportunity can be difficult indeed. The problems which have arisen are very complex and strongly rooted in our entire cultural system. Although it is the opinion of these authors that the petroleum industry is deeply concerned with providing truly equal opportunities to all applicants and employees, there is also within the industry a deep distrust of governmental action as it affects the operations of the industry. It may well be true that the changes in employment practices which are necessary would not have occurred without the pressures of government.[47] But how should the government best approach companies such as those in the petroleum industry to bring about the needed changes? The approach taken has caused serious resentment throughout the industry and the problem apparently has still not been resolved.

There may, in fact, be a cause for conflict built into the relationships between the agencies responsible for enforcement of policy. Many firms must now work with up to five separate agencies: one each representing city and state interests and three federal groups—

47. This hypothesis has been applied to industry generally, and is not directed solely toward the petroleum industry.

the Defense or Interior Departments, the OFCC, and the EEOC. Each is responsible basically for the same problems, but no one will accept the other's investigation or facts. Even the federal agencies do not cooperate. Added to these agencies are the numerous private groups and researchers (like the authors!) who hope to further their particular projects through company cooperation. It is understandable, therefore, that firms are reluctant to provide the extensive time and information demanded by the government. As a consequence, these demands have tempered industry's willingness to cooperate with government efforts. As government employees gain experience in dealing with industry, they have been able on occasion to improve their relationship with industry, but the interagency jealousy and competition promise to continue causing problems.

Discussions with management personnel indicate that government pressure has also affected the relationship between foremen and their subordinates. Prior to the enactment of government policy in this area, the only recourse open to Negro employees who felt they had been discriminated against by their superiors was to file a grievance through union channels. There has been general reluctance to take complaints of this nature through the white employee-controlled grievance procedure. Now government complaint investigators welcome purported discrimination charges from workers. Several executives have stated that it was their belief that government employees have on occasion induced previously content employees to file complaints against their firm. Although a significant number of these complaints are clearly instances of discrimination, many that have been filed are just as clearly attempts by disgruntled employees to compensate for their own inefficiency or bad behavior. Regardless of the cause, however, the firm must cooperate with the investigating agency through to the disposition of the case.

Not only have the unjustified complaints cost companies vast amounts of time and effort, but they have also weakened the position of the foreman. He must be especially careful, and is often reluctant, in carrying out disciplinary action against Negro employees. The resentment previously felt by Negro employees as white employees received favored treatment now has developed in white employees. The cost of providing equal opportunity to Negroes has been high but few responsible leaders would argue that the result is not worth the cost.

SOME PERSPECTIVES

The petroleum industry has incurred many problems and high costs to provide improved opportunities for Negroes but, thus far, the results have been very discouraging. A few occupations have afforded Negroes significant job opportunities. Unfortunately, most of the jobs in the industry simply do not have sufficient openings occurring to provide jobs to more than a token number of Negro applicants. Moreover, the inordinately long seniority ladders have prevented even highly qualified Negro applicants from gaining better positions as quickly as the public would desire.

There is little question that the industry has practiced discrimination in the past but it now is exerting great effort to rectify the results of these practices. Jobs in the industry provide good salaries and security to employees and their families. The Negro's progress into these jobs will, however, be exceedingly slow and difficult. In view of the changes that have occurred, it is understandable that problems and frictions have developed, and will probably continue to develop.

CHAPTER VII.

Factors Affecting Negro Employment

At various points throughout this study several factors have been discussed which affect Negro employment in the petroleum industry. To summarize this study the major factors will be re-emphasized.

EMPLOYMENT TRENDS

Employment is no longer expanding in the petroleum industry. Most units operating in crude exploration and production, pipelines, and refining have experienced steady or declining employment for several years. Traditionally in our country this has meant that Negro employment declines at a disproportionately rapid rate. Now, however, the popular axiom that the Negro is the "last hired and first fired" is no longer true in the petroleum industry. Negro applicants for both salaried and production jobs are turned away only if they cannot meet even minimal qualifications. There have, in fact, been cases in which discrimination has been used to favor the Negro. The industry is urgently trying to recruit Negroes who meet the high selection standards demanded by the technology. It is significant to note that the gains in the utilization of Negro employees represent a reversal of the declining employment trend.

The gains in Negro employment and upgrading in the petroleum industry have unfortunately been held below those of many other industries by the lack of job opportunities. In refining many plants are only now initiating their first hiring programs since the layoffs of the late 1950's. Many plants still maintain recall right for employees laid off during that period. Employment opportunities occur only when a new plant or facility is opened, or when separations cause too many openings for efficient operation. Additions to production work crews, black or white, will continue to be small in number for the foreseeable future.

Job Qualifications

Not only has there been a decline in overall demand for labor, but possibly more significant for the Negro is the upgrading of hiring standards. There are no jobs for applicants with low ability or little education. Everyone being hired must have the potential to be promoted as they gain seniority. Although Negroes formerly gained many jobs in the industry as laborers without possessing normal qualifications, the practice of hiring men with little expectation of promotion has been frowned upon by both government and by Negro pressure groups. Forcing each new hire to meet the extremely high selection standards necessary in the industry has decreased the number of Negroes that can be hired, and will continue to do so until Negroes catch up with whites in education and training.

The best opportunities for male Negroes will unfortunately be in those occupations for which so few are as yet qualified, the managerial and professional positions. The industry is continually trying to recruit the highly educated personnel needed to manage the complex petroleum industry. The unfulfilled demand for scientists, engineers, and other technically-oriented college graduates had forced the industry to consider all applicants for several years prior to the recent demands for equal opportunity. Both the quality of the educational programs, high school and college, available to Negroes, and the major areas of study traditionally chosen by Negroes have worked to his disadvantage in obtaining employment in the industry. Even now many of the Negro college graduates hired have majored in areas other than the scientific fields which are often necessary for success in the industry. The well-educated Negro can therefore expect continued opportunities throughout the industry.

Sales is a particularly promising job area for the Negro graduate in liberal arts or the social sciences. Negro salesmen were hired hesitantly at first only to serve the Negro community. Recently most of the major firms have eliminated this practice to a great degree and are utilizing Negroes for general sales work.

Negro females will probably experience the greatest advancement over the next few years. Clerical employees working in data processing find demand so much greater than supply in the petroleum industry that they are often hired with little or no training in the field. The industry has been compelled to begin its own training programs in order to obtain sufficient employees. Unlike training programs for production workers which may take two years or more to complete, programs to train key punch operators and other related occupations are short, inexpensive, and ideal for adding Negroes quickly to the payrolls. Unfortunately, these jobs are largely for females.

Until Negro education and training are improved to meet the needs of the petroleum industry, Negroes will continue to be at a decided disadvantage in their quest for the limited jobs available. The petroleum industry must require skill and educational attainments that proportionately few Negroes now possess. In view of the nature of the equipment, its great cost, the expense of error, and the hazard of fire, there cannot be compromise with legitimate skill requirements. Acquiring skills and education is a time-consuming process, so that upward job movement in this industry will continue to lag as long as the Negro educational and skill gap endures.

LOCATIONAL AND REGIONAL FACTORS

The petroleum industry has traditionally been a southern-based industry. Although the efficiency of locating near consumer markets has drawn many units out of the South, a large number of employees, particularly in managerial positions, have come from regions in which segregation and discrimination were once accepted practices. The racial employment practices which featured the petroleum industry until the 1950's were typical of the regions in which employment units were located. Our national atmosphere has become favorably disposed to the elimination of these attitudes and practices, but as always the mores of a region and the people growing up within it cannot be changed quickly.

The southern attitude toward racial equality has been felt also in the legal environment affecting petroleum industry employment practices. Highly industrialized northern states have generally had fair employment practice laws many years before similar action was taken by Congress. Although these laws have often not changed practices as radically as their sponsors had hoped, they have helped employers coming under their jurisdiction to recognize the problem, and have quelled opposition to altering discriminatory practices. Prior to the Civil Rights Act of 1964, Negroes in the South had no protection of this nature.

A final locational factor affecting Negro employment in the petroleum industry is the small town and rural setting of many drilling rigs, pipeline control points, and product distribution centers. The concentration of Negroes in cities, lack of good public transportation, and housing discrimination, all tend to reduce Negro participation at these units. Even the refineries which are located near major population centers have often been unable to induce Negroes to endure the transportation problems from the center-city areas to the refinery, a distance which often exceeds twenty-five miles, and for which adequate public transportation is often unavailable.

UNIONS AND SENIORITY

The major unions active in the petroleum industry have had little direct effect on Negro employment and upgrading. The OCAW, Teamsters, and Operating Engineers, have each had incidences of discrimination in the past but currently the sentiment of the leadership has favored equal employment opportunity. This statement is not necessarily true for each local union. Nor is such a positive approach taken by each of the many independent unions. In every case, however, the relatively weak influence of local unions in employee relations matters of this nature has permitted management to avoid costly disputes over this issue.

In OCAW, particularly, a tradition of democracy's weak national leadership and fear of local revolts has prevented national leaders from interfering with discriminatory local practices. The existence of the Civil Rights Act has reduced overt local union opposition to the elimination of discrimination, but national union leaders are not likely to push too hard for Negro rights because of fear of political opposition if they do.

The seniority clauses in union contracts have, on the other hand, now become a particularly detrimental restraint on rapid Negro advancement. Seniority districts are generally very narrow with little movement from department to department. With the low turnover in the industry, this means that twenty years' seniority or more may stand between the recent Negro hire and the top jobs. Moreover, the discrimination in the past has been perpetuated in many cases because Negroes, who do transfer out of the labor department, find themselves at the bottom of the departmental seniority list. Unless such Negroes are given a departmental seniority credit for the years in which they were denied the opportunity to bid on better jobs, or permitted to utilize plant seniority for bidding, the abolishment of segregated seniority will serve only a limited purpose.

GOVERNMENT AND CIVIL RIGHTS PRESSURE

Although government pressure to improve racial employment practices by loss of government contracts has been a threat more than a fact, the pressure of government looking over the industry's shoulder has undoubtedly been a positive factor. The government can ill afford to decrease or alter its petroleum product consumption patterns. On the other hand, the loss of a government contract by any of the major oil concerns would have little serious effect on sales revenue. Therefore, the government has thus far carried out its usual investigation program but has relied to a great extent on the industry to correct its own problem areas. Nevertheless direct exertion of government pressure has been the catalyst for change ever since World War II.

Closely allied with government pressure has been that of civil rights groups. In Philadelphia, for example, boycotts led by Negro church leaders proved quite effective in encouraging positive action. The torrid retail competition among oil companies makes each major concern anxious to avoid antagonizing any consumer group. The great threat of government pressure thus far is bad publicity which is so difficult to live down.

The deep resentment in the petroleum industry against the barrage of government inspections is, of course, found in all industry today. On successive days, one plant may be inspected by a state human relations commission investigator, then one from the Equal Employment Opportunity Commission, the Office of Federal Contract Compliance, and finally the Defense Department. Each wants the same information; each declines to accept the findings of another; three can find no cause, but one may, and a long quasi-legal battle then develops. The lack of coordination is aggravating and unnecessary. That the same impact on awareness and need for improvement could be accomplished by a coordinated agency approach seems obvious. Indeed, one cannot disagree with industry spokesmen in this and other industries that more might be gained with a coordinated agency approach because less resentment and better cooperation would be forthcoming. Yet despite these bureaucratic tangles, each period of improvement for Negroes has seen the federal government an active agent in inducing the improvement or at least emphasizing its need.

MANAGERIAL POLICY

Management is now fully cognizant of the exigency of improvement in the position of the Negro in the petroleum industry and the rest of the nation. There, of course, exists among the companies and executives of the industry a divergence of views and opinions on the response that the industry should provide to the demands of government and Negro influence groups. Generally the managements have remained reluctant to offer anything but meaningful, career employment opportunities. Most firms have been understandably reluctant to provide preference in any situation to Negroes. It is fair to say, however, that many industrial leaders in the petroleum industry now have a strong moral commitment to equal opportunity. Weaknesses in the employment policies and practices of the several companies still exist, but the changes which have been gradually initiated by the industry have improved employment opportunities for Negro employees and applicants decidedly during the past decade.

Increased efforts to implement desired programs are often made difficult by the industry's continued reliance on autonomous action by companies and executives. Traditionally petroleum companies have acted independently. Now they remain disinclined to offer any but token cooperation to national and regional programs. Independent action for which the firms receive full credit seems more agreeable to industry traditions. The magnitude of the problem seems unfortunately to negate the effectiveness of this philosophy.

The firm belief in autonomous or decentralized control of operations has also made it difficult to change totally the practices in the employment system which may still be causing discriminatory results. The employment policies and practices at the various facilities have often been solely the responsibility of management at that unit. This can be particularly damaging at the smaller locations where hiring and job assignment may be performed by supervisory personnel who have not been adequately trained for these responsibilities, and whose prime accountability is for other aspects of the facilities' operations.

Corporate officials working on minority employment problems have too often been given only advisory authority in this area, and their effectiveness consequently is limited. Mounting pressure for results is gradually forcing petroleum concerns to delegate the necessary, centralized authority to these officials, and as such pressure continues, further centralization can be expected.

Petroleum industry managements are today well aware of their racial employment problems. Having long enjoyed a reputation for farsighted and progressive personnel programs, they have become conscious of the seriousness of the Negro employment problem and the vital necessity of deriving a solution. Given the industry's sensitivity to public opinion, its past record of problem solution and its general desire to avoid possibly costly controversy with government, management can be expected to continue to increase its efforts to improve opportunities for Negroes. Nevertheless, the institutional and economic factors reviewed in this study emphasize that progress will be slow rather than dramatic.

Part Seven

THE NEGRO IN THE CHEMICAL INDUSTRY

by

William Howard Quay, Jr.

with the assistance of

Marjorie C. Denison

LIST OF TABLES

APPENDIX TABLES

CHAPTER I.

Introduction

The chemical industry in the United States comprises basic chemical producing companies, chemical operating divisions of conglomerates and firms in related fields, and the producers of specialty chemical products. It is illustrative of the problems of Negro employment in a research-oriented industry characterized by rapid technological progress and extensive diversification of products. Negro employment is affected not only by industry growth and subsequent creation of jobs, particularly in white collar categories, but also by the level of automation, by the degree of skill necessary to perform production functions, by union membership practices, and by government employment policy toward minorities. The specific policies of corporate management not only adapt to the social, economic, and political climate, but vary according to particular managerial desires, inclinations, and insights.

This study will examine the problems of Negro employment in the chemical industry and their effect on employment policy and practices. Research was conducted during the years 1968 and 1969 and consists of data collection and interviews with corporate and government officials, supplemented by such published sources as were available.

CHAPTER II.

The Chemical Industry

The chemical industry encompasses a diversity of markets so broad as to play a significant role in nearly all segments of our economy. Synthetic fibers, explosives, synthetic rubber, plastics, alkalies, solvents, antifreeze, dyestuffs, paints, and many basic and intermediate, organic and inorganic chemicals for countless industrial uses are produced by an industry which is more realistically a group of subindustries. With technological progress, new chemicals become competitive with products of companies in other industries; and as other industries find chemical uses for by-products of their own processes, they enter into competition with the basic chemical producers.[1] The result is an industry which defies definitive boundaries.

A small group of diversified chemical producers led by E. I. duPont de Nemours dominates the industry. Specialty chemical producers, such as Diamond Alkali, Air Reduction, and Texas Gulf Sulphur concentrate in limited areas; and recent years have seen the increase in large chemical producing divisions of conglomerates and companies in related fields, such as oil refining. W. R. Grace is placing major emphasis on agricultural chemicals, while Eastman Kodak has challenged in the synthetic fibers market. Drug, paint, cosmetic, and rubber tire companies are examples of extractive operations rather than basic chemical producers and will not be studied in depth for this report.[2]

The collection of statistical data is complicated by the complex nature of the industry. The governmental standard industrial classification system (SIC) divides the chemical industry into eight subindustries under the overall classification of chemicals and allied products

1. Alfred E. Kahn, "The Chemical Industry," in *The Structure of American Industry,* ed. by Walter Adams (New York: Macmillan Company, 1961), pp. 234 and 237.
2. See Parts Five and Six.

as set forth in Table 1. As previously noted, companies using primarily extractive processes are not emphasized in this study. Most employment and market data will, however, contain figures from these companies.

Research emphasis will be on industry racial employment and the policies of the major chemical producers. Company statistics and those from the Manufacturing Chemists' Association, Inc. and government agencies will be used whenever appropriate.

INDUSTRIAL STRUCTURE

Sales of chemicals and allied products reached $46.5 billion in 1968 comprising 5.4 percent of gross national product and 7.7 percent of all manufacturing industries' sales.[3] During the period 1958 to 1963, chemicals maintained an annual growth rate in sales of 6.5 percent compared to 4.9 percent for all manufacturing industries, and have continued steady growth to accommodate ever-increasing demand. Population estimates indicate that by the year 1990, the United States will consume in a few months what the chemical industry now produces in one year.[4] Table 2 summarizes the sales data.

TABLE 1. *Standard Industrial Classification Number 28: Chemicals and Allied Products*

SIC No.	SIC Classification
281	Industrial inorganic and organic chemicals (alkalies, chlorine, industrial gases, coal tar crudes and intermediate products, inorganic pigments)
282	Plastics materials and synthetic resins, synthetic rubber, synthetic and other man-made fibers, except glass
283	Drugs
284	Soap, detergents, and cleaning preparations, perfumes, cosmetics, and other toilet preparations
285	Paints, varnishes, lacquers, enamels, and allied products
286	Gum and wood chemicals
287	Agricultural chemicals
289	Miscellaneous chemical products (adhesives and gelatin, explosives, printing ink, carbon black)

Source: *Standard Industrial Classification Manual,* Executive Office of the President, Bureau of the Budget (Washington: Government Printing Office, 1967).

3. U. S. Department of Commerce, *Survey of Current Business.*
4. *Standard and Poor's Industry Surveys,* "Chemicals, Current Analysis," February 24, 1966, pp. C23-C24.

TABLE 2. *Chemical Industry Sales and the National Economy 1960-1968 (Billions of Dollars)*

Year Ending December 31	Total Gross National Product	Sales of: Manufacturing industries	Sales of: Chemicals and allied products	Chemicals and Allied Products Sales as Percent of: GNP	Chemicals and Allied Products Sales as Percent of: Manufacturing industries
1960	$503.7	$369.6	$26.6	5.3	7.2
1962	560.3	399.7	29.4	5.2	7.4
1964	632.4	445.6	33.6	5.3	7.5
1966	747.6r	538.5r	40.8	5.5	7.6
1968	860.6	603.7	46.5	5.4	7.7

Source: U. S. Department of Commerce, *Survey of Current Business.*

r Revised.

Research and development activities are essential to the chemical industry in meeting this demand as well as being a corporate requisite for successful market competition. Expenditures on research and development were $1.45 billion in 1967, about two-thirds being allocated to human resources.[5] Chemical companies spend an estimated 4 percent of sales on research, almost three times that of general manufacturing industries.[6]

Industry production has been rapidly increasing, while prices have lagged behind the rise in the wholesale price index for all commodities (food and farm products excepted). Price stability has long been a dominant philosophy within the industry; however, more immediate influences on prices have come from improved production techniques lowering costs and the growing competition from nonchemical companies and foreign imports. Over one-half of the fifty largest chemical companies in the western world are not American owned.[7] Table 3 summarizes chemical industry price and production indexes for the years 1960 to 1968.

TABLE 3. *Indexes of Wholesale Prices and of Production for the Chemical Industry and the National Economy 1960-1968*

	Wholesale Price Index (1957-1959 = 100)		Index of Production (1957-1959 = 100)	
Year Ending December 31	Chemicals and allied products	All commodities	Chemicals and allied products	All manufacturing
1960	100.2	100.7	116.6	108.9
1961	99.1	100.3	123.3	109.7
1962	97.5	100.6	136.1	118.7
1963	96.3	100.3	148.6	124.9
1964	96.7	100.5	159.6	133.1
1965	97.4	102.5	173.4	145.0
1966	97.8	105.9	193.2	158.6
1967	98.4	106.1	203.8	159.7
1968	98.2	108.7	221.6	166.8

Source: U. S. Department of Commerce, *Survey of Current Business.*

5. *Ibid.*, February 27, 1968, p. C24.
6. Kahn, *op. cit.*, p. 259.
7. *Standard and Poor's Industry Surveys, op. cit.*, November 3, 1966, p. C26.

Large scale enterprise dominates the industry because of the emphasis on technology and because of the economics of scale in production and research. Costs are lower per unit of capacity in large plants with their highly mechanized and automated installations of autoclaves, filter presses, evaporators, and vats.[8] In 1966, 4,091 chemical establishments employed 1,085,058 persons.[9] The twelve largest diversified chemical producing companies employed 580,153 persons in 1968,[10] the majority being employed in chemicals and allied products' operations. Table 4 lists the twelve largest chemical companies during 1968 of which nine have annual sales over one billion dollars.

TABLE 4. *The Twelve Major Diversified Chemical Producing Companies, 1968*

Company[a]	Sales[b] ($000 omitted)	Employees	Headquarters City
E. I. duPont de Nemours	$3,481,206	114,100	Wilmington, Del.
Union Carbide	2,685,921	100,448	New York City
Monsanto	1,792,938	59,848	St. Louis
Dow Chemical	1,652,493	47,400	Midland, Mich.
Minnesota Mining and Manufacturing	1,405,046	58,193	St. Paul, Minn.
Allied Chemical	1,278,071	35,700	New York City
Celanese	1,255,826	38,706	New York City
American Cyanamid	1,023,231	35,365	Wayne, N. J.
Olin Mathieson	1,002,085	31,000	New York City
Hercules, Inc.	718,037	34,700	Wilmington, Del.
Stauffer Chemical	478,283	10,829	New York City
Rohm and Haas	423,361	13,864	Philadelphia
Total	$17,196,498	580,153	

Source: *Fortune,* Vol. LXXIX (May 15, 1969), pp. 168-175.

[a] The companies listed are those primarily engaged in the chemical industry. W. R. Grace, FMC, and chemical divisions of major oil and tire companies are not included although their chemical sales and employment may exceed some of the companies listed.

[b] Sales and employment include both chemical and nonchemical operation.

8. Kahn, *op. cit.,* p. 242.
9. Data in the author's possession.
10. *Fortune,* Vol. LXXIX (May 15, 1969), pp. 168-175.

E. I. duPont de Nemours is significantly the largest firm in the industry, but competition has become intense. Celanese, for example, increased its sales almost 550 percent from 1956 to 1966 compared to an increase of just over 150 percent for duPont. Historically, duPont research has developed patent protected products, such as cellophane and nylon, enjoying an exclusive market while returning an average of 10 percent on gross operating investment. In 1967 duPont's return on gross operating investment had dropped to the level of its chief competitors because of the aggressive marketing and highly sophisticated research activities of such companies as Monsanto, Dow, Hercules, and Celanese.[11] By 1968, however, duPont had turned around with a return on shareholder equity equal to 14.5 percent—considerably less than its previous records, but, according to *Fortune,* better than the return of most other large producers. Meanwhile, although the sales of Celanese continued upward, it suffered a net loss of $77 million in 1968 as a result of its liquidation of unprofitable and marginal foreign plants and investments.[12]

As previously mentioned, chemical operating divisions of conglomerates and firms in related industries are prominent in the chemical market. W. R. Grace and Food Machinery Corporation (FMC) both with annual sales over $1 billion and employment over 50,000 persons are emphasizing chemical production.[13] Petroleum and rubber companies such as Mobil, Humble, B. F. Goodrich, and Uniroyal, Inc. have established major chemical producing divisions.

Although the chemical industry covers a vast line of products and comprises many diverse corporations, the bulk of industry sales are those listed in Table 1 under "industrial inorganic and organic chemicals" and "plastics materials, synthetic rubbers, and man-made fibers."[14] Continued growth in these major areas as well as in the entire industry with its more than 10,000 separate and distinct products will be of particular importance to the Negro quest for improved employment opportunities.

11. Gilbert Burck, "DuPont under Pressure," *Fortune,* Vol. LXXVI (November 1967), p. 137.
12. John Davenport, "The Chemical Industry Pushes into Hostile Territory," *Fortune,* Vol. LXXVIII (April 1969), pp. 108-114, 156-162; and *Wall Street Journal,* February 20, 1969.
13. *Fortune,* Vol. LXXIX (May 15, 1969), pp. 168-175.
14. Jules Backman, *Competition in the Chemical Industry* (Washington: Manufacturing Chemists' Association, Inc., 1964), p. 2.

MANPOWER

The chemical industry employed 3.9 percent of all manufacturing industries' production workers in 1962.[15] Total employment in the industry during 1968 was 1031.9 thousand persons of whom 610.6 thousand were production workers.[16] Long-term chemical employment is expected to increase at the rate of 2 to 2.5 percent per year, with the number of mathematicians, physicists, chemists, and agricultural scientists increasing at a higher rate[17] The professional nature of these nonproduction jobs presents a serious problem for the relatively large number of Negroes who have not achieved higher levels of education.

Employment is concentrated in the "industrial inorganic and organic chemicals" and "plastics materials, synthetic rubbers, and man-made fibers" subindustries, totaling just over 60 percent of all those employed in the industry during 1968.[18] Table 5 presents chemical employment by subindustries for the years 1960 to 1968.

Occupational Distribution

The occupational distribution of the industry reflects a near balance between white and blue collar workers. In our 1966 sample of 4091 establishments, white collar employment numbered 495,872 persons out of the industry total of 1,085,058. Scientists, chemists, engineers, and other professionals comprised 22 percent of the industry's white collar employees. A large clerical force made up over 30 percent white collar employment. The relatively high proportion of white collar workers, over 45 percent of total industry employment, engaged in research, clerical, technical assistance, sales, and managerial functions, limits the industry's ability to employ persons without the required skills and education.[19]

15. Jules Backman, *Chemicals in the National Economy* (Washington: Manufacturing Chemists' Association, Inc., 1964), p. 68.
16. U. S. Bureau of Labor Statistics, *Employment and Earnings and Monthly Report on the Labor Force,* March 1969, Table B-2, p. 60.
17. *Standard and Poor's Industry Surveys:* "Chemicals, Basic Analysis," October 22, 1964, p. C25.
18. U. S. Bureau of Labor Statistics, *Employment and Earnings Statistics for the United States, 1909-68,* Bulletin No. 1312-6, pp. 643-675.
19. Data in the author's possession. Total industry employment for 1966 is different from that determined by the Bureau of Labor Statistics. This difference is believed insignificant since we are primarily concerned with proportions and trends.

TABLE 5. *Chemicals and Allied Products Industry Total Employment by Subindustry, 1960-1968*[a] *(In Thousands)*

Average for Year Ending December 31	Industrial Inorganic and Organic Chemicals	Plastics Materials, Synthetic Rubbers, and Man-made Fibers	Cleaning and Toilet Preparations	Agricultural Chemicals	Miscellaneous Chemicals; Gums and Wood Chemicals[b]	Drugs; Paints and Allied Products[b]
1960	284.3	154.6	91.2	45.9	80.4	171.9
1961	281.8	154.4	94.5	46.9	80.0	170.6
1962	282.9	165.4	96.4	48.6	82.2	173.0
1963	284.6	175.4	98.1	50.8	81.1	175.4
1964	288.4	181.7	101.5	51.4	78.5	177.1
1965	290.1	193.7	105.6	53.2	80.8	184.4
1966	303.5	205.7	109.3	55.0	93.9	194.1
1967	314.8	204.9	112.4	56.6	110.8	203.0
1968	317.0	215.1	116.7	56.5	116.5	210.2

Source: U. S. Bureau of Labor Statistics: *Employment and Earnings Statistics for the United States, 1909-68,* Bulletin No. 1312-6, pp. 643-675; *Employment and Earnings,* March 1969, Table B2.

[a] Differences in employment totals exist between the Bureau of Labor Statistics and data in the author's possession. It is felt that these are of negligible consequence since proportions and trends are the main point of concern.

[b] These subindustry classifications have been combined only for purposes of this table.

Blue collar workers in the same sample numbered 589,186, with 47.0 percent of these classified as semiskilled operatives.[20] The automated and highly mechanized production facilities, although not strictly repetitive in a production line sense, allow a routinized work process controlled by specific and thorough procedures. Since operating errors can result in substantial product losses, and since the work environment is potentially hazardous, a high degree of mental alertness is required. Extensive training is conducted by the companies in the industry to minimize these risks.

Craftsmen are employed in most maintenance and repair categories with emphasis on electricians, machinists, mechanics, pipefitters, and plumbers. Over 33 percent of the industry's blue collar workers in our sample were craftsmen in 1966. Laborers and service workers made up only about 20 percent of the industry blue collar workers.[21]

The data in Table 6 present the occupational distribution in the chemical industry as represented by the 4,091 establishments in our sample for the year 1966. The largest occupational groups are the operatives and craftsmen. Unskilled workers, laborers and service workers, account for just over 10 percent of all employees. Negro

TABLE 6. *Chemical Industry Occupational Distribution of Employees, 4,091 Establishments, 1966*

Occupational Group	Number of Employees	Percent of Total
Officials and managers	116,122	10.7
Professionals	110,214	10.2
Technicians	68,049	6.3
Sales workers	49,696	4.6
Office and clerical	151,791	14.0
Total white collar	495,872	45.8
Craftsmen (skilled)	195,388	18.0
Operatives (semiskilled)	276,921	25.5
Laborers	88,196	8.1
Service workers	28,681	2.6
Total blue collar	589,186	54.2
Total	1,085,058	100.0

Source: Data in the author's possession.

20. *Ibid.*
21. *Ibid.*

employment is concentrated in the operative, laborer, and service worker categories.[22] Although the operative is of critical importance to plant operation, increasing automation may decrease the number of these jobs and will probably raise skill requirements. Laborers and service workers are traditionally the lowest paid job categories, and the first to be eliminated by automated processes.

Earnings and Unionization

Earnings in the chemical industry, although above the average for all manufacturing industries, are not of the same magnitude as the high wages in the steel, automobile, and aerospace industries. Average hourly and weekly earnings for chemicals and allied products during 1964 were $2.80 and $116.48, respectively, versus $2.53 and $102.97 for all manufacturing industries.[23] By 1968, average chemical industry wages for production workers had risen to $3.26 per hour and $136.27 per week.[24] Table 7 lists average hourly and weekly

TABLE 7. *Average Hourly and Weekly Earnings of Production Workers in All Manufacturing Industries and in Chemicals and Allied Products, 1960-1968*

	Average Hourly Earnings		Average Weekly Earnings	
Year Ending December 31	All manufacturing industries	Chemicals and allied products	All manufacturing industries	Chemicals and allied products
1960	2.26	2.50	89.72	103.25
1961	2.32	2.58	92.34	106.81
1962	2.39	2.65	96.56	110.24
1963	2.46	2.72	99.63	112.88
1964	2.53	2.80	102.97	116.48
1965	2.61	2.89	107.53	121.09
1966	2.72	2.99	112.34	125.58
1967	2.83	3.10	114.90	128.96
1968	3.01	3.26	122.51	136.27

Source: U. S. Bureau of Labor Statistics: *Employment and Earnings Statistics for the United States, 1909-68,* Bulletin No. 1312-6, pp. 640-641 and *Employment and Earnings,* March 1969, Table C-2, p. 94.

22. *Ibid.*
23. *Employment and Earnings Statistics, 1909-68,* pp. 640-641.
24. *Employment and Earnings and Monthly Report on the Labor Force,* March 1969, Table C-2, p. 94.

earnings for production workers in all manufacturing industries and in the chemical industry from 1960 to 1968.

The highest earnings in chemicals and allied products subindustries are in industrial inorganic and organic chemicals, averaging $3.62 per hour and $152.76 per week for production workers in 1968. Second highest earnings are in the plastics materials, synthetic rubbers, and man-made fibers classification, $3.22 per hour and $136.53 per week for production workers in the same year.[25] These subindustries are the largest employers of chemical production workers as noted in Table 5.

Since World War II, nonwage or fringe benefits have increased in relative importance throughout the economy. Pension plans, health and welfare plans, and pay for time not worked (including holidays) are among today's most popular fringe benefits. In 1963, pensions, welfare funds, and other wage supplements equaled 14.2 percent of wages and salaries in the chemical industry, compared to 11.1 percent for all manufacturing industries.[26]

Chemical production requires intensive use of capital and inanimate energy with low intensity of labor. Capital investment per employee is among the highest in all manufacturing industries. The development of unions, consequently, has been less dynamic than in most mass production industries. No single union occupies a dominant role, and a far smaller proportion of workers are in unions than in industries such as steel, rubber, automobiles, and aluminum. National unions play a minor role at duPont, having a total membership of only about 4 percent of the hourly workers in 1967, while about 56 percent of the hourly employees belonged to independent local unions.[27]

The largest unions in the chemical industry are District 50, formerly of the United Mine Workers, the Oil, Chemical and Atomic Workers Union, and the International Chemical Workers Union. Table 8 lists the total membership of these unions by the year 1966. The first is independent; the latter two are affiliates of the AFL-CIO.

25. *Ibid.*
26. Jules Backman, *Chemical Prices, Productivity, Wages, and Profits* (Washington: Manufacturing Chemists' Association, Inc., 1964), p. 39.
27. *Ibid.*, p. 34, and E. I. duPont de Nemours and Company, Inc., interview with Employee Relations Department executives, July 9, 1968.

TABLE 8. *Membership of the Major Labor Unions in the Chemical Industry, 1966*

Union	Total Membership[a]
District 50 (formerly of the United Mine Workers)	232,000
Oil, Chemical and Atomic Workers	165,329
International Chemical Workers	93,000

Source: U. S. Department of Labor and union records.
[a] Membership includes employees in industries other than chemicals.

INDUSTRIAL LOCATION

Chemical plants are located throughout the United States with a heavy concentration in the northeastern states. Table 9 presents

TABLE 9. *The Eleven Largest Chemical Labor Market Areas, 1967*

Labor Market Areas	Chemical Industry Employment (thousands)	Percent of Total Chemical Industry Employment
Total chemical industry employment	1,002.4	100.0
Total eleven largest labor market areas	418.8	41.8
Total major northeastern labor market areas	236.4	23.6
Standard metropolitan statistical areas		
New York-Northeastern N. J.[a]	144.2	14.1
Chicago-Northwestern Ind.[a]	55.7	5.6
Philadelphia, Pa. (-N. J.)	41.6	4.2
Wilmington, Del. (-N. J.)	34.7	3.5
Los Angeles-Long Beach, Calif.	27.9	2.8
St. Louis, Mo. (-Ill.)	24.0	2.4
Houston, Texas	21.7	2.2
Detroit, Mich.	19.2	1.9
Cincinnati, Ohio	17.1	1.7
Cleveland, Ohio	16.8	1.7
Buffalo, N. Y.	15.9	1.6

Source: Total U. S. Employment: U. S. Bureau of Labor Statistics, *Employment and Earnings Statistics for the United States, 1909-68,* Bulletin No. 1312-6. Major Labor Market Employment: U. S. Bureau of Labor Statistics, *Employment and Earnings Statistics for States and Areas, 1939-67,* Bulletin No. 1370-5.

Note: Baltimore, Md., Charleston, W. Va., and San Francisco-Oakland, Calif. all had more than 10,000 employed in the chemical industry. Many other SMSA's have chemical employment up to 10,000 persons.

[a] Standard consolidated area

chemical industry employment in the eleven largest chemical labor market areas, and also shows the major northeastern markets comprising 23.6 percent of total industry employment in 1967. The spread of chemical employment is illustrated by the lack of dominant concentration in any standard metropolitan statistical area (SMSA), except the New York-Northeastern New Jersey, standard consolidated area. The eleven labor markets employed 40.3 percent of the industry total, but chemical plants are also found near small towns where they often are the prime employer. There are relatively few large chemical plants; instead a great number of smaller plants are scattered about the country. The duPont facilities in Deepwater, New Jersey, employed about 7,000 persons in 1967, their largest plant employment in the company.[28]

The expansion of chemical facilities, usually to city outskirts and rural areas because of waste removal and large space requirements, could well lessen Negro employment opportunities since many Negroes are concentrated in center cities, and often public transportation to these outlying areas is inadequate at best.

28. E. I. duPont de Nemours and Company, Inc., interview with Employee Relations Department executives, July 9, 1968.

CHAPTER III.

Negro Employment in Chemicals Prior to 1960

The American chemical industry evolved into the dynamic industrial enterprises that we know today during the first half of the twentieth century as the requirements of industrial self-sufficiency, dictated by participation in two World Wars, forced heavy investment in domestic chemical production. The number of chemical workers increased from about 18,000 in the year 1899 to 688,000 in 1945, with chemical employment expanding more rapidly than the average of all manufacturing industries.[29] This tremendous demand for labor provided Negroes with job opportunities in chemical facilities throughout the United States, including the South where many new plants were being located.

THE PRE-WORLD WAR II ERA

The 1930's are most significantly characterized as years of depression, but because of the chemical industry's function of supplying essential commodities, and the economic cushion provided by its widely diversified products, the decline in chemical output and employment was substantially less than the decline in total industrial activity.[30] However, the industry had less need for the unskilled, where we can assume most Negroes had gained employment. The semiskilled and skilled workers had considerably greater employment security since production requirements demanded the services of those who had craft skills and operational experiences.[31]

29. Jules Backman, *Chemical Prices, Productivity, Wages, and Profits* (Washington: Manufacturing Chemists' Association, Inc., 1964), pp. 32, 79.
30. Jules Backman, *Chemicals in the National Economy* (Washington: Manufacturing Chemists' Association, Inc., 1964), p. 41.
31. Robert L. Taylor, "The Chemical Industry," in *The Development of American Industry*, ed. by John G. Glover and William B. Cornell (New York: Prentice-Hall, Inc., 1946), p. 528.

Chemical industry employment reached 439,845 persons by the year 1940, including 39,987 nonwhites of both sexes.[32] Although nonwhite females achieved only a token representation of 1.3 percent of the total industry employment, nonwhite males made up 10.8 percent of chemical employment.[33] Plant expansion in the South and the migration of many Negroes from the South to northern industry[34] probably accounted for this relatively high proportion of nonwhite employment. Table 10 summarizes employment in the chemicals and allied products industry beginning in the year 1940.

Although Negroes enjoyed substantial representation in the chemical industry, their work was concentrated in the semiskilled operative and unskilled laborer and service worker categories, a condition which continues into the late 1960's. Table 11 shows that in the South during 1940, 74.1 percent of nonwhites in the chemical industry were employed as laborers, while 19.5 percent were employed as operatives. Although the occupational distribution varies in the selected northern cities of New York, Chicago, and Philadelphia, the lowest combination of both operative and laborer categories still accounted for at least 60 percent of nonwhite chemical employment. In relation to the overall pattern of chemical employment, nonwhites were generally overrepresented in the unskilled and semiskilled blue collar and service occupations and underrepresented in skilled, clerical and sales, managerial and professional categories.

Table 11 also reveals some regional differences, showing nonwhites in the South to have been overwhelmingly in the laborer category compared to the northern cities where generally a higher proportion of nonwhites were employed as semiskilled operatives. This differential may be partially explained by the higher level of education attained by northern nonwhites shown in Table 12, but is most likely the result of managerial adherence to regional employment customs.

WORLD WAR II DEVELOPMENTS

Chemical industry growth during World War II was rapid with more than 100,000 additional workers employed in organic chemicals

32. The overwhelming proportion of nonwhites are Negro.
33. *U. S. Census of Population, 1940,* Vol. III, *The Labor Force,* Part 1, Table 76.
34. Eli Ginsberg, "American Democracy and the Negro," in *The Negro Challenge to the Business Community,* ed. by Eli Ginsberg (New York: McGraw-Hill Book Company, 1964), pp. 10-11.

TABLE 10. *Chemicals and Allied Products Industry*
Total Employed Persons by Color, Race, and Sex, 1940-1960

	All Employees				Male				Female			
		Nonwhite				Nonwhite				Nonwhite		
Year	Total	Total	Negro	Percent Negro	Total	Total	Negro	Percent Negro	Total	Total	Negro	Percent Negro
1940	439,845	39,987	39,736	9.0	362,241	38,984	38,754	10.7	77,604	1,003	982	1.3
1950	655,740	55,980	55,230	8.4	525,150	51,690	51,030	9.7	130,590	4,290	4,200	3.2
1960	857,786	53,766	51,573	6.0	693,724	48,501	46,858	6.8	164,062	5,265	4,715	2.9

Source: *U. S. Census of Population:*
1940: Vol. III, *The Labor Force,* Part 1, Table 76.
1950: P-E No. 1D, *Industrial Characteristics,* Table 2.
1960: PC (2) 7F, *Industrial Characteristics,* Table 3.

Table 11. ***Chemicals and Allied Products Industry***
Occupational Distribution of Total and Nonwhite Employment for the South and Selected Cities, 1940

Occupation	South				New York				Chicago				Philadelphia			
	All Employees	Percent of Total	Nonwhite Employees	Percent of Total Nonwhite	All Employees	Percent of Total	Nonwhite Employees	Percent of Total Nonwhite	All Employees	Percent of Total	Nonwhite Employees	Percent of Total Nonwhite	All Employees	Percent of Total	Nonwhite Employees	Percent of Total Nonwhite
Officials and managers	6,909	4.9	37	0.1	2,475	8.1	4	0.6	1,146	6.7	11	2.0	474	5.3	4	0.6
Professionals	7,507	5.3	51	0.2	2,589	8.5	21	3.2	1,281	7.5	29	5.2	887	10.0	15	2.2
Sales and clerical	20,655	14.7	328	1.0	13,029	42.9	107	16.1	5,956	34.9	41	7.4	2,523	28.4	26	3.9
Craftsmen and foremen	17,981	12.7	576	1.7	1,745	5.7	28	4.2	1,470	8.6	31	5.6	945	10.6	24	3.6
Operatives	47,724	33.8	6,458	19.5	8,258	27.2	296	44.4	4,858	28.4	197	35.4	2,642	29.7	208	31.0
Laborers	36,458	25.9	24,528	74.1	1,650	5.4	108	16.2	1,944	11.4	182	32.7	1,143	12.8	327	48.7
Service workers	3,015	2.1	946	2.9	484	1.6	97	14.6	373	2.2	62	11.2	241	2.7	61	9.1
Occupation not reported	807	0.6	177	0.5	170	0.6	5	0.7	58	0.3	3	0.5	42	0.5	6	0.9
Total	141,056	100.0	33,101	100.0	30,400	100.0	666	100.0	17,086	100.0	556	100.0	8,897	100.0	671	100.0

Source: *U. S. Census of Population 1940*, Vol. III, *The Labor Force*, Part 1, Table 82, and Part 5, Table 20.

alone for the production of explosives.[35] Employment in chemicals and allied products grew with product demand, increasing from 371.0 thousands of workers in 1939 to 668.0 thousands in 1945. Production workers increased from 252.0 thousands to 518.0 thousands during the same period.[36] Expanding employment meant more jobs for Negroes; however, they remained concentrated in the unskilled and semiskilled blue collar occupations. Their relative lack of education, as shown by Table 12, and minimal training, in addition to racial discrimination, continued as major obstacles to Negro admission to the skilled worker occupations and to salaried employment.

The migration from rural areas to the cities was accelerated by the demands of a wartime economy. Although Negroes were moving into center city, as illustrated in Table 13, chemical facilities were

TABLE 12. *Percent Nonwhite and White, Ages 25-29 Who Have Completed High School but Not College in Selected States and Regions,[a] 1940-1960*

State and Region	1940 Nonwhite	1940 White	1950 Nonwhite	1950 White	1960 Nonwhite	1960 White
New Jersey	11.0	23.6	21.1	40.6	29.9	41.6
New York	14.4	24.1	25.3	40.4	31.8	37.6
Illinois	16.6	27.6	25.3	40.4	26.9	41.5
Pennsylvania	12.3	25.4	23.8	42.8	32.9	46.9
Ohio	16.2	33.4	24.8	43.1	30.0	42.9
Texas	8.7	22.7	13.7	27.3	25.8	32.6
California	27.1	35.6	33.1	40.6	33.5	35.6
Michigan	n.a.	28.7	21.7	40.4	29.9	42.6
North Carolina/Virginia	5.0	20.2	8.3	23.7	20.8	34.4
Delaware/Maryland/D. C.	10.2	26.2	19.6	39.7	25.8	36.6
Appalachian States	7.9	17.4	13.9	25.6	22.3	32.1
Deep South	3.1	20.2	5.3	24.3	15.0	34.9

Source: U. S. Bureau of the Census, *Population Trends in the United States, 1900 to 1960,* Table 6.

[a] In 1960 the proportion of Negroes that finished college was about one-half the proportion of whites that finished college.

35. *The Chemical Industry Facts Book* (Washington: Manufacturing Chemists' Association, Inc., 1953), p. 100.

36. *Ibid.*, p. 3.

TABLE 13. *Nonwhite Population of Central Cities and Outside Central Cities in Selected States and Regions, 1940-1960 (in thousands)*

State and Region	1940 Central City	1940 Outside Central City	1950 Central City	1950 Outside Central City	1960 Central City	1960 Outside Central City
New Jersey	91	105	138	133	248	194
New York	487	62	808	83	1,214	156
Illinois	290	55	514	91	848	144
Pennsylvania	333	111	486	126	671	153
Ohio	264	40	416	56	659	72
Texas	285	104	392	127	644	113
California	90	26	302	137	591	254
Michigan	169	26	347	69	581	93
North Carolina/Virginia	311	134	370	169	496	157
Delaware/Maryland/D. C.	367	64	523	88	762	107
Appalachian States	296	78	355	73	416	93
Deep South	768	504	962	514	1,198	583

Source: U. S. Bureau of the Census, *Population Trends in the United States, 1900 to 1960,* Table 2.

continuing to expand on the city outskirts and in the country, thus limiting the access by Negroes to chemical jobs.

Early Union Influences

Unionism came to the chemical industry with the passage of the National Industrial Recovery Act in 1933 and the birth of the CIO in 1935. District 50 (an affiliate of the United Mine Workers until 1968) was founded in 1936, and together with the National Council of Chemical and Allied Industries Unions, the Oil Workers International Union, the Textile Workers Union of America, the United Rubber Workers, and various independent local unions, represented about 40,000 workers by collective agreements in 1942, almost 35 percent of the industry.[37] By the end of World War II, in addition to those unions already active in organizing chemical employees, the International Chemical Workers Union and the United Gas, Coke,

37. U. S. Bureau of Labor Statistics, *Collective Bargaining in the Chemical Industry, May 1942,* Bulletin No. 716, July 1942, p. 2.

and Chemical Workers (later to merge with the Oil Workers International Union to become the International Oil, Chemical and Atomic Workers Union) were conducting organizational efforts within the industry.[38]

The chemical companies frequently dealt with from two to four major unions and with many single-plant independent unions. Even by the year 1961 only about 40 percent of the industry's workers were represented by unions other than the independent locals.[39] Because of this amalgam of labor unions, particular union racial policy has played a relatively minor role in racial employment policies. Segregated locals were existent in almost all major unions at this time, however, indicating that unions in effect accepted and tended to institutionalize the *status quo*.[40]

NEGRO EMPLOYMENT, 1945-1960

The chemical industry continued its expansion after World War II despite employment slumps in 1946 and during the recession of 1958. By the year 1951, shortly after the outbreak of the Korean War, chemical employment surpassed the World War II high and increased into the 1960's. Many of the new jobs were provided by the rapidly developing plastics, synthetic fibers, and synthetic rubbers subindustries. Although Negroes numerically increased their employment in the chemical industry into the 1950's, they could no longer maintain the 9.0 percent of total chemical employment which they experienced in the 1940's (see Table 10).

Postwar Transition, 1945-1950

Chemical employment decreases in late 1945 and during 1946 were mostly in explosives where over 100,000 workers were laid off. A steadily increasing output smoothed the general transition from wartime to a peacetime economy, such that the shift from military to civilian markets allowed greater volume production with fewer workers per ton of output. Improvement in labor productivity was

38. J. Wade Miller: "Collective Bargaining in the U. S. Chemical Industy," in Arnold R. Weber (ed.), *The Structure of Collective Bargaining* (New York: The Free Press of Glencoe, Inc., 1961), p. 205.
39. *Ibid.*, pp. 205-206.
40. U. S. Bureau of Labor Statistics, *Collective Bargaining in the Chemical Industry, May 1942*, p. 12.

made possible by new plants and more efficient equipment.[41] Thus, even with postwar layoffs which involved many Negroes and white workers of low seniority, industry output continued upward.

Employment in chemicals and allied products quickly recovered from the postwar slump and reached 655.0 thousands of persons by 1948. The recession of 1949 saw a major decline in chemical employment to 618.0 thousands, but one year later in 1950 employment jumped dromatically.[42] Table 10 shows chemicals and allied products employment numbering 655,740 persons in 1950, of whom 55,230 were Negroes comprising 8.4 percent of the total. Negroes had numerically increased their employment in the chemical industry since 1940, but their percent of total chemical employment showed a downward trend. This trend is probably attributable to major increases in white collar employment, primarily, clerical, sales, and research, during the postwar industrial boom.[43] Negro educational handicaps were critical restrictions on their taking advantage of these opportunities, and in chemicals, as well as in most industry, there was little attempt on the part of managements to employ those who were qualified. Plant expansion outside the periphery of cities as Negroes continued their migration to center city raised further barriers to Negro employment because of the gradual decline in public transportation, the relative scarcity of automobiles in Negro families, and discrimination in suburban housing and consumer credit.[44]

The Korean War to 1960

Increasing economic demand for chemical products, greater plant expansion, and rising employment were generated by the United States commitment in Korea.[45] Although the chemical industry is noted for

41. U. S. Bureau of Labor Statistics, *Employment Outlook in the Industrial Chemical Industry,* Bulletin No. 1151 (Washington: Government Printing Office, 1953), pp. 29-30.
42. Backman, *Chemical Prices, Productivity, Wages, and Profits,* p. 79.
43. Charles E. Silberman, *Crisis in Black and White* (New York: Random House, 1964), p. 40.
44. On these problems in general see: U. S. Bureau of Labor Statistics, *The Negroes in the United States: Their Economic and Social Situation,* Bulletin No. 1551, 1966; and *Social and Economic Conditions in the United States,* Report No. 332, 1967; Karl E. and Alma F. Tauber, *Negroes in the Cities* (Chicago: Aldine Publishing Company, 1965); and J. R. Meyer, J. F. Kain, and M. Wohl, *The Urban Transportation Problem* (Cambridge, Massachusetts: Harvard University Press, 1965), pp. 144-170.
45. *The Chemical Industry Facts Book,* p. 3.

its ability to increase output without proportionate increases in employment, plant expansion raised employment in chemicals and allied products to 707.0 thousands in 1951.[46] The war in Korea started an employment boom that resulted in the lowest unemployment level since World War II. By 1952 employment had jumped to 730.1 thousands and, except for a slight drop in 1954, continued upward to 810.0 thousands in 1957.[47] Although Negroes continued to suffer higher unemployment than whites,[48] it can be assumed that employment prosperity provided more Negroes with jobs.

The recession of 1958 caused a drop in chemical employment to 794.1 thousands, but by the end of 1959, 809.2 thousands were employed, about the 1957 level.[49] The industry's resilience to economic slowdown was once again demonstrated by this brief and relatively small decline in employment during a recession that lasted three years or more for many industries.

Negro chemical employment in 1960, however, showed ominous signs despite the industry's overall well-being. Table 10 shows chemicals and allied products employment increasing over 200,000 persons to 857,786 from the year 1950 to 1960. Negro employment for the same period declined over 3,000 persons to 51,573, and the Negro percentage of total industry employment dropped to 6.0 percent. The prime reason for this trend seems to have been the expansion of employment in those occupations in which Negroes were underrepresented rather than in occupations in which Negroes were concentrated, and the failure to open up the better jobs to black workers.

Occupational Distribution and Regional Differences, 1960

Negroes continued to be concentrated in the unskilled and semiskilled employment categories in 1960. Table 14 shows male and female nonwhite occupational distributions in the chemicals and allied products industry. The majority of nonwhites were employed as semiskilled operatives, comprising a respectable 9.6 percent of total operative employment. However, nonwhites were overrepresented in

46. Backman, *Chemical Prices, Productivity, Wages, and Profits*, p. 79; and U. S. Bureau of Labor Statistics, *Employment Outlook in the Industrial Chemical Industry*, p. 31.
47. Backman, *Chemical Prices, Productivity, Wages, and Profits*, p. 79.
48. Daniel Patrick Moynihan, "Political Perspectives," in Eli Ginsberg (ed.), *The Negro Challenge to the Business Community*, pp. 76-77.
49. Backman, *Chemical Prices, Productivity, Wages, and Profits*, p. 79.

TABLE 14. *Chemicals and Allied Products Industry*
Total Employed Persons, Occupation by Color and Sex, 1960

Occupation	All Employees			Male			Female		
	Total	Nonwhite	Percent Nonwhite	Total	Nonwhite	Percent Nonwhite	Total	Nonwhite	Percent Nonwhite
Managerial	58,632	342	0.6	54,630	322	0.6	4,002	20	0.5
Professional	134,255	2,412	1.8	119,697	1,989	1.7	14,558	423	2.9
Clerical	132,304	3,154	2.4	46,345	2,320	5.0	85,959	834	1.0
Sales	47,975	243	0.5	45,487	103	0.2	2,488	140	5.6
Craftsmen	142,581	3,610	2.5	139,452	3,408	2.4	3,129	202	6.5
Operatives	257,085	24,555	9.6	211,238	21,917	10.4	45,847	2,638	5.8
Laborers	48,115	13,152	27.3	46,612	12,931	27.7	1,503	221	14.7
Service	19,556	4,745	24.3	16,361	4,058	24.8	3,195	687	21.5
Occupation not reported	17,283	1,553	9.0	13,902	1,453	10.5	3,381	100	3.0
Total	857,786	53,766	6.3	693,724	48,501	7.0	164,062	5,265	3.2

Source: *U. S. Census of Population, 1960,* PC(2) 7A, *Occupational Characteristics,* Table 36.

the unskilled, low-paying laborer and service worker occupations where they respectively made up 27.3 percent and 24.3 percent of the total employment in these categories.

The increased reliance on automated equipment created a greater demand for workers in maintenance and repair occupations.[50] Craftsmen were the second largest occupational category in 1960, as they are today, yet nonwhites constituted only 2.5 percent of industry craftsmen.

Expanding white collar employment provided little opportunity for the Negro in the chemical industry for reasons previously discussed. In 1960 neither managerial nor sales occupations admitted more than 0.6 percent nonwhite employees. Professional employment, the third largest occupational category in the industry, had only 1.8 percent nonwhite employees. A booming clerical work force was only 2.4 percent nonwhite. Salaried work was still largely closed to Negroes in 1960.

Nonwhite women had significantly greater representation for their sex than did men in the craft and sales occupations, although their largest number of jobs were as semiskilled operatives. Nevertheless, the occupational distribution for nonwhite women generally followed the same pattern as that for nonwhite males. Laborer and service worker categories were overrepresented, while nonwhites in the higher-paying craft and white collar jobs, especially clerical, were underrepresented.

Regional Data, 1960

Negro employment in chemicals and allied products is also presented on a state and metropolitan basis by Tables 15 and 16. Negro chemical employment was numerically highest during 1960 in the states of New Jersey, New York, and Illinois, although the southern states of South Carolina and Virginia maintained the largest percentage of Negro employees, followed by Illinois, Tennessee, and Texas. The southern states, however, experienced a decline in the percentage of Negro employees between 1940 and 1960, and in most cases a decline in numerical Negro employment between 1950 and 1960. Job opportunities for Negroes in the chemical industry during 1960 were more favorable in the northeastern states as indicated by a

50. *Employment Outlook in the Industrial Chemical Industry,* p. 32.

TABLE 15. *Chemicals and Allied Products Industry*
Total Employed Persons by Race, Selected States, 1940-1960

State	1940[a] Total Employees	1940[a] Negroes Number	1940[a] Negroes Percent	1950 Total Employees	1950 Negroes Number	1950 Negroes Percent	1960 Total Employees	1960 Negroes Number	1960 Negroes Percent
New Jersey	51,740	1,307	2.5	74,891	3,413	4.6	93,084	4,867	5.2
New York	58,307	832	1.4	77,212	3,322	4.3	85,653	4,569	5.3
Illinois	30,309	1,272	4.2	45,404	3,793	8.4	57,620	4,289	7.4
Pennsylvania	31,260	933	3.0	42,778	2,112	4.9	59,011	2,636	4.5
Tennessee	17,701	2,681	15.1	33,509	3,548	10.6	43,378	2,625	6.1
Ohio	27,175	900	3.3	39,952	2,290	5.7	56,267	2,578	4.6
Texas	9,375	1,754	18.7	29,141	3,559	12.2	46,970	2,782	5.9
California	17,920	113	0.6	30,139	990	3.3	45,143	1,377	3.1
Michigan	19,050	170	0.9	30,577	557	1.8	40,909	849	2.1
Virginia	20,617	3,234	15.7	28,908	3,735	12.9	31,982	2,705	8.5
Delaware	9,266	230	2.5	14,533	625	4.3	21,096	764	3.6
West Virginia	15,166	84	0.6	21,739	267	1.2	25,566	232	0.9
Missouri	11,000	390	3.5	15,757	965	6.1	21,675	1,178	5.4
Indiana	8,390	328	3.9	17,447	838	4.8	24,747	1,125	4.5
South Carolina	4,274	2,967	69.4	5,015	2,082	41.5	12,571	1,807	14.4

Source: *U. S. Census of Population:*
1940: Vol. III, *The Labor Force,* Parts 2-5, Table 18.
1950: Vol. II, *Characteristics of the Population,* Parts 2-54, Table 83.
1960: PC(1) D, *Detailed Characteristics,* State Volumes, Table 129.

[a] Industry: "Rayon and Allied" and "Other Chemical and Allied."

TABLE 16. *Chemicals and Allied Products Industry*
Total Employed Persons by Race
Selected Standard Metropolitan Statistical Areas, 1950 and 1960

Standard Metropolitan Statistical Area	1950 Total	1950 Negro	1950 Percent Negro	1960 Total	1960 Negro	1960 Percent Negro
New York-Northeastern N. J.[a]	106,475	5,512	5.2	122,457	7,963	6.5
Chicago-Northwestern Indiana[a]	35,181[b]	2,843[b]	8.1	44,195	3,750	8.5
Philadelphia, Pa. (-N. J.)	26,851	2,083	7.8	40,261	2,697	6.7
Wilmington, Del (-N. J.)	17,124	703	4.1	24,242	910	3.8
Los Angeles-Long-Beach, Calif.	14,336	443	3.1	24,399	719	2.9
St. Louis, Mo. (-Ill.)	15,604	1,686	10.8	21,858	1,668	7.6
Houston, Texas	4,994	589	11.8	11,873	926	7.8
Detroit, Mich.	15,699	495	3.2	17,706	688	3.9
Cincinnati, Ohio	10,945	776	7.1	14,136	738	5.2
Buffalo, N. Y.	16,543	504	3.0	17,660	527	3.0
Cleveland, Ohio	15,159	707	4.7	17,363	904	5.2

Source: *U. S. Census of Population:*
1950: Vol. II, *Characteristics of the Population,* Parts 2-54, Table 83.
1960: PC(1) D, *Detailed Characteristics,* State Volumes, Table 129.

[a] Standard Consolidated Area.
[b] Porter County, Indiana not included in 1950.

continuing increase in the number of Negroes employed since 1940 and a relatively steady percentage of Negro employees in the chemical work force since 1950.

The major metropolitan areas in chemicals and allied products employment during 1960 are presented in Table 16. The largest of these labor markets, the New York-Northeastern New Jersey area, employed nearly three times the number of persons employed in the Chicago-Northwestern Indiana complex, which employs the second largest number of chemical workers. The highest percentage of Negro employment in chemicals, 8.5 percent, was found in the Chicago-Northwestern Indiana area, followed by Houston with 7.8 percent and St. Louis with 7.6 percent. Los Angeles-Long Beach, Buffalo, Wilmington, and Detroit had significantly lower percentages of Negro chemical workers. In all areas, except St. Louis and Cincinnati, Negro chemical employment increased between 1950 and 1960, but in over half the areas studied the percentage of Negroes employed in the chemical industry has declined over the same period.

TABLE 17. *Total Population by Race*
Selected Standard Metropolitan Statistical Areas, 1960

Standard Metropolitan Statistical Area	Total	Negro	Percent Negro
New York-Northeastern N. J.[a]	14,759,429	1,557,069	10.5
Chicago-Northwestern Indiana[a]	6,794,461	977,332	14.4
Philadelphia, Pa. (-N. J.)	4,342,897	671,304	15.5
Wilmington, Del. (-N. J.)	366,157	44,851	12.2
Los Angeles-Long Beach, Calif.	6,742,696	464,717	6.9
St. Louis, Mo. (-Ill.)	2,060,103	294,873	14.3
Houston, Texas	1,243,158	246,351	19.8
Detroit, Mich.	3,762,360	558,870	14.9
Cincinnati, Ohio	1,071,624	128,121	12.0
Buffalo, N. Y.	1,306,957	82,910	6.3
Cleveland, Ohio	1,796,595	257,273	14.3

Source: *U. S. Census of Population, 1960,* PC(1) D, *Detailed Characteristics,* State Volumes.

[a] Standard Consolidated Area.

A comparison of industry metropolitan employment with the 1960 population amplifies the above statistics, although the industry's limited ability to utilize the educationally and occupationally disadvantaged may be more the cause of any discrepancies than outright racial discrimination. Table 17 shows the percentage of Negroes in the population of the same eleven metropolitan areas. The chemical industry's low percentage of Negroes employed in Los Angeles-Long Beach and Buffalo is partially explained by the low percentage of Negroes in these areas. Wilmington and Detroit show greater discrepancies between the percentage of Negroes employed and percent in the population. Such discrepancies also exist in the Houston, Cleveland, and Philadelphia areas. The lowest ratios of percentage of Negroes in the population to percent employed in the chemical industry were in the New York and Chicago areas. It should be noted, however, that the preceding use of statistics is subject to significant flaws and should be used with caution. At best, the comparison of population to work force is only a general indicator of the racial employment trends, for it tells us nothing of such factors as skill requirements and capacity, plant location in relation to Negro residential areas, and other relevant factors.

The Nixon Committee Reports

President Eisenhower established the President's Committee on Government Contracts by Executive Order 10479. This Committee, chaired by Vice-President Nixon, investigated the employment practices of government contractors from 1957 to 1960, and made its findings available to federal contracting agencies. The Nixon Committee's intent was for employers to become "color-blind" in their employment policies and procedures.

In the 1957-1959 period the Nixon Committee met with management in a number of plants. The Committee concentrated its efforts largely in duPont company facilities, but also examined those of other concerns. The Committee findings show a much heavier percentage of Negroes in the southern chemical plants than in northern ones, but in the South, a concentration of Negroes in unskilled jobs. The Nixon Committee's merger reports on this industry for the years 1957 and 1958, as set forth in Table 18, support the conclusion, reached on the basis of census data, that the percentage of Negroes in the industry at this time ranged close to 6 percent, and that Negroes were concentrated in the blue collar jobs where automating was threatening their positions.

TABLE 18. *Chemical Industry Total and Negro Employment Eleven Establishments, 1957*

All Employees			White Collar			Blue Collar		
Total	Negro	Percent Negro	Total	Negro	Percent Negro	Total	Negro	Percent Negro
20,520	1,258	6.1	6,513	16	0.2	14,007	1,242	8.9

Source: President's Committee on Government Contracts (Nixon Committee) files.

CHAPTER IV.

Negro Employment and Affirmative Action in the 1960's

Negro employment in the chemical industry during the 1960's is the primary focus of this report. The factors examined in the preceding chapter continue to have restrictive effects upon the Negro's efforts to improve his economic condition. Increasingly technological job requirements, the continued rise in white collar employment and the relative stagnation of blue collar growth, chemical plant expansion outside center city, and lingering attitudes of racial discrimination limit the availability of jobs to the black community.

The 1960's, however, have brought a more aggressive attempt by corporate management to enlist Negroes into their work forces at a time of tight labor markets and labor shortages. Affirmative action programs, whereby management seeks out black employees and takes a more active role in their occupational development, have been motivated by a reappraisal of businesses' social responsibility, as well as by vigorous governmental pressures.

Chemical employment has grown steadily since 1960 when 828.2 thousand persons were employed. By 1968 industry employment reached 1031.9 thousand[51] with corporate manpower projections forecasting a continued upward trend. It will be recalled that the data in Chapter II predict a favorable economic future for the chemical industry. The future for the Negro worker in this vital industry, is discussed in the remainder of the chapter.

THE EARLY 1960's

Corporate attitudes toward the economic and social condition of Negroes began to swing from sympathy and concern to positive action

51. U. S. Bureau of Labor Statistics, *Employment and Earnings Statistics for the United States, 1909-68,* Bulletin No. 1312-6, p. 639.

during the early 1960's. The southern school crisis, resulting from the 1954 Supreme Court decision to prohibit segregation in all public schools, bus boycotts, and lunch counter sit-ins confronted the nation with the civil rights issue and Negro demands to share fully in American life. Governmental action under the President's Committee on Government Contracts (Nixon Committee) during the 1950's and the more stringent President's Committee on Equal Employment Opportunity established by President Kennedy in 1961, brought increasing pressure upon private industry to eliminate any form of discriminatory employment practice. A tightening labor market, after the resurgence of economic prosperity in the early 1960's, added pressures to employ fully the nation's manpower resources.

In 1962 most major chemical employers joined the Plans for Progress, a voluntary alliance of businessmen, formed originally as a part of the President's Committee on Equal Employment Opportunity to aid in the solution of employment and other community problems. Major policy statements were issued by members of this group prohibiting racial discrimination in the conduct of their businesses. Industry's efforts prior to the Civil Rights Act of 1964 were, however, primarily in the area of policy making with little progress made in actual employment results.

The EEOC Data for 1966

In early 1969, the Equal Employment Opportunity Commission published a summary of reports made to it in 1966 by employers of 100 or more, pursuant to the requirements of Title VII of the Civil Rights Act of 1964.[52] Table 19 sets forth the results of the EEOC tabulation for the Chemical industry in the United States.

The EEOC data cannot, of course, be strictly compared with those collected by the census of population. The former excluded employers of less than 100, and were submitted by employers based upon their records. The latter are based upon responses of individuals to census workers. Yet remarkably enough, the data based upon EEOC returns for 1966 in Table 19 and those based upon the census of 1960 in Table 14 reveal almost identical results. According to the census, 6.3 percent of chemical employees were Negroes in 1960; according

52. U. S. Equal Employment Opportunity Commission, *Job Patterns for Minorities and Women in Private Industry, 1966*. Report No. 1 (Washington: The Commission, 1969), Parts I, II, and III.

TABLE 19. *Chemicals and Allied Products Industry Employment by Race, Sex, and Occupational Group 3459 Establishments, Total United States, 1966*

Occupational Group	All Employees			Male			Female		
	Total	Negro	Percent Negro	Total	Negro	Percent Negro	Total	Negro	Percent Negro
Officials and managers	98,237	432	0.4	95,673	393	0.4	2,564	39	1.5
Professionals	89,470	687	0.8	84,810	577	0.7	4,660	110	2.4
Technicians	57,908	1,314	2.3	49,419	1,044	2.1	8,489	270	3.2
Sales workers	46,805	140	0.3	45,345	129	0.3	1,460	11	0.8
Office and clerical	124,033	2,202	1.8	33,164	907	2.7	90,869	1,295	1.4
Total white collar	416,453	4,775	1.1	308,411	3,050	1.0	108,042	1,725	1.6
Craftsmen (skilled)	150,632	4,378	2.9	149,270	4,274	2.9	1,362	104	7.6
Operatives (semiskilled)	245,418	23,487	9.6	197,466	20,858	10.6	47,952	2,629	5.5
Laborers	78,250	17,734	22.7	57,965	15,507	26.8	20,285	2,227	11.0
Service workers	25,161	5,747	22.8	21,927	5,139	23.4	3,234	608	18.8
Total blue collar	499,461	51,346	10.3	426,628	45,778	10.7	72,833	5,568	7.6
Total	915,914	56,121	6.1	735,039	48,828	6.6	180,875	7,293	4.0

Source: U. S. Equal Employment Opportunity Commission, *Job Patterns for Minorities and Women in Private Industry, 1966.* Report No. 1 (Washington: The Commission, 1968), Part II.

to EEOC, that percentage was 6.1 in 1966! Moreover, the EEOC occupational group percentage data follow closely those of the census. The conclusion seems unmistakable that, between 1960 and 1966, Negroes, at best, maintained their position in the industry, but certainly did not improve their status.

THE 1964-1968 FIELD SAMPLE

The data published by the EEOC are also broken down by state and by major Standard Metropolitan Statistical Areas (SMSA), which are cities and contiguous locations. We shall utilize the state data for our regional analysis below. The EEOC data, however, are based upon the period in late 1965 or early 1966, and therefore, do not reflect later trends and changes resulting from the impact of civil rights legislation and regulation and/or labor market developments.

Accordingly, data were gathered for this study for three years: 1964, 1966, and 1968. Although our sample is not as complete as that of the EEOC, it is broadly representative. Our data involve, with only very minor exceptions, the same companies and plants in 1966 and 1968, and these plus additional ones in 1964 so that the data for the three years are quite comparable. We are able, moreover, to utilize the 1966 EEOC data as a control to indicate any biases in our samples, and thus avoid any distortions resulting from sampling procedure. These will be noted where pertinent. The data gathered for this study are thus able to give an excellent picture of developments over a span of time in which both civil rights activity and legislation, and economic prosperity were at all-time high levels.

The basic data resulting from our field sample are set forth in the Appendix. Tables A-1 to A-3 provide the figures for the entire industry, nationwide, for the years 1964, 1966, and 1968 respectively. For convenience of analysis, the percentage of Negroes by occupational group and by sex, based upon these appendix tables, is shown in Table 20. The 5.0 percent Negro employment shown in Table 20 for 1966, as compared with 6.1 percent in Table 19, indicates that our field sample slightly underestimates the Negro ratio in the industry. This may result from the fact that our data are drawn heavily from the largest companies. Many companies having between 100 (the EEOC cutoff figure) and 500 employees, which was the minimum for most establishments in our sample, apparently have a slightly larger

TABLE 20. *Chemical Industry*
Percent Negro Employment by Occupational Group and Sex
Total United States, 1964-1968

Occupational Group	All Employees 1964	All Employees 1966	All Employees 1968	Male 1964	Male 1966	Male 1968	Female 1964	Female 1966	Female 1968
Officials and managers	0.2	0.2	0.4	0.2	0.2	0.4	0.2	0.4	1.1
Professionals	0.4	0.5	0.8	0.3	0.4	0.7	0.9	2.1	3.1
Technicians	1.2	1.5	2.5	1.2	1.5	2.3	0.8	1.5	3.5
Sales workers	0.3	0.3	0.7	0.3	0.3	0.7	—	0.4	0.5
Office and clerical	1.4	1.8	3.2	2.1	2.4	3.5	1.0	1.6	3.0
Total white collar	0.7	0.9	1.6	0.6	0.8	1.2	1.0	1.6	3.0
Craftsmen (skilled)	1.9	2.2	2.9	1.9	2.2	2.8	*	1.2	12.7
Operatives (semiskilled)	7.2	7.6	9.9	8.1	8.4	10.3	2.9	3.9	8.3
Laborers	25.5	25.8	22.4	27.7	28.5	25.2	3.6	5.6	8.5
Service workers	23.4	22.9	23.0	24.0	23.2	23.0	18.9	20.4	22.9
Total blue collar	7.7	8.0	9.2	8.2	8.3	9.2	3.4	4.7	9.1
Total	4.7	5.0	6.0	5.2	5.4	6.0	1.9	2.9	5.6

Source: Tables A-1–A-3.

* Less than 0.05 percent.

than average black employment ratio. This seems to be the only logical reason for the difference in 1966 between the 6.1 ratio of EEOC and the 5.0 percent in our sample. In discussing data in our sample, therefore, this slight underestimation should be borne in mind. In view of the fact that our concern is on trends, as well as existing ratios, the analysis will still be very pertinent.

The data in Table 20 represent 1964, 1966, and 1968 Negro employment in 280, 303, and 291 establishments respectively. The sample includes 38 percent of chemical employment in 1964, 37 percent in 1966, and 35 percent in 1968. Even assuming some underestimation in our data, and noting again the lack of comparability of our data, as well as those of EEOC, with census enumerations, it still does seem that in 1964, the downward trend of Negro employment in the industry, which commenced in the 1950's, was still occurring. The emphasis during the early 1960's, as in the late 1950's was on cost reduction and the substitution of improved methods and automatic equipment for labor. Negroes were concentrated in the lower-rated blue collar jobs, and were hence disproportionately displaced while better jobs were not open to them, or if they were, their disadvantaged backgrounds often prevented them employment.

By 1966, the trend had been turned around, and it has continued upward ever since. It seems obvious that Negro employment has not only surpassed the 1960 ratio, but is now trending upward well beyond that. Our field studies give clear indication that the trend was continued upward in 1969, and the affirmative action programs of the industry, described in a later section of this chapter, will probably insure this.

ANALYSIS OF OCCUPATIONAL GROUPS

A major difficulty with current occupational reporting is the classification of jobs into broad categories that do not represent the practice of a particular industry. It is, therefore, not uncommon for companies to disagree in their reporting into what group to place a job, or even to be unable accurately to place a job in a particular occupational group. Consequently, the occupational ratios in this report, or in any similar use of data, may not be precise, but they can be very helpful in revealing major occupational differences. An understanding of the problems of racial employment must include an analysis of these occupational categories, which are presented next.

Officials and Managers

Negroes are almost nonexistent in this critical occupational category, which includes all levels of industrial management from first-line supervision to the very top executive positions. Most Negroes in this grouping are at the first level of supervision, working as plant foremen in charge of racially mixed work crews, but probably not directing all-white units.

The highest managerial levels achieved by Negro workers are usually in employee relations and scientific research departments. The ranking Negro managerial positions are currently those of research laboratory manager and, in at least one case, manager of urban affairs and equal employment oportunity, an employee relations function. There is not one Negro in the top management of any major chemical firm known to the author.

Chemical management has been drawn predominantly from those employees with backgrounds in chemistry and engineering, and with professional degrees in business administration (MBA). Negroes who have had the opportunity to acquire such training in the past have instead chosen professions where greater potential for employment existed and therefore are not available for management consideration. Improvements have been made in the admissions of black students to programs in applied sciences and in graduate business administration, but the numbers involved are still quite small. Educational institutions are attempting to achieve better racial balance in their student bodies, but are faced with Negro suspicion that the opportunities are not truly available, and with the lack of qualified Negro applicants. Attitudes of mistrust after years of disappointment are not quickly overcome. Corporate recruiters are increasingly active on Negro college campuses and in seeking black students at predominantly white institutions. Notable success in gaining Negro managerial trainees has not been forthcoming, partly because of inadequate training, but also because of suspicion towards the motives of company officials. Young and talented Negro students fear being an "instant Negro," hired to demonstrate the unbiased personality of management.

A difficult cycle is in motion. Management wants to integrate its ranks with qualified members of minority groups. The trained Negro, in particular, is limited in supply and wants to see evidence of management's sincerity, that is, a substantial number of Negro managers. Management cannot demonstrate sincerity until it finds someone to hire and then promote. The dilemma is real and difficult. "Black power" is in part a cry for decision-making power in the conduct of American enterprise. There are few, if any, major decisions being made by Negroes in the chemical industry; and few Negroes in the industry with the requisite training.

Professionals, Technicians, and Sales Workers

Scientists, engineers, lawyers, and accountants are major representatives of the occupational category known as professionals. Basic and applied chemical research, engineering development of plant facilities, patent and corporate law, and accounting control procedures are critical functions to the success of a chemical manufacturer. Most of these occupations require advanced academic degrees which, we have already noted, relatively few Negroes possess.

Recruitment of Negro professionals is highly competitive because of the scarcity of candidates. This shortage often pressures firms into offering higher salaries to Negroes than those offered to white applicants. Many firms have refused to pay this premium on the grounds of equal treatment for all candidates of similar capabilities. These firms have not been notably successful in hiring Negro professionals. The extremely low ratio of Negroes in this occupational category reflects the above conditions.

Technicians are particularly essential to plant quality control procedures. The testing of batch samples is vital in determining if a product is chemically acceptable within specified tolerances. Modifications to existing process procedures are also analyzed in a laboratory setting which may include pilot plant facilities.

Job specifications call for a high school education or equivalent with mathematical and science abilities. Competition for jobs as technicians is very strong and only the high achievers in company testing and in their formal education are likely to gain employment in this category. Negroes, again, are at a disadvantage, especially if they have attended all-black schools without adequate quantitative curriculums, or inferior slum area institutions. Although Negroes are better represented in the technician category than in most other white collar occupations, they still accounted for only 2.5 percent of all chemical technicians in our sample in 1968.

Sales workers in the chemical industry are primarily industrial salesmen selling to other manufacturers. Consumer end-use sales are conducted by chemical divisions such as paints, drugs, and agricultural chemicals. It is in the sales category that racial prejudice is most apparent. The social nature of a salesman's work involving entertaining, meetings, and close working relationships with customers has caused chemical companies to fear the racial repercussions of a Negro salesman on company sales. In fact, customers have actually expressed their opposition to dealing with any chemical salesman who is black.

Some chemical producers have cautiously begun to introduce Negro salesmen into areas of liberal racial feelings. A Negro salesman in the South would be rare indeed, but they are employed on the West Coast and in the Northeast, with some inroads being made in border states such as Maryland. Even with the slow integration of sales forces, Negroes do not yet constitute 1 percent of chemical salesmen in our sample.

Office and Clerical

Office and clerical employment continues to grow steadily in the chemical industry. Increasing staffs of key punch operators, typists, stenographers, secretaries, purchasing personnel, bookkeepers, and personnel assistants dominate in this occupational group.

Negro employment here has made its greatest white collar gains, although the proportion in our sample was only 3.2 percent of all office and clerical employees in 1968. Difficulties are apparent in vocational training programs available to Negroes, and the competition for available Negro clerical employees is now severe. Moreover, the location of many chemical plants in outlying areas, rather than in center city, discourages center city dwelling Negroes from applying.

Poor schooling remains a key factor. Young typists are often surprised to learn on applying for a job that their new skills are inadequate or incorrectly taught. The employer must then decide if further development by the company is feasible and, if not, the applicant must be rejected. A rejection after hopes have been again raised is possibly more disastrous to improved understanding between the races than if the training had never been received in the first place. Certainly, it is most injurious to the morale of the applicant.

The explosion in computer programming short courses is an example of the problems of "aspiration level." With the obvious benefits of computer-based information systems and the shortage of programmers, many communities have witnessed the birth of computer institutes offering approximately six-month courses in programming and suggesting the opening of new and better job opportunities upon graduation. The graduates have, however, sometimes realized upon applying for a computer programming job that they did not learn enough relevant material in six months and that much of what they learned was clearly obsolete. High hopes have been shattered and the resultant despair may be more acute than before the promise of new opportunity was offered. Depth of despair could be related to the frequency of previous disappointment, which would be considerable in the case of many Negroes. Chemical companies are attempting to create more understanding among vocational schools and institutes concerning the actual skill requirements the employer is seeking. The need of the companies for employees and the availability of black candidates indicate that these problems will be overcome, although it will not be done without problems, or in a short period.

Secretarial work-study programs are available to Negroes and are popular with chemical companies as a means of increasing the supply of qualified clerical help. Since many clerical and office jobs are filled by women, a high turnover rate exists due to marriage, pregnancy, and travel requirements. A shortage of labor in this occupational category is added incentive to the employment of minority group members by the chemical companies.

Craftsmen

Craftsmen are the second largest occupational group in the chemical industry, growing in response to maintenance and repair demands of automated facilities. Mechanics, electricians, plumbers, pipefitters, and machinists are well represented in chemical plants. These jobs are often considered the elite of blue collar chemical occupations, yet the emphasis is more on general skilled capabilities as opposed to skilled specialties.

Recruiting is conducted primarily on the open market without regard for craft union affiliation. Graduates of Manpower Development Training Act programs and men with skilled military experience are sought as much as tradesmen. In addition, operatives and helpers are given upgrading opportunities.

Negroes, however, still face barriers to skilled employment. Craft union discrimination prevents many Negroes from obtaining the apprentice training so necessary for development of craft capabilities. Although white tradesmen may operate as free agents and seek employment in plants organized by industrial unions, Negroes are rarely able to represent themselves as apprentices or journeymen with the training that is implied in these designations because the oportunities have not been present.

The MDTA programs have frequently disenchanted Negroes by not providing sufficient job opportunities once training is completed. Many young Negroes cannot rationalize the value of long and rigorous training if no reward is forthcoming upon its completion.

Apprentice programs are not common in the chemical industry. Open market recruitment of workers already possessing the necessary skills has provided an adequate supply of skilled labor. In-plant on-the-job training is conducted in maintenance and repair departments, but these trainees usually have some degree of related experience prior to employment. Recent shortage of skilled labor, however, has put more emphasis on in-plant training and upgrading.

Maintenance and repair personnel are very protective of their jobs and fear massive inroads by black workers. The distaste of working one day for a black supervisor has been expressed in some walkout threats against possible selection of a Negro foreman.

These factors account for the low percentage of black workers in the craft occupations. Recent Negro self-help programs such as Opportunities Industrialization Centers, are attempting to provide the necessary training for skilled work, and with the cooperation of chemical employers are determined to provide jobs for graduates of their programs.

The increasing tendency of chemical companies to contract out all maintenance work mitigates against increased Negro craft employment. The maintenance function under such arrangements is performed by contractors dealing with the construction trade unions with persons employed for maintenance work as employees of the contractor, not of the chemical company. The lack of Negro representation in such unions and the general disinclination of such unions to accept racial integration point to continued difficulties in increasing the

Negro ratio as chemical industry craftsmen as the practice of contracting out maintenance expands.

Operatives

The largest occupational group in the chemical industry is operatives, consisting of semiskilled workers, some responsible for large investments in product and equipment. Chemical production is a continuous flow process controlled by a system of valves, gauges, and weighing devices. Operatives must possess sufficient mental ability to understand operating procedures and to react effectively in emergencies. Other operative classifications exist in shipping where the job of fork lift operator is common.

Most blue collar careers in chemical plants are oriented toward the operative functions. Recruitment is on the open market and selection criteria demand specified levels of mental training and ability. A high school diploma or equivalent and minimum general aptitude test scores are required for employment. These requirements are currently being re-evaluated to determine whether the cut-off level may be reduced.

Negroes are fairly well represented in these jobs, comprising about 10 percent of all chemical operatives. Entry requirements are among the lowest in the industry and the volume of jobs is the largest. Opportunities for promotion ultimately to the rank of foreman are best in the operative grouping. Wages are among the highest of blue collar categories. Negroes have traditionally been concentrated in the lower operative positions, but in recent years have been moving upward as a result of labor shortages and civil rights pressures.

Although Negroes currently have their best employment opportunities as operatives, future developments in automated facilities may reduce the number of blue collar jobs as machinery takes over functions now performed by workers. When an automated system becomes more closed in design, the opportunities for employment decrease and operational responsibility increases. Conversely, it is conceivable that automation may become so effective as to reduce the current demands on human ability; but if this situation occurs, job applicants may eventually face a restructured job, combining maintenance and repair functions with those of process operation, with responsibility for both product and equipment. One major chemical producer is already experimenting with such a job classification, although results are inconclusive. Skill requirements for this restructured job would increase beyond those of the current operative category. Unless Negro educational opportunities improve and company training covers more employees, the operative grouping could become closed to many Negro applicants, especially in new plants not bound by union agreements as to job classification. This is because new plants are likely to be the most completely automated and to structure jobs requiring all-around ability and/or special training. In view of the current emphasis on civil rights, companies moving in this direction may be expected to put considerable resources into training black employees.

Laborers and Service Workers

The smallest blue collar occupational categories are laborers and service workers. Traditionally, Negroes have been concentrated here and today comprise more than 20 percent of all chemical workers in each of these groupings. The concept of "Negro work" was based on a belief that colored people could only perform routine manual functions such as janitorial maintenance, messenger duty, some guard duty, and cafeteria service. All of these jobs were dead-end careers with no opportunity for bidding into operative or craft occupations. This condition exists today, except for the plant labor pools which serve as entry jobs for operator development.

The labor pool, once 100 percent black in some southern locations, has been increasingly integrated and revised to serve as a talent reservoir for plant operations. Routine tasks such as painting, grass cutting, and digging are still the job of laborers. Service in the labor pool, however, rarely exceeds one year as workers are promoted through seniority channels into lower-level helper and operative positions.

Major plant maintenance and expansion is subcontracted by most chemical firms, removing the need for large standing labor forces. The elimination of unskilled jobs has reduced the opportunities in chemical plants for the hard-core unemployed, but at the same time those who do gain employment now have the opportunity to advance into the higher-paying jobs. The decline in the proportion of Negroes in labor jobs in our sample between 1964 and 1968 indicates that Negro laborers are being upgraded.

Service positions remain limited in career development, although some jobs have channels for bidding into plant operations. The number of workers in this category is relatively small compared to most other occupational groupings and is more a class of specialties than a source of operational manpower.

The proportion of Negroes represented in these categories, although declining, is likely to remain high. Many of these workers are advanced in age without the skill or motivation to pursue new careers. Although efforts are being made to train and to upgrade those who have previously been discriminated against and who desire advancement, progress is limited by the nature of existing employees and the fact that they were employed to be laborers without thought of future advancement.

Negro Women in the Chemical Industry

Negro women are not well represented in the chemical industry. Their occupational distribution follows the same general pattern as that of male Negroes with underrepresentation in white collar jobs and overrepresentation in the lowest-paying blue collar groups.

The office and clerical category is predominantly female, but Negro women comprise merely 3 percent of these employees. Most Negro women are employed as blue collar workers in the traditional, routine operative, laborer, and service occupations of sorter, checker, janitress, cafeteria worker, and minor laboratory assistant. The tradition of black domestic help leads Negro women to seek these occupations, but racial prejudice is also a factor in preventing Negroes from joining other groups of female workers.

A high turnover rate is a common characteristic of female employment. Marriage and pregnancy contribute to heavy resignations. Transportation to outlying chemical facilities is also a hindrance to longterm female employment because of a lack of safe, comfortable travel facilities. Negro women are usually highly motivated to work, especially after they have a family, and are often more tolerant of transportation and working conditions than whites. Even so, lack of training for white collar positions and continuing racial prejudice have limited their utilization by the chemical industry.

LOCATIONAL FACTORS

Chemical facilities are often located near urban centers with large Negro populations. There is recent evidence that the Negro migration to urban centers is receding, and that some black families are leaving the inner city to escape despair and stagnant occupational opportunity, but with whites still moving to the suburbs, Negro urban ratios may well continue to increase.

As previously discussed, chemical facilities locate primarily on city outskirts in order to have adequate space for plant expansion, lower tax burdens, better waste removal, reduced effects of air pollution, and limitation of the effects of possible explosion. Plant employment often necessitates extensive daily travel from the cities or relocation in the suburbs nearer to the place of work.

Public transit service is becoming less adequate in meeting the demands of urban populations, reducing the Negro's opportunity to take advantage of chemical jobs. Attempts have been made to organize car pools, but few major firms are actively engaged in improving transit facilities. Bus lines find it increasingly difficult to employ drivers for center city routes where robberies and violence have become commonplace. The only alternative means of transportation for inner city residents is the private automobile, which, of course, requires a steady income to own and operate.

Housing in the suburbs is another barrier to the Negro. Suburban housing opportunities have often been closed to blacks except in those communities consciously supporting open housing. Besides the elimination of racial restrictions on suburban housing, the Negro aspirant must have sufficient income to afford the higher housing costs in the suburbs.

A few companies have been active in supporting state and local open-housing legislation; yet most have taken a hands-off approach. The major firms do, however, attempt to find desirable housing for black professionals being offered employment, especially in headquarters' cities.

Chemical companies remain mostly oriented strictly towards economic factors in plant location. Social responsibility in providing open housing and in improving urban transit is primarily in the discussion stage. The question of how involved in these matters a company should become is still largely unresolved.

REGIONAL AND PLANT SIZE COMPARISONS

Both the Equal Employment Opportunity Commission data for 1966, and our sample for 1964, 1966, and 1968 have been grouped for geographical comparisons. As in the data examined for the total

United States, the EEOC data are used as an indication of the accuracy of our sample. The regional data for our sample include all establishments represented in the total 1964, 1966, and 1968 data. Many companies, of course, have plants and offices in more than one region.

The dominant regions of chemical employment are the Southeast, Middle Atlantic, and North Central. Southwest and other Midwest regions have moderate chemical employment, with New England and the West Coast being relatively sparse in large chemical production facilities.

Table 21 summarizes our sample data for the three years by region and sex. In each area, the percentage of Negroes increased, with the Southeast having the highest ratio. Very substantial gains were made by Negro women, with the greatest of these advances being in the South and Midwest. Increased use of black women both in factory and office occurred in these areas, as labor markets tightened and civil rights pressures grew, but as we shall note, the employment gains were much more in blue collar, than in white collar jobs.

The percentage of Negroes is below the national average in the Middle Atlantic region, which includes for the purposes of this study, the great chemical concentrations not only in the New York-New Jersey Metropolitan areas, but those around Philadelphia, Wilmington, Delaware, and Baltimore. This is surprising in view of the great concentration of Negroes in these areas. An examination of the racial-occupational data for the regions is required prior to detailed comment on this phenomenon.

Tables 22-24 contain the occupational group and sex data for Negroes and total employment for the Northeast region, and its constituent areas, New England and the Middle Atlantic states, calculated from the 1966 data submission to the Equal Employment Opportunity Commission.[53] Tables 25-27 show the percentage breakdowns for the same groups and areas for 1964, 1966, and 1968, calculated from our field sample. As is the case with the national data, comparing our field sample for 1966 with the EEOC data indicates that our data underestimate the Negro ratio in the chemical industry of the Northeast.

53. U. S. Equal Employment Opportunity Commission, *Job Patterns for Minorities and Women in Private Industry, 1966.* Report No. 1 (Washington: The Commission, 1968), Part II. States selected are those with ten or more reporting establishments or those with at least five establishments and at least 2,000 employees.

TABLE 21. *Chemical Industry*
Percent Negro Employment by Sex and Region[a]*, 1964-1968*

Region	All Employees			Male			Female		
	1964	1966	1968	1964	1966	1968	1964	1966	1968
Northeast	3.9	4.1	4.8	4.3	4.5	5.1	1.8	2.3	3.6
New England	3.4	3.7	4.3	3.9	4.1	4.6	0.6	0.9	2.6
Middle Atlantic	3.9	4.2	4.8	4.4	4.6	5.1	1.9	2.4	3.7
South	6.0	6.3	7.3	6.6	6.8	7.4	2.0	3.6	6.9
Southeast	6.2	6.6	7.7	7.0	7.1	7.8	2.1	3.8	7.2
Southwest	4.9	5.2	5.4	5.1	5.4	5.6	0.6	1.4	2.4
Midwest	3.8	3.9	5.3	4.1	4.2	4.9	1.8	2.3	7.0
North Central	3.8	3.8	5.2	4.0	4.0	4.9	2.0	2.4	7.0
Other Midwest	3.9	4.4	5.4	4.3	4.8	5.0	1.5	1.9	6.7
West Coast	3.5	3.7	4.7	3.1	3.4	4.3	5.9	6.1	6.8
Total United States	4.7	5.0	6.0	5.2	5.4	6.0	1.9	2.9	5.6

Source: Appendix Tables A-1–A-33.

[a] Geographic definitions are as follows:

New England: Connecticut, Maine, Massachusetts, New Hampshire, Rhode Island, and Vermont.
Middle Atlantic: Delaware, Maryland, New Jersey, New York, and Pennsylvania.
Southeast: Alabama, Florida, Georgia, Kentucky, Louisiana, Mississippi, North Carolina, South Carolina, Tennessee, Virginia, and West Virginia.
Southwest: Arizona, New Mexico, Oklahoma, and Texas.
North Central: Illinois, Indiana, Michigan, Ohio, and Wisconsin.
Other Midwest: Iowa, Kansas, Minnesota, Missouri, Nebraska, North Dakota, Rocky Mountain States, and South Dakota.
West Coast: California, Idaho, Nevada, Oregon, and Washington.

TABLE 22. *Chemicals and Allied Products Industry Employment by Race, Sex, and Occupational Group 1046 Establishments in the Northeast Region, 1966*

Occupational Group	All Employees			Male			Female		
	Total	Negro	Percent Negro	Total	Negro	Percent Negro	Total	Negro	Percent Negro
Officials and managers	36,942	197	0.5	35,922	190	0.5	1,020	7	0.7
Professionals	41,682	425	1.0	38,949	357	0.9	2,733	68	2.5
Technicians	24,784	635	2.6	20,840	491	2.4	3,944	144	3.7
Sales workers	21,448	90	0.4	20,616	86	0.4	832	4	0.5
Office and clerical	60,144	1,383	2.3	15,630	530	3.4	44,514	853	1.9
Total white collar	185,000	2,730	1.5	131,957	1,654	1.3	53,043	1,076	2.0
Craftsmen (skilled)	47,956	2,083	4.3	47,346	1,999	4.2	610	84	13.8
Operatives (semiskilled)	83,774	7,124	8.5	66,360	6,196	9.3	17,414	928	5.3
Laborers	31,111	5,294	17.0	20,384	3,794	18.6	10,727	1,500	14.0
Service workers	10,584	1,828	17.3	8,997	1,585	17.6	1,587	243	15.3
Total blue collar	173,425	16,329	9.4	143,087	13,574	9.5	30,338	2,755	9.1
Total	358,425	19,059	5.3	275,044	15,228	5.5	83,381	3,831	4.6

Source: U. S. Employment Opportunity Commission, *Job Patterns for Minorities and Women in Private Industry, 1966.* Report No. 1 (Washington: The Commission, 1968), Part II. For limitations of data, see note 53, p. 45.

Note: For regional definitions, see Table 21, p. 652.

TABLE 23. *Chemicals and Allied Products Industry Employment by Race, Sex, and Occupational Group 135 Establishments in the New England Region, 1966*

Occupational Group	All Employees			Male			Female		
	Total	Negro	Percent Negro	Total	Negro	Percent Negro	Total	Negro	Percent Negro
Officials and managers	3,131	12	0.4	3,049	12	0.4	82	—	—
Professionals	3,020	31	1.0	2,866	27	0.9	154	4	2.6
Technicians	2,218	62	2.8	1,835	55	3.0	383	7	1.8
Sales workers	1,056	1	0.1	1,042	1	0.1	14	—	—
Office and clerical	4,391	55	1.3	1,006	15	1.5	3,385	40	1.2
Total white collar	13,816	161	1.2	9,798	110	1.1	4,018	51	1.3
Craftsmen (skilled)	4,347	148	3.4	4,267	147	3.4	80	1	1.2
Operatives (semiskilled)	8,430	605	7.2	6,488	431	6.6	1,942	174	9.0
Laborers	4,003	527	13.2	2,692	318	11.8	1,311	209	15.9
Service workers	822	86	10.5	729	72	9.9	93	14	15.1
Total blue collar	17,602	1,366	7.8	14,176	968	6.8	3,426	398	11.6
Total	31,418	1,527	4.9	23,974	1,078	4.5	7,444	449	6.0

Source: U. S. Employment Opportunity Commission, *Job Patterns for Minorities and Women in Private Industry, 1966*. Report No. 1 (Washington: The Commission, 1968), Part II. For limitations of data, see note 53, p. 45.

Note: For regional definitions, see Table 21, p. 652.

TABLE 24. *Chemicals and Allied Products Industry*
Employment by Race, Sex, and Occupational Group
911 Establishments in the Middle Atlantic Region, 1966

Occupational Group	All Employees			Male			Female		
	Total	Negro	Percent Negro	Total	Negro	Percent Negro	Total	Negro	Percent Negro
Officials and managers	33,811	185	0.5	32,873	178	0.5	938	7	0.7
Professionals	38,662	394	1.0	36,083	330	0.9	2,579	64	2.5
Technicians	22,566	573	2.5	19,005	436	2.3	3,561	137	3.8
Sales workers	20,392	89	0.4	19,574	85	0.4	818	4	0.5
Office and clerical	55,753	1,328	2.4	14,624	515	3.5	41,129	813	2.0
Total white collar	171,184	2,569	1.5	122,159	1,544	1.3	49,025	1,025	2.1
Craftsmen (skilled)	43,609	1,935	4.4	43,079	1,852	4.3	530	83	15.7
Operatives (semiskilled)	75,344	6,519	8.7	59,872	5,765	9.6	15,472	754	4.9
Laborers	27,108	4,767	17.6	17,692	3,476	19.6	9,416	1,291	13.7
Service workers	9,762	1,742	17.8	8,268	1,513	18.3	1,494	229	15.3
Total blue collar	155,823	14,963	9.6	128,911	12,606	9.8	26,912	2,357	8.8
Total	327,007	17,532	5.4	251,070	14,150	5.6	75,937	3,382	4.5

Source: U. S. Employment Opportunity Commission, *Job Patterns for Minorities and Women in Private Industry, 1966.* Report No. 1 (Washington: The Commission, 1968), Part II. For limiitations of data, see note 53, p. 45.

Note: For regional definitions, see Table 21, p. 652.

TABLE 25. *Chemical Industry*
Percent Negro Employment by Sex and Occupational Group
Northeast Region, 1964-1968

	All Employees			Male			Female		
Occupational Group	1964	1966	1968	1964	1966	1968	1964	1966	1968
Officials and managers	0.2	0.3	0.5	0.2	0.3	0.5	0.4	0.9	1.8
Professionals	0.5	0.6	1.0	0.5	0.5	0.9	0.9	1.9	3.1
Technicians	1.5	1.9	2.5	1.6	1.9	2.4	1.3	2.0	3.1
Sales workers	0.4	0.4	0.7	0.4	0.4	0.8	—	—	—
Office and clerical	1.9	2.3	3.7	3.2	3.2	4.7	1.3	1.9	3.3
Total white collar	1.0	1.2	1.9	0.9	1.0	1.4	1.2	1.8	3.2
Craftsmen (skilled)	4.1	4.1	4.7	4.1	4.1	4.7	—	—	2.2
Operatives (semiskilled)	6.5	6.9	8.6	7.3	7.7	9.8	1.6	1.8	2.3
Laborers	13.4	14.1	12.2	14.7	15.6	13.5	3.5	4.4	6.1
Service workers	17.9	16.3	19.3	17.6	15.9	18.4	19.2	18.9	24.0
Total blue collar	7.1	7.3	8.3	7.5	7.6	8.8	3.6	3.8	4.8
Total	3.9	4.1	4.8	4.3	4.5	5.1	1.8	2.3	3.6

Source: Appendix Tables A-4–A-6.

Note: For regional definitions, see Table 21, p. 652.

TABLE 26. *Chemical Industry*
Percent Negro Employment by Sex and Occupational Group
New England Region, 1964-1968

	All Employees			Male			Female		
Occupational Group	1964	1966	1968	1964	1966	1968	1964	1966	1968
Officials and managers	0.3	0.3	0.3	0.3	0.3	0.3	—	—	—
Professionals	0.7	0.7	0.6	0.5	0.6	0.5	2.7	3.0	1.4
Technicians	3.5	3.6	4.3	4.2	4.2	4.6	—	0.8	2.1
Sales workers	—	—	—	—	—	—	—	—	—
Office and clerical	0.7	1.1	1.8	0.8	1.8	0.8	0.7	0.9	2.2
Total white collar	1.0	1.2	1.4	1.0	1.2	1.2	0.7	1.0	2.1
Craftsmen (skilled)	4.2	5.2	4.9	4.2	5.2	4.9	—	—	—
Operatives (semiskilled)	5.3	5.6	7.4	5.7	6.0	7.5	0.5	0.5	5.0
Laborers	5.1	5.5	5.8	5.4	5.9	5.7	—	—	7.6
Service workers	12.8	11.7	16.2	14.0	12.8	17.6	—	—	—
Total blue collar	5.3	5.8	6.8	5.5	6.1	6.9	0.3	0.3	5.3
Total	3.4	3.7	4.3	3.9	4.1	4.6	0.6	0.9	2.6

Source: Appendix Tables A-7–A-9.

Note: For regional definitions, see Table 21, p. 652.

TABLE 27. *Chemical Industry*
Percent Negro Employment by Sex and Occupational Group
Middle Atlantic Region, 1964-1968

	All Employees			Male			Female		
Occupational Group	1964	1966	1968	1964	1966	1968	1964	1966	1968
Officials and managers	0.2	0.3	0.5	0.2	0.3	0.5	0.5	1.0	1.8
Professionals	0.5	0.6	1.0	0.4	0.5	0.9	0.7	1.8	3.2
Technicians	1.4	1.7	2.3	1.4	1.7	2.2	1.4	2.1	3.1
Sales workers	0.5	0.4	0.8	0.5	0.5	0.8	—	—	—
Office and clerical	1.9	2.3	3.8	3.4	3.3	4.9	1.3	1.9	3.3
Total white collar	1.0	1.2	1.9	0.9	1.0	1.4	1.3	1.9	3.3
Craftsmen (skilled)	4.1	4.0	4.7	4.1	4.1	4.7	—	—	2.4
Operatives (semiskilled)	6.6	7.1	8.7	7.5	7.9	10.0	1.7	1.9	2.3
Laborers	15.5	15.7	13.3	17.2	17.5	15.1	4.0	4.8	5.9
Service workers	18.3	16.6	19.5	18.0	16.1	18.5	20.0	19.9	24.8
Total blue collar	7.4	7.4	8.5	7.7	7.8	9.0	3.8	4.0	4.8
Total	3.9	4.2	4.8	4.4	4.6	5.1	1.9	2.4	3.7

Source: Appendix Tables A-10–A-12.

Note: For regional definitions, see Table 21, p. 652.

The small chemical industry of New England is concentrated largely in the southern area of that region. Most New England Negroes live in this area, but the percentage of blacks in Connecticut or Rhode Island, while increasing, is substantially less than in any of the Middle Atlantic states. Yet the latter region, with its enormous chemical industry concentration and its much higher percentage of Negro residents, has a ratio of Negroes barely larger than does New England. Indeed, the Northeast area remains below the national average in its percentage of black employees, with the ratio increasing between 1964 and 1968 at about the same rate, but slightly slower, than did the national ratio.

Several factors account for the Northeast situation. Among them are the large number of central offices and research centers in this region, which employ only salaried employees, and few Negroes. Also, many of the plants in this region are located away from the cities where the black population is concentrated. Nevertheless, even with these difficulties, it does appear that the chemical industry in this area was perhaps slow to put its affirmative action programs into effect and has had difficulty in opening up jobs on a quantitative basis.

Within the occupational structure, however, the Northeast area compares favorably with the national picture. In the salaried groups, the Northeast Negro ratios are equal to or superior to the national ones, and 4.7 percent of the craftsmen were black in 1968 in the Northeast as compared with 2.9 for the nation as a whole. Actually it is in the bottom three categories that the Northeast falls behind. It is thus apparent that employers in this region have concentrated in upgrading and in recruiting Negroes in the better jobs, rather than in quantitative recruitment in recent years.

The South remains the region of highest Negro percentage employment. Table 28, based upon the 1966 EEOC reports, shows this ratio at 8.6 percent. Table 29 shows that our field study again underestimates the ratio in this area.

The South leads in utilization of black chemical workers primarily because of their heavy concentration in the lowest-skilled classifications. Some progress in the better jobs is indicated by Table 29, but all salaried groups and the craftsmen category had a smaller percentage of Negroes than nationally in 1968. The reverse was true in the three lowest-skilled categories especially in the traditional Negro jobs of laborer and service worker.

Plants in the Southeast (Table 30) had both a higher Negro ratio and a better representation in the salaried and craftsmen groups than did those in the Southwest (Table 31). The plants in the latter area are found mainly in Texas in association with the petroleum industry. Our study of the latter pointed up the long segregation pattern and the difficulties of altering it.[54] The Southwest also had a large Mexican-American minority, who as Negroes, are likely to be found in the lowest occupational groups.

Table 32 contains the EEOC 1966 data for the Midwest, which find this area below the national average in totals, but actually only because there is a lower representation in the lowest categories. The lack of Negro population in some Midwestern areas may well account for this difference.

Comparing the 1966 EEOC percentages in Table 32 with those from our sample in Table 33, we find a decided underestimation of

54. See Part Six, especially Chapter V.

TABLE 28. *Chemicals and Allied Products Industry*
Employment by Race, Sex, and Occupational Group
971 Establishments in the South Region, 1966

Occupational Group	All Employees Total	All Employees Negro	All Employees Percent Negro	Male Total	Male Negro	Male Percent Negro	Female Total	Female Negro	Female Percent Negro
Officials and managers	30,262	94	0.3	29,856	93	0.3	406	1	0.2
Professionals	22,369	52	0.2	21,834	40	0.2	535	12	2.2
Technicians	16,331	288	1.8	14,360	237	1.7	1,971	51	2.6
Sales workers	5,054	13	0.3	4,910	11	0.2	144	2	1.4
Office and clerical	23,527	316	1.3	8,092	207	2.6	15,435	109	0.7
Total white collar	97,543	763	0.8	79,052	588	0.7	18,491	175	0.9
Craftsmen (skilled)	65,809	1,282	1.9	65,588	1,275	1.9	221	7	3.2
Operatives (semiskilled)	86,595	10,177	11.8	69,086	9,343	13.5	17,509	834	4.8
Laborers	19,822	8,913	45.0	17,822	8,589	48.2	2,000	324	16.2
Service workers	6,993	2,615	37.4	6,434	2,358	36.6	559	257	46.0
Total blue collar	179,219	22,987	12.8	158,930	21,565	13.6	20,289	1,422	7.0
Total	276,762	23,750	8.6	237,982	22,153	9.3	38,780	1,597	4.1

Source: U. S. Employment Opportunity Commission, *Job Patterns for Minorities and Women in Private Industry, 1966.* Report No. 1 (Washington: The Commission, 1968), Part II. For limitations of data, see note 53, p. 45.

Note: For regional definitions, see Table 21, p. 652.

TABLE 29. *Chemical Industry*
Percent Negro Employment by Sex and Occupational Group
South Region, 1964-1968

Occupational Group	All Employees 1964	All Employees 1966	All Employees 1968	Male 1964	Male 1966	Male 1968	Female 1964	Female 1966	Female 1968
Officials and managers	0.1	0.1	0.3	0.1	0.1	0.3	—	—	—
Professionals	0.1	0.2	0.4	0.1	0.2	0.4	0.8	2.9	3.8
Technicians	0.7	1.0	2.0	0.7	1.0	1.8	0.1	1.0	3.1
Sales workers	—	—	0.4	—	—	0.4	—	—	—
Office and clerical	0.6	1.1	2.3	1.0	1.6	2.6	0.4	0.9	2.2
Total white collar	0.3	0.5	1.0	0.3	0.4	0.8	0.4	0.9	2.3
Craftsmen (skilled)	0.9	1.3	2.0	0.9	1.3	2.0	*	1.0	3.0
Operatives (semiskilled)	7.9	8.5	11.0	9.2	9.7	11.6	3.1	4.6	9.1
Laborers	44.7	46.9	41.5	46.5	48.7	43.5	2.2	11.6	13.6
Service workers	34.6	33.4	32.4	34.9	33.4	32.2	29.8	32.6	36.4
Total blue collar	8.7	9.1	10.2	9.6	9.7	10.3	2.9	5.2	9.4
Total	6.0	6.3	7.3	6.6	6.8	7.4	2.0	3.6	6.9

Source: Appendix Tables A-13–A-15.
Note: For regional definitions, see Table 21, p. 652.
* Less than 0.05 percent.

TABLE 30. *Chemical Industry*
Percent Negro Employment by Sex and Occupational Group
Southeast Region, 1964-1968

Occupational Group	All Employees 1964	All Employees 1966	All Employees 1968	Male 1964	Male 1966	Male 1968	Female 1964	Female 1966	Female 1968
Officials and managers	0.1	0.1	0.3	0.1	0.1	0.3	—	—	—
Professionals	0.1	0.2	0.5	0.1	0.2	0.4	1.0	3.3	4.3
Technicians	0.7	1.0	2.0	0.8	1.1	1.8	0.1	1.0	3.2
Sales workers	—	—	0.3	—	—	0.3	—	—	—
Office and clerical	0.6	1.1	2.4	1.0	1.6	2.8	0.3	0.7	2.1
Total white collar	0.3	0.5	1.1	0.3	0.5	0.8	0.3	0.8	2.3
Craftsmen (skilled)	1.0	1.5	2.3	1.1	1.5	2.3	*	1.0	3.1
Operatives (semiskilled)	8.2	8.7	11.4	9.7	10.2	12.3	3.1	4.6	9.1
Laborers	40.9	42.4	36.7	42.9	44.3	38.7	2.2	11.6	13.6
Service workers	37.0	35.6	34.5	37.4	35.6	34.3	31.9	34.8	37.7
Total blue collar	8.9	9.3	10.5	10.0	10.0	10.7	2.9	5.2	9.5
Total	6.2	6.6	7.7	7.0	7.1	7.8	2.1	3.8	7.2

Source: Appendix Tables A-16–A-18.
Note: For regional definitions, see Table 21, p. 652.
* Less than 0.05 percent.

TABLE 31. *Chemical Industry*
Percent Negro Employment by Sex and Occupational Group
Southwest Region, 1964-1968

Occupational Group	All Employees			Male			Female		
	1964	1966	1968	1964	1966	1968	1964	1966	1968
Officials and managers	0.1	0.2	0.2	0.1	0.2	0.2	—	—	—
Professionals	*	0.1	0.3	*	0.1	0.3	—	—	—
Technicians	0.3	0.8	1.8	0.3	0.7	1.7	—	1.0	2.7
Sales workers	—	—	0.7	—	—	0.7	—	—	—
Office and clerical	0.8	1.5	2.1	1.0	1.3	1.6	0.7	1.6	2.4
Total white collar	0.3	0.5	0.9	0.2	0.4	0.7	0.6	1.5	2.4
Craftsmen (skilled)	0.3	0.5	1.1	0.3	0.5	1.1	—	—	—
Operatives (semiskilled)	6.1	6.4	7.5	6.1	6.4	7.5	—	—	—
Laborers	65.0	69.8	67.8	65.0	69.8	67.8	—	—	—
Service workers	22.8	22.6	21.9	23.3	23.0	22.0	—	—	12.5
Total blue collar	7.7	8.1	8.1	7.7	8.2	8.1	—	—	2.9
Total	4.9	5.2	5.4	5.1	5.4	5.6	0.6	1.4	2.4

Source: Appendix Tables A-19–A-21.
Note: For regional definitions, see Table 21, p. 652.
* Less than 0.05 percent.

Negro representation. The trends in the Midwest, as indicated in Table 33, show definite improvement in Negro employment each year. Gains were made in all categories except the bottom two, with the technicians, office and clerical, and craftsmen group rather significant.

Most Negroes residing in the Midwest live in the North Central area, which includes Cleveland, Detroit, Indianapolis, and Chicago, among other cities, or in the southern tier of Missouri and Kansas, including St. Louis, Kansas City, and Wichita. Data were collected for two subregions in the Midwest. The North Central area (Table 34) followed the same general pattern as the total Midwest. The "other Midwest" area, showed a concentration at the bottom jobs, much like the South (Table 35). The latter sample, however, is small and could be inadequate to be conclusive.

Table 36 shows the number and proportion of Negroes, by sex and occupational group for the West Coast states, as reported by the EEOC for 1966. The Negro proportion is small, but qualitatively follows the national patterns except in the three lowest groups. Here, as in the Southwest, there is a strong petroleum industry tie-up and

TABLE 32. *Chemicals and Allied Products Industry Employment by Race, Sex, and Occupational Group 999 Establishments in the Midwest Region, 1966*

Occupational Group	All Employees			Male			Female		
	Total	Negro	Percent Negro	Total	Negro	Percent Negro	Total	Negro	Percent Negro
Officials and managers	25,161	126	0.5	24,329	103	0.4	832	23	2.8
Professionals	21,179	167	0.8	19,975	142	0.7	1,204	25	2.1
Technicians	13,960	337	2.4	11,965	272	2.3	1,995	65	3.3
Sales workers	16,480	27	0.2	16,102	23	0.1	378	4	1.1
Office and clerical	32,486	424	1.3	7,632	133	1.7	24,854	291	1.2
Total white collar	109,266	1,081	1.0	80,003	673	0.8	29,263	408	1.4
Craftsmen (skilled)	28,954	850	2.9	28,552	838	2.9	402	12	3.0
Operatives (semiskilled)	61,646	5,509	8.9	50,234	4,775	9.5	11,412	734	6.4
Laborers	22,142	3,144	14.2	16,432	2,867	17.4	5,710	277	4.9
Service workers	6,330	1,145	18.1	5,349	1,052	19.7	981	93	9.5
Total blue collar	119,072	10,648	8.9	100,567	9,532	9.5	18,505	1,116	6.0
Total	228,338	11,729	5.1	180,570	10,205	5.7	47,768	1,524	3.2

Source: U. S. Employment Opportunity Commission, *Job Patterns for Minorities and Women in Private Industry, 1966.* Report No. 1 (Washington: The Commission, 1968), Part II. For limitations of data, see note 53, p. 45.

Note: For regional definitions, see Table 21, p. 652.

TABLE 33. *Chemical Industry*
Percent Negro Employment by Sex and Occupational Group
Midwest Region, 1964-1968

Occupational Group	All Employees 1964	1966	1968	Male 1964	1966	1968	Female 1964	1966	1968
Officials and managers	0.3	0.3	0.7	0.3	0.3	0.7	—	—	1.7
Professionals	0.4	0.6	1.0	0.4	0.6	1.0	0.4	2.0	2.7
Technicians	1.2	1.7	3.2	1.3	1.7	2.9	0.7	1.6	4.9
Sales workers	0.1	0.2	0.8	0.1	0.2	0.8	—	0.7	0.7
Office and clerical	1.1	1.7	2.8	1.3	1.6	2.3	1.0	1.7	3.1
Total white collar	0.7	0.9	1.7	0.6	0.7	1.3	1.0	1.6	3.2
Craftsmen (skilled)	1.5	1.7	3.3	1.5	1.7	2.8	—	5.0	18.4
Operatives (semiskilled)	6.8	6.8	8.7	7.2	7.2	8.0	3.1	3.3	13.0
Laborers	13.1	11.4	11.8	14.5	13.5	13.1	4.2	2.4	8.1
Service workers	16.3	18.3	17.0	17.0	18.9	17.2	10.1	12.8	16.3
Total blue collar	6.4	6.4	8.1	6.7	6.7	7.5	3.8	3.7	12.3
Total	3.8	3.9	5.3	4.1	4.2	4.9	1.8	2.3	7.0

Source: Appendix Tables A-22–A-24.
Note: For regional definitions, see Table 21, p. 652.

TABLE 34. *Chemical Industry*
Percent Negro Employment by Sex and Occupational Group
North Central Region, 1964-1968

Occupational Group	All Employees 1964	1966	1968	Male 1964	1966	1968	Female 1964	1966	1968
Officials and managers	0.1	0.1	0.6	0.1	0.2	0.6	—	—	2.1
Professionals	0.5	0.7	1.2	0.5	0.6	1.1	0.6	2.5	3.2
Technicians	1.4	1.9	3.3	1.5	1.8	3.0	0.8	2.1	4.9
Sales workers	0.1	0.3	0.9	0.1	0.2	0.9	—	0.7	0.7
Office and clerical	1.2	1.6	2.8	1.1	1.2	2.3	1.2	1.8	3.0
Total white collar	0.7	0.9	1.7	0.6	0.7	1.3	1.1	1.8	3.2
Craftsmen (skilled)	1.5	1.7	2.2	1.5	1.7	2.2	—	—	—
Operatives (semiskilled)	7.0	6.9	8.7	7.5	7.3	7.9	3.2	3.5	13.6
Laborers	10.9	9.3	12.7	12.1	11.0	13.9	4.1	2.8	9.3
Service workers	11.6	13.4	12.6	12.2	13.8	12.3	5.8	8.2	14.1
Total blue collar	6.1	6.0	7.9	6.3	6.3	7.2	3.6	3.5	12.4
Total	3.8	3.8	5.2	4.0	4.0	4.9	2.0	2.4	7.0

Source: Appendix Tables A-25–A-28.
Note: For regional definitions, see Table 21, p. 652.

TABLE 35. *Chemical Industry*
Percent Negro Employment by Sex and Occupational Group
Other Midwest Region, 1964-1968

	All Employees			Male			Female		
Occupational Group	1964	1966	1968	1964	1966	1968	1964	1966	1968
Officials and managers	0.6	0.9	0.9	0.6	0.9	0.9	—	—	—
Professionals	0.2	0.4	0.7	0.2	0.4	0.7	—	—	1.2
Technicians	0.8	1.2	2.9	0.8	1.3	2.6	—	—	4.9
Sales workers	—	—	—	—	—	—	—	—	—
Office and clerical	1.0	1.8	2.9	1.8	2.8	2.3	0.7	1.3	3.2
Total white collar	0.7	1.0	1.7	0.7	1.0	1.2	0.6	1.2	3.2
Craftsmen (skilled)	1.6	1.6	5.8	1.6	1.6	4.3	—	50.0	18.5
Operatives (semiskilled)	6.1	6.6	8.7	6.5	6.9	8.4	2.4	2.3	10.8
Laborers	24.6	19.2	7.8	25.9	21.8	9.7	4.5	—	3.4
Service workers	36.9	37.7	36.8	40.4	40.8	39.9	20.3	21.9	24.2
Total blue collar	7.6	7.9	8.9	7.8	8.1	8.4	4.8	4.7	11.9
Total	3.9	4.4	5.4	4.3	4.8	5.0	1.5	1.9	6.7

Source: Appendix Tables A-28–A-30.
Note: For regional definitions, see Table 21, p. 652.

competition for jobs by not only whites, but Mexican-Americans as well.

Turning to our field data, summarized in Table 37, we find, by comparing the 1966 percentages, a slight overrepresentation of Negro participation for our sample. The West Coast trends, like those in other regions, are uniformly upward in Negro job holding, except in the lowest categories where upgrading has reduced the Negro ratios.

Throughout this comparison of regional employment no reference has been made to the female worker. The small number of women included in these samples results in extremely volatile statistics as can be seen by close inspection of the tables. Any comparisons of female ratios would probably be misleading.

All regional samples showed commonality in the lack of Negro representation in white collar and craft categories although all regions increased their percentage utilization of Negroes in nearly all white collar, craftsmen, and operative categories between 1964 and 1968. This would suggest that geographical location and the associated cultural values are not the only critical determinants of Negro employment in the skilled and white collar jobs. Education and training are

TABLE 36. *Chemicals and Allied Products Industry Employment by Race, Sex, and Occupational Group 387 Establishments in the West Coast Region, 1966*

Occupational Group	All Employees Total	All Employees Negro	All Employees Percent Negro	Male Total	Male Negro	Male Percent Negro	Female Total	Female Negro	Female Percent Negro
Officials and managers	5,394	15	0.3	5,088	7	0.1	306	8	2.6
Professionals	4,017	43	1.1	3,830	38	1.0	187	5	2.7
Technicians	2,642	54	2.0	2,075	44	2.1	567	10	1.8
Sales workers	3,735	10	0.3	3,630	9	0.2	105	1	1.0
Office and clerical	7,530	76	1.0	1,671	34	2.0	5,859	42	0.7
Total white collar	23,318	198	0.8	16,294	132	0.8	7,024	66	0.9
Craftsmen (skilled)	6,842	152	2.2	6,713	151	2.2	129	1	0.8
Operatives (semiskilled)	11,518	652	5.7	9,940	519	5.2	1,578	133	8.4
Laborers	4,686	377	8.0	2,840	251	8.8	1,846	126	6.8
Service workers	1,152	152	13.2	1,052	137	13.0	100	15	15.0
Total blue collar	24,198	1,333	5.5	20,545	1,058	5.1	3,653	275	7.5
Total	47,516	1,531	3.2	36,839	1,190	3.2	10,677	341	3.2

Source: U. S. Employment Opportunity Commission, *Job Patterns for Minorities and Women in Private Industry, 1966.* Report No. 1 (Washington: The Commission, 1968), Part II. For limitations of data, see note 53, p. 652.

Note: For regional definitions, see Table 21, p. 652.

TABLE 37. *Chemical Industry*
Percent Negro Employment by Sex and Occupational Group
West Coast Region, 1964-1968

	All Employees			Male			Female		
Occupational Group	1964	1966	1968	1964	1966	1968	1964	1966	1968
Officials and managers	—	0.1	0.1	—	0.1	0.1	—	—	—
Professionals	0.3	0.8	0.5	0.2	0.6	0.3	1.6	3.0	3.6
Technicians	1.4	1.6	2.8	1.6	1.7	3.0	—	—	—
Sales workers	—	—	0.8	—	—	0.8	—	—	—
Office and clerical	1.8	2.4	4.6	1.5	2.2	4.0	2.0	2.5	4.8
Total white collar	0.9	1.1	1.7	0.7	0.9	1.2	1.6	2.2	4.1
Craftsmen (skilled)	0.9	1.4	1.4	0.9	1.4	1.4	—	—	—
Operatives (semiskilled)	8.4	7.7	11.2	7.3	7.8	11.8	13.2	7.0	7.6
Laborers	14.6	22.9	20.3	14.3	14.0	15.4	18.2	46.5	37.2
Service workers	14.0	16.4	11.1	13.9	15.9	10.6	15.0	20.0	16.7
Total blue collar	6.0	6.3	7.9	5.2	5.5	7.4	13.5	14.8	12.4
Total	3.5	3.7	4.7	3.1	3.4	4.3	5.9	6.1	6.8

Source: Appendix Tables A-31–A-33.

Note: For regional definitions, see Table 21, p. 652.

vital essentials for these occupations, and Negroes have long been handicapped in acquiring these qualifications; and those who have been qualified, only recently have had the necessary opportunities.

Plant Size

In our comments relating to the generally higher proportion of Negroes found in the EEOC data than in our 1966 sample, it was suggested that smaller plants (that is, those having less than 500 employees) may have a generally higher proportion of Negroes than larger ones. The reason for this is that the smaller plants are usually simple process operations, which have a high percentage of laborers or low-rated operatives, and to which are attached a minimum office, professional, and managerial complement. Given the concentration of Negroes in the lower blue collar jobs and their lack of representation in the white collar occupations, which are found in proportionately larger numbers in the bigger plants, one would expect a higher proportion of Negroes in small facilities.

TABLE 38. *Chemical Industry*
Percent Negro Employment by Size of Establishment and Region, 1964-1968

Region	Large Establishments (Over 2,500 Employees in 1966)			Small Establishments (500-700 Employees in 1966)		
	1964	1966	1968	1964	1966	1968
Southeast	6.1	6.1	7.2	27.8	26.7	27.0
	5.8	7.1	8.7	22.4	20.4	23.8
	7.2	9.4	16.5	13.1	13.0	13.8
	1.7	3.7	4.4	0.2	0.2	0.5
	0.8	0.8	1.3	17.5	18.2	17.8
				0.2	0.6	1.2
Southwest	0.3	0.4	1.0	0.5	0.6	1.2
				7.3	6.3	7.5
Middle Atlantic	1.8	2.2	2.4	11.0	12.0	13.1
	4.8	4.5	5.1	6.6	10.2	11.9
	3.4	3.1	3.0	1.7	1.7	1.8
	0.3	0.4	0.9	1.4	1.9	4.3
				7.9	2.1	2.8
				0.9	0.2	2.3
				1.2	2.4	2.0
				0.2	0.8	1.8
North Central	0.1	0.2	0.3	0.2	0.1	0.2
				1.5	1.8	4.3
				27.0	29.1	29.7
				1.0	2.6	2.5
				2.2	2.7	4.3
				2.7	3.2	3.2
				7.4	0.9	2.1
				6.2	5.6	8.9
				1.6	2.4	3.2
				—	0.8	1.1
Other Midwest	2.8	2.8	3.7	1.8	1.4	6.0
				4.6	2.9	4.3
West Coast		none		1.3	1.2	3.1
Total	2.6	3.0	3.8	6.5	6.1	7.0

Source: Data in author's possession.

Our sample is mostly based on plants having 500 or more employees. The EEOC data includes employers of 100 or more. That the difference in Negro participation may well be a function of plant size is indicated by comparing the large plants in our sample, defined as those employing 2,500 or more, with small ones employing 500-700 persons. Table 38 shows the relevant data for the two groups by regions.

With few exceptions, the smaller plants have a larger Negro proportion. The character of the work and the nature of the occupations associated with plants of various sizes thus are significant factors in determining the rate of Negro employment.

AFFIRMATIVE ACTION

Data above do not show the extent to which companies are moving to increase Negro participation. Indeed it is highly possible for data, unless all factors are considered, to mislead. The Negro participation in the better chemical industry jobs remains small. Past discrimination is difficult to overcome. It is, however, worth noting that chemical companies are increasing their "affirmative action" to comply with the objectives and spirit of the federal civil rights policy.

Types of Affirmative Action

Affirmative action programs can be as many and varied as dedicated leaders have the imagination and capacity to make them. All such programs should exhibit a positive effort to go beyond nondiscrimination and achieve full utilization of minority manpower. The major emphases of current program involvement are on company employment policy and on general community assistance.

Corporate equal employment policy appears in various forms, but most companies have built on their original Plans for Progress pledges and have expressed equal opportunity in all facets of their employment procedures. Personnel manuals, plant notices, intracompany correspondence, labor management agreements, company publications, and help-wanted advertising are traditional methods of communicating company policy. Group discussions with supervisory personnel and internal EEO audits have proved useful in insuring that the intent and purpose of these policies are met throughout the organization.

Some firms employ managers specifically to coordinate their EEO efforts.

Affirmative action is most apparent in the aggressive recruiting of minority groups. In addition to recruiting efforts through employment agencies, high schools, and employee referral, affirmative action is taking chemical companies into the ghettos, working through civic organizations and ghetto leaders to seek black workers. The help of local leaders is often essential to encourage the hard-core unemployed and disaffected youth to believe conditions are truly more hopeful than before. Company recruiters are visiting an increasingly large number of Negro schools and colleges in search of the skilled, professional, and managerial talent so important to this industry. Yet, the companies are still suspect to only token hiring and must prove through actual results that equal opportunity does exist. Chemical employers often hire Negro applicants in preference to equally qualified whites in an effort to discredit the charge of "tokenism."

Selection devices, especially testing and the high school degree requirement, are being re-evaluated. The question is being asked, "Is the high school diploma a necessary requisite for this job and for future advancement?" Companies are finding the diploma may not be essential to satisfactory performance in the entry position and, with adequate training, not necessary for advancement.

Testing, always a controversial device, is under attack by some Negroes as violating the Civil Rights Act of 1964 by fomenting "systemic discrimination," whereby cultural differences can screen out otherwise qualified applicants. Many firms are analyzing their tests not only for reliability but also for cultural bias which reduces test validity. Cut-off scores have been lowered in many cases, and sometimes the entire test has been rejected as not valid.

Training of employees previously considered unqualified for employment is becoming more common in the chemical industry as employers seek to qualify new workers beyond the dead-end labor categories. As previously noted, chemical process operators must be able to control the continuous product flow without significant possibility of quality damage or jeopardization of personal safety. Companies are investigating and in some instances utilizing threshold training where new employees receive formal education in verbal, literary, and mathematical skills to qualify them for formal job training at entry-level positions. It is believed once employees are qualified at this level further on-the-job and formal training will be possible.

Secretarial work-study programs are popular in the chemical industry. A number of firms have provided untrained women with the opportunity to study part-time at company expense while they hold jobs within their present ability. Many such part-time employees have become full-time employees for the sponsor company upon completion of their training.

Seniority and promotional channels increasingly are being restructured to enable upward movement for all employees, a more feasible expectation once employees become qualified through equal training and experience opportunities. The chemical industry's traditionally high regard for education and training in fulfilling its job requirements should provide excellent opportunities for employee mobility.

Chemical companies have joined cooperative employment efforts of the business community, such as the National Alliance of Businessmen's pledge to hire a specified number of hard-core unemployed. This particular program has confronted some chemical employers with their lack of job opportunities for this group and their lack of preparedness to undertake threshold training on a large scale.

Affirmative action in corporate employment takes many forms not presented here, from even more imaginative utilization of disadvantaged workers to complete integration of plant facilities, such as change houses, in which walls have been torn down and locker assignments juggled to insure no outward discrimination.

Major community assistance by chemical firms is not widespread within the industry, but some firms are investing heavily in educational and civic efforts to bring prosperity and stability to community life. Financial support to and management involvement in community affairs is believed by some firms to provide indirect and long-run returns to their businesses. A stable, prosperous community is good for business.

Aid to education through financial grant, scholarships, and use of company facilities and training aids are very much in evidence. Work in the sciences receives the strongest backing, especially chemistry. Career motivation programs enlist members of the chemical industry to aid in the counseling work of city high schools. Programs designed to get people out of the ghetto into educational and occupational channels are receiving more support. Local Upward Bound programs and the Street Academy in New York City have chemical employees among their active participants. The successful Opportunities Industrialization Centers, originated in Philadelphia by the Reverend Leon Sullivan, are spreading to many major cities and receiving the help of the chemical industry.

Negro self-help activities have received enthusiastic moral support by the chemical industry, but some insecurity exists as to the motives of black leaders and the economic feasibility of black-operated subsidiaries. At this writing no formal plans have been made known by the major chemical companies for black subsidiaries or significant participation in other self-help activities.

Affirmative action in company employment policy is stimulated by government pressures, although defense contracts are not as vital to chemical companies as to those in predominantly defense industries. It is also stimulated by a moral commitment of top management to help eliminate racial injustice. This commitment by management is encompassed by the Plans for Progress mentioned earlier in the report. Formed voluntarily in 1962, the Plans for Progress now includes most major chemical manufacturers. Much of the community action work by the industry has been done under this banner. Although in the early 1960's Plans for Progress signatories may have felt that merely espousing nondiscrimination in employment was sufficient, considerably more active efforts have been made by the same companies since 1964.

Chemical management is faced, however, with its personal attitudes toward black people. Can equal opportunity programs be visualized as an economic investment, opening up new manpower resources, or are they seen as unpleasant costs to be eliminated as soon as a quota is reached and socio-political pressures ease to an acceptable level?[55] This question must be resolved before real progress can be made through affirmative action.

UNION IMPACT ON RACIAL POLICY

As we have seen in Chapters II and III, the labor movement is fragmented in the chemical industry although many plants are totally organized. The major unions, the Oil, Chemical and Atomic Workers,

55. For an analysis of this question, see Part Four, Chapter VII.

District 50, and the International Chemical Workers, are supplemented by the Teamsters, Operating Engineers, Textile Workers, Rubber Workers and many other national and independent local unions.

Union policy has little formal impact on company utilization of Negroes. Most labor agreements contain nondiscrimination clauses, and the segregated local is now almost nonexistent. Some corporate officials have indicated, however, that union leaders may exert informal pressures on management to go slow on integration or else expect deteriorating labor relations.

The attempt by government and management to provide equal opportunity in employment has sometimes been met by resistance from local communities, primarily in the South where social mores limit the Negro "to his place." The candidacy of ex-Governor George C. Wallace for President of the United States in 1968 brought to the surface the working class fears of black competition for white jobs. Nevertheless, few overt instances of backlash have been uncovered in the chemical industry perhaps because its traditional job stability has softened fears that an increase in jobs for Negroes will mean layoffs for whites.

Intraplant Movement and Seniority

Union-management seniority agreements are mostly determined on a departmental basis for promotion and plant-wide for layoff. Under law, the union is required to bargain equally for all its members regardless of race, and indications are that this is taking place, negating the practice of locking Negroes into dead-end promotion channels such as the black labor gang.

Promotional channels are open to all employees including Negroes, although some dead-end jobs remain. Service occupations such as janitors, cafeteria workers, and plant watchmen are usually outside normal lines of progression. Most employees are hired as laborers, but remain in the labor gang for only a short time. Management's intent is to upgrade labor pool personnel into the operative categories as jobs become available, which is the primary reason for the educational and mental ability selection requirements.

Critical to the speed of upward movement for all workers is the turnover rate of employees in the top blue collar jobs. Helpers and low-ranking operatives may wait many years for these positions to open. Plant expansion will speed upward movement with the creation of more jobs. However, the normal pace of progression beyond the first-level operative positions slows the upward progress of Negroes.

Seniority is important in the chemical industry for the advancement and layoff of production workers, especially in unionized plants. Job bidding is the common means of upgrading hourly workers and most decisions are based on departmental seniority. Negroes have gained access to some higher jobs through these departmental seniority progressions.

Plant-wide seniority usually governs layoff. This can, and has, affected Negroes adversely, for it permits higher-rated workers to bump down into the least skilled jobs where Negroes are concentrated, provided the higher-rated workers have more plant seniority. Layoff provisions, as in industry generally, do not permit upward bumping when work is curtailed. Thus a laborer with longer plant seniority cannot displace a shorter service man in an operative job unless the laborer has previously worked in that operative job. On the other hand, a longer service operative can displace a shorter service laborer although the operative has never worked as a laborer. Given the concentration of Negroes in the labor groups, this system, although not conceived with race in mind, tends to work hardship on Negroes.

Moreover, the departmental seniority system governing promotions has tended to maintain Negroes in lower-rated groups, not only since they have traditionally been (although not recently) the last hired, but also because until recently they have been hired mainly for departments with the lower-rated jobs. A departmental seniority system therefore tends to confine Negroes to these lower-rated departments even when their seniority exceeds that of white workers in jobs in higher-skilled departments.

Chemical employers are attempting to achieve more equitable racial distribution within departments and occupational groups by altering their hiring policies and by concentration on the promotion of qualified Negroes. There is no apparent union resistance to such moves. It will, however, be many years before these policies show large-scale results, given the rate of employment in the industry and the extent and qualifications of Negro employment.

Job bidding for promotion by workers in the next lower job classification is common in the chemical industry. Some employers have indicated they will select Negroes over whites with comparable seniority. Even though seniority lines do not now restrict Negro upgrading more than that of whites, some Negroes still avoid bidding on jobs where they might be subjected to discrimination within the new work group.

In the 1960's Negroes have experienced an accelerated opening of seniority lines to upward movement and are increasingly protected by plant-wide provisions in case of layoff. Yet the threat of economic recession remains very real to the black worker. His progress notwithstanding, the Negro will still suffer heavy unemployment during economic slowdown since many remain at the bottom of seniority lists.

THE GOVERNMENT ROLE IN EQUAL EMPLOYMENT OPPORTUNITY

Public policy on discrimination in employment was pronounced by President Roosevelt during World War II with two executive orders, 8802 and 9346, banning discrimination in employment by government contractors. Presidents Truman and Eisenhower continued this policy with similar executive orders, the latter's Executive Order 10479 in 1955 establishing the President's Committee on Government Contracts (Nixon Committee) to which reference was made earlier. Executive Order 10925 of 1961 expressed President Kennedy's resolve to remove racial barriers in employment by establishing the President's Committee on Equal Employment Opportunity with powers to withhold government contracts for noncompliance with his nondiscrimination order. President Johnson's Executive Order 11246 in 1965 which substituted the office of Federal Contract Compliance for the President's Committee on Equal Employment Opportunity, and that of President Kennedy in 1961, required not only nondiscriminatory employment practices by government contractors, but also "affirmative action" to overcome the effects of past discrimination.

The Civil Rights Act of 1964, although a landmark statute in the civil rights movement, has had less impact on employment practices than have the executive orders. The Equal Employment Opportunity Commission (EEOC) formed under this act investigates individual charges of discrimination and seeks employer conciliation, resorting to court action if such conciliation is not forthcoming. Most major chemical employers have felt this agency has not been instrumental in motivating companies to remove racial employment barriers even though many decisions have been unfavorable to the employer. The individual nature of each case as it applies to single workers or small groups does not have the impact of a plant-wide compliance review made pursuant to the Presidential Executive Orders by the Office of Federal Contract Compliance (OFCC) or government contracting agencies such as the Department of Defense or the Atomic Energy Commission.

The OFCC, established under President Johnson's Executive Order 11246, and reporting to the Secretary of Labor, has frequently been described along with the contracting agencies as being helpful to chemical employers in their attempts to comply with government policy. No contracts have thus far been withheld from the major chemical producers, yet compliance violations have been found. Although the chemical industry is not heavily reliant on government contracts, OFCC pressure is a prime mover in accomplishing equal employment opportunity.

Thirty-eight states have Fair Employment Practices (FEP) laws developed since the original New York law of 1945. Noticeably absent in passing such legislation are many southern states. Chemical employers are often faced, therefore, with three investigatory agencies, the EEOC, OFCC, and state commissions. In addition, separate investigations are made by federal contracting agencies and by city human relations commissions. An apparent lack of coordination among these agencies creates confusion for the employer as to what is expected and by whom.

Another source of employer confusion has been a lack of formal guidelines from these agencies as to what is required. "Affirmative" and "positive" action prior to 1968 were left mostly to individual interpretation, and it is not uncommon for an employer to find his interpretation not sufficiently affirmative or positive in the eyes of the government agency.

Government pressures have probably been necessary for significant action to be taken in removing racial employment barriers and in removing previous injustice, even though many chemical firms had expressed nondiscrimination policies prior to government action. In an industry not readily vulnerable to consumer boycotts, government pressure is added insurance that affirmative action will be taken.

CHAPTER V.

Determinants of Industrial Policy

This study has attempted to discuss and consolidate the major issues in the development of equal employment opportunity in the chemical industry and in the determination of industrial employment policy. These issues will be summarized in the following remarks.

DEMAND FOR LABOR

The demand for labor in the chemical industry continues to increase, especially in the white collar and skilled occupational groups. A continued upward trend in chemical employment is forecast by nearly all the major firms.

As our economy seeks a full employment level of output, employment opportunities will be available to the Negro labor force, and may even exceed, the existing manpower supply. Chemical companies continually explain that there are more jobs than there is qualified talent to fill them. Improvement in Negro educational and training opportunities will be vital to their taking advantage of these jobs. The threat of economic slowdown and recession is very real to the black worker. Negroes still remain low on seniority rosters and even with their recent employment gains, many will be the first to face layoff. This may further harden their feeling of despair and exclusion from sharing in white affluence.

JOB STRUCTURE AND PLANT SIZE

Although white collar employment continues to increase, blue collar jobs are experiencing static growth if not some slight downward trend. The more secure jobs all require a high degree of skill which is a barrier to Negro employment, especially for the hard-core.

The supply of Negro labor is generally classified as unskilled with low educational and training experience. Ghetto mores make it difficult for the black worker to adjust to work discipline, such as promptness, regular attendance, and efficiency requirements. Negroes are further burdened with a distrust of the sincerity and motivation of white management's efforts to open promising career paths. It is also difficult for members of both races to discard past discriminatory attitudes and accept the existence of equal opportunity. The concept of "Negro work" is rapidly disappearing, but Negroes previously hired with the capability for only dead-end menial tasks are finding it nearly impossible to take advantage of the better jobs offered them. A fresh start such as is possible in new plants will be very beneficial in meeting the aspirations of new members of the Negro work force.

The chemical industry may better apply its efforts to provide qualified Negroes with jobs by concentrating on the traditionally closed white collar and skilled blue collar categories than to increase the concentration of Negro employees in semiskilled and unskilled blue collar occupations. Substantial Negro representation in sales, managerial, and other white collar jobs as well as in the skilled trades will go far effectively to develop a society where all races share equally.

Because small plants tend to have a larger percentage of unskilled labor and smaller salaried complements, they are likely to have a higher Negro population. This seems a function of past practice, discrimination, and education, and is likely to be true for many years to come.

GOVERNMENTAL PRESSURE

Government pressure to accelerate equal employment opportunity in the chemical industry has been both necessary and helpful in the attempt to achieve a fully integrated society. Industrial consumers, not the public, are the primary direct customers of chemical manufacturers, eliminating pressures on company sales as an effective device for social change. A resort to violence is not acceptable to the public interest, thereby requiring a combination of government and managerial pressures to bring about the necessary change. Although the chemical industry is not primarily reliant on government contracts, the government is an important customer and can require compliance with its equal employment policy.

Government efforts must, however, recognize the high skill and safety requirements inherent in chemical production. Improper analysis of employment conditions by government inspectors might force employer acceptance of marginal or unqualified employees into occupations where severe harm could be done to equipment, product, and personal safety.

The appeal of racial grievances to the Equal Employment Opportunity Commission, although protective of minority rights, has its adverse effects on intraplant efficiency and cannot be viewed as an optimum solution to eliminating employer unethical racial practices. The third party nature of such a grievance procedure tends to further undermine corporate authority on the foreman level, already eroded by the presence of union contract provisions. Negro employees must have reason for confidence that justice can be attained within the plant through union and employer action.

Although government pressure is often necessary to effect needed social change, the peaceful and private resolution of conflict is essential to a continuance of free enterprise and a free society. Nevertheless, until that is achieved, redress from the outside is probably essential to progress.

SENIORITY AND UNIONISM

Departmental seniority in promotions combined with plant-wide seniority in layoffs tends to work against the integration of Negroes in the industry, because of the concentration of Negroes in the lower-paying jobs and past discriminatory practices in hiring. Departmental seniority may confine Negroes to the departments in which they are concentrated, which include the lower-paying and lower-skilled jobs. Plant-wide seniority in layoffs permits Negroes to be bumped by higher-rated personnel in other departments. Chemical companies, however, are making special efforts to reduce the adverse effects of seniority on the Negro, through increased training and the encouragement of Negroes to bid on higher jobs. In addition, Negroes have received preference when higher jobs are open and seniority is similar to that of white candidates.

Unions do not have universal representation in the chemical industry and, other than jointly determining contract provisions with management, do not formally affect the utilization of Negroes within chemical establishments. Informal pressures against rapid integration of the work force by union members may exist in some plants, but overt action is rare. The challenge to union-management relations is the balancing of Negro employment and upgrading with equitable treatment of white workers.

LOCATIONAL AND REGIONAL FACTORS

Chemical plant location on city outskirts and in rural areas is not favorable to easy access by those Negroes who have migrated to the center cities. Although there is some indication that this migration has slowed, the bulk of Negro labor in the Northeast, Midwest, and West Coast regions is concentrated in the cities. The South is more accurately described as rural with a wide dispersion of small towns and medium-sized cities. Negro populations in these regions seem to be more favorably located in relation to chemical plant location.

The slum dwelling Negro faces two major locational barriers to chemical employment. If he is without ownership of a private automobile, he must rely on an increasingly inadequate system of public transportation to get to work. The only alternative is to relocate nearer the job, but he is then faced with all-white suburban neighborhoods which remain inhospitable to black neighbors. The support of open housing and adequate public transportation are important policy issues for chemical management to consider. Even then, however, economic factors will continue to inhibit changing dwelling trends.

MANAGERIAL POLICY

Chemical management has generally embraced the need to overcome past racial injustices and to provide equal employment opportunity for Negroes. Affirmative action in company employment efforts and contributions to community betterment all indicate a firm commitment by top management. Problems still remain, however, in implementing racial policy through middle management and first-line supervision which are primarily occupied with the daily operation of the enterprise and the more routine pressures of this responsibility.

Management has learned through disappointing experience of the need to make employment promises only when they can be kept. To raise the aspiration level of those who have been long deprived and then not fulfill these commitments threatens substantially to set back racial understanding. The admission of Negroes to critical decision-making positions within middle and top management will be a major contribution to improving this understanding.

CHAPTER VI.

Concluding Remarks

The Negro in the chemical industry has served to illustrate a most critical social dilemma. Much of our nation's efforts to resolve this crisis are spent in argument over terminology, such as "black power" and "white racism," and in defending ourselves for past conduct. Each of these labels has extreme as well as moderate connotations. The acceptance of the historical evidence that white society has been a major contributor to the deprivation of the Negro, and realization that the black minority must have an effective role in making the decisions which affect their lives are both necessary conditions to solve these problems which affect us all, regardless of race.

Business does have a social responsibility. In a complex, technologically exploding society, free enterprise can exist prosperously only in a stable and affluent environment. The function of the business firm is to produce goods and services as efficiently and profitably as possible, but this role is irrelevant if social conditions generate violence, poverty, and repression.

Appendix

TABLE A–1. *Chemical Industry*
Employment by Race, Sex, and Occupational Group
280 Establishments in United States, 1964

	All Employees			Male			Female		
Occupational Group	Total	Negro	Percent Negro	Total	Negro	Percent Negro	Total	Negro	Percent Negro
Officials and managers	40,586	73	0.2	40,083	72	0.2	503	1	0.2
Professionals	35,162	124	0.4	33,871	113	0.3	1,291	11	0.9
Technicians	22,496	263	1.2	19,973	244	1.2	2,523	19	0.8
Sales workers	7,930	21	0.3	7,646	21	0.3	284	—	—
Office and clerical	40,349	564	1.4	13,349	283	2.1	27,000	281	1.0
Total white collar	146,523	1,045	0.7	114,922	733	0.6	31,601	312	1.0
Craftsmen (skilled)	71,241	1,330	1.9	68,847	1,329	1.9	2,394	1	*
Operatives (semiskilled)	93,445	6,764	7.2	77,948	6,317	8.1	15,497	447	2.9
Laborers	17,707	4,515	25.5	16,112	4,457	27.7	1,595	58	3.6
Service workers	9,300	2,180	23.4	8,313	1,993	24.0	987	187	18.9
Total blue collar	191,693	1,478	7.7	171,220	14,096	8.2	20,473	693	3.4
Total	338,216	15,834	4.7	286,142	14,829	5.2	52,074	1,005	1.9

Source: Data in author's possession.

* Less than 0.05 percent.

Note: For regional definitions, see Table 21, p. 652.

TABLE A–2. *Chemical Industry*
Employment by Race, Sex, and Occupational Group
303 Establishments in United States, 1966

Occupational Group	All Employees			Male			Female		
	Total	Negro	Percent Negro	Total	Negro	Percent Negro	Total	Negro	Percent Negro
Officials and managers	42,335	102	0.2	41,788	100	0.2	547	2	0.4
Professionals	36,768	179	0.5	35,424	151	0.4	1,344	28	2.1
Technicians	23,901	361	1.5	20,899	317	1.5	3,002	44	1.5
Sales	6,737	23	0.3	6,481	22	0.3	256	1	0.4
Office and clerical	39,036	721	1.8	12,456	293	2.4	26,580	428	1.6
Total white collar	148,777	1,386	0.9	117,048	883	0.8	31,729	503	1.6
Craftsmen (skilled)	72,372	1,568	2.2	72,209	1,566	2.2	163	2	1.2
Operatives (semiskilled)	102,426	7,823	7.6	84,170	7,112	8.4	18,256	711	3.9
Laborers	17,508	4,516	25.8	15,454	4,401	28.5	2,054	115	5.6
Service workers	9,400	2,152	22.9	8,492	1,967	23.2	908	185	20.4
Total blue collar	201,706	16,059	8.0	180,325	15,046	8.3	21,381	1,013	4.7
Total	350,483	17,445	5.0	297,373	15,929	5.4	53,110	1,516	2.9

Source: Data in author's possession.

Note: For regional definitions, see Table 21, p. 652.

TABLE A–3. *Chemical Industry*
Employment by Race, Sex, and Occupational Group
291 Establishments in United States, 1968

Occupational Group	All Employees			Male			Female		
	Total	Negro	Percent Negro	Total	Negro	Percent Negro	Total	Negro	Percent Negro
Officials and managers	43,766	188	0.4	43,197	182	0.4	569	6	1.1
Professionals	37,528	311	0.8	35,863	259	0.7	1,665	52	3.1
Technicians	23,543	583	2.5	20,194	466	2.3	3,349	117	3.5
Sales workers	6,610	48	0.7	6,400	47	0.7	210	1	0.5
Office and clerical	39,914	1,266	3.2	12,138	423	3.5	27,776	843	3.0
Total white collar	151,361	2,396	1.6	117,792	1,377	1.2	33,569	1,019	3.0
Craftsmen (skilled)	69,076	2,016	2.9	68,502	1,943	2.8	574	73	12.7
Operatives (semiskilled)	109,094	10,794	9.9	88,163	9,056	10.3	20,931	1,738	8.3
Laborers	17,731	3,970	22.4	14,745	3,715	25.2	2,986	255	8.5
Service workers	9,045	2,077	23.0	7,956	1,828	23.0	1,089	249	22.9
Total blue collar	204,946	18,857	9.2	179,366	16,542	9.2	25,580	2,315	9.1
Total	356,307	21,253	6.0	297,158	17,919	6.0	59,149	3,334	5.6

Source: Data in author's possession.

Note: For regional definitions, see Table 21, p. 652.

TABLE A–4. *Chemical Industry*
Employment by Race, Sex, and Occupational Group
97 Establishments in the Northeast Region, 1964

Occupational Group	All Employees			Male			Female		
	Total	Negro	Percent Negro	Total	Negro	Percent Negro	Total	Negro	Percent Negro
Officials and managers	14,617	28	0.2	14,387	27	0.2	230	1	0.4
Professionals	16,420	78	0.5	15,544	70	0.5	876	8	0.9
Technicians	9,037	139	1.5	7,854	124	1.6	1,183	15	1.3
Sales workers	4,473	19	0.4	4,386	19	0.4	87	—	—
Office and clerical	20,662	384	1.9	6,199	200	3.2	14,463	184	1.3
Total white collar	65,209	648	1.0	48,370	440	0.9	16,839	208	1.2
Craftsmen (skilled)	19,442	799	4.1	19,395	799	4.1	47	—	—
Operatives (semiskilled)	27,889	1,813	6.5	24,004	1,751	7.3	3,885	62	1.6
Laborers	6,373	856	13.4	5,664	831	14.7	709	25	3.5
Service workers	3,455	617	17.9	2,933	517	17.6	522	100	19.2
Total blue collar	57,159	4,085	7.1	51,996	3,898	7.5	5,163	187	3.6
Total	122,368	4,733	3.9	100,366	4,338	4.3	22,002	395	1.8

Source: Data in author's possession.

Note: For regional definitions, see Table 21, p. 652.

TABLE A-5. *Chemical Industry*
Employment by Race, Sex, and Occupational Group
102 Establishments in the Northeast Region, 1966

Occupational Group	All Employees			Male			Female		
	Total	Negro	Percent Negro	Total	Negro	Percent Negro	Total	Negro	Percent Negro
Officials and managers	15,027	45	0.3	14,809	43	0.3	218	2	0.9
Professionals	16,743	102	0.6	15,856	85	0.5	887	17	1.9
Technicians	9,607	182	1.9	8,378	158	1.9	1,229	24	2.0
Sales workers	3,792	16	0.4	3,694	16	0.4	98	—	—
Office and clerical	19,629	443	2.3	5,687	184	3.2	13,942	259	1.9
Total white collar	64,798	788	1.2	48,424	486	1.0	16,374	302	1.8
Craftsmen (skilled)	20,771	858	4.1	20,726	858	4.1	45	—	—
Operatives (semiskilled)	29,627	2,049	6.9	25,735	1,977	7.7	3,892	72	1.8
Laborers	6,438	906	14.1	5,569	868	15.6	869	38	4.4
Service workers	3,599	585	16.3	3,123	495	15.9	476	90	18.9
Total blue collar	60,435	4,398	7.3	55,153	4,198	7.6	5,282	200	3.8
Total	125,233	5,186	4.1	103,577	4,684	4.5	21,656	502	2.3

Source: Data in author's possession.

Note: For regional definitions, see Table 21, p. 652.

TABLE A–6. *Chemical Industry*
Employment by Race, Sex, and Occupational Group
95 Establishments in the Northeast Region, 1968

Occupational Group	All Employees			Male			Female		
	Total	Negro	Percent Negro	Total	Negro	Percent Negro	Total	Negro	Percent Negro
Officials and managers	15,070	71	0.5	14,842	67	0.5	228	4	1.8
Professionals	17,042	170	1.0	15,984	137	0.9	1,058	33	3.1
Technicians	9,423	234	2.5	8,244	198	2.4	1,179	36	3.1
Sales workers	3,606	27	0.7	3,551	27	0.8	55	—	—
Office and clerical	20,246	744	3.7	5,399	255	4.7	14,847	489	3.3
Total white collar	65,387	1,246	1.9	48,020	684	1.4	17,367	562	3.2
Craftsmen (skilled)	17,877	842	4.7	17,831	841	4.7	46	1	2.2
Operatives (semiskilled)	26,958	2,319	8.6	22,640	2,218	9.8	4,318	101	2.3
Laborers	5,741	699	12.2	4,700	636	13.5	1,041	63	6.1
Service workers	3,260	628	19.3	2,755	507	18.4	505	121	24.0
Total blue collar	53,836	4,488	8.3	47,926	4,202	8.8	5,910	286	4.8
Total	119,223	5,734	4.8	95,946	4,886	5.1	23,277	848	3.6

Source: Data in author's possession.

Note: For regional definitions, see Table 21, p. 652.

TABLE A–7. *Chemical Industry*
Employment by Race, Sex, and Occupational Group
13 Establishments in the New England Region, 1964

Occupational Group	All Employees			Male			Female		
	Total	Negro	Percent Negro	Total	Negro	Percent Negro	Total	Negro	Percent Negro
Officials and managers	1,067	3	0.3	1,059	3	0.3	8	—	—
Professionals	1,371	9	0.7	1,298	7	0.5	73	2	2.7
Technicians	684	24	3.5	575	24	4.2	109	—	—
Sales workers	258	—	—	236	—	—	22	—	—
Office and clerical	1,263	9	0.7	373	3	0.8	890	6	0.7
Total white collar	4,643	45	1.0	3,541	37	1.0	1,102	8	0.7
Craftsmen (skilled)	1,821	77	4.2	1,816	77	4.2	5	—	—
Operatives (semiskilled)	2,861	152	5.3	2,647	151	5.7	214	1	0.5
Laborers	1,281	65	5.1	1,201	65	5.4	80	—	—
Service workers	273	35	12.8	250	35	14.0	23	—	—
Total blue collar	6,236	329	5.3	5,914	328	5.5	322	1	0.3
Total	10,879	374	3.4	9,455	365	3.9	1,424	9	0.6

Source: Data in author's possession.

Note: For regional definitions, see Table 21, p. 652.

TABLE A–8. *Chemical Industry*
Employment by Race, Sex, and Occupational Group
13 Establishments in the New England Region, 1966

	All Employees			Male			Female		
Occupational Group	Total	Negro	Percent Negro	Total	Negro	Percent Negro	Total	Negro	Percent Negro
Officials and managers	1,144	3	0.3	1,135	3	0.3	9	—	—
Professionals	1,325	9	0.7	1,259	7	0.6	66	2	3.0
Technicians	743	27	3.6	618	26	4.2	125	1	0.8
Sales workers	154	—	—	144	—	—	10	—	—
Office and clerical	1,224	14	1.1	339	6	1.8	885	8	0.9
Total white collar	4,590	53	1.2	3,495	42	1.2	1,095	11	1.0
Craftsmen (skilled)	1,481	77	5.2	1,477	77	5.2	4	—	—
Operatives (semiskilled)	2,807	158	5.6	2,607	157	6.0	200	1	0.5
Laborers	1,005	55	5.5	935	55	5.9	70	—	—
Service workers	266	31	11.7	243	31	12.8	23	—	—
Total blue collar	5,559	321	5.8	5,262	320	6.1	297	1	0.3
Total	10,149	374	3.7	8,757	362	4.1	1,392	12	0.9

Source: Data in author's possession.

Note: For regional definitions, see Table 21, p. 652.

TABLE A-9. *Chemical Industry*
Employment by Race, Sex, and Occupational Group
12 Establishments in the New England Region, 1968

Occupational Group	All Employees			Male			Female		
	Total	Negro	Percent Negro	Total	Negro	Percent Negro	Total	Negro	Percent Negro
Officials and managers	992	3	0.3	986	3	0.3	6	—	—
Professionals	1,170	7	0.6	1,101	6	0.5	69	1	1.4
Technicians	678	29	4.3	583	27	4.6	95	2	2.1
Sales workers	113	—	—	111	—	—	2	—	—
Office and clerical	945	17	1.8	261	2	0.8	684	15	2.2
Total white collar	3,898	56	1.4	3,042	38	1.2	856	18	2.1
Craftsmen (skilled)	1,268	62	4.9	1,263	62	4.9	5	—	—
Operatives (semiskilled)	2,117	156	7.4	2,037	152	7.5	80	4	5.0
Laborers	861	50	5.8	795	45	5.7	66	5	7.6
Service workers	234	38	16.2	216	38	17.6	18	—	—
Total blue collar	4,480	306	6.8	4,311	297	6.9	169	9	5.3
Total	8,378	362	4.3	7,353	335	4.6	1,025	27	2.6

Source: Data in author's possession.

Note: For regional definitions, see Table 21, p. 652.

TABLE A–10. *Chemical Industry*
Employment by Race, Sex, and Occupational Group
84 Establishments in the Middle Atlantic Region, 1964

Occupational Group	All Employees Total	All Employees Negro	All Employees Percent Negro	Male Total	Male Negro	Male Percent Negro	Female Total	Female Negro	Female Percent Negro
Officials and managers	13,550	25	0.2	13,328	24	0.2	222	1	0.5
Professionals	15,049	69	0.5	14,246	63	0.4	803	6	0.7
Technicians	8,353	115	1.4	7,279	100	1.4	1,074	15	1.4
Sales workers	4,215	19	0.5	4,150	19	0.5	65	—	—
Office and clerical	19,399	375	1.9	5,826	197	3.4	13,573	178	1.3
Total white collar	60,566	603	1.0	44,829	403	0.9	15,737	200	1.3
Craftsmen (skilled)	17,621	722	4.1	17,579	722	4.1	42	—	—
Operatives (semiskilled)	25,028	1,661	6.6	21,357	1,600	7.5	3,671	61	1.7
Laborers	5,092	791	15.5	4,463	766	17.2	629	25	4.0
Service workers	3,182	582	18.3	2,683	482	18.0	499	100	20.0
Total blue collar	50,923	3,756	7.4	46,082	3,570	7.7	4,841	186	3.8
Total	111,489	4,359	3.9	90,911	3,973	4.4	20,578	386	1.9

Source: Data in author's possession.

Note: For regional definitions, see Table 21, p. 652.

TABLE A-11. *Chemical Industry*
Employment by Race, Sex, and Occupational Group
89 Establishments in the Middle Atlantic Region, 1966

Occupational Group	All Employees Total	All Employees Negro	All Employees Percent Negro	Male Total	Male Negro	Male Percent Negro	Female Total	Female Negro	Female Percent Negro
Officials and managers	13,883	42	0.3	13,674	40	0.3	209	2	1.0
Professionals	15,418	93	0.6	14,597	78	0.5	821	15	1.8
Technicians	8,864	155	1.7	7,760	132	1.7	1,104	23	2.1
Sales workers	3,638	16	0.4	3,550	16	0.5	88	—	—
Office and clerical	18,405	429	2.3	5,348	178	3.3	13,057	251	1.9
Total white collar	60,208	735	1.2	44,929	444	1.0	15,279	291	1.9
Craftsmen (skilled)	19,290	781	4.0	19,249	781	4.1	41	—	—
Operatives (semiskilled)	26,820	1,891	7.1	23,128	1,820	7.9	3,692	71	1.9
Laborers	5,433	851	15.7	4,634	813	17.5	799	38	4.8
Service workers	3,333	554	16.6	2,880	464	16.1	453	90	19.9
Total blue collar	54,876	4,077	7.4	49,891	3,878	7.8	4,985	199	4.0
Total	115,084	4,812	4.2	94,820	4,322	4.6	20,264	490	2.4

Source: Data in author's possession.

Note: For regional definitions, see Table 21, p. 652.

TABLE A-12. *Chemical Industry*
Employment by Race, Sex, and Occupational Group
83 Establishments in the Middle Atlantic Region, 1968

Occupational Group	All Employees			Male			Female		
	Total	Negro	Percent Negro	Total	Negro	Percent Negro	Total	Negro	Percent Negro
Officials and managers	14,078	68	0.5	13,856	64	0.5	222	4	1.8
Professionals	15,872	163	1.0	14,883	131	0.9	989	32	3.2
Technicians	8,745	205	2.3	7,661	171	2.2	1,084	34	3.1
Sales workers	3,493	27	0.8	3,440	27	0.8	53	—	—
Office and clerical	19,301	727	3.8	5,138	253	4.9	14,163	474	3.3
Total white collar	61,489	1,190	1.9	44,978	646	1.4	16,511	544	3.3
Craftsmen (skilled)	16,609	780	4.7	16,568	779	4.7	41	1	2.4
Operatives (semiskilled)	24,841	2,163	8.7	20,603	2,066	10.0	4,238	97	2.3
Laborers	4,880	649	13.3	3,905	591	15.1	975	58	5.9
Service workers	3,026	590	19.5	2,539	469	18.5	487	121	24.8
Total blue collar	49,356	4,182	8.5	43,615	3,905	9.0	5,741	277	4.8
Total	110,845	5,372	4.8	88,593	4,551	5.1	22,252	821	3.7

Source: Data in author's possession.

Note: For regional definitions, see Table 21, p. 652.

TABLE A–13. *Chemical Industry*
Employment by Race, Sex, and Occupational Group
98 Establishments in the South Region, 1964

Occupational Group	All Employees			Male			Female		
	Total	Negro	Percent Negro	Total	Negro	Percent Negro	Total	Negro	Percent Negro
Officials and managers	15,785	20	0.1	15,657	20	0.1	128	—	—
Professionals	10,196	10	0.1	10,074	9	0.1	122	1	0.8
Technicians	7,535	49	0.7	6,699	48	0.7	836	1	0.1
Sales workers	598	—	—	578	—	—	20	—	—
Office and clerical	9,616	62	0.6	3,873	40	1.0	5,743	22	0.4
Total white collar	43,730	141	0.3	36,881	117	0.3	6,849	24	0.4
Craftsmen (skilled)	38,396	333	0.9	36,066	332	0.9	2,330	1	*
Operatives (semiskilled)	41,792	3,314	7.9	32,896	3,041	9.2	8,896	273	3.1
Laborers	6,885	3,076	44.7	6,609	3,070	46.5	276	6	2.2
Service workers	3,354	1,162	34.6	3,156	1,103	34.9	198	59	29.8
Total blue collar	90,427	7,885	8.7	78,727	7,546	9.6	11,700	339	2.9
Total	134,157	8,026	6.0	115,608	7,663	6.6	18,549	363	2.0

Source: Data in author's possession.

Note: For regional definitions, see Table 21, p. 652.

* Less than 0.05 percent.

TABLE A–14. *Chemical Industry*
Employment by Race, Sex, and Occupational Group
112 Establishments in the South Region, 1966

Occupational Group	All Employees			Male			Female		
	Total	Negro	Percent Negro	Total	Negro	Percent Negro	Total	Negro	Percent Negro
Officials and managers	16,760	24	0.1	16,593	24	0.1	167	—	—
Professionals	11,067	22	0.2	10,930	18	0.2	137	4	2.9
Technicians	8,500	84	1.0	7,309	72	1.0	1,191	12	1.0
Sales workers	73	—	—	55	—	—	18	—	—
Office and clerical	9,381	106	1.1	3,664	57	1.6	5,717	49	0.9
Total white collar	45,781	236	0.5	38,551	171	0.4	7,230	65	0.9
Craftsmen (skilled)	38,290	492	1.3	38,192	491	1.3	98	1	1.0
Operatives (semiskilled)	48,181	4,078	8.5	36,298	3,528	9.7	11,883	550	4.6
Laborers	6,565	3,077	46.9	6,246	3,040	48.7	319	37	11.6
Service workers	3,381	1,128	33.4	3,188	1,065	33.4	193	63	32.6
Total blue collar	96,417	8,775	9.1	83,924	8,124	9.7	12,493	651	5.2
Total	142,198	9,011	6.3	122,475	8,295	6.8	19,723	716	3.6

Source: Data in author's possession.

Note: For regional definitions, see Table 21, p. 652.

TABLE A–15. *Chemical Industry*
Employment by Race, Sex, and Occupational Group
112 Establishments in the South Region, 1968

Occupational Group	All Employees			Male			Female		
	Total	Negro	Percent Negro	Total	Negro	Percent Negro	Total	Negro	Percent Negro
Officials and managers	17,718	47	0.3	17,510	47	0.3	208	—	—
Professionals	11,109	49	0.4	10,927	42	0.4	182	7	3.8
Technicians	8,235	163	2.0	6,962	123	1.8	1,273	40	3.1
Sales workers	521	2	0.4	514	2	0.4	7	—	—
Office and clerical	9,485	221	2.3	3,660	94	2.6	5,825	127	2.2
Total white collar	47,068	482	1.0	39,573	308	0.8	7,495	174	2.3
Craftsmen (skilled)	38,049	769	2.0	37,885	764	2.0	164	5	3.0
Operatives (semiskilled)	55,912	6,157	11.0	43,001	4,988	11.6	12,911	1,169	9.1
Laborers	6,195	2,572	41.5	5,782	2,516	43.5	413	56	13.6
Service workers	3,096	1,003	32.4	2,934	944	32.2	162	59	36.4
Total blue collar	103,252	10,501	10.2	89,602	9,212	10.3	13,650	1,289	9.4
Total	150,320	10,983	7.3	129,175	9,520	7.4	21,145	1,463	6.9

Source: Data in author's possession.

Note: For regional definitions, see Table 21, p. 652.

TABLE A–16. *Chemical Industry*
Employment by Race, Sex, and Occupational Group
79 Establishments in the Southeast Region, 1964

Occupational Group	All Employees			Male			Female		
	Total	Negro	Percent Negro	Total	Negro	Percent Negro	Total	Negro	Percent Negro
Officials and managers	12,541	16	0.1	12,422	16	0.1	119	—	—
Professionals	7,993	9	0.1	7,891	8	0.1	102	1	1.0
Technicians	6,066	45	0.7	5,328	44	0.8	738	1	0.1
Sales workers	596	—	—	576	—	—	20	—	—
Office and clerical	7,904	48	0.6	3,191	33	1.0	4,713	15	0.3
Total white collar	35,100	118	0.3	29,408	101	0.3	5,692	17	0.3
Craftsmen (skilled)	29,899	310	1.0	27,572	309	1.1	2,327	1	*
Operatives (semiskilled)	37,300	3,042	8.2	28,419	2,769	9.7	8,881	273	3.1
Laborers	5,813	2,379	40.9	5,537	2,373	42.9	276	6	2.2
Service workers	2,796	1,035	37.0	2,611	976	37.4	185	59	31.9
Total blue collar	75,808	6,766	8.9	64,139	6,427	10.0	11,669	339	2.9
Total	110,908	6,884	6.2	93,547	6,528	7.0	17,361	356	2.1

Source: Data in author's possession.

Note: For regional definitions, see Table 21, p. 652.

* Less than 0.05 percent.

TABLE A-17. *Chemical Industry*
Employment by Race, Sex, and Occupational Group
89 Establishments in the Southeast Region, 1966

Occupational Group	All Employees			Male			Female		
	Total	Negro	Percent Negro	Total	Negro	Percent Negro	Total	Negro	Percent Negro
Officials and managers	13,303	17	0.1	13,146	17	0.1	157	—	—
Professionals	8,648	20	0.2	8,528	16	0.2	120	4	3.3
Technicians	6,776	71	1.0	5,690	60	1.1	1,086	11	1.0
Sales workers	71	—	—	53	—	—	18	—	—
Office and clerical	7,598	80	1.1	2,959	48	1.6	4,639	32	0.7
Total white collar	36,396	188	0.5	30,376	141	0.5	6,020	47	0.8
Craftsmen (skilled)	29,691	450	1.5	29,595	449	1.5	96	1	1.0
Operatives (semiskilled)	43,150	3,757	8.7	31,293	3,207	10.2	11,857	550	4.6
Laborers	5,489	2,326	42.4	5,170	2,289	44.3	319	37	11.6
Service workers	2,809	999	35.6	2,628	936	35.6	181	63	34.8
Total blue collar	81,139	7,532	9.3	68,686	6,881	10.0	12,453	651	5.2
Total	117,535	7,720	6.6	99,062	7,022	7.1	18,473	698	3.8

Source: Data in author's possession.

Note: For regional definitions, see Table 21, p. 652.

TABLE A-18. *Chemical Industry*
Employment by Race, Sex, and Occupational Group
89 Establishments in the Southeast Region, 1968

Occupational Group	All Employees			Male			Female		
	Total	Negro	Percent Negro	Total	Negro	Percent Negro	Total	Negro	Percent Negro
Officials and managers	14,407	40	0.3	14,210	40	0.3	197	—	—
Professionals	8,457	41	0.5	8,293	34	0.4	164	7	4.3
Technicians	6,535	133	2.0	5,373	96	1.8	1,162	37	3.2
Sales workers	377	1	0.3	370	1	0.3	7	—	—
Office and clerical	7,575	181	2.4	2,910	82	2.8	4,665	99	2.1
Total white collar	37,351	396	1.1	31,156	253	0.8	6,195	143	2.3
Craftsmen (skilled)	29,473	676	2.3	29,310	671	2.3	163	5	3.1
Operatives (semiskilled)	49,965	5,713	11.4	37,079	4,544	12.3	12,886	1,169	9.1
Laborers	5,234	1,920	36.7	4,821	1,864	38.7	413	56	13.6
Service workers	2,588	892	34.5	2,434	834	34.3	154	58	37.7
Total blue collar	87,260	9,201	10.5	73,644	7,913	10.7	13,616	1,288	9.5
Total	124,611	9,597	7.7	104,800	8,166	7.8	19,811	1,431	7.2

Source: Data in author's possession.

Note: For regional definitions, see Table 21, p. 652.

TABLE A–19. *Chemical Industry*
Employment by Race, Sex, and Occupational Group
19 Establishments in the Southwest Region, 1964

Occupational Group	All Employees			Male			Female		
	Total	Negro	Percent Negro	Total	Negro	Percent Negro	Total	Negro	Percent Negro
Officials and managers	3,244	4	0.1	3,235	4	0.1	9	—	—
Professionals	2,203	1	*	2,183	1	*	20	—	—
Technicians	1,469	4	0.3	1,371	4	0.3	98	—	—
Sales workers	2	—	—	2	—	—	—	—	—
Office and clerical	1,712	14	0.8	682	7	1.0	1,030	7	0.7
Total white collar	8,630	23	0.3	7,473	16	0.2	1,157	7	0.6
Craftsmen (skilled)	8,497	23	0.3	8,494	23	0.3	3	—	—
Operatives (semiskilled)	4,492	272	6.1	4,477	272	6.1	15	—	—
Laborers	1,072	697	65.0	1,072	697	65.0	—	—	—
Service workers	558	127	22.8	545	127	23.3	13	—	—
Total blue collar	14,619	1,119	7.7	14,588	1,119	7.7	31	—	—
Total	23,249	1,142	4.9	22,061	1,135	5.1	1,188	7	0.6

Source: Data in author's possession.

Note: For regional definitions, see Table 21, p. 652.

* Less than 0.05 percent.

TABLE A–20. *Chemical Industry*
Employment by Race, Sex, and Occupational Group
23 Establishments in the Southwest Region, 1966

Occupational Group	All Employees			Male			Female		
	Total	Negro	Percent Negro	Total	Negro	Percent Negro	Total	Negro	Percent Negro
Officials and managers	3,457	7	0.2	3,447	7	0.2	10	—	—
Professionals	2,419	2	0.1	2,402	2	0.1	17	—	—
Technicians	1,724	13	0.8	1,619	12	0.7	105	1	1.0
Sales workers	2	—	—	2	—	—	—	—	—
Office and clerical	1,783	26	1.5	705	9	1.3	1,078	17	1.6
Total white collar	9,385	48	0.5	8,175	30	0.4	1,210	18	1.5
Craftsmen (skilled)	8,599	42	0.5	8,597	42	0.5	2	—	—
Operatives (semiskilled)	5,031	321	6.4	5,005	321	6.4	26	—	—
Laborers	1,076	751	69.8	1,076	751	69.8	—	—	—
Service workers	572	129	22.6	560	129	23.0	12	—	—
Total blue collar	15,278	1,243	8.1	15,238	1,243	8.2	40	—	—
Total	24,663	1,291	5.2	23,413	1,273	5.4	1,250	18	1.4

Source: Data in author's possession.

Note: For regional definitions, see Table 21, p. 652.

TABLE A-21. *Chemical Industry*
Employment by Race, Sex, and Occupational Group
23 Establishments in the Southwest Region, 1968

Occupational Group	All Employees			Male			Female		
	Total	Negro	Percent Negro	Total	Negro	Percent Negro	Total	Negro	Percent Negro
Officials and managers	3,311	7	0.2	3,300	7	0.2	11	—	—
Professionals	2,652	8	0.3	2,634	8	0.3	18	—	—
Technicians	1,700	30	1.8	1,589	27	1.7	111	3	2.7
Sales workers	144	1	0.7	144	1	0.7	—	—	—
Office and clerical	1,910	40	2.1	750	12	1.6	1,160	28	2.4
Total white collar	9,717	86	0.9	8,417	55	0.7	1,300	31	2.4
Craftsmen (skilled)	8,576	93	1.1	8,575	93	1.1	1	—	—
Operatives (semiskilled)	5,947	444	7.5	5,922	444	7.5	25	—	—
Laborers	961	652	67.8	961	652	67.8	—	—	—
Service workers	508	111	21.9	500	110	22.0	8	1	12.5
Total blue collar	15,992	1,300	8.1	15,958	1,299	8.1	34	1	2.9
Total	25,709	1,386	5.4	24,375	1,354	5.6	1,334	32	2.4

Source: Data in author's possession.

Note: For regional definitions, see Table 21, p. 652.

TABLE A-22. *Chemical Industry*
Employment by Race, Sex, and Occupational Group
75 Establishments in the Midwest Region, 1964

Occupational Group	All Employees			Male			Female		
	Total	Negro	Percent Negro	Total	Negro	Percent Negro	Total	Negro	Percent Negro
Officials and managers	9,513	25	0.3	9,381	25	0.3	132	—	—
Professionals	7,651	33	0.4	7,420	32	0.4	231	1	0.4
Technicians	5,093	63	1.2	4,662	60	1.3	431	3	0.7
Sales workers	2,839	2	0.1	2,662	2	0.1	177	—	—
Office and clerical	9,468	107	1.1	3,077	40	1.3	6,391	67	1.0
Total white collar	34,564	230	0.7	27,202	159	0.6	7,362	71	1.0
Craftsmen (skilled)	12,130	187	1.5	12,113	187	1.5	17	—	—
Operatives (semiskilled)	22,200	1,506	6.8	19,765	1,431	7.2	2,435	75	3.1
Laborers	4,291	560	13.1	3,692	535	14.5	599	25	4.2
Service workers	2,313	376	16.3	2,066	351	17.0	247	25	10.1
Total blue collar	40,934	2,629	6.4	37,636	2,504	6.7	3,298	125	3.8
Total	75,498	2,859	3.8	64,838	2,663	4.1	10,660	196	1.8

Source: Data in author's possession.

Note: For regional definitions, see Table 21, p. 652.

TABLE A-23. *Chemical Industry*
Employment by Race, Sex, and Occupational Group
78 Establishments in the Midwest Region, 1966

Occupational Group	All Employees			Male			Female		
	Total	Negro	Percent Negro	Total	Negro	Percent Negro	Total	Negro	Percent Negro
Officials and managers	9,847	32	0.3	9,697	32	0.3	150	—	—
Professionals	8,033	48	0.6	7,779	43	0.6	254	5	2.0
Technicians	5,020	83	1.7	4,506	75	1.7	514	8	1.6
Sales workers	2,852	7	0.2	2,712	6	0.2	140	1	0.7
Office and clerical	9,439	158	1.7	2,922	48	1.6	6,517	110	1.7
Total white collar	35,191	328	0.9	27,616	204	0.7	7,575	124	1.6
Craftsmen (skilled)	12,006	200	1.7	11,986	199	1.7	20	1	5.0
Operatives (semiskilled)	23,192	1,586	6.8	20,898	1,510	7.2	2,294	76	3.3
Laborers	4,348	497	11.4	3,525	477	13.5	823	20	2.4
Service workers	2,249	411	18.3	2,030	383	18.9	219	28	12.8
Total blue collar	41,795	2,694	6.4	38,439	2,569	6.7	3,356	125	3.7
Total	76,986	3,022	3.9	66,055	2,773	4.2	10,931	249	2.3

Source: Data in author's possession.

Note: For regional definitions, see Table 21, p. 652.

TABLE A-24. *Chemical Industry*
Employment by Race, Sex, and Occupational Group
73 Establishments in the Midwest Region, 1968

Occupational Group	All Employees			Male			Female		
	Total	Negro	Percent Negro	Total	Negro	Percent Negro	Total	Negro	Percent Negro
Officials and managers	10,103	69	0.7	9,987	67	0.7	116	2	1.7
Professionals	8,463	87	1.0	8,094	77	1.0	369	10	2.7
Technicians	5,268	169	3.2	4.429	128	2.9	839	41	4.9
Sales workers	2,223	17	0.8	2,076	16	0.8	147	1	0.7
Office and clerical	9,461	268	2.8	2,853	65	2.3	6,608	203	3.1
Total white collar	35,518	610	1.7	27,439	353	1.3	8,079	257	3.2
Craftsmen (skilled)	11,932	388	3.3	11,568	321	2.8	364	67	18.4
Operatives (semiskilled)	24,738	2,152	8.7	21,273	1,702	8.0	3,465	450	13.0
Laborers	5,603	660	11.8	4,114	540	13.1	1,489	120	8.1
Service workers	2,491	424	17.0	2,087	358	17.2	404	66	16.3
Total blue collar	44,764	3,624	8.1	39,042	2,921	7.5	5,722	703	12.3
Total	80,282	4,234	5.3	66,481	3,274	4.9	13,801	960	7.0

Source: Data in author's possession.

Note: For regional definitions, see Table 21, p. 652.

TABLE A–25. *Chemical Industry*
Employment by Race, Sex, and Occupational Group
60 Establishments in the North Central Region, 1964

	All Employees			Male			Female		
Occupational Group	Total	Negro	Percent Negro	Total	Negro	Percent Negro	Total	Negro	Percent Negro
Officials and managers	6,862	8	0.1	6,757	8	0.1	105	—	—
Professionals	5,098	27	0.5	4,917	26	0.5	181	1	0.6
Technicians	3,591	51	1.4	3,223	48	1.5	368	3	0.8
Sales workers	2,529	2	0.1	2,354	2	0.1	175	—	—
Office and clerical	6,379	76	1.2	2,134	23	1.1	4,245	53	1.2
Total white collar	24,459	164	0.7	19,385	107	0.6	5,074	57	1.1
Craftsmen (skilled)	9,356	144	1.5	9,340	144	1.5	16	—	—
Operatives (semiskilled)	17,329	1,208	7.0	15,355	1,144	7.5	1,974	64	3.2
Laborers	3,607	392	10.9	3,052	369	12.1	555	23	4.1
Service workers	1,890	220	11.6	1,717	210	12.2	173	10	5.8
Total blue collar	32,182	1,964	6.1	29,464	1,867	6.3	2,718	97	3.6
Total	56,641	2,128	3.8	48,849	1,974	4.0	7,792	154	2.0

Source: Data in author's possession.

Note: For regional definitions, see Table 21, p. 652.

TABLE A-26. *Chemical Industry*
Employment by Race, Sex, and Occupational Group
62 Establishments in the North Central Region, 1966

Occupational Group	All Employees			Male			Female		
	Total	Negro	Percent Negro	Total	Negro	Percent Negro	Total	Negro	Percent Negro
Officials and managers	7,422	11	0.1	7,300	11	0.2	122	—	—
Professionals	5,418	38	0.7	5,214	33	0.6	204	5	2.5
Technicians	3,491	65	1.9	3,113	57	1.8	378	8	2.1
Sales workers	2,698	7	0.3	2,559	6	0.2	139	1	0.7
Office and clerical	6,752	110	1.6	2,094	25	1.2	4,658	85	1.8
Total white collar	25,781	231	0.9	20,280	132	0.7	5,501	99	1.8
Craftsmen (skilled)	9,137	153	1.7	9,119	153	1.7	18	—	—
Operatives (semiskilled)	18,487	1,276	6.9	16,539	1,208	7.3	1,948	68	3.5
Laborers	3,398	315	9.3	2,690	295	11.0	708	20	2.8
Service workers	1,796	240	13.4	1,650	228	13.8	146	12	8.2
Total blue collar	32,818	1,984	6.0	29,998	1,884	6.3	2,820	100	3.5
Total	58,599	2,215	3.8	50,278	2,016	4.0	8,321	199	2.4

Source: Data in author's possession.

Note: For regional definitions, see Table 21, p. 652.

TABLE A–27. *Chemical Industry*
Employment by Race, Sex, and Occupational Group
58 Establishments in the North Central Region, 1968

Occupational Group	All Employees Total	All Employees Negro	All Employees Percent Negro	Male Total	Male Negro	Male Percent Negro	Female Total	Female Negro	Female Percent Negro
Officials and managers	7,694	47	0.6	7,597	45	0.6	97	2	2.1
Professionals	5,768	67	1.2	5,485	58	1.1	283	9	3.2
Technicians	3,806	127	3.3	3,149	95	3.0	657	32	4.9
Sales workers	1,995	17	0.9	1,850	16	0.9	145	1	0.7
Office and clerical	6,910	193	2.8	2,195	50	2.3	4,715	143	3.0
Total white collar	26,173	451	1.7	20,276	264	1.3	5,897	187	3.2
Craftsmen (skilled)	8,541	192	2.2	8,539	192	2.2	2	—	—
Operatives (semiskilled)	19,990	1,738	8.7	17,250	1,366	7.9	2,740	372	13.6
Laborers	4,542	577	12.7	3,374	468	13.9	1,168	109	9.3
Service workers	2,034	256	12.6	1,721	212	12.3	313	44	14.1
Total blue collar	35,107	2,763	7.9	30,884	2,238	7.2	4,223	525	12.4
Total	61,280	3,214	5.2	51,160	2,502	4.9	10,120	712	7.0

Source: Data in author's possession.

Note: For regional definitions, see Table 21, p. 652.

TABLE A-28. *Chemical Industry*
Employment by Race, Sex, and Occupational Group
15 Establishments in the Other Midwest Region, 1964

Occupational Group	All Employees Total	Negro	Percent Negro	Male Total	Negro	Percent Negro	Female Total	Negro	Percent Negro
Officials and managers	2,651	17	0.6	2,624	17	0.6	27	—	—
Professionals	2,553	6	0.2	2,503	6	0.2	50	—	—
Technicians	1,502	12	0.8	1,439	12	0.8	63	—	—
Sales workers	310	—	—	308	—	—	2	—	—
Office and clerical	3,089	31	1.0	943	17	1.8	2,146	14	0.7
Total white collar	10,105	66	0.7	7,817	52	0.7	2,288	14	0.6
Craftsmen (skilled)	2,774	43	1.6	2,773	43	1.6	1	—	—
Operatives (semiskilled)	4,871	298	6.1	4,410	287	6.5	461	11	2.4
Laborers	684	168	24.6	640	166	25.9	44	2	4.5
Service workers	423	156	36.9	349	141	40.4	74	15	20.3
Total blue collar	8,752	665	7.6	8,172	637	7.8	580	28	4.8
Total	18,857	731	3.9	15,989	689	4.3	2,868	42	1.5

Source: Data in author's possession.

Note: For regional definitions, see Table 21, p. 652.

TABLE A-29. *Chemical Industry*
Employment by Race, Sex, and Occupational Group
16 Establishments in the Other Midwest Region, 1966

Occupational Group	All Employees			Male			Female		
	Total	Negro	Percent Negro	Total	Negro	Percent Negro	Total	Negro	Percent Negro
Officials and managers	2,425	21	0.9	2,397	21	0.9	28	—	—
Professionals	2,615	10	0.4	2,565	10	0.4	50	—	—
Technicians	1,529	18	1.2	1,393	18	1.3	136	—	—
Sales workers	154	—	—	153	—	—	1	—	—
Office and clerical	2,687	48	1.8	828	23	2.8	1,859	25	1.3
Total white collar	9,410	97	1.0	7,336	72	1.0	2,074	25	1.2
Craftsmen (skilled)	2,869	47	1.6	2,867	46	1.6	2	1	50.0
Operatives (semiskilled)	4,705	310	6.6	4,359	302	6.9	346	8	2.3
Laborers	950	182	19.2	835	182	21.8	115	—	—
Service workers	453	171	37.7	380	155	40.8	73	16	21.9
Total blue collar	8,977	710	7.9	8,441	685	8.1	536	25	4.7
Total	18,387	807	4.4	15,777	757	4.8	2,610	50	1.9

Source: Data in author's possession.

Note: For regional definitions, see Table 21, p. 652.

Table A-30. *Chemical Industry*
Employment by Race, Sex, and Occupational Group
15 Establishments in the Other Midwest Region, 1968

Occupational Group	All Employees			Male			Female		
	Total	Negro	Percent Negro	Total	Negro	Percent Negro	Total	Negro	Percent Negro
Officials and managers	2,409	22	0.9	2,390	22	0.9	19	—	—
Professionals	2,695	20	0.7	2,609	19	0.7	86	1	1.2
Technicians	1,462	42	2.9	1,280	33	2.6	182	9	4.9
Sales workers	228	—	—	226	—	—	2	—	—
Office and clerical	2,551	75	2.9	658	15	2.3	1,893	60	3.2
Total white collar	9,345	159	1.7	7,163	89	1.2	2,182	70	3.2
Craftsmen (skilled)	3,391	196	5.8	3,029	129	4.3	362	67	18.5
Operatives (semiskilled)	4,748	414	8.7	4,023	336	8.4	725	78	10.8
Laborers	1,061	83	7.8	740	72	9.7	321	11	3.4
Service workers	457	168	36.8	366	146	39.9	91	22	24.2
Total blue collar	9,657	861	8.9	8,158	683	8.4	1,499	178	11.9
Total	19,002	1,020	5.4	15,321	772	5.0	3,681	248	6.7

Source: Data in author's possession.

Note: For regional definitions, see Table 21, p. 652.

TABLE A-31. *Chemical Industry*
Employment by Race, Sex, and Occupational Group
10 Establishments in the West Coast Region, 1964

Occupational Group	All Employees			Male			Female		
	Total	Negro	Percent Negro	Total	Negro	Percent Negro	Total	Negro	Percent Negro
Officials and managers	671	—	—	658	—	—	13	—	—
Professionals	895	3	0.3	833	2	0.2	62	1	1.6
Technicians	831	12	1.4	758	12	1.6	73	—	—
Sales workers	20	—	—	20	—	—	—	—	—
Office and clerical	603	11	1.8	200	3	1.5	403	8	2.0
Total white collar	3,020	26	0.9	2,469	17	0.7	551	9	1.6
Craftsmen (skilled)	1,273	11	0.9	1,273	11	0.9	—	—	—
Operatives (semiskilled)	1,564	131	8.4	1,283	94	7.3	281	37	13.2
Laborers	158	23	14.6	147	21	14.3	11	2	18.2
Service workers	178	25	14.0	158	22	13.9	20	3	15.0
Total blue collar	3,173	190	6.0	2,861	148	5.2	312	42	13.5
Total	6,193	216	3.5	5,330	165	3.1	863	51	5.9

Source: Data in author's possession.

Note: For regional definitions, see Table 21, p. 652.

TABLE A–32. *Chemical Industry*
Employment by Race, Sex, and Occupational Group
11 Establishments in the West Coast Region, 1966

Occupational Group	All Employees Total	All Employees Negro	All Employees Percent Negro	Male Total	Male Negro	Male Percent Negro	Female Total	Female Negro	Female Percent Negro
Officials and managers	701	1	0.1	689	1	0.1	12	—	—
Professionals	925	7	0.8	859	5	0.6	66	2	3.0
Technicians	774	12	1.6	706	12	1.7	68	—	—
Sales workers	20	—	—	20	—	—	—	—	—
Office and clerical	587	14	2.4	183	4	2.2	404	10	2.5
Total white collar	3,007	34	1.1	2,457	22	0.9	550	12	2.2
Craftsmen (skilled)	1,305	18	1.4	1,305	18	1.4	—	—	—
Operatives (semiskilled)	1,426	110	7.7	1,239	97	7.8	187	13	7.0
Laborers	157	36	22.9	114	16	14.0	43	20	46.5
Service workers	171	28	16.4	151	24	15.9	20	4	20.0
Total blue collar	3,059	192	6.3	2,809	155	5.5	250	37	14.8
Total	6,066	226	3.7	5,266	177	3.4	800	49	6.1

Source: Data in author's possession.

Note: For regional definitions, see Table 21, p. 652.

TABLE A–33. *Chemical Industry*
Employment by Race, Sex, and Occupational Group
11 Establishments in the West Coast Region, 1968

	All Employees			Male			Female		
Occupational Group	Total	Negro	Percent Negro	Total	Negro	Percent Negro	Total	Negro	Percent Negro
Officials and managers	875	1	0.1	858	1	0.1	17	—	—
Professionals	914	5	0.5	858	3	0.3	56	2	3.6
Technicians	617	17	2.8	559	17	3.0	58	—	—
Sales workers	260	2	0.8	259	2	0.8	1	—	—
Office and clerical	722	33	4.6	226	9	4.0	496	24	4.8
Total white collar	3,388	58	1.7	2,760	32	1.2	628	26	4.1
Craftsmen (skilled)	1,218	17	1.4	1,218	17	1.4	—	—	—
Operatives (semiskilled)	1,486	166	11.2	1,249	148	11.8	237	18	7.6
Laborers	192	39	20.3	149	23	15.4	43	16	37.2
Service workers	198	22	11.1	180	19	10.6	18	3	16.7
Total blue collar	3,094	244	7.9	2,796	207	7.4	298	37	12.4
Total	6,482	302	4.7	5,556	239	4.3	926	63	6.8

Source: Data in author's possession.

Note: For regional definitions, see Table 21, p. 652.

Part Eight

CONCLUDING ANALYSIS

by

HERBERT R. NORTHRUP

LIST OF TABLES

CHAPTER I.

Summary and Conclusions

Studying particular industries tells us not only about those industries, but also, if the industries are representative, can provide some general conclusions as well. Table 1 compares the racial occupational breakdown of all industries reporting to the Equal Employment Opportunity Commission in 1966 and those in manufacturing industries so reporting, with our combined 1966 field sample of the industries studied herein.

The Commission's data include excellent coverage of manufacturing industry employing 100 persons or more, but considerably less complete coverage in many other types of businesses. Since our six basic industries are almost exclusively manufacturing (petroleum is not completely so), a comparison of our 1966 field sample data with the EEOC manufacturing reports is an appropriate test of its representative character.

Table 1 shows that our combined sample for 1966 includes about 25 percent of all manufacturing employees, attesting to the significance of the six industries, and to the size of our samples in each. Moreover, the proportion of Negroes in our data follows closely the general trend for all manufacturing, being slightly higher in all occupations except officials and managers, where it is equal to the EEOC manufacturing data. (In white collar occupations, our field sample Negro proportion is below that of all industries reporting to EEOC, except in sales; the reasons for this, we hope, will be clarified after our nonmanufacturing studies are completed.)

The six industries studied are not only large industries dominated by major concerns, but in addition our samples stressed coverage of the major companies. Hence our findings must be considered most applicable to large enterprise, which, of course, sets the pace in racial policy matters. The composition of our sample also affects its coverage in the different occupational groups. For example, the six industry sample

TABLE 1. *Six Industries Field Sample Comparison with All Industries and Manufacturing Industries by Race and Occupational Group, Total United States,[a] 1966*

	All Industries Reporting to EEOC			Manufacturing Industries Reporting to EEOC			Six Industries Combined Field Sample[b]		
	Total	Negro	Percent Negro	Total	Negro	Percent Negro	Total	Negro	Percent Negro
Officials and managers	2,077,663	18,106	0.9	878,497	4,991	0.6	289,605	1,878	0.6
Professionals	1,689,886	22,333	1.3	670,818	3,732	0.6	338,310	2,249	0.7
Technicians	1,137,952	46,503	4.1	448,217	6,563	1.5	147,731	2,368	1.6
Sales workers	1,796,574	42,417	2.4	346,136	4,160	1.2	59,193	1,534	2.6
Office and clerical	4,264,770	151,105	3.5	1,307,982	26,193	2.0	397,203[c]	11,839	3.0
Total white collar	10,966,845	280,464	2.6	3,651,650	45,639	1.2	1,232,042	19,868	1.6
Craftsmen	3,626,470	130,543	3.6	2,199,536	82,343	3.7	569,913	21,527	3.8
Operatives	6,499,351	702,234	10.8	5,020,500	531,586	10.6	1,101,818	175,861	16.0
Laborers	2,465,901	523,970	21.2	1,623,100	297,509	18.3	157,120	40,215	25.6
Service workers	1,952,135	452,036	23.2	247,082	53,521	21.7	70,597	17,249	24.4
Total blue collar	14,543,857	1,808,783	12.4	9,090,218	964,959	10.6	1,899,448	254,852	13.4
Total	25,510,702	2,089,247	8.2	12,741,868	1,010,598	7.9	3,131,490	274,720	8.8

Source: U. S. Equal Employment Opportunity Commission, *Job Patterns for Minorities and Women in Private Industry, 1966*. Report No. 1 (Washington: The Commission, 1968), Part II; and data in authors' possession.

a. Excludes Alaska and Hawaii.

b. Automobile, aerospace, steel, rubber tire, petroleum, and chemical industries.

c. This figure included a few sales workers in the automobile industry.

includes about 50 percent of all professionals in manufacturing because of the high proportion in this occupational group, especially in aerospace, but also in petroleum and chemicals; and less than 10 percent of the laborers because so few in the six industries are found or classified in this low status. The sales function is also underrepresented among the six industries because few in automobiles or aerospace (including those who do the selling!) are so classified.

Despite being less than perfect, our field sample does provide an excellent mirror of the racial occupational profile of basic manufacturing industry, particularly large industry. We believe also that the racial policies and problems of the industries which have been described and analyzed in the preceding pages are typical of American large enterprise. Therefore, it is useful to summarize the findings of the six industry studies in the light of thirteen of the fourteen hypotheses concerning Negro employment which were set forth in the initial chapter of this volume. (The fourteenth concerns service industry employment and does not, of course, pertain to the findings in this volume.)

THE DEMAND FOR LABOR

Except for rubber tires, all of the industries studied showed an increase in the percentage of Negro employees between 1964 and 1968 (Table 2). For three of these industries—automobiles, aerospace, and chemicals—this was a period of increased employment. The demand

TABLE 2. *Six Industries, Percent Negro Employment, 1964-1968*

	1964	1966	1968
Automobiles	10.5[a]	13.6	14.5
Aerospace	3.1	4.8	5.4
Steel	12.7	12.8	13.3
Rubber Tires	8.6	8.1	8.3
Petroleum	2.3	3.7	3.9
Chemical[b]	4.7	5.0	6.0

Source: Data in authors' possession.

a. Estimated.

b. Our field data probably underestimate the Negro employment proportion in chemicals by one to two percentage points because very few smaller companies, as discussed in Part Seven, are covered by the sample.

for labor was rising and affirmative action could be accomplished in a period of economic advancement. Automobiles, already a large employer of Negroes, moved forward with rising demand to become probably the largest employer of Negroes of any industry, and the major manufacturing industry with the highest percentage of blacks studied thus far.

The percentage of Negroes in aerospace is small, although given the more than 1.4 million persons employed by the industry in 1968, a 5.4 percent ratio involved about 800,000 jobs. The 1960's was a period of great expansion, enabling it to increase its Negro proportion despite difficulties of education and training. The probable decline in the industry's employment since 1968 could be a serious loss for black workers, especially as we shall note again below, because of the qualitative aspect of this labor force, both in the country as a whole and in the South where the industry has been a significant factor in opening up key jobs to Negroes.

The chemical industry has long been a large employer of Negroes, but only for unskilled jobs. The 1950's, however, represented a low point in the share of Negro jobs in the industry as unskilled work was automated out of existence and better jobs not offered to blacks. The period since 1964 featured a reversal of these policies, aided substantially in its effectuation by continued expansion of the industry and a consequent increased demand for labor.

The three other industries—steel, petroleum, and rubber tires—had a more difficult task in attempting to expand Negro employment from 1964 to 1968. The steel industry's competitive position has been under siege since the mid-1950's. Competition of substitute materials and foreign steel have reduced product demand and profits; and new processes and automation further helped to eliminate nearly 100,000 industry jobs after 1955. New hiring, therefore, has been on a very limited basis. As a result, the steel industry, once far ahead of the automobile industry in the number and proportion of Negroes, fell behind the latter in the key labor shortage and civil rights era of the 1960's.

Petroleum employs the smallest percentage of Negroes of any of the industries analyzed. It historically employed few blacks except as laborers in southern refineries. Moreover, in the mid-1950's employment in the industry, as the result of a vast program of methods and technical improvements, turned downward. Since then employment has continued downward, or been stable, except for some very recent small increases. New hiring has been very small with the exception of the office and clerical group which is commented upon below. Product demand has grown, but automation continues to curtail labor demand and limit the capacity of affirmative action programs to show substantial results in altering the industry's overall historical racial employment pattern.

The rubber tire industry has been able to expand production while reducing labor requirements during most of the years since World War II. Moreover, it has substantially reduced employment in older plants while adding capacity in new facilities. Its high wages and low labor demand have given the industry the capacity to employ on a highly selected basis. Only in the last few years has the industry taken affirmative steps to avoid "selecting out" the bulk of the Negro applicants who might be expected to be, on average, less qualified than the whites. Meanwhile, the elimination of laboring jobs by automation and denial of fair employment and fair seniority provisions, especially in some southern plants, reduced the proportion of Negroes in the industry prior to 1966.

Improvement in the economic status of Negroes thus is likely to depend upon a rising demand for labor. Some progress can occur in an industry in which employment is not expanding, particularly in a period of general tight labor markets, especially when, as in the 1960's, there is also great stress on civil rights and affirmative action to obtain that improvement. Without, however, employment expansion, it is obvious that changes in employment patterns are likely to be modest at best.

THE NATURE OF THE WORK

That the nature of the work is extremely significant in determining the degree of Negro employment is readily apparent from our six industry studies. The occupational mix, the character or relative unpleasantness of the work, and the pattern of occupational progression are all significant in this regard.

The Occupational Mix

Table 3 shows that in aerospace and petroleum, more than one-half of the employees are salaried. On the other hand, almost three-quarters of the employees in automobiles, steel, and rubber tires are in the

TABLE 3. *Six Industries, Percentage Distribution of Employees by Occupational Group, 1966*

Occupational Group	Automobiles	Aerospace	Steel	Rubber Tires	Petroleum	Chemicals
Officials and managers	7.9	9.1	8.3	8.5	10.5	12.1
Professionals	5.4	22.8	2.4	5.1	13.4	10.5
Technicians	2.6	8.1	2.3	3.0	5.0	6.8
Sales workers	—	0.1	0.6	2.1	10.8	1.9
Office and clerical	9.8[a]	16.5	8.6	9.5	19.4	11.1
Total white collar	25.7	56.6	22.2	28.2	59.1	42.4
Craftsmen	13.6	20.9	23.9	14.8	18.5	20.7
Operatives	54.5	19.7	37.1	49.7	17.5	29.2
Laborers	3.4	1.0	15.0	4.1	3.5	5.0
Service workers	2.8	1.8	1.8	3.2	1.4	2.7
Total blue collar	74.3	43.4	77.8	71.8	40.9	57.6
Total	100.0	100.0	100.0	100.0	100.0	100.0

Source: Data in authors' possession.
a. Includes the few classified as sales in the industry.

blue collar occupations. Chemicals is in the middle, with 42.4 percent white collar and 57.6 percent blue collar.

Given this occupational mix and the disadvantaged status of Negroes, reviewed in Part One, insofar as educational attainment, training, and industrial experience are concerned, one would expect that the proportion of Negroes would be highest in automobiles, steel, and rubber tires, lowest in aerospace and petroleum, and chemicals above the latter two, but below the first three. Of course, this is precisely the case (Table 2).

Both steel and automobiles provide a large proportion of jobs which can be done satisfactorily by persons of limited background and education and with minimum training. The fact that the automobile industry expanded in the 1960's permitted it to put thousands of blacks on its payrolls even though many had no previous plant experience and little schooling. Steel, of course, did not have the jobs available, not because of the nature of the work, but, as already noted, because of declining or stable employment, especially in the blue collar area.

The rubber tire industry is again, a special case not only because of declining labor demand, but because of the industry's high wages and concentration on employee selection processes that, with significant exceptions, took little or no note of black worker problems prior to 1966. Intense competition of white workers for its jobs and declining demand for labor, have offset the fact that the rubber tire occupational mix is about the same as automobiles or steel.

The chemical industry historically employed large numbers of Negroes in laboring and lower-rated operative jobs. Automation eliminated many of these classifications and more complicated equipment upgraded others. The trend is now toward an increase in craftsmen and top-rated operatives and a further decline in laboring and lower-rated operative work. Meanwhile, administrative and research requirements have expanded the white collar positions. Changing demand for labor eroded the Negro's position in the chemical industry in the 1950's. Even though the demand for labor continues upward and key companies have been stressing affirmative action, the proportion of Negroes in the industry is likely to lag until Negro education and training more nearly equals those of whites.

Aerospace has an unique occupational mix: the largest group is professionals; the second, craftsmen; the third, operatives; and the fourth, office and clerical. Product safety and reliability mitigate against the use of untrained or inexperienced personnel. Moreover, the type of education and training required is often attained only after considerable time has elapsed. On the other hand, the industry has developed remarkable training capability. It increased its ratio of blacks by recruiting a high percentage of available Negro professionals and by extensive recruitment and training in the operative, craftsmen, and clerical occupations. Few, if any industries, have worked harder at equal employment and affirmative action programs. Yet occupational realities would seem to insure that its proportion of Negroes will continue for many years to lag behind industries with occupational mixes similar to those of the automobile industry.

Petroleum, insofar as Negro employment is concerned, has at least three immediate major impediments: a historical failure to pursue equal employment policies; declining, or at best, stable employment demand in most sectors; and an occupational mix oriented toward salaried and craft jobs. The three largest occupational groups are, in order, office and clerical, craftsmen, and operatives. The first has offered the industry its most successful equal employment thrust, as will be discussed below. Requirements of skill and experience, bolstered by need to handle expensive equipment and to safeguard against the ever present fire hazard, plus the lack of employment expansion, all work to keep Negro employment at a low ebb in the industry.

The racial occupational mix for 1966 and 1968 in the six industries is summarized in Table 4. An examination of each of the categories reveals further significant variations. For example, it is not surprising, in view of past history, that there are few Negro "officials and managers." Most so classified are actually line supervisors. It is to be expected, therefore, that the industries with the highest percentage of blacks overall might well have the highest percentage of black supervisors. Our data show that is just about the situation.[1]

In the professional field, aerospace has the most professionals and both the highest percentage of professionals to all employees (Table 3), and the most and highest ratio of Negroes. (Indeed the 21 companies in our aerospace sample employed about 40 percent of all Negro professionals in manufacturing industry in 1966!) Rubber tires, with the smallest number of professionals ranks second with chemicals, with petroleum and automobiles close behind; but the comparisons are misleading since the tire data include only 54 Negro professionals as compared with 311 in chemicals, 350 in petroleum, and 1,598 in aerospace. In the technical group, the data also do not reveal significant comparative differences, but again the numbers in aerospace—1,308—far exceed those in the other industries.

Sales is an occupational group in which Negroes find difficulty in gaining acceptance. Of great significance are the social aspects of selling and feared or actual customer reactions. The high percentage shown for rubber tires is completely misleading. Included therein are almost all personnel in tire stores, including tire changers! Actually, there are few actual sales personnel employed by tire companies.

The petroleum industry has done the best job in both sales and office and clerical of the six industries. These are the main areas of employ-

1. The only exception is that aerospace has a slightly higher ratio than chemicals. The reader is, however, reminded that our data probably slightly underestimate the black representation in the chemical industry because of lack of coverage of companies having 100-500 employees.

TABLE 4. *Six Industries, Percent Negro Employment by Industry and Occupational Group, United States, 1966 and 1968*

Occupational Group	Automobiles		Aerospace		Steel		Rubber Tires		Petroleum		Chemicals[a]	
	1966	1968	1966	1968	1966	1968	1966	1968	1966	1968	1966	1968
Officials and managers	1.2	1.4	0.4	0.6	1.0	1.3	0.6	0.9	0.2	0.3	0.2	0.4
Professionals	0.6	0.7	0.8	0.9	0.2	0.5	0.3	0.8	0.6	0.7	0.5	0.8
Technicians	1.2	1.5	1.9	2.1	1.4	2.2	1.3	2.1	1.3	1.7	1.5	2.5
Sales workers	(b)	(b)	0.3	0.6	0.3	0.3	7.5[c]	5.0[c]	2.4	2.7	0.3	0.7
Office and clerical	3.8	4.4	2.8	3.4	2.3	2.9	1.4	1.9	3.9	4.8	1.8	3.2
Total white collar	2.1	2.4	1.5	1.7	1.4	1.9	1.4	1.6	2.0	2.4	0.9	1.6
Craftsmen	3.0	3.3	4.6	5.4	5.9	6.3	2.3	2.8	1.9	2.2	2.2	2.9
Operatives	20.2	21.3	11.9	13.5	17.8	18.7	11.6	12.8	6.8	7.3	7.6	9.9
Laborers	27.6	29.1	22.4	20.7	27.7	28.7	17.1	22.8	19.7	18.0	25.8	22.4
Service workers	27.2	27.3	22.2	23.2	19.1	20.0	30.4	29.2	24.2	21.5	22.9	23.0
Total blue collar	17.6	18.6	9.0	10.0	16.1	16.7	10.8	11.7	6.3	6.2	8.0	9.2
Total	13.6	14.5	4.8	5.4	12.8	13.3	8.1	8.3	3.7	3.9	5.0	6.0

Source: Data in authors' possession.

a. See Part Seven for analysis of possible 1-2 point downward bias in sample.

b. Few sales personnel combined with office and clerical.

c. Includes many nonsales personnel; actually very few Negroes in this classification are really sales.

ment expansion in the industry, and are tied in with the industry's efforts in consumer and credit card sales, and include also computer programming and data processing. The success of the petroleum companies in these areas gives them a white collar ratio equal to automobiles and superior to the others; yet this industry has the lowest overall Negro employment proportion. The concentration of employment in the top salaried categories where relatively few Negroes are as yet qualified keeps the salaried ratio of aerospace low although it employs more Negro professional and technical personnel than the five other industries combined.

In the blue collar area, all industries show a disproportionately heavy concentration in the bottom jobs. Only petroleum and chemicals show a less than 10 percent Negro representation in operatives. Both industries require considerable education, background, and training for such positions because of complicated controls and, especially for petroleum, fire hazards.

The craftsmen situation finds steel in the lead, with aerospace second. One reason for this is the nature of the progression systems discussed below. For steel, another reason is that the industry utilizes a large number of bricklayers, a trade in which Negroes, especially in the South, have traditionally been very strong. Most craftsmen in other industries are concentrated in the metal, electrical, and mechanical trades—crafts in which, contrary to the trowel trades, Negroes have been traditionally excluded since their inception. Historically, industries have not looked to Negroes to fill these craft jobs, and Negroes have not been trained to do so.

The relatively high percentage of black aerospace craftsmen is the result of conscious training and upgrading on the part of the industry, which has used its great training capability for this purpose. Thousands of Negroes have been upgraded by this industry into craft jobs for which they traditionally have not been sought. Even if such employees are laid off as a result of cutbacks in the industry, they will have acquired valuable skills much sought after in the labor market.

Character of the Work

Occupational mix is not the only aspect of work nature affecting the extent of Negro employment. One reason why Negroes made an early entrance into steel is because of the dirty, unpleasant, and backbreaking work. Negroes broke into automobiles in the paint and foundry departments, into rubber tires in the mixing rooms, into chemicals in the mixing and yard work, into petroleum as yard laborers, etc. As some of these unpleasant and backbreaking jobs were eliminated by machines, Negro worker representation typically declined. On the other hand, new, clean, pleasant, and light type of work, such as airplane manufacturing before World War II, was closed to Negroes.

The tendency of unpleasant or physically hard work to attract a disproportionate number of Negroes is not easily ended, although the extent may lessen. Especially in full employment periods, those who can find work elsewhere will do so—and whites, because of better education and training, are more likely to avoid the unpleasant jobs whereas Negroes for the opposite reason, and because discrimination is by no means wiped out, are less able to do so.

Pattern of Occupational Progression

The manner in which employees move from one job to another is largely determined by the industrial structure. The automobile, steel, and aerospace industries offer examples of quite different patterns. In automobiles movement is on a broad basis because production jobs are quite related in terms of training requirements, skills, and processes. Long narrow progressions from the lowest operation to the top are largely absent because the process does not require such training. Consequently, there is broad movement in the industry, even arrangements for plant transfers.

The steel job progression is quite different. It features long narrow seniority lines, with slow upward movement. Competence learned in one department, for example, blast furnaces, does not necessarily equip a person to work in another, for example, rolling mills. Once a worker starts up one roster, he has generally determined his area of employment as long as he remains in the industry. This is especially important for Negroes, for they have traditionally been placed in some departments (blast furnaces) and excluded from others (rolling mills). Given such a practice within a structure like steel, great difficulty is encountered in altering the pattern because an employee in the blast furnace department who desires to transfer must start at the bottom of the rolling mill hierarchy, and this could involve loss of pay and seniority. In contrast, lateral transfers in the automobile industry are common because the extent of special knowledge or experience required there makes them feasible, whereas in steel it does not.

But the steel system of progression has its salutory effects on Negro employment also. Table 4 shows that the steel industry has the highest percentage of Negro craftsmen among the six industries. One reason is that Negroes, although concentrated in particular departments, were able to work themselves up to high-rated, skilled positions within those departments. In many cases, their concentration in the bottom rungs of the occupational ladder insured that they would have little or no competition later from whites for the top jobs.

In the aerospace industry, training is all important for upgrading because, by the very nature of the business, new techniques, methods, materials, and processes must be learned in order to handle new jobs. Promotion depends more on competence and work mastery after special training, than it does on automatic job progression with on-the-job training. With the emphasis on civil rights, this training capacity aided the industry to train and to upgrade large numbers of Negroes so that its craftsmen's ratio is second only to steel among the six industries.

We thus conclude that the nature of the work is an extremely important determiner of the Negroes employed. This is especially true because of past discriminatory practices which confined Negroes to particular jobs or areas of work; and because of their disadvantaged educational attainment, training, and industrial experience. To the extent that these can be mitigated, the nature of the work becomes indifferent. Unfortunately, it would appear that a considerable period of time will elapse before the impact of past discrimination is totally eliminated and before true educational and training equality is achieved.

TIME AND NATURE OF INDUSTRY'S DEVELOPMENT AND COMMUNITY MORES

The timing and nature of an industry's development and the impact of community mores are perhaps more significant as a determiner of racial employment policy for such industries as textiles or paper, which are to be discussed in a subsequent volume on *Negro Employ-*

ment in Southern Industry, than they are for those industries analyzed in this volume. The hypotheses do, however, have pertinence here also. Five of the six industries achieved major growth during or just after World War I. They adopted the racial mores of the day, utilizing Negroes largely in unskilled work, and in general, not varying from what then seemed appropriate employment policy. When they opened southern facilities, they followed southern mores and community patterns in employing Negroes. Petroleum, which is heavily southern oriented, adopted quite rigid segregation patterns, as did the steel industry, especially in the Birmingham area.

Henry Ford, of course, and to a lesser extent, Harvey Firestone, were exceptions. Ford, true to his image as both an individualist and a friend of the underdog, opened up jobs to Negroes in the 1920's on a then unprecedented equalitarian scale. But Ford operated completely within southern mores in the South. Firestone, on the other hand, did not open the better jobs to Negroes in the North, but provided a substantial proportion of jobs to Negroes in the South. Of significance, of course, is that Ford's plants in the South were only assembly operations—before World War II considered strictly white men's work, and operated that way nearly everywhere but at Ford's River Rouge complex near Detroit. Firestone, on the other hand, had mixing room and heavy laboring jobs in the South, then typical Negro work.

The steel racial occupational composition still reflects the earlier racial job mores. The blast furnaces remain the black departments and few, if any, Negroes have made any dents in the all white rolling mill areas. In automobiles, foundries and paint shops remain as black as ever, but Negroes are now as common on Detroit assembly lines and in other factory jobs as are whites. In the South, the bar to Negro assembly line workers is slowly crumbling, but it was not breached before the 1960's. Also in the South, the traditional use of Negroes as laborers continues to feature chemical and petroleum plants especially, but those in other industries also. Few whites in the South will accept such jobs. It still violates the mores of the region.

The Southern Data

Table 5 shows the percentage of Negroes in each occupation for the six industries in the South for 1966 and 1968. Steel leads in Negro utilization in the South by far, having a black percentage almost

TABLE 5. *Six Industries, Percent Negro Employment by Industry and Occupational Group, South Region, 1966 and 1968*

Occupational Group	Automobiles		Aerospace		Steel		Rubber Tires		Petroleum Refining[a]		Chemicals[b]	
	1966	1968	1966	1968	1966	1968	1966	1968	1966	1968	1966	1968
Officials and managers	0.8	0.6	0.3	0.5	0.3	0.3	0.3	0.6	0.1	0.2	0.1	0.3
Professionals	0.6	0.7	0.6	0.7	0.3	1.3	—	—	0.2	0.2	0.2	0.4
Technicians	2.7	3.1	1.4	1.8	0.8	4.2	0.9	3.1	0.6	0.8	1.0	2.0
Sales workers	—	—	—	0.5	—	—	—	—	—	—	—	0.4
Office and clerical	2.9	3.3	3.0	3.8	1.2	2.5	1.1	1.6	0.3	1.1	1.1	2.3
Total white collar	1.9	1.9	1.4	1.8	0.7	1.8	0.6	1.1	0.3	0.5	0.5	1.0
Craftsmen	0.4	0.4	2.3	3.2	7.4	7.8	2.1	3.4	1.7	2.2	1.3	2.0
Operatives	12.4	13.6	8.3	10.0	31.9	35.8	12.6	12.9	21.0	27.0	8.5	11.0
Laborers	14.9	16.2	42.1	36.4	62.8	50.8	40.7	50.5	78.4	69.0	46.9	41.5
Service workers	24.4	25.4	35.5	38.0	28.2	26.5	66.9	60.7	45.3	45.0	33.4	32.4
Total blue collar	12.2	13.2	6.9	7.8	28.4	26.6	13.5	13.5	12.8	15.0	9.1	10.2
Total	9.7	10.3	3.7	4.4	22.5	21.3	11.4	11.5	9.3	10.7	6.3	7.3

Source: Data in authors' possession.

a. Author's estimates for 1968; regional breakdowns not available on comparative basis.

b. See Part Seven for analysis of possible 1-2 point downward bias in sample.

double that of rubber tires, which is slightly ahead of automobiles and petroleum refining. Chemicals and aerospace bring up the rear.

Looking at the occupational content, it becomes clear that all the industries have a large overconcentration in the bottom two categories, although automobiles less so than the others. The large number of Negro laborers and service employees accounts for the heavy Negro employment, and the relative insignificance of these classifications reduces the Negro ratio for such industries as aerospace and chemicals, and to a lesser extent, automobiles.

Steel's southern black ratio is worthy of further comment. Its nearly 8 percent black craftsmen's percentage is the result of two already noted facts: the movement up the progression in heavily black departments like blast furnaces; and the utilization by the industry of trowel trades craftsmen in which Negroes have been prominent in the South since slavery days. In addition, the substantial increase in the ratio of operatives between 1966 and 1968, and the decline in that of laborers and service workers, support the findings that considerable upgrading occurred in this period. Finally, again it should be noted that steel's Negro utilization is far ahead of automobiles in the South partially because the latter industry has only assembly plants there which used Negroes sparingly and discriminatingly before 1960. The early origin of the steel industry in the South, antedating the jim crow period and the traditional use of Negroes therein is in contrast to the beginnings of the automobile industry in the 1920's and its acceptance of Negro exclusion as proper industrial mores.

In the white collar occupations, steel does not rank first. In terms of numbers, the lead belongs to aerospace, although automobiles' overall percentage is slightly ahead. Petroleum, which has done so well nationally in the salaried area, operates like an old fashioned southern industry in the white collar area; little had been accomplished in the South in the salaried occupations of the oil industry.

Rubber tires show up surprisingly well. Actually, as was made clear in Part Five, these data reflect one plant, Firestone's Memphis facility, which has a substantially larger percentage than any other southern tire plant.

It is thus quite clear that the data for the South reflect both the industry origin and the community mores there. Even after taking into account labor demand and occupational mix, they reveal special characteristics not found in other parts of the country.

CONSUMER ORIENTATION AND IMAGE CONCERN

In the late 1950's, a superintendent of a General Motors southern plant brushed aside integration demands with the remark that the company was in business for profit, not social innovation. A few years later, General Motors was, like most companies, integrating its facilities. Companies which sell to consumers usually align their marketing and racial policies very carefully. They are more likely to be on the lookout for means to avoid offending any group, and especially majority opinion. Thus, they desire to move slightly ahead, but not too far. It is not unusual for such companies to work assiduously behind the scenes in a community to work out problems. Racial unrest can alienate a group, alter buying habits, and is generally bad for business.

Boycotts by Negro church groups against one oil company in Philadelphia in the early 1960's alerted the entire industry to the danger. Their affirmative action really began then. Competition for oil products at the retail level and the visibility of the oil companies resulted in a fundamental reappraisal of the industry's posture.

Steel and rubber tires are not especially consumer oriented even though the latter does sell tires at retail under company brand names. The steel industry is the dominant one in Birmingham; yet there is little evidence that racial improvements were high on its agenda there until difficulties arose and literally got out of hand. The steel industry is not used to dealing with the public in its marketing, selling as it does only to other producers. As a large employer of Negroes, it questioned what else were its responsibilities until forced by government to take a sharper look at its racial occupational patterns and community relations.

Rubber tire companies are oriented toward producer sales. They did little to alter employment policies before the early 1960's either in general employment practices, or in eliminating segregation in the South, with one exception.

The chemical industry is mainly not consumer oriented, although most large companies do have consumer sales. They too waited until the 1960's before giving special attention to what was happening to their Negro employment percentages. Concern with marketing—racial employment relationships do not seem to have been great before then.

Aerospace is a special case. With government as its big customer, and dependent on the tax dollar, its companies react not only to governmental power, but to consumer image. In matters such as this, they "market" their image by numerous activities, and a direct concern to be well considered by all groups.

Ford and Firestone

Individual entrepreneurs react differently. Ford did what was different and the public appreciated it. To a lesser extent, Firestone did likewise. Their individualist images permitted them to adopt unique policies without fear of adverse marketing impacts. Insofar as their racial policies were concerned, it may well be that their activity indicates that other companies were too timid.

Today Henry Ford II has assumed a public stance as an outspoken advocate of fair employment. There is no evidence that this visibility has sold more or less cars. It is quite possible that such stances are no longer controversial. On the other hand, none of the industries involved here, except possibly petroleum at the retail level, are easily subject to boycotts or other marketing intimidation.[2] In our forthcoming volume on service and retail trade, this aspect will be treated in a different and more vulnerable environment.

MANAGEMENT ETHNIC ORIGIN

We have virtually no evidence on the impact of management ethnic origins or nonracial policies. In one of the six industries, a major company has been dominated by a Jewish family for many years and is a leader in equal opportunity in that industry. This, however, is the only case which we have observed.

COMMUNITY CRISES

Community crises have resulted in companies re-examining their racial policies and becoming more concerned about shortcomings in equal employment opportunity. The Detroit riot of 1967 caused all the automobile companies to redouble their efforts not only to employ

2. The Southern Christian Leadership Conference annually attacks General Motors and declares a boycott. The effect is generally considered nil.

Negroes, but also to employ the hard-core and previously considered unemployable. The Birmingham confrontations a few years earlier led to a reappraisal by the steel companies of their employment policies and of their role in the community. Still earlier, the actual or threatened school closings to preserve segregation in the South found many major companies actively supporting those who felt this much too high a price to pay for tradition. Industry needs competent personnel, but without adequate schools, high-level people will not live or work in a community.

Companies located in the South were asked about the school crisis in relation to their racial employment policies. Most felt that it had resulted in a liberalization of the latter. As an aerospace executive noted:

> I was out making speeches to the effect that schools must stay open, integration or not. Each time, a voice from the floor demanded to know how many Negro managers were in my company. I was determined to be able to answer such a question affirmatively. Our first Negro foreman was promoted soon thereafter.[3]

Industry cannot operate at maximum efficiency if crisis and chaos exist in the community. Often the crisis occurs before industry moves into action. A riot, a threatened school closing, or a series of confrontations take their toll of output, productivity, sales, and profits. No wonder, then, that such events cause a re-examination of racial policies. In the 1960's, that meant more and better jobs for Negroes. Whether such would always be the case remains uncertain.

NATURE OF UNION ORGANIZATION

All of the industries involved in this volume deal primarily with industrial unions; there are some craft organizations in petroleum and chemicals, a few in aerospace[4] and virtually none in automobiles, steel, and rubber tires. Our analysis of the impact of unions on company racial policies, therefore, does not include the craft organizations which have often been antagonistic to fair employment practices in

3. Interview, June 1967.
4. The International Association of Machinists and Aerospace Workers was founded as a craft organization of railway mechanics, but it organizes aerospace (and many other) employees on an industrial basis.

industries such as railways or building construction. Moreover, the industries involved herein were not unionized prior to the 1930's; hence, racially restrictive practices of older unions did not become entrenched as they did in craft oriented industries.

By and large, unions in these six industries initially tended to accept the racial policies of industry, and modify them only slightly. None of the unions attempt to control hiring (except insofar as seniority rules require preference to those laid off). In general, therefore, hiring has remained a management prerogative. Moreover, none of these industries are unionized to a significant degree in the white collar occupations, except for Chrysler in automobiles. Hence, policies affecting salaried employees are almost exclusively those of management.

Promotion policies in the blue collar jobs are more affected by unions, but tend to follow the upgrading traditions established by industry to meet the needs of its manufacturing processes. This is especially true in an industry like steel which features long, narrow progressions. When the steel industry was unionized, the Steelworkers' Union successfully aided Negroes in progression lines to obtain promotions to which their seniority entitled them, whereas formerly they were sometimes passed over; but this union also negotiated agreements containing discriminatory seniority provisions that, together with employer hiring policies, restricted Negroes to certain job classifications and departments. Moreover, union codification of the practices of the 1930's and 1940's tended to institutionalize the status quo of those periods. In recent years, the national officers of this union have worked with management to eliminate the most discriminatory seniority provisions and to integrate many company departments; but they have not been sympathetic to modifying the basic seniority approach which requires an employee to give up seniority in one department and start at the bottom of another if he desires a transfer to a situation which eventually will provide better wages and/or opportunities.

Thus the union in the steel industry, despite policies which have welcomed Negroes as members and supported their rights to upgrading, has also, by institutionalizing some past practices, tended to help to perpetrate the results of past discrimination. The problem is now involved in cases being considered both by the Office of Federal Contract Compliance and by the federal courts. It would be surprising if the outcome of such litigation did not result in the application of the "rightful place" doctrine already established in litigation involving the tobacco and paper industries.[5]

The United Automobile Workers has assumed a vigorous equalitarian posture in the automobile industry. Moreover, the combination of the wide seniority system which befits the industry and the UAW's policies have greatly enhanced Negro employment opportunities. Yet, fearful of the separatist tendencies of its craftsmen members, even the UAW has been treading softly toward increasing opportunities for Negroes in these jobs. In aerospace, the UAW plays a less significant role, first, because its strength in this industry is considerably less, and second, because promotion seniority is less important in an industry where training and ability are so important. The UAW has, however, generally supported equal opportunity and affirmative action in aerospace whereas its rival union in this industry, the International Association of Machinists and Aerospace Workers takes a laissez-faire attitude. The IAM once excluded Negroes entirely; now it welcomes their membership but generally does not interfere either with management or local union policies.

In a study of union racial policies published in 1944, the senior author of this volume found that "National union control of such policies as admission and promotion is likely to prove of more benefit to Negroes than local control."[6] This finding is clearly affirmed by the present study. The Rubber Workers Union, for example, like the IAM, is highly decentralized. By first accepting, and then modifying departmental seniority (both for nonracial reasons), this union initially helped to confine Negroes to certain departments, and then aided their integration throughout all plant operations. But the national union was too weak to prevent southern locals from adopting departmental seniority policies based upon race, and was even helpless while violence in one case enforced discrimination, and in another case, a long court fight was undertaken by a local to stave off fair representation of black union members.

5. See *Quarles v. Philip Morris,* 279 F. Supp. 305 (E. D. Va. 1968); and *United States v. Local 189, United Papermakers and Paperworkers, Crown Zellerbach Corp. et al,* 282 F. Supp. 39 (E. D. La., 1968); affirmed F. (2d) (C. A. 5, 1969). The cases are discussed in Herbert R. Northrup: *The Negro in the Paper Industry,* and *The Negro in the Tobacco Industry,* Reports Nos. 8 and 13, in the Racial Policies of American Industry series.

6. Herbert R. Northrup, *Organized Labor and the Negro* (New York: Harper and Bros., 1944), p. 238.

Unions in the petroleum and chemical industries are not strong and play no significant role in the industries' racial policies. In petroleum, the Oil, Chemical, and Atomic Workers initially followed southern customs with jim crow locals and contracts continuing discriminatory wage schedules. The national opposed these policies, but needed governmental aid to effectuate change. OCAW was unable to enforce nondiscrimination in the South, and jim crow locals were not eliminated until recent years.

Union policies in these six industries have thus had some salutory and some negative effects but more often have not been dynamic elements of change. As representative organizations, propensities to move forward are often estopped by electoral realities. The union is, on balance, more likely to go along with change in racial policies than to instigate it.

IMPACT OF TECHNOLOGY

Technological development seems to have adverse effects on Negro employment, not because it is racially oriented, but because Negroes have been concentrated in the unskilled jobs which have been the easiest to automate. This certainly was the case for Negroes in the chemical and petroleum industries in the 1950's. Moreover, discrimination is often compounded in such instances because those displaced either are not given the opportunity for alternative employment, or because of educational and training deficiencies—again often a product of discrimination—cannot qualify to operate machinery and equipment.

In automobiles, expanding employment and continued demand for semiskilled labor has more than offset any technological displacement. But in rubber tires, technology has actually reduced employment, and especially eliminated unskilled jobs where Negroes have been concentrated, while at the same time production has increased. Aerospace technology has created vast numbers of new jobs of so complicated a nature that those with limited educational backgrounds often cannot be utilized. On the other hand, this technology has paved the way for expansion of the aircraft and aircraft engine businesses in which thousands of Negroes have found jobs.

In the steel industry improved technology, competition from other industries, and from foreign competition have reduced the work force, and further such reductions are likely. Moreover, Negroes may be disproportionately displaced in the future because of new automated processes outmoding current blast furnace operations, where Negro employment is concentrated. An alleviation of the industry's seniority system may be necessary to avoid this possibility.

The impact of technology is thus varied, but it can be adverse when it affects Negroes who are concentrated in departments or occupations. This is especially the case if those affected are unskilled and not qualified for jobs requiring more training or educational background; or if because of discrimination, rigidly narrow seniority provisions, or both, they are denied transfer rights to other jobs.

INDUSTRIAL LOCATION

The increased concentration of Negroes in center city areas, combined with the decentralization of industry and the lack of urban transit, have tended, as discussed in Chapter II of Part One, to increase the difficulties of Negroes to obtain jobs. The aerospace industry, by the very nature of its product, must locate away from population concentrations and there is no doubt that this has reduced Negro employment opportunities in many aerospace facilities. The same tends to be true of new chemical factories and petroleum refineries. Their odors and other characteristics commend locations outside of cities. (Older ones are often surrounded by slum areas in which Negroes dwell; the odors depreciate housing nearby.) Urban transit from center city to such locations is usually lacking or inadequate.

Now tire factories are also being located in small towns and in other nonurban areas. Many of these in the Midwest are not near Negro population centers; those in the South are. An automobile is needed to work in such factories, but hiring standards and policies have been more important in maintaining a low Negro percentage than has been location.

Steel and automobile plants are found, by and large, in areas where Negroes dwell and location has not been a serious hindrance to their employment. These industries have a long history of employing large numbers of Negroes, and attract black workers, as well as whites, who often commute long distances. In the automobile industry, particularly, the work force uses the industry's product for long rides to work. In all industry, however, women clerical employees do not commute long-distances. Plants located far from Negro population concentrations usually have few Negro female employees. The center city jobs available to Negroes are increasingly female jobs—those in offices, banks, etc. For these they have no need to travel to the suburbs and in any case cannot and still fulfill their marital or family obligations.

More significant is the fact that the Negro hard-core and teenage unemployed find it difficult to travel to jobs. Lack of knowledge of where jobs are and how to get there, and lack of opportunities close to home are factors contributing to the unemployment rates among these groups.

THE ROLE OF GOVERNMENT

In 1944, the senior author of this volume concluded that governmental action was essential if increased opportunities were to be made available to Negroes.[7] The information developed for this volume and others in this series all support the view that this is the case. Governmental assistance on equal opportunity encourages those who support the idea in principle but fear reprisal for making it a fact, and compels those who disagree to act anyway. Strong governmental pressure was needed to open up salaried positions and many craft jobs as well; and strong governmental pressure has been needed to eliminate segregation of facilities and, more significantly, segregation of work in the South. There can be no question that governmental action was required to insure progress in the 1960's.

Government action, however, is not singly-directed, nor can it perform miracles. Thus in aerospace, government must be concerned with effective procurement and absolute product reliability, as well as with equal employment opportunity. In all industry, government programs achieved much greater success than would otherwise have been the case because of the high employment and tight labor markets. If large scale unemployment had existed, government action would have had some success, but not nearly that which did occur.

Finally, it is very likely that government action in the equal employment area would be more successful if duplication and interagency rivalry could be curbed, and if the nature of different industries were considered. Duplication not only harasses and antagonizes employers, but also wastes compliance agency money and efforts. As a result, some companies are repeatedly inspected, others are ignored.

7. *Ibid.*, pp. 238-251.

By familiarizing themselves with the nature and structure of various industries, the compliance agencies could concentrate their efforts on the areas where the most potential for increased Negro employment exists. Thus, by examining the occupational breakdowns, employment trends, training needs, locational problems, and the other variables discussed herein, effective means of increasing Negro employment become clearer. No two industries are exactly alike. Approaching industries by understanding the needs of their production processes affords the greatest opportunities for effective utilization of government compulsion toward equal opportunity. It is hoped that the information contained in this volume and others in this series will aid in developing the most rational government-industry relationship toward the goal of equal opportunity.

MANAGERIAL POLICIES

As the reader will realize from the discussions in this volume, many of the decisions of mangement in regard to racial policies (as well as in regard to the conduct of other phases of business) are largely determined by a complex of internal and external pressures which are beyond managerial control to alter substantially. The state of the labor market, the production process, the occupational hierarchy, and many extraneous factors, particularly government pressures, cannot easily be changed by managerial action. Often, too, plant location is either given or determined by production or market requirements. Community mores and their impact are often also beyond managerial control, although large businesses in small communities can indeed, and have, affected them substantially.

Even given these constraints, the fact remains that top managements are able to, and have, on numerous occasions, made substantial alterations in racial employment patterns. Henry Ford proved that Negroes and whites could and would work together on assembly lines, and that whites would even work under black supervisors. McDonnell Aircraft refused to have segregation in its St. Louis facilities because McDonnell insisted on operating without it. Lockheed was the first to employ large numbers of Negroes in a Southern California aircraft plant and the first to join Plans for Progress. The consistently high percentage of Negroes in Firestone's Memphis plant is the result of the decisions of the Firestone family management.

The commitment of managers to fair employment varies over the entire spectrum. Yet we have found that in many industries it is not controversial. Few thoughtful persons deny a man's right to employment in accordance with his abilities. Some, however, are more courageous and more innovative than others. Not all managers are willing to risk employing Negro managers or sales personnel in customer sensitive areas—yet, some have with good results, and some have seen such innovations fail but have tried again. Innovators in racial employment policies are as necessary to progress as are those in other business endeavors. Progress in the future toward equal opportunity in practice will continue to depend in part, as it has always in the past, upon the innovations of individual managers and their interest and commitment to equal opportunity, operating as they must, within the constraints imposed by the internal and external pressures which bear upon business organization and operation.

The demand for labor must exist; but where it does, innovative management has shown that it often can develop the means to utilize those in our society who in the past have been denied their "rightful place" in our nation's great industrial complex.

Indexes

Index: Part One

INTRODUCTION AND OVERVIEW

INDEX: PART TWO

AUTOMOBILES

INDEX: PART THREE

AEROSPACE

Index: Part Four

STEEL

INDEX: PART FIVE

RUBBER

Index: Part Six

PETROLEUM

Index: Part Seven

CHEMICALS

INDEX: PART EIGHT

CONCLUDING ANALYSIS